STUDIES IN
JEWISH
THOUGHT

A Publication of the Leo Baeck Institute

STUDIES IN JEWISH THOUGHT

An Anthology of German Jewish Scholarship

Selected, Edited, and Introduced by Alfred Jospe

Wayne State University Press   Detroit, 1981

Library of Congress Cataloging in Publication Data
Main entry under title:

Studies in Jewish thought.

Includes bibliographical references and index.
1. Judaism—History—Addresses, essays, lectures.
2. Judaism—Doctrines—Addresses, essays, lectures.
3. Mendelssohn, Moses, 1729–1786—Addresses, essays,
lectures. I. Jospe, Alfred, 1909–
BM43.S78   296   80-29338
ISBN   08143-1676-X

CONTENTS

Editor's Note   7

Introduction   9

Wissenschaft des Judentums: Two Prefatory Statements
1. On Rabbinic Literature (excerpts)   *19*
Leopold Zunz
2. A Century of Wissenschaft des Judentums (excerpts)   *26*
Ismar Elbogen

Clarifying Fundamentals
3. Does Traditional Judaism Possess Dogmas?   *41*
Leo Baeck
4. Establishing Norms for Jewish Belief   *54*
Julius Guttmann
5. Jewish Piety and Religious Dogma   *70*
Max Wiener

Religious Truth and Philosophical Quest: Medieval Syntheses
6. The Purpose of Human Existence as Seen by
Greek-Roman Antiquity and the Jewish Middle Ages   *115*
Isaak Heinemann

7. The Concept of Kavvanah in the Early Kabbalah *162*
Gershom G. Scholem

8. Judah Halevi and al-Ghazali *181*
David Hartwig (Zvi) Baneth

9. Maimonides's Attitude toward Jewish Mysticism *200*
Alexander Altmann

10. Maimonides's *Guide* in World Literature *220*
David Kaufmann

11. Scientific Allegorization during the Jewish Middle Ages *247*
Isaak Heinemann

12. Leone Ebreo, Renaissance Philosopher *270*
Hiram Peri

13. Religion and Science in Medieval and Modern Thought *281*
Julius Guttmann

Revelation and Reason: The Challenge of Modernity

14. Mendelssohn's Concept of Judaism *343*
Fritz Bamberger

15. Mendelssohn's *Jerusalem* and Spinoza's
Theologico-Political Treatise *361*
Julius Guttmann

16. Moses Mendelssohn on Education and the Image of Man *387*
Alexander Altmann

17. Moses Mendelssohn and the Religious Forms of Judaism
in the Nineteenth Century *404*
Max Wiener

Contributors *417*
Index *425*

EDITOR'S NOTE

The spellings and transliterations of names, places, and titles of books follow the patterns used in the *Encyclopaedia Judaica,* except when authors preferred a different usage.

The documentation accompanying the essays presented particular editorial problems. Several essays were written without notes; in some other cases, the notes have not been included in this volume because of the difficulties connected with reproducing their foreign-language quotations (especially those in Greek and Arabic). However, the notes for Isaak Heinemann's essay, "The Purpose of Human Existence as Seen by Greek-Roman Antiquity and the Jewish Middle Ages," may be consulted either in the German original or in an English translation available in manuscript at the Leo Baeck Institute, New York City. For notes and sources of David Baneth's "Judah Halevi and al-Ghazali," the reader may consult the Hebrew translation in *Keneset,* vol. 7 (Jerusalem: Mossad Bialik, 1941–42). In order to make the notes to the remaining essays useful, the original diversity of forms has been silently emended and regularized, as far as was reasonable and possible, to conform to the publisher's usual house style. Where essays are presented in a slightly abridged form, the notes have been renumbered accordingly; those few notes which also carry letter designations reflect the author's own later additions to his original notes.

INTRODUCTION

Alfred Jospe

he beginnings of systematic Jewish studies ante-
date the emergence of the movement known as *Wissenschaft des Judentums* ("The Scientific Study of Judaism") in nineteenth-century western
Europe. The scholarly investigation of various aspects of the literature,
history, and language of the Jewish people has a long history among Jews
and non-Jews. But it was in western Europe and primarily in the orbit of
German-speaking Jewry that the Jewish tradition was first exposed to the
full impact of the intellectual, social, and political forces of modernity and
faced their challenge to the religious foundations and structure of Jewish
life. The Wissenschaft des Judentums is a direct product of this encounter
with modernity and one of the initial and most far-reaching responses to
it. Its beginning is marked by the publication of Leopold Zunz's "On
Rabbinic Literature" ("Etwas über die rabbinische Literatur") in May,
1818, although the term itself appears for the first time in 1822 in the title
of the *Zeitschrift für die Wissenschaft des Judentums,* which Zunz edited.

The present volume offers a representative selection from the contributions of the Wissenschaft des Judentums to the field of Jewish philosophical and religious thought, all of which were originally published in
German periodicals. While it is not the first collection of such essays—
Kurt Wilhelm's two-volume anthology, *Wissenschaft des Judentums im
deutschen Sprachbereich* (Tübingen, 1967), published under the auspices
of the Leo Baeck Institute, is a pioneer effort in the field—the selections
in this volume are presented for the first time in English translation.[1] The
wealth of material that might have been included made a high degree of
selectivity inevitable. Primary consideration was given to sources which

9

have retained their importance for the study of significant trends and issues of scholarly interest. Some of the essays may no longer be the last word in research with regard to a particular issue or thinker, but they were the first word, and they remain valuable for the ways in which they outlined the issues, assembled the data, analyzed trends, and opened or charted the path to further research. Others, replacing views long cherished, presented new approaches and vistas and continue to offer challenges to present-day scholarship. Material that is badly dated or very specialized has been excluded, nor has material been included solely because it might serve as a memorial to the past, as an evocation of the past for its own sake. Nevertheless, I am painfully aware that much that should have been included had to be omitted because of limited space.

The Wissenschaft des Judentums itself has been the subject of extensive research probing the factors contributing to its origin, the tasks it set out to serve, its scope and limitations, and the multiplicity of motivations that nourished its growth—all reflecting a still-continuing quest for definition and conceptual clarity.[2] A number of key articles have already become available for the English-speaking reader.[3] Two classic statements on the Wissenschaft des Judentums have, however, not been translated until now: Zunz's pivotal "On Rabbinic Literature," which, though unfortunately written in a somewhat tortured style and in a language that was still groping for the right word and clarity of conceptualization, broke new ground; and Ismar Elbogen's reassessment, "A Century of Wissenschaft des Judentums" ("Ein Jahrhundert Wissenschaft des Judentums"), first published more than one hundred years later. They are presented here as prefatory selections in order to complement the existing resources on the Wissenschaft des Judentums and to enable two of its most representative expositors themselves to speak about its origin, development, scope, and meaning.

The three essays in the section called "Clarifying Fundamentals" address questions of fundamental importance to Judaism: whether norms for Jewish belief exist and, if they do, from what source they derive their authority. Traditionally, Jewish beliefs "found expression primarily in the form of prayer and the recital of the *Shema*."[4] However, from Philo and especially from the early Middle Ages on, numerous attempts were made to meet the challenge of unbelief, heretical views, and, in particular, Greek philosophy, by the formulation of articles of faith that would define the character of Judaism and offer guidance on what constitutes the essence of Judaism. The debate over whether Judaism possesses "dogmas," a set of authoritatively formulated binding beliefs, became especially pronounced in the past two hundred years as a result of Judaism's entry into the general society and the immediacy and impact of its encounter with the religions of the West. The problem has remained one of the key issues in the quest for conceptual clarity about the character of the Jewish religion.

Leo Baeck's essay illustrates his basic approach to Jewish life, which involves what may be called a distrust of final formulations and a conviction that the place occupied elsewhere by dogmatics is, in Judaism, taken by Aggadah and, later, by religious philosophy. In subtle disagreement with Baeck's view, Julius Guttmann argues that the formulations of Jewish belief are established not through norms set by some ecclesiastical authority (in this respect he agrees with Baeck), but by tradition, by the community's belief which emerges as something final and definite that every member of the community is expected to affirm. Max Wiener, the first liberal theologian to reaffirm and restore the particularistic dimension of Jewish thought and experience on theological grounds, in analyzing the relationship between personal piety and religious dogma, maintains that an indispensable element of Jewish piety has always been a concern for the preservation of the Jewish people, and that the source of Jewish belief and norms is not metaphysics but history. These essays initiated a discussion in the *Monatsschrift für Geschichte und Wissenschaft des Judentums,* in which Isidor Scheftelowitz of Cologne and Felix Goldmann of Leipzig also participated, that is remarkable for the penetrating depths to which these questions were examined.[5]

Isaak Heinemann, in analyzing the encounter of Greek and Jewish culture in late antiquity and the early Middle Ages in the light of their views of the purpose of human life, provides the transition to medieval Jewish philosophy, the area to which Jewish scholars in Germany made their single most important contribution, both as historians and as systematizers. The topics in this section range from the encounter of Judaism with Hellenism to Jewish mysticism and Judaism's representative responses to the Kalām, Neoplatonism, Aristotelianism, and Renaissance thought. Heinemann's study illustrates his general approach, which, in opposition to that of earlier scholars, insists that Jewish philosophical and ethical thought must not be seen as "autarkic," as isolated from broad philosophical trends and unaffected by them, but rather as reflecting the cross-fertilization of Jewish and other cultures (in Heinemann's own essay, Greek culture).

Gershom Scholem, in a characteristic example of his multifaceted explorations of the concepts and symbols of the Kabbalah, analyzes one of the documents that are indispensable for an evaluation of its mystical character and shows that the Jewish form of the *unio mystica,* the basic act of mysticism, makes its appearance in the conception of the kavvanah of prayer. The primary focus of Jewish philosophical thought during the Middle Ages, however, was not mysticism but the tension between religious truth and philosophical truth and the relationship between the two.

Their identity was denied by Judah Halevi, who, as David Baneth points out, made revelation autonomous, maintaining that religious life constitutes a world that is wholly sui generis; he thus posited a sharp distinction between the philosopher who seeks the God of Aristotle with his intellect and the believer who senses and perceives the God of Abraham out of his deepest yearning. Alexander Altmann deepens the analysis of the tension between Jewish rationalism and mysticism by establishing, in "Maimonides's Attitude toward Jewish Mysticism," that philosophy and Jewish mysticism are based on fundamentally different existential attitudes, and that Maimonides, though speculative mysticism was not alien to him, represents "the antipole of Jewish mysticism." Maimonides's attempt to harmonize Judaism and Aristotelian philosophy, though the cause of bitter controversies for a century after his death, not only became a centerpiece of Jewish philosophical thought, but also exerted a far-reaching influence on non-Jews, including St. Thomas Aquinas, as is shown in David Kaufmann's survey.

In addressing himself to allegorization, another mode of Jewish literary and spiritual expression, Isaak Heinemann submits that in it religious motives acted in unison with scientific motives, and that a study of medieval Jewish allegorization is a valuable contribution both to the history of biblical exegesis and to clarification of the transformation which occured in Jewish group sentiment under the influence of Greek scientific teaching. Hiram Peri, illuminating still another facet of Jewish thought, explores the intellectual world of Leone Ebreo, whose philosophy occupies a singular position on the borderline between Jewish thought and Neoplatonic mysticism. In the concluding essay in the section, Julius Guttmann offers a survey of the attempts by representative thinkers from the Middle Ages to Kant to resolve the tension between religious and theoretical knowledge, and he finds that religious truth is not that of objective knowledge, but personal certitude, which is nevertheless trustworthy and relates man to a world of truth which represents an autonomous realm of objectivity.

The studies in the third section, then, their thematic diversity and methodological differences notwithstanding, reveal a unifying trend. They show not only the openness of Jewish thought to external stimulation and influences, but also the resilience and creativity with which it sought to preserve its distinctiveness through the selection, reinterpretation, or transformation of adopted ideas and their absorption into a new creative synthesis. The influence of Maimonides, the towering medieval Jewish philosopher and codifier, permeates most of the essays explicitly and extensively.

As Judaism entered the intellectual world of modern Europe, it necessarily encountered the contemporary trends of European philosophy and culture. Moses Mendelssohn, standing at the threshold of Jewish modernity, exemplified in his own life and thought the forces and tensions confronting the Jew in his transition from his medieval state to modernity—the tensions between personal piety and historically formed norms, between his stance as *homo religiosus* and his modern rationalism, between the particularistic and the universalistic dimensions of his tradition, between his effort to achieve full integration into western culture and to avoid surrendering the religious content and forms of Judaism. The issues engaging Mendelssohn's attention have remained the key issues confronting the contemporary Jew, and the essays in the fourth section examine Mendelssohn's concept of Judaism, his concepts of man and of *Bildung,* his philosophical and Jewish position in *Jerusalem* as compared with Spinoza's in the *Theologico-Political Treatise,* and his influence on the development of the forms of Jewish religious life and thought in the nineteenth century.

The present volume draws its selections only from one area of concern to the Wissenschaft des Judentums. For this reason the editor and the Board of the Leo Baeck Institute hope it will be followed by a series of similar anthologies presenting, in translation, representative essays in Jewish history, biblical studies, rabbinics, liturgy, Hebrew language and literature, and other areas.

The preparation of this volume has benefited greatly from the assistance of a number of individuals. I want to record my deep gratitude to the Board of the Leo Baeck Institute for its sponsorship of this project, and above all to its president, Dr. Max Gruenewald (who suggested this project to me), and its vice-president, Dr. Fritz Bamberger, for their ever-ready counsel and the constancy of their encouragement in connection with every aspect of the work. I am equally indebted to Dr. Alexander Altmann (Newton Centre, Massachusetts) and Dr. Nahum N. Glatzer (Watertown, Massachusetts) for their counsel in the selection of material and their patient responsiveness to my many questions. I also wish to acknowledge, with warm appreciation, helpful suggestions received from Dr. Hans Liebeschuetz (Liverpool, England; now deceased); Dr. Michael Meyer (Cincinnati, Ohio); Dr. Jakob Petuchowski (Cincinnati, Ohio); Dr. Jehuda Reinharz (Ann Arbor, Michigan); Dr. Hanns G. Reissner (Princeton, New Jersey; now deceased); Dr. Lou H. Silberman (Nashville, Tennessee); Dr. Ernst Simon (Jerusalem, Israel); and Dr. Hans Tramer (Tel Aviv, Israel; now deceased). Rabbi Theodore Wiener (Washington, D.C.) rendered valuable assistance by drafting a partial translation of one of his father's essays; Dr. Stanley Weber (Hamilton, Ontario, Canada) translated material which we hope to use in a later volume. Dr. Fred Grubel (Leo Baeck Institute) was thoroughly helpful in numerous technical details. I also wish to thank Dr. Leon Weinberger (University of Alabama) for his efforts on behalf of this manuscript and his valuable editorial advice. Finally, I want to record my gratitude to Mr. Myron Weinstein (Hebraic Section, Library of Congress) for his ever-ready kindness in tracing and verifying sources, and to Dr. Sherwyn T. Carr (Wayne State University Press) for her patient and painstaking efforts in seeing the manuscript through to print.

In an article in the *Allgemeine Zeitung des Judentums*, David Kaufmann wrote: "Can the demand be deemed unreasonable that, when the best names [of the intellectual and scholarly world] are mentioned, the Jews and their spirit will not be forgotten?"[6] Kaufmann expressed a concern shared by many of the early spokesmen of the Wissenschaft des Judentums, who labored in the hope that the Jewish contribution to history and literature would remain alive and gain proper recognition as a valuable strand in the texture of human civilization and of man's effort to understand himself and the world. In the same way, we hope this project will continue to keep alive and fruitful the efforts of generations of German-speaking scholars to deepen the understanding and demonstrate the vitality of the Jewish intellectual heritage for their own time and for generations to come. Their efforts have produced a wealth of new knowledge on which Jewish scholarship continues to build. No history of the Jewish intellectual effort can ignore the products of this Wissenschaft which, in the words of Salman Rubaschoff (later known as Zalman Shazar), writing in *Der jüdische Wille* in 1918, "is the most important gift which German Judaism has made to the whole of Jewry."[7]

Notes

1. Excerpts from Zunz's "Etwas über die rabbinische Literatur" have been published in English translation in Paul R. Mendes-Flohr and Jehuda Reinharz, eds., *The Jew in the Modern World: A Documentary History* (New York and Oxford: Oxford University Press, 1980), pp. 196–204; these excerpts, however, are partly drawn from different portions of the essay than those included in this volume.
2. A nearly complete bibliography of the primary and secondary sources on the origin and development of the Wissenschaft des Judentums is contained in Michael A. Meyer, *The Origins of the Modern Jew* (Detroit, Mich.: Wayne State University Press, 1967), pp. 240–43. Additional studies include Alexander Altmann, *Jewish Studies: Their Scope and Meaning Today* (London: Hillel Foundation, 1958); Salo W. Baron, *History and Jewish Historians* (Philadelphia, Pa.: Jewish Publication Society, 1964), pp. 47–58; Ismar Elbogen, "Die Neuorientierung unserer Wissenschaft," *Monatsschrift für Geschichte und Wissenschaft des Judentums* [hereafter *MGWJ*] 62 (1918):81–96; Nahum N. Glatzer, "The Beginnings of Modern Jewish Studies," in Alexander Altmann, ed., *Studies in Nineteenth-Century Jewish Intellectual History* (Cambridge, Mass.: Harvard University Press, 1964), pp. 27–45; Robert Gordis, *Jewish Learning and Jewish Existence—Retrospect and Prospect,* Leo Baeck Memorial Lecture 6 (New York: Leo Baeck Institute, 1963); S. Maybaum, "Zur Wissenschaft des Judentums," *MGWJ* 51 (1907): 641–58; Meyer, *Origins of the Modern Jew,* pp. 144–82; Gershom G. Scholem, *Devarim*

be-Go (Tel Aviv, 1975), pp. 59–63, 385–403; Solomon Schechter, *Seminary Addresses and Other Papers* (New York: Burning Bush Press, 1959), pp. 173–94; Lou H. Silberman, "The University and Jewish Studies," in Leon A. Jick, ed., *The Teaching of Judaism in American Universities* (New York: Ktav Publishing House, 1970), pp. 9–16; Ernst Simon, *Brücken* (Heidelberg: Verlag Lambert Schneider, 1965), pp. 47–58; Luitpold Wallach, "The Beginnings of the Science of Judaism in the Nineteenth Century," *Historica Judaica* 8 (1946):33–60; Kurt Wilhelm, ed., *Wissenschaft des Judentums im deutschen Sprachbereich*, 2 vols. (Tübingen: J. C. B. Mohr, 1967), 1:1–58.

3. Immanuel Wolf, "On the Concept of a Science of Judaism," *Yearbook of the Leo Baeck Institute* 2 (1957):194–204; Leopold Zunz, "Scholarship and Emancipation," in Nahum N. Glatzer, ed., *The Dynamics of Emancipation* (Boston, Mass.: Beacon Press, 1965), pp. 10–14; reprinted in Nahum N. Glatzer, ed., *Modern Jewish Thought: A Source Reader* (New York: Schocken Books, 1977), pp. 12–15; Abraham Geiger, "A General Introduction to the Science of Judaism," in Max Wiener, *Abraham Geiger and Liberal Judaism* (Philadelphia, Pa.: Jewish Publication Society, 1962), pp. 149–70; reprinted partially in Robert Chazan and Marc Lee Raphael, eds., *Modern Jewish History: A Source Reader* (New York: Schocken Books, 1974), pp. 62–77; and Gershom G. Scholem, *The Messianic Idea and Other Essays on Jewish Spirituality* (New York: Schocken Books, 1971), pp. 304–13.

4. Alexander Altmann, "Articles of Faith," *Encyclopaedia Judaica*, 1:654.

5. Wilhelm, *Wissenschaft des Judentums*, 1:51.

6. Vol. 55 (1891), pp. 161–62.

7. Quoted in Wilhelm, *Wissenschaft des Judentums*, 1:58.

WISSENSCHAFT
DES JUDENTUMS:
TWO PREFATORY
STATEMENTS

1
ON RABBINIC LITERATURE
(excerpts)

Leopold Zunz

part from all interest engendered by their age and content, the awe-inspiring [literary] remnants of the period when the ancient Hebrew culture was flourishing owe their true significance to chance: as a result of the revolutions [for example, Christianity] which had their origin in the [ancient] Jewish nation and which had no less an impact upon the Jewish people than upon the rest of the world, those remnants were designated as the "Hebrew canon" and established, as it were, the foundation of the Christian states. Later it was the steadily advancing progress of the sciences which did its part: based on these few [biblical] books, there developed an intellectual productivity whose scope is more admirable than that of the Greeks, inasmuch as it created its riches out of far scantier material.

The later products of the Hebrew nation, however, never gained this kind of recognition. Having declined politically as well as intellectually, for a long time the [Jewish] people seemed to have lost its productivity and was satisfied to engage in a sometimes more, sometimes less successful exegesis of the sparse writings of that earlier, better period. When the shadows of barbarism gradually receded from the darkened earth and light also began to shine upon its widely dispersed Jews, a new, alien culture [*Bildung*] was grafted upon the remnants of the ancient Hebrew one, and intellectual efforts as well as the passage of the centuries transformed both into the type of literature we call "rabbinic."[1]

Starting with the Reformation and as a direct consequence of the flowering of classical studies, there began a spirited study of the biblical books, combined with, we might say, an eager curiosity about the Orient. Hence men pursued the study of rabbinic wisdom for an entire century with great passion—which, however, ceased suddenly and perhaps forever as the intellectual products of their own country, richer and more congenial, began to capture their minds and stimulate their emotions. Indeed, rabbinic literature declined to the same degree to which European literature flourished and Jews began to be active in it. Even those writings of the past fifty years which can still be classified as rabbinic literature have merely borrowed the latter's language as an easily available garb of erudition for [new] ideas, a fact that ought to prepare [us] for a time when rabbinic literature will have ceased [completely] to exist.

But precisely because we see that the Jews of our time—to speak of German Jews only—are ever more widely using the German language and reaching out for German culture, thus carrying postbiblical [neuhebräische] literature to its grave (often perhaps without wanting or suspecting it), scholarship demands [of us] an accounting of an era that has come to a close. Now, when no new publication of importance is likely to block our perspective; when we have at our disposal larger subsidies than those available to scholars of the sixteenth and seventeenth centuries; when a higher cultural niveau leads us to expect a more enlightened treatment; and when Hebrew books are not yet as hard to obtain as they might be in the year 1919—now, we believe, it is our duty to engage in a comprehensive study of that era. This duty is even more weighty because it seems quite possible that a few passages [of those ancient writings] may provide us with an answer to the complicated question about the fate of the Jews. In order to arrive at balanced results, it is not enough to consider merely political and religious factors and the influence they exerted from without. One must also know the nature of the instrument [needed for research], and one must have learned how to use it.

To know any theories, be they juridical, theological, or economic, about today's Jews is to know the Jews at best partially. Only the ideas set forth [in the classical sources] as well as a knowledge of that era's mores and intent [Willen] can introduce us into the spirit [of Judaism]. Every reckless so-called improvement is being avenged by distorted results; hasty innovations serve only to assign a higher value to the old and, worst of all, to the antiquated. In order, therefore, to know and to discriminate between the old that is useful, the antiquated that is harmful, and the new that is desirable, we have to make every deliberate effort to study the people and its political and moral history. What until now has proved most disadvantageous is the fact that the case of the Jews has been treated like their literature: both have been attacked with a biased fervor, and both are valued either too highly or too little.

It is not in order to unravel a twisted knot on which more skillful fingers may go to work that we have digressed from our people's literature to its civic existence. Having in a few strokes outlined their impact upon each other, we now return to [our] literature, seeking elucidation about its origin and substance, its relations to its older as well as to its contemporary sisters [in the literary family], its present condition [*Vorrath*], and its particular character. In this quest we may here or there happen upon some smaller lamps, but they do not always contain sufficient or good oil, and our eye seeks in vain the light of the sun.

How does it happen, one may well ask, that at a time when magnificent, all-encompassing vistas have opened up, allowing all sciences and man's every endeavor to be illumined by brilliant rays of light; when one travels to the remotest corners of the world, studies the most esoteric languages, and neglects no material that might be useful in building up our store of wisdom—how does it happen that our scholarship alone must languish? What is it that keeps us from acquiring a thorough knowledge of rabbinic literature, from understanding it properly, explicating it felicitously, evaluating it correctly, surveying it with ease?[2]

Since only diversified, numerous, and good preliminary studies will enable us to reach a high [scholarly] plateau, the question reverts once again to the lack of such studies. Hence in our response, we must explore what we actually mean by "preliminary studies," and we must prove that there truly is a dearth of them. After we have attempted to explain this phenomenon, it will finally become evident that with this demonstrated lack of preparatory works we can never gain full clarity about the subject matter under consideration, let alone produce perfect results.

By "preliminary studies" we mean those literary works which either cover an entire field of scholarly research merely to a certain extent [*theilweisse*] or else deal with one of its segments in depth. In the latter group, each detail is properly investigated; each problem of scholarship is at least clearly outlined for possible solution by some future scholar; each noteworthy discovery is used to advance our knowledge; and even the most difficult passage is elucidated by critical analysis. The so-called *editiones principes*—insofar as they represent more than mere reproductions of manuscripts—as well as good translations, reliable manuals, biographies, and similar items can rightfully claim to be called "preliminary studies."

But we think we must give a higher rating to those works which cover an entire field of scholarly research, enriching it by their significant findings or transforming it by their new insights—works which deal with the literature of entire centuries if not millenia, leaving imprints of their giant strides wide enough to be followed by a hundred others. To this group belong, for instance, expositions of philosophical systems, histories

of individual doctrines, [the study of literary] parallels, specialized libraries, and so on.

Nevertheless, commendable and useful as all these efforts may be,
they will, in their preoccupation with detail, never be equal to the higher
task, much like the workman who does not see the enormous porphyry
mountain for the pebble he has picked up and polished, and who, resting
after having finished his work, self-satisfiedly tootles his own horn about
the beautification of nature which his hands have wrought. But the man
who regards a people's literature as the entrance gate to an understanding
of that people's cultural development throughout the ages—noting how,
moment by moment, its character is being molded both by its natural
endowment and by influences from without (that is, by external and
internal forces); how fate, climate, customs, religion, and chance interact
in a friendly or hostile manner; and how, finally, the present emerges as
the necessary result of all those phenomena interacting in the past—such
a man stands truly in awe before this temple of the gods, modestly waiting to be taken into its forecourt and hoping to enjoy the majestic view
from the height of its dome, once he will have become worthy of it.

This height, however, will be reached only by him who takes the
trouble of climbing, though even he can render an adequate account of
the whole only after he has looked at all of its parts with the eye of the
initiate. This kind of perspective will enable him to realize that our scholarly efforts have to deal with many areas, each of which must be cultivated lest the whole be distorted due to fundamental errors. If, then, we
take a closer look at our vast subject matter in order to explore and
organize it in accordance with the principles of literary criticism, we see
that these principles assist us in our work in three ways. We acquire the
competence to recognize and evaluate the given thought, the mode of its
communication, and the type and nature of our knowledge of it. On this
basis, we develop a tripartite theory of criticism: the *doctrinal,* dealing
with ideas; the *grammatical,* dealing with language; and the *historical,*
dealing with the history of these ideas from the time they were committed
to writing to the day that brought them to our attention. . . .

The indifference with regard to rabbinic literature is of a dual nature. Either one is not interested in scholarship as such (and nothing can
be done about that) or one's lack of interest concerns rabbinic studies
alone, possibly on the assumption that they are useless, or not worthwhile, or liable to spoil one's [literary] taste. Or it is assumed that one
cannot get far with them, that they are godless,[3] or even that they will
nowhere be well received. Such neutral indifference usually degenerates
into contempt, and it is by no means an uncommon phenomenon that
scholars are completely opposed to these studies.

. . . But more reprehensible than this indifference, more outrageous than this contempt, is the prejudice with which this subject has frequently been approached—a prejudice grounded not in love but in hatred. Anything that could be regarded as testimony against Jews and Judaism, even on the flimsiest evidence, was considered a welcome find.[4] Scholars would pick out some half-understood passages from this or that source so as to expose their age-old opponents to public scorn. And until about one hundred years ago, one could not find a single case of a learned doctor who might have culled from the writings of the Hebrews the beautiful and good they contain in order to present the Jews in a positive light.[5] . . .

The fanatic negativism that existed on the outside could also be found within [the ranks of Judaism], and carelessness, stemming from familiarity with the material, led not infrequently to the destruction of some of the most significant works and robbed otherwise sober minds of the ability to judge the material under consideration without bias.[6] Even where there was goodwill, classical education [hence evaluative competence] frequently was lacking. Vice versa, many scholars sinned because of their inability to enter into the Hebrew spirit and to develop a sense of empathy with the author.[7]

The fact that many Jews in our day are lost to the study of rabbinic literature is, however, due to plain ignorance, the consequence of ever-decreasing instruction in the Hebrew language. This decrease results in part from the realization that Hebrew studies offer poor career opportunities, in part from easier access to other kinds of study, and in part from a most praiseworthy turn to the arts and crafts, agriculture, and military service. But it is due also to a coldness toward religion in general and to one's ancestral literature in particular; to the irrational fear that occupation with that literature might be considered disgraceful; and to a good-natured lack of thoroughness, about which we shall have to say more later.

An additional reason, however, is that the material itself presents difficulties which drive even an expert Hebraist to more congenial occupations—difficulties such as, for instance, the scant availability of codices; the rather limited hope for professional advancement and for earning one's daily bread; problems connected with the Jewish book trade; the example of one's surroundings; and the need for additional studies, since competence in Hebrew alone is seldom sufficient. On the other hand, people also have the not uncommon illusion that a few glances into German writings suffice to make one a scholar. This, together with today's compulsion to write, produces the kind of men who remain standing at a halfway point, hesitant to pursue their studies with any zeal, or who, being ill-prepared, present us with Hebrew writings which are merely damaging to real scholarship and burden us with useless material. The one is sinning against interpretation, criticism, and, worst of all, against methodology;[8] the other deals with his topic only superficially and not with the respect it deserves. In fact, he shows as little respect for scholarship and his readers as he does for a work's integrity and completeness. A third "scholar" makes it still easier for himself by starting his work as if he already had the data he ought to be looking for, so that he can then delightedly announce that he found them;[9] a fourth such shuns even the effort to try his hand at this work, because his predecessors failed to provide him with preliminary studies. Thus one of the statements in the Pirke Avot is once again confirmed: "One transgression leads to another."

Given all these factors, it seems self-evident why we do not yet possess, nor soon will possess, an adequate Hebrew literature, for even equipped with all the talent, knowledge, and resources that are required, we always produce new ideas and subject matter in the treatment of ideas. Bibliography, critical analysis of the way the material is handled, and history are produced not merely by scholarship but also by history itself. And just as we incorporate into the world of scholarship "objective" material that was originally the subjective treatment of an earlier idea, so our own mastery of the world of scholarship will produce for us and posterity new material to be reworked in turn. . . .

Notes

"On Rabbinic Literature," translated by Alfred and Eva Jospe, first appeared as "Etwas über die rabbinische Literatur" (Berlin: Maurer, 1818); reprinted in *Gesammelte Schriften von Dr. Zunz* (Berlin: Louis Gerschel, 1875), pp. 3–31. The notes have been renumbered; the original numbers and pages are given in brackets.

1. [3n1] One ought to use this designation only for writings whose authors or content are rabbinic. In the final analysis, the title "rabbi," which politeness bestows upon everyone, means less than the title "doctor" [Ph.D.]. Why not "postbiblical" or "Jewish" literature?

2. [5n1] We are not afraid of being misunderstood. Here the entire literature of the Jews is established in its totality as an object of scholarly inquiry, and we are not concerned with the question whether its total content also can or should be a norm for our own judgments.

3. [23n1] Similar objections have already been raised against Hebrew literature in general. Cf. Hirt's *Orientalische Bibliothek,* 2:358ff., where de Rossi defends it against old Forster (died 1556). In the same work (1:221), a reviewer complained (in 1772) about the steadily decreasing number of professors who knew rabbinics.

4. [24n1] The index to Schickard's *Ius Regium,* edited by Carpzevious, contains the following item: "Chronologia Judaeis Odiosa—477." However, the text merely mentions the Messiah calculation. Claude Chappelain published a *Mare Rabbinicum Infidum* (Paris, 1667) about the different interpretations and divergent citations.

5. [24n2] Even Fr. Becker evaded it. What he described as noble patriotism and valor in the case of the Samnites [Sabines], Spartans, Carthaginians, Peruvians, and Germans became wretched obstinacy and despair in relation to the Jews.

6. [24–25n4] Thus years ago a foolish rabbi had the single extant manuscript of Luzzatto's Psalms burned out of zeal for the Davidic Psalms. Converted Jews frequently

sought to endear themselves through fanatic persecutions; read, for example, the publication by Friedrich Brentzin (formerly Samuel) with the horrible title *Jewish Cast-off Snake Skin* (Oettingen, 1814). Where are Manasseh ben Israel's *Tractatus de Scientia Talmudistarum* and *Defensio Talmudis?* Where are Sabbato Ambron's *Pancosmosophia* and the rabbinic library he had started? What about Aristobulus, whose works, says D. de Rossi, are in Florence and the Benedictine monastery in Mantua but never became accessible to him? . . .

7. [25n1] In order to see things correctly, it is necessary to be completely at home in the language. One can hardly have confidence in a scholar who may be great in theoretical matters if he does not establish his competence: for example, when Montfaucon (*Diar. Ital.*, p. 408) says, "de Esau liber Rabbinicus cujus exordium ani hatzair—ego Seir." Mendelssohn, too, is wrongly judged in Hirt's *Orientalische Bibliothek*, 1:71–72.

8. [26n1] Even better scholars are not free from such sins. Otherwise, how could Carpzov have included the Maharil's entire Jewish letter of divorce in his *Ius Regium?* . . .

9. [26n2] All ancient Hebrew writings can be used to produce more and weightier testimonials for rather than against the claim that women enjoy a position of respect among the Jews. One can, of course, also find nonsensical statements. What matters, however, it what has found general approval and has established itself as corresponding to the weight of the total body of tradition.

2
A CENTURY OF WISSENSCHAFT
DES JUDENTUMS

(excerpts)

Ismar Elbogen

he term "Wissenschaft des Judentums" has been in use for about a century. As far as can be determined, it was employed for the first time in 1822 in the title of the *Zeitschrift für die Wissenschaft des Judentums,* edited by Leopold Zunz.[1] . . .

Zunz had chosen the name carefully. It was meant to designate a new cause. In this way he characterized the contrast to Jewish learning as earlier practiced. At no time did Judaism lack scholars or erudition, but it has been estranged from science for several centuries. Since the battle over the writings of Maimonides and the admissibility of the study of philosophy in the thirteenth to fourteenth centuries, science had visibly lost ground. Everything which transforms knowledge into science had vanished from Jewish learning. Jewish knowledge was one-sided; it limited itself almost exclusively to talmudic literature and cultivated even this field . . . only within a narrow sector. The Wissenschaft des Judentums wanted to proceed systematically, to encompass the totality of the expressions of Jewish life and to present the full scope of its intellectual creativity. The old Jewish learning was Judeocentric, contemplating all things Jewish as self-sufficient and divorced from the rest of the world; the Wissenschaft des Judentums rejected this one-sidedness, recognized the interrelationship of all intellectual forces, and attempted to explore and explain the connections between Jewish and non-Jewish phenomena and their mutual interplay through adaptation and rejection. The old Jewish learning was tied dogmatically to belief in an inviolable tradition and the authority of its representatives; the Wissenschaft des Judentums considered itself independent, wanting to subject its material to free and unbiased critical analysis and not to accept any result merely on faith and trust, without having investigated its origin and premises and the methods of its transmission. The old Jewish learning proceeded in accordance with the dialectic method and remained unworldly; the Wissenschaft des Judentums wanted to be realistic and demanded concreteness and a sense of actuality. It was not satisfied with the accumulation of knowledge, but also demanded its classification, linkage, and evaluation, as well as its validation through the use of concepts commonly accepted in scholarly discourse. The old Jewish scholarship was a pious vocation, a part of Jewish religiosity; the Wissenschaft des Judentums did not recognize any purpose outside itself and did not want to be anything but a contribution to the knowledge of the development of the human spirit, a branch of science in general. It is the immortal merit of Leopold Zunz to have liberated the study of Judaism from its unworldly one-sidedness and dogmatic confinement, and to have raised it to the rank of a scholarly discipline, thus subsuming it under the sciences as a whole.[2]

The line of demarcation cannot be drawn sharply enough, nor can it be emphasized sufficiently, that the Wissenschaft des Judentums was a new creation, representing a break with the old learning and demanding a fundamentally different method. We must not let ourselves be deflected from this realization by a slanted attitude which is widespread today. We live in an age of mass adoration. Wherever masses of Jews are crowded together, Jewish learning and Torah study in the old style have maintained themselves. As much as that strong intellectual activity in the midst of the worst social misery and under the most severe political pressure deserves our highest admiration, as little is the erroneous romantic notion justified that that kind of scholarship alone bears genuine Jewish character and that the Wissenschaft des Judentums constitutes a deviation. Popular opinion can never constitute the yardstick for science; the concern of the masses, as a rule, is dogmatic bias rather than critical thought. Even though the Jewish spirit is never quite at ease with blind obedience to the words of a master, a total subordination to given authorities, and though, therefore, criticism had never died out completely in the Jewish academy, it nevertheless remained entangled in details. It was not practiced in terms of general principles, and it lacked a grounding in broad scientific training, or else it was placed on the index. [The argument] that the attitude of strictly orthodox circles toward general education has changed is not decisive. Isolation from alien knowledge had already become less rigid during the Enlightenment, and in the course of the past 120 years the invader has gained some ground—but the new insights are only tacitly tolerated, and the old hostility against all exoteric education has not been abandoned in principle. A compromise under the slogan "Torah and Wissenschaft"[3] would do damage to both components: the issue is not that a science is added from the outside to the study of Torah, resulting in an aggregate, but that the study of Torah is permeated by the spirit of critical scholarship. The union between Jewish learning and science can prosper only when it is legitimate, not when it is merely morganatic. The question of which practical consequences result from this union (whether, for example, it helps to refute attacks from scientific circles) is no longer a problem of Wissenschaft; its only concern is knowledge; it does not have to ask what the consequences of knowledge for life may be. Orthodoxy and Wissenschaft are mutually exclusive, even though once in a while orthodox scholars have made valuable individual contributions to Wissenschaft.

To be sure, the Torah study of the East European academies has not remained completely unchanged either. The revolutions in Jewish intellectual life during the past century could not pass by the yeshivot of the East without a trace. They may have been able to lock out the spirit, but not the creative products of the new Wissenschaft. The immense enrichment of Jewish literature, the increase of interpretative studies, had to make their influence felt, had to produce a widening of the horizon and an expansion of the material of learning, and ultimately it even had to overcome the old method. The effect of the new era also makes itself felt in that the young students of the old Talmud schools, when they awaken to independent thinking—if they do not become completely alienated from this cultural background—take refuge in the Wissenschaft des Judentums, and in this way many a new thought gains entry into the old system.

During the past decades, modern Hebrew literature has frequently communicated the thinking of the new age to those who were educated in the old tradition. The poets and storytellers writing in modern Hebrew have proven themselves as pioneers of the modern spirit and simultaneously brought knowledge of the results of the Wissenschaft des Judentums to the masses, but the rapid progress of the revival of the Hebrew language created a new stylistic problem. In contrast to traditional Jewish learning, which employed the Hebrew language almost exclusively, the Wissenschaft des Judentums preponderantly used the vernacular for its publications, following the example of the Jews in the orbit of Arab culture. This facilitated the task of making the products of the Wissenschaft des Judentums accessible to all scholarly circles, but it made communication between the Jews of various countries more difficult. As long as the use of the German language was predominant, a widespread acquaintance of Jews with the Wissenschaft des Judentums could be expected. But when due to the cultural progress and the migrations of the Jews new languages began to be used, the apprehension was justified that the products of the modern Wissenschaft des Judentums would share the fate of their predecessors in the Arabic language and sink into oblivion. More recently, the spread of Hebrew has made such progress that it may once again be considered the common language of the Jews. Its use, therefore, becomes a vital question for the Wissenschaft des Judentums. Only in this way can it find the response which a science needs for its continuous development and which it has lacked until now. Only in this way will it be able to preserve its connection with living Judaism. To be sure, it must not loosen its relationship with general science and abandon the use of European languages. It must rather—something not without analogy—prepare itself for bilingualism.

The name "Wissenschaft des Judentums" did not strike roots immediately. Zunz himself chose it only after some vacillation. He entitled his first work "On Rabbinical Literature," although he sketched in it in broad outline the task of the later Wissenschaft des Judentums. The society whose driving spirit he was took the name "Verein für Cultur und Wissenschaft der Juden" (1819–24); the journal of this society introduced the name "Wissenschaft des Judentums" (1822). With the rapid decline of the society the name fell into limbo; one did not hear it for a long time, and once in a while even read in Zunz's writings "jüdische Wissenschaft" in its stead. Younger comrades-in-arms, such as Abraham Geiger, even deliberately turned away from this designation and took a sharp polemical position against Zunz's views.[4] The use of the name was resumed only when Zacharias Frankel (1801–75) founded his *Monatsschrift,* but he devalued the term by naming his publication *Monatsschrift für die Geschichte und Wissenschaft des Judentums* ["Monthly Journal for the History and Scientific Study of Judaism"], as if the history of Judaism were not part of the Wissenschaft des Judentums. However, the designation struck roots in Berlin in the circle from which the Hochschule für die Wissenschaft des Judentums eventually emerged. On December 26, 1869, the decision was made to found a Hochschule, but because of the Franco-Prussian War it could not be opened until May 6, 1872.[5] Although numerous obstacles stood in the way of the thriving development of the Hochschule, its name has popularized the term "Wissenschaft des Judentums." It asserted itself gradually and has found unquestioned acceptance in newer establishments, such as the Gesellschaft zur Förderung der Wissenschaft des Judentums (1902) and the Akademie für die Wissenschaft des Judentums (1918–19).

However, this name has been adopted only in German and not in other languages.[6] The nature of the subject itself may be the reason for which it could not be adopted elsewhere. Only in German usage has the designation *Wissenschaft* been employed for individual scientific disciplines. It was especially the term *Altertumswissenschaft* ["science of antiquity"], created by his own university teachers, which served as Zunz's model.

Paralleling his high esteem for that branch of scientific studies, Zunz's ideal was to create, through its Wissenschaft, high regard for Judaism in the eyes of the educated, Jews and non-Jews alike. In his mind's eye he saw the enlightened and noble spirits among his coreligionists rally around it, as they once had done with talmudic studies. This appeared to him as the surest guarantee for the continuity of Judaism under the changed conditions of modernity; from its recognition he expected the fulfillment of the fondest dream of his age, the civil and social equality of the Jews.[7] Although Zunz's expectations remained unfulfilled, and although participation in the Wissenschaft des Judentums always remained restricted to a small circle and it developed only into a specialized discipline, its founding was, nevertheless, a providential deed for modern Judaism. It proved itself as a cultural force of the highest rank. The thorough improvement of the system of Jewish education and scholarship, the transformation of the Jewish view of life, the religious renewal, and—not least—the enlightenment of public opinion about Jewish ways and Jewish destiny are due to its efforts.

The Wissenschaft des Judentums was introduced by Zunz's first work, "On Rabbinic Literature." Although the term was not used there, the problem was clearly perceived, and whatever was worth knowing in Jewish literature was indicated. Unsuspected perspectives opened themselves to research.[8] Zunz was the driving force behind the Verein für Cultur and Wissenschaft der Juden, which sought to arouse interest in the scientific exploration of Judaism in wider circles, and, besides other ventures, founded the *Zeitschrift für die Wissenschaft des Judentums,* of which, however, ony one volume saw the light of day. Zunz became its editor as well as its most important collaborator. Each one of his studies touched upon a different side of the Wissenschaft des Judentums in a manner significant for its method. His "Solomon ben Isaac, called Rashi" (pp. 277–384) was a trailblazer as the first scientific attempt in Jewish literature to write the biography of a scholar. "This sure mastery of richly developed material, this illuminating penetration of dark, inaccessible territories, the instructive and enlightening passage through the halls of Jewish medieval literature—this was a delight and stimulation which, to be sure, intensified the thirst even more than it quenched it," was Abraham Geiger's description, one generation later, of the impression this work made upon a youthful seeker.[9] The lamentable failure of the society, the complete collapse of all his hopes, discouraged Zunz; only his firm faith in the vitality of the Wissenschaft des Judentums rescued him from despair.[10] In quiet seclusion, under the most difficult material conditions, he worked vigorously on *The Sermons of the Jews* [*Die gottesdienstlichen Vorträge der Juden*], the publication of which caused a stir in the scholarly world. The Wissenschaft des Judentums had demonstrated its legitimacy among the sciences. Zunz's work was compared with the pathbreaking achievements of Boeckh and Grimm.[11] "Since the days of Spinoza," wrote the Philo scholar Gfrörer, "no such good and thorough study has been written by a Jew."[12]

Zunz's endeavors unexpectedly evoked an echo in Eastern Galicia, the very echo which he had painfully found missing among the Jews of Germany. The dense clouds of Hasidism darkened the land, and the obscurantists confronted the friends of enlightenment in a life-and-death struggle. Nachman Krochmal (1785–1840) "became a Mendelssohn for Galicia, as it were."[13] A man of versatile education and linguistic knowledge, he felt particularly attracted to philosophy and finally became so captivated by Hegel's writings that his teaching appeared to him to be "the philosophy among philosophies" and stimulated him to seek out its foundations in Judaism. His profound intellect turned first to the problem of Jewish history, and he sketched its development in broad outline. He did not live to expose his thoughts to public scrutiny; he had formulated them in individual essays which he wanted to collect in a book about "purified faith." In keeping with his last will, they were edited a decade after his death by Leopold Zunz, who, echoing the title of Moses Maimonides's magnum opus, named it *Guide for the Perplexed of the Time* [*Moreh Nebukhe ha-Z'man*]. Even though this rare spirit withheld the results of his thinking from wider circles, he nevertheless was in close contact with a group of distinguished disciples. "For more than one of them, Krochmal's conversations, particularly regarding the critique of history, became igniting sparks." . . .

The entire domain of the Wissenschaft des Judentums—what does it embrace and what does it exclude? The answer to this question, the precise definition of the concept "Wissenschaft des Judentums," is even today beset with difficulties because it has hardly been clarified until now. At the beginning of Abraham Geiger's lectures entitled "A General Introduction to the Wissenschaft des Judentums" ["Allgemeine Einleitung in die Wissenschaft des Judentums"]—the only detailed treatment of the subject in our possession[14]—we read that "it is not necessary to establish a strict definition of the Wissenschaft des Judentums." Until the present time this fundamental need has generally been brushed aside with the same indifference. Even where the establishment of curricula for the

Wissenschaft des Judentums was at stake, no one started with a firm conception or aimed at a definite goal. Geiger was certainly correct when he remarked that definitions are the most difficult part of the inquiry when they are expected to cover the concept and present it vividly, yet one cannot agree with his view that definitions prove mostly unproductive for the understanding of scientific disciplines.

It must, of course, be admitted that in our case even the name contains a certain vagueness. We have stated before that it is used only in the German language. But the German term, too, is somewhat obscure. It has been said that the designation *Wissenschaft vom Judentum* ["science about Judaism"] would be more appropriate.[15] This would be highly compatible with the definition which Geiger eventually offers, after all.[16] "The Wissenschaft des Judentums is the contemplation of the unique direction of spiritual life, operating in a particular circle, which indeed founded, developed, and proclaimed Judaism far and wide and preserves its vitality to this hour." This definition is certainly too narrow and does as little justice to the full scope of the Wissenschaft des Judentums as does the proclamation of its goal as "the full comprehension of the content of religious thought which fills Judaism and infuses it as its unique life force."

But why such a complicated definition? Is there, to choose an analogy, a *Wissenschaft des Christentums* or *vom Christentum* ["science of" or "about Christianity"]? The *Wissenschaft vom Christentum* is called "Christian theology." Geiger, in his younger years, spoke about the same subject under the title "Introduction to the Study of Jewish Theology" ["Einleitung in das Studium der jüdischen Theologie"].[17] But if one rejects the view of Judaism as an exclusively religious community and sees in it a national phenomenon, we do not find it an analogous designation either. Nobody speaks of a Wissenschaft of Germanism or Gallicism; science knows only Germanic or Romanic philology or employs such appellations as "Germanistics," "Slavistics," and so on. As a matter of fact, today one frequently encounters the terms "Judaistics" and "Judaist." Nevertheless, one must keep in mind that such names emphasize the exploration of language and literature and leave the history, philosophy, religion, legal system, and so forth of those nations to other disciplines, while "Judaistics" is supposed to include all of them. Moritz Lazarus, the founder of ethnopsychology, explained in one of his addresses in his capacity as chairman of the board of trustees of the Hochschule für die Wissenschaft des Judentums that *Judentum* may not be endowed with a meaning analogous to *Christentum* or *Deutschtum* ["Germanism"]; it is more like *Altertum* ["antiquity"].[18] Just as the scientific study of antiquity goes beyond philology and encompasses the total life of the ancient nations, the Wissenschaft des Judentums would have to encompass "all the products and destinies of the Jewish spirit." Zunz may have had something similar in mind, to judge by the evidence in his first study, "On Rabbinic Literature."[19] Similarly, his close friend Immanuel Wolf (later Wohlwill) introduced his essay, "On the Concept of a Science of Judaism" ["Uber den Begriff einer Wissenschaft des Judentums"] with the words, "When one speaks of a Wissenschaft des Judentums, it is self-evident that here the word 'Judaism' is understood in its most encompassing meaning, as the embodiment of all the conditions, peculiarities, and achievements of the Jews, in relation to religion, philosophy, history, legal system, literature as such, civic life, and all human affairs—but not in that more limited sense in which it means only the religion of the Jew."[20] However, aside from the fact that *Judentum* and *Altertum* are never analogous in any way and that the word combination *Judentumswissenschaft* ["science of Judaism"] is never used, the legitimacy of *Altertumswissenschaft*, as it is customarily understood, is itself not free of challenge.[21] Above all, we must not overlook the difference that antiquity lies before us as a closed chapter, whereas Judaism exists in the flux of development, experiences problems as an actual, living organism, and poses tasks for scientific research which are alien to *Altertumswissenschaft*.

The interpretation of the term does not lead us to our goal; we must search for the concept, the thought which forms its basis, and ask for the pertinent justification of the name. What is the task peculiar to the Wissenschaft des Judentums; what is the foundation of its separate claim? When we survey its individual components, we find that all of them belong to other disciplines in the formulation of their problems and in their methods. With regard to Jewish history, the faculty of the University of Berlin stated in an expert opinion how little purpose would be served

> by tearing Jewish history out of its scientific connection with general history. As long as the Jews formed a state in world history, their history belongs to the history of antiquity and, even aside from ample lectures in the theological faculty which refer to the Old Testament, lectures about ancient history do justice to its world-historical significance. Since the Jews have ceased to form a state, their history has become a part of general cultural history.

One may consider the last sentence too narrow, but it is indisputable that the history of the Jews in the dispersion forms a part of the history of each particular country, and that it is the task of sociology to explore their life as a community and in the community. The philosophy and theology of Judaism certainly can become objects of scientific research only as special divisions of general philosophy and theology. Hebrew and Aramaic linguistics are subdivisions in the sphere of Semitic philology,

and Hebrew or Aramaic literature belongs precisely there, even though
the study of the Bible, because of its special significance, has become a
main subject of theology. Biblical scholarship, as we have seen, today has
deeper roots in Christian (particularly Protestant) theology than in the
Wissenschaft des Judentums. The Talmud, if we disregard its language
and consider only its content, belongs to the history of law, religion, and
culture. Even rabbinic literature was the exclusive domain of the Wissenschaft des Judentums only as long as it remained closed to Christian
scholars and was not a subject of sufficient interest to them. This condition, however, ended long ago. Christian scholars—not the least because
of the resources which the Wissenschaft des Judentums offered then—
have taken hold of this field and produced respectable results in it. [Her-
mann] Strack's *Introduction to the Talmud and Midrash* [*Einleitung in
Talmud und Midrasch*] (to point to just this one example) is a work
indispensable to every scholar in this field; it was in no way intended to
be a contribution to the Wissenschaft des Judentums. Just as little did the
author desire to serve the Wissenschaft des Judentums through the Semi-
nar on Postbiblical Judaism which he founded and which is a branch of
the theological faculty of the University of Berlin. Thus all the subjects
which are treated in the Wissenschaft des Judentums have their place
elsewhere, and though their rights to autonomy may not be recognized
and may even be reduced, this negative appeal does not yet offer a
methodical foundation for a separate science.

    If the fusion of all these segments from various fields of knowledge
into a new discipline, as well as its concentration into a unified whole and
its demarcation against other scientific disciplines, are to be justified,
such justification can only be derived from service to a living Judaism,
from the effort to further the understanding and continuing development
of a living Judaism on a historical basis. When [Heinrich] Grätz met Zunz
for the first time and was introduced to him as the author of a [scholarly
work in the field of] Jewish history, the latter exclaimed with some irrita-
tion, "What, another Jewish history?" Whereupon Grätz promptly replied, "Indeed, but this time a *Jewish* one."[22] If this bon mot has a
methodological meaning, it can only be that Grätz did not want to exca-
vate dead bones or accumulate scholarly notes as a learned explorer of
the past, but rather that he wanted to describe the historic development
of Judaism as a member of a living organism, as a feeling Jew for whom
the Judaism of all ages and countries formed an entity. Here we have the
decisive factor in the concept "Wissenschaft des Judentums"—it is the
science of living Judaism, standing in the stream of development as a
sociological and historic entity.

    The Wissenschaft des Judentums, therefore, is a purpose-directed
science whose parts form a whole—not because the idea of science de-

mands it, but because these parts advance the solution of a practical task. The case is entirely the same with disciplines such as medicine and law; they too consist of components which are organically connected only through the purpose which they are designed to serve. An analogous development has recently taken place in a field related to Judaism, namely in the highly emphasized study of Islam. Older Arabists restricted themselves chiefly to the study of the Arabic language and literature as a subdivision of Semitic philology. However, political and economic developments during the past few decades created such extensive new contacts with the Muslim world and with the life and culture of today's followers of Islam that scholarly expositions in this area became imperative. These investigations broke through the framework of philology and acquired the dignity of a separate discipline as Islamic studies.[23] In the same way, the Wissenschaft des Judentums also extends beyond the limits of philology, just as had been planned by Zunz. Even though it counts the most careful historical-philological investigation of the sources and discovery of facts among its tasks, it pursues this research not as a purpose in itself, not to resurrect past eras and dead monuments of literature, but in order to uncover the foundations on which the present time was built. Living Judaism is and remains its goal. It must provide the focal point toward which all rays are directed; it must provide the dominant thought which ties the bond of unity around the multiplicity of materials and investigations.

Every purpose-directed science is threatened by the danger that its individual subdivisions strive for expansion and autonomy without consideration for the ultimate goal. A phenomenon like Judaism, of such long historical duration, so widely dispersed, and of such strong cultural interests, frequently offers the temptation to scientific research to lose itself in other fields. Hence concentration cannot be demanded urgently enough. The Wissenschaft des Judentums must know its place; it must not wish to deal by itself with all the areas with which Jews came into contact in the course of millennia, else it would have to become universal science or lapse into dilettantism. To be sure, the borders are fluid; a fixed line of separation cannot be established, but the most important points of view must be carefully considered. In a purpose-directed science there is no area which does not require specialized studies in the relevant sciences in order to be treated thoroughly. Nevertheless, the distinction must be made whether closely related branches of knowledge are involved, or only remote areas which in turn require specialized training. Work in the history of the Jews can be done only by someone who is trained in general historical research; whoever wants to do work in the field of Jewish law must master legal science. The Wissenschaft des Judentums cannot avoid working in these fields because Judaism has developed its own legal system and has experienced its own history.

The activities of Jews in the various sciences is an entirely different matter. In order to discover the participation of Jews in the development of mathematics or medicine, special studies in these fields are required. But there is no such thing as Jewish medicine or Jewish mathematics. The Wissenschaft des Judentums needs the result of such studies insofar as they concern Jewish cultural history, but it is unable by itself to deal with these questions, which are completely outside the field of the social sciences. Even problems which touch Judaism most intimately cannot always be subjects of independent investigation. There is no question of greater actuality than the race question; a person's attitude in this area frequently influences his judgment on Jews and Judaism. Nevertheless, the Wissenschaft des Judentums cannot possibly burden itself with the entire complex of problems inherent in anthropology, of which the question of a Jewish "race" forms only a small segment. It must rather rely on the research and conclusions of others and use these, as far as it needs them, for its own purposes. The same applies to numerous questions in the fields of political and economic history as well as sociology (although these fields are more closely related to the Wissenschaft des Judentums), for here too it would be necessary to master enormous masses of material in order to judge a problem that is quite peripheral to the native territory.

One may expect a clarification of these questions of delineation through the planned Hebrew University in Jerusalem. It can be assumed that a Jewish university will not neglect facts relating to Judaism or treat them tendentiously to the detriment of Judaism, as is often done in scholarly circles. Here one will be able to create the ideal condition that each science, based on its own problems and methods, explores the Jewish factor within its own sphere. Thus it will unburden the Wissenschaft des Judentums, deliver completed results to it, and free it from the necessity of providing a good deal of clarification. Yet even today, before this future hope is fulfilled, the Wissenschaft des Judentums is faced with the duty to clarify what it requires for its purposes and what it can dispense with, what is central and what peripheral.

In this it must be guided by an awareness of its obligation to serve living Judaism, to comprehend it as an entity in the totality of its spatial and temporal phenomena, and to contribute to its understanding, preservation, and continuous development. "Judaism lives," said [Heymann] Steinthal in his address on the occasion of the twenty-fifth anniversary of our institution, "and has to testify to its life through its practical as well as its theoretical creativity; it lives, and so it has to continue to evolve, to form its teachings ever more profoundly and comprehensively. It is an inexhaustible well out of which something new can always be drawn. . . . Wissenschaft des Judentums is to us not only a history of our past, but the plan of our future dictated by Judaism."[24]

Notes

"A Century of Wissenschaft des Judentums," translated by Karl Richter, first appeared as "Ein Jahrhundert Wissenschaft des Judentums," in *Festschrift zum fünfzigjährigen Bestehen der Hochschule für die Wissenschaft des Judentums* (Berlin, 1922), pp. 103–44. Some notes have been renumbered; the original page and note numbers are given in brackets.

1. Berlin, 1923; the first segment was distributed in early 1922.
2. The content of these thoughts is also expressed in Immanuel Wolf's introductory essay to Leopold Zunz's journal; cf. esp. pp. 13, 16ff., 23–24. For the Talmud schools of that time, see, for example, Isaac H. Weiss, *Zikhronotai* (Warsaw, 1895), esp. pp. 69–72; Dubnow's *History*, 2:239.
3. *Jeschurun* 7 (1920):505–6.
4. *Der Israelit des 19. Jahrhunderts, Literarische Blätter* 1 (1846):4ff.
5. *Lehranstalt für die Wissenschaft des Judentums: Rückblick auf ihre ersten fünfundzwanzig Jahre (1872–1897)* (Berlin, 1897), pp. 1, 9, 37.
6. The French use the expression "études juives," as they also speak of "études grecques" or "études historiques." Lay people also sometimes use the term "science juive"; to be sure, one may speak of "sciences historiques et philologiques" (Renan), but hardly of science in connection with a particular people. The Larousse *Grand Dictionaire universel du XIX siècle,* 15:1517, calls Zunz "hébraisant." The Italians speak of "studi rabbinici" or "studi ebraici" (compare "ricerche ebraiche," "teologia ebraica"). Samuel David Luzzatto entitled one of his books *Giudaismo illustrato.* In English, where the word "science" is used mostly in connection with the physical sciences, one finds "science of Judaism" only as a translation. Israel Abrahams explains it as "critical investigation of Jewish literature, hymnology and ritual" (*Encyclopaedia Brittanica,* 28:1056), which does not quite cover the concept. It corresponds better to "scientific study of Judaism." More recently, Americans speak of "Jewish lore," "Jewish (Hebrew) learning," "Jewish research." Circumlocutions are used in Polish; in the Russian Jewish encyclopedia and in Dubnow's *History* one finds the term "Jewish science." In Hebrew, "Ḥokhmat Yisrael" is used in contrast to "Torat Yisrael," which applies more to traditional learning. Above the entrance of the Hochschule is the inscription, "L'Torah ul'Ḥokhma, der Wissenschaft des Judentums."
7. "The equality of the Jews in custom and life will emerge from the equality of the Wissenschaft des Judentums" (Leopold Zunz, *Zur Geschichte und Literatur,* p. 12; *Gesammelte Schriften* [Berlin, 1875], 1:59).
8. Cf. *Monatsschrift für Geschichte und Wissenschaft des Judentums* [hereafter *MGWJ*] 62 (1918):83–84.
9. Abraham Geiger, *Nachgelassene Schriften,* ed. Ludwig Geiger (Berlin, 1875), 1:303–4.
10. Cf. Adolf Strodtman, *Heinrich Heine's Leben und Werke,* 2 vols. (Berlin and New York, 1867, 1869), p. 317.
11. August Gfrörer, *Serapeum,* vol. 7 (Leipzig, 1846), p. 45.
12. August Gfrörer, *Geschichte des Urchristenthums,* vol. 1, *Das Jahrhundert des Heils* (Stuttgart, 1838), p. 5.
13. Zunz, *Gesammelte Schriften,* 2:153–54.
14. [138n69] Geiger, *Nachgelassene Schriften,* 2:39.
15. [139n70] "M. Steinschneider," in Felix Perles, *Jüdische Skizzen,* 2d ed. (Leipzig, 1912), pp. 51–52.
16. [139n71] Geiger, *Nachgelassene Schriften,* 2:39.
17. [139n72] Ibid., pp. 4–5.
18. [139n73] Among the documents in the archives of the Hochschule.
19. [139n74] Cf. *MGWJ* 62 (1918):85–86.
20. [140n75] *Zeitschrift für die Wissenschaft des Judentums,* p. 1.
21. [140n76] Cf. Eduard Meyer, *Geschichte des Alterthums* (Stuttgart, 1884), 2:27.
22. [141n77] See Philip Bloch in *MGWJ* 3 (1904):314.
23. [142n78] See the lead article in *Zeitschrift für Islamkunde,* vol. 1.
24. [143n79] Heymann Steinthal, *Über Juden und Judentum,* ed. G. Karpeles (Berlin, 1906), p. 248.

CLARIFYING FUNDAMENTALS

3
DOES TRADITIONAL JUDAISM
POSSESS DOGMAS?

Leo Baeck

hether Judaism, in its form of belief, is a religion without dogmas is a question that has often been raised.[1] That this question has so rarely found an adequate answer is mostly due to the fact that that which should have been done first, namely to establish what is meant by a "dogma," was not done. Inasmuch as "dogma" was thus used almost exclusively in a colloquial sense, it should not be surprising that the answer to our question also remained in the realm of the vague or rhetorical.

That people usually felt they were exempted from the requirement to start with a conceptual definition of the term is probably attributable to a kind of tradition—the long and widely held belief that Moses Mendelssohn had posited the principle that Judaism was a religion without dogmas. This, however, holds true only to a limited extent. What Mendelssohn had set forth is something different, something much more comprehensive. He altogether denied that Judaism was a revealed *religion* in the true sense of the word and attributed to it only revealed laws and revealed truths of history. Judaism was to him a pure religion of reason.

> As far as its major tenets are concerned, the religion of my fathers knows no mysteries which we have to accept on faith rather than comprehend. Our intellect can quite comfortably start out from the well-established primary principles of human cognition and be sure that it will eventually encounter religion on the same road.[2]

I recognize no eternal verities except those which can not only be comprehended by the human intellect but also be demonstrated and verified by man's reason. . . . I consider this view an essential aspect of the Jewish religion and believe that this teaching represents one of the characteristic differences between Judaism and Christianity. To sum it up in one sentence: I believe Judaism knows nothing of a *revealed religion* in the sense in which Christians define this term. The Israelites possess a *divine legislation*—laws, commandments, statutes, rules of conduct, instruction in God's will and in what they are to do to attain temporal and eternal salvation. Moses, in a miraculous and supernatural way, revealed to them these laws and commandments, but not dogmas, propositions concerning salvation, or self-evident principles of reason. These the Lord reveals to us as well as to all other men at all times through the nature of things but never through the spoken or written word. . . . People have usually paid little attention to this distinction. Supernatural *legislation* has been mistaken for a supernatural *revelation* of religion.[3]

A historical truth on which this people's legislation was to be founded, as well as laws, were to be revealed here, at Sinai, but no eternal religious truths.[4]

The divine utterances had as their sole purpose to appoint Israel to be God's possession above all other peoples, so that it should be to him a holy people above all other peoples of the earth. As regards rational doctrines, Israel is not specially favored above the other peoples.[5]

Inasmuch as the area of revelation was thus limited to law and history, the concept of religious revelation was basically discarded and the distinctively religious element eliminated from what is specifically Jewish. Judaism had become a mere addition of "law" and deistic natural religion.[6] This was the only way in which Mendelssohn thought he could join what he wanted to possess together: the freedom of his religious and cognitive doctrines on the one hand, and the determination to maintain the Law and his connection with the community on the other. But the specific question under discussion here—whether there are dogmas in Judaism—receives no consideration, although his Judaism, lacking all creedal statements, is of course also nondogmatic.

It is understandable that sooner or later opposition to the Judaism which he taught had to arise, and it is characteristic that it was voiced most vigorously by uncompromising Reform Judaism. Because it gave up old ties, it became essential for Reform to seek new ones in order to secure a foundation for the religious community, and a formulated credo seemed to guarantee that. Moreover, it is characteristic of a purely rationalistic view of religion—and such a view is the starting point of Reform—that it endeavors to erect a system of creedal doctrines, a creedal structure. In contrast to Mendelssohn, therefore, there was a greater readiness to acknowledge an obligation toward belief than toward law.

The sharpness with which, for instance, David Einhorn turned against Mendelssohn is characteristic.

> To claim that Judaism has no specific doctrines at all and that it does not even obligate its members to acknowledge one of its cognitive principles means to deprive this community of its very foundation, of every spiritual focus; and Mendelssohn could surely not have rendered his cause a worse service than by appealing to the testimony of history. Freedom from dogma is so little known to historical Judaism that the Talmud includes him who denies the divine revelation of even a single letter of the Torah in the category of *minim*, who, as is well known, are not exactly to be treated with consideration. And the Talmud denies eternal life even to such Noahites who, although most scrupulously fulfilling the duties incumbent upon them, regard these duties merely as emanating from reason but not from a supernatural divine revelation. . . . . In the light of these facts, we must most vehemently protest against the notion that Judaism, in contradiction to innumerable passages in its divine documents, lacks the character of a revealed religion and, furthermore, possesses no dogmas [which alone would ensure] that no religious view, no matter how constituted, would be able to nullify its inner connection with Judaism, or rob religious acts of their value.[7]

Samuel Holdheim fought against Mendelssohn's theory with the same determination.

> The assertion that Judaism is only legislation and not a religion, that it reveals only laws and ordinances and not eternal religious truths, is of such a kind that it must expect the strongest opposition. . . . . Judaism has revealed not only laws but *reasons for the laws,* and what else are these reasons if not ideas, truths, doctrines, dogmas, religion in the true sense of the word! . . . . The commandment "Ye shall be holy" is, admittedly, only a law. But the reasons—"because I, the Eternal One, your God, am holy"— is a revealed religious truth without which man can neither have virtue nor attain eternal bliss. If this is not religion, then we really do not know what Mendelssohn means by religion.[8]

Later on Leopold Löw, in a circular letter called "Jewish Dogmas" ["Jüdische Dogmen"], aligned himself with Einhorn and Holdheim, without, however, mentioning the latter.[9] This letter also treats the question primarily from the historical side, for which he adduced important material. In addition, he introduced the concept of "liturgically sanctioned dogmas," that is, "such dogmas to which a place is assigned in the liturgy and which, in this form, express the religious belief of the synagogue in a way that is pregnant with meaning."[10] In view of the fact that a reformed prayer book was in existence, he was consistent enough to speak about a twofold Jewish dogma, one orthodox and one reformed, reaching the conclusion that "just as the orthodox liturgy is a faithful interpreter of orthodox dogmas, so the reformed liturgy is a faithful interpreter of the dogmas of the reformation. Both liturgies protest loudly and solemnly against the doctrine of nonexistence of dogmas."[11]

The disquisitions of these three men, and especially that of Löw, already contain everything essential which has since been said against the absence of dogmas in Judaism.[12] For them, opposition to Mendelssohn was a part of the fight for their reform; they wanted to authenticate their reform through articles of faith.

The only member of this circle who took a different position on the question of dogmas was Abraham Geiger. He had first explained his position in a brief essay, "On Jewish Philosophy" ["Über jüdische Philosophie"], even before Löw wrote his letter about "Jewish Dogmas," although Löw characteristically does not refer to it. He was the first to proceed from a definition of "dogma," explaining:

> Judaism has no dogmas, that is, it has no articles of faith which have been solemnly proclaimed as eternal, inviolable truth by an assembly with legally binding power representing the whole community, the denial or doubt of which would place him who negates them outside the fold of the ecclesiastical community. Such a solemn agreement has not taken place in Judaism. However, at all times statements have been regarded as so indubitably fundamental to Judaism that everyone who doubted them was designated as a *kofer ba-ikkar,* as a "denier of the fundamental root," and the ban proclaimed against such men amounted to a declaration of expulsion. However, Judaism did not go any further either in the systematization of the beliefs or in the prosecution of the negator, and this was in no way because it "guaranteed freedom of thought," but because it was too powerless.[13]

Geiger came to the same conclusion in an exhaustive polemic against [Manuel] Joël's pamphlet, *Toward an Orientation Regarding the Problem of Ritual* [*Zur Orientierung in der Cultusfrage*].[14] Referring to the question what portions of the prayer book constitute "the expression of dogmatic views," Joël had explained: "Questions of cult are always only secondary. Wherever cultic questions are present, dogmatic questions must have preceded them, and not merely dogmatic questions but, to be precise, dogmatic solutions."[15] Accordingly, he arrived at the following principle for Judaism:

> Each positive religion has certain dogmas which are considered fixed and with the denial of which a member of that religion ceases to profess it. The statement that Judaism has no dogmas, if left as indefinite as it usually is, surely has not been adequately thought through. Without a dogma of any kind, probably no positive religion could come into existence. . . . The most that could be said—truly for the benefit of Judaism—is that it did at no time come to a dogmatic formulation of all articles of faith, regarded as final by all.[16]

Geiger turned especially against this last sentence. "Very well: dogmas without dogmatic fixation, conceptions without conceptual exactness, that simply means—nothing."[17] Point by point, he then sought to refute Joël's argument. However, he too most decidedly rejected Mendelssohn's doctrine.

> It was, indeed, an unhappy idea of Mendelssohn's to posit the principle that Judaism possesses no doctrinal truths but merely laws, statues. . . . That was a sentence of death for Judaism, which he thereby pronounced to be a skeleton without an animating soul. But it was at the same time a fundamentally wrong view, for Judaism has entered into history precisely with new ideas which transformed the entire world of thought and perception.

However, he held to the rejection of dogmas. "It never came to the dogmatic fixation of any statement of faith. . . . Doctrine is present as idea but simply not as dogma."[18]

It is characteristic that he, the only one who had given a definition of dogma, was also the only one in this whole group who understood Judaism as a religion without dogma.

But what then is dogma? In its original usage in Greek and Latin, it means "order," "decree." It is used this way for official regulations in the political sphere. In the Greek Bible it is, therefore, the translation of the diverse expressions for the edicts of the kings of Babylon and Persia;[19] the Gospels and Acts of the Apostles speak of the emperor's "dogma." Similarly, in the language of philosophy, the term is used for the axioms, the principles which, so to speak, are the decrees of cognition. Thus Cicero speaks of "the decrees of wisdom which the philosophers call dogmas."[20] That is why, when ancient philosophy accepted Christianity, when it became the philosophy of Christianity, it called its statements of faith "dogmas" (*coelestis philosophiae dogmata*)[21] and distinguished between these dogmas and ethical principles. Gregory of Nyssa, for instance, juxtaposed *to ēthicon meros* ["the ethical dimension"] and *tēn tōn dogmatōn akribeian* ["the rigid discipline of dogma"].[22] In the Middle Ages, the word "dogma," though still used, recedes in scholarly usage. Only the theology of the last centuries has taken it up again and given it its specific meaning.[23]

The Catholic church, which is of course the true locus of dogma, established a definitive definition of the concept at its last council. "With divine and Catholic faith, all these matters are to be believed"—that is, the faith commanded by God and taught by the church demands that all matters are to be believed "which are contained in the word of God, be it communicated in writing or through traditions, and which are put forward by the church as divine, be it through solemn decision or through the regular and common *magisterium*."[24] This statement indeed provides the clear and exact definition of dogma. The following characteristics in it are held to be essential: first, that it proffers the content of a revelation, whether it be taken from an inspired scripture or from an inspired tradition; further, that here is a regulative determination of the church, a *propositio ecclesiae* (that is to say, that the authority empowered to make decisions and impose obligations stands behind it). The *propositio* must be added to the *revelatio*. And finally, and this is of course inherent in the *propositio*, that the statement has a precise conceptualized form.

Protestant theology gives, by and large, the same definition. Thus H. H. Wendt, in his *System of Christian Doctrine* [*System der christlichen Lehre*] writes: "The concept 'dogma' in its strict sense denotes a doctrine belonging to Christian belief, conceptually formulated and raised in the ecclesiastical community to authoritative validity."[25] [Martin] Rade, in his *Creedal Doctrine* [*Glaubenslehre*] says: "*A doctrine backed up by authoritative power. No matter whether by state or church authority. This alone is the total concept of dogma.*[26] Similarly [Ernst] Troeltsch. He calls dogma "the doctrinal statements which the church has officially formulated in its great doctrinal pronouncements since the Nicene Council, together with parts of doctrine contained only in traditions and in the thinking of communities and generally recognized."[27] Accordingly, he adds: "The old Protestantism has, in this sense, no dogma because it does not go back to councils and to tradition, nor does it possess an infallible institution for the fixing of dogma."[28] [Adolf] Harnack gives a similar definition, except that his primary emphasis is on conceptual clarity.

> Ecclesiastical dogmas are the doctrines of the Christian faith, conceptually formulated and cast in scientific form for apologetic purposes, which deal with the knowledge of God, of the world, and of the salvation brought by Christ, and which thus represent the objective content of the religion. The Christian churches teach them as the truths contained in Holy Scripture (as well as in traditions) which circumscribe the *depositum fidei* and the acknowledgment of which is the condition of the salvation which religion promises. . . . The conceptual formulation is part of the essence of dogma.[29]

But he too emphasizes the need for a dogma-forming authority, and the preconditions of dogma are "the infallible *magisterium* of the church, the infallible apostolic doctrine and constitution and . . . the infallible apostolic canon of Scripture."[30]

Thus there is also agreement here that the concept of dogma is essentially determined by the finality of the formulation, ecclesiastical authority, and the contents of revelation, as well as possession of the correct belief and of salvation founded upon it.[31] Hence the definition, recently given in an essay by [Isidor] Scheftelowitz, that "dogmas are irrefutable articles of faith on the acceptance of which correct belief depends"[32] seems inadequate. Missing here is, first of all, the determination of what endows one article of faith, in contrast to others,[33] with the character of irrefutability. Who, in other words, can establish dogma? Further missing is the essential criterion constituted by the conceptual formulation. It is also inexact to speak of "acceptance" of articles of faith on which "correct belief depends." Acceptance is executed by authority empowered to make pronouncements; on the basis of this pronouncement of the authority, the true believer merely performs the obediently faithful acceptance, so that the Catholic church is largely satisfied with the mere submission, with *fides implicita.*

Once the definition is established, the question whether Judaism has dogmas is really already answered. For this is the only question here. That Judaism, in opposition to Mendelssohn's assertion, is a *revealed religion,* that it has its own characteristic religious tenets which struggle, especially in times of intellectual controversy, to find expression in new ways and for which new boundaries are being staked out time and again—this will by now hardly be questioned by anyone. No one doubts that Judaism conceives of itself as possessing a revelation and Holy Scriptures; that it proclaims the one unique God and finds in the fulfillment of His commandment the meaning of being human; that it demands the imageless worship of God; that it preaches the purity of the soul and atonement and promises a life in eternity; that it places his fellow man before man; that it teaches the election of Israel; and that it indicates as its realization also the messianic goal, the future. No one doubts that all this is peculiar to Judaism and to no other religion in the same manner. The objection is raised only against the claim that Judaism possesses dogmas, and the objection is based simply on the exact meaning of the term.

This meaning shows that Judaism possesses no dogmas, if for no other reason than that it lacks the authoritative institution which would have been empowered to proclaim creedal statements as dogmas and to enforce them as such. To be sure—and this objection is being raised[34]— the Sanhedrin existed for several centuries during which it was entitled, as the central authority, to speak in the name of the total community. But that the Sanhedrin could not establish "irrefutable religious doctrines" is really already shown in the fact that its decisions, in principle, were considered as refutable, as revokable,[35] whereas it is, of course, in the nature of an authority which creates dogmas that its decisions, in principle, are regarded as final.[36] Add to that the fact that we have little information about such "decrees fixed by the Sanhedrin," whereas it is indispensable for a dogma to be promulgated as such. And simply to declare a sentence from the Mishnah as "a decree fixed by the Sanhedrin" will hardly do either.

However, the Mishnah contains the sentence which denies a share in the world to come to those who claim that the doctrine of resurrection is not biblical and that the Torah is not from God. It is significant that side-by-side with these the Mishnah also mentions as ineligible for partaking in the world to come such lightly sketched figures as the Epicurean and, according to Akiva's opinion, also him who reads nonbiblical writings and him who, in the name of God, mutters healing incantations over a wound.[37] But, above all, this sentence is to be grouped with similar ones, such as that in the Mishnah which in still sharper language denies eternal life to those "who speculate about that which is above and that which is below, that which was before and that which will come after, and are thus without reverence before the glory of God."[38] The comparison shows that what we have here are not "decrees fixed by the Sanhedrin" nor dogmas, but merely expressions of condemnation of doctrines, trends, and customs which were at that time considered objectionable.

Actually, another sentence in the Gemarah is probably far more characteristic because it furnishes, in fact, an article of faith fixed by a special decision on the part of an authority empowered to speak. It is above all to this doctrine that those who support the existence of dogmas should have referred, and it is strange that they always pass over it in silence. It is the sentence which would make a doctrine out of pessimism. "It has been voted upon and decided: it would be better if man had not been created."[39] This sentence meets an essential precondition of dogma, yet it shows clearly that in Judaism even the "majority of religious leaders forming an authority"[40] does not yet create a dogma.

But apart from the question to what extent both the Sanhedrin and the Mishnah would have wanted to render decisions with regard to belief, one thing that is essential for the formation of dogmas at that time is missing: the exact formulation of creedal concepts. Whereas the formation of concepts in the area of Halakhah is penetrating and specific down to the smallest detail, it is lacking in the area of Aggadah. A conceptual formulation of creedal tenets evolved in the Near Eastern-European world always only as the result of an immediate encounter of the various religions with Greek philosophy. Therefore we find in Philo formations of concepts which could furnish material for dogmas,[41] but we do not have them in Palestinian Judaism because its relationship to Greek philosophy was not as close and far more intermittent. For the same reason, we find them again among medieval Jewish thinkers, and it is no coincidence that this was when articles of faith begin to be drawn up. They could not be turned into dogmas, however, for the ecclesiastical authority was lacking, just as the conceptual formulations had been lacking when, at the time of the Sanhedrin and of the constitutional academy, an authority empowered to make decisions could possibly have existed. Both preconditions together—the existence of an ecclesiastical authority empowered to formulate decrees and a conceptualization directed towards the *depositum fidei*—were given in the ancient Near Eastern-European world only in the church.[42] Therefore Harnack touches upon a decisive point when he emphasizes that "dogma is, in its conception and completion, a work of the Greek spirit on the soil of the Gospels"[43] (except that the reference should more accurately be to New Testament-Pauline thought rather than to the Gospels).

Thus, historically, dogma is something specifically Christian and ecclesiastical, and not only historically, but also in accordance with its essential character. Dogma appertains to the church as such. Hence the question whether Judaism possesses dogmas becomes another question, namely whether an ecclesiastical character pertains to Judaism. Something that is peculiar to the church as the divine institution for the mediation of salvation is that it, and not the individual in it, is the proper subject of belief. The *church* believes, and the individuals believe this belief of the church; they believe, as the sentence cited above says, *fide catholica;* they believe because it is the belief of the church.[44] Because the church in this manner defines the belief of all who are part of it, it must fix the dogma, this authoritative irrefutable expression of the belief of all, this *quod ubique, quod semper, quod ab omnibus*. There is no true church without dogmas. The tradition which the church guarantees and through which the church itself is guaranteed is therefore the tradition of dogmas, tradition of the right belief. Only what is dogma or can become dogma is true tradition.[45]

Judaism has never formed a church; it has, according to its essence, fashioned the community. The conceptual starting point in the church is the believing church; in the community, it is the faith of the individual. Every individual, by right and obligation, is the bearer of belief; therefore the individual, not the church, is the bearer of tradition, and that tradition, in turn, is not a mere transmission of tenets but also includes the demand to inquire. Possession is preceded by searching. This commandment to inquire is the opposite of dogma. Where dogma is transmitted, inquiring in the Jewish sense would become a sin against the church.

There is an even deeper reason why the church possesses dogma. The church, as guardian of the sacrament, is the preserver of salvation. Where salvation conditional upon the sacrament is promised, where in this manner redemption is said to be granted through the possession of the sacraments, there dogma is something indispensable, because there the meaning of the sacrament has to be brought before the believer in a definite conceptual form. An ecclesiastical sacrament cannot be depicted without a dogma. This salvation demands knowledge of salvation; each soteriological religion demands *gnosis*, the perception of the mystery of redemption; error here would be death. Therefore the believer has to be presented with the final irrefutable knowledge, namely the dogma.

Like the sacrament, the dogma also must be received. And where this receiving of the dogma as the word of God gains its special significance, as it does in Protestantism, and where religion truly becomes a denomination [*Konfession*], there the conceptual formulation of the accumulated beliefs possibly becomes something even more decisive. The confession of faith becomes the central point of religion. Here it is not, as is the case for instance in Maimonides's Thirteen Articles of Faith, a popular summation of the findings of the philosophy of religion. It is rather that which membership in the church offers in a real sense—the means by which the believer receives salvation. The confession of faith is something indispensable because through it the denomination confirms its own self-awareness.

Here we also have the innermost reason for which so many representatives of Reform Judaism took pains to attribute dogmas to Judaism. They wanted to transform their Judaism into a Jewish *Konfession* which could have its place alongside the Christian denominations. And, therefore, they wanted to formulate Jewish articles of faith which—and which alone—would distinguish their Jewish denomination from the others. For this purpose, they have surrendered an utterly essential aspect of the difference, namely that Judaism is no church and no mere denomination and, therefore, also has no dogmas. Out of his sensitivity for the peculiarly Jewish, which he also proves elsewhere, Geiger has, in contrast to many with whom he otherwise went along, rejected Jewish dogmas. And even though Mendelssohn, because of his theory that Judaism was no revealed religion, was led astray and in turn led astray those who followed him, he stayed on the right path by refusing to look for a church and its creed in Judaism.

The place elsewhere occupied by dogmatics is, in Judaism, taken by Aggadah (those supposedly dogmatic sentences of the Mishnah are in reality aggadic sentences) and later by religious philosophy. Study and inquiry were always extended to doctrine too, and rightfully so, for the principles always counted for more than the expression. One not only tolerated the Rambam next to the Rabad, but placed them side-by-side; the books of these two became as one book. It is perhaps the strongest proof for the inner strength of Judaism that, in all investigating and searching, through all the changing epochs, the creedal principles remained stable and firm, and that one always found oneself again with their help. They stood fast, without outward props. Jewish doctrine carried within itself, as did the entire community of Israel [*die Gemeinde des Judentums*]—to vary an often cited expression—the strong ferment of composition.

Notes

"Does Traditional Judaism Possess Dogmas?," translated by Elizabeth Petuchowski, first appeared as "Besitzt das alte Judentum Dogmen," *Monatsschrift für Geschichte und Wissenschaft des Judentums* 70 (1926):225–36. It was published in a revised form in Leo Baeck, *Aus drei Jahrtausenden*, 2d ed. (Tübingen, 1958); reprinted in Kurt Wilhelm, ed., *Wissenschaft des Judentums im deutschen Sprachbereich* (Tübingen, 1967), 2:737–49.

1. The author's exposition of [the place of] dogmas in Judaism in his book *Das Wesen des Judentums* (1st ed. Berlin, 1905), pp. 5–6, has been treated in a number of essays by Isidor Scheftelowitz, Felix Goldmann, and Julius Guttmann in *Monatsschrift für Geschichte und Wissenschaft des Judentums* [hereafter *MGWJ*] 70 (1926):65ff., 433ff., 440–41, and ibid., 71 (1927):241–42. The following comments refer to Scheftelowitz's contribution.
2. "Betrachtungen über Bonnets Palingenesie," in *Gesammelte Schriften*, ed. C. B. Mendelssohn (Leipzig, 1843–44), 3:164. [*Jubiläumsausgabe*, 7:95; Alfred Jospe, trans. and ed., *"Jerusalem" and Other Jewish Writings by Moses Mendelssohn* (New York, 1969), p. 154.]
3. *Gesammelte Schriften*, 3:311; emphases in accordance with the first edition of 1783, 2:30ff. [Jospe, *"Jerusalem" and Other Jewish Writings*, p. 61.]
4. Adapted from *Gesammelte Schriften*, 3:320.
5. See *Bi'ur* to Exod. 20.
6. See Mendelssohn's letter to Elkan Herz, July 23, 1771, in *MGWJ* 3 (1859):173. "We no longer add anything to natural religion except commandments, statutes, and righteous laws." Cf. Salomon Ludwig Steinheim, "Die Glaubenslehre der Synagoge," in *Die Offenbarung nach dem Lehrbegriff der Synagoge* (Leipzig, 1856), 2:viii. "This reforming rationalism, which dates its inception back to M. Mendelssohn and his school, had (while the orthodox were led by the nose by the mystics and mythologists) built its temples everywhere where there was talk of everything except of revelation."
7. David Einhorn, *Des Prinzip des Mosaismus und dessen Verhältnis zum Heidentum und rabbinischen Judentum* (1854), pp. 11–12. Cf. Michael Creizenach in Abraham Geiger's *Zeitschrift für jüdische Theologie* 1 (1835):39–40.
8. Samuel Holdheim, *Moses Mendelssohn und die Denk- und Glaubensfreiheit im Judentums* (Berlin, 1859), pp. 30–31. Creizenach puts forward a similar argument in the essay cited in n. 7 above. About the necessity of a declaration of faith in a religious community, see Holdheim, *Moses Mendelssohn*, pp. 34, 39, 42–43. His sentence about revealed truth without which man can have neither virtue nor eternal salvation sounds almost Augustinian.
9. "Jüdische Dogmen" (1871), in Leopold Löw, *Gesammelte Schriften*, ed. I. Löw (Szegedin, 1889), 1:133–76. Previously (1858) Löw, in an essay about "the fundamentals of the religion of Israel," had maintained the same standpoint ("Ben Chananya," in ibid., p. 31). See also Löw, "Hamafteah" (1855), ibid., pp. 330ff.
10. "Jüdische Dogmen," pp. 171–72; the expression, however, was coined by the unnamed theologian against whom Löw polemicizes. Cf. also Manuel Joël, *Zur Orientierung in der Cultusfrage* (Breslau, 1869), pp. 9–10.
11. "Jüdische Dogmen," p. 174. A few sentences cited from a report by Louis Binstock to the Central Conference of American Rabbis are particularly characteristic for the way in which bonds through articles of faith are to take the place of bonds through the commandment. However, the report was received with opposition. "And what the Pharisees did with Halachas in their day, we Reform Jews must do with dogmas in our day. If we would preserve Judaism in all its nobility and purity, we must have Halachas or dogmas that shall be definite and clear so that not only all Israel but all people shall know what we think and believe—dogmas that shall be issued by an authorized representative body and shall not be subject to change except by that body—dogmas that shall be mandatory upon all members of our progressive faith, upon rabbis as well as laymen, . . . dogmas that shall regulate uniformly and universally the religious belief and practice of every rabbi and layman in Reform Judaism" (*CCAR Yearbook* 35 [1924]:261).

12. Solomon Schechter's essay, "The Dogmas of Judaism," is particularly valuable and rich in historical materials (*Studies in Judaism* [Philadelphia, 1896], 1:179–80). Schechter closes with the words, "It is true that every great religion is 'a concentration of many ideas and ideals,' which make this religion able to adapt itself to various modes of thinking and living. But there must always be a point round which all these ideas concentrate themselves. This centre is Dogma." Cf. Jakob Guttmann, "Über Dogmenbildung im Judentum" (1894), who also treats the question essentially historically, and Siegmund Maybaum, *Methodik des jüdischen Religionsunterrichts* (Breslau, 1896), pp. 41–42.

13. *Jüdische Zeitschrift für Wissenschaft und Leben* 1 (1862):278–88.

14. Ibid., 7 (1869):2–3.

15. Joël, *Zur Orientierung in der Cultusfrage*, pp. 9, 13.

16. Ibid., p. 10. See a similar view in Heymann Steinthal, "Die Idee der Weltschöpfung," *Jahrbuch für jüdische Geschichte und Literatur* 2 (Berlin, 1899):43; reprinted in *Über Juden und Judentum* (Berlin, 1906), p. 128: "The question has been raised whether the religion of Israel has dogmas. If it has doctrinal statements, if it is not without content, it is bound to have dogmas, and the idea of creation is such a dogma. But what the religion of Israel does *not* require is the fixing of dogma in writing."

17. *Jüdische Zeitschrift für Wissenschaft und Leben* 7 (1869):7.

18. Ibid., pp. 7–8, 9–10. The conclusion that dogmas in Judaism should be rejected is also reached in valuable expositions by Martin Schreiner, *Die jüngsten Urteile über das Judentum* (1902), pp. 68–69, and Felix Perles, *Boussets Religion des Judentums* (Berlin, 1903), pp. 115–16.

19. Thus Dan. 2:13; 3:10; 3:12, and passim; cf. Aquila to Deut. 33:2 and Symmachus to Hab. 1:7.

20. Cicero, *Acad. Quaest.*, 2,27: "Sapientia neque de se ipsa disputare debet neque de suis decretis, quae philosophi vocant dogmata, quorum nullum sine scelere prodi potest."

21. Vincent de Lérins, *Comm.* 29. Cf. *Letter to Diognetus* 5,3.

22. Ep. 24.

23. Karl Hase, *Hutterus redivivus* (Leipzig, 1833), 2:18–19; Paul Lobstein, *Einleitung in die evangelische Dogmatik* (Freiburg im Breisgau, 1897), pp. 7–8.

24. Vatican Council [I, 1869–70], Session 3, chap. 3: "Fide divina et catholica ea omnia credenda sunt, quae in verbo Dei scripto vel tradito continentur, et ab Ecclesia sive solemni judicio sive ordinario er universali magisterio tanquam divinitus revelata proponuntur."

25. H. H. Wendt, *System der christlichen Lehre* (Göttingen, 1907), p. 13. Similarly Matthew Arnold in *Literature and Dogma* (cited by Binstock, p. 250; see n. 11 above): "Dogma means not necessarily a true doctrine but merely a doctrine or system of doctrine determined; decreed; received."

26. Martin Rade, *Glaubenslehre* (Gotha, 1924), 1:4; cf. ibid., p. 9. Cf. also Baur, *Geschichte der christlichen Kirche,* 2d ed. (1863), 2:217: "Once the dispute has taken this turn, the victorious party gathers together in the format of a general synod and elevates its opinion to the status of a resolution of the Catholic church. It is, then, the church which renders the last and highest decision; hence in it, the church, lies also the principle of truth. What it declares to be true must be generally recognized as truth; but it does not become truth because it has been declared such by the church. Rather, the church can pronounce only what in itself, objectively, was already present as truth."

27. In his *Soziallehren der christlichen Kirchen und Gruppen* (Tübingen, 1912), p. 209, Troeltsch describes these latter more precisely as "latent dogmas"; by this he means doctrinal statements for which all the conditions necessary for their official formulation and promulgation were present, but which had not yet been promulgated.

28. Troeltsch in *Religion in Geschichte und Gegenwart* (1910), 2:105. Cf. Troeltsch, *Soziallehren,* p. 172: "Through theocracy the church has achieved unity of dogma and unity of canon law which would not have come about without Constantine, and which was enforced through the power of the state, not through the immanent logic of the dogmatic idea."

29. Adolf Harnack, *Lehrbuch der Dogmengeschichte*, 4th ed. (Tübingen, 1909–20), 1:3 [translation based on that of Neil Buchanan in *History of Dogma* (New York, 1961), 1:3, which, however, was prepared from the third German edition].

30. Ibid., p. 9n; cf. p. 16. Cf. also Wilhelm Hermann, "Christlich-protestantische Dogmatik," in *Kultur der Gegenwart* (Berlin, 1906), p. 583. For Hermann, "the idea of a revealed doctrine is the most important aspect of dogma"; then added to this is "the ratification approved by the ecclesiastical authorities." Cf. Horst Stephan, *Glaubenslehre: Der Evangelische Glaube and seine Welt* (Giessen, 1921), pp. 10–11.

31. Leo Baeck, *The Essence of Judaism*, trans. Victor Grubwieser and Leonard Pearl (Frankfurt am Main, 1936), pp. 4–5. "It becomes [a dogma] only when definite formulas have been worked out in clear cut conceptions, and have been declared binding by an established and competent authority, as signifying the religious deposit, in the acceptance of which lie orthodoxy and salvation."

32. *MGWJ* 70 (1926):66.

33. Cf. the distinction which, for instance, Luther made in *De capt. Babyl. eccl.* (ed. Clemen, 1:438): "quod sine scripturis asseritur aut revelatione, opinari licet, credi non est necesse."

34. "My investigation is not based on views of individual rabbis—these views usually did not attain legal force—but primarily on regulations fixed by the Sanhedrin" (Scheftelowitz, *MGWJ* 70 [1926]:66).

35. Mishnah 'Eduyoth I,5; cf. V,5.

36. Cf. Harnack's discussion of Seeberg in *Lehrbuch der Dogmengeschichte*, 1:7n.

37. Mishnah Sanhedrin X,1.

38. Mishnah Ḥagigah II,1. The expression "v'khol shelo ḥas al k'vod kono" ["And whosoever gives no thought to the honor of his Maker (it would be better for him had he not come into the world)"] has become a *terminus technicus* for these forbidden speculations. Cf. Gen. R. I,7 and p. Ḥagigah 77c.

39. B. 'Erubhin 13b.

40. Scheftelowitz, *MGWJ* 70 (1926):67.

41. Cf. the five creedal statements which Philo posits at the end of *De opificio mundi* (pars. 170–71; I,41–42); cf. also Mendelssohn, "Betrachtungen über Bonnets Palingenesie," p. 164, about the three fundamentals of the Israelite religion.

42. On the dogmatic peculiarity of Islam, and especially the principle of consensus (of the *idschmâ*), see Ignaz Goldhizer, "Die Religion des Islam," in *Kultur der Gegenwart*, vol. 1, no. 3, p. 1.

43. Harnack, *Lehrbuch der Dogmengeschichte*, 1:105–6.

44. Cf. Leo Baeck, "Romantische Religion," in *Aus drei Jahrtausenden*, 2d ed. (Tübingen, 1958), pp. 75ff. ["Romantic Religion," in *Judaism and Christianity*, trans. Walter Kaufmann (Philadelphia, 1958), pp. 189ff.].

45. Cf. Ferdinand Christian Baur, *Geschichte der christlichen Kirche*, 2d ed. (Tübingen, 1863), 2:217. "Tradition and church are, if one inquires into the principle of the dogmatic truth, identical concepts; what is valid for one of these concepts is also valid for the other."

4
ESTABLISHING NORMS FOR JEWISH BELIEF

Julius Guttmann

n the instructive and stimulating discussion con-
ducted by [Leo] Baeck and [Isidor] Scheftelowitz [in vol. 70 of *Monatsschrift für Geschichte und Wissenschaft des Judentums; MGWJ*] on the
question whether there are dogmas in traditional Judaism, the two agreed
that only those tenets which are laid down as generally obligatory should
be recognized as dogmas. Thus the problem of dogma in Judaism centers
on the question whether, and in what form, Judaism has established
norms for the content of Jewish belief. The answer to this question represents an important step toward the clarification of the problem. That
Judaism has its own characteristic beliefs is self-evident; only Mendelssohn's paradoxical thesis that Judaism is not a revealed religion but revealed legislation could make it appear necessary to submit detailed
proofs for what was self-evident. The question whether or not Judaism
has its characteristic religious notions hardly presents a serious difficulty.
Nevertheless, there is a definite need to investigate the extent to which
these conceptions have been fixed and set down as obligatory for all Jews.
This question has been largely neglected due to the laxity of much of the
earlier literature, which Baeck rightly criticizes for its failure to distinguish between dogmas and conceptions of belief in general.

Despite their common point of departure, Baeck and Scheftelowitz
differ, partly in their terminology, partly in matters of substance. Though
they share a basic view, they disagree on terminology in their definitions
of the concept "dogma." Scheftelowitz is satisfied to use as his criterion

that a tenet is universally binding, and he defines dogmas as "irrefragable religious doctrines whose acceptance is a condition for being regarded as orthodox" (*MGWJ* 70:66). Baeck not only considers this definition formally inadequate (because it does not indicate the authority which confers "irrefragability" upon specific religious doctrines), but he also conceives dogma substantively more narrowly, in accordance with the usage in Christian theology. However, I believe both scholars consider the terminological problem to be much simpler than it actually is. As Baeck correctly points out, what can be demanded of a definition of dogma is that it be unambiguous and that it conform to scholarly usage. However, it seems to me that this usage is not as consistent as Baeck assumes. Of course, I do not consider it admissible to rely on the fact, as Scheftelowitz does (p. 433), that the term "dogma" is occasionally used by scholars in the field of religion without terminological precision. But in Christian theology too, there are substantial disagreements with regard to the definition of dogma. If Baeck holds that, in order to be classed as a dogma, a religious belief must have been set down as irrefragable by an authority whose "rulings, on principle, are regarded as final" (p. 746), he finds support in the impressive authority of [Adolf] Harnack, who likewise cites the "infallibility of the [Catholic] church" as a prerequisite for the designation of a belief as a dogma and who, for this reason, refuses to classify Protestant doctrines as dogmas. It is known, however, that Seeberg, Loofs, and, more recently, O. Ritschl, do not agree with him on this point.[1] [Martin] Rade's definition, which Baeck cites and which accepts both secular and ecclesiastical powers as authorities in a position to formulate dogmas, differs with Harnack's interpretation.

There is greater consensus when it comes to Baeck's other criterion, the conceptual formulation of dogmas. But plausible though this criterion appears to be, it has been virtually abandoned by [Ernst] Troeltsch, who accepts as "latent dogmas" even those teachings which are contained solely in tradition or exist only in the spirit of the community and are generally affirmed by it.[2]

These differences in interpretation obviously are also significant for the question whether the religious doctrines of Judaism may be characterized as dogmas. Using a broad interpretation of this concept, it seems permissible to say that Judaism has at least some rudiments of dogma. However, the options between the various definitions of dogma are a matter of scholarly expediency, and since these options are determined by the requirements and cognitive goals of Christian theology—to which the concept of dogma is indigenous—the final choice must be left to the latter. Nor can we expect much profit from a detailed study of the implications which the various attempts at defining dogma may have for the evaluation of doctrinal formulations in Judaism. I shall therefore disregard the question of terminology and confine myself to an examination of the question whether, and if so in what manner, the religious concepts of Judaism have ever been set down as normative for all Jews.

It is to this problem that the previously mentioned difference in substance between Scheftelowitz and Baeck addresses itself. Scheftelowitz characterizes Judaism's religious concepts as dogmas because he is convinced that the Jewish religion possesses a quintessence of authoritative doctrines which, though not formulated in fixed, unchangeable terms, have been unequivocally defined in accordance with their spirit and must therefore be accepted by every Jew (p. 67). Baeck, on the other hand, in rejecting the concept of dogma in Judaism, asserts that Judaism, as a communal religion, is based on the "faith of the individual," whose "searching and inquiry" also "extend to the Torah." The following remarks attempt to clarify this difference.

I

In his argument against the existence of dogma in Judaism, Baeck cites the fact that the religious doctrines of Judaism were never authoritatively defined. This fact also plays a decisive role in our inquiry because it demonstrates that no attempt has ever been made by an authority in Judaism to set down systematically the quintessence of those religious doctrines which are binding on every Jew. The best proof of this is the passage in Mishnah Sanhedrin X,1—frequently cited in discussions of the question whether Judaism has dogmas—stating that anyone who does not believe in resurrection and the divine origin of the Torah will have no portion in the world to come. The Mishnah thus seems to confer universally binding force on these two tenets. However, it is not the intention of the Mishnah to designate these two tenets as the only ones binding on all Jews; it merely singles them out from among a multitude of basically similar tenets in order to counter the influence of certain heretical views. Moreover, the Mishnah in no way intends to ascribe a primary position to these two principles. In the case of the belief in the divine origin of the Torah, such a position cannot possibly be intended even in the sense in which, say, the proclamation of a dogma by the Catholic church bestows official sanction upon a religious truth that had already been accepted as valid. The Mishnah presupposes the validity of these two principles and states merely that anyone who denies them thereby excludes himself from the community of Israel. This is even more true in the case of certain religious truths whose validity is demonstrated by the fact that they have been incorporated into communal prayer. Here too the intention is not to set down a religious truth as a dogma, but to give expression to certain religious convictions that are shared by the entire community. Thus, contrary to Scheftelowitz's assumption, we have nowhere an act creating dogma. In making this statement, we are not simply emphasizing a scholarly nuance but are clarifying a fact of fundamental importance. In Jewish tradition there is no authoritative fixation or finalization of beliefs; tradition takes certain beliefs of the community for granted as something given and merely gives expression to them as the need arises.

Consequently—and this is an extremely important consequence—Judaism nowhere presents an exhaustive statement of beliefs held by the entire community. It is taken for granted that there is indeed a religious truth which is valid for all members of the Jewish community, but this truth is nowhere explicated systematically. The boundary line between the unchangeably permanent and the variable elements is nowhere clearly drawn. In fact, it is impossible to trace such a boundary line in accordance with the talmudic tradition. This difficulty has arisen in connection with every attempt to set forth the substance of Jewish faith in dogmatic form. We first encounter it in the discussions of our medieval religious philosophers about the basic teachings of Judaism. Maimonides is criticized by later scholars for the fact that, in the compilation of his Thirteen Articles of Faith, his selection of these specific doctrines from the totality of Jewish religious teachings had not been based on clearly discernible principles. Yet when these thinkers themselves attempt to formulate the basic tenets of Judaism, they rely mainly on subjective criteria. They are unable to find any guidelines in talmudic tradition. Even if we were to assume that they view the difference between the basic doctrines and the other religious truths of Judaism as having merely methodological (but not dogmatic) significance, they still would have to come to grips with the talmudic statements about beliefs binding on all Jews—if they were able to find such statements. The same problem also confronts more recent attempts to determine the binding beliefs of Judaism on the basis of talmudic tradition. One may possibly contend that there is such a thing as "dogma" in Judaism, but one would be hard put to specify what the "dogmas" of Judaism are. This quandary is quite evident in the adventitious and unsystematic nature of Scheftelowitz's list of "dogmas." However, the fault lies not with Scheftelowitz, but in the fact that it is impossible to extrapolate a system of universally accepted religious truths from the available material.

This lability in the quantity of the religious truths generally accepted as binding on all Jews is associated with a similar, though lesser, lability in content. Even those doctrines which are regarded as binding are, for the most part, not defined in such unequivocal terms as to assure their uniform comprehension. In this respect, the absence of a fixed text is of the utmost significance. Inasmuch as the doctrines of Judaism have never been formulated authoritatively, Judaism has a potential for an infinitely greater freedom of interpretation and development in the content of its beliefs than has the Christian church. This can be readily documented from as early a source as the talmudic Aggadah, but it is, above all, medieval religious philosophy which demonstrates that authoritatively accepted doctrines can be thoroughly recast under the influence of a completely different system of metaphysics. Gersonides is not the only one to assert that the notion of an eternal uncreated matter can be harmonized with the biblical doctrine of creation. Maimonides, who defends the belief in the biblical account of creation against Aristotelianism, admits the possibility of an even more profound transmutation of this doctrine than that posited by Gersonides when he claims that it would be possible to reconcile the text of the Bible with the theory of the eternity of the world if a strictly philosophical proof for this theory were required. The doctrine of divine omniscience and the closely related belief in divine providence have undergone no less drastic transmutations. According to ibn Ezra and Gersonides, God's knowledge is limited to the universal [the general order of forms]; it does not encompass the individual qua individual, but only as a link in the general order of being. Finally, the belief in immortality—which, probably because of the competing belief in resurrection, has been left oddly incomplete in the Talmud—is frequently understood in terms of the philosophical doctrine of the eternity of the "acquired intellect": that is, only the philosopher is considered immortal, and in a manner to boot that hardly suggests the survival of the individual soul. Such freedom of speculation about traditional beliefs would not have been possible had they ever been set down in an authoritatively fixed conceptual form.

However, contrary to widely held opinion, the foregoing must not be interpreted to mean that Judaism offers complete freedom of belief.[3] It is not correct to assume that the traditional conceptions of belief were deliberately formulated this way in order to permit relative freedom for the development of religious thought. Nor, indeed, does Judaism have freedom of belief in the basic accepted meaning of the term. In principle, traditional Judaism considers certain religious beliefs as authoritative. This applies, above all, to the belief in the divine origin of the Torah. The acceptance of this belief is demanded of every Jew; its denial is considered a heretical rejection of Judaism itself. Given this claim for the factualness of the divine revelation, it is no longer permissible to ask on what authority this belief is based; this "formal religious principle" is the very principle by which the concept of religious authority is constituted. Wherever there is such a thing as an authoritative religion, the principle of authority is of necessity primal and final. That the belief in the divine origin of the Torah and, in a wider sense, in the divine origin of the entire

Scripture has this binding force in traditional Judaism can be seen without difficulty (if indeed proof is needed) from the fact that this belief is the basic assumption for the validity of the religious law, whose binding force rests solely upon its divine origin. Without this theoretical underpinning, the Halakhah possesses no practical authority. Of course, it would seem that this principle is contradicted by the statement that universally binding norms exist only in the Halakhah, while there is complete freedom in the Aggadah. However, this seeming contradiction shows merely that even this statement cannot be accepted without qualifications. The concept of Aggadah, which is defined in purely negative terms and embraces the entire nonlegal part of the Law, obviously includes elements of utterly different religious significance. If Aggadah is so defined as to subsume the ultimate religious truths, which alone validate the Halakhah, it becomes clear that the principle of aggadic freedom cannot be applied to them. This doubtless is also the view held by tradition as a matter of course. It is, however, characteristic that the religious truths which are considered binding on all Jews are nowhere explicitly separated out as a sphere of their own. This fact alone is sufficient to show that any act to fix religious tenets is completely foreign to our tradition.

For our present purposes it is sufficient to point out that the belief in the divine origin of the oral tradition has the same claim to acceptance by Jews as has the written law. It is in this belief that the authority of all laws not contained in Scripture itself is grounded. The Talmud expresses this idea clearly when it characterizes as contemptuous of the word of God everyone who denies that any one of the generally accepted interpretations of the Law is of divine origin (Sanhedrin 99a). The Talmud's lack of concern for precise definitions of its dogmatic presuppositions is, of course, strikingly evident here. The Talmud is emphatic in its insistence on belief in the divine origin of the oral tradition, but it is difficult to derive from the Talmud a definitive understanding of the boundaries of this revealed oral tradition: what is of divine and what of human origin. The various statements in the Talmud on this subject are often mutually contradictory, and in some cases represent an indistinguishable blending of serious assertion and aggadic playfulness. It is, therefore, not surprising that the commentators of the Talmud represent diametrically opposed views on important questions, such as whether the halakhic precepts, derived from the Torah with the help of the traditional rules of interpretation, were divinely revealed or created by the sages, or whether they are to be taken literally or merely as an allusion.[4]

At any rate, it can readily be seen that this conception of belief in revelation establishes the authoritative character of religious truth as such. Along with belief in the divine origin of the written and oral laws, every Jew is expected to affirm the truth of their contents. Revelation and

tradition alike contain religious truth as a given fact, and every individual
is bound to this given belief held by the entire community. The only
purpose of a person's search and inquiry is to ascertain the true meaning
of that religious truth. No matter how much latitude may thus be left for
the development of individual religious thought, religious truth is consistently presented as a given fact. This was clearly recognized in the medieval discussions of the problem of dogma. Simeon ben Ẓemaḥ Duran, and
Joseph Albo after him, explicated the consequences inherent in the principle that the Torah is of divine origin along the lines just mentioned. The
mere fact that a particular teaching contradicts the Torah does not brand
its proponents as heretics as long as they believe themselves to be in
agreement with the Torah. On the other hand, a deliberate questioning of
any part—no matter how insignificant—of the Torah is regarded not as a
pardonable error but as a heretical revolt against the authority of
revelation.[5] Thus, neither the latitude allowed in the interpretation of the
meaning of revelation nor all the attempts to accomodate revelation to
the doctrines of philosophy invalidates the steadfast belief that revelation
constitutes the firm and inviolable norm of religious faith.

However, this axiomatic conviction seems to have no practical significance as long as there is unrestricted freedom for the interpretation of
revelation. Here too the statements of our religious philosophers during
the late Middle Ages on the basic teachings of Judaism are instructive,
though they are, of course, based not on historical but on normative
points of view. Whereas Maimonides, in formulating his Thirteen Articles
of Faith, was motivated primarily by his interest in rationalizing Judaism,
Ḥasdai Crescas and those who followed him sought to set down the
principles of belief out of a desire to confine the philosophical interpretation of Scripture to fixed boundaries. A reinterpretation of the basic
principles of belief is not permissible. These principles, therefore, differ
from the other components of the Torah not only in their logical position
but also in their dogmatic validity. The criterion for the selection of these
particular basic principles is the fact that they are the precondition for the
concept of revelation itself.[6] (Crescas, however, accepts this criterion only
for his principal category of dogmas.) This conceptual deduction of universally binding beliefs from the principle of divine revelation reflects an
interrelationship which also exists in historical reality. Historically seen, a
number of religious beliefs were inextricably linked with the Jewish belief
in divine revelation—beliefs which shared its authoritative character and,
like it, did not need to be formulated explicitly in dogmatic terms in order
to command adherence from the community. Thus the conviction that
Judaism's religious truth is given in the Torah for all time does not dissolve itself into a mere postulate; rather it is fulfilled by a series of

religious ideas which, by virtue of their linkage with the belief in revelation, themselves constitute a firm element of faith. Concepts such as divine providence, reward and punishment, and miracles, to name only a few, remained unassailably valid and had to remain so as long as the divine origin of the Torah was accepted as the basis of Jewish belief. Not even the freest philosophical reinterpretation of Judaism has ever negated these principles as such. It merely reinterpreted them, a procedure which was, of course, regarded by its opponents as incompatible with the concept of revelation.

Similar authority was, however, vested also in other beliefs which were not so intimately bound up with the principle of revelation. The beliefs in the Messiah, immortality, and resurrection have not only remained unchallenged but were considered unchallengeable. The messianic hope was so clearly expressed by the prophets that to doubt it was utterly unthinkable. The concept of resurrection was secured against any challenge by the Mishnah, which equated the rejection of this belief with the denial of the divine origin of the Torah. But it was primarily their expression in congregational prayer that turned these religious convictions into elements of a generally obligatory religious tradition. While their incorporation into the liturgy was not motivated by the intention to establish them as dogmas, the effect nonetheless was to confer upon them a dogmalike distinction.[7] The same holds true for all the other cases we have cited. The authority of tradition is imparted to the beliefs which were clearly expressed in the authoritative traditional sources.

In recapitulation, we can say that the foundations for Jewish beliefs are not established through norms set by some official authority. At the same time, the authoritative character of revelation and tradition serves as the binding force of the community's religious beliefs. If we search talmudic literature for statements explicitly granting dogmatic status to certain tenets, we find, at best, a haphazard conglomeration of data. The character of Jewish belief can be determined only on the basis of belief in revelation and of the ideas permeating Jewish worship. The notion that these fundamentals of Jewish belief should be singled out is alien to religious life as such, which considers itself bound to truth as transmitted by tradition, without attempting to analyze the components of that truth. As a result, as we have already pointed out, there is no firm line of demarcation between bindingly fixed and variable elements. Even the content of the former is open to various interpretations. It is the elasticity of this bond [between religious life and tradition] that has permitted a relative latitude in the development of Jewish religious thought and has frequently created the impression that Judaism offers complete freedom of belief.

II

The facts outlined in the preceding section are highly informative about the religious character of Judaism. The norms for religious belief in Judaism are determined entirely by the concept of revelation. In this and all other respects, authority is based on the fact that Judaism is a scriptural religion and that "Scripture"—divine revelation promulgated for all time in the sacred book—rules as the supreme authority in every area of life. This, to begin with, establishes the historical character of the concept of revelation. Revelation in Judaism is a historical event which is the source of religious truth. All subsequent religious life conceives itself as being bound up with that origin and accepts the religious truth as a given fact. Things are entirely different in those religions which perceive revelation as a recurring process, as a continuously renewed communication from the deity imparted to certain individuals by virtue of their personal state of grace or addressed to holders of specific religious offices. In either case, religious life is dominated by the personal authority of the recipient of the revelation, and the process of divine communication in principle remains uncompleted. In such religions, no matter how factual their historical traditions may be, religious life is not grounded in history. Preexilic Israel also knew such forms of religious authority: the authority of the prophet, resting on the call he received, and that of the priest, resting on the authority of his office. It is not necessary for our purposes to investigate the attitude of prophet and priest toward the authority of historical revelation during preexilic days. The development which begins with the Exile permits only historical revelation to survive as the supreme authority. Revelation, be it through prophet or priest, is considered to have ended. Thus it becomes itself a part of history, and the definition of revelation as historical fact is, with full consistency, projected back into the interpretation of the past. The prophecy of Moses founding the Jewish religion is sharply distinguished from the teachings of the later prophets; it is the norm binding upon prophets and priests and, indeed, upon every adherent of Judaism in all fundamental religious questions. The revelation communicated to Moses establishes the validity of the religious norm as obligatory for all time.[8]

This historical view of revelation provides the basis for the formation of a much firmer, or at least more stable, authority than does the notion of an ongoing process of divine revelation. An even stronger impetus in this direction is given when revelation is set down in writing. Customs, usages, or the traditional ideas of a religious community that are fluctuating and changeable are firmed up once they are given a literary form. The scriptural religions, which view a sacred document as the norm for every aspect of religious life, constitute, indeed, a special category in the development of religious authority by making it possible to capture a religious idea firmly and to allow it to exert a historical influence in a manner that would hardly be possible otherwise. Judaism has carried through this principle of scriptural authority with particular determination. Even its concept of tradition, despite the possibilities it offers for the reinterpretation of the scriptural text, has basically served to reinforce the authority of Scripture.

The extent to which this formal principle of scriptural authority also leads to the establishment of norms for the content of belief depends, of course, on the contents of the holy writings. Hence the development of Judaism is also determined by the contents of the Bible, which includes not only religious laws but also the revelation of a world of religious ideas complete in itself. Though these ideas appear in the Bible as products not of intellectual reflection but of purely religious intuition, they are stated with unmistakable clarity, as opposed to the figurative imagery and fantasies of mythology. Rooted in the concept of a supernatural God-Creator, they are set forth by the Bible, even to the deluded pagans, with a claim to exclusiveness not known before in religious history, as *the* one religious truth. After the principle of scriptural authority is fully developed, this exclusive claim to truth is of necessity applied not only to the revealed divine law, but just as much also to revealed religious truth as the nucleus of Jewish doctrine. Revealed religious truth thus becomes the norm for the community's religious beliefs, which are regarded as expressions of the truth set down in Scripture. This does not, of course, preclude the continued development of the ideas contained in the Bible any more than it arrests the evolution of religious law. But once this principle of tradition has gained ascendancy and such later concepts as the beliefs in resurrection and in retribution after death are classified as part of the original tradition and vested with its authority, and once the principal features of that tradition have been formulated, the belief of the community emerges as something final and definitive which every member of the community is expected to affirm.

Norm-setting in Jewish belief comes to a halt at this stage; the substance of Jewish belief has never been set down in the form of dogmas. An explanation frequently given for this state of affairs is that Judaism has lacked an authority which would be in a position to evolve dogmas and to determine their content. Baeck, in his more far-reaching attempt at an explanation (p. 748), pursues a similar direction when he says that Judaism has not been able to develop dogmas because it is, by its very nature, a communal religion in which the faith of the individual is the starting point and the bearer of tradition. However, the character of Judaism as a communal religion need not have precluded the development of dogmas, as can be seen from the development of Jewish religious law. There too the conceptual starting point is the individual; nevertheless, norms have evolved in religious law down to the minutest detail. To be sure, Baeck is correct when he says that the principle of authority, which is basic to the [Catholic] church, is alien to Judaism as a communal religion. The individual does not receive the truth from the hands of the church, but is himself the direct recipient and bearer of the divine teaching. However, when it comes to interpretation of the divine law, he is not autonomous but bound to the authentic interpretation. This principle, which the Talmud can derive from the text of the Torah, makes it possible to develop an authority on the basis of the communal religion, a uniform way of regulating the religious life of the members of the community.[9] This principle is the initial foundation for the authority of the Sanhedrin. However, the Sanhedrin's authority differs sharply from that of an ecclesiastical body in that it can demand acceptance of its rulings not because of the power it possesses in its own right, but because it is the sole body legitimized by the Torah to interpret the Law. At the same time, the application of this principle makes it possible to regulate religious practice even after the disintegration of every Jewish central authority and organizational unity by placing the authority into the hands of scholars qualified by their expertise. This type of authority, emerging from the soil of communal religion, is by its very nature applicable both to questions of religious law and to problems of dogma; thus it also would permit an authentic interpretation of the Torah with regard to dogma. But the Talmud does not do this, and later teachers of the Law are unable to make up for this omission because their own authority is founded solely on the Talmud. Thus Judaism at that point indeed lacks an authority that could formulate dogmas. During the talmudic era, however, the external conditions that would permit dogma formation are definitely present.

That this development does not occur is attributable not to the structure of the Jewish religious community, but to the content of Jewish religiosity. This fact has been pointed out repeatedly and, in the main, I can subscribe especially to Baeck's statements on this subject (pp. 747–48). Talmudic Judaism knows none of the specific factors which could motivate the formulation of a formal creed. The method of norm-setting described earlier is entirely sufficient for the preservation of the communal unity of belief, because disputes on dogma which would necessitate a definite ruling hardly ever arise. The defense against opposing religious trends from without or against dissident trends within (such as Sadduceeism, Christianity, or antinomian Gnosticism) call for other methods than authoritative statements of Jewish dogma. At the most, the immediate task at hand is to shore up the community's belief in specific disputed religious doctrines. But these trends never cause religious conflicts within talmudic Judaism itself. The differences in aggadic speculation on basic religious questions do not touch on the tenets which are thought to constitute the collective faith of the community, and therefore they do not require an authoritative ruling.

But this brings us to yet another, more profound, consideration. Judaism does not require dogmatic status for the content of its faith because it does not attribute to its tenets the salvational significance which motivated the development of dogma in Christianity. Judaism also considers the belief in God, in His Law, and in His promises as basic elements of piety and thus as prerequisites for salvation, but the concept of salvation through faith, be it in the sense of the Christian doctrine of vindication or in the sense of a gnostic concept of faith, is alien to Judaism. Accordingly, Judaism has no reason to formulate the content of correct belief conceptually and to set it down authoritatively. The acceptance of belief in the contents of the Torah and of the oral tradition, which Judaism demands of its adherents, does not presuppose a conceptual explication of these contents. Characteristically, this state of affairs changes during the Middle Ages when, under the impact of Aristotelianism, the correct knowledge of God is made a precondition for communication with Him and for eternal life. The objective of Maimonides and of some of his successors in fixing the dogmas of Judaism is to set down that correct perception which leads to salvation. The intellectualization of the concept of belief leads to the fixing of the content of belief. While talmudic Judaism also reflects frequently on the content of belief, these reflections never probe belief as such. Judaism remains a naive religion in its talmudic phase and thus lacks any impulse to produce a conceptual explication of its contents.

III

Notwithstanding the changes which traditional Judaism has experienced since the talmudic era, we have been able to treat it as a unified whole. The form of norm-setting which we have described is so closely intertwined with the Jewish belief in the revealed law and in the oral tradition that, along with that belief, it has survived all changes and continues to exist in present-day Judaism wherever belief in the divine origin of the written and oral laws in accordance with the traditional concept of revelation still constitutes the basis of religious life. Today we actually no longer have the options for the interpretation and reinterpretation of the biblical text which medieval rationalism could use in complete confidence. Stricter philological adherence to the biblical text has at the same time resulted in a more stringent adherence to religious concepts. Thus it is far more difficult today to reconcile, for instance, the theory of evolution in the natural sciences (or even only the current theories concerning the age of the earth) with the biblical account of creation than it was for a medieval thinker to bridge similar contradictions in his time. But this study is not the place for a detailed investigation of the problem or of possible ways of resolving it.

However, we must still show briefly that this situation changes radically once the belief in the verbal inspiration of the Torah and in the Sinaitic origin of the oral tradition is discarded. As this form of belief in divine revelation is surrendered, the Bible, and especially the oral tradition, cease to be norms of belief in the sense that every passage in them is authoritative and binding. By its very nature, the freer concept of inspiration, which replaces the idea of verbal inspiration, no longer requires adherence to the literal text of the Bible. Moreover, the world of Jewish belief can be examined in the light of historical development, making it evident that these beliefs have gone through a process of thoroughgoing evolution in the Bible itself and that important religious principles of Judaism are of postbiblical origin. In this respect, the consequences of abandoning the ancient supernaturalist concept of revelation in Judaism are basically the same as in the Christian churches. This fact is not always clearly recognized because, in Judaism, these consequences affect the area of religious law much more strongly than they do the creedal content. In contrast to Christianity, the struggle between religious movements in Judaism occurs primarily in the area of religious law, not in the sphere of dogma. The basic ideas of biblical monotheism—the belief in man's moral freedom, in his predestination for an eternal life, and in the coming of the kingdom of God—are shared by all branches of Judaism. A reading of the crucial passages in a modern presentation of the beliefs of Judaism will hardly reveal the religious group to which the author belongs.

Nevertheless, the break with the authoritative concept of religion has by no means been without consequences in respect to dogma. Parallel to the development in the Christian churches, Judaism's attitude toward the biblical accounts of creation and of miracles has changed. Without going into detail, I want to mention merely two factors which have played a significant role in the struggles about reforms in the Jewish prayer book: the abandonment of belief in resurrection and the changes in belief in the messianic future. The belief in physical resurrection has not been able to stand its ground anywhere without the support of the dogmatic authority of tradition; indeed, it has vanished almost entirely from the consciousness of many Jewish circles. Already during the Middle Ages Maimonides clearly attached little significance to it. However, he considered it as an equivalent of dogma; it remained in force as a component of the traditional doctrine of Judaism. The belief in a messianic era per se is common to all trends in Judaism, but its content has undergone an essential change. Its most obvious manifestation is that the belief in a personal Messiah had been given up, leaving only the belief in a messianic era. But the transformation of the messianic idea goes much farther. The idea that God's messianic kingdom will be established by a single miraculous act from Heaven and will replace the present world order has vanished together with the belief in a personal Messiah. The messianic kingdom of God is regarded as the ultimate goal toward which the moral and religious development of mankind is striving. This recasting of the messianic idea into the ideal of moral-religious progress—for which there certainly is no lack of foundation in Jewish tradition—has profound implications. Above everything else, it has given Judaism a completely new orientation to the present-day world: today's world will not be replaced by an entirely new messianic world in which Israel's destiny will be realized, nor is it merely the arena in which Israel must suffer and prove itself worthy of future redemption. The present-day world itself is to evolve into a messianic world, and it is in this world, the here and now, that Israel has a religious task to perform. In this way, a religious basis for the integration of Judaism into the world of modern culture and for its active participation in worldly concerns is established.

But no matter how much significance one attaches to this change in the content of Jewish belief, the facts remain that in principle the link with the authority of tradition has also been broken in matters of dogma and that the traditional form of norm-setting in Jewish belief has lost its foundation. Felix Goldmann's essay, "The Dogmatic Foundations of the Jewish Religion" ["Die dogmatischen Grundlagen der jüdischen Religion"] (*MGWJ* 70:440ff.), though containing much that is valuable, errs in principle inasmuch as it blurs this contrast and seeks to define dogma in a way which will accommodate the diverse interpretations equally well. To this end, Goldmann bases his theory of dogma on a concept of the divinity of the Torah which drops the principles of verbal inspiration and the imperishable validity of all its teachings, retaining merely the unifying and binding force of its "spirit" (p. 445). It is, of course, impossible to impose such a construction on traditional Judaism. No matter how old the principle of verbal inspiration is—and it doubtlessly long antedates Rabbi Akiba and was already taken for granted in the dispute between the Pharisees and the Sadducees—the fact is that it has reigned supreme in traditional Judaism ever since it first emerged, and one cannot simply ascribe to traditional Judaism a concept of the divine origin of the Torah of "different, deeper significance." For a historical understanding of traditional Judaism, such a liberalized interpretation of the divine character of the Torah is undoubtedly misleading. As a matter of fact, Goldmann's concept only appears to be historical. In reality, he intends it to be normative; that is, he wants to hold on to the religiously important core concept of inspiration in order to determine, with its help, that component of Jewish doctrine which continues to be valid.

The motivation for this attempt is entirely justified. The abandonment of the original principle of authority makes it necessary for Jewish theology to find new means of identifying its beliefs as Jewish and of differentiating clearly between what is Jewish and what is not. This problem has not become very significant within Judaism itself, because there has, indeed, been no change in the fundamental principles of Jewish belief, and the unity of belief (to the extent that it is still determined by religious factors) has remained intact. However, this does not alter the theoretical significance of the problem. Its solution lies in the definition of the concepts "spirit" or "essence" of Judaism, which more recent Jewish religious philosophy has rightly adopted as the basis for its researches. The Jewish character of our belief is guaranteed by its harmony with the spirit and essence of Jewish doctrine. However, these concepts present enormous theoretical difficulties. As similar discussions in Christian theology show, a clear definition of the concept "essence" is an extremely complicated task which we cannot even begin to undertake in the present study.

To conclude these reflections, only the following still remains to be said: contrary to what Goldmann frequently seems to imply, the concept of "essence" cannot help in establishing new authoritative norms for the content of Jewish belief. The criteria by which it can be defined are internal and, as such, necessarily "subjective." If this is true for the purely historical definition of the essence of Judaism, it is all the more true for the application of that definition to norm-setting. This subjectivity obviously rules out an authoritarian fixing of belief. Even in instances in which its separation from the old principle of authority has left the substance of belief unaltered, its validity undergoes a fundamental change. Not only the acceptance of the truth of its contents, but also the affirmation of the Jewish character of the principles of belief become a matter of personal insight and religious conviction. This is increasingly apparent as one comes to realize that the essence of Judaism does not consist of a series of individual tenets, but of a unified fundamental religious conviction which is the very basis of these tenets and which alone gives them their religious meaning. To extract this religious conviction from its conceptual and ideational expression is the crucial task involved in defining the essence of Judaism—a definition which alone makes it possible to comprehend the multiplicity of individual tenets as the expression of *one* religious spirit, and to discuss the unchanging religious content in the changing conceptual forms in which it manifests itself.

The definition of "essence" is therefore also the basis for any decision whether a given doctrine is inextricably linked with the essence of Judaism. This formulation of the task at hand underscores even more strongly the subjective nature of any definition of the essence of Judaism— a subjectivity, however, which need not create fear of arbitrariness and individual whim. In place of a theoretical substantiation of this fact, may it suffice to point to the actual result of studies made to date, studies which have essentially followed the procedure outlined here and which, through this process, have arrived at a remarkable consensus in their conception of Judaism. But even more significant than this accord in the scholarly definition of Jewish belief is the unity which has survived in Jewish belief itself. The inner bond with the basic religious beliefs of Judaism which has taken the place of external norms for these beliefs has proven strong enough to preserve the uniform religious basis of Judaism.

Notes

"Establishing Norms for Jewish Belief," translated by Gertrude Hirschler, first appeared as "Die Normierung des Glaubensinhalts im Judentum," *Monatsschrift für Geschichte und Wissenschaft des Judentums* 71 (1927):241–55; reprinted in Kurt Wilhelm, ed., *Wissenschaft des Judentums im deutschen Sprachbereich* (Tübingen, 1967), 2:753–68.

1. For the Loofs controversy, see Albert Hauck, ed., *Realenzyklopädie für protestantische Theologie und Kirche*, 3d. ed. (Leipzig, 1896–1913), 4:760ff.
2. Cf. the sources cited by Baeck, *MGWJ* 70:746.
3. As early an authority as Abraham Geiger opposed this view in *Jüdische Zeitschrift für Wissenschaft und Leben*, vol. 1 (Breslau, 1862).
4. Cf. Abraham Geiger, *Nachgelassene Schriften*, ed. Ludwig Geiger (Berlin, 1875), 1:102ff.; Saul Kaatz, *Die mündliche Lehre und ihr Dogma*, 1:30ff.
5. Simeon ben Ẓemaḥ Duran's introduction to the Commentary on the Book of Job, chap. 9 (*Sefer haHashgaḥah* [called *Ohev Mishpaṭ*]).
6. Cf. Julius Guttmann, "Religion und Wissenschaft im mittelalterlichen und im modernen Denken," in *Festschrift zum 50-jährigen Bestehen der Hochschule für die Wissenschaft des Judentums* (Berlin, 1922), p. 152.
7. Leopold Löw, *Gesammelte Schriften*, ed. I. Löw (Szegedin, 1889), 1:171, and in a similar vein Scheftelowitz, *MGWJ* 70:71, rightly cite the significance of "liturgical sanctioning" for religious doctrine. The objections to the use of this observation in the sense of its definition of dogma can be seen from the text itself.
8. The passage in the Talmud stating that no prophet is authorized to add anything new to the Torah (Megillah 2b) refers directly only to the halakhic sphere; however, it clearly shows that the later prophets basically were subordinate to the Mosaic revelation upon which the Jewish religion is based.
9. Sifre to Deut. 17:10–11; Babylonian Talmud, Sanhedrin 87a; cf. Mishneh Torah, Hilkhot Mamrim, chap. 1.

5
JEWISH PIETY AND RELIGIOUS DOGMA

Max Wiener

[In his introductory section, omitted here, Max Wiener distinguishes between religious feeling and *Weltanschauung,* the conceptual formulation of a religious world view based on specific articles of faith. He points out that conserving, and conservative, ties of emotion remain even after the intellectual content to which this emotion was attached has disappeared: Jews are able to remain Jews by sentiment even after the Jewish Weltanschauung has lost its power of conviction for them. Yet Weltanschauung, defining or embodying what it conceives to be the nature of religious truth, is an indispensable dimension of religion. On the other hand, there can be no genuine religious feeling without the experience of the reality and activity of a Godhead that is beyond the horizon of the intellect and excludes everything that is Weltanschauung, dogma, or scientific proof. Therefore the question is whether, if at all, the gap between the religious and the intellectual spheres, between Jewish piety and religious dogma, can be bridged.]

edieval religious philosophy arose from the practical need to establish the truth of the Jewish faith against the objections of philosophy and the criticism of the other great religions, especially Islam. When Judaism had to adjust itself to the new scene after its emancipation in the nineteenth century in central and western Europe, losing itself more and more in the surrounding social structure, absorbing the European spirit in its various national nuances and thus assimilating the world's culture, it was compelled to look into its own character, to come to terms with itself, and to give to itself and others a clear account of how it saw and experienced itself. It had a perfect right to define itself as a religion. But in the case of Judaism this definition was a generalization of the vaguest kind. For when people discovered that the most potent ingredient in Jewish religious life was the conviction of the divine election of the Jewish people, and that it was the entire community of the children of Jacob which was the bearer of piety, it became apparent that this definition of its own nature made Judaism something altogether different and not merely a special kind of religiously tinged Weltanschauung—that is, an intellectually elaborated conception of the highest Being. Such a conception could, of course, serve as a valid Jewish response to the general questions raised by mankind concerning the meaning and purpose of life; in competition with Christian, Buddhist, or philosophical solutions it could well hold its own and even emerge triumphant as the true solution—true in the sense of metaphysical knowledge. That the content of Judaism and its historical development entitle it to appear in the arena of philosophically formulated religious systems and present its answer to the ultimate problems of existence as *the* answer cannot be doubted. In this respect, it is merely one religion among all others. The question is, however, whether this self-definition as a Weltanschauung, which accidentally has remained confined to the members of one people, does justice to Judaism's true character—whether Jewish strivings receive their impulse exclusively from this religious view that presents Judaism as a mixture of metaphysical-ethical notions about God and the world.

Yet this approach is merely a bypath. The main road to an understanding of Jewish piety must start from the fundamental fact that the Jewish religion is professed only by members of the Jewish ethnic group [*Menschen des jüdischen Stammes*]. What conclusions ought to be drawn from this fact? In modern times, extreme Jewish nationalists have gone so far as to claim that the palpable manifestations of Jewish piety—our symbols and ceremonies, the regulations governing food and clothing, the holidays that celebrate historical events, the sacred regimen of the Law—are nothing but expressions of national life. Yet this claim says too little or too much. Too little, for we merely state the obvious when we point out that religious observances and expressions, like any other manifestation of man's inner life, retain some of their eggshells and show the marks of their origin. The soul of an ethnically circumscribed group is naturally reflected in its creations. That the Jewish religion is the product of Jews and bears the stamp of their character is certainly no big discovery.

But this trite and obvious statement is frequently taken to mean something entirely different, and indeed, far more different than can be justified from the ethnic point of view and an analysis of the religious idea as such. Jewish self-awareness never characterized itself as exclusively national. It did not regard itself merely as a functional framework for a variety of cultural phenomena, but saw itself (and this essentially constituted its individuality) as filled with a clear and definite content, namely a religious content. Only because it claimed sole possession of this religious content on the basis of its ethnic self-limitation, living in the belief that it was chosen by a special dispensation to the service of God, did it become conscious of having a special, indestructible identity. Whether or not the Jews should thus be defined as a "people" is a matter of semantics. At any rate, it is impossible to understand the term "people" here in any other sense than as a group of individuals who feel ethnically united because of their common origin and fate, but whose spiritual self is profoundly and emphatically formed by their special relationship to God.

It is, however, a grave error on the part of those who hold this "national" view to identify the essence of religion solely with ethnic customs and usages involving distinctive dress, national drinks, or similar social habits. This degrading definition fails to recognize that it was Judaism which first experienced the primacy and centrality of the religious idea, adopted monotheism with passionate devotion, and made itself its spokesman to the world. Judaism realized, of course, that the unsurpassable significance of this affirmation was subjective, that it sprang from its own soul. Yet it placed the objective validity and absolute dignity of this highest Being above all natural events. The reduction of religion to national mores nullifies the demand insisted upon and fulfilled by Judaism itself that religion must be a matter of conviction and conscience.

Motivation by conviction or conscience, however, does not imply that the core of religion must be comprehended as a Weltanschauung whose validity is judged by the truth concept of science. We have already noted that the experience of divine revelation as the source of piety defies description. From this point of view, mysticism, as a spiritual attitude that makes no compromise with the conditions of life or with our knowledge of the empirical world, represents the perfect type of pure religiosity.

What, then, is the relation between the historical phenomenon of Judaism and the epistemological foundations of religion discussed here? Mysticism, understood as a complete, closed system of piety, plays a less significant role in Judaism then elsewhere. From its very beginning, Judaism strongly emphasized a piety that is governed by obedience to the Law. Consequently, a certain spirit of rationalism captured the Jewish soul, and an aversion to mysterious doctrines of faith, as contrasted to pious conduct, characterized Judaism from its earliest days. If we wanted to investigate the reason for this constancy of mind and heart, inherent in Judaism from its birth to the present—a constancy that made for the unity of its life and the inner harmony of its personality—we would find it to be its preference for clear and distinct ideas and its dislike of mystical obscurity. That this passion for clarity has been among Judaism's most abiding possessions throughout the centuries need not be demonstrated here in detail, for no

one is likely to dispute it on historical grounds. We shall here merely touch
upon the results and the current status of this development.

The abundant references in the Torah and especially in Deuteron-
omy to the wisdom, reasonableness, and evident power of the Law
("Law" there is anything but a means of dictatorial coercion to obedience, exacted by the sovereign will of an almighty God) created at the
very beginning of Jewish existence an atmosphere of clarity and pervaded
its subsequent history. If Israel would be faithful in observing the commandments of its God—all of them wise and truly life-enhancing—it
would gain the admiration of all other nations. The basic principles of the
covenant that binds the Holy One with Israel are clear and convincing;
He is the one and only God, creator of heaven and earth: Israel is His
people, upon whom He has bestowed countless benefits and from whom
He demands obedience to His will, which is revealed in commandments
easily comprehended by a perceptive mind. Moreover, there is the event
that took place at Sinai for all eyes to behold. Can there be anything
more compelling to the mind and heart than the experience of this people
with the living God? These were the foundations that appeared to all
later generations as secure and unrejectable. Man's reason had no cause
to doubt them.

The mainstream of the Jewish spirit flowed into Talmudism and
Rabbinism. Both are so deeply embedded in the practices of religious life
as set forth in the Law, and both breathe in the air of the Torah so
naturally and matter-of-factly, that it would never occur to them to question their own presuppositions. They undoubtedly sharpened the intellect
and made it an ever-keener instrument as they analyzed and dissected,
with painstaking care, the meaning and implications of the Law. However, the intellect was not employed to examine the roots of this religious
reality and to comprehend its principles, but only to elucidate and elaborate the Law, the foundation of all life and all Jewish existence.

Thus there emerged a vast system whose ramifications encompassed
all facets of man's quest for God as well as the plethora of his relations to
the world and his fellow men. Strict rationality ruled within this system.
Logic, though often adapted to the needs of legalistic-religious thought,
was enlisted to deepen and refine the knowledge of the divine Law. But
this religious world, which extended into all areas of life and conformed
to its own inner rationality, rested on an altogether different basis: the
belief that the Law was communicated to Israel through the miracle of
revelation. Regardless of how we may define the relationship between
divine reason and human reason with regard to the content [of rev-
elation], and even assuming that God's revelatory will is in principle
comprehensible to human understanding, the real basis of the Law is its
rootedness in the transcendent, in miracle, in revelation. No matter how

deeply man might penetrate the meaning of the Torah, divinity, in its full meaning as an emanation from another world and from its highest Being, was attributed to the Torah. Human wisdom was legitimized and authenticated only by the extent to which it corresponded to the teaching that comes from God.

The revelation that was given to Israel alone must be distinguished from the original revelation that was imparted to the children of Noah prior to the Mosaic legislation, and through them to all mankind. The Noachian revelation is nothing but a metaphor expressing the conviction that the seeds of morality dwell within the human spirit and that man possesses the inborn capacity to recognize the essential meaning of ethical precepts and to practice them. This is a mythologizing version of what is known in philosophy as the doctrine of innate ideas, but here it is expressed by an oriental mind that can visualize knowledge only as something that is inculcated from without, and that cannot conceive of the existence of a teaching without the existence of a teacher to impart it. A consciously felt distinction between the divine and the human, between this world and the next, is hardly perceptible.

Yet it was this distinction which Judaism felt to be the very basis of its historical consciousness—*the experience of an entire people* to whom the divine Spirit, the one and only God, reveals himself in a supernatural manner. Jewish religious feeling, in its pure form, undistorted by interpretations, means the acceptance and inner appropriation of the tradition of that experience of a heroic age by the Jews of later generations. True, according to this historical view the generations that do not belong to the era of the founders and of the prophets, and thus were not contemporaries of the classical revelation, appear to be excluded from the experience of having received the divine message directly. That miracles and other extraordinary forms of divine intervention could occur was, of course, considered possible, and indeed probable, by postbiblical Judaism, just as it was by every non-Jewish religious community. But since the emphasis of religious interest was from the very beginning placed on the *content* of the divine word, on the Torah as the law of life, and since this content could not be changed either by adding or by subtracting—its essential function being to serve as a practical guide for the existence of an entire people—the revelation of the Torah and the devotion of the faithful to the tradition of that event remained the focal point of Jewish experience. What we have is the belief in a historical event and in its enduring effect, as experienced in the observance of the Law and its practical application at all times and in all walks of life.

This attitude is far removed from mysticism. But it is no closer to the rationality of a religious Weltanschauung. If there is an absolutely irrational element in mystical "illumination" as seen from the standpoint of natural thought, we might speak in the case of Judaism of a "historical-metaphysical irrationalism," insofar as its self-consciousness is rooted in the thesis that God bestowed His special grace upon it alone. The irrational element lies in this restriction. The effects of this fortuitous historical event that extended far beyond the classical period of revelation, and the unbroken devotion to its meaning whose consequences determined the content of Jewish religiosity, demonstrate its enduring vitality. We must bear in mind that we are here confronted with two utterly different levels of self-understanding: the Christian view of the supernatural revelation of God in Christ as the road to salvation for all mankind, and the Jewish view that restricts the giving of the Torah to Israel. Christian universalism contains a rational core in its belief in the salvation of mankind—that is, of the individual. If human nature is as Pauline psychology defines it, man's salvation can logically not be achieved in any other way. Thus we find that theology assumes the dominant role at the very birth of this new Pauline religion of salvation. This is what we mean by "rational Weltanschauung," and in this sense it has always remained the basis of Christianity and deeply affected the Christian mystical experience of the living God. In Judaism the mystery lies elsewhere: greater emphasis is placed upon the human aspect. Why did God choose Israel from among all the nations? Why, even in its faithlessness, has it remained God's firstborn? This is what we mean by the term "historical-metaphysical irrationalism," in contrast to an intellectual irrationalism regarding which the two religions do not differ in principle.

This, then, is the essential nature of Jewish being. We can comprehend it more clearly if we consider the absurdity of the claim that this particularism, as it exists in Jewish consciousness, is meant to be nothing but a preliminary step toward a larger truth: that the Jewish people, having given the world the monotheistic ideal of the One God, has completed its task and can now disappear among the surrounding nations that have appropriated this truth. On the contrary. An indispensable element of Jewish piety has always been the preservation of the people that descended from the patriarch Abraham, the progeny of those who heard the divine voice at Sinai and thus were duty-bound to keep the covenant with God, as were all later generations. Ethical universalism in Judaism did not come into being, as may superficially appear, by way of theoretical deduction from the abstract idea of the uniqueness of God. In Judaism, the spirit of human universality was not the product of thought, as we find it among the Stoics or among the philosophers of the European Enlightenment; it was a feeling that sprang from the heart. This emotion was most passionately felt by the prophets; in the boundless devotion with which they, the chosen of the children of Israel, worshiped the God of Israel, He grew into infinity. This strong feeling of exclusiveness, of having been chosen by God, the mightiest of all powers, from among all the nations, gave birth to that ardent fervor that characterized the piety of the prophets and to that intense passion that extended their goal—God—to infinity. Obedience, fidelity, and gratitude to God were to know no limits. A sense of deep obligation thus enters the soul of the people. This earnestness is the true origin of all moral conduct. Once it takes hold of men's hearts, the barriers that initially impede the flow of moral energy from one people to another must fall. We shall have occasion to discuss this matter further.

In any case, it will not do to define the relationship between the universalism of content and the particularism of the Jewish community as if the universal validity of the religious idea—the only God, creator and sustainer of the world and of mankind—had to break through the barriers that enclosed the original community of believers. Israel's election, the unique distinction bestowed upon Israel by a divine act of grace, never signifies something that is merely provisional, conceived teleologically as a preparatory step on God's part which will lead to the illumination of all mankind. One might similarly feel tempted to interpret the messianic idea as if it represented the unlimited extension of God's relationship to man per se, to mankind as a whole. This intention is no doubt inherent in the messianic idea, and the coexistence of the particularistic and universalistic elements in Messianism should not prevent us from recognizing the purity of hope for the union of all mankind under the one God in the latter. Messianism is merely the full and conscious completion of what is already contained in the monotheistic idea of God, namely, that the meaning of the one God is realized only when He becomes the God of all. But this does not cancel what is posited in the original idea of the Jewish religion—that Israel, in a special manner, always remains God's people. Nowhere does this appear more distinctly than in Isa. 49:6, the clearest expression of prophetic universalism: "It is too little that you should be My servant in that I raise up the tribes of Jacob and restore the survivors of Israel· I will also make you a light of nations, that My salvation may reach the ends of the earth."

That the moral content into which this religion can be distilled is and must be the concern of all men goes without saying. It is this self-evident character of the moral content that constitutes its dignity, its universal eminence. But seen from within and as experienced by Jewish consciousness, it must appear utterly unacceptable that the Jewish people, as God's servant and as the special object of God's actions, should disappear. All of this emerges with utmost clarity from the prophet's words. This is true of all references, messianic and otherwise, in the prophetic discourses and in the biblical-talmudic writings which deliberately seek to bridge the gap between Israel as God's people and the heathen world. There is no need to cite these references in detail. Specific references drawn from this vast and comprehensive literature do not prove very much, especially since the spirit of particularism can be documented with the same philological-historical fidelity. Since the time of the prophets, the idea of one humanity, united by the consciousness of one God, has always been present in the Jewish soul. The crystallization of this idea engendered an ethical broad-mindedness which, in the face of Judaism's historical experience of being excluded, compelled it to participate in the life and culture of other nations, always reminding it of its unconditional moral obligation to the individual non-Jew. This religious-ethical universalism, however, could in no way affect the most distinctive characteristic of Jewish piety: to regard the preservation of the Jewish people, the natural carrier of this piety, as a holy obligation.

Thus we find here a type of religion that is sui generis. Its ethnic basis distinguished it from that type that proclaims the predestination of the elect, as found in the doctrine of grace in Puritanism and in orthodox Islam. Moreover, prophetic and talmudic Messianism and universalism never went beyond a merely relative differentiation of the elect, Israel, and the nonelect, the other nations. Judaism not only did not recognize but absolutely rejected any distinction between the blessed and the damned, for it held that the pious of all nations have a portion in the world to come. In both [Judaism and Calvinism], the divine will is a decisive factor, but the Calvinistic doctrine of grace is harsher than the Jewish principle of election. In the former, grace can also be bestowed on individuals, in principle making possible the gradual inclusion of all into the community of the elect. Actually, however, the possibility of extending this religious principle to all mortals is expressly rejected. In this respect, there is no basic difference from Judaism. However, an essential difference is immediately apparent when we consider that in Calvinism man is conscious of individual grace and of the divine voice calling to him when he leads a life that is willed by God, a life to which all men are summoned but which only a few—because God so wills it—succeed in leading. Moreover, a strong activist element, whose effects are evident in historical experience, is a potent ingredient in the moral character of those who believe that they are participating in grace. Such an impulse to energetic activity is also found in Jewish religiosity, but since in it the believer is subject to God's commandments not as an individual but because he belongs to the community of the elect, the energy that flows into the individual soul can only come from the deep feeling of a collective vocation imbedded in ethnic consciousness.

Thus Judaism, according to its self-image, is an organism in which ethnic and religious consciousness interpenetrate. Neither is permitted to become predominant. On the one hand, we must reject the tendency to regard Judaism merely as the sum total of its religious teachings and of the practical maxims that flow from them—of teachings, in other words, that are objectively valid, that can be dissociated from those who promulgated them, and that were accidentally professed by a people united by a common origin, so that it becomes possible to compare a Jewish denomination [*Konfession*] to a Christian denomination or that of any other group.

Nor does the opposite view do justice to the actual situation, the view that reduces Judaism to an ethnic religion and regards its peculiar relation to the divine as merely one of the many manifestations, more interesting perhaps than the others, of the folk-soul. That there is a psychological-historical standpoint from which the situation may and perhaps even must be so regarded is obvious and has already been stressed. The first view appears possible when theological-metaphysical speculation endeavors to erect a system from elements of the Jewish religion. Our primary interest, however, is in neither of these two views, but in the phenomenological aspect: what does the living, concrete Jewish consciousness say to us? This interest requires that we give full consideration to the uniqueness of the phenomenon of ethnic feeling, involving at the least a sense of common descent from those who received the original revelation, and that we regard it as the indispensable condition of religious life which, in its devotion to one God, recognizes the unity of mankind as an essential directive force of its practical conduct.

In other religions, people are born into a church and find themselves, as they emerge from childhood, in the arms of an institution that receives them with its rites and symbols, its prayers and hallowed traditions, thus making them an organic part of its corporate life. At first sight there may seem to be no difference between someone who is bound by the decision of his parents and forefathers to such a community and a Jew who is similarly bound to his community. A sharp difference comes to light, however, when we consider the specific religious character of the feeling of solidarity signified by the idea of *k'lal Yisrael*.

This feeling of solidarity in Judaism could be reduced to the combined effects of two elements: first, an ethnic unity that is fortified by the homogeneity or the common fate of individuals and groups that come from the same geographic area; second, the general formative power of the religious idea that makes for social cohesion, apart from its concrete content. The socializing and solidifying force of these elements is beyond question, but it does not exhaust the peculiar religious coloration of the world Jewish community. It was not the cumulative effect of similar personal convictions concerning God's sovereignty, the nature of the transcendent, that created our religious community, but the fact that the individual, even in religious matters, is placed in the concrete reality of a living spirit and that the actual life patterns of the bearers of the tradition become their experiential context.

Needless to say, personal conviction is also demanded. The Jew must not only acknowledge God, he must also seek to know Him. But he is also required to adopt the outlook of the religious community as such. Judah Halevi's dictum that the revelation and election at Sinai, addressed not to an individual prophet but to the entire people, obligated the entire Jewish nation as such to bear eternal witness to the truth of the one God, accurately expresses what the Jewish religion has at all times considered to be its true vocation. Traditional religious law does not recognize the conversion of a Jew to another religion. This is also true of Catholic ecclesiastical law. The difference is, however, that Catholicism regards all mankind as potentially Catholic and has always endeavored to realize the possibility, whereas Judaism, specifically defined as a religion, has, notwithstanding exceptions, limited itself to the descendants of the patriarchs. To be sure, the institutional and sacramental character of the Roman faith may in effect appear quite similar to Judaism in that the significance of personal conviction recedes behind the authority of the church. But its fundamentally universal character, which places objective truth above subjective truthfulness and brands error as a sin, negates any true similarity. Conversely, we would do violence to the facts if we were to conclude, because of the zeal with which our Law watches over those bound to it by birth, and even over those who have freed themselves from it inwardly, that we are dealing merely with an example of national or social self-assertion. The primary motivation is religious: every member is required by the God of Israel to observe the commandments promulgated by Him. To transgress them is a sin. And the most grievous sin is to throw off the yoke of heaven and, by worshiping other gods, deny its validity in principle.

The discussion of the controversial question whether present-day Judaism in central and western Europe is essentially national or religious in character can be advanced only if we keep in mind that the Jewish religion has been content to remain a minority religion and, indeed, a religion that is strictly confined to those who feel themselves united in an ethnic relationship. This firmly established point enables us to clarify the relationship between pious emotion and a religious view of the world. We have already indicated that ideas concerning God and life, which as such resist all attempts to confine them to circumscribed groups, did not create the religious community of Judaism. We have to assume a primeval experience that united the one God and the one tribe, Israel. We need not discuss the fact that this condition is itself the result of a historical development whose traces are evident in the earliest documents. For even if the belief in YHWH as the only real divine power, the creator of the world, was preceded by a preliminary stage in which He was regarded as the sole tribal god beside those of other nations, we already find in the earliest accounts in the Pentateuch, side-by-side with this view, a more highly developed universal view acknowledged [by later generations] as the specifically biblical consciousness of God, without which the systems of Christianity and Islam, both based on the religion of the Old Testament, could hardly have arisen. This basic view not only remained intact in rabbinic Judaism but also received strong emotional support that emerged as a reaction to the political and social debasement experienced by the Jews in the Diaspora. It represents the fundamental datum in their religious consciousness.

If we should characterize it according to its psychological content and the significance it has for its disciples, we must say that it is not a doctrine that is subjectively felt as a personal experience. It is only as a member of the group, as a child of a tribe whose election is anterior to his existence, that the individual Jew participates in this truth. This truth is based on the feeling of certitude with which a historical fact is accepted and its irrationality acknowledged, without any attempt at metaphysical reconstruction or interpretation. This consideration is the decisive factor, for Jewish piety is not kindled by the flame of faith in metaphysical facts but by the psychological appropriation of empirical-historical facts. Here we have the clearest expression of the conjunction of the ethnic and the religious communities. Just as the wellsprings of Israel's religious life, the summons to Abraham and the giving of the Torah at Sinai, were conceived as purely historical events, so the pious consciousness is always oriented primarily around events in the community, in which the ways of divine guidance are, of course, recognized and gratefully acknowledged. The most eloquent testimonies of this attitude are our prayers, whose kernels have come down to us from the time of the Mishnah and which, in their later expanded formulations, are ethnically oriented (except for some medieval religious-philosophical poetry, which cannot alter the general character of our prayers as a whole). The Eighteen Benedictions with their characteristic opening phrase that has become a standard formula of invocation, "Our God and God of our fathers"; the constant references to the central event in Jewish religious history, the giving of the Torah at Sinai; the equally stereotypical reference to the Exodus from Egypt as the birth of God's people, made possible only through the gracious intervention of the Eternal—in short, all the events that we are accustomed to designate as "national" produce an emotional stance that differs fundamentally from the stance produced by a narrow, metaphysically oriented Christian religiosity. It is no valid objection to claim that similarly well-known "universalistic" expressions, such as the formularized characterization of God as lord of the world and creator of heaven and earth, or the fervent hope that all idolatry and superstition might vanish from the earth and that all creatures might unite to do the will of God, reflect a more broad-minded outlook. For before one speaks of two tendencies in Judaism, one should bear in mind that the belief in election with its apparently particularistic consequences is possible only on the conceptual basis of a religious universalism. Of that Being who was nothing but a tribal god and who, therefore, could care only for those who knew and worshiped Him, only some fragments of tradition have come down to us.

In a minority religion the feeling of solidarity among the faithful is not based solely on their sense of shared religious unity and piety. A special sociological element is added to the general consciousness of religious unity. Sharing in one faith, quite apart from its content, itself creates a powerful bond which becomes stronger the deeper the soul's interest in religion. In the history of religious persecutions it is not an uncommon phenomenon that the persecuted sever all bonds that tie them to their homeland—political, cultural, social, economic—and emigrate to new countries for no other reason than to be free to live in accordance with their religious convictions. Where this motivation is strong enough, it proves to be superior to any other impulse. Yet it is individual conviction (which must, of course, be shared by many others) which accounts for this breakaway from all other existential relationships and for a new orientation which is consciously guided only by the religious impulse.

Judaism possesses an additional peculiarity: the notion that the conviction of the individual involves a relationship to the community. The feeling of *k'lal Yisrael* means more than just an active sympathy that extends to all coreligionists who have the same relationship to God. It also differs from the empathy, deepened by a tragic common fate, for all brothers and sisters who trace their descent to the patriarch Jacob.

God—this is the Jewish self-image—has chosen this people from among all the nations. I belong to this chosen tribe and take part in the precious possession that has given my community its lofty position. This idea of being chosen signifies the rule of democracy within the community and a feeling of aristocratic pride towards the outside. This coincides in part with the attitude to oneself found in Puritanism. But in Judaism, condemned to a pariah existence on the outside, this feeling appeared even more strongly by contrast. Every Jew is a comrade to every other Jew. It is one thing, of course, to live under the same national flag, whose principal function is to demonstrate its unifying power to outsiders, or to participate in a common faith that seeks to unite all mankind under its symbols but whose cohesive power decreases in proportion to the geographic dispersion of its believers. But Jewish solidarity is an entirely different thing. One Jew is a pledge or guarantee for the other, because all derive their dignity and significance from the fact that they are, in a special way, regarded by God as a community.

The general conception that we are God's children and made in His image—the conception on which ethical monotheism bases the unity of the human race—is therefore developed in an exemplary manner within a small segment of mankind. The universal significance of this idea has never been absent from Jewish consciousness. Indeed, world-embracing monotheism has its roots in the human soul which, in its fervent love of God, experiences the relationship between God and man as one of mutual devotion and confidence and sees God as the bond encompassing all spirits. However, the notion that they are God's children is not a theoretical principle or dogma for Jews, but something directly experienced in historical events by the individual as a member of his ethnic group. Hence Jewish society as a living community was able to imbue this religious ethic with a vitality not found in any other ethico-religious system whose practice is far removed in time from the heroic period of its founders, prophets, and martyrs.

The ethical doctrines of even the most divergent religions are so similar in their demand for the same virtues—loyalty, goodwill, benevolence, helpfulness, compassion, forgiveness—and in their censure of the same vices—vindictiveness, cruelty, brutality, overweening conceit—that a fair-minded and discerning critic would not play off one faith against the other. The question, rather, is whether and by what means a religion is able to erect a system of practical conduct on this common theoretical basis. It is a generally recognized fact, deeply ingrained in the consciousness of the people among whom we live, that the Jew, at least in his conduct towards other Jews, displays feelings of brotherliness, loyalty, rectitude, and sympathetic concern which the others exhibit in their own circle only on the rarest occasions. Even the caricatures of these attitudes illustrate the validity of this point. It is as characteristic for the Jewish *shnorrer* to be brazen as it is for the Christian beggar to be humble and modest, showing clearly the matter-of-factness with which the Jew takes the benevolence of another Jew for granted and even as his inborn right. This fact is well known. Its source is the peculiarly religious solidarity inherent in Judaism. For the chosen people, every one of its children is significant in God's sight. This places every individual in a double role: as the bearer of a special obligation and as the object of exceptional concern on the part of his fellow man.

Less known but no less worthy of serious consideration is another consequence of this attitude—the specific coloration that Jewish individualism receives from the Jewish religion. Since this religion represents itself as an experience that is deeply imbedded in the consciousness of an entire people, and since all revelations imparted to the various prophets derive their significance from the meaning they possess for the people as a whole, it was generally assumed that for biblical piety it was the community which should be designated as the proper carrier of religiousness. Religious individualism, which is grounded in a reciprocal relationship between God and the individual soul is [assumed to be] (and this is the usual thesis of Christian scholars) a product of the Exile, emerging after the destruction of national independence, the abolition of the sacrifical cult, and the separation of the people from the cultic institutions that had flourished on the soil of the Holy Land in order to make room for a new religious feeling that had its roots in prayer, in personal dedication to religious traditions, and in the dogma of the resurrection of the flesh and the doctrine of personal retribution. This was said to be the preparation for the proclamation of the kingdom of God by Jesus, who, without denying explicitly the superior status of the Jewish people, was to replace Jewish ethnic solidarity once and for all with the recognition of the infinite worth of the individual human soul and the salvation of the individual personality by postulating the freedom of every human being.

This crude typification, however, fails to take into account what we know of ancient times and from the testimony of past as well as our own Jewish experience: the antiindividualistic, impersonal content of pious feeling and thought. In short, the social character of religion, in the postexilic and rabbinic period, was no less pronounced than before. This is especially evident in the eschatological hopes that are of such immense importance for practical faith. How important is the resurrection of the dead, an individual hope, compared to that cardinal article of faith, the idea of messianic redemption imparted to the entire people?

Besides the observance of the prescriptions of the Torah required of every individual, the intellectual penetration and appropriation of God's Law is a decisive criterion of piety. But the efficaciousness of the study of the Torah rests on the objectivity of its truth, a truth that need not first be acquired through a personal inner struggle of the soul, but rather is accepted without question as the one possession shared by all the children of the covenant.

Judaism, which has never departed from its social basis, nevertheless attaches great importance to the individual by preserving a sense of solidarity that endows individual effort with greater significance and enhances the worth of the individual soul that labors for the common good. Even the obstinacy and willfulness of the Jewish people, which had already been felt and censored by its first leader, are, in both their good and bad senses, transferred to its individual members who, conscious of their participation in the national cause, derive from them a deepened sense of human worth.

The elevation of society elevates the individual as well. Personal elevation, however, also means an elevation of personality. The emphasis which the children of the covenant place on loving care and sympathetic concern, on a feeling of mutual consideration and respect, helps to create a focus on the individual. The abstract principles of the moral law which, isolated from the soul's natural inclinations, hovers above us as "the Law," may indeed help to define the moral personality as such. But the universally valid values that it sets up, with its insistence on their uniform application in all instances and its consequent disregard of all individual differences, will contribute very little concretely to the development and improvement of a person's moral character. The concept of duty in rational ethics, in endeavoring to create ethical personalities by establishing the validity of universally identical maxims, overlooks or neglects the worth of the individual qua individual. The idea of moral duty always presents the danger of creating uniformity, especially when, as is proper, this idea defines the maximum and not the minimum duty. In contrast, the conduct of individuals in Jewish society is distinguished by a sense of genuine comradeship on the part of men of flesh and blood, not for the sake of a rational idea, but out of a feeling of genuine respect for the peculiarities and even the whims of one's neighbor. A sense of discipline is not among the distinguishing marks of the Jewish character. But this lack of formality and organizability is, in the final analysis, derived from a certain innate quality of the individual Jewish soul, and it often obliterates the boundary between inner conviction and plain willfulness.

Differentiation and individualization are concepts whose exact meaning can be determined only after the goal or direction of these processes has been ascertained. When we, therefore, say that we find Jewish people in relation to their environment to be exclusive and individualistic, we merely indicate the framework; the concrete contents of differentiation still have to be filled in. There is no need to dwell on this aspect of the matter. We merely want to point out that Jews as such, as they appear to an outsider, tend to keep aloof from the herd and, in remarkable contrast to the strongly developed peculiarity of the [Jewish] people as a whole, exhibit an astonishing variety of individualistic views and personal convictions. This is by no means an unmixed blessing. The deplorable factionalism and the divisive partisanship which often plague even small groups arise for the most part from this obdurate temper. Likewise, unbelief, skepticism, and certain destructive tendencies which are (not always without justification) attributed to certain circles of emancipated Jews who have dissociated themselves from their spiritual roots doubtless stem at least in part from the fact that excessive individualization has prevented their involvement and integration into a structured social organism. And the revolutionary zeal that motivates many Jews to join radical movements aiming at social regeneration in politics, economics, and the creative arts may be attributed—apart from other, including even religious, motives—to a subjectivism to which the formative influence of his piety has accustomed the Jew. We must not forget that a phenomenon as complex as the Jewish spirit is the product of numerous internal and external factors.

The feeling of being especially close to God is a double-edged sword. This was already evident in Jewish history in the days when the God of the prophet Amos admonished the people: "You only have I known of all the families of the earth; therefore I will visit upon you all your iniquities." A latent chauvinism is always present when the consciousness of a unique and exclusive relationship to God lies at the center of religious feeling. This pitfall has not always been avoided. It is obvious that the elated feeling of having been chosen by God must at certain times have led to an outright rejection of everything foreign and to an overly self-conscious underestimation of all outside influences. Self-righteousness may very well be the unavoidable psychological consequence of every monotheistic faith that holds to the exclusive truth of its own conception of God. As soon as religion has developed what it considers a true concept of being and understands the demands which arise from what it considers to be the real meaning of life, intolerance is unavoidable, at least in theory. But this process can also give rise to intolerance in practice, something which no community has experienced in its own flesh more painfully than that of the Jew. The disfranchisement of the Jews, their relegation to pariah status at the hand of the ruling churches over a period of fifteen centuries, left an ineradicable imprint on Jewish self-consciousness: the persecuted reacted by rejecting the spirit that revealed itself in such shameless defamation and lack of humaneness. And there was still another reaction. Quite apart from their justified pride in their own ethical teachings and their profound effect on moral conduct in daily life, the oppressed, precisely because they were oppressed, felt superior to those whom they know only as oppressors. This is, indeed, the way in which all despots and persecutors condemn themselves: the victims, because of their innocence in one particular respect, conclude that they are morally superior in all respects. The rulers are immune to feelings of bitterness or revenge. The resentment of the tormented finds compensation in total rejection of the tormentor.

It is precisely when we are dealing with the difficult relations between Israel and the strangers—relations that cannot be summed up in a precise formula which is valid for all periods, but which fluctuates in response to different circumstances and epochs and in accordance with the character and temperament of those who deal with the issues—that we see how Jewish self-consciousness defines itself in distinctly religious, and not in national, terms. Only because God gave Israel the Torah is Israel superior to the other nations. It owes its wisdom and moral strength not to any hidden natural disposition or "racial" trait, but solely to its readiness to accept the sacred revelation. Israel was redeemed not at the Red Sea, when it became a people after the Exodus from Egypt, but at Sinai. God commanded Moses to write down the Torah in seventy languages so that all the nations could receive it, and it was given in the open desert so that all could hear the divine message. All nations have a share in it, and not only Israel, as Israel might have assumed had it received the Torah in the land of Canaan. According to God and the Law, it is the possession of all who are willing to accept it.

Over against the universalistic tendency of this Aggadah (and there are many like it), we have, of course, the fact that Israel alone was willing to accept the Torah. But if this acceptance is understood to involve a sacred responsibility on the part of those who have undertaken to bear its yoke and obey its commandments, then possessing it is no reason for chauvinistic boastfulness. The idea that the Torah is a gift of grace, a road that leads to blessedness and salvation, recedes behind the idea that the "People of the Book" have been charged with an arduous task—to love God with all their heart, with all their soul, and with all their might. On the other hand, God's Law and God's people are so closely related that the two are regarded as inseparable, a thought expressed by the Aggadah (Avodah Zarah 2b,3) when it relates that God tipped Mount Sinai over the congregation of Israel like a vault and said, "If you accept the Torah, it will be well with you; but if not, you will here find your grave." Or, when God created the world, He concluded a pact with the forces of nature to the effect that they shall endure only on condition that Israel accepts the Torah; if not, chaos shall return. The obvious intention of such legends is to point out that the ultimate goal of revelation is the moral penetration of the universe and that nature is merely the arena for the enactment of the divine commandments. At the same time, the legends show clearly that the Torah, for whose sake the visible world was created, is dependent on Israel for its acceptance and fulfillment. The two belong together: Israel is chosen because it accepted the divine revelation, and it accepted it because it was chosen. Cause and effect cannot be completely separated here.

After this characterization of the specific nature of "national" as seen by Jewish religiosity, we must turn to still another issue. What is meant by "universalism" in Jewish piety? What does it demand of us? And how does Judaism solve the problems implied in these questions?

An accurate answer requires that we clarify once again the twofold meaning of the monotheistic experience of God as represented by Judaism. More than anywhere else, one must be extremely careful here not to weave rational thoughts into conclusions which may be logically tenable but which are irrelevant to the world of experienced reality. True, belief in the existence and sovereignty of the one and only God, who is the God of all men, can culminate in the idea of one all-embracing humanity—that is, the idea of universal love and righteousness. Moreover, the concept of the all-embracing brotherhood of man certainly corresponds to the idea of the highest Being who is felt to be the sovereign guardian of all nations and a righteous, benevolent father. Nevertheless, the practical ethical universalism of Judaism, conscious of what is in its soul, is less the result of abstract deduction and speculation than it is the product of the sense of humanity with which it had been imbued.

This is the double effect of Jewish monotheism. One might call it "extensive" and "intensive." It is extensive insofar as it eradicates idolatry, superstition, hero worship, and the adulation of power through the idea of the One, and insofar as it banishes dualism, demonology, and all the monstrosities of mythological fantasy, because all honor is due to this One alone. It is intensive insofar as it created in Jewish consciousness (as long as it remained uncorrupted) a dedication to the divine, an overpowering force of religiousness, which could perhaps still be found in the early and heroic periods of other faiths, but never in a large tribe throughout the millennia of its history. The God whose greatness was such that the whole universe was barely sufficient to constitute a domain worthy of Him became the unique possession of the Jewish people. This intense relationship with God, who, as the unique and only One, exerts this overwhelming influence on man, was the radiant source of the rules governing man's conduct. We can safely say that the thrust of the community's religious will created a high standard of ethical conduct in the Jewish people, so that the commandment to love one's fellow man— literally, one's neighbor within the tribe—was in large measure fulfilled. This was surely a consequence of God having become an inner possession, a God whose perfection and holiness manifested themselves above all in the commandment given to man.

Since this view of God made for a high degree of humaneness and culminated in the lofty thought that "the children of Israel are merciful and the children of the Merciful One," it was psychologically inevitable that such an intense feeling of humanity should transcend the confines of the Jewish people and apply to all people. Love, goodness, justice, benevolence, sympathy, and compassion cannot be confined within definite boundaries. Men cannot be taught to love their compatriots and hate their enemies; they treat everyone either with humanity or inhumanity. In saying this we do not mean to close our eyes to the obvious inhumanity of religious fanaticism and nationalistic chauvinism. Israel in particular is not unacquainted with their effect. But here we simply want to point out that where religion, as happened so successfully in Judaism, could instill in the people the idea of having been chosen by God—an idea which culminated in the development of exemplary ethical conduct and a sense of human dignity—the influence of such an elevated moral sensitivity will not be limited to the ethnic community, but will have a profound impact on society as a whole. In this respect, Judaism created a type of human being that can conceivably also be encountered in some of the smaller Protestant sects.

How, then, can the relationship between particularism and universalism in Judaism be clearly defined? And how can we show the true significance for the whole of mankind of a religiosity that is inseparably embedded in an ethnic basis?

It would be pointless, as we have already indicated, to try to arrive at an answer statistically by quoting passages from a variety of documents supporting either the one or the other emphasis. Only the results of personal experience or a sympathetic receptivity to the deep impulses that stir the Jewish soul can help clarify the problem. And this approach will show how an ethnic solidarity that is rooted in religion can generate a high regard for the individual personality, a regard that finds expression in a lived pattern of moral conduct. It will show such a reverence for the dignity of man, such a respect for the innate and inalienable rights of one's fellow man, such an intense sense of obligation to the other person, that the meaning of one's belongingness to the ethnic group finds its completion only in an individualism which manifests itself in a sense of mutual consideration.

We merely have to think of the strict admonition in rabbinic ethics against the frivolous or even malicious humiliation of another person, an admonition that to the present day is heeded and felt to be a duty in the delicate treatment of the poor and needy.

The respect that is accorded to the individual as a child of God is the origin of the impulse leading to the universality of the spirit which embraces all mankind. The path leading from the humane feeling that created a love for his neighbor in the soul of the Jew, a love born of the conviction that his tribe was chosen by God, to the idea of an all-embracing, unified humanity—this was the path of Jewish universalism. It remains meaningful and effective only as long as the ethnic consciousness that stems from the feeling of belonging to this God-chosen people is not weakened, but deepened in the service of mankind. What is vital for our understanding of ourselves is not the lixiviation of the Jewish content, a process of selection that extracts the singular and characteristic and leaves behind the sediment of the human-universal, but the deep appreciation of that which is truly ours and which discloses the universally valid human element that lies at the core of the Jewish personality.

Whether this conception of the religious and ethical elements in Judaism is to be called "universal" or "particularistic" need not trouble us. Whoever endeavors to see things as they are, and not as they could, should, or might be, and permits himself to be guided, in his investigation of Jewish problems, by an unbiased study of the situation itself, and not by the dictates of Christian theological polemics, will not at the mere sound of the phrase, "the restrictive nationalism of the Jewish religion," turn pale with shame because of the alleged inferiority of his faith, which has indeed remained within the confines of an ethnically related people. He will instead ask himself in what sense the juxtaposition of the universal and the particularistic is justified at all.

A fatal error seems to have crept into the discussion of this problem, an error that begins with an illicit confusion of religious and moral motives. To speak of "moral universalism" makes, of course, good sense. The term simply refers to the validity of the moral command for the generality of mankind. Incidentally, the principle that "charity begins at home" is not hereby excluded. On the contrary, it is included as an indication of the fact that the universality of the moral community can be realized only gradually, step by step. Such a moral universalism can be the product of religious conviction, the tender blossom of every lofty-minded piety. Religion itself, however, in its original form and properly distinguished from its moral effects (that is, from interhuman relationships) remains primarily the encounter between God and man—man touched and captured by God's grace. The question how interhuman relationships are formed is a secondary issue; it is not a necessary component of the original meaning of religion. This is clearly evident in mystical devotion, in which the consideration of one's fellow man is completely absent and the absorption of the individual soul by the infinite constitutes the entire content. That specific rules of social conduct could be derived from this position is obvious; after all, masses of people do exist and cannot be completely ignored. But the religiosity to which I am referring, like every religiosity, takes another path. The questions it asks are: How can I endure before God? How can I, who have been chosen and called by God, receive His grace? Why was I chosen, and why has His grace descended upon me and not upon others who may be just as worthy to receive it? All these questions may be subjects of further reflection, but they are not contained in the original revelation.

It is precisely the consciousness of Judaism which became aware of God's grace as a tribe and as the seed of Abraham, and thus provided a clear illustration of what is meant by the awakening of the religious spirit. Its particularism is only a special case of that kind of delimitation that the power of the religious spirit delights to make. It is ethnically circumscribed while preserving the full thrust and power of the religious motif. European students of Buddhism, turning away from western fanaticism and priestly proselytizing, have admired the smiling composure with which India's piety, joyful and secure within itself, neither offers nor commends itself as a model. Its ethical radiations are beneficial to all who come under its influence. Teachings and beliefs may at times be propagated, as was done by the founder and his disciples, but one who does not accept them is neither outlawed nor excommunicated.

Judaism certainly has very little similarity to the spiritual style of the Gautama and his disciples, but this confidence in one's own being, the religious self-assurance that does not succumb to a *rage de nombres* and seek "proof" for its truth in the large following it attracts, is not something for which Judaism should be reproached, least of all by a Jew, out of fear that a religion would otherwise be unable to lay claim to universalism.

Universalism, as we have stated before, is not a feature that is characteristic of the religious life; it is not a religious but an ethical concern, having to do with a theoretical Weltanschauung and the struggle for a correct metaphysics. Its command, which is urgent and ineluctable, is fulfilled by Judaism through the ethical impulses that are derived from its relation to God. Nothing more appropriate can be cited to document this fact than the biblical accounts of creation and, above all, that magnificent passage in Amos (1:3–2:16) in which the prophet castigates the surrounding nations for their sinful acts, upbraids the Moabites because they burned the bones of the king of Edom into lime (while not forgetting the sins of the Edomites), and finally reproaches Judah because it rejected the Torah of the Eternal One, did not keep its statutes, and let itself be led astray by false gods whom the forefathers had already followed. Here Judah's attitude to the divine Law is naively and matter-of-factly—and, therefore, with greater effect—characterized as constituting the very essence of its character. Nevertheless, all the nations are subject to the divine commandment to practice justice, faithfulness, and mercy.

This, we believe, spotlights the decisive element in this controversy. The question can, of course, be raised whether an ethical position that is rooted in a particularistic kind of religiosity is able to evoke and foster that generosity of heart and mind which appreciates and reveres in all human beings the image of the one Father and Creator. Hence the scholars who have established the humane character of Jewish ethics deserve recognition and gratitude. This task, however, does not require us to disregard the national component in the Jewish religion—that is, its conscious restriction to an ethnically circumscribed segment of the total human community—or, indeed, to look upon it as something shameful which one blushes to mention or which one seeks to invalidate with specious arguments when others mention it. On the contrary, we will have to bear in mind a fact which, because of its consequences, is of decisive importance: the dichotomy, encountered throughout history, between the catholicity of the religious idea (that is, its claim to universal validity and the general recognition it actually enjoys), on the one hand, and its failure to apply this principle universally in the treatment of real people, on the other. To brand unbelievers as perfidious and atrociously wicked simply because they do not have the right belief seems to be as compatible with religious universalism as it is incompatible with ethical universalism. Indeed, it is a reversal of it. In contrast to this, an attitude of modest renunciation and quiet restraint that does not compromise one's ideals or weaken one's convictions will more readily open the soul to the larger world that includes all mankind.

We have thus traced that which is alive in the Jewish soul, its truly living pious emotions, in order to ascertain Judaism's real attitude toward the idea of humanity, and not a distilled version of it. We have thereby defined the true meaning of Jewish monotheism and attempted, in the study of this single but highly important example, to clarify the distinction between our approach and the method of rational theology which may be described as a dogmatic view. The most prominent and historically most influential representative of this view is Maimonides. His religious doctrine, most concisely formulated in his Thirteen Articles of Faith, serves the requirements of philosophical systematization far more than it serves as a testimony to the specifically religious spirit. First, the foundation of religion, the doctrine of God, is derived from pure reason; then the specific Jewish teachings on revelation, prophecy, and Torah are joined to this rational theology. Thus the whole enterprise emerges as a fusion of metaphysical and irrational historical elements. One feels that the Jewish religious doctrines were worked into the general framework of a rational faith, and that the thinker's intent was not so much to present the Jewish view as it was to give a biblical-talmudic coloration to the principles of philosophical religion. The Thirteen Articles of Faith certainly reflect their author's convictions, but they fail to authenticate the religious consciousness of Judaism, quite aside from any objections we might have to their content.

Here we can see how difficult and even misleading it is to pour Jewish religious teachings into the mold of creedal statements whose contents always give the impression of something foreign, something that touches man from the outside. This difficulty is particularly evident in the statements regarding the Torah. To be sure, they are true for the pious soul. However, the opposition to the formulation of these truths was instinctively correct, for it was felt that such a detached formulation of a truth cannot do justice to the "givenness," the given reality of life itself. For the Jew, the Torah was part of this natural givenness of life, so that he was hardly conscious of its separate existence. With all due respect to the intellectual formulation of the creedal elements by the great systematizer, it is nevertheless true that the Torah was for the Jew a reality of such elementary force, and the belief in its divine origin and in the binding character of its statutes was so deeply woven into the very fibers of the Jewish soul, that there was no real need to present this fact to the believer in the guise of an article of faith which confronts him with a demand. An activity that has become an integral part of daily life, such as the Torah, need not and indeed cannot be proved. And this was the way the givenness of the Torah was experienced by the Jewish community; it had become part of its life.

The conspicuously practical character of the Torah is a permeating influence on the Jewish soul. Torah is Law, rules of conduct in man's daily life. We therefore do not agree with those Jewish critics who, under the influence of polemical arguments that come from without, protest against the characterization of the Torah as Law. A doctrine whose sole aim it is to capture the will and to subject it to its moral and legal norms can reasonably not be called anything else than Law. The Christian struggle against the Law stems from the Pauline distinction between ritual and morality. Judaism knows nothing of such a distinction: the goal of the Law is always the moral command. Indeed, herein lies the strength of the Jewish position.

We are not concerned here with the content of the Law or with the duality of ritual and ethos, but with the nature of legalism itself as an essential part of Jewish piety. The Christian, and especially the Protestant, struggle against the Law has its real source in the basic view of grace found in the Gospels: in place of "should" we are to put "be" or "must." He who has experienced God's grace receives a new character by virtue of which the principle of love operates directly within him like a natural force.

In contrast to this view we have the imperativistic ethic which demands an unceasing struggle, an ever-renewed wrestling on man's part to attain his ethical ideals. It points up his inner contradictions. It stresses the ever-present danger that he may relapse into sin and urges unceasing vigilance against it. It recognizes that man's will, directed toward the good, can be fortified by the constancy of his actual striving for the good. But it insists that it is this never-ending tension which reveals the true nature of the moral life, a life that can never be the product of mere habit but, to be possessed, must always be won anew.

The doctrine of grace, on the other hand, regards the new Adam as the steadily flowing source of ethical conduct. Whoever is in a state of grace lives a new life under God's merciful dispensation. There is a polemical argument that seeks to cast aspersion on the moral integrity of Jewish insistence on the Law by claiming that it must lead to a greedy expectation of rewards. But there is, at least in principle, an effective answer to this insinuation. The saying of Antigonus of Sokho (Avot 1:3) that not the pursuit of profit but the awe of heaven should inspire the true servant of God, and the admonition that "all that you do, you shall do out of love," have numerous parallels. There are, of course, no less frequent references to retribution as part of the world order. But there is no serious argument to prevent us from interpreting these references as pedagogic expedients. One need not even go so far as Maimonides does when he interprets the eschatological promises (an article of belief that is basic to all religions) in conformity with his ideal of the highest good, so that hardly anything of its original and obvious meaning remains, and when he then justifies this misconstruction on the ground that it is the evident pedagogical intent of these biblical and talmudic passages. For as long as religion remains a set of instructions of how to achieve felicity, man's eyes will always be turned towards the fate that awaits them as they walk in the way of the Lord.

One must appreciate the depth of the difference that has emerged between Judaism and Christianity with regard to the nature of men's actions. The Law is law for the man of action; its significance within the structure of Jewish piety merely reflects the significance which this piety attaches to practical conduct. If it seems at times that the study of the Torah, unceasingly recommended throughout talmudic literature, is regarded as more important than its application, we find that this judgment is usually retracted at the last moment or is more precisely defined so as to mean that the study of the Law is but the indispensable condition for the performance of the practical duties demanded by God. No more than this is meant by the dictum that the ignorant person cannot be pious. The assertion that the study of the Torah outweighs every other activity is, no doubt, a sincere reflection of the attitude of rabbinic Judaism. However, there is no need to view it as a personal statement of faith on the part of the exponents of the rabbinic tradition. It should, rather, be understood as the expression of the psychological fact that those for whom life under the Law had become a matter of course, a subject no longer requiring discussion, should all the more direct their attention to the law's presuppositions, the knowledge of the Torah and its anchorage in the spirit. The joy of theorizing and the primacy of knowledge over activity were not foreign to medieval Judaism. But where they appear in their purest form, as they do in Maimonides, it is evident that something other than the talmudic high estimation or overestimation of study accounts for their presence. The influence of Aristotelianism and Neoplatonism, the predilection for contemplation that found its ideal in the idea of God enjoying the highest bliss in self-reflection, diverted Judaism from its basic course. When we compare Judaism with the contemplative religiosity that grew out of Greek wisdom, we are struck by the fact that there is an exact reversal of means and ends. The superiority accorded to dianoetic, discursive thought over ethical virtues, which Maimonides took over from Aristotle, means that man's perfection of himself in the area of practical morality is the *conditio sine qua non*, the indispensable basis on which man's higher life, truly turned to God, ultimately can be erected. The talmudic saying, "the study of God's teaching counterbalances all," regards this as the only path that leads to the ultimate goal, to a life lived in accordance with the will of the Highest.

Proving oneself through action, observing the Law in fulfillment of the divine command, is the meaning of Jewish piety as well as its direct expression. In the light of this basic fact, the distinction between the cultic-ritualistic and the ethical content of the Torah—though highly significant in itself—occupies a secondary place, especially when compared with the ethics of grace in the Gospels. Paul, in whose reinterpretation of the evangelical ideas we first become keenly aware of their distance from Jewish teachings, sets the Law over against the idea of salvation, disregarding in principle the distinction between the particularistic national form of worship and the universal ethical command. Even if Hillel's commentary reducing the entire Law to the precept of loving one's neighbor had fallen into disuse—that is, if Judaism had renounced the ceremonial Law root and branch—the opposing views would have remained in all respects: on the one hand, the view of man with trust in his power to act and, on the other, the view of the individual who is deprived of the power of independent action and who acquires positive significance only when quickened by divine grace.

This affirmation of the central position of the Torah as the object of the Jew's practical will sums up his relationship to belief. In order to fulfill its commandments and to let himself be guided by its statutes every moment of his existence, he must necessarily believe in its divinity. Its rational and irrational precepts, the *ḥukkim* and *mishpatim*, the revealed and rational commandments, form a unity. Whoever fulfills them is conscious of having fulfilled the demands of the divine will. But all of this is not a reasoned Weltanschauung grounded in a specific theory, nor is it a flight into the inner recesses of the soul or confined to the heart's yearnings. That this belief contains metaphysical convictions, elements of reasoning, attempts to validate the content of belief intellectually, follows from the fact that every real act of will presupposes this kind of inner disposition in order to be regarded as an act that is willed by the subject himself. The metaphysics of belief is, however, reduced to a minimum. A member of the tribe of Jacob cannot possibly affirm the truth of the revelatory character and divine origin of the Torah without at the same time confirming the meaning of this dogma by fulfilling its precepts. Jewish existence is life lived under the commandment. Jewish religiosity does not originate in the affirmation of the truth of some specific intellectual propositions (which in turn lead to a specific attitude towards life), which is the way that Christian piety may have to be understood; it arises from the actual observance of the Law, which, as faith-inspired deed, unites soul with soul in a common activity. Life is set aflame by life, not by some speculation about the "true nature" of God and man.

The discipline generated by the habitual performance of religiously consecrated deeds, the observance and symbolism of the customs and rites that are handed down from generation to generation in the concrete activities of daily life—these are primary experiences that have an immediate impact upon human consciousness. It may well be possible to explain these observances as products of the historical experiences of the Jewish people. Nevertheless, their historical origin always remains secondary to their performance. This is evident, for example, in the scene in the Pesach Haggadah where the father is confronted by the four questioners. The obvious symbolism of the Seder evening is, of course, the point of departure: the service which the Jew has to render to God finds its historical motivation in the fact of the liberation from Egyptian bondage and in the divine precepts connected with that event. However, this service must here as elsewhere be performed punctiliously and with painstaking care if it is to be valid and acceptable to God.

The ceremonial Law defines itself nearly always as a symbolic reference to religious truths and to decisive moments in the history of God's people. It is not subject to attenuation or substitution; it is always a means, never an end in itself, nor does it ever in itself perform a redemptive or sacramental function. Nowhere in Judaism do we find, as we do in other religions, remnants of magic or taboo beliefs in connection with our often quite complex rites and ceremonies. When the Talmud looks forward to the messianic era, it envisages the possibility that these statutes and ordinances may lose their force, since their goal—the elevation and moral perfection of mankind—will then have been realized. It is undoubtedly true that numerous precepts which constitute "the fence around the Law" owe their existence solely to the consideration that God's people, dispersed as it is to all corners of the earth, could only be preserved if at every moment it remained conscious of the difference separating it from the nations around it. Thus, there are enough reasons to indicate that the Law never became an object of abstract idolatry. But the Law had to be kept, and it was kept, for it retained its validity, together with all its ramifications, as the emanation of revelation; and revelation remained the source of the Law even when the reasons for the observance of the ordinances and precepts were evident and their clearly expressed ends might conceivably have been attained in some other way. The rites of Pesach or the Feast of Tabernacles that are meant to remind us of the miraculous experiences of the people when it was redeemed from Egyptian bondage or wandered in the desert, the regulations concerning the fringes and phylacteries that are meant to direct our thoughts to God and His Law, the dietary laws designed to keep alive the consciousness of holiness and of Israel's separateness—all show that they derive their validity from the divine will.

This fact actually leaves open the possibility that the divine legislator could conceivably agree to an abrogation or reformation of the Law. But since the inviolability of the Law was axiomatic for the Torah, the Talmud, and the religious consciousness oriented around them, and notwithstanding the theory that the Law will be abrogated with the advent of the messianic era, the thought of such a possibility is merely an expression of the eminently active, action-oriented character of Jewish piety. It seems as if the idea of the unchangeable validity of the Law implied that there is also a demand for an absolutized, unchangeable, divinely ordained human character, for we must always bear in mind that a ritual or ceremonial precept can only be understood as a link in a life system whose entire goal is the moral development and sanctification of the individual Jew. Here we can rightly say, "In the beginning was the deed." But the goal also is verification through the deed.

It is interesting to note that even so contemplative a theorist as Maimonides, who placed the idea above the deed, was unable to resist the basic attitude of the Jewish spirit and, therefore, expressed the content of faith in the form of required duties. In the *Hilkhot yessodei ha-Torah,* the Israelite is enjoined to acquire the knowledge which is the basis for rational fulfillment of the divine command. No teachings concerning the existence of God and His essence, no theories concerning providence or the creation of the world, are set forth as theoretical presuppositions or as doctrines to be accepted; Maimonides deliberately chooses the formula of a halakhic precept. "The knowledge of this subject, that is, the existence of God and the governance of the world by Him, is a positive commandment, for it says: 'I am the Lord, your God'; and he who thinks that there exists another divine being transgresses a negative commandment, for it says: 'You shall have no other gods beside me'" (I,6). Although this formula expresses merely a basic doctrine, it is significant that it takes the form of a halakhic precept.

Even more striking than Maimonides's halakhic approach is the original passage in the Decalogue itself. Monotheism, as was self-evident for a theoretical, Weltanschauung-oriented mind, is a truth that can be taught and even demonstrated. It is an article of *faith* if we go back to its source in revelation; it is an object of scientific *knowledge* if we focus on its certitude which, though evident, can be clarified by demonstration. But this instructive-doctrinal truth, strangely enough, is presented in the form of a precept. It is not the product of theoretical disputations; it is nothing but the practical application of a doctrine. "You shall not make for yourself a sculptured image, or any likeness," for, as we must assume, when you do make "a sculptured image, or any likeness of what is in the heavens above, or on the earth below, or in the waters under the earth," you will worship a god other than your God, who is a jealous God who tolerates no other form of worship but that which is due to Him alone, and who visits the iniquity of the fathers upon the children. The dogma of God's unity is thus introduced in the Torah itself, not in the form of an article of faith but, corresponding to its life-directing spirit, as a commandment for the Israelite to worship that God alone who, for him, must be the Only One.

Two attempts were made in our history to distill a system of dogmatics from the biblical and talmudic writings. The professed aim of medieval religious philosophy was to rationalize the religious content in its totality. It wanted to make the motives that led the divine legislator to promulgate the religious Law as transparent to human reason as possible, in the same way in which it attempted to explain the teachings of revelation regarding God's existence, His essence, and the creation of the world and its meaning, and make them comprehensible to man's natural understanding. But at the height of its powers in the Aristotelian period, its theoretical, speculative character caused it to focus its principal interests more and more on the concept of God and His relation to man and the world. If a comprehensive system of dogmatics did not thus emerge, it was not because it was uncongenial to the Jewish spirit of that day and to its peculiar attitude toward religious problems which, at least among the Jewish Aristotelians, was inclined to dogmatic formulation, but rather because of external circumstances. The Jewish community lacked the ecclesiastical structure whose rule and guidance alone can establish a system of dogmatics.

The second attempt to create a Jewish theology was made in the nineteenth century in central and western Europe, when, in the wake of civil and political emancipation, a religious liberalism undertook to make Judaism a religious community in the sense of a mere denomination [*Konfession*]. Once again, the theoretical element, the Weltanschauung, came to the fore, just as it had done eight hundred years before. From Moses Mendelssohn to Hermann Cohen, the attempt was made to separate the doctrinal element of Judaism from its concrete physical base in the Jewish community. Philosophy became the criterion of the Jewish religion. One compared this religion with Kantian ethics and was proud to discover that it was almost as pure and objectively convincing as the morality of the categorical imperative. One praised the spiritual, unmythological character of Jewish monotheism and interpreted the messianic thought of the prophetic writings as the symbolic expression of the unending progress of the human race. The optimistic character of Jewish religiosity was stressed in distinction to the pessimism inherent in the Christian doctrine of salvation, and its freedom of the will in contrast to the soul's abasement in the doctrine of original sin. The denunciation of the sacrificial cult by the prophets and their prediction of the imminent downfall of the Israelite state and the Temple, which God would bring to pass in order to manifest His holiness, were interpreted as the revelations of an ethical universalism that had risen above the inferior forms of particularistic backwardness. This reformative theology was thus led to conceive the "essence" of Judaism to be a Weltanschauung, a religious confession that had outgrown its antiquated and irrational ceremonial law, a law rooted in a narrow nationalism and in which the unessential and external trappings of religion had become the central and most distinctive feature. Although this interpretation of Judaism was not always explicitly stated, it formed the basis of the religious trend we have described. The religiously interested laymen lived wholly in this belief, which fully justified their contempt of traditional Jewish life-forms, insofar as they felt any need to defend their progressive views.

What can we say to all of this? The entire purpose of our reflections has been to show that Judaism did not exhaust itself in its Weltanschauung as a doctrine, and that the form in which Jewish piety expressed itself was not belief, but life itself. We must clearly keep in mind that the abstract and theoretical elements which people thought could be used to construct some system of dogmatics do not exist as general beliefs divorced from their concrete roots in man's soul. They can only be comprehended as the intellectual condensation of Jewish emotion. It should be made clear, in other words, that it is not objectively correct doctrines— doctrines that are derived from the idea of an absolute religion or from an unconditionally comprehensible ethical system—which impart a rational character to the Jewish view of life, but that the validity and certitude of this religiosity are derived from different sources.

What is the monotheism of the Bible? The significance of this idea for Jewish sensibility must be carefully analyzed, since the doctrine of the uniqueness of God is the foundation of our faith and has always been acknowledged as such. No one will dispute the fact that Israel, in the early periods of its history, worshipped YHWH only as its tribal god, as may still be glimpsed in a number of biblical accounts. This henotheism made YHWH its national god to the same extent that the numina of other nations became their rulers. When the national hero, David, innocently complains that King Saul's unjustified anger against him compels him to flee the country and serve strange gods (1 Sam. 26:19), his complaint reveals merely a naive national sentiment without any indication that he is conscious of the uniqueness and singularity of God. The prophets inveigh against this parochial view. Amos (3:2, 5:18) pours his scorn on the thoughtless exuberance of national sentiment created by military victories, and Hosea (9:1) admonishes the people, "Rejoice not, O Israel, unto exultation, like the peoples, for you have gone astray from your God." In neither instance do we find any indication that the masses are conscious of the difference that separates them from the heathens, a sense of difference that both prophets strive to awaken. In the same prophetic sense, Israel is praised by Bileam as the tribe that lives apart and does not count itself among the heathens. The multitude no doubt believes that a close bond unites God and his people; they belong to one another; nothing can separate YHWH from what is His own. Speculative fantasy might portray this God as the mightiest and as the Only One. Had He not created the world and all that is therein, Israel and all the nations? He *could* be the God of all. In reality, however, He remained the God of Israel alone in the way in which His presence was actually felt and experienced. Nothing is further from the intent of the prophetic religiosity than to establish a mere intellectual relation between Israel and YHWH, who is clearly felt to be the God of the universe. The prophets might repeatedly castigate the sinful and faithless nation and predict its downfall and destruction, and YHWH as the avenger of His honor might wish to turn His eyes away from the transgressors and their wickedness. But the feeling that this unique people of Israel is under the special protection of this one God, and that the two belong together, is basic to the religious consciousness, including that of prophetic Israel. This sense of unique relationship characterizes biblical monotheism. Neither in its beginnings nor at the height of its development, nor in personalities such as Amos, Hosea or Isaiah 1 and 2, does it reveal any trace of reflection or speculative construction with regard to doctrine. Its primary aim is not to present a theory of ethical monotheism whose truth is intellectually acknowledged and which kindles a flame of emotion, as we find it, for example, in the Christian doctrine of salvation, in which Christ is the instrument of grace and man's knowledge that the redeemer exists kindles his feeling that he stands in need of redemption. In Judaism, the relationship of God to man is direct and not derivative. The individual Jew is as certain of this direct relationship to God as he is of his life among his own people.

This relationship has in no way been affected by the destruction of the state, the loss of national independence, and the dissolution of the theocracy that was concentrated in Jerusalem. The talmudic-rabbinic period of Judaism reveals fundamentally the same consciousness of God which we find in the prophetic period. There is, of course, a hardening of the national-religious consciousness, a feeling of strangeness towards other people, and a greater awareness of widespread persecution as a result of the people's indomitable will to live as Jews in accordance with its own principles. The progressive development of pious folk customs and their official designation as God-ordained laws erected a high wall around Jewry. This isolation and seclusion from the outside world, which was the fundamental experience of the Jewish soul for two thousand years, received its religious meaning from the fact that the Jewish people, precisely because of its isolation, continued to consider itself as the only true worshiper of the one God. The monotheistic consciousness was in no way severed from the experience connected with its origins. On the contrary, new sources of feeling were opened up. The naive sense of peoplehood and the simple devotion to a unique God who had revealed Himself and who appeared in the canonized Holy Scriptures were replaced by life lived under the Law, and the certainty and serene fidelity with which the Law was accepted, the matter-of-factness with which it was observed, created a new basis of existence that had its roots in the immutable will of God.

The aim of the philosophy of religion was to prove the existence of God, to determine the correct meaning of His singularity and uniqueness, to clarify the knowledge of His essence and make it comprehensible within the limits of man's finite reason—all of which falls within the domain of theory, speculation, dogmatics, and doctrinal interpretation. These activities have their proper place on the battlefield of ideas where Jewish belief struggled with Islamic or Christian doctrine for the recognition, or in the defense, of its truth. But this philosophy had detached itself from Judaism as a community of men of flesh and blood far more extensively than Christian speculation had from the Christian community. This can be seen, for instance, in the history of Jewish Scholasticism. Jewish philosophy arose, fructified by the Arabic-Islamic spirit, developed its bold constructions for centuries, always under the influence of foreign ideas, and then vanished. It was a passing phenomenon, the product of a special fate and peculiar historical constellation, with whose dissolution it disappeared. True, it drew for its nourishment on the substance of the Jewish spirit, but it did not become part of that substance and had no lasting effect on its development. Nowhere is this seen more clearly than in the dogma of monotheism that we have been considering.

How much space is taken up by the doctrine of attributes from Saadiah to Maimonides, by the scientific attempts to establish the oneness of the divine Being and His incomparability in the sight of all creatures! That the tools for this conceptual work were borrowed from Greek thought and Arabic Scholasticism is not relevant here. But the immense energy expended on these speculative investigations, the one-sided and indeed exaggerated position which the metaphysical doctrine of God occupies in the whole system of Maimonides's religiosity, can in no way be explained by the historical development of Jewish piety. The principal biblical source for the doctrine of attributes is the simple utterance, "Hear O Israel, YHWH is our God, YHWH is one." It served for many centuries as the Jewish confession of faith, consecrated by martyrs' flames and the last breath of dying men. No other utterance reveals so clearly the mood of Jewish submission to God. But it contains nothing which would justify the ingenious distinctions and refined subtleties projected into it by the religious metaphysics of medieval Judaism. On the contrary, this philosophical speculation read into the *Sh'ma* a meaning that could not possibly be found in it by any biblical or genuinely Jewish understanding. Regardless of whether "one," the last word of this verse, originally had a henotheistic connotation or contained from the very outset the full force of monotheistic conviction—renouncing the worship of all strange tribal gods and rejecting every dualism of the divine principle, as Isaiah 2 did—the fact remains that, for the pious Jew, it has the meaning of "uniqueness" and not of "oneness." All the subtlety of the Jewish Aristotelians was expended on problems that might have been significant for Islam and Christianity, but it contributed little to the conceptual clarification of what the religious consciousness of the Jew, as nourished by the Bible and the Talmud, felt in a vague and inarticulate manner. Jewish Aristotelianism had a perfect right to do this for polemical reasons, directed not only against those strange religions but also against certain mythologizing fantasies which, under the influence of those religions, attempted to graft foreign thoughts and tendencies onto its own religious consciousness. But it aspired to much more than self-defense on a broad religious-philosophical basis. By adhering closely to the biblical text and by claiming to be the final authority in the exegesis of the holy writings and to represent the genuine philosophical understanding of the biblical words and of the idea of God that is only vaguely present in the consciousness of the people, it converted philosophical knowledge into dogma. The Christological speculations of the philosophizing ecclesiastical writers were justified, for the essence of Christianity is speculation, complex metaphysical argumentation regarding the relations of God the Father to God the Son, and of the confluence of the divine and the human in Christ. In Christianity, there is a pressing necessity for the intellectual elaboration and conceptual clarification of these subtle ideas that are an indissoluble part of Christian piety. There was, however, no reason to expand the simple thought that there is but one God for all of mankind into an elaborate conceptual analysis of the doctrine of attributes. This is not to deny that there was an independent intellectual interest in determining the essence of the God concept and that general philosophical concerns press for a clarification of the various elements inherent in the idea of God. Our central point simply is that the specifically Jewish consciousness of God does not find adequate expression in a discussion of the principle of uniqueness. It appears, if we may thus formulate it, that the vacuum created by the silence of the Torah and Talmud regarding the metaphysical nature of the Jewish God was filled by speculations that were indeed compatible with the religiosity of the Torah, but in no way required by it.

This is true, however, not only for the cardinal principle of monotheism in its abstract form, but also for the other tenets of the Jewish religion. If we turn to the second group of Maimonidean principles, we find the doctrines that deal with prophetic revelation, the towering figure of Moses, the divine communication of the Torah, and its immutability and eternal validity. In these principles we have the condensation of what Israel believes to be the heart of its historical experience. But what was the nature of this experience of God's revelation by the prophets, and what, especially, was the nature of Moses' incomparable closeness to God? Was it empathy, a deep sensitivity to the rapture of those visionaries, or was it a reflex of the illumination that suffused the prophetic soul? Nothing of all this! Maimonides's doctrine of prophecy, it is true, attempts to base the connection between the consciousness of the prophet and the divine spirit on certain psychological conditions of the human intellect in general, and on metaphysical assumptions regarding the active intellect that emanates from God. By asserting that the condition of the unenlightened sage's soul—his intellectual and moral capacities and achievements—is a precondition for being seized by the divine, he erects, as it were, a pillar in the terrestrial sphere of the bridge that leads to the absolute. For Maimonides, this structure supports the road that leads to the edge of the terrestrial world, where a spirit like Aristotle or perhaps he himself can safely stand. One could call this a mystical point of view arrived at by rational means.

In this respect, however, Maimonides can hardly be said to be representative of the Jewish spirit, for he expressly reserves this privileged position for a few exceptional sages. Even in his view, belief in the divinity of prophecy does not mean an inner condition which one can acquire or at least clarify through a kind of imitation of the prophets; it is simply acceptance of the fact, attested to by reliable tradition, that such revelations had taken place at a given time. But what is the living proof that attests to the reliability of this chain of tradition? This is for Maimonides, as it is for all Jews to whom the religious Law is the very breath of existence, the ninth Article of Faith: the eternal validity of the Torah. The immediacy of the tradition of religious life, the conscientious and fearless fidelity to one's own history, the personal response to the deep-rooted moral and ritual commandments of the biblical Law, which from time immemorial have been the natural expression of Jewish existence—and together with these the feeling of being physically a part of the Jewish people, deeply conscious of its God-ordained particular position in the world—created the necessary disposition of the soul, the experience of what was dogmatically formulated as the immutability of the Mosaic Law. If we consider the matter carefully, we see that the prophets, headed by Moses, were people who at some time in the past were deemed worthy by God to receive the revelation. But the dramatic experiences of the soul and the passionate beliefs of the heart do not cling to historic reminiscences, however impressive and amazing they might be, but rather to some curcial spiritual event which is directly experienced and has the power to move the mind and the will here and now. Objectively, Maimonides is no doubt justified in formulating principles constituting Jewish piety, and in the selection of the [second group of] principles discussed above he reveals a deeper insight into the characteristic nature of the piety of his people than in those where the doctrinal content of abstract monotheism is formulated. But it is precisely in those principles that express the fundamental nature of the biblical doctrine of revelation that we find the actual historical meaning of Jewish religious consciousness. The ethical, social, and legal commandments, the ceremonial Law, the symbolism, the ancient inherited customs of worshiping God—in short, everything that presents man with a challenge and whose binding force has been attested to by actual deeds since time immemorial—are what the soul of the people feels to be the essence of religion and the real significance of life itself. Nowhere has the primacy of the practical remained so little a pious wish as in Judaism.

The theoretical and practical influence of the third group of dogmas laid down by Maimonides is more difficult to determine. They deal with the general relation between God and creation, with providence and retribution, and, finally, with the eschatological doctrines concerning the coming of the Messiah and the resurrection of the dead. Maimonides's attitude toward the fantasy-filled descriptions of life after death is highly instructive, for it indicates the significance he attached to them in his own mind. His remarks on this subject in the commentary to Mishnah Sanhedrin X,1 show, at any rate, that he failed to find the clarity which a fundamental article of faith ought to have in these intricate and often contradictory ideas. As his cautious presentation shows, he sees in them nothing but symbolic paraphrases and forms into which proper thinking can introduce whatever has been approved by rational investigation. He later made ample use of this method in his doctrine of immortality. By making the condition of the human soul after death dependent on the degree of insight achieved by the active intellect during a person's lifetime, he deprives the immortal spirit of personal consciousness. It is absorbed by the supraindividual reason. In the final analysis, therefore, it does not matter that immortality is a privilege reserved for selected sages.

This view also seems to negate the eudaemonistic character of the eschatological belief in retribution.

But Maimonides is not Judaism, and his theory can in no way be harmonized with the actual beliefs of the people. What are these beliefs with regard to the expectation of immortality and to that distinctive quality ascribed by religious literature to life hereafter and to the messianic hope? It may be said that the belief in retribution and the rule of divine providence is deeply rooted in the Jewish soul which has not been touched by modern enlightenment. So is the hope in the coming of the Messiah and the restoration, through him, of the people of Israel on their ancestral soil. The prayers which contain these notions and which beseech God to hasten the day of His promised redemption attest to the fact that these hopes and beliefs are expressions of genuine piety.

But these same prayers also show that the redemption awaited for the Jewish people, and indeed for all mankind, was more ardently longed for than were personal happiness and individual salvation. The religious instinct is deeply concerned with man's fate in this world and with the salvation of his immortal part in the world to come. A just balance between here *or* there, and preferably between here *and* there; the assurance that we can influence destiny by good works; the possibility of erasing or rendering less injurious the consequences of previous errors by pious acts pleasing to God; the visible effects of retribution on the growth of character and personal conduct—these ideas have been very powerful in the unbroken tradition of Jewish piety, and among Christians as well. Pious casuistry has frequently tempted some less high-minded believers in God to view the relationship between deed and reward according to a mathematical calculus that makes obedience to the divine Law seem to be the most prudent and profitable course to attain personal happiness as well as material advantages. Between this utilitarian piety and the devotion of a man who, like Job, in silent submission to God's will leaves the granting and withholding of salvation in His hands, there have always been many gradations and nuances of intensity among both the Jews and other nations. The peculiar Jewish form of belief in providence, however, is not expressed in this general doctrine of retribution, but rather in those eschatological hopes for the coming of a Messiah who will redeem the people from misery and the yoke of foreign oppressors. One might call this a dogma, provided this term is understood merely as the description of the content of a general kind of faith.

But this idea, too, though at first glance it seems to represent a theory, is interwoven with the living historical consciousness of its bearers. Just as the people feel at every moment of their waking existence that they constitute a historical community and comprehend all truly significant events only as the children of this community, so also they regard the future and the salvation it is to bring as a common possession. Nor is mankind as such forgotten in this messianic belief. The righteous of all nations have a portion in the salvation that is to come. The world order to be established by the Messiah is the name of God will bring peace to the entire human race. But what we are concerned with here is neither the specific content of the universalistic and particularistic elements in the passages just mentioned nor an exploration of the unresolved tensions inherent in their coexistence. Our purpose is to show that the religious metaphysics of Judaism, wherever it has remained an integral part of the spirit of the people, is rooted in the historical life of the nation. The messianic hope is on the same plane as the remembrance of the Exodus from Egypt. Its content is not a supratemporal, transcendent reality, but the concrete reality of human existence and events experienced as historical fate.

Thus we find that it is always the historical existence of the people rooted in reality, and perhaps the unity of all men, that is at the center of Jewish consciousness. This is surely different from a vain and thoughtless self-admiration, the apotheosis of one's own group, or even the self-glorification of humanity. What it means is—and the purpose of the present study has been to point this out with utmost clarity—that it is not possible to arrive at a true understanding of Judaism and the Jewish religion if their spiritual content is sublimated from the very outset, reduced to evaporating abstractions, and represented as a universal human view of life [*Lebensanschauung*].

Our attention should be focused not on the objective spirit nor on a set of doctrines concerning the nature of the divine and the human (doctrines which could be deduced by interpretation, reinterpretation, symbolism, omission, or condensation), but on the reality of the soul, on the concrete events that have shaped the individuality of the Jew. This is completely misunderstood by the rationalistic view that arose with the Emancipation when it reduces the whole complex of Judaism to those elements which can be distilled into ideas and doctrines concerning God or ethical conduct. This rationalism is an offspring of the Deism of the seventeenth and eighteenth centuries, a late-born child that cannot hide the decrepitude of its progenitors and their lack of originality.

What is the nature of the mood and outlook of the movement known as the religious Enlightenment, which, in the West and especially in German Judaism, stands in opposition to traditionalism? Its positive meaning, which becomes most obvious in its rejection of obsolete and superfluous ritualistic forms, manifests itself in the attempt to develop the seeds of the universal-human elements, which are an essential dimension of Judaism, into a universally valid Weltanschauung. The struggle against allegedly or actually outworn forms, which more radical efforts soon extended into a rejection of the traditional forms of Jewish worship and life generally; the secularization of the individual Jew (that is, his separation from the religious-ethnic matrix in which he had been embedded until then); the reduction of Jewish Weltanschauung to a teachable content; the aversion against the national aspects of Judaism, directed not only against the political restoration of the Jewish people on its ancestral soil and the creation of an independent Jewish culture in the Diaspora, but also involving a rejection or at least mistrust of the concrete living elements of religiosity (for instance the language of the Hebrew prayers)—all these signify a deconcretization, as it were, of Jewish life, and a dilution of its religious reality.

We need not necessarily raise any objections to these initial attempts to tear religiosity from its traditional historical moorings. On the contrary, to transcend the historical can be a symptom of renewed vigor and vitality. If, during the Middle Ages, the destroyed portal of a Gothic cathedral was replaced by a new structure in the Romanesque style because the latter style had become dominant, it would make little sense to criticize the period for its ignorance or lack of architectural style. On the contrary, we ought to admire the artistic taste and resourcefulness of an age that could give wings to such an imaginative and original conception. If, instead of a Romanesque church portal, it had introduced a stylistically impeccable Gothic structural part, whose overall conception was more suitable for a town hall than a house of worship, we would find it more questionable than praiseworthy. A temple should remain a temple. In short, the opposition to Jewish tradition; the readiness in principle to abolish or demolish numerous forms of Jewish religiosity that have lost their meaning and become obsolete; the lowering or total dismantling of the fence built around the Law; the assertion of the right to delete old prayers and introduce new ones—these can only appear commendable to a thoughtful person and a truly free spirit, provided the basis on which the meaning of this entire life-form rests is not ignored or interpreted away. This basis is the individual Jew in the actuality of his relationship to the Jewish people as a whole; it is not a Weltanschauung, a doctrine of God, a view concerning the meaning of existence and the significance of life's values providentially devised by the Jews for the benefit of all mankind.

The reduction of Judaism to a Weltanschauung, however, was the tendency of Jewish reformative rationalism. As a consequence, it committed its initial error when it attempted to reform Jewish religious life with the help of science. The relationship between these two cultural realms has already been discussed in the first part of this essay and need not be repeated here. Our present concern is to show how this approach destroys the fundamental meaning of Jewish existence. For psychological-historical as well as ideological reasons—it wants to abolish or purify certain aspects of religion—the rationalistic tendency must emphasize the *weltanschauliche* aspect of religion. It wishes to be regarded as the religious constitution of emancipated Judaism, of an ethnic group whose members become more and more integrated into the civil, economic, political, and general intellectual structures of the surrounding world. This development may be inevitable as the Jews become increasingly involved in the world around them. However, besides this obvious and unavoidable tendency to assimilation, there also exists a conscious motive that quickens the development. This motive, too, tends to re-form the Jewish religion, for it is now considered necessary to isolate the specifically human activities of the individual Jew so that he can be integrated more easily into the social groups around him. Therefore, the Jew had to be freed from the complications involved in the observance of the religious laws whose claims had bound him with amazing power in every sphere of life.

Freedom, as is well known, has two aspects: freedom *from* something and freedom *for* something. The reform movement overlooked, or at least did not sufficiently comprehend, that an intellectual structure, especially when it is deeply rooted in the human soul, consists not of different layers neatly arranged side-by-side, but of interrelated and mutually integrated elements.

Two consequences seemed possible here. One was the assimilation of the Jew as an individual. As [the Judaism of] the individual Jew was emptied of all specific content which until then had given him his distinctive character and complexion, and as the religious and ethnic bonds and the living historical associations that had connected him to his roots were severed, the road to full assimilation seemed to be open. It meant that the Jews who had dissociated themselves from Judaism could now enter freely into the national and cultural life of the people around them. As personal traditions grew weaker and the will to take part in the beckoning culture around them grew stronger, a large number of Jews did indeed lose their Jewish distinctiveness and attachment to their history. In recent years, the need for baptism as an admission ticket to modern culture has substantially decreased, at least where membership in a specific "confession" ceased, in response to an increasing emancipation from traditional religions, to be taken for granted.

A second consequence was the assimilation of the Jewish religion as such. It resulted indirectly yet very effectively in a general weakening of Jewish life. By assimilation, we mean the attempt to define the specific nature of the Jewish religion in accordance with a general concept of religion and to stress selectively those elements which, following the model of Christianity, can be considered as Weltanschauung. Whenever we have mentioned the term "dogma" in this essay, we have indicated that it is necessary to understand it not in its technical, theological sense, which, according to established usage, defines it as an article of faith, formulated and officially adopted by ecclesiastical authority, but in the less rigorous meaning of a religious opinion which is more or less widely accepted and which reflects convictions whose truth is asserted by religious metaphysics. It is in this sense that the modern rationalistic treatment of the Jewish religion can be said to aim at "dogmatization" or, more exactly, seeks to restrict Judaism to a Weltanschauung. The more Jewish life lost its distinctive nature under the impact of the leveling force and inescapable assimilative influence of European culture, the greater became the tendency to reduce Judaism to a confession. "Confession," literally, means "acknowledgment," an acknowledgment of the truth and validity of certain principles with regard to which alone it differs from other religions. Just as the Deists felt they had discovered the essence of true religion, whether natural or rational, by renouncing the distinctive features of the individual Christian confessions and ultimately by discarding the irrationality of the apparently basic dogmas, including even the Trinity (thus reducing the entire meaning of piety to the belief in the one wise and beneficent God and His rather vaguely defined retribution), so did the rationalistic Jewish approach attempt to define the essence of the Jewish religion.

This was and still is a legitimate undertaking, provided this essence is not sought in some world of ideas but, in accordance with the special character of Judaism, in the midst of pulsating life itself. Instead, however, we find that the discussion of these issues—treated only sparingly in systematic works and far more in popular devotional literature and sermons—limits itself exclusively to a presentation of a universal-ethical Weltanschauung. The aim is to show that the Jewish religion, in its spiritual struggle against the overwhelming influence of Christianity, can hold its own by virtue of its comprehensible and indeed more rational conception of God and man. Thus a body of doctrines—doctrines by content if not by definition—is articulated, modeled after the ethical and metaphysical principles of Christianity in the sense that, for polemical reasons or for the sake of self-defense, the character and the content of Judaism are determined by their contrast to Christianity: there the Trinity, here the one God and pure monotheism; there original sin and salvation through an intermediary, here freedom of personality and independent decision; there the appropriation of saving grace through faith, here the direct struggle of the human soul for God-given salvation through the observance of His commandments; there the curse of the Law, here a blessing for him who can fulfill it; there the denial of the world, here the affirmation of life; there pessimism, here optimism.

It cannot be denied that the sources of the Jewish religion—its literary documents as well as its expressions of living piety—in general justify such juxtapositions. Nor need we overlook the fact that, from the standpoint of a natural moral sensitivity and a simple religious view of the world, the Jewish beliefs appear incomparably clearer and more convincing to a mind that has not been twisted by a dogmatic upbringing. But even if we admit the truth of these principles with respect to Jewish thought and feeling, the question remains whether this formulation accurately reflects the religious content of Judaism. We cannot dispose of this question by referring to the fact that Christianity arose out of Judaism, as if the metaphysical dispute between the two were nothing but a return to the original position from which the daughter religion had departed. In the first place, the daughter religion did not arise only as a deliberate revolt against its historical origin, as shown, for example, by the opposition of Pauline theology to the Law; Greek ideas, too, contributed substantially to the development of its doctrine. Secondly, when Christianity dissociated itself from its historical roots in a small people in order to devote all its energies to the spiritual conquest of the world, it detached itself from the very foundation of life which the existence of the Jewish people has always constituted for the Jewish religion. A conclusion is inevitable: the description of a belief, however clearly drawn, historically accurate, and faithful to the self-attestation of piety, can never capture the inner essence of Judaism, which is as dependent on the life of the soul as it is on the content of the mind.

An instructive example illustrating the relationship between these two realms can be found in the utterly different attitudes of two eminent thinkers of our people, Solomon ibn Gabirol and Baruch Spinoza. Both are philosophers of religion, and their religious philosophies—their metaphysical speculations—have nothing to do with the intellectual content of biblical and rabbinic Judaism. For several centuries Gabirol's work was actually taken as the product of a non-Jew, until scholarly research rectified the error. And yet this completely un-Jewish thinker is, next to Judah Halevi, our greatest religious poet and, in his hymns composed for religious worship, a sublime interpreter of the deepest Jewish emotions, of the joys, sorrows, hopes, and fears that bind us to one another. Spinoza's speculative system is not farther removed from Judaism than Gabirol's, but in his innermost heart Spinoza is a bitter foe and relentless accuser of his brethren. He is no longer inspirited by the sincere love of Jewish existence that sustained Gabirol. The case of Spinoza has had, of course, its predecessors and its successors, and it is not an isolated or surprising phenomenon in our history.

How then can we explain the religious poet Gabirol, whose heart is indissolubly tied to the soul and fate of his people? How can he appear as a stranger in his philosophical works and even in his theological speculations, yet prove himself as the truest son of the beliefs and manners of his forefathers in his personal life and in the devotion of his heart? The explanation is that we are dealing with two different matters here. It is one thing to follow the wisdom of the heart and have a sense of rootedness, of identity with one's own people, with real people of flesh and blood, and it is quite another thing to construct theories by which the free-roaming intellect, moving in a bloodless realm of abstraction, detaches itself from its existential basis. The processes of thought, the systematic development of ideas—notwithstanding the fact that ideas as such possess logical autarky and independence—are rooted, especially in the case of a philosophical genius, in a profound sense of and feeling for life. They are, to a large extent, a projection of emotion into the realm of the mind. Nevertheless, the fact remains that a theory-oriented mind can easily detach itself from the concrete concerns of human life. For the "feel" for life as it is lived [*Lebensgefühl*] that gives wings to his thinking is for the most part something highly personal and individual.

In contrast to this individualized attitude, the emotions which transformed the un-Jewish thinker Gabirol into a poet deeply attached to his people reflect his consciousness that he was part of his people, belonged to it, and as a member of this historic group shared its way of worshiping God.

We encounter this phenomenon everywhere. The Jewish idea can be understood only when we personally identify ourselves with the deeds, the suffering, and the fate of its bearers. When the strong influences of the Kabbalah threatened to disrupt the Jewish community and turned men's minds from the traditional paths of Judaism, the children of Israel did not desert their common tent, for stronger than all speculations about divine truths and the fascination of secret knowledge was the abiding fidelity to the law of life kept by the Jew with his whole heart and soul.

The source of Jewish belief is not metaphysics but history governed by God's goodness, which, the people felt, guided it along a special path. This history is more significant than the elaboration of ideas and views of life which it produced, for it deals with the real life of real persons, the life of a people sensing itself to be chosen by God to serve Him in a particular way. It is the notion of election which constitutes the decisive, ever-renewed reference to the reality of the people's existence. With this revelation, the pre-Mosaic Israelite religion emerged into the light of history, promising the special care of the one God to the descendants of Abraham. This is the knowledge that sustained prophetic, talmudic, and rabbinic Judaism—not mystical reveries or speculative doctrines of God, but the special fate and specific task of the chosen people. The Torah and the prophets speak of the living God, the God of the fathers who is also the God of the children. These two characterizations are closely related, for the Jew can prove and justify himself before God only in his history, that is, only by the conscious identification with the work and fate of his people, the Jewish community. That the Jew should not be confined within the narrow compass of a small people, and that his eyes should not be denied an unobstructed view of the world beyond this people's walls, is made possible by the God of Israel, the God whom the Jew worships and who has always remained for him the Only One, the God of all mankind.

Notes

"Jewish Piety and Religious Dogma," translated by Noah J. Jacobs and Alfred Jospe, first appeared as "Jüdische Frömmigkeit und religiöses Dogma," *Monatsschrift für Geschichte und Wissenschaft des Judentums* 67 (1923):153–67; 225–44; 68 (1924):27–47.

RELIGIOUS TRUTH AND PHILOSOPHICAL QUEST: MEDIEVAL SYNTHESES

6
THE PURPOSE OF HUMAN EXISTENCE AS SEEN BY GREEK-ROMAN ANTIQUITY AND THE JEWISH MIDDLE AGES

Isaak Heinemann

[Isaak Heinemann raises the question of how the purpose of human existence may be determined as the key to the examination of a larger problem: the meeting of Greek and Jewish culture in late antiquity and the Middle Ages and the mutual effects of this encounter. In the first part of his study, not included here, Heinemann points out that the question of the purpose of man emerged in Aristotle's early writings under the influence of Anaxagoras' teleological approach and of the ideal of the theoretical life among the disciples of the aging Plato. According to Aristotle, man exists for the sake of contemplation, of intellectual activity. While Aristotle's interest in this question waned, it gained new significance in the Stoa in connection with the transcendent conception of teleology; the early Stoics already placed the practical ideal next to Aristotle's theoretical ideal. Their successors related the problem of purpose to the inquiry into the essence of man. Still within the Stoa, tendencies emerged to conceive the theoretical as well as the practical ideal primarily in a religious sense, that is, as a connection with God through perception of the kindred Divine and as preservation of the soul's purity. This inclination was, however, fully unfolded only in the gnostic-cathartic ideas of Neoplatonism and Hermeticism. Elsewhere antiquity, in its later stages, fluctuated between a mainly theoretical and a mainly practical conception. Although the commentaries on Aristotle offered nothing substantially new, they contributed to the emergence of a definition of man as a "thinking being," of a transcendent teleology and, in conjunction with it, of the concept of thinking as our "purpose."]

The lines of development which originate in classic antiquity extend, notwithstanding Spengler, into the Middle Ages. They

115

can be found in the orbit of Christian culture as well as that of Islamic culture, to which the representatives of Jewish philosophy belong. But while comprehensive presentations have traced the development of numerous ideas and forms of style through Hellenism and the Christian Middle Ages into modernity, they nearly always disregard Islamic-Jewish thought. Someone will, for instance, write the history of the concept of *logos* from Heraclitus to the modern age without giving any thought to the fundamental significance of this concept for Gabirol and Judah Halevi and their Arab models. Someone else will survey the history of dialogue from Plato to the Renaissance and beyond, yet fail to make any reference to [Abu Hamid] al-Ghazali's *Scales of the Righteous* [*Qustas el Mustaqim*], a notable precursor of Hans Sachs's conversation between the shoemaker and the canon, or Gabirol's *Fountain of Life* [*Mekor Hayyim*], or Judah Halevi's *Kuzari* [al-Hazari]. Similarly, comprehensive presentations mainly limited to antiquity, such as [Rudolf] Hirzel's far-reaching treatment of the concept of *talio* ["retaliation"], take note of postbiblical Judaism only as far as its sources are written in Greek. Certain exceptions—studies in the postbiblical era undertaken with the help of Jewish experts, such as [Eduard] Norden's discussion of ancient forms of prayer, [Wilhelm] Roscher's studies of the concept of "the navel of the earth," and especially [Franz] Dornseiff's treatment of *gematria* [numerology]—raise the expectation that tracing ancient lines of development through the orbit of Jewish intellectual life will enable us to recognize important historical connections which are of equal concern to the classical and the Judaic scholar.

The fruitfulness of such examinations should be particularly evident when we consider the history of a question which is linked to the ultimate problems involved in the concept of a world view on which both Greek and Jewish culture, each in its own way, have taken a position. This should shed light on the extent to which the formative forces of antiquity continued to influence medieval Judaism and were in turn affected by what Judaism had to offer.

From this point of view I seek to trace the history of an important question regarding the view of life through ancient and medieval Jewish culture—a question which has been touched upon only twice by classical scholars and has not yet been treated by the expositors of the Jewish Middle Ages. The present study is conceived and written in such a way that it can be read and examined by experts in both fields. Thus, since the second part is based on the analysis of the most important ancient systems presented in the first part, the attempt [of the second part] to establish a relationship between Bahya and Hermeticism, Gabirol and Porphyry, and to comprehend Maimonides's relationship to Aristotle with greater precision, may also be judged by the classical scholar. The principles set forth in the concluding remarks touch upon concerns in both fields of research. . . .

I

The problem of "human purpose" has several aspects that require consideration. The "purpose" [*Bestimmung*] of a being can be understood passively. Thus people say that the animal is "destined" to serve man; man, according to Goethe (as before him according to Epictetus, *Diatribai* II,10,6), is "destined to suffer." But an examination of the doctrine of purpose in this passive sense is unrewarding, because it does not matter whether or not an optimistic, pessimistic, or even fatalistic view of life makes use of the formula that "we are here for something."

The belief in a purpose of man in an active and meaningful sense—that is, the belief that a specific theoretical or practical conduct is prescribed for us as the ultimate goal of our endeavors—is a variant of the belief in a "goal" of our striving which, in contrast to ethical nihilism, appears wherever an "ought"," a general human obligation, is acknowledged and its content, in contrast to a naive faith in authority, is discovered through reflection. If one wishes to call such a doctrine concerning the goal of life a "doctrine of purpose" [*Bestimmungslehre*], one will discover that it can be found in every important ethical system. Originally, however, the question "what have we been created for?" does not aim only at our "ought" as such. The issue will be raised and elucidated here only . . . as the question of our purpose. This question is based on the premise that the "ought" does not originate in our subjective will alone (depending, for instance, on the systematic gratification of our striving for happiness), but that it corresponds to the goals of that power to which we owe our existence and, above all, our particular disposition. Its special premise, besides the general premises of every theory of obligation, is the acknowledgment of an ultimate ground, conceived as goal-directed, for the existence and thusness [*Sosein*] of man. In a system such as that of Epicurus, there is of course room for a quest after the *telos,* the ultimate goal of man striving for happiness, but the question of our purpose would be impossible there. Nietzsche, in his last period, was able to raise the question of the meaning of life—and, accordingly, the "meaning of earth"—but not the question of man's purpose. The goals of this ultimate metaphysical ground must be intelligible to us if we hope to arrive not only at the acknowledgment of a revealed task, as the Bible does, but also at a scientifically examined concept of our purpose.

The discovery that every doctrine of purpose rests upon three premises—belief in an ultimate "ought," in a metaphysical ground of the world's existence, and in the intelligibility of its goals—is important for our analysis because it will enable us to understand the appearance and disappearance of the problem in the period of history with which we are concerned here. Moreover, it will show how the preponderance of the one or the other premise results in different ways of posing and solving the question. . . .

II

The Bible is far more strongly interested in the question of the meaning of life than is hellenic thought. Nevertheless, the doctrines about the purpose of man which we find in Judaism and, as far as I may judge, in Christianity and Islam, do not go back to the Bible, but to a hellenic stimulus in some form. This may sound strange, but it becomes clear as soon as we consider the fact that a doctrine of purpose in the strictest sense must also deduce man's "ought" from his existence. But this never happens and cannot happen in the Bible. There the "ought" is determined by God's commandment which, regardless of whether it is comprehended as external or internal revelation, is in no way based upon our nature since, on the contrary, our inborn faculties and inclinations drive us often enough toward paths He does not desire. Passages such as Isa. 43:21, "I have formed this people for Myself, and they shall proclaim My praises," state nothing about a religious aptitude of Israel which would be the cause of its purpose. They contain, if one wants to put it this way, a doctrine of vocation, not a doctrine of purpose. The saying of the Mishnah, "If you have studied much Torah, do not take pride in it, for to this end you have been created," describes in the same way only an obligation based upon history.

As far as I can tell, there is only one passage in early Jewish literature in which one could with some justification see a doctrine of purpose in the hellenic sense. We find it in the Book of Enoch (69:3).

> The name of the fourth (angel) is Penemue. He has taught man how to work with ink and paper, and through this many human beings have sinned . . . from eternity to eternity. For human beings have not been created that they confirm their loyalty in this manner through stylus and ink. For human beings have been created like the angels, so that they may remain just and pure. All-annihilating death would not have touched them; but through this knowledge they perish.

Here written communication among human beings is considered unnatural (and therefore anti-God) in the sense of Cynicism and its opposition to all artificially created forms of human intercourse. Because we are born pure, we are also created for a pure life without any particular cautionary measures. This doctrine has probably been passed on by Cynicism, though we are not able to gain an entirely clear picture of the original position.

However, it may be rewarding to take a quick look at those concepts which emerge in connection with our doctrine and have effected Judaism. It would have been impossible for a prophet or the Psalmist to ask why God created the world. The question is found several times in the Apocalypse of Baruch, and the answers, "for the sake of human beings," or "for the sake of the just," make it evident that the familiar Stoic teleology has here been adopted and ethically developed. A further step in the development of our doctrine is reached in the popular midrashic interpretations of the opening words of the Bible. God had created the world "for the sake of the beginning," namely "for the sake of the Torah which is called beginning," or "for the sake of Israel which is also described as a beginning." All these are probably aftereffects and further developments of the Greek concepts.

A further question emerges in connection with the problem of purpose: the question of who we are. In Greece, especially after Panaetius, it is linked with the Delphic statement, but it was probably too abstract for ancient Judaism in this particular form. In a more concrete form it can be found in Seneca (*Epistolae* 82:6): "Man knows where he goes, whence he comes, and what is good and bad for him." Posidonius probably is Seneca's source, and one would have to answer in accordance with his view that the self, the *daimon,* stems from that world and returns to it and, therefore, has to keep itself pure on earth. In the same sense and presumably under the same influence, Porphyry also . . . speaks of the man "who has clearly comprehended who he is, whence he comes, and where he will go." But just as self-knowledge, conceived in Posidonius's sense as the perception of our God-relatedness and godliness, already has been transformed by his disciple Philo into the perception of our worthlessness (out of the same motives from which the same doctrine emerges in Baḥya ibn Paquda, the Turkish poet Omar ibn Sulaiman, and Pascal), so the Mishnah transforms our question into an admonition. "Mark well three things, and you will not fall into the clutches of sin: know whence you came—from a putrid drop; where you are going—to a place of dust, worms, and maggots; and before whom you are destined to give an account and reckoning—the King of Kings." On the other hand, the reflections about the peculiarity of man's bodily structure, which are also present in the Midrash, remain without connection with the doctrine of purpose.

Norden had already suspected that there was originally a link between the admonitions for self-perception and the problem of purpose in
the light of certain gnostic passages which also concern us, in view of
Gnosticism's considerable influence upon Judaism. There too the Greek
formulation of the question is continued with complete independence: the
task of life does not ensue from our natural being, but from participation
in *gnosis,* which we obtain by being accepted into the mysteries. Thus the
young man in the Acts of Thomas thanks God, "who has taught me to
explore myself—to perceive who I was, who I have now become and in
what way, so that I may become again who I was." Bishop Clemens, too,
wants to derive gratitude to God only from consideration [of the ques-
tion] "from which matter we come, who we were, and how we were
shaped while entering into this world: that out of grave and dust the
Creator and Master introduced us into His cosmos." Adversaries, for
him, are people "who do not know whence, by whom, and to what end
we have been called." That such questions were originally part of a larger
context is shown by the fortunately preserved fragment of the writings of
the Gnostic Theodotus, in which some people in recent years have
wanted to see the leitmotif of Gnosticism: "Not baptism alone liberates,
but also the knowledge who we were and what we have become, where
we are and where we have arrived, whence we run to and from what we
are being freed, what birth is and what rebirth." Admittedly the Greek
formulas shine through more clearly here than in the passage quoted from
the Mishnah, yet not even here does it come to [the formulation of] a
doctrine or purpose in the hellenic sense. Nevertheless, we may note even
now that the old connection between those questions and the problem of
purpose is preserved in Ghazali.

> You shall strive for knowledge of your true being: what you are, whence
> you have come, where you are going, and to which end you have come into
> this caravansary for these few days, for what you have been created, what
> your happiness consists of and through what you become happy, and what
> your misery consists of and through what you become miserable.

The development of a Jewish doctrine of purpose was particularly encour-
aged by the fact that the commentaries on Aristotle which had greatly
influenced the Jewish Middle Ages revealed that a remarkable extension of
the peripatetic views had taken place. Above everything else, the commentaries reflected the victory which the transcendental teleology of the later
Peripatos and the Stoa had won over Aristotle's immanent and vitalistic
teleology. Thus a commentator on the *Metaphysics,* of whom one certainly
does not have to expect any original thought, writes, "The other beings
have been given the faculty of thought only for the purpose of the preservation of life, but man has received the sciences for the sake of the preserva-

tion of life as well as for the sake of thought itself." Given such an inclination to infer the existence of a God-willed purpose from the presence of an
advantage, and given also the connection of purpose-directed cause and
essence in the Peripatos, it had to become highly significant that the same
commentaries, again deviating from Aristotle yet also linked again to a
development begun in the Peripatos, defined man as the "thinking being."
This (and, of course, profound changes in the view of the world and of life)
is the reason why the "perfection" of man—in deviation from the all-
embracing ideal of Aristotle, which considered all sides of our humanity—
was placed exclusively into the intellectual sphere which, in contrast to the
animals, forms our specific nature. That the distance from this point to the
theoretical concept of purpose, which we shall meet so frequently in the
Middle Ages, was very short is shown by the sentence of a Syrian who is
already dependent on Arab Aristotelianism.

> Wisdom is the perfection of the human soul through perception of the
> existing things in accordance with the aptitude which nature has given it to
> this end. Indeed, . . . we have been created either for its perception alone
> and not also for action, or for both simultaneously.

It was quite natural that the Greek doctrine of purpose became significant
for Islam for the same reason for which it gained significance for Judaism.
Since this significance cannot be treated exhaustively here, we shall deal
with it only to the extent required to make evident the intermediary role
of Islam for Jewish thought. When Allah says in the Koran, "I have
created demons and human beings for nothing else but to serve Me," we
find in this sentence as little of a doctrine of purpose in our sense as we
do in the previously mentioned biblical verses. After all, "Many among
the demons and human beings have been created for hell" [Sura 7,178].
But these words come so close to Greek views (especially to those passages of Asclepius according to which obedience to God is among the
obligations of our life), that it seems plausible that the rationalizing exegesis of the Koran saw in the verse a doctrine of purpose after the Greek
model. "Reason is the servant of the heart, and the heart is created for
contemplation of the divine beauty. In doing this, the heart is a true
subject and servant of God; and this service is meant in the saying of
God" (here follows the verse from the Koran quoted above). Somewhat
more rationalistic than Ghazali was in these words, though probably
under his influence, a Turkish poet of the fifteenth century interprets the
verse as follows: the words "that they shall serve Me" are to mean "that
they know Me," and he adds the explanation, "as one serves God the
Exalted, one must through knowledge also reach the goal of cognitive
certitude. For the purpose of the worship of God is this: 'Serve your Lord
until cognitive certitude comes to you' " [Sura 15,99]. The road to this

knowledge of God goes through the knowledge of the self: "Whoever knows his soul, knows his Master."

A similar interpretation was given to a traditional dictum (*hadîth*) of the tenth century, according to which God says, "I was a treasure of kindness and excellence, yet did not know such things. Then I wanted to recognize their value. Had I not formed creation, the marvels of creation would have remained hidden from Me." The closing words were quoted as follows: "Thus I formed creation so that I should be known," and these words were taken to mean that "the knowledge of truth is found only in man." Thus the purpose of creation is not God's knowledge of Himself, but man's knowledge of Him.

We find the first Jewish solution of our problem in a statement by an unimportant eclectic compiler who nevertheless has a certain historic significance as the first among the Jewish thinkers known to us—Isaac Israeli (about 900 C.E.). In connection with the doctrine of purpose-directed causes (not with the intention to offer a new presentation of ethical problems), he wrote:

> If one asks what man is here for, one must give the following answer: because man is formed out of a natural body, he is the tool of the rational soul, so that, with his help, it may distinguish the truth of the things and work with him according to reason. But if one asks why man is a rational being, one must answer: so that he may distinguish between good and evil, true and false, that he may abide by truth and justice, worship God and acknowledge His rule, stay away from every impure deed, and receive God's reward for it. This [reward] consists in union with the upper soul, in order to gain from its light the light of intelligence and the splendor of wisdom. On this rung man reaches spirituality in linking himself to the light which emanated directly from the power of God.

This doctrine is obviously Neoplatonic (not in Plotinus's sense, but in that of Porphyry). It will be more adequately discussed in connection with our more explicit treatment of other Jewish Neoplatonists; for this reason we omit its discussion here. But it is instructive that this first Jewish doctrine of purpose already shows a pronounced eschatological character. Moreover, it is significant that the eschatology itself obviously shows Greek influence. For if "the paradise, recompense, and blissful rest" of man can be found in the union with the divine light, whereas the sufferings which the soul, burdened by sin and therefore incapable of ascent, endures in the fiery glow of the sphere are meant to represent Gehenna, we evidently have here more than merely the influence of the theoretical ideal of life and, of the reinterpretation of the myths of Hades, which had been popular since Posidonius. Here man's condition in the beyond obviously is not conceived as the execution of the freely made verdict of a judge, as in Jewish and New Testament eschatology, but as the necessary consequence of our life here on earth. To what extent the preponderance of the eschatological component of the world view and the strict causal connection between our actions here and our destiny in the beyond have contributed to the elimination of the obstacles inhibiting the appearance of a doctrine of purpose in the Bible is a question that can be answered only by a comprehensive survey of the Jewish Middle Ages. But it is instructive even now that the causal conception of our destiny in the beyond (in other words, a doctrine of purpose) is absent from the writings of Saadiah, Israeli's more important contemporary. Like the teachers who instructed him in the Kalām, he saw the question of the beyond exclusively from the perspective of God and His justice. For him, that we receive reward and punishment there is an entirely free act of God—that is, a miracle. He considers man as the immanent purpose of the world and the will of God as its transcendent purpose; in contrast to man's, God's will requires neither any utility for its motivation, nor God's wish to reveal His wisdom in the sense of the previously mentioned *hadîth*, nor His intention to benefit man. A unified doctrine of human purpose is, however, not developed.

On the other hand, we find discussions of the question of purpose at about the same time in Gabirol and Bahya. They are especially valuable because they cast a clear light upon the ways in which hellenistic teachings penetrated Jewish philosophy.

Bahya's discussion is found in the dialogue between soul and reason in the third book of *Duties of the Heart* [Ḥovot ha-Levavot]. After the soul, with deep shame, has recognized its lack of devotion to God and its indolence in His service, it asks reason "what its hidden rationale may be, and to what purpose it dwells in the world." But in a certain sense it anticipates the answer by expressing the fear that it may fare like that king who was elected only for one year and, at its conclusion, had to bid farewell to all his riches, unlike the other [king] who, in the same situation, had as many possessions as possible transferred abroad and therefore was able to enjoy them later. The latter's action presupposes that the guideline for our actions, reflecting the perception of and regard for our purpose, shall guarantee us simultaneously our well-being in the beyond. Reason expressly assures us that the soul becomes receptive to its instruction about the divine intention only though a concept of this world like that manifested in the parable. Meanwhile reason replies only to the question of purpose.

> The question of your particularity is this: for your distinction and well-being, the Creator formed you out of nothing in the community of spiritual beings, in order to elevate you and to raise your stature to the stature of those who belong to Him and of the pure ones among those who are close to the splendor of His light. But you are only capable of this elevation after

three events: first, the removal of the veil of folly from you and your illumination through His knowledge; second, your examination and trial whether you decide in favor of obedience or disobedience to Him; third, your torment in this world and your steadfastness in His troublesome service in it in order to elevate you to the stature of the high and steadfast ones. Such elevation cannot be your lot as long as you are in your first condition. But the wisdom of the Creator forms this universe for your use and a palace resembling Him with the five gates of the senses. (Here follows a detailed description of the body.) He provided you with two counselors (reason and passion) and two scribes (for good and evil deeds), as well as with numerous subordinates, and says to you: "Whatever I have submitted to you in this world cannot elevate your self, but only touch it from the outside, as the shell touches the little chick. If you are sensible and understand the intention I have for you, I let you reach the height of the pure who belong to Me, bring you close to My love, and clothe you with the brilliant splendor of My grandeur. In the case of disobedience, I punish you severely. If you are in doubt how to conduct yourself, ask your intellect for advice."

No scholar familiar with hellenistic literature will be able to read this dialogue without being strongly reminded of Hermeticism. Because its influence on Islamic thought, and indeed even on the interpretation of the Koran, has been demonstrated and most likely has influenced the study of the soul handed down over Bahya's name, we shall have to examine whether old [Johann Jacob] Reiske was entirely wrong when the single hermetic study in the Arabic language published until now [*Hermetis Trismegisti de castigatione animae libellus* (Bonn: Bardenhewer, 1873), with Latin translation] reminded him of Bahya's *Duties of the Heart*. To do this, we shall have to compare Bahya with the abovementioned study as well as with hellenistic Hermeticism. Whatever else is said about Arab Hermeticism is colorless and of as little value to us as Christian Hermeticism.

Since Bahya and the Arabs could at best find the content of the hermetic writings useful only after making substantial changes, we start by considering its form. The dialogue as we find it in Bahya is very rare in Arabic literature. On the other hand, it not only is prevalent in Greek-Roman Hermetica, but also is explicitly in evidence in Syrian Hermetica. The soul is being addressed. Exactly the same thing happens in the Arab Hermetica. This is particularly striking since we do not find any completely valid parallels to such discourses with the soul in either hellenistic or Jewish prose. We probably have to reckon with a gnostically transmitted echo of an older concept for which psyche was a deity. At any rate, the Arab study demonstrates that addresses to the psyche were customary in Islamic Hermetica. The Arab [writer] gives no information about the person who is speaking. But one has only to read the opening words of the seventh address. "How long shall I drive you, O Soul, upon the path of salvation, while you seek to drive me upon the path of misfortune, though I do not let myself be tempted to follow your path? When the difference between us is so great, we must separate, each of us going his own way." These words (in which, by the way, the older form of dialogue retained by Baḥya still shines through) are unintelligible if one assumes that the soul is being addressed by a writer whom she had never tried to seduce and whose "separation" from her is hardly felt as something threatening. They are, rather, based on a model in which the *nous* spoke to the soul, as in Baḥya (in the sense of the thought, familiar from Plotinus, that the *nous* is united with the soul except when she deserts it). Indeed, immediately before this passage we read that the soul can escape death only be being joined with the *nous* and by obedience to it. The refusal to be obedient, therefore, causes the *quo usque tandem* of the seventh address. Hence not only the addressee but also the speaker are identical here and in Baḥya.

But now the question arises: who [or what] is this *nous*? Is it man's individual faculty of thought, or is it world reason personified? We cannot expect a completely precise answer from our two authorities. It is quite obvious that we deal in both cases with one of those concepts floating between the concrete and the abstract, between person and attribute, which, according to [Wilhelm] Bousset's telling remark, "have to be assigned respectively to theological or theosophical speculation which mediates between folk belief and rational reflection." A closer examination shows, however, that both authors are personally inclined toward an individual and abstract concept of reason, but under the influence of their predecessors assign to it functions which are justified only when reason is conceived as general and concrete. Thus the Arab probably understood the "I" of the seventh address, which wants to protect itself from temptation by the soul, to be individual. Yet it evidently speaks as an infallable messenger from the "world of reason" to which the soul is supposed to return; and although Baḥya, in paragraph 5, introduces "our reason" as the speaker, the infallibility which is there ascribed to reason and the highly respectful way in which the soul addresses it are hardly compatible with the insight into the inadequacy of individual thought emphasized so strongly, especially by Baḥya. Therefore, despite the transformation that is easily understandable in monotheists, an older concept shines through in which the *nous* spoke as personally conceived world reason. Such instructive addresses of the *nous* are, however, in evidence in Hermeticism a number of times. And our Arab [author] makes it possible for us to go back still another step. At the end of the first address, he calls the *nous* "the noblest interpreter" of the supreme being. This designation, which is also found in the hermetically influenced pseudo-Baḥyanic study, goes, of course, back to the equation of *Hermes* and *hermeneus* ["herald"; "interpreter"] which we, to disregard Plato's allusion, are able to trace back to the second pre-Christian century (and probably have to consider as the chief motive for the literary activity of the god Hermes). Strangely enough, however, it retreats into the background in Greek-Roman Hermetica but is preserved in the writings of the Church Fathers and especially of the Gnostics. This would harmonize excellently with [Richard] Reitzenstein's assumption that we have here a study that was worked over by the Gnostics.

In the light of this consideration, the introductory words of our dialogue gain their correct meaning in Baḥya. He explains at the beginning of paragraph 5 that he wishes "to deal with awakening through reason in the form of questions and answers." This awakening is "man's inspiration by God by means of his reason." Since this [statement] obviously is the introduction to the address that follows, the source from which Baḥya draws these words must have intended to refer to individual but not to universal reason, which it then designates as mediator and awakener. If we do not want to confuse this "awakening to cognition" with that "arousal to action" with which experts in the language of biblical and Jewish medieval poetry are familiar, we shall have to acknowledge that what applies to awakening applies just as much to mediating: here too is a concept to be traced back into pre-Christian times, which seems to emerge only once in Greek-Roman Hermeticism in connection with another image. This concept was preserved among the Naasites who, in the above-mentioned passage, see in Hermes simultaneously the "mediator" and the "awakener from sleep." Thus a critical analysis of the sources shows that "mediation" and "awakening," as they are connected in Baḥya, belong together as witnesses for the aftereffect of a gnostically revised hermetic manuscript.

If we therefore look first only at the form of both writings and their probable models, we can obtain an overview of a development which leads to a steadily increasing fading of a primal mythical form: the dialogue of two divine beings (assuming that Reitzenstein's theory is correct) turns into a discourse between world *nous* and the human soul. This is turned by Baḥya into a discussion between individual reason and individual soul, while the Arab [writer] leaves us with an admonition of reason to the soul, and Pseudo-Baḥya chooses the customary form of a treatise.

Baḥya reminds one of Hermeticism more strongly than does the Arab, not only in the form of the dialogue but also in his tone. We are assured three times that a secret shall be communicated, and it is stressed emphatically that the soul "in its previous condition" had not been able to fulfill its purpose. This genuine tone of mystery is apparently lacking in the Arab who, with a lateral glance toward different hermetic writings, explains in his preface that he wishes not only to elucidate the teachings of Hermes but to support them with clear arguments in such a way that every healthy mind will have to accept them. But he too is aware that the sages may turn only to souls capable of seeing and hearing, and, as we know, he is prepared to reject defiant souls.

Baḥya also is closer to the older Hermeticism in the content of his views. Although both writers have completely blurred the dogmatic content of original Hermeticism and have established a connection with philosophical (especially Neoplatonic) teachings, they do not make the salvation of the soul—as we shall immediately see in Gabirol—dependent upon methodical investigation. For the Arab [author], it is not through skilled logical operations that the soul achieves closeness to God, but through rejection of lassitude, through struggle against love of this world, through separation of what is essential to it from what is alien to its essence, and through the endeavor to enlist friends for the beyond even now. To be sure, these characteristics are not characteristic only of Hermeticism, nor is it characterized solely by its emphasis on the singling out of a class of "pure human beings" who may hope for an honored place in the beyond, as implied by the self-designation of the Pure Brethren, whose alleged dependence on Hermeticism has remained totally unsubstantiated. But these concepts are found not only in the Arab Hermetic; Judah Halevi too seems to know them from hermetic sources, since even according to the report of his Peripatetic the souls of the perfect ones achieve communion in the beyond with "Hermes, Asclepius, Socrates, Plato, and Aristotle." Thus his eschatology (one must pay attention to the sequence of the names) is certainly linked to hermetic concepts.

We can, however, obtain more definite results by examining the three conditions of immortality posited by Baḥya. The first is "the removal of the veil of folly and your illumination through its recognition." The first image too is found literally in the hermetic dialogues, next to the admonition to the soul—preserved by the Arab—to shed the robe of the body. It can conceivably be explained as a version of this image that has become dimmer over the years. The *photismos* ["enlightenment"] through the *gnosis* of God also is a hermetic demand. Secondly, Baḥya declares that examinations are necessary in order to find out whether the soul remains constant in obedience. While nothing about such a meaning of the examinations is known to me in hermetic literature, we do know that Hermeticism—in contrast to Neoplatonism, with which a number of the concepts mentioned before would be in accord—adopted the demand of obedience to God in its doctrine of purpose. Thirdly, "God chastises you to raise you to the rank of the high ones, the constant ones, of whom it is said: 'Serve the Eternal One, O His angels.' " It is remarkable that a pious Jew describes suffering as *conditio sine qua non* for complete bliss. Even more remarkable is that the concluding words compel us to assume that the soul not only becomes more blessed than it is on earth, but is elevated to the rank of superhuman beings. Yet the goal which Hermeticism promises is to become Godlike through cognition, and the ascent is preceded by painful purifications on earth and in the beyond. The sufferings are perceived simultaneously as punishment and as a means to the ascent.

Thus an examination of the form, tone, and content of Baḥya's dialogue leads us to the same result: a hermetic script has been drawn upon, either directly or in an adaptation which enables us to recognize its character even more clearly than does the [text of the] Arab Hermetic that has been preserved. Whereas the latter only grants that man has been created solely for "knowledge and action" (the Arabic play on words will occupy us further), Baḥya's source poses the question entirely in the sense of the dialogue of Asclepius: to what end have we descended to earth? The solution ensues in the spirit of Hermeticism, though probably also under the influence of that mystery of the redemption of the psyche of which we have spoken: we dwell on earth not in order to remain what we are, but to raise ourselves to a superhuman height. Contemplation of the world helps us toward awareness, trials lead us to perseverance, and suffering to purification. Baḥya could, of course, not use the central idea—that of elevation to the rank of a *daimon*—and allowed it to shine through only very dimly. But his soul, wide open to every kind of genuine piety, perceived the religious nature of this world view (and especially its moral demands) as something akin to and likely to further that internalization and deepening of religious life which he sees as the objective of his little book. He believed he could square it with his Judaism not only to keep the dialogue form of the model, but also to preserve the exhilarating stimulus produced by the ray of light falling upon this world from the secrets of the beyond. Most of what we read in III,5–10 has probably been derived from his source, since Hermeticism clearly also taught that illumination through God is needed and that an examination of our situation in the world leads to an awareness of far-reaching dependence, but not at all to complete determinism. Of course, we are unable to get a clear picture of the thought processes of the model. Baḥya himself hints that he has greatly abbreviated it. . . .

Certain as it is that Baḥya links himself to antiquity, it is just as certain that a systematic look at his efforts enables us to recognize their medieval character.

The ancient doctrines of purpose had already sought to demonstrate the validity of the forces to whose service each individual thinker had dedicated his life. For some it was the advancement of science, for others some generally beneficial work which gains a deeper motivation through the belief that we have been destined or created for this or that. In the Middle Ages, these life forces, which expect to be directed by a doctrine of purpose, are joined by religion, not only in Posidonius's sense, as a purely personal need, or even merely in the hermetic sense, as the motivating force of a community based upon free association, but as the sovereign of life who approaches us with a demand for submission. Baḥya attempts to validate religion on the following premise: not only are the "Duties of the Heart" incomparably more important than the "Duties of the Limbs"—indeed, they are the essential duties of religion—but the purpose of the purification of the heart is [the attainment of] eternal bliss. Therefore our striving for bliss is what determines our purpose. Here the first of the previously described three ways is entered, the way originating in ethics: what we envision as the goal of our obligation is considered to be the command of a higher will. But the second, teleological, consideration is immediately added: man's spiritual and physical makeup and his condition—that is, his placement into a lowly existence on earth and thus even his external fate—are understood in the light of this purposiveness. And according to the third way, this concept becomes closely associated with the image of God as the kind father who, at the same time, directs us strictly toward the right path.

If we allow ourselves to rely upon Baḥya's words, his doctrine of purpose would deprive both scientific research and moral action of the last vestige of their autonomous value, which even Hermeticism seems to grant them. To be sure, whoever wishes to understand the man and his influence must be clear in his own mind that here too the formula does not reflect the form without change. While in Hermeticism genuine striving for the beyond insufficiently transforms the formulations of science, it seems that in Baḥya the high valuation of the beyond originates essentially in a disdain for the *dunja,* the world with its self-centered bustle, alienated from God and in need of a religio-moral structuring of life.

The question of purpose is also of great significance for Gabirol. It is prominent even in his religious poetry.

Do not let me ascend in the midst of my days
until I have prepared what I shall need for the road
and provender for the day of the journey;
and if I left the world as I entered it,
and returned to my home naked as I had emerged from it,
for what should I then have been created
and summoned to behold trouble?
Then it would have been better had I remained there,
than to have left to increase sin and multiply guilt.

The contrast with Job 1:21, which Gabirol of course had in mind and which considers it the inescapable destiny of man "to return naked as he had emerged," demonstrates clearly the development of the view of life that has taken place. Life here has no intrinsic meaning; its meaning lies in the fruit which it produces for the beyond. As in Baḥya, it is to help us to a perfection which we could otherwise not reach. But why it can help us to attain perfection is left open by the *Royal Crown* [*Keter Malkhut*]. Nor are we helped much further by a hint in his ethical treatise, according to which the world was created for the sake of man, but man has the duty to raise himself to the highest possible rung and to employ his senses only for the necessities of life, because God has lent them to him for this purpose.

On the other hand, the thinker speaks with perfect clarity in his chief metaphysical opus. He begins his *Fountain of Life* with the admonition of the teacher to the student, who has made good progress through the "quality of his talent" and his eagerness for knowledge, to turn to the "ultimate question," the question for what man has been created. After a short exchange regarding the methodology to be used, the student, without referring to the teacher's preceding words, poses the question: what should man strive for in this life? The answer: since cognitive intelligence is the best part of man, cognition is the most worthwhile goal. Particularly worthwhile kinds of cognition are: first, self-knowledge, for since man's nature comprehends and penetrates everything external to himself and everything is subservient to his power, he advances from self-knowledge to universal knowledge; second, recognition of the purpose-directed cause for whose sake he has been created. He must eagerly pursue it, for in this way he reaches blissfulness. Such a cause must exist because the divine will moves everything; it is the "union of his soul with the higher world, so that everything may return to its own kind." We reach this cause through knowledge and action, for through these the soul unites itself with the higher world. That is to say: knowledge leads to action, and action liberates the soul from what is alien and harmful to it and leads it back to its own nature and essence. In fact, knowledge and action redeem the soul in general and purify it from its dimness and darkness; and thus the soul returns again to its higher world.

When the student asks for proof that the purpose-directed cause of our existence lies in knowledge and action, two lines of thought are developed (though they actually demonstrate only knowledge as our purpose). The first asserts that it starts with a definition of man; stating the general principle that actual perfection is always the purpose-directed cause of potential perfection, it concludes that thought is perfection and, therefore, the ultimate purpose of the soul. According to the second line of reasoning, which is merely hinted at and probably inserted from another source, the fact that we are destined for knowledge follows from the doctrine of the transformation of the elements into the sense organs, the tools of the perceiving soul and its secret and manifest power.

Now, asserts the student, we actually ought to examine the continuity of the soul, what effect the knowledge it absorbs has upon it, and what knowledge does or does not remain with it after its separation from the body. These investigations, however, belong to psychology. "Right now I must ask what kind of knowledge it is for the sake of which man has been created." The knowledge of all things according to their nature, answers the teacher, especially the knowledge of the first substance which carries and moves him. To be sure, we can not acquire this knowledge as knowledge of the essence, but only from its effects, since the first essence is totally dissimilar from us and without limits.

The conclusion of the work corresponds essentially to this definition of the goal by demanding, though without mentioning a purpose set by God, the ascent into the world of the spirit and from there into the world of divinity. This ascent guarantees liberation from death and union with the source of life, but can only be achieved through separation from the world of the senses and immersion into the sphere of intelligible things.

These lines of thought have been interpreted to imply that Gabirol raised the question why man had not remained in the beyond but had been transferred to the earth. Consequently the thinker was not spared the reproach that he had "not answered the question." This error stems from the attempt to explain Gabirol's Neoplatonic views merely in terms of their connection with Plotinus and the Arabic Pseudepigrapha, and not with the Greek successors of Plotinus, who were much better known to Islam. Plotinus does indeed raise the question about the reason for our descent, but not the more general question about man's purpose. The truth is that Gabirol has posed the question of our descent in the previously mentioned, but apparently heretofore unconsidered, passage of the *Royal Crown* and hinted there at an answer along Baḥya's lines of thought, namely, that sojourn on this earth enables the soul to collect provisions for the beyond. In the *Fountain of Life,* however, the question is not answered because it has not been raised. Gabirol's standpoint is not that of Plotinus but rather that of Porphyry, of whose commentary on Aristotle's *Categories* the form of Gabirol's work reminds us just as unmistakably as Baḥya's dialogue does of Hermeticism. Furthermore, the step which Porphyry took in the direction of Aristotle manifests itself not only in the way the question is posed, but just as much in the answer. The purpose of our life, according to the line of reasoning repeated by Gabirol, lies exclusively in theory, because the *nous* is that which is best within us and because, according to the commentaries on Aristotle, it follows from the definition of man as a (potentially) thinking organism (which, of course, Gabirol also presupposes) that his perfection lies in the actualization of the intellect. Insofar as man thereby simultaneously attains bliss, the Aristotelian ideal of theoretical eudaemony is revived anew. On the other hand, the Neoplatonic doctrine of being, in contrast to Aristotle's, limited contemplation to the sphere of the spiritual, even to an explicit turning away from the world of the senses.

Something else follows from the presuppositions of the Neoplatonic epistemology, according to which like can only be recognized by like. Since cognition must depend on the union of subject and object, cognition of the pure substances must, therefore, rest upon self-recognition of a soul resembling them. [What follows], on the one hand, [is] the identification of the urge for knowledge with the religious yearning for a closeness to God which assures immortality; on the other hand, there is the moral demand for the "deed," but not in the Aristotelian sense of effect upon the outside world—[rather, it is] understood cathartically, as in Porphyry, as the fruit and condition of cognition. What we have here is what we find in Proclus, according to whom "the virtues follow one another: the dianoetic follow the ethical ones, and the ethical the dianoetic." In the same way, just as according to our passage the deed follows cognition, and just as even man's connection with the world of the senses, correctly utilized, helps the soul achieve clarification and purification, so the contemplation of the intelligible substances can succeed only when we "purify ourselves from contamination by sensual impressions and free ourselves from the bonds of nature." Abstraction and catharsis, after all, are merely different symptoms of the anagogy of the soul to its original divine source. The posing of the question is un-Platonic, and so is the solution, insofar as the notion of an ascent through the intelligible into the divine and consequently the possibility of ecstasy are merely intimated. Gabirol himself, whose feeling about the distance between man and God was strengthened and deepened by his scientific studies, must surely have been able to conceive of union with the ultimate entity only as *communio,* not as *unio.*

That this doctrine of the goal of life remained for Gabirol not just an empty phrase and formula, but in fact gave direction to his life, is shown in his secular poetry. Precisely because it is tied to entirely different conventions than his philosophical writings—and convention means a great deal to Gabirol—it is highly instructive to see how the same ideal of a science leading to knowledge and moral purity finds expression, not only in the brilliant hyperbolic language of a poetry informed by Arabic models, but also in the sober formulas of scholastic deduction. It is only in his poetry that we learn of the sacrifices with which the poet had to purchase his dedication to this science. Love of knowledge has already blanched the cheek of the sixteen-year-old, though a young man's cheek ought to glow as the sun-drenched rose. In the course of the years he is drained of his physical strength because he "links light as well as dark hours to his work." Time cripples his eagle's wings, without, however, preventing him from diving into the sea of wisdom and bringing up its pearls. He—who is in need of friendship as hardly anyone else—must even leave his friends because they do not understand his best. Even his joy in poetry turns into bitterness because the fools call "his fullness meager." One understands why he has written his *Fountain of Life* in such a way as to find not only Jewish readers. He knows it: "the more thought, the more sorrow." Yet despite sacrifice, pain, and loneliness, he clings to genuinely human strivings: "Should I abandon wisdom, since the spirit of God created the bond between me and her?" Even more characteristically: "Who frees himself from desecration cannot loosen the belt of reason . . . he does not desecrate his own heart, lowering himself to grass and thorns." "Desecration" (Gabirol uses the term for religious defection) of one's "own heart" (referring, according to Sufic language, to that essential core of man which Democritus and Posidonius call *daimon*) is for him, therefore, defection from science. Whoever barters her "luminous robe," her "purple mantle," for the dress of the world already stands as high above the dumb fools as man stands above the animal, and he knows that in the other world God will separate the wise from the fools.

It is not surprising that Gabirol's poetry emphasizes the theoretical aspects of the ideal of life more strongly than the moral-cathartic ones; only the former were in need of explicit defense. To be sure, it seems that the beginning of the *Fountain of Life* is based on two sources, one closer to the peripatetic, the other closer to the Neoplatonic ideal. In particular, the passage already discussed, which offers a proof but does not carry it through, shows that Gabirol has not completely succeeded in harmonizing the two. One reason may be that the doctrine of purpose is sometimes substantiated peripatetically by the concept of the superiority of thought and sometimes by eschatological considerations. Yet the fissure does not go very deep, because the thinker is already acquainted with the view of the Arabic Aristotelians that certain elements of knowledge guarantee continuity in the beyond. Moreover, he believes in a very intimate mutual relationship between catharsis and thought, which has of course also influenced the ideal of his poetry. The syncretism of Plotinus's successors is revived in him. However, the contrast to Baḥya is clearly evident, and it is notably reinforced in the writings of his opponents—here the enemies of science, there coldhearted teachers of the Law. Just as Gabirol's ethical manual cites a number of Greek names, in contrast to Baḥya who consciously quotes only Moslems (Gabirol wants to heal the sickness of the soul, while Baḥya makes far-reaching concessions to Islamic asceticism), so Gabirol's work, despite his eschatology, shows the emergence of a scientific passion which appears the more worthy of its original Greek source the harsher the sacrifices with which his satisfaction had to be bought.

Gabirol's kindred spirit, Joseph ibn Ẓaddik, asserts unambiguously, "Man has been created for the sake of wisdom." But how remote this view is from that of Aristotle becomes clear through the addition that the sensual (or the "primary," as Joseph, joining Gabirol in following Plotinus, calls them) substances and accidences have only been impressed upon him, so that through these, whose existence he easily recognizes, he may arrive at the knowledge of the spiritual ("secondary") ones. Therefore, only the science of the suprasensual has value; the remark regarding the relative value of sensual knowledge could conceivably be connected with Joseph's wish to determine not only the purpose-directed cause of our existence, but also that of our sojourn on earth—as Gabirol does in the *Royal Crown*. At any rate, wisdom is restricted to knowledge of the suprasensual. But even with this limitation, which of course comes considerably closer to religion, wisdom is not an end in itself. For man, according to the following proof of the previous assertion, has been created only in order to partake of the delights of the future world. But the path to this participation leads through the deed (that is, through service of God, as Joseph apparently adds to the excerpts from his source); since the only path to the deed is through wisdom, wisdom is the cause of his creation. That wisdom is the source of the good deed, and that we therefore must trace the actions of the unbelievers back to the weakness of the animalistic soul is shown by the following explanation: we comprehend the eternal, universal substances for the sake of wisdom, in order to recognize universal existence and especially the science dealing with the highly praised first substance. The action which follows from it is the selfless moral deed. While others act decently out of lust for gain and power, the philosopher loves the good for its own sake, for he strives to arrive at true unity; true unity and the truly good, as the philosopher has often taught, are identical. This, therefore, is the foundation and source of good action.

After Joseph has demonstrated the duty to imitate God's ways from biblical passages, justice, to which wisdom directs us, is denoted as the second important foundation. Both imitation and justice point to two further "foundations": trust in God and humility. There are no qualities of the wise soul which are not contained in these four. Hence the task of philosophy is [to lead to] the knowledge of the Creator as the true, one, eternal, just, beneficient, and merciful God, but the fruit of philosophy and the action which results from it and bears witness to it is the closest possible adaptation to His activity. It is for this that we shall receive the promised reward.

These teachings represent an attempt at an eschatological transformation of the rationalistic doctrine of purpose in Peripatos, which is linked to the peculiarity of man in such a way that rationalism prevails in the formulation, but eschatology in the substance. To be sure, [the definition of] our purpose—in distinct contrast to Baḥya—is entrusted to science, which, just as in Gabirol (according to the Stoic model), starts from self-knowledge. But what is significant is not only that, again as with Gabirol, science and deed "free us from enslavement to nature" in this world, but that science already has received exclusively religious meaning in the introductory remarks. It is not understood, as it is in Gabirol in agreement with the peripateticizing commentators of Aristotle, as comprehension of things according to their essence, but in agreement with the Platonists as *homoiosis theo* [*imitatio dei*]. Even though the merit of thought is acknowledged, our scientifically determined purpose is not derived from it, but exclusively from the eschatological benefit which science contributes through the medium of ethical purification. This eschatologization of the scientific ideal leads ibn Ẓaddik to a highly novel version of the concept of cognition. When God says regarding His attributes, "I, the Eternal One, establish mercy, righteousness and justice on earth," and adds, "for in this I delight, says the Eternal," this means "this is what I demand of you, nothing else: for the creatures, all of them, exist through justice." Such words closely approach the ethicalization of the concept of God as achieved in Neokantianism by Hermann Cohen, who refers to similar prophetic passages; yes, knowledge of the good God and "clinging to the good" are related to such an extent that one could well speak here of a kind of ethical *gnosis* (in contrast to the metaphysical *gnosis* of Christianity).

When, therefore, the Aristotelian traits of the earliest Neoplatonists recede into the background in ibn Ẓaddik, [Abraham] Ibn Daud moves them into the foreground. When a thing reaches a certain perfection through gradual progress, we may say that it represents the intended purpose-oriented cause. Thus, primal matter is not here for its own sake, but that it may serve as the foundation of the elements. But the elements, too, are here only for the sake of the coordinated bodies; among these the lowest rungs are occupied by minerals and gasses, higher rungs by plants, then animals, then man: therefore he is the intended goal of the "world of nature." But if we apply the same process of reasoning to the powers of man, it follows that his vegetative and animalistic powers are there only for the sake of the highest, the power of reason. This, in turn, is of a twofold nature: turned upward, it receives instruction from the angels; turned downward, it masters the other powers by preventing every excess and every disorder.

But now the author, without stating it explicitly, applies his method for the third time to the creations of reason, the sciences. They also are ordered according to steps; their purpose (we must add, the purpose of the highest among them) is the science of God. From here it becomes evident how foolish human beings are who are totally preoccupied with the care of the body. But the same also applies to those who are satisfied with fostering individual sciences. They resemble the slave who is able to gain his freedom through a pilgrimage to Mecca but loses sight of his journey while he fashions a rope in case his water gourd should be ruptured. Our goal must therefore remain the knowledge of God, which, however, in this life is restricted to knowledge of His existence, not of His essence.

Whereas Gabirol's doctrine of purpose of Neoplatonic, not Platonic, Ibn Daud's is peripatetic, but not Aristotelian as such. It is peripatetic in its view of the relationship of knowledge and deed, and, therefore, in its position regarding the controversy between 'ilm and 'amal [knowledge and action] which strongly occupies Arabic philosophy as a whole. Although, following Aristotle, a "practical part of wisdom" is also acknowledged, action does not possess any cathartic significance through which it could gain autonomous value and, in accordance with Neoplatonic epistemology, could become a precondition of cognition. As Ibn Daud assures us in his preface [to The Exalted Faith (Emunah Ramah)], only those for whom his book has not been written could do without philosophical writings, because only the deed is truly the goal of philosophy. Thus the rational element prevails against the eschatological, which shines through faintly only in the comparison taken over from Ghazali. That scientific thinking constitutes our purpose is not immediately proven through its meaning for our bliss, but through its inner value. To be sure, the teleological method employed here is not truly Aristotelian, but, as we know, was developed only in the later Peripatos and in the Stoa. Moreover, Aristotle showed much more interest in empirical knowledge than would appear in Ibn Daud. But the devaluation of the encyclia in favor of a religiously conceived philosophy had already begun in the early Stoa, and it may have been favored not only by the general trend of medieval thought, but also by Ibn Daud's personal predisposition.

The influence of Ibn Daud's personality on his position becomes even more evident in juxtaposition to Moses Maimonides, who draws upon the same philosophical sources but has an utterly different personality.

He treated the question of man's purpose twice: as a youth in the introduction to his Mishnah commentary, and as a mature man in his chief philosophical work. The presentation of the question in his early work offers one of the significant expositions which abound in his Mishnah commentary, this first attempt to interpret a halakhic work philosophically. The author creates the opportunity for this by mentioning the rabbinic dictum that "God owns nothing in this world except the four ells of the Halakhah." Although this passage, in its literal sense, opposes the view of science (the questions of Halakhah are, after all, insignificant beside those of metaphysics), its meaning appears profound and true when one assumes that the rabbis hold the philosophical view that one may proclaim ultimate truths to the multitude only in allusions. (According to Maimonides, this view is already worked out in the Bible.)

The ancients, so Maimonides begins, discovered that everything must have a purpose for the sake of which it exists. As far as human artifacts—for example, a saw or an axe—are concerned, this statement requires no proof. It is different with regard to the works of divine art and the wisdom of nature. Among them, there are some whose purpose-directed cause may be easily found. In others it is disclosed only through profound reflection. Still others require the gift of prophecy for their discovery—for example, we are hardly able to say why some ants have wings and others do not. However, when it comes to noteworthy creatures whose functions are obvious, we recognize their purpose the more distinctly the wiser we get. When Solomon "spoke about trees, from the cedar of Lebanon to the hyssop, . . . about beasts, birds, creeping things, and fishes" (1 Kings 5:13), his statement, which was admired as a sign of special wisdom, is taken to mean the cognition of their final cause.

In general, one might say that everything in the sublunar sphere is here only for the sake of man: thus the animal for his nourishment and other uses (for carrying burdens, riding, or other yet unexplored purposes). Likewise the plants: in every generation the usefulness of herbs and fruits, the use of which was still unknown to our forebears, is disclosed to us. . . . But after we have found that the purpose of all these things is the existence of man, we must explore further for what man is on earth and what his ultimate purpose may be. Careful investigation has shown that man can produce numerous things (in contrast to the palm which can only produce dates, or the spider which can only spin webs); but one can also discover that his ultimate purpose is only one, and that the other aspects of his productivity exist only to make his existence possible and fulfill the one purpose—that he may indeed perceive the intelligible things in his soul and conceive the truths as they are. For man cannot possibly be born for eating, drinking, begetting, for the building of walls or for the dignity of kings, for all these are accidents which he encounters. Moreover, he shares these functions with other living beings. Wisdom, on the other hand, adds something to his essence and raises him from a contemptible to an honorable level. Whereas he previously was a human being only potentially, he now becomes one in actuality. Man, before he thinks, equals the animal, from which he is distinguished only by thought, as the thinking organism—"thinking" to be understood as the perception of the intelligible things. But the most worthy among the intelligible things is the soul's concept of the unity of God, because all other kinds of wisdom serve merely as initial exercises for the attainment of divine wisdom. Meanwhile, the perception of intelligible things requires avoiding an excess of physical pleasures, for the first insight we must acquire is that the soul is suppressed by the comfort of the body and vice versa. When man pursues his lusts, loves the splendor of the senses, and makes his reason subservient to his cravings, . . . the power of God (reason) cannot appear in him, and he is only a piece of matter swimming in the "Ocean of Hyle."

We see, therefore, [Maimonides continues,] that the purpose of our world and of everything that fills it is a wise and good human being. When, therefore, an individual clarifies for himself the concept of wisdom and action ("by wisdom I mean the comprehension of truths, as they are, through reason and the attainment of all truths comprehensible to man; by action I mean a correct, well-regulated attitude toward the physical, without submerging oneself in pleasures to which one surrenders only as far as the preservation of the body and harmony of character demand it"), [he achieves] the sought-for purpose. This is known not only through the prophets, but also through the sages of the other religions who do not know the prophets yet know nonetheless that man is perfect only when he combines wisdom and (righteous) deed. It is sufficient to point to the word of the most outstanding philosopher: God has intended for us to be understanding and excellent; for when man is knowledgeable and understanding but dedicated to his lusts, he is in truth not knowledgeable, because it is the first doctrine of science that one surrenders to physical enjoyments only as much as is required by the needs of one's body. Thus the prophet too reproached him who boasts of his wisdom but does not obey the Law and follows the inclination of his soul. But a God-fearing man whose conduct of life shows exemplary moderation, yet who is devoid of wisdom, is also imperfect (though superior to the former), because his actions are not based upon the foundation of truth and righteousness. Therefore our sages say, "The boor is no fearer of sin". . . ; and whoever says of an unlearned person that he is pious contradicts the clear decision of the sages just as much as he contradicts reason. Therefore we find in the Torah the commandments "we shall teach them" and "we shall do them," giving priority to instruction over deed because one reaches the deed through wisdom and not wisdom through deed. This is what is meant by the dictum of our sages that learning leads to doing.

Yet there still remains a question. One could reply to us: you have said that divine wisdom created nothing in vain; that of all the creatures in the sublunar sphere man is the most valuable; and, finally, that it is the purpose of man to conceive the intelligible things in his soul. Why, then, has God created all those human beings who conceive no intelligible things? Moreover, we see that the largest part of humanity, bereft of wisdom, follows its lusts, while a wise, temperate person is an extraordinary phenomenon and can be found only in the course of many generations. To this we answer: there are two causes for their existence. The first one is that they serve that one (the wise man). For if all people were to devote themselves to wisdom and philosophy, the world would become desolate in a short time and humanity would die out, because man is very helpless and needs many things. Hence he would have to learn how to plow, harvest, thresh, bake, and make vessels in order to provide for his subsistence. . . . When, then, should that (wise) man find time to study and to acquire wisdom? For this reason unwise ones have been created for the performance of those labors, so that wisdom may be possible at all . . . . and therefore our sages described them as "people of the soil" because they are here only for the cultivation of land. But if one objects that many an unreasoning person is at ease and receives service from others, perhaps even from wise men, we have to remind ourselves that the houses which he arranges to be built and the orchards which he causes to be planted may some day benefit the wise man. Ben Soma, too, looking at the multitude streaming up to the Temple Mount, said in this sense, "Praised be He who created all these to serve me." After all, he was unique in his generation.

The second reason for the existence of unwise people is that the number of sages, according to divine wisdom, has to be small by necessity, and in the face of necessities which the first wisdom has determined, one cannot ask why they are so constituted. Why are there nine spheres of the stars, seven planets, and four elements? Our sages, too, have stated this repeatedly. Thus Rabbi Simeon bar Yoḥai said about his generation, "I saw only few people of high rank; if there are two, they are I and my son." According to this, the mass of people is created to live together with the person of rank. And although you might assume that this argument is easier [to accept] than the first one, it is in truth more important; for you see that God has permitted the unbelievers to remain in the (Holy) Land so that they may live together with the favored people, as it is written: "I will not drive them out before you in a single year lest the land become desolate." For this reason our sages have also distinctly taught, "What is the meaning of the biblical verse, 'and this is the whole man'? The whole world has been created for his sake"—that is, to live together with him. From everything we have discussed it becomes evident that the sole ultimate purpose of this world of growth and decay is the perfect human being, who in the manner which we have described combines wisdom and (righteous) deed.

It is fascinating for the expert in the development of our problem to note how closely Maimonides, in the basic thought of this treatise, approaches the (to him completely unknown) train of thought of the young Aristotle. . . . This closeness exists even in those aspects which are not found in [Aristotle's] didactic writings, though there too a teleological point of view was connected with the ideal of the "theoretical life," just as thought, for Maimonides, appears not only as the greatest advantage, but also as "the purpose of man's existence" (in contrast to the other functions, which are given to him only for the preservation of the life which has its meaning exclusively in thought). But this unconscious coincidence is, of course, based to a considerable extent on the transformations which the understanding of the didactic writings had experienced at the hands of the commentators. . . . These transformations explain the deviations not only from the later Aristotle, but from Aristotelianism as such. They conceived teleology wholly transcendentally, in the sense of the later Peripatos and the Stoa. At any rate, Maimonides neither goes as far as Saadiah, who was "infected by the Kalām," nor as far as Gabirol, who was probably under the indirect influence of a passage from the Koran. Both of them place man in the center of the entire universe. He even differs distinctly from Ibn Daud, insofar as his genuine scientific bent senses precisely the difficulties which are posed to an anthropocentric teleology by, for instance, the existence of poisonous plants.

On the other hand, rationalism helps him to discover the special purpose of man in a way similar to that of Ibn Daud, though differing from Aristotle's rationalism. Maimonides was certainly aware of his ties to the *Nicomachian Ethics*, which asks for "the work" (*ergon*) of man and does not want to see it in the functions which man shares with the lower organisms, instead demanding its connection with thought.

Maimonides follows his hellenic model in this basic rationalist position, willingly and out of deepest conviction. Nevertheless, the passage also reveals highly instructive differences. They are, first of all, those of the technique of thinking. Aristotle's view, which is fixed upon reality, proceeds from the image of the living person. He saw no reason to give a definition of man in his ethical writings. For Maimonides, the definitions of man and of science which he found in the commentaries form the pillars of his structure of thought, and between them he permits the conceptual pairs of substance and accident, *dynamis* and *energeia* ["potency and act"] to play back and forth. But just as the scholastic technique of thought one-sidedly continues the hellenic trend toward abstraction, which found its completion in Aristotle's time (and especially in his person) through the joy of contemplating the sensual, so the content of the definitions—drawing on individual passages from Aristotle and yet in profound contrast to the development of his later, mature years—permits the abstract meaning of scientific work and of life to emerge overly strongly. Man is the thinking being; thought is abstract thought as metaphysics practices it. Hence only the metaphysician may be properly called man [*Mensch*], while for Aristotle thought lifts man above the human, and the objection can be raised whether we may strive for such closeness to the gods at all. But while a Neoplatonic trend is evident in this exclusive valuation of abstract metaphysical knowledge, Neoplatonic eschatological concepts have an even more definite effect upon the view of scientific work. For Aristotle, study and action are variants of energy; specifically, theoretical energy is basic to our feeling of happiness. The Arabic antithesis of *'ilm* and *'amal* has no sharp edge here: *man 'alima, 'amila* ("whoever studies, acts"), Aristotle would have said.

It is different with Maimonides. Of course, he also knew the joy of the genuine scholar and, in contrast to ibn Zaddik, he rejected the definition of wisdom as "approach to God." But for this theory, knowledge and act are opposites. The value of thought does not lie in the satisfaction it gives us, but, as he hints here and states openly in the *Guide for the Perplexed* [*Moreh Nevukhim*], in the fact that it first forms the passive *nous* and then, by means of the inseparable connection between it and the active *nous,* helps us to gain special divine care in this world and bliss in the beyond. Thus Aristotle starts entirely from this-worldly eudaemony, calling it the theoretical ideal divine only to the extent that *nous* is divine, but not because it somehow links us to the universal deity. He knows nothing of any bliss after death and, therefore, assigns great significance for eudaemony to health and fate. Maimonides, however, perceives eudaemony not so much as religion as a metaphysical substitute religion, which, by repressing sensual in favor of suprasensual knowledge—indeed, by suspecting that the body is an enemy of the intellect—reveals Neoplatonic influence. As a matter of fact, he seems to refer to a Neoplatonic work which parades under Aristotle's name. Yet it is odd how sharply Maimonides, in the last portion of his treatise, draws a line between thinking and nonthinking people. To be sure, the allusions he makes in this passage, which is designed for lay people, [indicate] that he is aware that the reader will not completely understand his point of view, but that the reader will nevertheless not find it difficult to accept the fact that he derives the existence of nonthinking human beings from an ultimate mystery of the will of the divine power. (This actually is not an explanation, but the abandonment of an explanation.) We are able, however, to complement these allusions. According to Judah Halevi's Peripatetic, the philosophically talented person reaches through thought "the highest step accessible to man, the lowest rung of the angels" by uniting himself with the active *nous.* Such philosophers form a kingdom of their own, so to speak, just as the kingdom of man stands above the animal kingdom and the animal kingdom above the kingdom of plants. As has long been known, this is the doctrine of the *Guide* regarding the favored people for whom alone bliss is reserved, although Maimonides, like his predecessors, referred to the philosopher, in contrast to Judah Halevi, who referred to the prophet. Nevertheless, in accordance with their common basis, both are concerned with the question why there are not only favored people. Maimonides resolves this difficulty by creating another difficulty: he introduces the question of the small number of the spheres in order to demonstrate that the divine plan is beyond questioning. Judah Halevi answers with the counterquestion: why are there also animals? We have to be satisfied with the statement that the world is constructed in steps which, as Judah's more complete presentation makes clear, are the result of hereditary and climatic necessities to which the divine power also is bound. The disclosure of the thought which Maimonides had in mind and at which he deliberately only hinted—his belief in the special position of favored man—moves Maimonides's ideal of life into unexpected closeness to the hermetically influenced thought processes of Baḥya, of which we have spoken. This is no accident. Baḥya, as his open-mindedness toward the Kalām shows, clearly was not touched by genuine Aristotelianism, and Maimonides was not familiar with any serious hermetic writings. What reverberates in both is ultimately the idea of divine man which Aristotle and Hermeticism adopted from Platonism and its aftereffects: the idea of the man who somehow stands close to God in his essence, yet is also worthy of special divine help, particularly in the cognitive sphere. Since Philo, this idea has always had a special attraction for religious persons. The remarkably ascetic coloration of the ethical ideal [in Maimonides], where the well-being of the soul is predicted upon deadening the physical (in hardly compatible contrast to Maimonides's view elsewhere, particularly in the very moderate ethics of *Eight Chapters* [*Shemoneh Perakim*], written at the same time), indicates that this passage was affected by mystical trains of thought whose view was not quite identical with that of Maimonides. When the author continues that a life of the senses prevents the "divine force" from coming to light, adding in explanation, "I mean 'reason,' " it becomes evident that he revised a model which did not quite correspond to his views. When, in conjunction with this statement, lower man is called "a piece of matter, swimming in the Ocean of Hyle," the assumption may not be too daring that the hermetic concept of "hylic man" could have had an indirect influence on that mystic source.

Maimonides steadily clung to this doctrine of the goal of human life insofar as he saw metaphysical knowledge as the bond between man and God. This conviction, expressed in the *Mishneh Torah*, both in individual statements and especially in the prefatory "Book of the Knowledge of God," causes him in the *Guide* to assign to religion and its laws the exclusive purpose of reinforcing this spiritual bond and to see the purpose of Israel's existence in the preparation of humanity for the pure worship of God. The *Guide* does not essentially deviate from the Mishnah commentary when it enumerates four steps of perfection (material, physical, moral, and intellectual-religious), of which the two lower ones, though of lesser value, are still not considered obstacles to the higher steps, among which the intellectual is elevated above the morally active even more strongly than in the Mishnah commentary.

However, a certain change of view seems to occur in the famous discussion in the *Guide* about the purpose of the world. To be sure, a comparison of the passages is difficult because of the different ways they pose the question. The concern of the Mishnah commentary is to establish a philosophical goal of life and to warn us against a literal understanding of the statement that God owns nothing in the world except the four ells of the Halakhah; the philosophical work examines the justification of the question about the meaning of the world. The two treatises agree to the extent that in the early work man cannot be designated as the purpose-directed cause of the whole world, while the *Guide* also maintains that some things in nature have been created for the sake of others and that man, to a certain extent, can be considered the purpose-directed cause of the lower world. However, not only is the purely religious formulation that man's purpose is service of God rejected here, but his existence and essence, as well as those of nature as a whole, are derived from the ultimately inexplicable will of God. The [influence of the] immanent teleology of Aristotle's writings also is quite evident in the explanation of the lower organisms. It has long been assumed that this line of thought was influenced by ibn Rushd; acquaintance with his writings, in which the purely anthropocentric concept had been abandoned, may have caused Maimonides to reexamine the view of his younger years.

The genuinely Aristotelian traits, however, seem to stand out in the *Guide* in much purer form than in his early essay. This phenomenon, viewed as a whole, is not to be traced back to literary influences, but more likely is a return on Maimonides's part to his own natural predisposition. He had a much stronger kinship with the scholarly idea of the true Aristotle than with those Neoplatonists and Hermetics whose interpolations, interpretations, and elucidations dimmed the image of "the philosopher" for him. As his life's work demonstrates, he experiences the theory-connected eudaemony of the master and appreciates research not solely for its eschatological implications. "Had Torah not been my pleasure and had science not let me forget my sorrow, I should have perished in my woes"—these words from a well-known letter, in which the Torah may have been mentioned first out of consideration for the addressee, characterizes him completely. And his interest in science is not restricted to the metaphysical; it also encompasses medicine and teaching of the

Law (*fiqh*). The latter [is among his interests] not only insofar as it contributes to bliss in the beyond (else he would have restricted himself, as Jacob ben Asher later did, to laws applicable to his own time, and would not have taken infinite pains to include the laws regarding purity, sacrifices, and rules of the Temple), but also out of the truly Aristotelian need for organic contemplation, for logical illumination of sensual appearance, and for an understanding of the general formative laws of nature in the empirically given details. (For the Middle Ages, history, too, is nature.) His scientific interest, indeed, goes far beyond metaphysics and its empirical auxiliary sciences; the hope for the beyond which can be based only on metaphysical knowledge constitutes at best a weak side-motif to the restless urge for research, which finds its reward in itself.

In summary, one might characterize Maimonides's doctrine of purpose as a resumption of the young Aristotle's, provided we keep in mind that the concept of theory had in the meantime been transformed by Neoplatonic thought. In both cases, the theoretical ideal of life presents itself as the personal confession of the thinker and is in complete harmony with his life's work. But it transcends this personal dimension: first, in its contemplation of the organization of man (in Maimonides perhaps even more strongly than in Aristotle), because intellectual activity, not only because of its later development but also because of its significance for the nature of man, may appear as his task; and secondly, in its conception of a God who essentially (as in the later Aristotle) is intellectually satisfying as the ideal of theoretical perfection, yet is conceived simultaneously in the religious sense as calling us to *imitatio dei*. Thus the threefold strand is again woven together; from the ethical, the physical-teleological, and the metaphysical-religious point of view, thought—that is, the conception of ultimate metaphysical and ethical truths—appears to emerge as the definition of man's purpose.

Nevertheless, this doctrine was not considered adequate by later generations.

While Levi ben Gershom does not deal with questions of ethics in his philosophical work and refers in his introduction only briefly to the significance of metaphysics for theoretical and practical eudaemony, [Hasdai] Crescas shows a strong interest in our problem. Since, as he says, Maimonides had rejected the question of the ultimate purpose of the entire creation, he wants first to examine the purpose of the Torah, for he is certain his great predecessor will agree that a creation of divine reason must have such a purpose even more surely than the work of man. But while Maimonides does not hesitate to acknowledge that the Torah has several purposes, Crescas believes on logical grounds that the four individual goals—purification of insight, moral elevation, salvation in this world, and salvation in the next—must serve an all-embracing single goal, regardless of whether it is identical with one of the individual goals. For him, such a single goal is man's love of God. This goal is served by thought (which does not find its meaning in itself or in the creation of an "acquired *nous*"), as well as by prescribed action, especially by the observance of the laws of holiness which Christianity quite unjustly rejects as not binding. This love, which grows out of right thinking and doing, leads by necessity to union with God, whose essence is love and pleasure in benevolent action (not in thought), and consequently also to bliss in the hereafter. But this bliss is, of course, by no means a higher goal than love. The division of the ultimate purpose remains: seen from man's point of view, the purpose of the Torah is education to love; from the point of view of divine goodness, its purpose is guidance to bliss.

But after the ultimate purpose of the Torah has been recognized, the question may also be raised how it is related to the ultimate purpose of the world. Indeed, [he says,] it is quite obvious that the ultimate purpose of both is of the same kind, since both aim at the realization of the "good." When this "good" is a generic term embracing many "kinds" and "individualizations," it can be asserted further that the good for whose sake all of creation and the Torah exist is of the same "kind," since everything in creation exists because of eternal duration or for the furtherance of eternally enduring essences, just as the Torah also wants to help us toward eternity. In fact, the ultimate purpose of the lower world and that of the Torah are identical according to their "individuality," because the final end of the lower world is man, whose purpose, the realization of the love of God, coincides completely with that of the Torah.

This view [of Crescas's position] is supported by the hint that the world represents a unified whole, just as it does for Maimonides, and that a unified purpose therefore has to be presumed for it. Inasmuch as God is essentially good, this purpose can only be the realization of the good. Maimonides believed that the assumption of a purpose of the world contradicts tradition and reason—on the premise of the eternity and the createdness of the *hyle*—but the opposite is true. The thought of a God who creates without purpose is intolerable, as is the *physics* ["nature"] of Aristotle which "forms nothing without purpose." The sentence in the prayers, "If He is just—what does He give you?," quoted by Maimonides, merely states that doing right can never give us a claim to divine pardon and justification, but it does not say anything about the purposelessness of the world. Therefore Maimonides does not want to consider human piety as the ultimate purpose of creation, because God does not derive any advantage from it and because regardless of the advantage man receives from it, the question still remains why a being capable of piety has been created at all. The answer is that the ultimate purpose of the creation of man is the realization of goodness, which represents the essence of God. These arguments appear so compelling to Crescas that he comes to the conclusion that Maimonides did not deny the existence of a purpose of the world, but merely wanted to demonstrate how difficult it was to prove it.

Crescas could actually have quoted several statements of his great adversary in support of hiw own views. The *Guide* (III,13) undoubtedly emphasizes the rejection of a naive anthropocentric limitation, not the denial of the purpose of the world as such. In fact, since Maimonides expressly establishes a parallel between God's activity in law-giving and in nature and views the opinion that God could carry out "playful action" (action without serious intent) as blasphemy, he explains openly that there is "a definite goal for every event in nature, whether we recognize it or not," and he criticizes "ignorance regarding the first aim of the Creator, which consists in helping all potential existence to actual existence, because existence is undoubtedly better" and because "the heavenly beings" (certainly God) "always create only the good." Crescas could also have found proofs for the belief that man approaches God through love—certainly in the *Mishneh Torah*, though probably less in the *Guide*.

Nevertheless, there remains a profound difference between the two men's views. Crescas apparently sensed it. The God of Maimonides still is essentially Aristotle's Unmoved Mover. The activity Maimonides ascribed to Him is not rooted in His essence. What brings Him bliss is not activity but a theoretical attitude, though of course one cannot attribute human "thought" to Him. It remains completely inexplicable how a God so conceived could possibly derive any kind of satisfaction or gratification from His effect upon the world or from a particular conduct of man. Therefore, as certain as it is that Maimonides believes in a goal-directed meaning of divine activity, it is just as certain that a structural gap remains in his attempt to explain creation out of a purely theoretical ideal being. [This logical gap is] in contrast with his view that specific details [which we still lack] in our understanding of nature and of the [religious] commandments could possibly be clarified as our knowledge increases. But this gap becomes doubly sensitive for religious thought, which is interested specifically in ascertaining God's share in human life and which, in addition, can hardly feel satisfied with the ideal—analogous to the rationalistic conception of God—that man's purpose is pure thought.

It is at this point that Crescas had to begin to introduce his changes. He felt himself to be the advocate of Judaism vis-à-vis the Greek and his misguided disciples, but sensed at the same time the scientific need for a consistent and necessary deduction of all events from the ultimate cause strongly enough to assert it against the interest and tradition of religion in the question of divine and human freedom of will. Thus he replaces Aristotle's *nous,* which we can at best recognize but not love in any way, with the creative goodness of Plato's *Timaeus* and, consequently, the theoretical ideal of life with the doctrine that our final purpose is love. The new aspect of this change is, of course, that the demand of love is *not* something which is set before us. It occupies a very important place in nonphilosophical Judaism, particularly in connection with the daily affirmation of Deut. 6:5 and the interpretation of the Song of Songs. Among the philosophers, Bahya dedicates the last book of his *Duties of the Heart* to it; Judah Halevi sees the difference between the God of religion and the God of speculation in our ability to love the former, while the latter is reached only by knowledge; Gabirol likes to describe the supreme being as "Goodness"; and Maimonides presupposes an "intoxication of love" in the worshiper of God. And—this goes without saying—Islam also knows the love of God, and not only Sufism, whose statement, "Whoever knows God loves Him," has actually attained the status of a proverb. But only Crescas transforms the concepts of God and of communion with God in such a way that true love may be comprehended as *imitatio* of a scientifically knowable God as well as a means of eschatological connection. Only in this way is he able to preserve a rightful place for love within a scientific world view. What Bahya calls love is in truth a wholly numinous feeling which reveals aspects of the *tremendum* as strongly as those of the *fascinosum*. Especially in the tenth book, it is not the feeling of love that is essential for him, but concentration upon the beyond, from which alone light may fall upon this world and our duties in it. Maimonides, following Ghazali, assigns scientific meaning to the Sufic saying (which was meant gnostically) that "we can love God only with our reason. According to our knowledge our love is great or small. Therefore man must devote himself as strongly as possible to science, which lets him know his Creator." Hence, as the *Guide* shows even more distinctly, scientific cognition constitutes the genuine goal of our striving. For Gabirol, cognition leads to union with God. Judah Halevi, on the other hand, declines to use science in order to perceive the God of love in nature after revelation has taught us to perceive His goodness.

In contrast [to these thinkers], Crescas discovers in the God of the Platonic *Timaeus* (conceived as imageless), who creates the world out of envy-free goodness, an *Elohim* with the features of YHWH (to use Judah Halevi's concepts), a scientifically knowable God who yet is sufficient for the religious yearner. He does not arrive at a union with Him (as demanded by the Middle Ages) as the rationalist does, based upon the statement that like fuses with like (*nous* with *nous*), nor, as the Sufi does, through mystical union, but through the scientific-religious belief of Empedocles in the unifying and creative power of love.

Thus he arrives at a completely unique solution of our much-discussed problem. Neither Plato nor Neoplatonic thought uninfluenced by the Peripatos ever expressed themselves with regard to our question. On the other hand, Crescas, without rendering a clear account of this to himself, goes back to Plato and thereby gains a twofold advantage. First, the purely intellectualistic central concept of metaphysics is replaced by a concept that has a stronger voluntaristic coloration and thus gives his world view greater completeness. Secondly, from this vantage point the most important basic concepts of religion lend themselves to scientific formulation: by necessity, God appears as personality, since cognition as such can also be directed toward the nonpersonal, and the personal character of the God of the Aristotelians fades away much more completely than they themselves realized. On the other hand, love, despite Spinoza, is by necessity directed toward the individual (assuming that I do not do violence to the term and especially to the emotion): God appears as supremely kind personality and thus becomes a model for man. His relationship to the world, filling in the above-mentioned gap, becomes clearly recognizable and thereby fruitful as the foundation of religious thankfulness. Man approaches Him not, as with Maimonides, from his chamber of study, but through immediate communion fortified by pious action. The metaphysical ersatz religion which dominated Maimonides's system, though not his personal piety, is replaced by true religiousness with its closeness to life and fullness of life. Though it may sound paradoxical, his reaching back to Platonism makes it possible for Crescas to assign much greater significance to historic religion for the fulfillment of our purpose. (Most recent studies of Plato esteem its religious motives much more highly than was previously the case.)

The idea of a creating God recommended itself to the Jew who appreciated labor, for the same reason for which it was repulsive to the Greek and the Roman; Crescas also knew how to justify ritual law out of the meaning of life. To be sure, his predecessors had already sought to do this. In fact, the peculiarity of the medieval solutions lies in the attempt to take historic religion into account in formulating the doctrine of purpose. Like his predecessors, Crescas cannot comprehend religion phenomenologically and in the fullness of its forms, but, corresponding to the medieval mode of thought, must posit a unified meaning of these forms (that is, of the doctrines and the laws). But unlike Baḥya, he does not see this meaning one-sidedly in education for the beyond nor, as Maimonides did, in the communication of purely metaphysical knowledge (to mention merely those attempts at a solution which are most distant from each other), but in tying the bond of love between man and God. In this solution, the teleological point of view—the second point we mentioned in our introductory statement—recedes into the background, inasmuch as there is no attempt to derive the yearning for love from the organization of man. But the yearning for union with God in this world and in the beyond is perceived as man's most powerful striving. Its realization constitutes our task. God Himself, however, is not only the Kind One who wants to lead human beings to the supreme good; he also is the Giver of the Torah whose purpose is conceived to be the education of man for the love of God and the ever-renewed reinforcement of the bond of love.

Thus historic religion has an entirely different meaning for Crescas than it has for Baḥya, whose doctrine of purpose hardly gives any consideration to the Torah, or for Maimonides, for whom this doctrine can only be of very indirect help. This twofold rootedness of Crescas's God concept—in Platonism and in the Torah—makes his impact upon the Renaissance and Judaism understandable. That a Jewish philosophy of the Renaissance did not come into being, and that the Jewish spiritual kin of Platonism expressed their view of life in the semiphilosophy of the Kabbalah, may have to be ascribed primarily to the exceedingly sad act of providence which caused the pen to slip so early from the hand of this eminent thinker.

Joseph Albo's solution is far less independent. In the second chapter of the third section [of his *Basic Principles* (*Sefer ha-Ikkarim*)], he develops the notion that the final goal of man must lie in the spiritual sphere. Every natural being has a distinctive value which distinguishes it from other beings. This value, which is found in every species, is simultaneously the purpose-directed cause of its existence in the form which characterizes its particular species. Because man belongs to the natural beings—and since he is the worthiest of these beings, creation reaches its completion through him—there must also be for him a distinctive value related to the form that determines his species. This value cannot lie in man's vegetative or perceptive power, since this would mean that the perfection of the donkey and the pig would be equal to that of man. His perfection must rather lie in those qualities by which he surpasses the animals. Since we now see that he possesses the power and aptitude, far beyond the potential of the animals, to receive intelligible truth, to create the sciences, and to lead them from their potentiality to their actuality, the perfection of man must depend on this intellectual power. Because this power is divided into a theoretical and a practical faculty, the perfection of man seems to rest more upon the theoretical than the practical part, for the latter is, as we know, related to his natural constitution. Besides, all thought which did not serve a practical purpose would otherwise be meaningless. But this would contradict our constitution and the general view, since everyone agrees that labors of the mind are more meritorious than manual labor. Moreover, our enjoyment is the greater the more intellectualized its foundations. It is, therefore, greater in our visual and auditory impressions than in those of our lower senses. The reason for this, which Albo demonstrates in an exegetical exposition, is that "through the use of these two senses the potential in man achieves actuality." Whereas the chair or the animal attains its entelechy at the moment of its origin, perfection is given to man only as a disposition. In this respect, "his preeminence over the beast is as nothing"; that is, it is not yet an actual one, and "the day of his death," on which he reaches his relatively highest perfection, is to be preferred "to the day of his birth."

Consequently, one would have to expect that Albo, together with the [Greek] philosophers, sees our purpose in the development of our intellect. But against this view and the doctrine of immortality on which it is based, he raises the objection that only a very few individuals are able to reach this goal and that it might perhaps not be reached at all in some generations, so that the creation of a large portion of mankind would be utterly without purpose or meaning. Besides, the auxiliary science of mathematics does not possess the significance which this doctrine of purpose must ascribe to it. Above all, since our thinking, especially in the field of metaphysics (as shown by the divergent opinions of the philosophers), is certainly not free from errors, this doctrine cannot assure anyone of his immortality. One must rather begin with the assumption that every being needs to perform certain actions in order to reach its perfection. Only from this point of view does the course of the stars become understandable. What kind of actions, however, serve our perfection and the achievement of our goal is hard to say; they cannot even be recognized with full certainty from the joy which the soul, originating in God, experiences in certain actions, because temperaments differ too much. Therefore God has communicated to us through His prophets what is pleasing to Him "in order to guide man toward the ultimate human goal." This end is served especially by the Torah, not only through its teachings and those commandments which we fulfill only because they were given to us by the divine will, but also through its judicial statutes which, in contrast to civil laws with which they sometimes appear to be identical, are being practiced in obedience to the divine law-giver.

Some phrases in the fourth book are not completely in accord with these expositions, as, for example, when we read in connection with the doctrine of retribution that "the soul is a spiritual essence with the faculty of cognition in order to serve God but not" (as the Aristotelians have taught) "with the faculty of cognition as such" (since, as was also mentioned before, at most one among thousands achieves this cognition). "Consequently, when man derives any cognition from the worship of God by gaining an insight or knowledge pertaining to God, be it great or small, he reaches through this—I mean through this cognition from the worship of God—a higher rung among the gradations of the beyond." To be sure, these discussions agree with those of the third book, to which they point expressly, that the perfection of man is being placed into the

actualization of his potentiality and that a combination of the philosophical ideal of thought as our purpose with the traditional ideal of religion is
being attempted. But aside from the fact that the third book does not
discuss the potentiality of man with the same acuity as is done in the
fourth book, the relationship of the scientific-intellectualistic element of
the doctrine of purpose to the religio-cultic one obviously is conceived
differently. According to the third book, the worship of God serves our
intellectual perfectability. Admittedly we do not understand how this is
possible, but this is equally unknowable in regard to the stars and the
influence which their movement is supposed to exert upon themselves
and the spirits of the spheres. The fourth book reverses the position:
thought stands in the service of obedience, which seems to guarantee bliss
at least as much as thought itself does.

Thus Albo's theory reminds us of that of Crescas, insofar as he also
seeks to establish the Torah as *conditio sine qua non* for the achievement
of the goal of life. The context in which the problem is raised is the same
for both, too. But in the treatment of the issue, Albo's approach turns
out to be not a continuation of Crescas's approach but a contrast to it: in
the "light" of God an independent thinker bridges the gap between science and religion—and not merely of historical religion which is his immediate concern—by positing love as the supreme goal acceptable to
both; and drawing skillfully on the most significant creations of the scientific as well as the religious *Eros,* he forms an image of the world and of
faith in accordance with this goal concept. The merit of the *Basic Principles* is that they uphold the right of science and illumine the difference
between Judaism and Christianity in a particular way. However, their
author lacks the scientific power to construct a coherent philosophical
system, notwithstanding his sagacity and homiletic gifts.

III

Even though our assemblage of proof texts is certainly in need of
completion, . . . it may well permit even now a survey of the history of
our problem. . . . While biblical and apocryphal literature shows hardly a
trace of the doctrine of purpose in our sense, and the literature of the
Mishnah and early Christianity was influenced only by the demands of
self-knowledge and its attainment, the Jewish thinkers of the Middle
Ages show a strong interest in a scientific doctrine of purpose. All
answers are based on the premise that the purpose for which God has
created man (or sent him down to earth) corresponds to his essence in a
twofold way: the yearning for happiness which lies within him and is
conceived in purely eschatological terms determines the direction of his

striving; the capacity to think and act which God has bestowed upon him determines the way to this goal. Within this general view, four main types can be distinguished. For the hermetic type, represented by Baḥya, the purpose of our having been sent to earth is to elevate us into beings of a favored kind. Perception of our secret, obedience, and constancy in enduring purifying tribulations lead to this goal. In the sense of the syncretistic Neoplatonism of a Porphyry, Gabirol (like Israel and ibn Ẓaddik) sees our purpose in the knowledge of God, which we attain with the help of self-knowledge as well as cathartic virtues; both bind us to God. Aristotelianism, professed by Ibn Daud and especially by Maimonides, bases the priority of metaphysics less upon its eschatological value than upon its superiority over the other sciences, which are subservient to it. Right action shows its value not by any immediately redeeming effect, but by its correspondence to reason and by protecting our devotion to science from disturbances. The Platonizing solution of Crescas sees the meaning of existence in the unfolding of love to which performance of the divine commandments educates us; Albo seeks to combine this latter thought with that of Aristotle.

Thus a continuous line of development seems to lead from the young Aristotle to the last thinkers of the Jewish Middle Ages, and the specific relationship of individual Jewish thinkers to particular Greek systems becomes evident. The significance which a Greek method of raising questions and their Greek answers had for the Jewish Middle Ages proves strikingly that it is utterly impossible to follow David Neumark in regarding philosophical thought in Judaism primarily as a continuation of an internal Jewish development. But it would certainly be no less one-sided to underestimate the significance of Judaism for the ultimate ethical goal-setting of the medieval thinkers. Here we are thinking not so much of the limitations imposed upon the philospher by the letter of an authoritative literature (which, as we know, was considerably loosened by the medieval interpretation of Scripture), but of the effect of religion on his entire existential position, in the sense in which even in Kant's system the Puritan heritage asserts itself. Even Philo, who of all of Jewish literature knows only the Torah and does not let its actual meaning affect him, is entirely influenced by Judaism in his religious and—more strongly than has previously been recognized—in his ethical attitude. This is true to an even higher degree of men who were influenced both by the entire biblical-rabbinic literature and by the greatly reinforced disciplines of religious life. The strength and direction of this Jewish influence are particularly evident in a comparison of Jewish and Islamic ethics which are subjected to the same hellenic influence. True, it was possible to translate many an Islamic study into Hebrew without many changes and to replace without great difficulty quotations from the Koran with passages from the Bible or Midrash. But agreement has its limits. If one compares not only certain Jewish writers (for instance Saadiah or Baḥya) with their Arab models, but the entire literature of the Jewish Middle Ages with its Islamic counterpart, it becomes clear how consciously Judaism has eliminated the ascetic and ecstatic traits of the Muslims. While it may, therefore, be possible to write a history of epistemology in Judaism without mentioning any other than the hellenic roots of Jewish thought, the discussion of a problem of *ethics* imperatively requires consideration of the Jewish components, because these ethics, as Maimonides's letters and Gabirol's poetry show, were not intellectually contrived but [existentially] experienced—they were related to that depth [of feeling] which is affected by religion.

Consequently, the claim made by all Jewish philosophers of religion that they offer a Jewish ethics must in no way be viewed as a deception. Their ethical teachings—hence also their formulations of the doctrine of human purpose—must be understood out of the interaction of Greek and Jewish culture. [Jewish ethics] cannot be understood adequately if one merely stresses the transforming effect which in one or the other was caused by Jewish feeling (for example, in Baḥya or Gabirol). The problem must be seen as a whole: how was such a synthesis of the fundamentally quite diverse life goals of the Jews and Greeks possible in the Middle Ages? What historic change brought these cultures so close to each other that they could enter into a productive association? Above all, since a development in the sense of the natural sciences did not take place here, and the later forms did not replace the earlier ones but merely took their place beside them, how was it systematically and psychologically possible for the Greek and Jewish formulations of goals to coexist and interact within the same thinkers?

These questions obviously lend themselves to a solution only when we keep in mind the total effect of Greek culture upon the Jewish Middle Ages. Thus we shall have to go beyond the discussion of the doctrine of purpose in some points. This is, of course, not the place to broach the total problem. Moreover, the "reception" of hellenic culture does not represent as unified a process as is often assumed. Hence the preferential treatment of individual lines of hellenic influence is quite justified.

Greek ethics influenced Judaism under different conditions than obtained in the case of the other religions. The lack of belief in a mediator and of any inclination to propagandize by force made Judaism more open-minded and receptive to kindred elements in pagan ethics than was possible in Christianity. When Baḥya cited pious non-Jews on almost every page in his popular work, he could point to the fact that the Bible and Talmud explicitly demand the imitation of good non-Jewish models. The influence of hellenic science upon Judaism—beginning relatively late—had both a beneficial and an impeding effect: there was no need to make room for the mediating activity of the *logos* which had become flesh, but hellenization also cannot be linked to the initial stages of religion and thus invoke the example of renowned Church Fathers. Completely new paths have to be broken. This process succeeds only because of a change on both sides, [as the result] of a movement of the two cultures toward each other, which can be indicated here as far as our theme demands it.

[We can see that] the spiritualization of the ideals of life in Greece . . . was paralleled by a kindred process in Israel, provided we focus our attention upon the people, and not upon eminent intellects. The change finds expression in the words of the prophet: "Let not the wise man glory in his wisdom, neither let the mighty man glory in his might, let not the rich man glory in his riches" (Jer. 9:22). As a result, a spiritualization of the concepts held by the people takes place: a Hellene or a Jew in the fullest sense is created by a process of refinement which may be learned from the sages of each tribe. But while spiritualization leads Anaxagoras to the scientific ideal, the sole values acknowledged by Jeremiah are those of morality and piety. These values have just as little to do with scientific investigation as the ideal of the young Aristotle has to do with action and with religion (though he certainly was a religious person).

The confluence of these ideals in the doctrine of purpose in the Jewish Middle Ages, which has a scientific and a religious coloration but also shows a strong eschatological tint, could only occur as the result of a process in which Greek science adopted religious elements, Jewish piety assumed scientific form, and eschatology gained a strong influence on both.

The first of these processes has often been described. Norden in particular showed in his *Unknown God* [*Agnostos Theos*] how the *ennoia theou,* the [intellectual] comprehension of God, turned into *gnosis,* which had originally been alien to hellenic thought. Similarly, the strong emphasis which the Stoa placed on the practical as well as the theoretical goals of life tended to narrow the gap between the Greek and Jewish views even further—the more, for instance, Posidonius tended toward a religious validation of moral action.

But the biblical *da'at Adonai,* cognition as recognition of God, could not maintain its plain meaning either. The religious ideal of the postbiblical period demands both the study of the Scriptures and pious deeds, but certainly not any methodologically scientific approach, despite the replacement of graphic biblical images by precisely formulated concepts, and despite the derivation of individual decisions from strictly regulated proof texts and deduction from legal principle. Nevertheless, there evidently is now a demand for a considerable measure of intellectual work in addition to the demand for piety and morality. Just as in

Hellas, the bliss of study is also experienced here in different modes of thought, and it is sanctioned by religion even though the sanction might refer more to the subject than to the method. Alongside the hellenic discussion regarding the value of theoretical and practical eudaemony, there is the talmudic question whether study or action merits preference. Thus it happened that the very primitive rationalism of the ninth-century thinkers was not considered revolutionary in its method, and just as "study" had been central originally, so methodical study . . . became an essential part of the religious task of life. Just as the Midrash cannot imagine the patriarchs without "academies," so all religious philosophers of the Middle Ages, with the single, characteristic exception of Judah Halevi, consider the *da'at Adonai* demanded by the Bible as "knowledge of God" in a strict scientific sense. Accordingly, when Maimonides, referring to occasional praise of metaphysics in the Talmud, merges religious and scientific devotion in his ideal image of the "metaphysician in the prayer shawl," the convergence has been completed. In Greece the ideal of the *episteme* ["scientific knowledge"] assumes a gnostic coloration, while in Judaism an originally religious setting of goals gains scientific meaning.

But in both cultures a turn toward eschatology was added to this strange convergence. As old as the belief in an afterlife was in both, it was still a long time until the concept of life on earth as an antechamber to the beyond, or even as a prison from which we step into the freedom of the other world, began to influence the leading intellects. But the consolidation of eschatological belief in late antiquity not only brought East and West more closely together—since the ultimate goal of striving, the attainment of eternal bliss, was now the same for both—but it also reached decisive significance for our specific problem, the doctrine of purpose.

It is no accident that a doctrine of purpose is not found in Judaism where, as in Judah Halevi, the eschatological meaning of our earthly conduct retreats behind the task to develop in this world a kind of religious "superhumanness" [*Übermenschentum*] based on certain geographic-physiological premises, or where, as in Saadiah, our destiny in the beyond does not appear as necessary consequence and continuation of life in this world, depending rather on a "miracle," the free verdict of the divine judge. These views can quite naturally lead to a doctrine of obligation, as they do in the Bible, but not to a doctrine of purpose in our strict sense, because it is impossible to understand why our natural constitution should direct us more to obedience than to disobedience. All Jewish medieval doctrines of purpose are, therefore, colored eschatologically and based on the premise that man, by dint of his God-given powers and with God's help, is able to gain not only a certain claim upon future life before God's judgment seat but future life itself. Only on this premise is it possible to enter the teleological path to the doctrine of purpose and to define our purpose as the unfolding of that supreme faculty which is granted to us and which is served by all our other faculties, the faculty of gaining a future life.

The knowledge that the gnostic-eschatological turn of Greek thought became hardly less significant for Judaism than for Christianity inevitably leads to another question: which of the Greek systems had the greatest influence upon the view of life of the Jewish Middle Ages? So far this question has been raised only as part of a more general inquiry into the reception of Greek philosophy by Judaism. Since the influence of the Aristotelian didactic writings upon logic and basic concepts of the philosophy of nature is obvious, as is the influence of the *Enneads* upon the theory of the formation of the world (and not merely upon the theory of the Neoplatonists), [scholars] simply wanted to consider the mature Aristotle and Plotinus as the instructors of medieval Judaism. [They] sensed, of course, the difficulties which resulted from these thinkers' attitudes toward religion. Aristotle dissociated himself more and more from the religious attitude of his early years; Plotinus preferred not to go to the gods, but rather have them come to him—and dealt with them partly in connection with the extremely complex problem of Gabirol and partly by presenting the view of life in Aristotle's early writings, which had an eschatological coloration, but were unknown to the Middle Ages. Compared with this view, it is truly liberating to observe how much Jewish medieval thought was influenced by a kind of questioning for which there can be room neither in the *Enneads* (in which not every chapter stems from Plotinus) nor in Aristotle's didactic writings, and how small the influence was which the characteristic qualities of both thinkers—the self-satisfaction of the scientific sense of research in Aristotle and the ecstasy of Plotinus—had upon the Jewish Middle Ages. The stream of Greek thought which nourished and fructified the Jewish Middle Ages is, of course, also fed by tributaries of Aristotelian and Plotinic origin as far as the formulation of practical goals is concerned. But the effect of the tributaries has been at least as strong as that of the wellsprings. Thus the treatment of our question by the Stoa through its adoption of the practical demand, its reinterpretation of teleology, and its synthesis of its inquiries into the purpose and essence of man has had an especially great influence upon the Jewish Middle Ages, difficult though it was to ascertain the immediate effects of this school of thought. Similarly, the turn Posidonius took toward eschatology appears anew in its historic significance, and it is also possible to identify the share of the religious aspects of Platonism and the popular hope for a future life in its hermetic setting. However, the extraordinary esteem which Aristotle enjoyed among the Jews of the Middle Ages rests only to a small extent on the continuing influence of his didactic writings, but to a large degree on a twofold misconception for which the syncretism of late antiquity is to blame: he was seen, as has long been recognized with regard to his doctrine of the soul (it is similarly true of his teleology) through the spectacles of his "interpreters"; people believed they discovered the deep, esoteric meaning of his view of life in writings which in truth grew out of the soil of completely different schools.

Insight into the historic process of the convergence of Hellenism and Judaism—which was, of course, strengthened by such reinterpretations—facilitates the solution of the question of the inner relationship between the elements of Greek and Jewish culture in the systems of Jewish medieval philosophers and of the mutual effect of Greek and original Jewish thought.

In the main, this mutual effect has been eclectic, exactly as in Philo. The Jew rejects Atomism as well as Scepticism (particularly in its metaphysical and ethical aspects) and, in contrast to Islam and Christianity, the radical ascetic demands of Hellenism. Above all, he senses the religious and ethical forces which are at work in Greek thought as far as they correspond to his own piety. In Aristotle's and the Stoa's proofs for the existence of God he finds supports for his own beliefs. Plato's admonition to let thought rule over the lower faculties of the soul and the Aristotelian teaching of the primacy of the intellect become foundations of his ethics. The devaluation of this world into an illusory world in Neoplatonism validates the otherwoldly yearning of religion and the veneration of the supranatural. To be sure, this picture of Greek culture is one-sided, but it has been the one painted by all observers who approached Hellas not as objective scholars but as disciples (up to and including Walter Otto), and it undoubtedly made possible the acceptance of the most significant of those Greek thinkers known to the oriental Middle Ages.

On the other hand, Greek science motivates the philosophically trained Jew to emphasize the universal human foundations and obligations of religion. There was no one-sidedness in this emphasis. [Such Jews] knew how to maintain the belief in revelation and to prove it with the help of hellenistic lines of thought; even a rationalist like Maimonides certainly did not neglect the study of the ritual laws. However, it was a wholesome reaction against one-sidedness in the opposite direction—against the danger, which threatens every (especially every persecuted) religion, of seeking God only in the revelation, history, and ethical teachings of its own community. Bahya's *Duties of the Heart* and Gabirol's *Royal Crown* truly represent the ethical conviction of the prophets and the natural piety of the Psalms in their own time's forms of thought.

   This selectivity on both sides of course could not prevent conflicts between the two worlds at some points. That original contrast between the two forms of spiritualization in Jeremiah and Anaxagoras—leading, in the one case, to an appreciation of plain and humble piety, and in the other to the bold flight of methodical investigation—still had its aftereffects in the Middle Ages; indeed, it had to have them precisely because the oldest documents enjoyed the highest esteem and could not completely lose their original meaning, notwithstanding every possible kind of interpretation. Thus conflict arises, not only between individual doctrines of Greek and Jewish origin, but, above all, about the ways in which to approach God. This conflict makes itself felt especially in the doctrine of purpose: the rationalists (Saadiah and especially Maimonides) see in the piety of the masses, which is the result of revelation, a substitute philosophy for the eternally immature; Judah Halevi considers philosophy valid as a surrogate religion for the religiously untalented, just as the rules of poetry are meant for those not gifted "in the art of verse-making"; and Crescas believes he finds in religious *Eros* a supreme goal concept which stems from science but fully satisfies religious feeling.

   A further differentiation occurs in connection with the question about the relationship between action in this world and destiny in the beyond. Crescas in particular represented with extraordinary vigor the belief, based on Hellenism, in a causally necessary connection—that is, in our ability to gain afterlife; Saadiah follows a religious conception according to which God's justice and forbearance guide His judgment over us. The contrast between the two worlds which constitute the framework of perception for these thinkers shows its effect even in Maimonides's question whether doing good out of inclination or out of self-mastery deserves preference, in the contrast between his rejection of the ethics of the "golden mean" in favor of modesty, and in the strong sense of ego which speaks out of his letters (as it does out of Gabirol's poetry).

   It can easily be seen that in all these points much more is at stake than differences of dogmatics. Hellenism has become a threat to the basic attitude of Jewish piety, if not of every religion. It is understandable that it was unable to exert a deep and lasting influence upon Judaism in the questions we touched upon.

   Strangely enough, however, we find that . . . there are other cases in which Greek concepts were simultaneously reinterpreted and reinforced as a result of their adoption by Judaism. This applies especially to the three roots of the doctrine of purpose. The belief in an ethical meaning of life, the teleological conclusion, the attempt to comprehend the world out of the essence of God—all of these have meant for the Jew, by reason of his much more personalized concept of God, something else (indeed much more) than they did for the Hellene. For the latter, the task of understanding the world out of God has always had a certain boldness; for the Jew, the striving for such understanding belonged to the dominant and self-evident ideas of his religious thinking. The belief in a task of life had a much more definite meaning for him who, according to the beginning of a very unphilosophical work [*Shulḥan Arukh*], "shall rouse himself every day like a lion for the service of his Creator." The teleological conclusion, too, pointing to the traces of divine activity in nature, had particular persuasive force for the worshiper of a personal God whose grandeur is proclaimed by the heavens, but also witnessed in the history of mankind and especially in the history of one's own people. Thus, when taken over by Judaism, the roots of the belief in purpose become considerably more concrete and meaningful, and the formulations, even where they are taken over literally, begin to sound fuller and more definitive. In fact, the system becomes more integrated since all its parts spring from the same metaphysical premise. At the same time, the certitude of the basic doctrines is heightened because they seem to receive confirmation by revealed teachings. On the other hand, the fundamental convictions of the Jew—belief in a world-ordering God and in a goal of life desired by Him—gain scientific substantiation and reinforcement through reference to observation and lines of thought that were independent from revelation. Indeed, while revealed in ancient forms of language and thought, they attain for the Middle Ages (as far as it was accustomed to systematic thought) not only the force of persuasion but also full relevance for life only through their adaptation to the mode of speech and the world view of the later period.

Thus Greek plants took root in the soil of Jewish thought, and Jewish ones in Greek thought, in such a way that the juices of one culture rose in the branches of the other and affected the color and taste of the fruit. This curious symphesis—not merely synthesis—of both cultures led to the result that the problem of purpose became perhaps even more popular in Jewish than in Greek thought and that the answers to the problem were felt to be entirely Jewish—and with a certain justification could so be felt.

This happened, for instance, in conjunction with the theory regarding the numerical value of the letters of the alphabet which, as young as it was on Jewish soil, was disseminated to such an extent that the most recent compiler heads the chapter which he devotes to it with the (shall we say Jewish?) word *gematria* [Dornseiff, *Das Alphabet,* 2d ed., pp. 91ff.]. The same happened to the etymological method with which the Stoa influenced Philo and Romanticism influenced (Isaac Bernays and) S. R. Hirsch, for whom it has infinitely greater significance in its application to the sacred tongue of the Bible than it has for Chateaubriand and Z. Werner. It was, of course, historically unjustified that he saw it as the foundation of his entire conception of the Jewish doctrine of faith and felt it to be a Jewish, even the uniquely Jewish, method of research, because etymology, as the belief that it is possible to arrive at the *etymon,* at general truth, through discovery of original meaning, did not originate in Jewish soil. Nevertheless, his view was objectively well founded because the new method, in the manner in which his deeply religious nature employed it, made the thought content and the linguistic garb of Jewish literature doubly valuable to him.

In the same way we must understand and appreciate that the thoughts of the Greek philosophers which affected the Jewish Middle Ages were considered alien only to a minimal extent, even by thinkers who, like Crescas and Judah Halevi, confronted the Greek with suspicion. This complete "naturalization" of numerous philosophical doctrines was substantially furthered by the fact that oriental translators successfully rendered all technical scientific terms [with one exception: *hyle;* Hebrew *hiyuli*] in their own languages. It therefore became possible not only to erase the most obvious outer traces of alien origin, but also to permeate the adopted concepts with the spirit of one's own language and mode of thought. This is why works that ultimately date back to Greek thought, yet were written out of the Jewish soul, found readers far beyond the circle of friends of science. Even today thousands of plain people are edified by Bahya's *Duties of the Heart.* For the same reason, such Greek wisdom as could be adopted by Jews could also be transplanted into poetry, so that Aristotle's saying, "the first in thought is the last in realization," could find its place in the lyrics of the Sabbath, and Gabirol's *Royal Crown* is still read today in numerous houses of God during the holiest night of the year. The genuinely alien word has no place in true poetry, nor does the purely alien thought. [True poetry] can only master that which has been internalized, regardless on which historical soil it grew.

Thus an understanding of its historical convergence with Greek culture and of its inner relationship to it seem to provide us with a psychological understanding of the Jewish intellectual effort in the Middle Ages. The belief that there is a far-reaching affinity between Greek and Jewish thought on which it is based turns out to be a fiction of which the philosophers are unaware, but whose correctness they have proven through demonstration of its fruitfulness. It is precisely the history of the problem of purpose which shows how they were able to transform alien thought in such a way that they considered it their own, and how their own could continue to have its effect upon their intellectual efforts and feelings. If the scholar considers it his task to establish distinctions between cultures, the living person will always endeavor to infuse the power of selected spirits of all peoples and times into his own veins. And the living person is right. . . .

Notes

"The Purpose of Human Existence as Seen by Greek-Roman Antiquity and the Jewish Middle Ages," translated by Karl Richter, first appeared as "Die Lehre von der Zweckbestimmung des Menschen im griechisch-römischen Altertum und im jüdischen Mittelalter," *Bericht des jüdisch-theologischen Seminars Fraenckelscher Stiftung für das Jahr 1925* (Breslau, 1926), pp. 1–104. For notes and bibliographical references, see the German original or the English translation on deposit in manuscript form at the Leo Baeck Institute, New York City.

The German title of this study can be taken to refer to doctrines defining man's purpose as well as to the way this purpose can be determined. Since the study deals primarily with the first aspect, the English title was rendered accordingly.

7
THE CONCEPT OF KAVVANAH
IN THE EARLY KABBALAH

Gershom G. Scholem

I

t is well known that Jewish kabbalistic literature is in many respects markedly different from the mystical writings of the non-Jewish world. In describing their inner spiritual worlds, the Kabbalists were to a large extent guided by a pronounced theosophical interest as well as by an interest in the process in which God manifests Himself— conceived as a process which, as it were, was taking place within God Himself. To these interests must be added a strong aversion to a detailed treatment of strictly mystical matters, events, and experiences, though not because the Kabbalists were unfamiliar with the religious experiences of mystics the world over. The living experience of God in the depth of one's soul, or in whatever other way one may describe the goal of mystical longing, is a primal human experience that existed in rabbinic Judaism as a primary human phenomenon, just as it did elsewhere. The only difference, aside from the specific Jewish or non-Jewish forms of expression of such experiences, is the will to their expression and literary communication. Whether it is because the contrast between mystical experience and a concept of God that emphasized the aspect of Creator and Law-giver was felt especially keenly in Jewish life, or for other motives, it is certain that kabbalistic literature exhibits a marked reserve and reticence precisely where other mystics stammer most assiduously—in the communication of autobiographical details and in attempts at a conceptual definition of religious processes, even when expressed (as indeed they must necessarily be) in paradoxes.

These [kabbalistic] documents, often found in the most remote places, are all the more valuable for the student of Jewish mysticism because they have abandoned this reticence somewhat or even completely, thus enabling us to catch a glimpse of an inner world that tended to remain hidden in mystery. Though such documents are by no means rare, they exist almost entirely in manuscript, and in any case the Kabbalists would hardly ever have permitted them to appear in print. Unfortunately, we have good reason for assuming that much has been lost: the diary of Issac of Acre, most of the prophetical writings of Abraham Abulafia, the revelations of Joseph Taitazak in Salonika, and others [although some manuscripts, originally considered lost, have turned up since this article was first published]. In a series of studies over a number of years I have endeavored to make such documents available, for they are indispensable in evaluating the mystical character of the Kabbalah. In the following study I hope to be able to present some particularly valuable evidence of this nature.

In "Kawwana, the Struggle of Inwardness in Judaism," H. G. Enelow undertook to interpret the concept of kavvanah in Jewish literature.[1] He also attempted to demonstrate how the general concept, seen in later Judaism as "sustained devotion throughout prayer," acquired mystical coloration and significance in the Kabbalah.[2] It is understandable that the highly revealing evidence regarding the nature of kavvanah as a mystical absorption in prayer should have been unknown and inaccessible to Enelow at that time. Even the Zohar contributes little to the definition of the concept, which the Kabbalists of the thirteenth century associated with *kavvanah*, "intention." What is specifically new in the kavvanah of the Kabbalists is not clearly stated nor as sharply defined here as is the case in other early sources.

The doctrine of special meditations and of a special absorption in prayer, the path traversed by mystics when absorbed in the Word, has been an essential part of kabbalistic tradition since it first appeared in Provence around 1200. There is undoubtedly a direct historical and substantive connection between this kabbalistic conception of kavvanah and the "Secrets of Prayer" that had come down to the twelfth-century German Hasidim from earlier sources. While an extensive literature of commentaries to the prayers provides a good deal of information about the nature of these mystical, mostly numerological "secrets," these writings do not make clear whether such mystical numerology found a place in the prayers themselves (perhaps in certain meditations), nor do they clarify the precise meaning which such [numerological] reflections might disclose about the connection of the prayers with certain names of God and other things (formulas, biblical verses with the same numerological values). However, as far as I can see, the circle [in Germany] did not succeed in formulating a definite concept of kavvanah. The only reference to kavvanah as a religious concept in the mysticism of German Hasidism is in a work of Eleazar of Worms (ca. 1200),[3] who states that kavvanah in the benedictions is directed to what he calls the "holiness" of God (in contradiction to His "greatness"), which is the "glory" of God devoid of all shape or form.[4] It is this formless holiness of God in which prayer loses itself, and we understand what is meant when we read immediately thereafter that this "holiness" is indeed no form, but a voice (conceived in the sense of Deut. 4:12: "Ye heard the sounds of words but perceived no shape—nothing but a voice"). Holiness—which is קול דיבור, divine voice and divine word—is here the object of reflection and absorption in kavvanah.[5] In fact, it already appears to denote a profoundly mystical concept of kavvanah which is closely related to that of the Kabbalists. In prayer the word of man, in its purest form, interlocks itself with the Word of God, or, to use the more exact terminology of the literal meaning of kavvanah itself, it is "aligned" with the Word of God. In the words of prayer, the finite human word strives to attach itself to the infinite divine Word. Here, then, kavvanah already denotes a definite path, not simply the intensity and concentration of prayer in general. However, no doubt there were direct relations between the circle of Eleazar of Worms and the Provençal Kabbalists; it has become increasingly clear that it is impossible to view these circles as completely separate from one another, as has long been the custom in the literature on the subject.

II

The first significant Kabbalist to emerge somewhat clearly as a mystic from the fragments of his writings that have come down to us . . . is Isaac the Blind, the son of Abraham ben David in Posquieres, an exact contemporary of Eleazar of Worms.[6] He is also the first from whom we have not only reliable traditions concerning details of kavvanot in certain prayers, but also a statement about the meaning of the performance of kavvanah which alone makes those special instructions comprehensible.[7] This first significant statement about kavvanah as meditation possessing a specific character is found in Isaac's doubtlessly authentic commentary to the still unpublished Sefer Yezira,[7a] which is one of the most important but also one of the most difficult documents of the early Kabbalah.[8] Isaac comments on the meaning of prayer in connection with the words of the text (chap. 1:8): "Lock your heart that it may not brood." I shall endeavor to translate the very difficult passage accurately by rendering the term *midda,* used by Isaac, in accordance with the usage in the *Sefer Bahir—* where it has the various meanings of "quality," "hypostasis," "manifestation," "mode" of the Infinite, of God—as "potency."[9] The passage reads:[10]

> *That he may not brood*—concerning that which is hidden to thought, lest he fall into confusion.[11] For (only) from that which he comprehends is he able to recognize also that which he cannot comprehend. And to this end the potencies arose.[12] For language comprehends only that which comes from him(?)[13] since man is unable to grasp the potency of the (divine) Word[14] and the letters of the alphabet, but only its (the language's) potency itself.[15] And there are no potencies outside of the letters of the alphabet.[16] And all the sublime[17] potencies are given to be meditated upon.[18] For every potency (arises)[19] from a potency above it, and they are given (or transmitted by tradition) to Israel in order to meditate from the potency that appears in the heart (of the worshiper) to meditate up to the Infinite (to the *Ein-Sof*). For[20] there is no path to (true) prayer other than that whereby man is absorbed (sucked, drawn)[21] by means of finite words (into pure thoughts) and in his thinking rises to the Infinite (*Ein-Sof*).

This difficult passage reflects the peculiar views and terminology characteristic of Isaac and his circle. The potencies are the *sefirot,* the *modi* (literally, "measures") through which the Infinite, *Ein-Sof,* acquires dimension, in which the limited and the Limitless are united. The totality of these divine potencies, which arise from the primal Idea, from "pure thought," is the *logos, dibbur,* the divine Word which dissolves itself or is also concealed in the "letters" of the alphabet as the ultimate elements of all being. The "words," *devarim,* are here not only the finite words of human speech, but at the same time denote the infinite Words of the divine *logos* or *dibbur.* In Isaac's usage they are frequently identical with the *logoi* or *ma'amarot* which appear instead of the term *sefirot* in the oldest table of the divine potencies, the *Sefer Bahir.*[22] Above this "word" or these "words" stands, as the highest of all the manifestations of God, the *mahashavah,* "thought," the primal idea of God. In relation to its infinitude[23] all those *logoi* are of course finite: the *logoi, ha-dibburim,* Isaac comments on Yeẓira 1:4, "have dimension and number; thought, however, is without any dimension." In this sense, the last sentence of the passage quoted means not only that finite human words and human thought elevate the worshiped to the Infinite ("the divine predication," according to the mystics), it also means the inner path of this prayer in the kavvanah. By means of the *sefirot,* the relatively limited "words" are elevated to the unlimited pure "thought" and from there to the innermost core of the Ein-Sof itself, where thought originates. The divine potencies, *midot,* are then the object of "reflection" of meditation, wherein the worshiper addresses himself to the potencies indicated in the specific parts of the prayer[24] and "delivered" to the mystics, and wherein he finds, in his concentrated contemplation of the word, the "primal Word." In it he finds union with the infinite movement of divine thought itself, through which he rises to the Ein-Sof.[25]

There is no doubt that here, in the mystical conception of the kavvanah of prayer, the Jewish form of the *unio mystica,* the basic act of mysticism, makes its appearance; it contains those aspects of the *unio* which alone can become vital for a Jewish mystic. For this is certainly not a union of the essences of God and man, but the "short circuit of the will" (as I would like to call this process) that is brought about by kavvanah. For those early Kabbalists, the fixed text of prayer was the precious setting for the pearl of an experience of God, of a genuine *unio per voluntatis conformitatem* realized by means of kavvanah. Kavvanah is thus a process in which meditation concerning divine things in prayer takes place: in it the limited passes into the Limitless, and the two unite with one another. As man's thinking during prayer purifies itself completely of everything extraneous and distracting, it becomes capable of entering into God's "thought." It seems to me that if we are to find this distinction at all meaningful and acceptable, we must regard the contemplative movement of thought described by Isaac—an attitude which, according to his disciples,[26] he called מחשבה הדבקה , "thinking that is attached (to God)"[27]—not as an intellectual but as a voluntaristic act, in keeping with the sense of the word *kavvanah.*[28]

It should be emphasized, however, that in distinction to the ultimate meaning of kavvanah as defined in the Yeẓira commentary, there is not a single kavvanah in the various but essentially identical versions of Isaac's kavvanot which actually reaches up to Ein-Sof. They merely name the various potencies and their connections to which the special kavvanot address themselves in specific prayers; they are hence concerned, at least in the form in which they express themselves, only with the first stage of the process defined above: the manner in which the worshiper is ushered into the world of "primal words."[29] They are silent with respect to the second stage. Needless to say, an unmediated and explicit kavvanah directed to Ein-Sof itself, in the stricter meaning of the concept, does not exist for Isaac nor the entire early Kabbalah that came after him. This development of the kavvanah concept, which eventually dominated the thirteenth-century Kabbalah, must have been preceded by earlier stages, as is evident from an ancient and no doubt authentic report concerning a controversy in which the father of Isaac the Blind, the famous Abraham ben David (Rabed), was involved.[30] The authenticity of that testimony is corroborated by the fact that its content in every way contradicts the Kabbalah that prevailed in the thirteenth century, and I know of no single case in which the Kabbalists showed any interest in inventing or falsifying traditions which deviated from their own world of ideas. The previously mentioned tradition contrasts the views of R. Jacob Nazir and Rabed concerning the kavvanot of the *Shemoneh-Esre,* and Nazir, in distinction to Rabed and his son, indeed upholds kavvanot directed to the "first cause" itself.[31] (The expression *Ein-Sof* was still unknown to that tradition.) Such a kavvanah cannot be found in the entire litarature of prayer mysticism in the thirteenth-century Kabbalah, nor could it be under the dominant concept of kavvanah described here. The extent to which this concept must have changed since the twelfth century is also evident from the writings of Meir ben Simeon of Narbonne, an opponent of the Kabbalah, who around the years 1235–45 reported that the Kabbalists of his time and region had declared that the kavvanah directed to the first cause in prayer (עלת כל העלות) was neither possible nor desirable—a view which made him highly indignant.[32]

III

This idea of kavvanah as a systematic absorption in the divine Will and the desire to be united with it forms the basis for the unpublished commentary to the prayers by Ezra ben Solomon (in fact, Azriel) of Gerona, a commentary that may more accurately be described as a collection of prescriptions for meditation.[32a] In the writings of this disciple of Isaac we already find God's "thought" replaced by His "will" as the medium of the *unio.* This is evident in many places, especially in his comment to the prayer *yehi razon* at the beginning of the morning prayer (from Berakhot 16b): "Those who comprehend the truth (the mystics) do not recite this prayer. For they themselves ascend from word to word until they reach the innermost Will; as it says: 'neither know we what we do' (2 Chron. 20:12). This means: after we have directed the words to a point where the word ceases" (to the wordless, literally: to the nothingness of the word), "we can add nothing more."[33] The bold formulation of this criticism corresponds completely to the view analyzed above. The individual petitions constituting the content of the prayer they had rejected lose their meaning for the mystics.[34] Directing (*hadrakhah*) one's words (again in the double sense indicated before) towards the "nothingness of the word," which is the *fons et origo* of the divine Will to which the Kabbalist surrenders himself in prayer and with which he is imbued[35] —this is the religious concern of prayer.

In the light of this deeply mystical view of prayer and of the stages traversed by the worshiper while absorbed in prayer, Azriel's book is one of the most valuable and instructive documents in all of kabbalistic literature. It shows the intensity with which mystical prayer was cultivated even in these early kabbalistic circles. At the same time, it bears eloquent testimony to the paradoxical but vigorous and vivid endeavors of those mystics who did not sever mystical prayer from the general communal liturgy, but sought to develop it from the context of its traditional form.[36] From the historical point of view, it is precisely the reciprocal relationship of these two forces that gave rise to the mystical concept of kavvanah and promoted its development. Kavvanah achieved (and this is demonstrated in an exemplary manner by Ariel's description of the meditations and absorption in prayer) what mysticism needs most if it is to establish for itself a central place within Judaism: it bridged the gap between the ancient forms of Jewish prayer and its new forms by planting the seeds of the new in the soil of the old. In this way, kavvanah did for a changed understanding of the religious act in prayer (and later of religious behavior in general) what, on a different plane and with different means, the symbol and symbolic exegesis did for a changed understanding of the Torah and the sources of revelation in general. It may not be inappropriate at this point to emphasize that the primary purpose of this study is to understand the religious meaning and content of the concept of kavvanah, and not to defend or reject it. Such an understanding, however, is all too frequently lacking in our scholarly literature on the subject, which prefers to indulge in wholesale rejection, and at times violent condemnation, of kavvanah.[37]

It is in keeping with the Kabbalists' mystical concept of the nature of prayer that they understand the talmudic definition of prayer as *avodah shebalev*, "God's service in the heart," in its pregnant mystical sense, and, by drawing on the meaning of *avodah* as sacrificial service in the Temple, gave it interpretations such as:

> Since the destruction of the Temple nothing was left but the great Name (of God). And the righteous and pious withdraw to live in solitude and achieve the unification of the great Name, and stir the fire on the altar of their hearts; and then all the *sefirot* arising from pure thought (contemplation) unite and join one another until they are drawn up to the Source of the endlessly sublime flame.[38]

The stirring of the fire in one's own heart instead of on the sacrificial altar, and its upward ascent to the Source of the divine flame—that seems to me in fact a valid formulation of what impelled the Kabbalists to formulate the doctrine of the mystical kavvanah in prayer.

How easy the transition from an unmystical to a mystical concept of kavvanah can be is seen most clearly in the classical definition of kavvanah as an indispensable element of prayer, a definition given by Maimonides in his great work on Halakhah[39]: "Kavvanah means emptying the heart (the mind of the worshiper) of all thoughts, and to think of oneself as if standing before the *Shekhinah* ['divine presence']. It is therefore appropriate that one should sit (quietly) for a brief interval before prayer so as to collect ('focus') one's thoughts, and then to pray serenely."[40] A great kabbalistic work on prayer mysticism, the *Or Zaru'a* of David ben Judah Ḥasid (a grandson of Nahmanides, ca. 1300),[41] also introduces the discussion of kavvanah with this definition (without, however, giving its source), but then immediately proceeds to give it a subtle mystical tinge.[42]

> The true kavvanah, however, consists in clearing the mind of all extraneous thoughts, these being corporeal desires . . . and then to reflect on intelligible and not on manifest matters,[43] and to think of oneself as standing before the heavenly *Shekhinah*, one's desires and soul united with the heavenly King, having eradicated all sensual feelings in oneself[44] in order to be united with the heavenly Light.

Here, then, the characteristic element of mystical concentration for contemplation[45]—the systematic dissociation from one's feelings and desires and the exclusive devotion to the highest good, the "heavenly Light," by a radical elimination of sense impressions and the thoughts engendered by them[46]—is explicitly included in the concept of kavvanah. Maimonides's definition thus all of a sudden becomes a strictly mystical one; he calls it the "true" kavvanah, no doubt in contrast to his earlier definition, a contrast of which he must have become conscious. The concept of kavvanah, however, is in no way exhausted by this general definition of its contemplative character, even for the author of *Or Zaru'a* himself; added to it must be the more exact definition of its linguistic character discussed in the previous section of this essay. We are dealing here with two different elements and levels of thought: the one refers to kavvanah as preparation for prayer; the other refers to it as the mystical activity in prayer itself. Only when the two are taken in conjunction do we obtain a complete understanding of what the early Kabbalists meant by this word.

IV

This concept of kavvanah took on its specific character at an early stage of its development, when it understandably was regarded as a criterion that determined the favorable reception of prayer and, therefore, as a guarantee that the prayer was heard. At this point a magical element began to make its way into the mystics' prayers, an element that gradually became more and more pronounced. Just as the student of the Kabbalah should not ignore its strictly mystical character in order to emphasize its abstruse elements, so also he should not commit the opposite error and overlook its strongly marked magical tendencies. The internal history of the Kabbalah is basically that of a never-ending confrontation, both friendly and hostile, between the attitudes of the mystic and of the magician. They have not only found expression in different currents of thought within the Kabbalah, but have often—at time in the strangest ways—coexisted and intermingled in individual Kabbalists.[47] The absolute separation of these two types, a separation that can be found in many influential modern works on mysticism (such as those of Evelyn Underhill or George Mehlis), should be undertaken only with strong reservations. It fails to account for the actual facts, not only in the Kabbalah but in large areas of the various historical forms of mysticism. The mystic's absolute devotion, passivity, and self-abnegation more easily turn into the magician's alleged characteristics of self-assertion, pride, and demiurgical presumption—even in the same person at times—than one would assume from the writings of these modern authors.[48] Indeed, one of the principal points where we can grasp such a conversion most clearly is in the kabbalistic conception of kavvanah, which in the case of many Kabbalists appears in the form of a basic concept of a magic of inwardness arising from strictly mystical conceptions. The magical light with which kavvanah illumines the path of the worshiper, as described in the most important piece of kabbalistic literature that we possess on the subject (its text will be given below), is highly ambiguous. The most complete description of the path and nature of kavvanah which we possess is, at the same time, the description of the most inward magic that subdues the secret worlds—and the path that leads from there to external, practicable magic is not far! The dialectical character of kavvanah comes into its own there for the first time.

The basic idea in all this is that the mystical "intention" can, in spite of everything, be reconciled with certain concerns of the worshiper and that, united with the divine Will, it "fulfills" not only the mystical kavvanah or intention but, at the same time, the intention that is directed towards a definite concern. Thus, the meaning attached to the reception of prayer by means of properly directed mystical kavvanah is described forcefully and in much detail by the renowned Spanish Kabbalist Josef Gikatilla (as early as shortly before 1300) in his introductory work to the symbolism of the *sefirot, Sha'arei Ora.*[49] The "potencies" of Isaac the Blind appear throughout this work in the symbolism and terminology of God's name. The kavvanah appeals to the "Name" in the words of the prayer, descending to deeper and deeper names, potencies, and *sefirot* worlds until he reaches the name אהיה, "I AM," which denotes the "place" of the Infinite (*Ein-Sof*). The place where kavvanah penetrates to the innermost manifestation of God (identified by Gikatilla with the essence of the Ein-Sof, but which is left separate and distinct by others) is called "the source of the will," and the prayer of him who reaches this far is granted. The innermost point to be pierced by kavvanah in order to have the source of the divine Will burst, "open up," and overwhelm the worshiper is designated as the letter *yod* in the Tetragrammaton; having reached this point, absorption in prayer leaves the level of expression and speech to immerse itself in the nameless, primordial fount of the Ein-Sof.[50] The magical element here is barely evident and is merely suggested: it is not only an immersion in the primordial source of the Ein-Sof but also an evocation of the Ein-Sof from the deep primordial fount of the Will, brought about by the prayer of the conversion into the prayer of the magician. Gikatilla, in a profound reinterpretation of the words of Psalm 130:1 ("Out of the depths do I call unto Thee") which he took from two passages in the Zohar[51] (without, however, indicating the source, something he fails to do everywhere in his work) understands the verse to mean not "out of the depths (where I am) do I call unto Thee," but "out of the primordial deep (in which Thou art) do I call Thee forth."

The most complete penetration into the mystical conception of kavvanah made by the magical element, however, is to be found in another document. In a large number of manuscripts of the Spanish Kabbalah there is a piece that is called שער הכוונה למקובלים הראשונים, "Chapter on the Kavvanah by the Early Kabbalists." This short piece gives a very exact and valuable description of what takes place in kavvanah. Its stylistic perfection is unrivaled in the literature of speculative Kabbalah, and this is no doubt because the author wanted to describe the magic of the kavvanah but simultaneously described its mystical nature at great length. The relationship of these two attitudes to prayer emerges here with unusual force and clarity. The mystical conformity of the will visibly changes over to a magical one, whose roots, it should not be forgotten, are by no means kabbalistic. Nevertheless, it is that definite magical note in the conformity of the will which finds its expression in one of the best-known sayings of the Pirke Avot. Rabban Gamliel, the son of R. Judah ha-Nassi, used to say: "Do His will as though it were thy will, so that He may do thy will as though it were His will. Set aside thy will for the sake of His will, so that He may set aside the will of others for the sake of thy will."[52]

The piece is written in Arabicized Hebrew, and its partly bombastic phraseology raises the question whether its style imitated Arabic sources. The terminology is only partly that of the thirteenth-century Kabbalists; it is in part unusual and even impenetrable. I surmise the piece was composed around 1280–1300, but I am unable to state by whom.[52a] At any rate, the connection of the kavvanah of the preparation for prayer with that of the prayer itself, as well as the theory concerned with the granting of prayers, are not described with such clarity before the end of the thirteenth century. The concluding remark could also refer to Abraham Abulafia's like-minded circle. The oldest manuscript is preserved in Isaak

Chelo's valuable collection, completed in 1328 in Lerida (Aragon), whose
text is given below.[53] To this manuscript, now found in the Laurentiana in
Florence (Plut. II, Cod. 41, fol. 222 a/b), I have also compared the
Vatican manuscript Urbinat. 31, fol. 186 (from 1405) and the manuscript
of the Casanatense 3134, fol. 37, but found there only a few insignificant
corruptions and omissions.[54] The text reads as follows:

שער הכוונה למקובלים הראשונים ז"ל

כל הקובע דבר בדעתו בדעתו קביעות שלם ישוב אליו עקר. על כן אם תתפלל ותברך או תרצה לכוין דבר
לאמתו דמה בדעתך שאתה אור וכל סביבותיך מכל פנה ומכל עבר אור. ובתוך האור כסא אור ועליו
כאיר נג"ה וכנגדו כסא ועליו האור הטו'ב. וכשתהיה ביניהם לנקום נקם פנה אל הנגה ולרחם פנה
אל הטוב. ומרצא שפתיך אל נכח פניו. ונטה לך על ימינו ותמצא אור שהוא אור בהי"ר. ועל שמאלו
ותמצא הדר שהוא אור מזהי"ר וביניהם ולמעלה מהם אור הכבו"ד וסביבותיו אור החיי"ם. ולמעלה
ממנו כתר האור המכתיר חפצי הדעות המאיר דרכי הדמיונת המזהיר זוהר המראות ואין חקר
ותכלית למאור. ומכבוד שלימותו רצון וברכה ושלום וחיים וכל טוב אל השומרים דרך ייחודו. ומן
הנוטים מדרכו האור שהוא מתעלם ומתהפך מדבר לתמורה בתוכחות מוסר וביושר לפי כוונת היודע
לכוין לאמתו בדבקות מחשבה ורצון הנמשך בחלומות חזקתו חזקתו מאין חקר. כי לפי התחזק כח הכוונה
למשוך חזק ברצונו ורצון בדעתו ודמיון במחשבתה וכח בהניעה ואומק בעיונו כשאין הרהור
וחפץ אחר מתערב בה ו'היא מתחזקת בעוצם הנהגתה למשוך משך הבא מאין סוף נגמר כל דבר
ומעשה לדעתו ולרצונו, אם ידע להקיף פאתי המוגבלים ורצון מחשבותיהם מן העקר אשר הם ממנו
ויתעלה עליהם בכח כוונתו ויעמיק כדי לסתור הדרך מעקרו ולחדש דרך לרצונו בכח כוונתו אשר
היא מכבדת שלימות האור המתעלם אשר אין לו מראה ולא דמיון ולא שעור ולא מדה ולא אומד ולא
גבול ולא חשבון ולא קץ ולא חקר ולא מספר ואין לו סוף בשום צד. והמתעלה בכח כוונתו מדבר
לדבר עד הגיעו לאין סוף צריך להנהיג כוונתו בדרך הנאות להשלמתו שיהיה הרצון העליון מתלבש
ברצונו לא שיהיה רצונו בלבד מתלבש ברצון העליון. שאין השפע כמעיין המתגבר שאינו פוסק אלא
כשהוא זהיר בהתקרבו לרצון העליון בעניין שיתלבש רצון העיון ברצון תאותו בהתאחד רצון העליון
ורצון השפל בהשואתו בדבקות האחדות ימשך השפע כדי כדי השלמתו. ואין השלמת רצון השפל
בהתקרבו לצורך עצמו כי אם בהתקרבו בהתלבש בו חפץ ורצון לגלות די ההשואה המתעלמת בסתר
תעלומה. ובהתקרבו על דרך זה אז רצון העליון יתקרב אצלו ויוסיף אומק בכחו וחפץ ברצונו לגמור
ולהשלים כל דבר ואפילו לרצונו נפשו שאין לרצון העליון חלק בו. ובדרך זה נאמר שוחר טוב יבקש
רצון. כי לפי הדבק רצונו בעניין הנאות לרצון העליון יתלבש בו החפץ וימשך לרצונו באיזה עניין
שיתחזק בו בכח כוונתו וימשיך השפע המכתיר סתרי החפצים וההרות בדרך חכמ"ה וברוח בינ"ה
ואומץ הדע"ת. וכפי אשר יתלבש ברוח ויבא כוונתו בדבריו ויעשה סימן במעשיו ימשוך השפע
מכח לכח ומסיבה לסיבה עד היגמר מעשהו ברצונו. ובדרך זה היו הראשונים שורין שעה אחת קודם
התפלה להעביר שאר המחשבות ולקבוע דרכי הכוונה וכח ההנהגתה. ושעה אחת בתפלה להוציא
הכוונה בדיבור הפה. ושעה אחת אחר התפלה להרהר היאך ינהיגו כח הכוונה הנגמר בדיבור בדרכי
המעשה הנראים. ומתוך שחסידים הם תורנו נעשית ומלאכתן מתברכת. וזה הדרך מדריכי הנבואה
שהמרגיל עצמו בה יעלה למדרגת הנבואה.

In the closest possible translation:

"Whoever fixes a thing in his mind with complete firmness, that thing
becomes for him the principal thing." Thus, when you pray and recite
benedictions, or (otherwise) wish to direct the kavvanah to something in a
true manner, then imagine that you are light and all about you is light, from
every direction and every side, and in midst of the light a stream of light,
and upon it a brilliant light,[55] and opposite it a throne and upon it a good
light;[56] and when you are standing among them and desire vengeance, turn
to the brilliance; and if you desire love, then turn to the good light, and let
what comes from your lips be turned to his countenance. And turn to the
right and you will find pure light,[57] to the left and you will find an aura
which is the radiant light.[58] And between then and above them the light of

glory, and around it the light of life.[59] And above it the crown of light that crowns the objects of thoughts,[60] illumines the paths of ideas, and brightens the splendor of visions. And this illumination is inexhaustible and unending, and out of its perfect glory come grace and blessing, peace and life for those who keep the path of its unity. To those,[61] however, who turn aside from its path, the light that conceals itself comes and transforms itself from a thing to its opposite, (and it appears to him at times) as a visitation and (at times) as true guidance.[62] (All this) according to the kavvanah of him who knows how to practice it in the proper manner: by joining thought to the will[63] that emanates in its full strength from the Unfathomable.[64] For in accordance with the intensity with which the kavvanah draws strength unto itself through its will, and will through its knowledge, and ideas through its thinking, and strength through its attainment,[65] and constancy through its reflection, (and indeed) when none of the other senses and desires are mixed with it, and its intensity increases from the power with which it is guided in order to draw unto itself the current (of emanation) that comes forth from the Infinite (according to the degree of such intensity of the kavvanah), every thing and every action takes place in accordance with his direction and will: if only he knows how to comprehend the limits of finite things and the intent of their ideas[66] from the principle[67] whence they are derived. He should then lift himself above them with the strength of his kavvanah and descend to the depths in order to destroy the (usual) path at its very root and clear a new path in conformity to his will: by the strength of his kavvanah which arises[68] from the perfect glory of the withdrawing light[69] that has neither form nor image, measure nor magnitude, extent nor bounds, neither limit nor ground nor number, and which is in no way finite. And he who in this manner lifts himself by the strength of his intention from one thing to another[70] until he reaches the Infinite must direct his kavvanah in a way that corresponds to that which he wishes to accomplish,[71] so that the upper will clothes itself in his will. For the stream of emanation[72] is only then like the inexhaustible fount that never ceases when, on approaching the upper will, it sees to it that the upper will clothes itself in the will of its desire. When the upper will and the lower will in its[73] identification, in its adherence to unity,[74] become one, then the stream gushes forth with sufficient strength to accomplish its intention. The lower will, however, does not fulfill its purpose when it seeks to favor its own needs, but only when it approaches the upper will, which clothes itself in it in order to manifest sufficient identification which (otherwise) conceals itself in the most secret of places. And when it approaches in this manner, then the upper will also approaches and imparts constancy to his strength, and to his will the incentive to accomplish and execute all, even if it be for his own need wherein the upper will has no part. This is the meaning of the verse: "He that diligently seeketh good seeketh favor" (Prov. 11:27). For to the extent to which his will adheres to an object that conforms to the upper will, the impulse (of the divine Will) clothes itself in it and draws itself up, as he (who directs it) wishes, towards the desired object to which he strives with the strength of his kavvanah. And he draws down the effluence that crowns the secrets of things[75] and essences[76] along the path of ḥokhmah and with the spirit of binah and the power of daat.[77] And to the extent to which he clothes himself with the spirit (pneuma) and elucidates his kavvanah with his words and erects a monument (to it) by his actions, he draws along the effluence from stage to stage and from cause to cause until his actions are completed in conformity to his will. And it was thoughts of this nature that the ancients used to meditate upon[78] for a brief interval before praying, in order to remove all extraneous thoughts and to determine the path of their kavvanah (during the prayer that followed) and the strength to be expended for its guidance. And similarly (also) a brief interval during the prayer in order to realize the kavvanah in articulated speech. And similarly a brief while after the prayer in order to meditate on how the power of the kavvanah that had been attained (terminated) in articulated speech could be directed into the paths of visible actions. And since they were truly pious, their Torah became deed and their work blessed. And this is the highest path of prophecy along which he who makes himself familiar with it is able to ascend to the rank of prophecy.

An element emerges in this description of kavvanah that is still missing in the other passages analyzed above: the symbolism of light, the meditation on the stages of the theosophical world of lights. If the ancient report[79] that Isaac the Blind "never glimpsed light" (that is, was blind from birth) is true, then the complete absence of light meditation in his works and its replacement by a noneidetic element such as the "names" of God is understandable. It is quite natural, however, that the element of actual visibility—light and color symbolism—should again assert itself.

These elements are occasionally juxtaposed virtually without connection, as they are in the text just cited. Sometimes, however, they are connected, and certain mystical meditations relating to color are combined with the kavvanah that is directed to the names of God. In a subsequent study I hope to be able to present clear proof for this development, a *responsum* on the kavvanah ascribed to Josef Gikatilla but in reality belonging to a later date. At any rate, the elements of this development are completely set forth in the present study.

To help us understand the turn that is here given to the theme of the conformity of the will, we must bear in mind that prayer as "sacrificial service of the heart" takes the place of sacrifice. However, in the mystical theory of sacrifice, which naturally played an important part for the Kabbalists, the word *qorban,* "sacrifice," was understood in its literal meaning as "drawing nigh" and unification.[80] An ancient work on the theory of sacrifice from the circle of Naḥmanides[81] already speaks (in the formulation also used here) of a "drawing nigh of the lower will to the upper will by means of sacrifice" as being its proper intention, but of course there are no definite magical components here, for sacrifice signifies to the author nothing else than self-sacrifice, the offering of one's will in conformity to the divine Will.[82] Such ideas could be applied with relative ease to the theory of mystical prayer. At any rate, a magical conception of what took place during sacrifice and prayer was sufficiently obvious to reemerge and reassert itself at critical points in the further development of such ideas.

Notes

"The Concept of Kavvanah in the Early Kabbalah," translated by Noah J. Jacobs, first appeared as "Der Begriff der Kawwana in der alten Kabbala," *Monatsschrift für Geschichte und Wissenschaft des Judentums* 78 (1934):492–518.

1. In the *Festschrift: Studies in Jewish Literature, Issued in Honor of Prof. Kaufmann Kohler* (Berlin, 1913), pp. 82–107. See also Martin Buber, *Die chassidischen Bücher* (Hellerau: Jakob Hegner, 1928), pp. 149–56. A dissertation on the subject by L. Breslauer (Kiel, 1921) is known to me only in the form of an excerpt of little value. Wensinck's Dutch work was inaccessible to me.

2. Kohler *Festschrift*, p. 86.

3. In Eleazar's *Sha'arei Ha-Sod ve-ha-Yihud ve-ha-Emunah*, ed. Jellinek, in *Kokhvei Yiẓḥak* 27 (1862):13.

4. ‏לכל יראי ה' יש לכוין כשהם מברכים ברוך ה' ומשתחוים ומודים ומכונים בלבם לאותו קדושתו לבד שהוא כבודו‎ ‏בלא דמות וצורה רק קול ודיבור.‎

5. I refrain from treating the character of these *logos* speculations of the German Ḥasidim in greater detail, confining myself to the question concerning the nature of kavvanah. We are here dealing with a mystical reinterpretation of Saadiah's concept of glory or of the holy spirit (in his Yeẓira commentary).

6. Cf. my preliminanary article on Isaac the Blind in the Hebrew festschrift for Bialik's sixtieth birthday (*Sefer Bialik* [1934], pp. 141–62).

7. His special notes on the kavvanot of the fixed prayers have been preserved by his students, especially Abraham ben Isaac Ḥazzan, the precentor in Gerona, at that time the center for mystics. Cf. Neubauer in the catalogue of Bodleian MSS, No. 1945, fol. 47b, and Steinschneider to MS Munich 92, fol. 216b and fol. 357[2]. These traditions give no particulars on the meaning of these meditations and the manner in which they took place.

7a. The Hebrew text has now been published as a supplement to my Hebrew lectures on the Kabbalah in Provence (Jerusalem: Akademon, 1963).

8. Of this commentary—which I found highly interesting, at least in those parts I was able to understand—no less than seven MSS are known to me, two of which (in the Vatican Fondo Ebr. 202 and in the Biblioteca Angelica in Rome, Fondo Antico Or. 46) are dated as early as ca. 1350. The best MS is the copy of Abraham Graziano in the library of the Hebrew Union College in Cincinnati. Cf. Steinschneider in the catalogue of MSS in Leiden, p. 96, who knew only a MS owned by J. Reifmann.

9. Cf. my translation to par. 92.

10. I append the passage in the original from MS Cincinnati, fols. 30–31. Whole lines are missing in the MS of the Vatican. I have added several important variations in brackets from this MS.

‏מלהרהר מן הנסתרות מן המחשבה פן יטרד. כי מתוך מה שהוא משיג יכול להכיר מה שאינו משיג ולכך נעשו‎ ‏המדות. שאין הלשון משיג אלא מה שהוא בא ממנו שאין אדם משיג מדת הדבור והאותיות אלא מדתה בעצמה‎ ‏[עצמה: .Vat] ואין חרק מן האותיות מדות. וכל המדות הנוראות נמסרו להתבונן [להתבונן מתוך מדה שבהן‎ ‏.Vat] כי כל מדה ממדה שהיא למעלה [מתמלאה: .Vat] ונמסרה לישראל להתבונן מתוך המדה הנראית בלב‎ ‏להתבונן עד אין סוף. כי אין דרך להתפלל אלא על ידי הדברים המוגבלים אדם מתקבל ומתעלה במחשבה עד אין‎ ‏סוף.‎

11. That is, he loses his spiritual balance. ‏נטרד‎ is often used in this sense.

12. As mediating between the comprehensible and the incomprehensible.

13. Difficult. If *lashon*, "speech," is here construed as masculine, which is possible, then *mimenu* could mean "that which comes out of it"—that is, out of the language itself. In that case, however, the change of gender in the continuation, where the feminine ‏מדתה בעצמה‎ in the context of the sentence can refer to nothing else than *lashon*, is indeed puzzling, even though such a change of gender in the same sentence is by no means impossible in medieval MSS. In this instance, however, the sentence can with equal justification be translated differently: "For speech comprehends only that out of which it comes" (‏מה שהוא [הלשון] בא ממנו‎). Then the thought would at least be comprehensible, for that from which speech comes is precisely its inner root, its potency. Thus at the beginning of the book Isaac explains the mystical essence of the letters in a similar manner, alluding to the secondary meaning of the word '*otiyot*, "that which is

to come" (Isa. 41:23 and elsewhere) as הדברים הבאים מסיבתם, as the essences that come forth from their root, or out of their primordial ground. The potency of the divine Word would then of course be distinct from that of the human word, and this is, in fact, Isaac's thought. It is not directly comprehensible, but can be comprehended by immersion in the potency of the human word. This seems to me the most acceptable interpretation of the passage, one that is also in keeping with the other thoughts expressed in it.

14. In all the texts of Isaac the Blind, *dibbur* always means the *divine* Word, even when there is no further addition.

15. Hence a lower potency.

16. The letters are partly the potencies themselves, partly the medium and the organs through which alone they are effective, and in which they are realized.

17. That is, divine. Another reading in the MSS, הנראות, "appearing," is not inappropriate in view of the continuation: from the lower potencies visible to the heart, meditation rises to the higher and hidden potencies.

18. התבונן is the proper *terminus technicus* of the early Kabbalah for "meditating"; cf. *Monatsschrift für die Geschichte und Wissenschaft des Judentums* [hereafter *MGWJ*] 71 (1927):118.

19. Text of the Vatican MS: "fills itself." The word is simply omitted in the later MSS.

20. This critical concluding sentence is missing in the Vatican MS, but its inclusion is warranted not only because it is in keeping with the other thoughts that are expressed, but also because of its characteristic Hebrew usage.

21. The term *mitkabbel* is one of the most characteristic in Isaac's mystical lexicon, and it was no longer used outside his circle. It occurs very often in the Yeẓira commentary, and seems to be a synonym of the mystical term *yanok,* "to suck at or out of something," a term that expresses the closest relationship of the two potencies. (The *derekh yenikah* stands higher in his estimation than the *derekh yediyah.*) For example, הויות המושגות המּתקבלות בהתעלותן or המצטייר והמתקבל מהמקום אשר חוצב משם דבר Just as in our passage, the words מתקבל ומתעלה appear here once more to explain the nature of צפייה, the spiritual vision:

הצפייה היא שכל סבה וסבה מתקבלת ומתעלה וצופה מסבה עליונה ממנה.

The precise use of the word in this sense is also found in the general description of mystical contemplation in Azriel's commentary on the talmudic aggadot, which I have published (*Kitbe Yad be-Kabbalah* [Jerusalem, 1930], p. 197). Is this terminology derived from Neoplatonic sources?

22. Bahir, par. 96 in my German translation (Leipzig, 1923). Cf. *Korrespondenzblatt des Vereins zur Gründung einer Akademie der Wissenschaft des Judentums* (1928), p. 15; and the article "Bahir" in the German *Encyclopaedia Judaica,* vol. 3.

23. This infinity of *maḥashavah* is already explicitly emphasized in *Sefer Bahir,* pars. 48, 53, 60, 103.

24. The special kavvanot transmitted by Isaac refer mostly to entire prayers; see also the critique published in Shemtob ibn Gaon's *Keter Shem Tob,* edited in *Ma'or va-Shemesh* [Livorno, 1839], fols. 35b–36b. But even in the early prayer commentary of his disciple Rabbi Aẓriel, the kavvanot of the principal prayers are for the most part indicated for individual words.

25. The rise of pure thought to the Infinite may perhaps be placed, together with the Catholic formula of prayer as *elevatio mentis ad deum,* as *anábasis nou pios theou,* wherein F. Heiler, *Das Gebet,* 2d ed., p. 291, finds "the peculiar character of mystical prayer aptly defined."

26. Isaak of Akko in *Me'irath Enayim,* MS München 17, fol. 140b: _____

שמעתי מפי חכם ירא שמים שראה החסיד הרב ר' יצחק בן הראב"ד ז"ל ששימש לפניו שאמר כי זה החסיד מימיו לא ראו עיני בשרו מאומה וכאשר רצה ללכת בשום מקום היה אומר לתלמידיו ההולך עמו כאשר נגיע סמוך לעבודה זרה מהר פסיעתך כאשר תוכל. וכל זה היה עושה מדעתו לכבור השם ית' שהיתה מ ח ש ב ת ו ד ב ק ה בו ומפני רוח הטומאה השוכן על הע"ז היה צריך להפסיק מחשבתו.

27. מחשבה דבקה refers to thought that is no longer active, but absorbed within itself, dedicated, and "adhering" to its source, which R. Ezra, the disciple of Isaac the Blind, described in great detail in his aggadot commentary (cf. Aẓriel's critique of the passage

in my *Kitbe Yad be-Kabbalah,* p. 197). It is also well described by Recanati to the Torah, Gen. 49:33. "When the pious retire in solitude and busy themselves with the highest mysteries, the formative power of their mind imagined them as if those things were engraved before them. If they bound their soul to the highest Soul, the things increased and exposed themselves before them of their own accord from the point of origin of their thought (literally, 'out of the nothingness of thought'), as if one were to open a stream of water and the water would spread further and further; for dedicated ('attached') thought is the source and the stream of water and the inexhaustible fount."

28. Not in vain does the Zohar in many places employ "will," as a translation and also at times as a synonym of a Hebraic כוונה.

29. As examples, I give two explanations of kavvanah to ברכו and to the ברוך of the benedictions. First, from *Ma'or va-Shemesh,* fol. 36a:

ברכו כשמזכיר את ה' מכוין לתפארת שיהיה מבורך מן הברכה וכשמחזירין הקהל לומר ברוך ה' המבורך יכוין כי ברוך לשון ברכות מים וברוך הוא הבריכה העליונה שהיא התשובה והמבורך שהוא מבורך מעצמו. לעולם הוא משך הברכה לעולם. ועד רמז לכלה הכלולה.

Second, from Ezra's [that is, Azriel's] Prayer Commentary, MS Parma (Stern 46), fol. 63b:

ברוך כלול מכל כח ממקור חיים ומן החיים ומאור החיים והוא ברוך ומבורך ומתברך כמעין הבריכה המתברכת שהוא מבורך מן המקור הנקרא ברוך.

30. In the light of the material known to us today, no more words need to be lost on the complete failure of Gross's attempt to exclude the Kabbalah from the spiritual world of Rabed (in "Die Mystik des Rabed," *MGWJ* [1874]:164ff.). His essay is a perfect example of hypercriticism that throws the baby out with the bath. Concerning the explicit testimony of Rabed's own son Isaak in his authentic letter to Naḥmanides, see my article in *Sefer Bialik,* p. 152.

31. MS Oxford 1646, fol. 116b:

קבלת ר' יעקב הנזיר ז"ל ג' ראשונות וג' אחרונות לעלה שבעלות ליוצר בראשית. קבלת הר"ר אברהם ז"ל. ג' ראשונות וג' אחרונות לבינה ואמצעיות ביום לתפארת בלילה לבינה כלם.

In MS Brit. Mus. Margol. 755, fol. 85b, the authorship of the two traditions is reversed. The terminology used in opposing יוצר בראשית and עלת העלות also appears in a famous passage in Abraham ben David, which, however, is not decisive in determining the authorship; the two were contemporaries and friends, and are even said to have lived as close neighbors (Posquières and Lunel). The text of the Oxford manuscript is favored by the fact that Isaac, the disciple of his father, cited these kavvanot to the *shemoneh essreh;* moreover, he theoretically rejects direct kavvanot.

32. Cf. the passage from the Parma manuscript of מלחמת מצוה ס' in *Sefer Bialik,* p. 148.

32a. A French translation of this text by Gabrielle Sed-Rejna has recently been published (Leiden, 1975).

33. In the MSS Parma (Stern 46), fol. 67a and Cambridge Dd. 4,2,3, fol. 3a, the original reads:

משכילי האמת אין אומרין יהי רצון לפי שהם מתעלין מדבר לדבר עד שיגיעו עד הרצון הפנימי ש' ואנחנו לא נדע מה נעשה כלומר אחר שהדרכנו הדברים עד אפס. דבר לא נוכל להוסיף.

In the Parma manuscript the passage עד שיגיעו עד הרצון is corrupt, but it is correctly cited in the Cambridge text.

34. Cf. Heiler, *Das Gebet,* p. 308: "To petition for the fulfillment of selfish requests also contradicts the mystical ideal of absolute congruity with God's will." Helier cites a very apt verse by Dshelal eddin Rumi: "To pray: Oh Lord, turn aside this fate, / Truly a sin against him who gave it." Yet this is precisely the content of the prayer יהי רצון, which Azriel rejects.

35. Cf. below, the passage from the work of Josef Gikatilla.

36. It is plain that prayers which were composed by mystics and which stemmed from the practice of the mystical prayer itself (concerning which much material is to be found in Heiler, *Das Gebet*) are, from the standpoint of content, form, and inner rhythm, basically distinct from the liturgical communal prayers. Nevertheless, one must emphasize, since it is also important for the Kabbalists' attachment to specifically Jewish forms, that in the early Kabbalah such unattached and independent mystical prayer plays a much less important role than the time-honored prayers of the liturgy, of the Siddur, which

were mystically recast in the kavvanah. Of course there was no dearth of such prayers, and we still possess quite a number, among them two contemplative prayers from the circle of Provençal Kabbalists that stem from around 1200. These prayers—which, moreover, were ascribed to tannaitic authorities—were from the start written in the symbolic language of the Kabbalists, and they express their contemplative content completely through themselves. There are no special kavvanot to such prayers.

37. I do not deal with the development of kavvanah in the later Lurianic Kabbalah in this study. The Lurianic concept of kavvanah contains some new aspects that are not even mentioned here. On the other hand, an understanding of the earlier concept is basic for it as well. It is precisely the excessive and exaggerated development of the Lurianic doctrine of kavvanah which called forth hostile criticism of the mystical kavannah and its violent rejection. (Not on the basis of its theoretical reasoning, which, it may safely be said, no one has read, but on the basis of its outer forms as they appeared in the typography of the later prayer books. This attitude is shared by the scholarly representatives of a "purified" religion of all "denominations," from the orthodoxy of A. Berliner through the moderate school of Grätz to the left-wing Reform of Enelow. Epithets such as "crack-brained" (Grätz) and "incomprehensible" (namely, to the outsider—as if that were an objection) are often encountered in this connection.

38. In an old kabbalistic homily, MS Berlin Or. Qu. 833, fol. 98a. The principal passage reads in the original:

והצדיקים והחסידים ואנשי מעשה מתבודדים ומיחדים את השם הגדול ית׳ ומאחזין את האש במדורת בית המוקד
בלבהם ואז מתוך המחשבה הטהורה התאחדו כל הספירות ויתקשרו זו בזו עד המשכם עד מעין השלהבת שאין סוף
לרוממותו.

"The fount of the unending sublime flame" is an image repeatedly used in the ancient writings of the Provençal Kabbalists of the Iyyun circle.

39. *Mishneh Torah*, Hilkhoth Tefilla IV,16. Cf. Sanhedrin 22a.

40. Hebrew: בנחת.

41. See concerning the book Marmorstein in *MGWJ* 78 (1934):39ff., and my remarks in *Kiryat Sefer*, 4:320ff.

42. MS Brit. Mus. Margoll. Nr. 771, fol. 5b:

אבל הכוונה האמתית שיפנה לבו מכל המחשבות הנכריות שהן תאוות גופניות ... ויסתכל במושכלות ולא
במפורסמות ויחשוב עצמו כאלו הוא עומד לפני השכינה העליונה ויהא תאותו ונפשו דבוקה במלך העליון
ויבטל עצמו מכל הרגשותיו כדי שידבק באור העליון.

43. A contrast that is very common in philosophical literature; the Kabbalists, however, did not always agree with the philosophers about the meaning of מפורסמות ("that which is evident or manifest"), at times meaning simply to refer to the perceptual world.

44. Or also literally: "detach yourself from all sense impressions."

45. Cf. Heiler, *Das Gebet*, pp. 291ff.

46. The soul systematically emptying itself of ideas plays an important role in the theory of contemplation in the works of Abraham Abulafia and his school.

47. They meet, for example, in Cordovero and intermingle in the works of Isaac Luria.

48. Abulafia's teachings concerning meditation on the names of God served the Kabbalah of the fourteenth to the sixteenth centuries as a prelude to ecstasy and, at the same time, as a theoretical basic science of "practical Kabbalah," of magic, without ever reconciling the inherent conflict of motives.

49. Ed. Offenbach (1715), fols. 40bff., where Hannah's prayer in 1 Sam. 2 is given as an example.

50. I cite only a few sentences from the lengthy but significantly formulated presentation as proof of what is stated in the text.

כי עלתה בתפלתה עד שם אהי״ה ומשם הפיקה רצונה ... ראוי להעלות כוונתו למעלה למעלה לפנים מן העולם הבא
עד מקום הכתר שהוא אהי״ה שהוא אין סוף ... דע והבן שאע״פ שאנו אומרים שהרוצה להשיג חפצו מאת ה׳ ית׳
יהיה מחכוון באותו השם הידוע משמותיו לאותו החפץ שהוא צריך אין כוונתו לאמור שיתכוון לאותו שם בלבד
ויעמוד אלא כוונתו לומר שיתכוון באותו השם שהדבר שהוא צריך תלוי בו וימשיך כונת אותו השם עד סוף עשר
ספירות שהוא המקור העליון הנקרא מקור הרצון וכשיגיע למקור הרצון אז יפיק רצונו ומשאלות לבו וזהו שכתוב
פותח את ידיך אל תקרא ידיך אלא יודיך כלומר שאתה פותח סוד יו״ד של שם הויה שהיא מקור הרצון אזי אתה
משלים רצון כל שואל ... שאדם צריך לההכוון בתפלתו ולעלות מספירה לספירה וממחפץ לחפץ עד שיגיע בלבו
למקור החפץ העליון הנקרא אין סוף ... ממעמקים קראתיך כלומר מאת המקור העליון הנקרא הנקרא אין סוף.

51. Thus Zohar II,63b: ... לאמשכא ברכאן מעמיקא דכלא בגין דינגיד ברכאן ממבועא דכלא
52. Abot II:4.
52a. I have come to recognize Aẓriel of Gerona as the indubitable author, two generations later!
53. Concerning him, see my article in the annual *Zion*, vol. 6 (1933).
54. Other MSS are, for example, München 240[8]; Brit. Mus. 777[4]; Parma, Perreau 86[7]; Jewish Theol. Sem. (New York) 837, fol. 43.
55. *'Or nogah*, according to Proverbs 4:18. It is evident from the continuation that he means primarily the "resplendent light" that is mentioned in the Merkaba vision in Ezekiel 1:4, and, indeed, in accordance with the nuance in which the early kabbalistic commentaries understand this verse. *Nogah* is there generally taken to be one of the four shells (*kelippot*) which, according to this verse, envelop the world of divine potencies and which the prophetic vision must first penetrate. (This is also the meaning given in the Zohar.) Moreover, "throne of splendor" (כסא הנגה) is called one of the potencies which in the literature of the Provençal Iyyun fill the Merkaba world. In *nogah*, grace and judgment intermingle.
56. That absolute good light of which Gen. 1:4 speaks.
57. *'Or bahir* again a concept (taken from Job 37:21) of the oldest kabbalistic light symbolism—which, incidentally, stems from Saadia. The distinctions of these gradations, as apparently imagined by the author, are no longer known to us. In the ancient literature the primal light is that of Gen. 1:4, the *'or bahir*.
58. In the literature of the Iyyun circle, *'or mazhir* is a kind of astral light in which the prophetic visions appear. Thus also further below: המזהיר זוהר המראות . Cf. the piece I published in *Kitbe Yad be-Kabbalah* from an old Merkaba commentary (before 1250).
59. This is also a very common symbol in kabbalistic writings.
60. The light that is the final goal of thought.
61. This sentence is extremely difficult. The מן is perhaps, as often in the Arabicized Hebrew of the Middle Ages, to be understood as partitive: to the portion of those who turn aside belongs the אור המתעלם. Hence, because of the sentence structure, the previous sentence would have to be similarly understood in its opening words (מכבוד שלימותו) , which is difficult to reconcile with the meaning that seems to express a genealogical relationship.
62. I understand יושר here in the sense of הישרה, the path to blessedness, in contrast to תוכחות מוסר, the punishment of those who turn aside from the right path.
63. By means of attachment and devotion, *devekut,* of thought and will to divine Thought and Will.
64. The Unfathomable, המשך ; the term המשך is one of the most pregnant expressions for "emanate" in the Kabbalah.
65. Namely, by arriving at the prime fount of the will or at the Infinite. הגיע is also partly used in this sense in the passages discussed earlier.
66. Or: the will inherent in their thoughts. רצון המחשבה is a turn of speech that occurs only in kabbalistic literature (among the Kabbalists of Gerona and their successors, and also in the Zohar).
67. *Ikkar* in kabbalistic usage combines the three meanings: "principle," "primal ground," "root."
68. Here the two concepts האור המתעלם and כבוד שלימות, which appeared above in opposition, are unified into one.
69. In the event that מן is to be understood as partitive, it is to be translated, "which belongs to (the perfect glory).
70. מדבר לדבר can hardly be understood here grammatically as "from word to word," but as "from one spiritual potency to another." *Devarim* are also the *sefirot.*
71. השלמה means the accomplishment of what had been the intent.
72. The stream of emanation that stems from the divine Will.
73. Of the will. For the Kabbalists, השואה means identification as well as identity.
74. Or: in the unification of oneness.
75. חפץ is here used confusedly in three senses: concern, volitional impulse, and object.

76. הויות is a term commonly used by Kabbalists for spiritual essence, substance. It is modeled on the concepts ουσία or *essentia*.

77. According to the Kabbalists, these three *sefirot* denote the stages of the emergence of the essences of all things from the mystical nothingness that preceded even "wisdom"; in God's "wisdom" they are concealed, in God's "reflection" they emerge, and in God's "knowledge" they acquire form (very often in the writings of the Kabbalists of Gerona).

78. Mishnah Berakhot V:1.

79. In the passage from Isaak of Akko cited above.

80. At first in *Sefir Bahir*, par. 78: "Why is sacrifice called *korban?* Because it brings the holy forms close to one another." This "bringing closer" is its unification with the theosophic organism of the divine manifestations.

81. In a Kollektaneensammlung that was edited as early as the thirteenth century and found, for example, in the Bodleiana 1945 and in Christ Church College 198 in Oxford. I quote from the latter manuscript, a copy of which I have before me.

82. Fol. 12b: מקרב רצון השפל ברצון העליון ע״י הקרבן וזה שנא׳ נפש כי תקריב מעלה עליו הכתוב כאלו הקריבו נפשו. Cf. for the conclusion of *Vayikra Rabba* to Lev. 2:1 (end). Even clearer, ibid., fol. 14a:

ודע כי ענין הקרבן לעלות רצון השפל כדי לקרבו ולייחדו ברצון העליון כדי ליחדו ברצון השפל כדי שיהיה הרצון העליון ורצון השפל אחד לפיכך השפל צריך לקרב לו רצונו ... וקושר רצונו בנפש קרבנו ומעלה עליו כאלו הקריב נפשו שני ונפש כי תקריב ורצון השפל מתקרב לרצון העליון מתרצה להשלים חפצי תאותו ענין שהקריב קרבנו בשבילו.

The striking formulation of the concluding sentence here reminds us of the text cited above and seems to me to indicate the point of transition from the mystical to the magical concept.

8
JUDAH HALEVI AND AL-GHAZALI

David Hartwig (Zvi) Baneth

ewish religious philosophy during the Middle Ages generally tends to view Judaism as the "religion of reason," as a doctrine which not only is nowhere in conflict with rational thinking, but in fact deals with the most important cognitions accesssible to our reason and with the highest practical postulates at which our reason can arrive. This cannot be said as readily of any other religion as it is of Judaism, with its uncompromising, consistent monotheism, emphatic insistence on the knowledge of God, vigorous accentuation of the purely ethical, and limited stress on otherworldly matters beyond the realm of rational thought.

Only one of the earliest Jewish religious philosophers represents an opposite point of view: Judah Halevi, who finds the essence of Judaism precisely in those elements which are outside the realm of human reason. He makes a sharp distinction between that which the human intellect has developed and can continue to develop out of itself and the content of the divine doctrine, which adds to it a newer, loftier dimension.

This peculiar conception cannot be adequately substantiated from the contents of Judaism, but it can be objectively understood if one considers the specific question which Judah Halevi poses. His problem, from the outset, is not Judaism's relationship to rational truth, but its relationship to the other religions and to the practical teachings of the philosophical systems. "Why just Judaism?" he asks. What is the special merit of this one religion, that I should hope to attain the goal of religion especially and indeed only, through Judaism? This merit could not have a rational basis, for if it did, the sages of all other nations would have had to arrive at Judaism by virtue of their own mental capacity. Therefore the merit of Judaism could be sought only in the superrational sphere, in a revelation by the Deity Himself embodied exclusively in Judaism.

Judah Halevi's approach can be understood in terms of the religious conditions of his era, an era in which there was a danger that among people trained in philosophy a general philosophical ideal of life would displace their interest in their own religion and that, being philosophical minds, they would consider the differences between the positive religions insignificant. Though Judah Halevi himself was considerably influenced by the theories of "philosophy"—this term was then used particularly to denote an Aristotelianism infused to a greater or lesser degree with Neoplatonism—his theory was decisively opposed to the rationalism of those adherents of "philosophy." Nevertheless, a man like Judah Halevi, more distinguished for his artistic creativity and emotional sensitivity than for intellectual acuity, would hardly have been able to resist the captivating influence of the world view which dominated his own intellectual circle, had not the theoretical foundations of that outlook already been shaken by a towering intellect. This was done about fifty years before the appearance of the *Kuzari* of Abu Hamid al-Ghazali, perhaps the most significant thinker and religious leader of Islam. David Kaufmann deserves the credit for having traced Judah Halevi's relationships to Ghazali's teachings in detail, but even Kaufmann overrated Ghazali's influence, so that gradually the erroneous impression arose that Judah Halevi's system was essentially a transplantation of Ghazali's ideas into the Jewish sphere. Indeed, some went so far as to refer to the author of the *Kuzari* as "the Jewish Ghazali." Thus, it should be of interest to compare the basic points of the doctrines of both men, as far as a comparison is possible, and also to underscore the differences between their philosophical and religious ideas.[1]

Ghazali's case presents a problem, for his numerous writings, dating from different periods of his life, contain many contradictory views and postulates. Scholarly accuracy would require that a detailed presentation of his doctrines be preceded by a careful chronological study of his works. Such a study has yet to be made. However, it seems that the contradictions in his writings were due even more to the conflicts in his character and the heterogeneity of the ideas that influenced him than to his inner development; not infrequently one and the same book contains ideas that are difficult to reconcile with one another. This, incidentally, is true also for Judah Halevi. But in Ghazali there is the added complication that he changes his language depending on the circles to which he addresses himself; he anxiously avoids anything that might endanger naive faith or that might disclose any of his inmost thoughts to a more serious student. The primary purpose of the present study is to compare the intellectual orientation of the two thinkers, not to examine the problem of their literary interrelationship. We shall therefore deal primarily with those passages in which we may expect to find expressions of Ghazali's deeper convictions, regardless of whether or not one might assume that the work in question was known to Judah Halevi.

The most distinctive feature common to both thinkers . . . has already been mentioned. It is their common critical rejection of the philosophers. Ghazali's penetrating work, *The Incoherence of the Philosophers* [*Tahafut al-Falasifah*], was not intended primarily as a refutation of Aristotelianism in the sense that it attempts to demonstrate that Aristotle's teachings were full of contradictions or led to absurd conclusions. For the most part it merely seeks to show that Aristotle's theses do not rest on immediately self-evident presuppositions, that they do not represent knowledge, but merely opinions. Ghazali's work is original in content but time-bound in form; in the manner of the Muslim theological Scholasticism, the Kalām, the material is fragmented into many individual questions which for the most part are treated dialectically, without method, clarity of arrangement, or a firm point of view, and repeatedly interspersed with arguments and disruptive queries. The author neither underscores basic principles nor analyzes his opponents' basic concepts, a procedure which would have obviated the necessity for entering into many details.

Judah Halevi is already in a position to base his own writings on the work of the great Muslim. It was no longer necessary for him, as it had been for Ghazali, to engage in subtle, painstaking studies in order to refute the philosophers' arguments in support of their heretical views. Judah Halevi has only two concerns: first, to diminish the enormous prestige which the Aristotelian doctrine still enjoyed; and second (and here he goes farther than Ghazali), to demonstrate that Aristotle's teachings are inadequate to satisfy the demands of religious and ethical consciousness. The first of these two objectives is served primarily by a series of critical comments which are partly appended to, and partly interspersed with, a summary presentation of the system of the philosophers. These are not far-fetched arguments in need of complicated proofs and dialectical zigzagging; rather, the author intended to present convincing, cogent objections calculated to show the adversary's weaknesses in full relief. Naturally the points with which he deals are largely the same as those which had also been attacked by Ghazali. Both authors share the same general viewpoints, just as they are motivated by the same basic tendency. But if one compares the reasoning of the two thinkers in detail, the surprising result is that in his polemics Judah Halevi turns out to be independent of his precursor in nearly every respect. It almost seems as if he deliberately avoided repeating the other thinker's arguments. But several differences in their conceptions of the points in dispute seem to indicate that Judah Halevi, when he wrote his work, no longer had Ghazali's treatise actually before him, but merely recalled its general outline.

One of the most detailed arguments in the *Kuzari* does not appear in Ghazali at all. We are referring to the doctrine of the four elements, which Judah Halevi cogently refutes as having no empirical basis. Following Hippocrates, he accepts only four fundamental qualities (heat, cold, wetness, dryness). However, it is only our thinking which dissolves all bodies into these primary simple elements. In reality they never occur unmixed. This idea represents an advance over that of Isaac Israeli, the oldest Jewish-Arabic philosopher who is well known to us, and whose work on the elements, like Galen's, attempts to interpret the Hippocratic theory of the fundamental qualities according to the Aristotelian theory of the elements and to support it with scholastic arguments.

Judah Halevi directs not only criticism but sarcasm at the attempt, common among the Arabic Peripatetics, to link the Neoplatonic theory of emanation with the Aristotelian theory of spheres—which is indeed an amazingly arbitrary construction. Every intellect (*nous*) emanating from the One supposedly emits another pure intellect when it thinks of the One, but emits a sphere when it thinks of itself. This process is supposed to recur in the second intellect and so on, until the tenth of these intelligences emits the transitory world. It was easy to dismiss this theory, which virtually amounted to a travesty of the profound Neoplatonic view and which offered a particularly suitable example that could be used to hurt the reputation of the philosophers (that was based on the claim that the exactness of their tenets could be substantiated scientifically). Ghazali apparently inspired the humorous remark that, if one wanted to be consistent, one would have to expect Aristotle himself (who was erroneously considered the originator of these assertions) to emit an intellect at some times and a sphere at others, depending on whether he was thinking of the First Being or of himself. In addition, however, Judah Halevi offers his own arguments in order to underscore the inconsistencies which mark this structure, quite aside from its arbitrary character.

This is not the place for a more detailed study of *Kuzari*'s theoretical arguments against the philosophers. Along with some unwarranted statements, [these arguments] contain many sound ideas, but they cannot compare in depth and thoroughness—nor are they intended to—with Ghazali's criticism in his polemical treatise. Judah Halevi's polemic is far more original and significant when he appeals not to the intellect but directly to religious sentiment and calls upon it to pronounce its verdict on the concepts of God and life goals of the philosophers. He makes a very sharp distinction between rationalistic and theistic concepts of God. For the philosopher, whose sole aim is to gain a speculative knowledge of the character of all things, God is merely one object of knowledge among many others; he considers ignorance of God as no more harmful than, say, a misconception about the position and form of the earth. He seeks God with his intellect, through the medium of logic. Thus, the God of Aristotle is different from the God of Abraham, whom the believer senses and perceives out of his deepest yearnings. His greatest joy is to be near Him; his greatest agony to be separated from Him. To such a God one can surrender with all one's soul, and one can go to one's death joyously for His sake. The philosopher, by contrast, has no incentive to tolerate so much as one petty annoyance for the sake of his God, who does not even have knowledge of His own existence. The ethics of the philosophers also lack a firm foundation because they do not believe in divine retributive justice; they demand moral conduct because this can best be combined with a life dedicated to cognition, but their demands, unlike those of religion, are not unconditional. Ghazali never emphasized the contrasts between philosophers and believers with the same clarity and acuity. His own mode of thinking is much too close to philosophical intellectualism for him to have been able to sense these differences so clearly.

The significance of the basic principles of Ghazali's critique of the philosophers has been overrated. He seeks to prove that the metaphysical systems of the Aristotelians and the Platonists are unscientific. He clearly recognizes their hypothetical character as distinct from the exactitude governing logic and the mathematical sciences, which the ancient Greeks had also developed. However, he does not dispute the admissibility of a scientific metaphysics as such. True, in his polemical treatise he narrowly restricts the knowledge attainable by rational means. Thus he refutes the philosophers' arguments for the immateriality and immortality of the human soul and for the "ensoulment" of the heavens, though he obviously considers these doctrines to be true. His refutation is clearly intended to remove these questions from the realm of rational cognition and to assign the response to them to another source of truth, revelation. In addition, he designates as misguided all speculation concerning the "how" of divine creation. However, he is dealing only with isolated questions, not with a basic separation of two distinct spheres of truth. On the other hand, when he goes so far as to refute even the proofs of the Arabic Peripatetics for the existence, unity, incorporeality, and so forth of God, he certainly does not do it with the same intention, but most probably in order to defeat his adversaries as devastatingly as possible, and perhaps also to show that their assumptions did not adequately prove the basic truths of religion. He apparently did not think that proofs for the major traditional dogmas which he himself sets forth in two of his works were exact. He merely ascribed relative value to them for practical apologetics. Still, he held that a chosen few might succeed in attaining ultimate certainty about the religious truths by absolutely exact proofs without any possibility of error. Thus one cannot say that there is a distinction between belief and knowledge. When Ghazali emphasizes that individual philosophers disagree over metaphysics, in contrast to their unanimity in matters of logic and mathematics, he [actually] refuses to posit as a criterion of knowledge that everyone understands an issue in the same way. After all, he himself reports that many defenders of Islamic dogmas believe they are obligated to attack even the mathematical sciences of the ancient Greeks. Indeed, at one point he expressly cautions against disdaining a science merely because its exponents are at odds with each other or lack competence.

Therefore Ghazali's attitude toward metaphysics is, in principle, neither critical nor completely skeptical; one can merely say that he shows a certain tendency toward skepticism. Virtually the same can be said of Judah Halevi. He completely agrees with Ghazali in his evaluation of the philosophers' metaphysics, in contrast to their logic and mathematics. He too does not confine his polemic to theories whose content he rejects, but also directs it against, among other issues, the proofs for the substantiality and immortality of the soul—a doctrine which he accepts and repeatedly utilizes but believes has not been cogently demonstrated. On the question of creation he even goes beyond Ghazali. While Ghazali apparently thinks that he can provide not only dialectical but also adequate philosophical proof for the origin of the world in time, Judah Halevi boldly asserts that the proofs for and against the eternity of the world counterbalance each other. If his motivation were not so different, one might be tempted to view this perception as a first step in the direction of Kant's antinomies. But the purpose of Judah Halevi's observation is not to interpret the conflicting proofs as indicating that the ultimate assumptions are wrong, but to show that the methods of pure reasoning are inadequate for dealing with this question. Accordingly, he also considers the rational arguments for the existence of God as generally inadequate. Relegating rational cognition to the background, he clears the way not for a separate sphere of religious truth but for his own proof, which bases the truth of Judaism on the miraculous events in Israel's history. Only miraculous incursions into the natural order constitute fully acceptable proof that the world is ruled by a power above this order, and can, at the same time, inspire the belief that it is this power that created the world.

There is a certain lack of clarity in Judah Halevi's attitude toward religious dogmatics arising from the fact that, without adding a critical word of his own, he incorporates in his work a brief excerpt from a dogmatic treatise by Ghazali, including the proofs for the existence of God and His attributes and for the creation of the world. Of course, he also indicates unequivocally that he is not prepared to give a blanket endorsement to these doctrines and proofs, which are not his literary property and which he does not use as such. It seems that, like Ghazali himself, he does not regard these explanations as certain knowledge, but considers them merely of practical value for strengthening belief in the hearts of those who have already lost the pure faith of childlike simplicity.

We see, then, that the two thinkers do not differ in principle in their attitude toward metaphysics. However, there is a considerable difference in their practical attitudes. True, certain metaphysical views form the background of Ghazali's religious doctrine. However, they do not play a crucial role, and they appear behind the veil of mysticism, not in the garb of exact science. In *Kuzari,* on the other hand, certain metaphysical concepts and basic Aristotelian views are used abundantly for the purpose of providing a philosophical foundation. This difference is attributable in part to the different tendencies of the two works. While most of Ghazali's writings merely want to awaken the religious impulse and channel it into the right path—in other words, to serve the purposes of practical theology—Judah Halevi also aims at the attainment of a specific cognitive goal. He wants to validate the truth of Judaism and, especially, to integrate the concept of Israel's chosenness with the scholarly world view of his time. As a physician, Judah Halevi must have early become familiar with Greek scholarship and must have moved in circles where the theories of the philosophers were regarded as the only true scientific perception of the world. Hence it is likely that he was more predisposed to this world view than Ghazali, who had been reared under the influence of entirely different ideas and who, from the very beginning, had viewed philosophy with suspicion.

For this reason, Judah Halevi, like the adherents of Greek philosophy whom he opposes, seeks to comprehend every development in the world with the aid of the Aristotelian categories of matter and form. He clings to the view that the forms, and thus the disposition, of all objects are dependent on the disposition of their constitutive matter, and that a higher form must always correspond to a more perfect mixture of the particles of matter. Thus matter is given an important role of its own as the basis for the differences between things. As a result, the idea of God in *Kuzari* takes on a more pronounced coloration than the author probably intended. Judah Halevi pursues the idea of God's unity until he arrives at the thesis that all things have been given the stamp of unity by God and that the differences between them are solely attributable to matter. This concept is grounded in the idea that God is the prime intellect which bears within itself all forms or essences as a unified order; it is only due to the differences in receptivity inherent in matter that forms become different from one another.

However, such an abstract concept of God cannot satisfy Judah Halevi's religious spirit. His theory of God as the form-giving prime intellect was a protest against the philosophical theory which denied that God acted directly upon the universe. But the concept of a deity whose operations are mechanical and completely dependent on the quality of matter cannot satisfy the needs of religious consciousness; nor can a deity whose activity is restricted to a one-time bestowal of form. For this reason Judah Halevi views God not only as the prime intellect but also as the soul, the spirit, of the universe—He is not merely the form-giver, but the one who preserves, guides, and cares for every creature. Side-by-side with the concept of a divine wisdom operating in accordance with fixed laws is the concept of a free creative will, creating "what pleases Him, as it pleases Him, and when it pleases Him," and capable of disrupting the processes of nature whenever He desires. It is true that these two conceptions are occasionally reconciled in the notion of an eternal will which is identical with the divine wisdom and which had already laid the foundations for miraculous happenings at the time of creation. But on the whole the two conceptions exist side-by-side, completely separate, as elements of two distinct basic directions in Judah Halevi's thinking, religious and scientific, each alternately coming to the fore without ever colliding.

Precisely this point demonstrates the difference in Ghazali's position. He places the problem of freedom or necessity in the workings of God on the razor's edge and sets out to prove that the "thusness" of the world cannot be explained in terms of mere rational necessity. Based on this premise, Ghazali insists that there must be a free divine will which ultimately determines the condition of things, for in his view the character of this will consists precisely in its ability to establish differences between things which are, in themselves, alike. From this vantage point he can far more decisively refute the philosophers' arguments against the creation of the world in time than can Judah Halevi. In principle, Ghazali, in explaining the changes and development of objects, can also dispense with the concept of dualism in matter and form (though both concepts do, in fact, occur frequently in his writings, in some instances under other designations). But Ghazali only appears to be defending the orthodox Muslim dogma of the unbounded freedom of divine activity. It is erroneous to regard the idea of the divine will as the decisive element in his concept of God. It is only in the context of dogmatics, in the strictly scientific marshaling of proofs, that he does not venture beyond this idea. Where he expresses his deeper convictions, he admits that there are limits to divine arbitrariness: first, the objectively given limit of what is possible (an element which occupies the place of matter in the Aristotelian system); and second, a limit set by the will itself—the all-embracing goodness of the deity. Much as Leibniz [was to do later], Ghazali formulates the thesis that the existing world is the best possible world, for, he argues, if God had been able but not wanted to create a better world, He would not be all good, but could be rightly charged with parsimony. However, if a better world were possible but God, with all His goodness, were unable to create it, He would lack the omnipotence which belongs to the concept of the deity. The purpose of the world's organism is "to realize the greatest possible measure of good, as required by God's goodness." God is He "who has necessary existence because of His essence, and through whom everything which can exist is called into being in the best of order and in the greatest perfection." Thus it is precisely Ghazali's religious concern that leads him to impose limits upon the divine will which, from a purely scientific point of view, could have been considered as not subject to limitations—the exact reverse of what we noted in Judah Halevi. At bottom, however, both thinkers agree in their deeper perceptions of God's activity; freedom and necessity coincide in God because the divine will, which is identical with all-goodness, has made it a law for itself to realize the best possible world order.

Aside from this similarity, traceable to their common roots in Neoplatonism, the two philosophers diverge sharply on a number of points. Ghazali recognizes no other activity than that of God. He clearly formulates the point, which we primarily associate with David Hume, that we can derive from experience only a repeated, "customary," temporal-spatial association, not a causal connection of objects. Although he thus eliminates empirical causality, Ghazali firmly upholds the principle of causality and carries it through consistently. All change and all that is changeable—in other words, the world in its totality—must have a cause. But those phenomena which we regard as causes must, in turn, have causes, a process repeated until we arrive at a first cause: hence God, the First Cause, determines all events in the world. Consequently, God alone is properly the true cause of all actions and effects. However, the eternal divine power does not operate without rules; it unfolds itself in chronological sequence in accordance with a fixed law. Its operation in every individual instance always depends on conditions that must be fulfilled in their entirety before any process can take place. The world is one gigantic mechanism. In fact, Ghazali repeatedly likens it to an ingenious water clock which strikes the hours, in whose mechanism the various parts move in a fixed sequence, but in which only one power, the gravity of water, operates. In the same manner the divine power alone governs the universe, but it does so in a well-calculated, immutable order.

The human will, too, can be no more than one small part in the mechanism of the universe. Man has no free will; when we say that man can make a choice or a decision, we merely mean that, after his intellect, of necessity, has found a certain course of action to be proper, man, also of necessity, finds himself wanting to take that course. In other words, an act of will is distinct from natural processes only in that it is preceded by conscious processes (as a condition of its realization) before it can be translated into reality. Man is capable of willing, but he cannot will whatever he wants. He can will only what God has determined for him.

Such a rigorous determinism was certainly compatible with Islam, whose meaning, as indicated by its very name, is "submission (to the divine will)." It did not noticeably conflict with popular religious awareness or the prevailing theology. Al-Farabi and Avicenna [ibn Sina], the leaders of Arabic Aristotelianism, also espoused determinism. Judaism, on the other hand, the religion of the pious deed, is founded upon free will and cannot be reconciled with a deterministic view without having violence done to it. As a result, virtually all Jewish thinkers, including Judah Halevi, have come out on the side of free will. Judah Halevi's attempt to uphold man's freedom of will without discarding the concept of divine omniscience and of God as the First Cause yields no useful idea and is without interest to the present study. A defense of the concept of free will was, of course, impossible if one shared Ghazali's rigorous mechanistic view of the world.

Indeed, the theory of causality advanced in *Kuzari* thoroughly differs from Ghazali's. Judah Halevi also attributes all being and becoming to God as the First Cause, but whereas Ghazali sees every phenomenon in the universe, no matter what its character, as virtually created by God, Judah Halevi speaks of gradations of divine influence even in natural events. Even the life and growth processes of plants and animals, processes which in their purposiveness and goal orientation still clearly bear the stamp of the world's divine governor, are not caused directly by God, but instead result from intermediate causes. Even further removed from the divine will are those phenomena which lack the stamp of purposiveness and owe their origin to accident. Such a graduated system of causality left more room for free will than did Ghazali's monolithic theory.

However, this approach was motivated by still another consideration. By characterizing natural phenomena as only indirectly derived from God, it becomes possible to distinguish them from supernatural events directly caused by God. The history of the Jewish people affords three distinct kinds of such supernatural events: acts of revelation, single miracles, and the miraculous, providential guidance of the people's destiny, which is dependent on its religious conduct rather than on accidental and natural causes. Judah Halevi's philosophical endeavor is to interpret these supernatural events (without weakening their uniqueness) analogously with natural processes in order to preserve the concept of a uniform world. Just as, in Aristotle's view, the operation of all natural forces is dependent on a specific disposition or potential of matter, so too are the workings of the divine power. Just as the seed of every creature stems from a creature of the same species, so too this supreme faculty must be inherited from someone endowed with it. The first man possessed it, and it lived on through various individuals during the generations that followed, until it was passed from Israel to all his sons and then to the entire people descended from them. However, the mere existence of a seed is not enough; a seed can grow only in the proper soil and with the proper care. Accordingly, the supernatural powers inherent in Israel can become effective only in the Holy Land and only by Israel's observance of the divine commandments. The supernatural, then, almost appears as merely a higher species of the natural. It is not distinct from the latter in its conditionality; however, it is above natural law and has the power to suspend it.

The difference between Judah Halevi's and Ghazali's conceptions of divine activity already indicates the most important external contrasts between their doctrines concerning religion. Judah Halevi sees supernatural phenomena as the correlate of the true religious life. That faculty which was granted only to one part of mankind—namely, to Israel—is nothing more and nothing less than the ability to lead a genuinely religious life. Therefore Judah Halevi's doctrine can be characterized in the conventional phraseology as "supranaturalist" and "particularist" (both closely linked), while Ghazali's differing concept of causality runs parallel with a tendency to religious universalism. Of course, Ghazali regards Islam as the true religion and bases his views as much as possible on the koranic revelation. But his religious theories, unlike Judah Halevi's, are not inextricably linked with his own religion by virtue of their essence. Given the role he assigns to revelation, it is irrelevant whether that revelation is the one communicated to Mohammed or some other revelation. In fact, prophecy could be eliminated entirely from Ghazali's doctrine without changing its substance materially. What he preaches and seeks to substantiate is essentially religion in general, almost in the modern sense of the term, without any relationship to the religious data of Islam.

This basic universalist attitude is not unique to Ghazali. He shares it with the main exponents of Muslim mysticism as well as Arabic philosophy, and it could develop most easily within Islam because Islam is less linked to specific historical facts than any other monotheistic faith. Mohammed's followers see him only as the last in a long line of prophets who emerged within various nations and who all proclaimed the true faith. Unlike the revelation at Sinai and the giving of the Torah in Judaism or the "salvific events" in Christianity, Mohammed's mission does not establish the faith. Incidentally, the structures of most of the systems of the Jewish religious philosophers show a tendency towards universalism, and Judah Halevi's unique achievement is precisely that he clearly recognized the problem of the special historic status of Judaism and attempted to solve it with the philosophical methods of his day. This lends, of course, an air of superficiality to his substantiation of the Jewish religion. His theory of Israel's special religious faculty bears an unmistakable resemblance to modern racial theories. But unlike those theories, which are outgrowths of a sense of racial superiority, his doctrine does not attempt to construct evidence that would fit the doctrine. Rather, it rests on the (for him) given facts, immediately evident and established by the Bible, according to which true knowledge of God, prophecy, and supernatural providence can be found only in Israel. Nevertheless, he is far from wanting to press this theory rigorously. Unlike Ghazali who, in keeping with Islamic dogma, excludes infidels from salvation, Judah Halevi, faithful to Jewish tradition, acknowledges that the righteous of other nations also have a share in eternal bliss. He even softens his basic notion by saying that a proselyte can be equal to a born Jew in every respect except for the ultimate supreme gift of prophecy, and he apparently feels that this last barrier also will fall in the days of the Messiah when, even as a seed acts to transform the soil from which it synthesizes its plant, Israel too will have transformed all the nations into its own likeness.

So far we have characterized only the surface aspects of the differences between the religious doctrines of the two thinkers. In order to come closer to the essence of this difference, we must briefly turn to those fundamental views of Ghazali which he himself attributes to "revealed knowledge" (that is, of mysticism) rather than to true science, and which he has drawn mainly from the Neoplatonic-Sufist sphere of ideas. As a rule—disregarding his more complex theories—Ghazali makes a distinction between two spheres of existence: one is the "world of the dominion (of the kingdom of heaven)" or the "world of the hidden"; the other is the "world of the governed" or the "world of the obvious." The first represents the realm of the spirit, the second, that of bodies. Only the first can be said to have existence in the true sense of the term; the second is merely a shadow, a reflection of the first. Everything that exists in the visible world must have a prototype in the invisible world; however, any one thing can have any number of prototypes, just as many terrestrial images may be assigned to one of the spiritual substances. Obviously Ghazali is speaking of a world of ideas operating as active intellectual substances in the Neoplatonic sense. The human "heart" (the term Ghazali usually uses for "soul," in line with Sufist usage) comes from the world of the dominion and is exiled into the world of bodies as into a foreign land. Thereby it receives the ability, and at the same time the duty, to elevate itself again into the spiritual realm and thus come close to God once more.

These views determine Ghazali's conception of religion in a twofold

way. The soul is bidden to free itself from its enmeshment in finite concerns and return to its original home. Thus we are dealing with a doctrine
of salvation. The home of the soul is the realm of ideas through which the
soul comes close to God. Therefore cognition becomes a basic element of
religiousness. Both elements are partly complemented and partly modified by motifs which originally differed from one another. The salvation
motif he sets forth, which at least in monotheism is not closely related to
the religious idea, recedes almost entirely into the background in the face
of the demand for an immediate surrender of the self to the deity through
renunciation of all earthly thoughts and aspirations. Ghazali justifies this
demand by ingenious reasoning. Hidden in every man's heart is the wish
to be a god in his own right, to be the almightly owner and ruler of the
whole world while remaining completely free and independent himself.
But this yearning can never be fulfilled, no matter how much man may
strive to amass worldly goods or gain dominion over the minds of others
by attaining fame and glory. All these goods are limited and transient,
sham values which can never satisfy him. Only in complete surrender to
God can he find peace; only by detaching himself from all earthly bonds
is he able to attain the freedom for which he longs; only in an all-
embracing knowledge of God can he find the unbounded, imperishable
good. This idea, carried to its logical conclusion, actually leads toward
pantheistic mysticism: man's striving after the attributes of the deity can
be truly fulfilled only when he becomes completely one with the divine
all-presence [*Allgottheit*]. Ghazali, however, does not draw this conclusion. Notwithstanding his proclivity to mysticism, his sober mind categori-
cally rejects pantheism and the notion of man's union with the deity. He
interprets the *fana* of Sufism, the absorption of the self in the divine
all-presence, psychologically as the state of the soul forgetting itself in
being entirely filled by God.

Cognition as religious content and value is central in another train
of thought which can be traced back to Aristotelianism. In this view, the
purpose or destiny God implanted into every creature is based upon the
unique characteristics of that creature, those traits which set it apart from
all other species. What distinguishes man from the lower forms of life is
his "heart," the seat of cognition and of rational volition. Ghazali places
the strongest emphasis on cognition. Action, at which the will is aimed,
takes second place for him; it exists only for the sake of cognition. Man's
true perfection consists in his knowledge, and the degree of bliss he will
attain depends on the level of cognition he acquires. The only insights
worth striving for are those which are universal, eternally valid, and
transcend the realm of the senses. They are united in the knowledge of
God, for the knowledge of God, of His attributes and works, embraces
the knowledge of all that exists; it is only in this relatedness to the deity

that knowledge has any value. Two paths lead to this knowledge. The one is the path of scientific study, of discursive thinking. There are few who can or should take this path: individuals who are endowed with great intellectual gifts and can begin their studies in early youth under the tutelage of a teacher of independent spirit. The other path is that of asceticism and spiritual vision. He who, by persistent self-discipline and by uprooting all worldly desires from his spirit, has cleansed the blight from the mirror of his heart will obtain in that mirror an unclouded view of the eternal truths, a reflection of the "preserved table"—that is, of the eternal divine world plan from which alone physical reality is derived.

This is the path which Ghazali preaches, the path to which he summons the faithful time and again in his great religious treatises and his many smaller works. However, he emphasizes that the cognition attained by these two paths is, in principle, the same; it differs neither in essence nor in its substrate (organ of cognition). This does not discount the possibility that the pursuit of one path might lead to the apprehension of some truths to which the other may not give access. Ghazali makes frequent references to a cognitive capacity which, he says, is granted only to prophets and divinely favored individuals, which is above the intellect just as the intellect is above the senses, and which is capable of perceiving things not accessible to the mere intellect. What he means is doubtlessly nothing but the intuitive perception attained by the purified soul. And when Ghazali implies that this exalted vision overcomes the limitations of the physical, material, and accidental, one may also interpret this as signifying the vision of pure ideas which, according to Plotinus, belong in different categories than the objects of the senses.

What, then, is the place of koranic revelation—that is, of positive religion—in this doctrine? Only now and then is revelation considered a significant source of cognition. For Ghazali there is no doubt that all of the more profound truths are contained in the Koran; in order to demonstrate this conviction, he compiled a treatise in which he systematically strings together the "pearls of the Koran." Yet he is aware that the crucial role belongs to exegesis, inasmuch as for the most part these truths do not lie exposed for all to see, but can be extracted only by thorough interpretation. True, one occasionally also finds the view that the human intellect, in order not to have to grope in the dark, must allow itself to be illuminated by the word of God. But Ghazali apparently does not consider the communication of truths to be the real purpose of the prophetic mission. Instead, he sees the essence of prophecy in practical doctrine. "The prophets are the physicians of the soul": this ancient adage constitutes the basis of his concept of positive religion. Revelation imparts to the prophets those means which are conducive to the purification of the heart but are not accessible to the intellect. Medical science makes use of remedies which, when properly compounded, produce cures, although our intellect is not capable of understanding the reasons. In the same way, the weakness and frailties of the heart can be healed only by painstakingly specified actions, whose potency we cannot grasp with our intellect but the prescriptions for which we must trustingly accept from the prophets. These prescriptions are the rituals prescribed by religious law down to the minutest details: the number of prayers, tithing, fasting, pilgrimages, and many others. Their efficacy consists in that they strengthen faith, fear of God, and the good in man, and that they banish evil. Hence they are aids to religious ethics. Ghazali's science of religion, the doctrine of religiously prescribed acts, occupies a place equivalent to, say, propaeduetics. Its relationship to cognition is characterized by the statement that "the rational sciences may be likened to nourishment; the science of revelation, to medicine." Cognition is the content of religious existence, the substance on which, in fact, the soul draws to form itself; it is through cognition that man has a share in the divine. Religious acts are conducive to perfection only in a negative sense, in that they remove the imperfections from the soul.

Both elements—withdrawal from the world and emphasis on the religious significance of cognition—are alien to Judah Halevi. The description of Jewish piety in *Kuzari* begins: "In our view, a pious man is not one who detaches himself from the world lest he become a burden to the world and the world to him, or lest he come to hate life, which is a gift of God. . . . On the contrary, he loves life and wants to live to a ripe old age because it affords him an opportunity to deserve the world to come." It is understandable that *Kuzari,* too, names the world to come, eternal life, as man's goal in contrast to his brief span on earth. However, Judah Halevi seeks to minimize as much as possible the difference between the pious Jew's life on earth and his life in the world to come. The pious Jew can already enjoy, right here in this world, the bliss of God's nearness, the goal to which all religions aspire.

For Judah Halevi also, this blissful communion with God is linked to the vision of a "higher world." He notes in *Kuzari* that on that highest level of existence truth can be apprehended without the exertion of study. But here we have merely vestiges of that Neoplatonic-Sufic thought which held powerful sway over the minds of that period and which Judah Halevi had not yet sloughed off. He nowhere describes cognition as a religious value in itself; nowhere does he call upon us to strive for knowledge, be it rational or mystical. It is precisely in this area that he feels himself decisively opposed to the peripatetic world view, and he rightly declares that the God for whom his soul is yearning is not the one concocted by the intellect of Aristotele. Ghazali's doctrine of the two paths, equating prophetic vision with mystical gnosis and scientific cognition, blurs the difference between these views of God.

According to Judah Halevi, the path to God is not through asceticism or a quest for cognition, but through pious deeds. By this he does not mean moral conduct in general. Since the moral law is grounded in our own reason, it cannot be religion in the specific sense of the term if we define religion as the path to God. Reason is that specifically human element which elevates man above the lower forms of life. It can raise him to the highest levels of being human, but not beyond them. Religion, on the other hand, seeks to elevate man above the human condition, to make him rise to a higher form of existence, to have him enter into the realm of the divine. Man, who is not even capable of seeing through the lower processes of nature, could never find his way alone to this transition into a higher form of existence. Only God can show the way, and he has indeed shown it to Israel by means of revelation—that is, through the ritual acts commanded by the Torah.

This is approximately the train of thought underlying Judah Halevi's particularism. He stands midway between the universalist rationalism of the philosophers and the Pauline Christian doctrine of grace. In the one, religious elevation depends entirely on the character of the individual, and particularly on his intellectual capacity; in the other, it is dependent exclusively on the arbitrary dispensation of God's grace. According to Judah Halevi, only the knowledge of the path must come from God; the religious goal is attained through the acts of the individual who is competent to act by virtue of a special mission. Ghazali combines all three motives in a peculiar fashion: like the philosophers, he grounds the religious impulse and the potential for elevation in the specific human condition, and he regards observance of the revealed religious law as an indispensable aid. However, man's actions and the religious level he attains are preordained by God—not, of course, through an arbitrary dispensation of grace, but through the law of the emanation of the greatest possible good.

Though Judah Halevi distinguishes between ethics and religion in the narrower sense, he does not dissolve their connection. Man's first duty is to obey the moral law through which he reaches perfection qua man. Without it, observance of religious law, which is intended to affect man's linkage with the divine, is worthless. In this sense, moral law prepares for religious law. Ghazali reversed this position. The cultic observance is a preliminary and aid to ethics; it serves the "purification of the heart." As he sees it, the deeds dictated by the intellect stand above those commanded by revelation alone. Judah Halevi's views, by contrast, are permeated by the idea that the doctrine communicated in a supernatural manner by the infinitely exalted deity must contain something higher than what human reason can attain.

Judah Halevi's notion that communion with God can be established by specified deeds performed at a specific time and place borders on undisguised magic but must be distinguished from it. These deeds are not sacramental symbols of whose meaning the faithful should, if possible, be aware as they perform the rituals. But they also are not mysteries wrested from the celestial powers in order either to compel them to descend or admit the soul of the adept into their own high places. What Judah Halevi means is the worship of God in its simplest form: a simple fulfillment of the will of God without first inquiring into the whys and wherefores. The perfectly pious person makes himself into a direct instrument of God on earth; his and God's will become one. Here is the point of closest contact as well as of sharpest disagreement between Ghazali and Judah Halevi. Both have as their goal complete surrender to God, but while the one merely wishes to share in the vision of the divine essence, the other wants to serve as an instrument in the inscrutable workings of God.

However, in Judah Halevi's view, piety does not exhaust itself in the devout performance of religious acts. The entire life of the pious man must be informed with religious impulses; every moment must be inspired by his awareness that he is standing before God. The central passage of *Kuzari* describes how this requirement is fulfilled in the life of the pious Jew. Here there are once again close affinities between Judah Halevi and Ghazali, but there are also typical areas of disagreement which emerge especially at this point.

We may stress two important differences. We have already noted that Ghazali's doctrine points toward asceticism, detachment from the world. His writings are pervaded by a stern and not infrequently gloomy strain. The primal motive of Islam—fear of terrible punishment in the next life—still occupies an important place in his thinking, at least with regard to the early stages of the religious path. True, this fear should be associated with hope for the goodness of God, but as long as man still knows himself to be a sinner, fear must predominate. Judah Halevi, on the other hand, unaffected by the influence of the cultural trends around him, perceives religious joy as the essential ingredient of Jewish piety. He lists the fear of God, the love of God, and rejoicing in God as the cardinal religious virtues, as it were, of Judaism, and he considers the rejoicing on festival days, as long as it is grounded in religious devotion, to be no less important than repentance and contrition on fast days. Rejoicing is an emanation of love, from which in turn flows a sense of gratitude to God.

Ghazali's piety, like religiosity based on asceticism and mysticism, is the piety of the individual. The task of every individual is to work on the purification of his own soul and, if he can, on the acquisition of eternal truths, either alone for himself or together with a few like-minded companions, but without connection with his people as a whole. It is true that the individual's moral duty is to work for the general weal as long as there is no one else to step into the breach, even if it means that he thereby jeopardizes the salvation of his own soul. However, the specific religious life of the individual is not dependent upon that of his people; in fact, he should, as much as his natural gifts permit, elevate himself above the religiosity of the masses. For Ghazali, there is a wide gap between the piety of the few God-seekers and the piety of the masses, who know only the literal text of the credo and the externalities of ceremonial practice.

Not so Judah Halevi. His theory of the special religious faculty granted to Israel already places the entire Jewish people on essentially the same level. The religious acts he stresses serve to unite the nation; intellectual differences remain insignificant. In Judah Halevi's ideal image of religious life during the period of the Temple, the individual is depicted as being carried by the piety of the masses, irresistibly drawn into the current of living religion. Judah Halevi emphasizes strongly that prayer must be communal prayer; it must include the entire community. God, whom he considers to be beyond the grasp of man as a philosophical concept, takes on personality in the God of Israel. Closely associated with this idea is the connection he establishes between the Holy Land and God as the "Lord of the Land." Just as a sizable part of *Kuzari* is devoted to the glorification of Palestine, so too the book ends with Rabbi Judah Halevi's resolve, notwithstanding all dangers, to go to the Holy Land, where alone it is possible to lead a perfect life consecrated to God. In the final analysis, the role which the people, the land, and religious acts play in *Kuzari* is not determined by the logical arguments described in this study, but by emotional associations in the poet's soul which find more adequate expression in his poetry than in his philosophical-polemical treatise. This role is grounded in a sense of nationhood, an innate attachment to all the elements of one's own existence.

Thus we see in Ghazali and Judah Halevi two profoundly different religious personalities. Ghazali's religious will reaches for that which is infinitely exalted, the infinitely remote, the totally abstract. It seeks to intellectualize itself completely by discarding everything natural, to objectify itself in order to come close to the first cause and quintessence of the spiritual, of true existence. Judah Halevi, groping, vacillating, and lacking conceptual clarity, searches for the most fundamental element which has been at work in the history of his people, which revealed itself most gloriously in the land of his ancestors, and whose reflection is still discernible in the simplicity of Jewish folk piety. He searches for the enigmatic supernatural, whose most profound mysteries lie concealed especially in the workings of nature, which cannot be comprehended intellectually and can be approached only by intuitive penetration. Just as Ghazali's doctrine is not tantamount to that of Islam, Judah Halevi's religiosity is not tantamount to that of Judaism. He ignores fundamental elements of Judaism, and those which he stresses are given a highly individualistic expression. Yet no other medieval thinker has succeeded equally well in grasping the essence of Jewish piety and overcoming the rationalism dominant in his time. For this reason, Judah Halevi is close to those trends in present-day Jewish life which seek to return to a living Judaism, while Ghazali is closer to the mystical tendencies of our age.

Notes

"Judah Halevi and al-Ghazali," translated by Gertrude Hirschler, first appeared as "Jehuda Hallewi und Gazali," *Korrespondenzblatt des Vereins zur Gründung und Erhaltung einer Akademie für die Wissenschaft des Judentums* 5(1924):27–45; reprinted in Kurt Wilhelm, ed., *Wissenschaft des Judentums* (Tübingen, 1967), 2:371–89. For sources and other annotations, see the Hebrew translation of this essay in *Keneset,* vol. 7 (Jerusalem: Mossad Bialik, 1941–42).

1. The most important aspects of the relationship between Ghazali and Judah Halevi have already been elaborated by Julius Guttmann in *Festschrift zum fünfzigjährigen Bestehen der Hochschule für die Wissenschaft des Judentums* (Berlin, 1922). David Neumark was the first to reject the assumption that Judah Halevi's philosophy was largely dependent on that of Ghazali; see particularly Neumark's monograph, *Judah Halevi's Philosophy in Its Principles* (Cincinnati, 1908). See also Emil Berger, *Das Problem der Erkenntnis in der Religionsphilosophie Jehuda Hallewis* (Berlin, 1916). The best recent source of information on Ghazali is J. Obermann's *Der philosophische and religiöse Subjektivismus Ghazzalis* (Vienna and Leipzig, 1921). The interpretation of Ghazali in the present study differs from that of Obermann in numerous respects. However, the intention of the present study is to place more emphasis on other aspects of Ghazali's character. The author wishes to acknowledge his indebtedness to all the works listed here. The problem of divine attributes, which is particularly complex and obscure in both thinkers, was deliberately passed over in the present study.

9
MAIMONIDES'S ATTITUDE TOWARD JEWISH MYSTICISM

Alexander Altmann

T he purpose of the present study is to investigate how close Maimonides comes to mysticism, that is, to that form of cognition which, broadly speaking, claims the capacity for a mystical union with the divine. This general concept of mysticism is so vague that it also may be said to cover Maimonides's ultimate philosophical stance, considering that he viewed the act of metaphysical cognition as a communion with God by means of the active intellect.[1] What we do intend to examine is Maimonides's attitude toward that type of Jewish literature which, in distinction to the halakhic-exegetical and philosophical-rational writings, represents a phenomenon that may be described as "Jewish mysticism," even though it is not genuinely mystical in the strict sense of the term.

The attitude of the Kabbalists toward Maimonides has been the subject of a number of studies in recent years. Gershom Scholem, in his literary-historical analysis of the well-known "conversion" legend, traced the changes in their attitude,[2] while Horodetzky recorded their statements about Maimonides all the way into Ḥasidism.[3] Yet so far no one has attempted a systematic inquiry into the objective relationship of Maimonidean philosophy to Jewish mysticism. Independent of the question whether, as legend has it, Maimonides turned to the Kabbalah toward the end of his life (a proposition no longer considered tenable after Scholem's cogent demonstration of how the legend evolved), one should inquire whether the structure or specific details of his system show points of contact or coincide with Jewish mysticism. Thus, irrespective of the biographical question whether to draw a distinction between the old and the young Maimonides, it seems necessary to make a serious investigation of the objective relationship. It should be kept in mind that mystics of the same era, such as Naḥmanides, feel spiritually close to Maimonides;[4] that Kabbalists of the first generation after Maimonides in particular consider him an outright Kabbalist and, like Abraham Abulafia, use his system as their starting point; and, finally, that time and again, down into the hasidic era, voices are heard claiming Maimonides for the Kabbalah. All these facts suggest the question whether the customary image of Maimonides as the great rationalist does not, indeed, require some revision or supplementation.[5] It should by no means be summarily concluded that Maimonides's rejection of practical mysticism implies the absence of a positive relationship with theoretical mysticism.[6] Even though it is established that Maimonides vigorously combated astrology, the writing of amulets, and all other forms of magic, it does not necessarily follow that speculative mysticism is alien to him. After all, even kabbalist literature contains passages rejecting magic.[7] Admittedly, a more serious objection is his negative attitude toward the liturgical poets (*payyetanim*).[8] Here he reveals a lack of understanding which cannot be interpreted as the expression of a purely pedagogical stance,[9] but which does demonstrate that Maimonides confronted one specific expression of mysticism, the liturgical hymn, without the slightest effort at appreciation. However, given the essentially magical purpose of the hymn, one could maintain that Maimonides may have rejected it not so much because mysticism was alien to him as because he was hostile to magic.[10] Yet the very fact that this open hostility did not prevent many Kabbalists from claiming him as their own makes it even more urgent to ask what the theoretical stratum is in which this sense of kinship is rooted.[11] The present study will attempt to shed light on this question from several points of view, without seeking to give it an exhaustive treatment. We shall reach the conclusion that Maimonides's system does indeed contain some formal elements of mysticism, which enabled mystics to relate positively to him. On the other hand, the question whether Maimonides should be classified as a mystic with respect to the structure of his teachings and attitudes will have to be answered all the more emphatically in the negative.

I

Formal Analogies to Jewish Mysticism

The Concept of "Secret" in Maimonides

As is well known, the esoteric nature of mystical teachings in Judaism is expressed by the terms *sod* ("secret"), *sithrey Torah* ("mysteries of the Law"), and their equivalents. Obscure though the historical origins of

Jewish mysticism are, and especially its connection with the various schools of prophecy, apocalyptic literature, and Gnosis, a definite esoteric posture, setting down a precise form of transmission, had evolved as early as the tannaitic period. The master-disciple relationship, a phenomenon typical of the sociology of early mysticism, appears in its developed form in talmudic statements relative to the well-known Mishnah Ḥagiga II,1.[12] This exclusive relationship between master and disciple definitely recalls the esoteric character of the hellenistic mysteries. Although an incursion into Judaism of pagan doctrines stemming from the mystery religions can be suggested only with great caution,[13] it appears that the hellenistic notion of "mystery" obtruded, in a formal way, upon the transmission of Jewish mystical doctrines. In view of the nonesoteric posture of normative Judaism,[14] it must be assumed that its form of transmission stemmed from the influence of the hellenistic "mysteries," a fact indicated also by the not infrequent occurrence of the Greek loan word *misturin* ("mystery"). To be sure, this term also is frequently used in a debased sense, but at times it retains its full value and conveys a meaning which, though not organically Jewish, is pregnant with its original signification.[15] Moreover, the fact that one can find a certain affinity to the mystery religions among the Therapeutae, a Jewish sect described by Philo (who refers to ascetic exercises in preparation for visions), also shows the powerful impact of these trends upon the Judaism of that period.[16] In all these mystical movements (among which Philo has to be counted), the master-disciple circle finds its true mystical object in the interpretation of the Torah, particularly of the *ma'aseh bereshith* ("account of creation") and the *ma'aseh merkavah* ("account of the chariot," that is, Ezekiel's vision of the upper world). Here the concept of the "secrets of the Torah" is definitely mystical in character and adapted to that of the "mystery." The appropriation of the secret is not a matter of mere theoretical knowledge, but, analogous to the meaning of the "mystery," is endowed with a transforming, pneumatic force.[17] Phenomenologically speaking, that which is hidden is sheltered with God. Accordingly, the concept of *sithrey Torah*, by reason of its meaning, must be classed with the root *str* in its biblical meaning ("to hide," "shelter"), which survives in rabbinic Hebrew but there also denotes the act of "tearing down," "destroying," "contradicting."

Maimonides takes both the concepts of *sod* and *sithrey Torah* and their specific areas of application, *ma'aseh bereshith* and *ma'aseh merkavah*, from talmudic tradition. In fact, he too considers them the central concern of his work. The elucidation of *ma'aseh bereshith* and *ma'aseh merkavah* is for him the essential content of his *Guide for the Perplexed* (*Moreh Nevukhim*).[18] At every turn he describes these disciplines as *sithrey Torah*, as "secrets," "hidden matters."[19] Yet the same terminology is used here to denote an additional aspect. Maimonides formulated his own entirely different concept of "secret." Abraham Abulafia, in his mystical-speculative commentary on the *Guide,* made the penetrating remark that for Maimonides the term *seter* has a double meaning: it means "secret" as well as "contradiction."[20] Abulafia's interpretation is based on the much-discussed passage in the Introduction to Part I of the *Guide,* in which Maimonides, in the seventh of the seven causes accounting for contrary or contradictory statements, links the phenomenon of contradiction with that of the secret. To talk about a secret means of necessity to talk in contradictions. Hence a contradictory statement points to a secret. Here the innermost motive of Maimonides's concept of *sod* is revealed. From contradiction the road leads to secret. It is not the mystic's need to grasp what is hidden beneath the veil of the written word, but the unsettling realization that there are contradictions between the literal meaning of Scripture and philosophical truth which drives Maimonides to develop his theory of the layers of esoteric and exoteric meaning. After all, he openly admits that he sees no reason to give a new meaning to the biblical text wherever its literal meaning is in harmony with the requirements of philosophy.[21] Only the presence of a contradiction demands the assumption of a deeper level of understanding. The theory of the secret is meant to explain the factuality of contradiction and to dispose of it. But once the contradiction is resolved, the secret as such has been abolished, for by its very nature the secret is merely logical, whereas the secret of mysticism is ontological, inextricably caught in contradictions that are anchored in the structure of the world itself.

It is, therefore, quite appropriate to interpret Maimonides's concept of "secret" in the sense of an esoteric "enlightenment" and to explain it in the context of the intellectual history of his time. The question as to the possible meaning of the esoteric tendency in a nonmystical system[22] can be answered adequately by emphasizing the elitist character of enlightenment during the Middle Ages. When mystics such as Shemtov ibn Gaon (late thirteenth to early fourteenth century) invoke Maimonides's esoteric position in support of their own views,[23] one can respond that this esotericism is grounded in the philosophical attitude of the time and is expressed in a specific theory about the limits of popular enlightenment.[24] Nevertheless, we must not overlook the fact that Maimonides adopts, albeit in a formal sense, an esoteric orientation whose legitimate place is in mysticism, thereby creating the impression of being a legitimate heir of the ancient schools of mysticism. In actual fact, he borrows from talmudic mysticism the elitist principle of selection for the transmission of nonmystical secrets. Hence the concept of the esoteric secret implies not merely that metaphysical cognition is beyond the reach of the masses, but also that it is reserved exclusively for a special circle of disciples which is not at all identical with the circle of philosophers. Thus, in addition to its "enlightenment" component, the definition of "secret" contains a formal mystical feature. This duality is explicitly set forth in the Introduction to Part III of the *Guide*.

> Understand, if you are of those that understand, the magnitude of those matters to which they directed us. They have amply made clear how secretly the "account of the chariot" was treated, and how alien it is to the mind of the common people. It has further become clear that even that part of it that a person graced with understanding did comprehend must not be taught, according to the Torah, except orally to one possessed of certain stated qualities and by communicating to him only "chapter headings."[25]

Nowhere do we find a theoretical reasoning substantiating this principle of tradition which pushes the esoteric character of metaphysical cognition far beyond the limits of a pedagogical measure in the interest of enlightenment. The reason for this lies in the fact that Maimonides simply adopted the principle of transmission that had had its legitimate place in the master-disciple relationship of the authentic talmudic-mystical tradition, and that he did so in a purely formal way, without being able to invest it with any mystical content. In Maimonides, the mystical character of *ma'aseh bereshith* and *ma'aseh merkavah* is a residuum of talmudic mysticism. It is from this mysticism that the specific solemnity which envelops the *mysterium* of the law is transferred to Maimonides, and it is this source which nourishes his profound emotional tie to the secret.

Creative-Elucidative Speculation

Research has thus far not paid sufficient attention to the fact that the doctrine of prophecy in Maimonides's system is paralleled by the doctrine of the "sage." According to Maimonides, a distinction should be made between the prophet, who is the harbinger of the secret,[26] and the sage, who is the legitimate interpreter of the prophet's message.[27] There is a formal analogy between the two. Both prophet and sage have certain qualities: the prophet must possess absolute human perfection, the sage a specific measure of intellectual and moral maturity.[28] To both the secret is imparted. The prophet receives the prophetic message from God by way of the active intellect; the sage receives it from a master who is in possession of the interpretative tradition (*Kabbala*).[29] It is here, as has already been pointed out, that the esoteric principle which Maimonides takes over from the mystical tradition finds its place in his rationalistic system.

At the same time, however, the fact that an alien formal principle has been adopted without being genuinely interwoven with the new fabric of thought has some radical consequences. Maimonides is forced to insist upon the application of the master-disciple principle to the transmission of the "secrets of Scripture" to the sage, but since he himself stands outside the chain of the original mystical tradition, he does not share in the transmission process. He frankly admits as much in the Introduction to Part III. Nevertheless, his awareness of this deficiency assumes momentous significance: it is transformed into determination to replace the tradition which is lacking by creative-elucidative speculation. He justifies this step by his conviction that lack of tradition is not his personal problem, but part of a condition afflicting his day and age as a whole— namely, the tragedy of the breakdown of the tradition that was meant to interpret the secrets of the Torah. He believes that, like the practically oriented Halakhah, the theoretical doctrine of Judaism once had an oral tradition, a metaphysics articulating the secrets of the Torah, but that even the Talmud and Midrash contain no more of it than a few fragments (I,71). He assumes that because of Israel's dispersion, such a living tradition no longer exists in his own day (II,11; I,71). Therefore, he can under no circumstances acknowledge that posttalmudic mysticism possesses an authentic tradition. His historical concept of the disintegration of the metaphysical tradition prevents him from taking such a view. If, in his opinion, even the talmudic era was no longer in full possession of the tradition, how could the pretentious mysticism of the Gaonic era command his confidence? One has to bear in mind that even in Halakhah Maimonides accepts as binding only halakhic literature up to and including the Talmud. To him, whose compendium of the entire Halakhah, the *Mishneh Torah,* explicitly sets the final seal upon the talmudic era, no posttalmudic Halakhah can be authoritative.[30] Thus, his statement that these metaphysical matters had never been set down in writing (Introduction to Part III) doubtless is intended as a barb aimed at contemporary mystical literature.[31] The character of the oral tradition concerning the metaphysics of the "secrets of the Torah" makes it impossible for Maimonides to accept the mysticism recorded in the literature of his time.

In full awareness of this lack of tradition and, indeed, impelled by this awareness, Maimonides proceeds to interpret the prophetic writings. He is entirely aware of the fact that his exegesis is open to questions.[32] But he dares to follow the path of creative spontaneity, thus demonstrating that it is possible to approach the realm of the "secrets" with a speculative-creative attitude. Maimonides shows in exemplary fashion how Ezekiel's vision of the *merkavah* may be explored philosophically. As much as he rejects the mystic contemplation which gives free reign to the imagination, he does accept that kind of *merkavah* interpretation which is based upon scientific premises. Even if, as will be shown further on, the result of such speculation may be anything but mystical, the subsequent development of Jewish mysticism can definitely invoke Maimonides in support of its venture to penetrate the "secrets of the Torah" contemplatively by using philosophical motifs. Even in instances in which its methods of thinking differ completely from those of Maimonides, it could still adhere to the Maimonidean tradition;[33] and even where Maimonides's constructions were in conflict with their authoritative traditions, the mystics did not need to view him as an opponent of their doctrines. They could, with the forbearance of those who held in their hands the tradition so sadly missed by Maimonides, replace the supposed with the true interpretation and do so without "pondering the wearying thought."[34]

By means of this activation the sage moves into the creative sphere on a level with the prophet, as it were. Of course, he could never replace the prophetic message. Yet he can at least attain the level of independent interpretation of the secret. Hence Abraham Abulafia's conception of the "prophetic Kabbala" (*Kabbala nevu'it*) may have evolved not so much in connection with Maimonides's theory of prophecy as on the basis of his doctrine and the demonstration that it was possible to replace tradition by spontaneous reconstruction.[35] The road that leads from reconstructing the meaning of the prophets to the construction of new prophecy is not very long.

Because the *Guide* claims to be nothing else but a venture to reconstruct the lost tradition regarding the "secrets of the Torah," Maimonides's image thereby takes on a quasi-mystical aspect. By seeking to start a new chain of initiates, he becomes a sage himself, a master of the tradition. Only from this point of view can the epistolary form of the *Guide* be fully understood. Its teaching method is tied to the law of double esotericism. The work does not address itself to the masses; what is more, it is intended to teach only a single expressly chosen disciple. Accordingly, it does not spell everything out in detail. The disciple must come to his own conclusions. Here Jewish mysticism encountered much of its own elitism. It was ready to look further into the allusions, having been authorized to do so by Maimonides himself.

II

The Speculative Content of the Secrets

What is the result of Maimonides's independent speculation, detached from the living mystical tradition of Judaism, regarding the secrets of the Torah? Are *ma'aseh bereshith* and *ma'aseh merkavah*, as viewed by Maimonides, to be classified as mystical in the sense of the literary-historical character of Jewish mysticism?

In many passages of the *Guide*, Maimonides defines *ma'aseh bere-*

shith as the "science of nature" and *ma'aseh merkavah* as the "science of things divine"—that is, things metaphysical.[36] An analysis of the doctrines which Maimonides associates with these disciplines clearly shows that they contain practically no mystical motifs. Neither his cosmology nor his specific theology goes beyond the Neoplatonic-Aristotelian system in a manner which would definitely utilize mystical motifs such as we might encounter, say, in the *Sefer Bahir*. Such motifs as the "cosmic tree,"[37] the "channels,"[38] and the *sefirot*[39] are entirely absent. There is no trace of the cosmogony of linguistic mysticism, the *A* and *O* of the Kabbala. Language, letters, and numbers lack any symbolic character. Languages, for Maimonides, are "matters of convention and not something natural, as has long been assumed by some."[40] In the context of this theory about the origins of language, the "sanctity" of the Hebrew tongue is given a completely unmystical interpretation.[41] The meaning of the various names denoting God is something "wherein there lies no mystery" (*khafā'*).[42] The only exception is the Tetragrammaton.[43] Yet when Maimonides, in interpreting it discusses also the talmudic tradition regarding the effect of the knowledge of the Name (b. Qidd. 71a), the doubtlessly gnostic-magic intent of this passage[44] is rendered completely innocuous.[45] In his explanation of the *merkavah* doctrine, too, we miss truly mystical tenets. For instance, the highly mystical concept of the patriarchs ("The patriarchs are the *merkavah*") which, derived from Gen. R. 47:8 and 82:7, already plays a significant role in Judah b. Barzilai, the *Massekhet Aṣilut,* and the *Bahir* as the classical formulation of a doctrine of mystical symbolism,[46] lacks any mystical character in Maimonides. Now and then Maimonides interprets it in the simplest manner by saying: "They [the patriarchs] carry the Throne of Glory within their hearts, since they comprehended Him in truth."[47] In this way, the realm of the secrets is deprived of essential components with which it was endowed by the mystical tradition.

Thus the fact that Abraham Abulafia believes he can develop from the *Guide* a plethora of mystical themes in his commentary on it is of no great significance. The number of secrets which he extrapolates from the text, giving the exact source for each, is thirty-six.[48] Nevertheless, his constant invoking of Maimonides, whose allusions he traces in the attitude of the master's disciple, imposes upon us the obligation to study the legitimacy of Abulafia's mystical interpretations of the Maimonidean doctrine. The following is an analysis of a case which may be considered a paradigm of Abulafia's mode of interpretation.

> With reference to Exod. 24:10, Maimonides (II,26) notes:
> This is a great mystery *(sirr 'aẓīm; sod gadol)*, and you should not consider of small account what the greatest sages of Israel have brought

to light concerning it: that it is one of the mysteries of being and one of the secrets of the Torah (*we-sether mi-sithrey ha-tora*). The verse is thus open to mystical interpretation. However, Maimonides's own explanation of the "secret" is completely unmystical. According to *Guide* I,5, the passage is solely intended to state the shortcomings of the visionary act described in Exod. 24:10, not to describe the manner of seeing. This vision, Maimonides said, was permeated with physical representations. According to *Guide* I,28, what was apprehended in this vision was the true reality of first matter, namely, its origin in God. *Livnat ha-sapir* ("transparency," not the white color) represents matter which is capable of receiving all forms, just as a transparent body is capable of receiving all colors (cf. *Guide*, III,4). The interpretation is continued in II,26, where a reference to Pirqey de R. Eliezer, chapter 3, is added: the prophetic vision refers to the nature of sublunar prime matter. *Livnat* signifies the terrestrial matter created from the snow beneath the divine throne. (Here, in contrast to I,28, *livnat* does denote "whiteness.")

Completely independent of this speculation on Exod. 24:10 is the interpretation given to Gen. 1:7. This passage too is counted among the "mysteries" (II,30). For its interpretation, Maimonides adduces the well-known passage in b. Ḥagiga 14b: "When you come to the stones of pure marble (*avney shayish ṭahor*), do not say 'water, water,' because it is written: 'He that telleth lies shall not tarry in my sight.' " Maimonides comes to the conclusion that there is one common matter to which Scripture refers as "water," but which is divided into three forms. One part was turned into the seas, one part into the firmament, and one part into the water above the firmament. The water above the firmament, however, is not actual but potential water. Hence Rabbi Akiba's utterance has a purely physical meaning. Maimonides cites Aristotle's *Metereologica* and the "men of science." Here is certainly no point of departure for any kind of mystical thought.

What happens to these exegetical points in Abulafia's interpretation? Abulafia (MS Munich 408, fols. 60a–61b) establishes a connection between the above-mentioned entirely separate speculations. He juxtaposes *livnat ha-sapir* with *even ha-sapir* (Ezek. 1:26), basing his analogy on the *Targum* version common to both, doubtless referring to *Guide* III,4, where, however, *livnat ha-sapir* and *even tarshish* (Ezek. 10:9) are said to have been translated in the same way by their respective *Targum*. But here *shayish* (b. Ḥagiga 14b) is obviously equated with *tarshish*. This equation makes it possible to establish a relationship between the speculations concerning *livnat ha-sapir* and *avney shayish*. The analogy, but at the same time the essential difference, between *even* ("stone") and *levena* ("brick") is ingeniously supported by the homiletical adduction of Gen. 11:3ff. But his analogically contrasted pair of concepts is then immediately transformed into a dualism. Both concepts become descriptions of the opposite potencies of the cosmic process. It is from them that the firm upper and fragile lower worlds, respectively, are created. Contrary to Maimonides's interpretation of Pirqey de R. Eliezer, to which Abulafia alludes, this does not mean a distinction between celestial and terrestrial matter—that is, a mere cosmological gradation—but the full breakthrough of the mystic conception of an ontological dualism. Light and darkness, life and death, strength and decay are the hallmarks of this contrast. Maimonides's gradation of the universe into the world of spheres and the sublunar world is given a new meaning, a new accent of existential interpretation. Abulafia obviously is not conscious of being excessive in his interpretation. However, it is clear that he goes beyond Maimonides's intent when he immediately defines light and darkness as allegories of "wisdom" (*hokhma*) and "folly" (*sikhlut*), whose connection is asserted in the "intelligences" (*sekhalim*) as the principle even of the celestial world, as opposed to God's pure sphere of light. This chain of thought terminates in the interpretation of snow as pure darkness, from which the terrestrial world is created. (*Guide* II,30, on the other hand, equates darkness with the elemental fire.) However, this darkness is identical with the "force of the motive power" (*koah ha-yeṣer*), which, given the statement *ki ha-yeṣer ḥakham,* in light of *Guide* II,14 (*ha-teva' ḥakham*), can only mean the "force of nature" (*koah ha-ṭeva'*). In other words, Abulafia constructs a doctrine of three grades which is completely alien to Maimonides: pure light (God); light mixed with darkness (the heavens); and pure darkness (the nature of terrestrial matter). (Cf. *'olam ha-yeṣira* as the fifth and last grade in Abraham bar Hiyya's system of five worlds of light; cf. Gershom Scholem in *Monatsschrift für die Geschichte und Wissenschaft des Judentums* 75 [1931]:172ff.) "Pure darkness" is "like snow that melts and turns into water, that is, it returns to its original state, namely, water in *potentia,* not in actuality." In this way Abulafia interprets the passage in b. Hagiga 14b in accordance with his own system. The passage cautions against equating the upper, here actual, waters with the lower, here potential waters—the exact reversal of Maimonides's view asserting the potentiality of the upper waters and the actuality of the lower ones. This reversal is also connected with Abulafia's interpretation of Hagiga 12a: "*Tohu* is the green line that encompasses the entire world and from which darkness went forth . . . *bohu* is the wet stones immersed in *tehom* from which water goes forth." According to this interpretation, the sphere of the stones had to be that of actual formation (especially if one considers that, along with the other Kabbalists, Abulafia interprets the passage in *Bahir* sec. 2 in the sense of matter (*tohu*) and form (*bohu*). (Cf. Scholem, *Bahir* sec. 2, n. 1.)

Thus there is a considerable difference between Abulafia's interpretation and Maimonides's actual exegesis. For Maimonides, the upper waters are something purely physical, whereas Abulafia regards them as a cosmic symbol. They denote the actual formative forces composed of polar elements (life-death, wisdom-folly, strength-decay) which discharge themselves upon the world of matter below. In other words, Abulafia has turned Maimonides's rationalistic, scientific interpretations into an allegory. The "secret," abolished by Maimonides, is restored, and in a thoroughly mystical manner.

This illustration—and the remaining *topoi* of the thirty-six secrets could be treated in a similar fashion—proves that Abulafia's mystical interpretation of Maimonides does not represent an extension or deepening of Maimonides's explicit thoughts, but rather a fundamental twisting, a *metabasis eis allo genos,* of his views. The ultimate reason for this lies in the fundamentally different attitudes of Maimonidean philosophy and Jewish mysticism.

III

The Difference in Basic Existential Attitudes

Difficult though it is to make a typological distinction between the contemplative mystic and the contemplative philosopher, it is possible to differentiate between the basic attitude of Jewish mysticism in its concrete form and that of the philosophical way of thinking. For, contrary to Neumark's construction, philosophy is as little the outgrowth of monotheistic thought from kabbalist mythology and in conflict with it as Kabbala is a mere relapse into *merkavah* mysticism.[49] Rather, both philosophy and Jewish mysticism are governed by two different, independent, and autonomously developing structures of thought. Hence their susceptibility to trends in intellectual history follows different laws. Though occupying the same cultural space (as for instance in Spain and Provence during the twelfth and thirteenth centuries), they are subject to different influences. As Hans Jonas puts it in the methodological introduction to his book on Gnosticism,[50] the fundamental mold [*Grundbefindlichkeit*] of existence is the primary factor determining the relevance of a given "motif." Seen in this light, there is no doubt that philosophy and Jewish mysticism are based on fundamentally different existential attitudes.[51]

To point out the essential difference at once: we are dealing with a divergence in existential attitude, which reaches its center in the relationship of the subject to the phenomenon of evil. In Jewish mysticism, evil is experienced as having real existence. The experience of the demonic character of existence is a decisive stimulus for speculation. A gnostic heritage is at work here. In the light of the studies of Hans Jonas, it can now be assumed with even greater justification than before that the intellectual revolution denoted by the term *gnosis* has left deep traces in Jewish thought. The apocalyptic element in the Bible, the Pseudepigrapha, and talmudic-midrashic literature attests to this. It seems to us that the actualization of this gnostic attitude is probably based on something deeper than a time-bound influence—namely, on the unique relationship with the demonic which is latent in man in general (probably as an aftereffect of experiences going back to primeval times).[52] Regardless of how Jewish mysticism has speculatively mastered the problem of evil,[53] the original sense of the reality of this phenomenon has survived.

Maimonides's position, on the other hand, represents the antipole of Jewish mysticism, inasmuch as the gnostic impulses inherent in the latter seem to have been completely expunged from his thinking. He is a harmonist through and through. In him, the biblical tradition which attributes the predicates of goodness and purposiveness to creation is combined with the classical Greek tradition of the harmony of the cosmos,[54] forming an exalted optimism, whose experiential force finds expression in his famous theodicy (III,12). The decisive factor in this harmonistic view is the concept of emanation. This concept occurs in both the cosmology and the prophetology as well as in the doctrine of divine providence, thus representing the central axis of the system. Since the same concept also has a significant function in Jewish mysticism, one might be tempted to assume their substantive identity. But it is precisely this shared concept of emanation which reveals the essential differences in their attitudes. This state of affairs can be traced historically to the fact that, even in its original Plotinian conception,[55] the definition of emanation is in fact ambiguous. It seems to us that it represents an unsuccessful attempt to achieve a compromise between the attitude of the Gnostics and that of Greek classicism. At any rate, the concept of emanation lends itself to interpretation in two directions: on the one hand, in the direction of the "lapsing primal pneuma" (that is, in the gnostic sense of a tragic destiny, decay from step to step); on the other hand, in the direction of the eradiating Primal One, which remains undiminished despite the emanations that issue from it and which, indeed, unfolds itself positively in the process of emanation.[56] One can sense the gnostic meaning when Plotinus asks why souls forget God, the Father, and answers his own question by assigning the blame to the descent of the soul (*Enneads* V,1). Thus, in Plotinus, metaphysical cognition has an explicit redemptive character which can only be understood in terms of gnostic yearning for redemption. The detachment of the soul from the world of the senses to the point of *ekstasis,* therefore, represents an act of restoration, a homecoming, a scaling of the heights of the pristine state.[57]

In Maimonides, this gnostic aspect of the concept of emanation and thus also of cognition is absent. Hence the dramatic character of metaphysical cognition in the sense of a mystery of redemption is missing. The function of cognition is the completely undramatic acquisition of immortality through the actualization of man's rational capacity.[58]

On the other hand, there is the possibility of interpreting Plotinus's concept of emanation harmonistically. Here the most important motifs are those of the "source of water" and the "light," and emanation fulfills the function of bringing all gradations of reality into contact with the One. The beauty of the spiritual cosmos is reflected even in the phenomenal world, in which the world soul has combined itself with matter. It is, therefore, precisely by virtue of emanation that the universe is an organic whole, one harmonious cosmos. Thus the Plotinian theodicy rests on the concept of emanation.[59]

Maimonides appropriates this function of the concept of emanation in a specific way. The limitations which he places on the Neoplatonic doctrine of emanation must not be construed to mean that he seeks to attenuate it. He defines emanation as the figurative expression of the fact that God's activity is the activity of an incorporeal being and, therefore, in contrast to the spatial limitations of physical effects, overflows freely in all directions. The Plotinian allegory of the "source of water" is adduced in *Guide* II,12 simply to point out that the workings of God are incorporeal. That Maimonides does not teach the emanation of the world from God[60] is already attested in the passage I,58.[61] However, it would be incorrect to deduce from his rejection of a dynamic pantheism that he has completely reinterpreted the concept of emanation. *Guide* II,12 expresses the specific meaning of the allegory of the source of water by stating that just as the source of water overflows and sends forth its bounty in every direction, so the action of God is incessant, and every substance which is ready to do so receives this influence, which is called emanation. Accordingly, the purpose of the concept of emanation is not to provide a theoretical explanation of creation as such, but to express the fact of the bond between God and the world, the eternal renewal of creation. It is therefore used above all where the "preservation and governance" of the world by God are mentioned. However, this is done to denote not merely the principle of existence (as in I,69) but, albeit in a conceptually undefined manner, the principle of life.[62] The world is governed and maintained by means of the forces emanating from the spheres and by means of the intelligences of the spheres, the angels (II,4–10). True, the concept of emanation is radically reshaped in this manner.[63] But we must not overlook the fact that it still retains one very essential function: it links God and the world and does this, entirely in the Plotinian spirit, by making a harmonistic theodicy possible. If God is He from whom "only the good overflows" (II,4), then "it may in no way be said of God that He produces evil" (III,10). But even matter, despite its association with privation, serves the eternal preservation of existence (ibid.). The demonic potencies—such as death, Satan, and the evil inclination—which play a role in mysticism are simply interchangeable terms for the privation of good that attaches to matter (III,22; II,30). Evil is simply the privation of good.[64]

This serene philosophy stands in diametrical opposition to that of Jewish mysticism, especially its gnostic phases, starting with the *Sefer Bahir*. The *Bahir* makes reference to *tohu* and Satan as positive principles (secs. 2, 9, 93, 109). The impact of this difference extends into the doctrine of attributes. Maimonides sees the stream of emanation as the quintessence of a causality whose nature can be described as "attributes of action" (I,58). True, these attributes encompass a multitude of divine attributes (*middot;* I,54): God's mercy as well as his jealousy, vengefulness, wrathfulness. Basically, however, this polar manifoldness is not carried through with sufficient intensity to provide a profound conception of the problem of the demonic in the world. The attributes of action are not grounded in God's essence but reside in the sphere of relation; they remain mere aspects of the divine as seen by man (I,54). In Jewish mysticism, too, the unknowability of the divine essence is not called in question. But while in Jewish mysticism the *sefirot* represent God unfolding Himself in the movement of His potencies and aspects, Maimonides narrows the scope of *middot* from a polar-ontological to a moral-practical realm. He does not acknowledge the numinous character of the biblical-talmudic God experience, which goes far beyond the borders of rationalism. For this reason, he is capable of summarizing the multiplicity of the *middot* in the collective concept, "emanation of the good." Jewish mysticism, by contrast, has not contented itself with this one-dimensional causality. The one direction of emanation becomes a multiplicity of potencies, those of the *sefirot,* which imply not merely the individuation of the one, unequivocal principle of causality, but qualitatively distinct gradations, archetypical structures of an axiological-ontological kind. Reality is not seen as unidimensional, but in perspective. Hence the phenomenon of emanation in Jewish mysticism does not have the character of a series or succession but of space, of multidimensionality. Seen from this perspective, it becomes possible to understand the symbol of the sefirotic tree and the odd localization of the principles in space.[65] The issue here is the ordering of the potencies according to their intertwined relationships, which cannot be comprehended in the image of a flow from one form to another. Maimonides sees the spheres in the unequivocal order of succession in the gradations of the emanations. Each of the *sefirot* of the Kabbala, on the other hand, despite the order of succession, relates directly to the *Eyn Sof;* they are relatively independent potencies within the total realm of manifestations. Only in this manner can the "left side" become independent so as to give scope to Original Evil, the "Other Side" (*sitra aḥra*), and a demonic "fall." Indeed, the "spheres" of Maimonides have nothing in common with the *sefirot* of the Kabbalah. The ten spheres of Maimonides are ontological gradations of being; the *sefirot* of the Kabbalah are theosophical attributes.

It is true that one can also find in Jewish mysticism the Plotinian-Maimonidean allegory of emanation as a "source of water" (*berekha*).[66] But there the substance of this emanation has the mystical meaning of a *berakhah.*[67] Yet this "blessing" is not a matter of course, something that flows forth naturally. While according to Maimonides the "water of the source" overflows freely in all directions, it is here directed into "channels." Thus, for instance, the letter *gimmel* symbolizes the conduit which receives the water from above and conducts it downward.[68] In this manner, the stream of grace can flow through the worlds without watering them, for it is only at the end of the conduit that the flow becomes efficacious. Thus the emanation motif no longer serves an all-embracing harmonistic theodicy but, rather, describes a mystery. Such an interpretation could evolve only within a frame of mind that still felt the tremors of the gnostic existential anxiety.[69] Here the demonic arouses the yearning for grace; here too is the point of origin of magic for which Maimonides can see no meaningful basis. According to Maimonides, God does not receive in return any benefits from the things under his governance; there is nothing that can affect him (I,72). With Maimonides, causality moves only downward, while the spatially conceived notion of causality in mysticism is in a position also to concede a role to the deeds of man.[70]

Notes

"Maimonides's Attitude toward Jewish Mysticism," translated by Gertrude Hirschler and Alfred Jospe, first appeared as "Das Verhältnis Maimunis zur jüdischen Mystik," *Monatsschrift für die Geschichte und Wissenschaft des Judentums* 80 (1936):305–30; reprinted in Kurt Wilhelm, ed., *Wissenschaft des Judentums im deutschen Sprachbereich* (Tübigen, 1967), 2:441–60.

1. Despite the ambiguous character of mysticism, attempts have been made to demonstrate the existence of one basic law for the mystical mode of thinking. See, for example, Rudolf Otto, *West-östliche Mystik* (1926), pp. 2ff., who, while recognizing the existence of "varieties of expression," asserts that all of mysticism is founded on a uniform basic attitude. In a similar vein, Georg Mehlis, *Die Mystik in der Fülle ihrer Erscheinungsformen in allen Zeiten und Kulturen* (1927), p. 22, has attempted to formulate a uniform definition of the character of mysticism. On the other hand, Joseph Bernhart, *Die philosophische Mystik des Mittelalters* (1922), p. 7, admits that "due to the vagueness and continuous evolution of these two concepts" a consideration of the relationship between mysticism and philosophy cannot be expected to yield final conclusions. Hans Leisegang, in *Religion in Geschichte und Gegenwart*, 2d ed., 4:355, gives a relatively precise definition; however, despite his interpretation of mysticism as grounded in the mysteries, his definition has a latitude which would allow for subsequent varieties of mystical phenomena.
2. *Tarbiṣ* 6 (1935), pp. 334ff.
3. *Moznayim* III, 4–5, pp. 441ff. In J. L. Fischmann [Maimon], ed., *R. Moshe ben Maimon*, 2:279ff., Z. M. Rabbinowitz presents, in a more popular vein, the positive attitude of the Kabbalists toward Maimonides.
4. Cf. Naḥmanides's letter to the French rabbis, *Qoveṣ Teshuvot ha-Rambam Ve-Iggerotav* (Leipzig, 1859), 3:8ff. (*Monatsschrift für die Wissenschaft des Judentums* 9 [1860]:184–95 [hereafter *MGWJ*]). [On the role of the Kabbalists in the conflict over Maimonides's writings, see now Gershom Scholem, *Ursprung und Anfänge der Kabbala* (Berlin, 1962), pp. 349–66.]
5. The catchword "rationalism" cannot be used to distinguish between philosophy and Kabbala, because theosophical Kabbala could be called "rationalist" with hardly less justification than can philosophy. Gershom Scholem, *Das Buch Bahir*, sec. 60, n. 2, in his interpretation of the nonvisual *maḥshava* which transcends the "purely visionary mysticism" of the Gaonic era, aptly speaks of a "mystical rationalism." On the other hand, scholars such as Joel and Leisegang have pointed to the "mystical" element—in the broader meaning mentioned above—that is inherent in many Greek systems.
6. We will not go into more detail in this study regarding Maimonides's negative attitude toward "practical Kabbala," because the facts are evident. Cf. I. Finkelscherer, *Mose Maimunis Stellung zum Aberglauben und zur Mystik* (1894). For the attitude of the Gaonim toward magic, see B. M. Lewin, ed., *Oṣar ha-Ge'onim*, 4:15–27; Martin Schreiner, *MGWJ* 35 (1886):314–19; E. E. Hildesheimer, "Mystik und Agada im Ur-

teile der Gaonen R. Scherira und R. Hai," in *Jakob Rosenheim Festschrift* (1931). [See also Georges Vajda, "Etudes sur Qirqisānī," *Revue des études juives* n.s. 6 (106) (1941–45):87–115.]

7. Indeed, as Gershom Scholem has pointed out, "the inner history of the Kabbala" shows a continual vacillation "in the struggle to determine how deep one should and could go in exploring the depths of the magic element" (*Der Jude*, 6:61).

8. Cf. *Moreh Nevukhim* I,59; A. Freimann, ed., *Responsa*, p. 328 and note.

9. Cf. the interpretation given in Isaak Heinemann, "Maimuni und die arabischen Einheitslehrer," *MGWJ* 79 (1935):143, n. 28 and his comment on Eppenstein. However, in the *responsum* cited by Goldziher, Maimonides speaks only of secular music, which, he says, leads men to stray from moral perfection. "The songs which the Geonim mention as permissible are hymns and songs of praise such as are also mentioned by the author of the *Halakhot*" (*MGWJ* 22 [1873]:179–80). Accordingly, the hymns (*divrey shirot ve-tishbaḥot*) are not halakhically forbidden, and Maimonides's rejection of the *payyetanim* is all the more significant.

10. For the meaning of the hymn, see Scholem, *Der Jude*, 6:61. For the history of the hymn in Jewish mysticism, see S. A. Horodetzky in *Kenesset Divre Sofrim l'Zekher H. N. Bialik*, 1:416ff. [See now Gershom Scholem, *Major Trends in Jewish Mysticism*, rev. ed., pp. 57–62; Scholem, *Jewish Gnosticism, Merkabah Mysticism, and Talmudic Tradition* (1960), pp. 20–30, 75–83, 103–17; Alexander Altmann, "Shirey Qedushah be-Sifrut ha-Hekhalot ha-Qedumah," in Edward Robertson and Meir Wallenstein, eds., *Melilah* 2 (1946):1–24.]

11. Despite its mystical coloration, Maimonides's religious sense of humility, to which Heinemann refers (*MGWJ* 77 [1933]:396ff.), cannot be considered an adequate explanation, even though, according to Koch, such a "theocentric posture" might have influenced a mystic like Meister Eckhart (J. Koch, "Meister Eckhart und die jüdische Religionsphilosophie des Mittelalters," in the 101st annual report of the Schlesische Gesellschaft für vaterländische Cultur [1928], p. 140).

12. See esp. the story about Rabbi Yoḥanan ben Zakkai and Rabbi Ele'azar ben 'Azariah in b. Ḥagiga 14b, and the parallel passage in p. Ḥagiga 9a, as well as analogous accounts in b. Ḥagiga 13a and p. Ḥagiga 9a. For the esoterical transmission of the Divine Names, see also Gen. R. 3:1 and Midrash on Pss. 104:4. It is clear, as M. Joel, *Blicke in die Religionsgeschichte* (1880), 1:151ff. has already shown, that the prohibition of cosmological and eschatological speculation which follows Mishna Ḥagiga II,1 dates from a later period during which it became necessary to check the influence of Gnosticism. But this did not in any way inhibit the development; it only served to intensify esotericism. For the qualities required in order to be entrusted with esoteric lore, see b. Ḥagiga 14a, b. Qiddushin 71a.

13. Cf. Isaak Heinemann's rebuttal of E. Norden and R. Kittel, *MGWJ* 69 (1925):337ff.

14. Particular attention should be given to the protests hellenistic Judaism made against the mysteries—for example, the interpolation of the LXX to Deut. 23:18(17), the polemics of *The Wisdom of Solomon*, and Philo's protests. See Isaak Heinemann, "Die griechische Quelle der 'Weisheit Salomons,' " in *Jahresbericht des jüdisch-theologischen Seminars Breslau* (1920), pp. 150ff.; *Philons griechische und jüdische Bildung* (1932), pp. 175, 452, 525. For the contrast between Judaism and the mystery religions, see also Michael Guttmann, "Beḥinat qiyyum und die-miṣwot," *Bericht des jüdisch-theologischen Seminars Breslau* (1930) and *MGWJ* 76 (1932):319ff.

15. A study of the passages cited in S. Krauss, *Griechische und lateinische Lehnwörter im Talmud, Midrasch, und Targum*, vol. 2 (1899; reprt. 1964) under the heading *misṭirin* (also *misṭurin, misturin*) shows that this term was used as follows: in Exod. R. 19:7, Tanḥuma *lekh lekha*, 19, it denotes election through the covenant of *milah* (to which some circles attributed magical powers); in Gen. R. 98:3 (M. Friedmann, ed., *Pesikta Rabbati* 21:105b), Tanḥuma *va-yeḥi*, 8, it denotes the secret date of the redemption; in Yalkut Ex. 171, the secret of the divine essence in connection with the mystery of the Name of God; in Gen. R. 50:9 (68:12; 78:2), Midrash on Pss. 9:7, the secret of the divine plans; in Tanḥuma *va-yera'*, 5 (*Pesikta Rabbati* 5:14b), the oral tradition which was intended for Israel alone; in Exod. R. 19:1, the mystery of

resurrection. It is commonly used in a wider sense to denote any secret, as in Gen.
R. 74:2; Lev. R. 32:4; Num. R. 20:2 (Midrash on Pss. 114:4); moreover, the term
ba'aley misturin occurs in Gen. R. 71:5 (Yalkut Gen. 126), where it denotes "the
silent," "the reticent." For the spelling and socioetymological origin of the term, see
Theodor-Albeck to Gen. R. 50:9 and 71:5. Note also the resemblance to *mesatrata* in
Dan. 2:22.

16. For a description of the Therapeutae, see Isaak Heinemann, *MGWJ* 78 (1934):10ff. and
Pauly, Wissowa, and Kroll, *Real-Enzyklopädie, s.v.* Heinemann assumes them to be the
link in intellectual history between the apocryphal mysticism of the Book of Enoch and
the Books of Hekhalot in the Gaonic era. [See now Ithamar Gruenwald, *Apocalyptic
and Merkavah Mysticism* (Leiden, 1979).]

17. For the magical power of the knowledge of the Divine Name, see b. Qidd. 71a; for the
elevation of the "initiated" into the state of pneuma, see b. Ḥagiga 14b. For further
references, see Ludwig Blau, *Das altjüdische Zauberwesen* (1898).

18. *Moreh Nevukhim* II,29; Introduction to Part III.

19. The Arabic text has the terms *sitrey tora* and *sod* in the original Hebrew, which clearly
shows that Maimonides deliberately based himself on tradition. In addition, the Arabic
terms *sirr* and *khafiyya* are frequently used to denote "secret" and "mystery."

20. This commentary (see Part II below), which is extant only in manuscript, is of extraordinary value for our systematic analysis, notwithstanding the fact that it transposes
Maimonides into a mystical key. For the present study I consulted the Hebrew MSS
Munich 341 and 408. The passage referred to above is found on fols. 71b–72b of MS
408.

21. *Moreh* II,25. It should be noted that, in admitting the reality of miracles, this principle
excludes mystical speculations of the kind engaged in by the Islamic *Bāṭinīya* (ibid.). It
also renders unnecessary mystical-cosmological speculations of the sort found in *Pirkey
R. Eliezer* (*Moreh* II,26). Our analysis of the concept of *sod* in Maimonides also sheds
light on the basic differences between the allegorisms of Philo and of Maimonides. Cf.
Isaak Heinemann, *MGWJ* 64 (1920):121 and "Altjüdische Allegoristik," *Bericht des
jüdisch-theologischen Seminars Breslau* (1935), pp. 75, 83ff.

22. Cf. Meir ibn Gabbai, *'Avodat ha-Qodesh* (Warsaw, 1883), fols. 151b, 153a.

23. Cf. the well-known passage in his *Migdal 'Oz* on *Yesodey ha-Torah* I,10, where he
refers not only to the legend of Maimonides's supposed "conversion" to Kabbala, but
also to Maimonides's esotericism. For the specific proof of the doctrine of the ten
angelic degrees, see the refutation by Scholem, *Tarbiṣ* 6 (1935), pp. 334ff.

24. See the penetrating investigations by Isaak Heinemann in "Maimuni und die arabischen
Einheitslehrer," *MGWJ* 79 (1935). This article presents an exhaustive analysis of the
Enlightenment component in Maimonides's concept of *sod*. For a characterization of
the medieval Enlightenment, see Leo Strauss, *Philosophie und Gesetz* (1935), pp. 88ff.
[See also now Leo Strauss, *Persecution and the Art of Writing* (1952). In his *Jerusalem
and Athens* (New York: City College, 1967), p. 10, Strauss writes: "In post-biblical
parlance, the mysteries of the Torah (*sithre torah*) are the contradictions of the
Torah"—a phrase that comes close to our formulation mentioned above.]

25. Cf. *Moreh* I, where the concept of "secrets of the Torah" is first defined in pedagogical-
rational terms, but where it is then added that even individuals with a scholarly background may be told only the basic concepts.

26. We follow here Leo Strauss's interpretation of the Maimonidean doctrine of prophecy.
This interpretation, based as it is on Moses Narboni's, places the prophets qualitatively
above the philosophers. In a similar vein, R. V. Feldman [in I. Epstein, ed., *Moses
Maimonides* (1935), pp. 85ff.] stresses the character of prophecy as that of a *scientia
intuitiva* (making a careful distinction between intuition and imagination), and so moves
Maimonides's doctrine of prophecy closer to Judah Ha-Levi's of the *amr ilāhī* (p. 99,
n. 1). It seems that the possibility of such an interpretation was frequently overlooked
during the Middle Ages. Cf. Naḥmanides (*Derasha*), cited in Ibn Gabbai, *'Avodat
ha-Qodesh*, 151a, 152a. Cf., however, the important passage in *Moreh* I,32, cited in
Botarel's commentary on the *Sefer Yeṣirah* (Warsaw, 1834), pp. 35ff.; also *Qoveṣ*
II,23b.

27. Cf. *Moreh* I,34: "He who has acquired an actual knowledge of the sciences is called 'wise in the arts.' " For examples of such authoritative interpretations of the mysteries of Scripture by the "wise men," see *Moreh* I,70; II,10; II,27; II,30; III,22.
28. *Moreh* I,33; I,34; I,62.
29. Thus Maimonides uses the term "Kabbala" simply to denote the form of transmission. As late a source as the *Sefir Bahir* does not know "Kabbala" in the "kabbalistic" sense. Cf. Scholem, *Encyclopaedia Judaica*, "Bahir," col. 976; Bahir, sec. 134. [See now Scholem, *Ursprung und Anfänge der Kabbala*, pp. 32ff. and passim.] See also D. Neumark, *Toledot ha-pilosofia be-Yisra'el*, 1:177. The belief that the prophetic writings can legitimately be interpreted only on the basis of an authoritative tradition also obtains in Arabic mysticism. According to the teaching of the esoteric *ṣūfī* exegetes, Mohammed confided the secret meaning of the revelation to 'Alī. "These teachings, communicated only to a select few, constitute the kabbala of Ṣufism" [Ignaz Goldziher, *Vorlesungen über den Islam*, 2d ed. (1925), p. 158]. The Arabic term for this kind of "tradition" is *naql*, which is also used by Maimonides (for example, in *Moreh* I,5; Munk, 16b; *Moreh* I,62; Munk, 79a). Maimonides employs the familiar term *taqlīd* to denote that "tradition" which imparts the most general theological truths to the broad masses (for example, in *Moreh* I,33; Munk, 37a; *Moreh* I, 35; Munk 41b, 42a). However, this sense of *taqlīd* (cf. Dozy, Suppl. 1881, p. 394, col. 2) must not be equated with the concept opposed by the polemics of the Ẓāhirites and al-Ghazālī (see Ignaz Goldziher, *Die Ẓāhiriten, ihr Lehrsystem, und ihre Geschichte* [1884], pp. 30ff., 201; and *Streitschrift des Gazālī gegen die Bāṭinijja-Sekte* [1916]). An authoritative principle such as the one represented by the concept of *taqlīd* in the Bāṭinīya sect is impossible in Judaism.
30. See A. Schwarz, "Das Verhältnis Maimunis zu den Gaonen," in *Moses ben Maimon*, 1:332ff.; see also W. Bacher, "Die Agada in Maimunis Werken," ibid., 2:131ff. For Maimonides's attitude toward the Aggada, see esp. *Moreh* II,30; *Qoveṣ* I,34b and II,26a.
31. That Maimonides was familiar with this mystical literature is clear from the vigorous fight he waged against it. He considered the *shi'ur qomah* mysticism to be the miscarriage of a preacher (*darshan*). Cf. H. Grätz, *MGWJ* 1 (1859):114. [See now Alexander Altmann, *Studies in Religious Philosophy and Mysticism* (1969), pp. 186ff.] Maimonides makes no mention of the *Hekhalot*, which Judah ben Barzilai considers to be on a par with talmudic material (cf. Neumark, *Toledot ha-pilosofia be-Yisra'el*, p. 175) and which Naḥmanides regards as based upon an ancient oral tradition to the Pentateuch (*Derasha* [Warsaw, 1875], p. 26). As early an authority as Saadia Gaon hypothetically denies that the *Hekhalot* were of talmudic character (Grätz, *MGWJ* 8 [1859]:109). Maimonides gives a good deal of attention to the *Pirkey de Rabbi Eliezer*, which he considers to be of tannaitic origin (see *Moreh* I,61; I,70; II,10). In *Moreh* II,26, we see, precisely as the result of this positive valuation, the considerable embarrassment which of necessity resulted from this collision with an out-and-out mystical conception. See also *Qoveṣ*, II,24b. However, the conception of light as *materia prima* is an ancient midrashic theme; see V. Aptowitzer, "Zur Kosmologie der Agada, Licht als Urstoff," *MGWJ* 72 (1928):363ff. [See now Altmann, *Studies*, pp. 128–39; Scholem, *Jewish Gnosticism*, pp. 56–64.] Notwithstanding Munk's doubts (1:75, n. 4), the conclusion of *Moreh* I,26 clearly shows that Maimonides was acquainted with the mystical writings about the permutations of the Divine Name. For the question whether Maimonides was acquainted with the *Bahir*, see Narboni to *Moreh* I,62; Scholem, *Das Buch Bahir*, sec. 80, n. 3.
32. "Yet it is possible that they are different and something else is intended" (Introduction to *Moreh* III, and conclusion of III,4).
33. It would therefore be no accident if, as Scholem holds in *Die Geheimnisse der Schöpfung, ein Kapitel aus dem Sohar* (1935), p. 17, the author of the Zohar had started out from studies of Maimonides. [Cf. Scholem, *Major Trends*, p. 195.]
34. Cf. *Kuzari* I,65. Mystics frequently stress this element to point up the "ease" with which they attain perceptions. Cf. Ibn Gabbai, *'Avodat ha-Qodesh*, p. 151; Abraham Abulafia, "Epistle on Philosophy and Kabbalah," in A. Jellinek, *Philosophie und Kabbala* (1854), 1:6ff. Conversely, *Bahir*, secs. 46 and 100, points out that error is inevitable, even in mystical contemplation.

35. Cf. Abulafia, "Epistle," p. 12, where reference is made to *Moreh* I,34, that is, to the chapter about the sage.
36. *Moreh*, Introduction; I,33; I,34; I,63; *Yesodey ha-Tora* II,11; IV,10.
37. Scholem, *Das Buch Bahir*, secs. 14, 15, 64, 67, 85, 118.
38. Ibid., secs. 13, 82.
39. Ibid., secs. 87, 89, 92ff., 102ff.
40. *Moreh* II,30 (Munk, II,71b). [For the background of this theory, see Bernard G. Weiss, "Medieval Muslim Discussions of the Origin of Language," *Zeitschrift der Deutsch-Morgenländischen Gesellschaft* 124 (1974):33–41.]
41. By Maimonides's pointing out that there are no Hebrew terms for obscene things (*Moreh* III,8; cf. the rebuttal of this theory by Naḥmanides, Commentary on Exodus 30:13; also Pseudo-Rabad to *Sefer Yeṣira*, I,10).
42. *Moreh* I,61.
43. Ibid. The passage in I,35, where the meaning of the divine names is inaccurately counted among the secrets of the᷒Law, probably also refers to the Tetragrammaton.
44. Cf. Joel, *Blicke in die Religionsgeschichte*, p. 121.
45. On the other hand, see the definitely gnostic accentuation of this talmudic passage in *Bahir*, sec. 80.
46. Cf. Neumark, *Toledot ha-pilosofia be-Yisra'el*, pp. 177, 181, 184.
47. *Qoveṣ* II,5b.
48. MS Munich 408 contains a list of these "thirty-six secrets." The formulation of these *topoi* in MS 408 is identical with that in MS 341.
49. Scholem has the merit of having replaced this construction with a religio-historical view of Jewish mysticism. See his "Zur Frage der Entstehung der Kabbala," in *Korrespondenz-Blatt der Akademie der Wissenschaft des Judentums* (1928). [See now his discussion of the general characteristics of Jewish mysticism in *Major Trends*, chap. 1, and esp. his remarks in *Ursprung*, pp. 6–9.]
50. Hans Jonas, *Gnosis und spätantiker Geist*, vol. 1, *Die mythologische Gnosis* (1934), pp. 1–91.
51. Neumark's reference to the frequent combining of philosophy and mysticism in one person does not constitute a rebuttal, because the leap or the evolution from one existential posture to the other is psychologically possible. One need only remember Schelling's transition from the philosophy of science to that of freedom. Under no circumstances can the fact that two objective structures are combined in one person lead to the conclusion that the two must be identical.
52. Cf. Edgar Dacqué, *Urwelt, Sage, und Menschheit* (1927), pp. 258ff.; Oskar Goldberg, *Die Wirklichkeit der Hebräer*, vol. 1 (1925).
53. Cf. Neumark, *Toledot ha-pilosofia be-Yisra'el*, pp. 173, 179. Neumark's attempt to trace an adumbration of the ṣimṣum doctrine in Maimonides also shows that Neumark basically ignored the crucial difference in attitudes.
54. For the Greek concept of harmony, see Jonas, *Gnosis und spätantiker Geist*, 1:519ff. For the intellectual and historical consequences of the Bible's de-deification of the world, see ibid., p. 176, n. 2.
55. Jonas's studies also point in this direction. On Plotinus, see Jonas, *Gnosis und spätantiker Geist*, 1:154, 168ff. [See now 3d ed. (1964).]
56. Plotinus himself sought to reconcile the "descending" and "unfolding" aspects of emanation (*Enneads* IV.8.5). C. Sauter, "Der Neuplatonismus, seine Bedeutung für die antike und mittelalterliche Philosophie," *Philosophisches Jahrbuch* (Fulda, 1910), pp. 371, 396, has already called attention to the contradictory character of the Plotinian concept of emanation.
57. Cf. *Enneads* IV.8.1ff.; V.9.2; VI.9.9.
58. Even Maimonides's Messianism is entirely devoid of the dramatic and apocalyptic meaning which presupposes that the world has descended into depravity (see *Hilkhot Melakhim* XII, and the antiapocalyptic chapter, *Moreh* II,29). For the redemption theme in Gnosticism, see Jonas, *Gnosis und spätantiker Geist*, 1:165, 196ff.
59. Cf. *Enneads* IV.8.3; IV.8.5–6.

60. Such an interpretation of his doctrine was rejected by Plotinus himself (*Enneads* VI.9.9). [For a fuller discussion of the Plotinian doctrine of emanation, see now, among others, J. M. Rist, *Plotinus: The Road to Reality* (Cambridge, 1967), and the studies by Heinrich Dorrie, Klaus Kremer, and Josef van Ess in Kurt Flasch, ed., *Parusia, Studien zur Philosophie Platons und zur Problemgeschichte des Platonismus. Festgabe für Johannes Hirschberger* (1965).]

61. "But unlike that of heat from fire," and so on. Concerning this phrase, see M. Steinschneider, *Alfarabi* (1869), p. 236; cf. Simon van den Bergh, *Averroes' Tahafut Al-Tahafut* (1954), 1:263–64.

62. God is *ḥey ha-ʿolamim*, the "Life of the Universe," *Moreh* I,69; I,72. On the *ʿaravot* as the seat of the principle of life, see *Moreh* I,70. General and particular providence as well as prophecy are likewise explained in terms of emanation (*Moreh* II,36ff.; III,17ff.).

63. Fritz Bamberger, *Das System des Maimonides* (1935), p. 98. Bamberger states that Maimonides has "completely stripped" the concept of emanation of its "dynamic character." It is true that God ceases to be the principle of becoming in the sense of the Aristotelian concept of form. However, in our opinion Bamberger did not give due weight to the important passage in *Moreh* II,12, where, in a thoroughly Plotinian manner, the principle of emanation is said to support the theodicy.

64. On Maimonides's conception of privation as opposed to Kalām, see Z. Diesendruck, "Le-musag ha-heʿder be-torat ha-Rambam," in *Abhandlung zur Erinnerung an H. P. Chajes* (1933), Hebrew sec., pp. 197ff.

65. Thus, the seat of evil is in the north (*Bahir*, secs. 9, 109).

66. Cf. *Bahir*, secs. 4, 82, 85, 89.

67. Cf. the etymological interpretation *berakha* = *berekha*, which is already found in the Midrash; see Scholem, *Das Buch Bahir*, sec. 90, n. 10.

68. Cf. *Bahir*, secs. 13, 82.

69. Cf. Scholem, *Geheimnisse der Schöpfung*, p. 38. For the terminology of *Bahir*, which frequently uses the verbs *heriq*, *shaʿav*, and *yanaq* instead of the philosophical terms *heʿeṣil*, *hishpiʿa* and their passive forms, see Scholem, *Das Buch Bahir*, sec. 56, n. 4; sec. 89. This terminology also admits of conclusions regarding the existential posture.

70. This contrast reveals the entire basic conflict between Maimonides and mysticism, which comes to the fore in the interpretation of religious law. However, this subject requires a separate study.

10
MAIMONIDES'S *GUIDE* IN
WORLD LITERATURE

David Kaufmann

erder and Goethe introduced us to the concept of
a world literature in the realms of aesthetics and poetry. However, this
concept had already been known and firmly established in the Middle
Ages in areas that dealt with the sciences and the theory of truth. Although that earlier period has frequently been decried as an age of darkness, there was no tendency to limit or confine culture and knowledge to
any one country, people, or religious faith. Looking back upon the
Middle Ages, we see Syrians and Arabs—particularly the latter—fall upon
the intellectual heritage of ancient Greece with that thirst for knowledge
and hunger for light so typical of aspiring civilizations, incorporating and
absorbing this heritage into their own language and paying idolatrous
tribute to the wisdom of the pagans, and especially to that of Aristotle,
the great teacher of Stagira. During a period which we view as pervaded
and darkened by the fanaticism of the Crusades, champions of Christianity and high-ranking dignitaries of the church hastened to the wellsprings
of their sworn enemies to fill their pitchers with the wisdom of the Muslims, which they bore off in triumph to their homes in the West. Nor did
Jewish thinkers, masters of Jewish literature, recoil from zealously
gathering up in the vessel of their own sacred tongue the spiritual oil
pressed by some of the most celebrated teachers in Christendom. Islam,
church, and synagogue seemed bent upon outdoing each other in their
efforts to transplant the wisdom of the heathens, the achievements of
antiquity, into their own literature. As a result, every creation of the

Greek spirit has been resurrected three times: first in Arabic, next in Latin, and finally in Hebrew.

Thus far, [Jewish scholars] have accomplished only the final third of the task, the compilation of an exhaustive survey of that initial rebirth of ancient scholarship. Notwithstanding the works of Jourdain, Wenrich, Leclerc, and Wüstenfeld, the Arabic and Latin literatures still lack a comprehensive volume such as the one on Jewish literature by Moritz Steinschneider, a monumental achievement which won him an award from the Académie des inscriptions in Paris.[1] But the main points in this development, the most significant facts in this history of intellectual conquests, can be readily surveyed. About 1050 we encounter the work of Constantinus Africanus, the Benedictine friar of Monte Cassino. This honored guardian of Galen's thought (Daremberg wanted to see a monument erected to him either on the hilltop of the monastery or on the shores of the Gulf of Salerno) introduced the writings of the Jew Isaac Israeli, the great physician and philosopher of Kairouan, into world literature by translating them into Latin. Throughout the twelfth century—the golden age of translations—we encounter Christians and Jews jointly devoting their skills to translating products of the Arab intellect. John Hispanus, of the Jewish Ibn Daud family of Seville, and Dominicus Gundisalvi, archdeacon of Segovia—both of them sustained and supported by their patron, Raymond, archbishop of Toledo—collaborated with unquenchable zeal to introduce the treasures of Arabic literature into the Christian world. The great master Gerard of Cremona, king of medieval translators, who died in Toledo in 1187 at the age of seventy-three, was not deterred by his clerical status from making extensive use of Jewish assistance in his almost febrile eagerness to complete his translations of Arabic literature. It is indeed typical of this era that, about the middle of the twelfth century, the Koran was translated into Latin at the request of Petrus Venerabilis, abbot of Cluny, and that the work was done by Petrus of Toledo, a Jew.[2] The finished translation was reviewed and edited for style by two priests, Robert de Rétines and Hermannus Dalmata, who were studying astronomy in Toledo at the time. De Rétines, an Englishman, was later to become archdeacon of Pamplona. As late as the thirteenth century, Michael Scot, the famous translator at the court of the Hohenstaufen emperor Frederick II, was aided in his work by two Jewish friends, Master Andrew and Jacob ben Abba Mari Anatoli.

The social and intellectual interaction between members of different religious faiths is reflected also in the great original creations of the thinkers of that era. As if in gratitude for the flood of light which spread from Toledo over all of western Europe, the schools of Christendom echoed with the illustrious names of the physicians, philosophers, astronomers, and mathematicians of the Arab world. In their veneration of

Aristotle, the Scholastics had also adopted his retinue of Arab disciples and interpreters, so that before long al-Kindi and al-Farabi, al-Ghazali and Avicenna, Avempace, and Averroës were discussed far more often in the disputes of the Scholastics than among their Muslim coreligionists. Notwithstanding their hatred of Islam, the Christian scholars were completely receptive to the influence of Muslim knowledge and listened with a blissful kind of naiveté to revelations from the very power which Christianity was preparing to sweep out of Europe.

In this chorus of foreign-sounding names we can also discern the Latinized appellations of many Jews whose works were swept up in the current of the translators' passion and were introduced to Christian scholarship in Latin garb. In some instances the Latin distortions of the authors' names caused the world to forget, or to fail to recognize, that these individuals were Jews. Thus, William of Auvergne mistook Solomon ibn Gabirol, author of The Fountain of Life [Mekor Ḥayyim] for a Christian because of his Arabic name, Avicebron. But even when a scholarly work was definitely known to be of Jewish authorship, this did not deter medieval savants from consulting it. There is no indication that Isac Judaeus (as Isaac Israeli was usually called), or Abraham Judaeus (the Latin appellation for both mathematician-astronomers, Abraham ibn Ezra and Abraham bar Ḥiyya), or Prophatius Judaeus (the Latin name for Jacob ben Mahir), to cite only a few of the Jewish names that passed into Latin literature, ever suffered on account of their cognomens.

The transplantation of these works by pagan, Muslim, and Jewish authors into the Latin language, the medium of world literature, may well have been facilitated by the fact that most of them were devoted entirely to scholarship which, independent of the religion of its exponents, did not assume a distinct position contrary to the prevailing religions. Only one book of clearly religious coloration and significance was found worthy of general acceptance into the literatures of its sister (or daughter) faiths, though it definitely was not a product of pure philosophical research, but a basic theological work in its own religion. This book deserves special consideration in any study of medieval cultural history. Completed about 1190 by the Jewish physician, philosopher, and polyhistor Moses ben Maimon (Maimonides), known in Arabic as Maimûni, the book was originally written in Arabic and entitled Dalátat al-Haîrîn: a "guide" for the "puzzled," "confused," "irresolute," or "perplexed." It was an attempt to harmonize philosophy and religion and to provide a philosophical foundation for Judaism's teachings.

The special position assigned to the Guide [Moreh] among other medieval translations, in contrast to works of pure scholarship, demonstrates history's judgment of the intrinsic value of an achievement which more recent generations no longer know how to appreciate. Contrary to an opinion expressed by Salomon Munk, who is usually objective and reliable, and accepted also by Friedrich Überweg in his *History of Philosophy* [*Grundriss der Geschichte der Philosophie*], it must be pointed out that most of the basic conclusions set forth in the *Guide* have had far-reaching significance in philosophy and, above all, in the history of religion. Every section in this work of three parts contains fundamental teachings, bearing the stamp of originality and perfection, which have made their way into literature and everyday life. They are seeds of free inquiry, ferments of illumination and progress, which must be recorded in the history of religious enlightenment as memorable triumphs of the spirit of philosophy. Part I contains a section of epochal importance for the history of the allegorical interpretation of many scriptural terms.[3] It is the portal, as it were, to the entire work, followed immediately by the historically most effective and consequential nucleus of the whole, the doctrine of negative attributes: the negation that anything positive can be said about the essence and the attributes of God.[4] This is a teaching of timeless significance for all monotheistic religions. The appreciation of the Kalām with which this part ends—a presentation of the second bloom of ancient atomism,[5] which is as ingenious as it is objective—has proven to be one of the most valuable documents for the history of medieval thought. The twenty-five propositions, offering judiciously considered arguments and proofs for the creation of the world and for the existence and unity of a creator, had a profound impact on the religious history of the Middle Ages and represent a kind of *Mécanique céleste* in a new meaning, a kinematics employed for theological purposes, a systematic continuation of the Stagirite's theory of constant motion, culminating in the affirmation of the existence and unity of a Prime Mover who created heaven and earth.

The core of Part II, on the other hand, is devoted to a venture at something which in modern parlance we might describe as the "psychology of prophecy." Here, for the first time in the history of religious thought, is a definitive and logical illumination of areas which until then had been considered out of bounds to theological inquiry. Part III is devoted more specifically to Jewish theology, dealing, aside from certain metaphysical and ethical explanations at its beginning and conclusion, primarily with the reasons for Jewish ceremonial law, thus securing the rights of human reason even in a territory where only tradition and blind submission had held sway before. Sustained by a universality of knowledge that strikingly reveals the versatility of his intellect, familiar also with the literature of superstition and pseudepigraphic fraudulence, and endowed with a sharp critical mind which evoked admiration even from a judge of the caliber of Alfred von Gutschmid,[6] Maimonides sets out to illumine the most obscure details of the Mosaic legislation and to demonstrate its historic significance by using the relevant literary sources to show its tendency to act as a defense against pagan concepts and rituals. Always taking it for granted that his readers had a grounding in philosophy, and viewing the teachings of science only as means, as theological armament, and never as ends in themselves, Maimonides was an Aristotelian of consummate training by the lights of his time. Thoroughly at home among the commentators of the "first teacher," familiar and intimate with al-Farabi—whom he held in high esteem—and with Avicenna, Maimonides created in his *Guide* a masterpiece of construction and execution, thought and presentation, whose value not even the changing spirit of the times could diminish. Never casting furtive glances beyond its sphere, the *Guide* is exclusively dedicated to Judaism, whose sources it brings into play constantly and in an original way, side-by-side with the basic rights and demands of innate reason. It was, therefore, natural that the *Guide,* as the finest example of its literary species, should have won respect and prestige even in those religious and literary circles from which one might have thought it would be debarred by virtue of its structure and intent.

I

The *Guide* among the Muslims

If we can rely on a report by Abdallatif, to whom we owe an excellent description of Egypt in the days of Maimonides, made accessible to wider circles by Silvestre de Sacy,[7] Maimonides emphatically refused to permit the publication of his *Guide* in Arabic characters. (Though composed in the Arabic language, the book had been written in Hebrew characters.) Maimonides was probably motivated by the feeling that Muslims might be offended by some of his observations, especially in the part dealing with prophecy, which he felt might be interpreted as being directed against Mohammed. However, Maimonides's prestige as personal physician to Sultan Saladin, and the fame of his book from the very beginning, were too great to make this precaution or prohibition effective. Abdallatif himself had read the book by that time, probably in an Arabic transliteration. Only a short time after the completion of the work, copies in an Arabic transliteration had turned up in southern France and had come into the hands of the author's first Hebrew translator, Samuel ibn Tibbon.[8] Fragments of one of the earliest manuscripts of the *Guide* in Arabic characters have been preserved at the Bibliothèque nationale in Paris. The fact that it was quoted in Arabic writings such as the *Theriac of the Spirits,* a work on Christian theology by the Coptic priest Rashid Abu'l Kheir, shows that the *Guide* had been widely circulated among non-Jews who wrote in the

Arabic language.[9] Before long, Arab writers began to make scholarly studies of it. Thus the work of Abu Abd Allah Muhammad ibn Abi Bekr al Tebrizi contains an Arabic commentary on the twenty-five propositions set down at the beginning of Part II of the *Guide*.[10] This commentary was subsequently circulated in two separate Hebrew translations. One of these, by Isaac ben Nathan of Cordova, also exists in printed form, but a comparison with extant manuscript versions shows it to be virtually useless because it is replete with errors. There is a tradition that one of the Muslim students of the *Guide*, one Abu Ali ibn Hûd al Mursi (so called from his native city of Murcia, Spain), a scion of the ibn Hûd Spanish royal dynasty, lived in Damascus during the second half of the thirteenth century.[11] A *sûfi* (ascetic Muslim mystic) steeped not only in the theology of Islam but also in the theologies of Christianity and Judaism, he associated with the Jews of Damascus, among whom this devout Muslim sometimes—in absentminded rapture—had a drop too much, and whom he led in the study of Maimonides's *Guide*. Bonafoux d'Argentières (Joseph Caspi) records in an account of his travels through the Orient (Tarascon, 1329) that, according to information he had received, Jews had been engaged by the Muslim universities in Fez to deliver lectures on the *Guide* to Arab students, and that Christians demonstrated their admiration for the *Guide* by having it translated.[12] As late as a century thereafter (ca.1430), Simeon ben Ẓemaḥ Duran, who had fled from Spain to Algiers in 1391, records in his encyclopedia of the sciences what Muslim theologians had told him personally: except for the views set forth in his teachings on prophecy, they subscribed to all the doctrines developed by Maimonides in his *Guide*. The book was probably even more widely read from the very outset by Arab physicians and philosophers who, as can be seen from the writings of the Arab medical historians, had always highly respected Maimonides. Al-Kifti, the famous author of a history of physicians,[13] was a close friend of Maimonides's favorite, Joseph ibn Aknin, who had the good fortune to be immortalized because Maimonides dedicated the *Guide* to him. The friendship between al-Kifti and ibn Aknin had been so intimate that, like Marsilius Ficinus and Mercafi after them, they vowed that whoever preceded the other in death would have to send reports from eternity to the survivor.

II

The Hebrew Translations of the *Guide*

Samuel ibn Tibbon

Less than ten years after publication of the *Guide*, Maimonides's admirers, notably Rabbi Jonathan Hakohen, asked Samuel ibn Tibbon, who lived in Lunel, the famed cultural and scholarly center of French Jewry, to make the best possible Hebrew translation of this latest work by the great master from Egypt. No translator had ever found himself faced with a challenge of similar difficulty. Though long familiar, through his father, Judah, with the art of translating from the Arabic, Samuel confronted insuperable difficulties and must have been tempted to give up in despair. With its limited, incompletely transmitted vocabulary, the Hebrew language is suited for the expression of perceptions and feelings, but not for abstractions and logical inferences. Lacking the syntactic resources of other languages, Hebrew from the outset seemed inadequate for the task. The translations of ethical, philosophical, and grammatical writings in which the Hebrew language was awakened to a new scholarly life by Judah ibn Tibbon were easily achieved compared to the endeavor now confronting Samuel: the translation of a work whose wealth of thoughts and concepts embraced all contemporary scientific disciplines and their standard terminologies. However, Samuel's training and the serious concentration with which he approached the material proved equal to the task. In the first place, he spared no effort to insure the accuracy of the text from which he would have to work. Maimonides himself had to confirm the accuracy of the collation which had been prepared in Fostat, upon Samuel's request, from his own manuscript. Samuel studied it thoroughly, reviewed it carefully for doubtful and questionable passages, and provided it with clear annotations. Where he encountered questions or doubts, the translator turned directly to the author for advice and clarification. As a matter of fact, he was not satisfied until he had been able to visit Maimonides at his place of work and receive the master's personal blessing and authorization to publish the work on which he had labored for so many years and with such devotion. On November 30, 1204, fourteen days before Maimonides died in Fostat, Samuel, in Arles, completed his translation of the *Guide*,[14] in which both he and the Hebrew language passed the master's test with flying colors.

Thus at one stroke the Jews of the West had acquired not merely the greatest achievement of the medieval Jewish spirit, but also the language in which they could continue to work and study in the spirit of this trailblazer. The translation, which immediately was disseminated in countless copies to the most distant lands, had an impact rarely enjoyed by any literary accomplishment. The rise of this sun brought a new dawn of scientific knowledge to the communities of Provence, northern Spain, and Italy. Nor did the enlightenment which penetrated the minds in those regions stop at the gates of the houses of study; it also made its way into the synagogues and everyday life. Sermons and scriptural exegesis were the first to reflect the impact of the new trend, which in fact represented a revolutionary change; suddenly the younger generation had acquired a new ideal of education. To be sure, such a profound reshaping of public opinion could not occur without a strong reaction; those whose theories had been refuted or had become outdated by this revolution turned in fury upon the torch which started the fire. But the impact of the *Guide* was so powerful and all-pervasive that its opponents' attempts to destroy it had no more than passing consequences. It is true that ibn Tibbon, who had opened the new movement, was denounced, and that the authorities burned copies of the book in the public squares of Paris and elsewhere. But the flames of these pyres only succeeded in adding yet another halo to this precious book, which by that time had become an imperishable treasure of Jewish literature and of the whole of Jewry. Both the Jews who had denounced it and the Christians who had condemned it were soon to be found among its admirers.

> The Dominicans had sat in judgment on Maimonides; the largest cathedral in Paris had contributed its largest altar tapers to light the funeral pyre for his works; but soon the minds of the celebrated Dominicans Albertus Magnus and Thomas Aquinas were to catch fire from the writings of Maimonides that had just been consigned to the flames.[15]

The *Guide* emerged from the dispute as from a trial by ordeal, unscathed and with greater prestige than before. Its praise was sung in enough poems and epigrams to fill an anthology.[16] The *Guide* itself became invulnerable and an object of reverence, even for opponents of philosophy and free inquiry. Commentary after commentary attempted to penetrate the deeper meaning of its expositions, and soon there was no country or generation that had not contributed a commentator of its own. The experts' reverent admiration was rivaled only by the esteem in which the book was held by connoisseurs: it was every collector's ambition to own a beautifully crafted parchment copy of the *Guide,* a demand which soon created a rewarding task for the skills of scribes and illuminators. Although many manuscripts disappeared after the invention of printing, a few splendid handwritten specimens of ibn Tibbon's translation have survived. Physically, they are downright lavish. The rich golden sheen of the initial letters, the colorful artistic ornamentations, the fine parchment, and the careful script show the love which patrons and artists alike devoted to the production and ornamentation of this book. Another eloquent testimony to the demand for the ibn Tibbon translation is the fact that it was one of the earliest products of the Hebrew branch of Gutenberg's art, an incunabulum most likely published before 1480. It is this translation, in its Venice and Sabionetta editions and their reprints, that has become the focus for the commentators who have devoted their attention to the *Guide* over the centuries.

Judah al-Ḥarizi

The ibn Tibbon translation had hardly begun to circulate when the poet Judah al-Ḥarizi received a commission, either from Marseilles or from Spain, to undertake a new Hebrew translation of the *Guide*. Because ibn Tibbon wanted to remain meticulously faithful to the original, his translation was too obscure, the Hebrew too awkward, labored, and interspersed with a motley collection of foreignisms and new terms, to be suited for popular use. It was a work only for scholars and specialists. The task now was to produce a new version that would be distinguished for the elegance of its Hebrew style. The man who undertook to devote his skill and talents to the *Guide* was the Spaniard Judah al-Ḥarizi. An expert in both Arabic and Hebrew, a master in Hebrew poetry, he had dared to contend with an artist like Hariri for the palm of facility in the infinite variety of the Maqamat style.[17] He was himself the author of a collection of poems describing the rogueries of strolling scholars, of which four known editions were to appear during his lifetime; several presentation copies of his collection have survived. However, this superbly gifted and masterful poet lacked serious purpose as well as knowledge of his subject matter. His procedure seems to have been to take one glance at the Arabic original, followed by two at the ibn Tibbon version. He retained the title which ibn Tibbon had given to his translation and also incorporated a number of Samuel's passages, unchanged, into his own new work, using the older translation as a guide whenever he came upon a stumbling block. Al-Ḥarizi's motto was elegance at any price. Just as he had sought to show in his own poetry that the language of Zion was capable of competing with that of the poets of Araby, so he now wanted to prove that in prose, too, the plain language of the Bible was equal to the subleties of the philosopher's artistic style. To give truth its due, it must be admitted that, artistically, al-Ḥarizi stood head and shoulders above his precursor. Some of his achievements in recoining archaic and coining new terms, in the felicitous application of existing terminology to new concepts, in versatility and pliancy, in syntactic clarity and organic structure, are unique. A comparative study of the two Hebrew translations from this vantage point will yield rare intellectual stimulation. But as far as a deeper knowledge and understanding of the original subject matter are concerned, it soon becomes obvious that this translator found greater satisfaction in the metamorphoses of Abu Said of Seruj than in the profundity of Aristotle. He sees nothing wrong with having Maimonides say that the Stagirite had proven the nonexistence of demons; he does not question the Arabic manuscript from which he worked and in which a copyist had erroneously put "demons" instead of "atoms." He translates proper names as conceptual terms. Thus, for instance, he renders the school of Abul Hasan Ali ibn Ismail al-Ashari, the illustrious founder of orthodox Muslim theology, as a group of sensualists. He uses "liver" instead of "heaviness," "chance" instead of "width," and "similarity" instead of "doubt." He renders "prejudice" as a "council of elders," and, with inexcusable irresponsibility, translates "planes of existence" as "brothers." Even if one makes allowances for the many pitfalls involved in the unvocalized Arabic text from which he was working, it is inexplicable why his translation should have been so full of errors. He also had ibn Tibbon's translation, and in each instance his deviation from the Tibbonite rendering should have given him pause. As a result, both enemies and friends of the *Guide* poured out upon him the full measure of their wrath. Samuel ibn Tibbon, in an index of terminology appended in 1213 to his own translation, heaped scathing criticism upon the work of his competitor. Even Abraham, the gentle son of Maimonides, could not abstain from reprimanding al-Ḥarizi for his carelessness. But al-Ḥarizi's work was literally damned in the dispute over the *Guide* itself, inasmuch as Maimonides's opponents shifted part of their ire from the author onto his translators, and especially onto the irresponsible poet.[18]

In the contest between these two translations, history has ruled against the later version. While ibn Tibbon's translation became one of the earliest publications in the history of Jewish printing, seven-and-a-half centuries were to pass and all but one manuscript copy of the al-Ḥarizi translation were to disappear before this work was first printed, in London in 1851. The fact that the one surviving manuscript (now in the Bibliothèque nationale) on which that printed edition is based dates back to 1234, the year it was completed in Rome, is proof that this translation too was disseminated widely and at an early date. However, even under the best of circumstances, a single manuscript is hardly an adequate basis for a scholarly edition, even when it is utilized with greater conscientiousness and critical skill than this one is. The Schlossberg edition (Vienna, 1876–79), which no longer enjoyed Simon Scheyer's valuable editorial assistance, has errors in almost every line, particularly in Parts II and III. The original manuscript on which this text is based could not possibly have contained so many errors. In this respect, too, al-Ḥarizi did not measure up to ibn Tibbon. Though al-Ḥarizi's translation was used in Spain throughout the thirteenth century and thereafter—even by Jewish authors, such as Naḥmanides[19]—it eventually fell into desuetude, so that its manuscript versions became increasingly rare.

On the other hand, al-Ḥarizi's translation had a historical impact which was far more remarkable than that of ibn Tibbon's work. It was from al-Ḥarizi's version that the *Guide* was translated into Latin and thus became part of world literature. As a result, his translation is to this day considered an important source for the scholarly investigation of the version which made the supreme creation of the medieval synagogue known to the Christian world. Because of its special significance in the history of civilization, but partly also because it is in many ways a brilliant success as a translation seeking to utilize the language of the Bible for the sophisticated expression of philosophical concepts, and thus is a monumental linguistic and literary work, al-Ḥarizi's *Guide* is deserving of a new critical edition.

III

The Latin Translation of the *Guide*

The *Guide* shares the fate of most great historical phenomena in that the exact date when it first entered the Christian world has remained obscure. All of a sudden we encounter traces of the impact of the book in clear-cut evidence of how it was received, without having so much as the shadow of a historic datum indicating the exact date of its translation, much less the identity of the person who did or stimulated the translation. All that can be established with certainty is that a Latin translation of the entire *Guide* was undertaken sometime during the first half, or perhaps as early as the first quarter, of the thirteenth century—in other words, shortly after the *Guide* had been translated into Hebrew. The outstanding exponents of medieval Scholasticism (which came into bloom under the direct impact of the first renaissance of Greek scholarship and its Arab continuators) demonstrated a thorough familiarity with the theological masterpiece by "Rabbi Moyses Judaeus" or Maimonides. Thus there can be no doubt but that a Latin translation of the *Guide* was already in use.[20]

The works of Alexander of Hales (d. 1245), who had produced the first comprehensive *Summa Theologiae* and was called "doctor irrefragibilis et theologorum monarcha," indicate that this great Franciscan Scholastic had occupied himself intensively with the *Guide;* it is a safe conclusion that the *Guide* had long since become a standard textbook for Christian theologians. It is noteworthy that Alexander, and even more so the Christian thinkers who followed him, were less interested in those parts of the book that contained matters of common interest to all monotheistic religions than they were in the expressly "Jewish" portions of Part III.

Deeper, and more verifiable, is the impact of the *Guide* on yet another philosopher of the church and contemporary of Alexander of Hales, William of Auvergne (d. March 30, 1248), who, as bishop of Paris, had been directly and personally involved in the burning of the Talmud in 1242.[21] Maimonides's *Guide* was his primary source of information on Judaism and Jewish literature. It was from the *Guide* that he derived his own views on the meaning of the Mosaic ceremonial laws, their antipagan tendency, and the moral value of the sacrifices. But it was also from the *Guide* that he took the canon by which Maimonides placed limits, as it were, upon the authority of the Stagirite: William considered Aristotle reliable on what transpires in the sublunary sphere down to the center of the earth, but by no means free of errors and mere conjectures when it comes to events beyond that sphere—that is, to questions of true metaphysics.

The impact of the original metaphysical teachings in the *Guide* on church philosophy first becomes apparent in the works of the great master of theology, Albertus Magnus (d. 1280), a Dominican who was called "doctor universalis."[22] The influence of the *Guide* upon the thought and method of this trailblazing teacher was even more profound than one might surmise from his numerous and often substantial quotations from "Moyses Aegyptius." It is discernible especially in Albertus's treatises on prophecy and creation. From Maimonides's views on prophecy, Albertus derived psychological insights into the problems of vision and true prophecy; from the *Guide's* teachings on creation, he took over critical investigations of the antinomian character of our cognition of creation and eternity.

But the Christian scholar most deeply steeped in Maimonides's work was Albertus's disciple, Thomas Aquinas (d. March 7, 1274), known as "doctor angelicus."[23] No part of the *Guide* escaped his painstaking attention, and his major works contain direct and indirect borrowings, quotations and rejoinders, making it clear beyond any doubt that this learned Dominican and powerful intellect was amazingly familiar with Maimonides's book. Thomas consistently finds Maimonides's views on the most important teachings of theology worthy of consideration, regardless of whether or not he agrees with them.

The French Dominican friar and great medieval encyclopedist, Vincent of Beauvais (d. 1264), also was familiar with the *Guide*.[24] His *In Speculum Maius*, a treasury of all branches of knowledge, includes quotations from the *Guide*, without, however, always citing their source.

Richard Simon[25] has already pointed out that Aquinas's disciple Thomas Bradwardine must have consulted a Latin translation of the *Guide* in the preparation of his own work, *De causa Dei contra Pelagium* (a book which also shows his familiarity with the *Fountain of Life* by "Avicebrol," Solomon ibn Gabirol).[26] John Duns Scotus, the great Franciscan Scholastic philosopher (d. 1308), was also well acquainted with the *Guide*.[27]

But the history of culture, even more than the foregoing facts, shows one noteworthy proof of medieval Christianity's keen interest in the *Guide*—namely, the special regard in which the book was held by the great Hohenstaufen emperor, Frederick II. He attracted Jewish scholars to his court, who served as translators and spread abroad some remarks which made Jews in other lands perpetuate his memory gratefully. The great warrior and statesman, the philosopher and heretic, appears much like a medieval rabbi whose ingenious interpretations are passed from mouth to mouth. Three observations in particular attributed to "Fridolic" (as he was popularly known) attest to his intensive preoccupation with the *Guide*. Thus he interpreted a rabbinical explanation which he had learned from the *Guide* to mean that the white snow beneath the divine throne symbolized the *materia prima* because, just as white can absorb all other colors, so it is capable of reflecting the world of forms. Frederick is also supposed to have expressed surprise that Maimonides, who so ingeniously tracked down the most hidden reasons for the Mosaic ceremonial laws, should have failed to furnish an answer to the greatest mystery of them all: the precepts of purification with the ashes of the Red Heifer [Num. 19]. And the emperor, entirely in the spirit of the master and again as a faithful disciple of the *Guide*, reportedly added the explanation that there was a custom among the people of India and the Sabaeans to burn lions, whose ashes purified the defiled but at the same time defiled those performing the sacrifice. Moses, according to the emperor, had incorporated this rite into his own code of laws, substituting the harmless heifer for the dangerous lion. The emperor also raised the question, probably in connection with Part III of the *Guide*, why wild beasts had been omitted from the list of animals fit for sacrifice under Mosaic law. His perceptive answer is supposed to have been that one could properly offer up to the Lord only personal property, whose sacrifice attested to the devotion of the individual making the gift.[28]

Nothing would seem easier than to associate Emperor Frederick himself, great patron of scholarly translations that he was, with the development of the Latin translation of the *Guide*.[29] But knowing the punctiliousness with which Jewish literature recalls even the smallest details of this emperor's personality, it is hardly likely that such a noteworthy fact— if indeed it were a fact—would have been forgotten or left unmentioned. It is more likely that the book was already extant in Frederick's time, in view of the fact that his Italian contemporary, Nicolo de Giovenazzo, founder of the Dominican abbeys in southern Italy, who had been inducted into the order by Saint Dominic himself, studied the *Guide* in its Latin translation with his friend Moses ben Solomon of Salerno.[30] The *Guide* was in all likelihood already well known and no longer regarded as a novelty. The first news of the book's appearance may well have come to the Christian world through the associates of Samuel ibn Tibbon himself, who, as we know, must have had numerous contacts with high dignitaries of the church, thanks to his father, Judah. However, the Latin translation of the *Guide* could not have originated in the south of France, ibn Tibbon's native land, because it is known that it would have been impossible during the early part of the thirteenth century to get Christians and Jews in that region to collaborate in the translation of Arabic writings, and a project of this order could not have been attempted without such collaboration. A more likely place would be Spain, cradle of some of the most important and extensive translations from Arabic literature, and particularly Toledo, the eastern gateway of all medieval scholarship, through which the light of knowledge spread across the civilized lands of the rest of Europe. It was to Toledo that Michael Scot came as a pilgrim—Michael Scot, who had made Averroës accessible to the western world and later joined Frederick II in his effort to master Arabic literature. There ecclesiastical and secular authorities worked together to bring the art of translation into unprecedented full bloom. The Catholic church had set up universities in Tunis and Murcia to recast the knowledge of Arabic and Hebrew into weapons for its missionaries and defenders. Eight Dominican friars were chosen to make the intensive study of these non-Christian literatures their life's work. It is said that even Alfonso the Wise ordered a translation of the Talmud and of the Kabbalah, the Jewish esoteric doctrine, as one of the many tasks which his restless, ambitious mind assigned to the skilled translators at his court. By that time, of course, the Latin translation of the *Guide* had long since become a permanent part of Christian scholarship; however, the fact that so many similar undertakings had originated in Spain may be taken as an indication that Spain also could have been the birthplace of the Latin *Guide*. The fact that a man like Raymond Martin, probably the most learned of the eight Dominican friars, made his own translation of those passages from the *Guide* which he quoted in *Pugio fidei*, his fundamental work of Christain apologetics,[31] does not prove that no other published Latin translation existed at the time, just as the independent translation of a passage from Plato by a contemporary philologist for inclusion in a book does not mean that Schleiermacher's work does not exist. All it means is that Raymond Martin preferred to arrive at his own interpretation of the original text without the crutch offered by another translator.

Thus we cannot answer the question where the Latin *Guide* of the Scholastics originated, and we would not have fared any better with regard to the second, even more urgent question—what became of that Latin translation?—had it not been for the work of Dr. Josef Perles.[32] This Munich rabbi, whom death snatched much too early from the world of scholarship, made a fortunate discovery which helped us to trace the whereabouts and subsequent history of this book. In the former Kaisheim Abbey, Rabbi Perles came upon a parchment codex, a folio volume of 124 sheets, now owned by the Königliche Hof- und Staatsbibliothek in Munich, which he recognized as the long-lost *Guide* in that Latin garb in

which it had first been introduced to the Christian world during the early
decades of the thirteenth century. Further research yielded another even
more significant discovery: a printed edition of this ancient handwritten
translation that has been in existence for over four-and-a-half centuries.
The Latin translation signed by Bishop Augustinus Giustiniani and published in Paris in 1520 turned out to be nothing more than a reproduction
(I will not call it an exact duplicate) of the old Latin manuscript discovered by Perles.

Giustiniani, bishop of Nebbio on the island of Corsica, one of the
most enthusiastic Renaissance collectors of books and manuscripts and
patron of Semitic languages and literatures, surely had never intended to
plagiarize another translator. He may simply have felt that, having
smoothed out some unkempt phrases or plucked away a bit of fluff here
and there, and having seen to it that the style of his edition should be
respectable, he had made enough of a personal contribution to justify
publication of the manuscript under his own name. Giustiniani, who was
a friend of Erasmus, Thomas More, and Pico of Mirandola, and who
prized his own fame as a scholar above his position as bishop and his
functions at court, probably discovered the ancient Latin manuscript in
his library and wanted to get it published as quickly as possible. Even
though the incredibly careless errors which mar this edition are chiefly the
fault of his copyists and typesetters, the work certainly did nothing to
enhance his reputation as an editor. The errors Justus Scaliger, with his
usual sharp eye for mistakes, had already listed in the sixty-second of his
letters contra Isaac Casaubon are by no means the most outstanding
examples of the pitfalls awaiting the unsuspecting reader of this edition.
Scaliger asserted that he could have listed countless others, such as the
translator's consistent confusion of *specialis* with *spiritualis, prophetia*
with *philosophia, bonitas* with *brevitas,* and *altitudo* with *aptitudo.* Ignorance of summaries and abbreviations customarily used in ancient manuscripts gave rise to annoying and at the same time ludicrous misreadings
and misinterpretations. Thus the word *communia* in the manuscript was
printed as *consequentia,* and *et solutionem* was transmogrified into *et
Salomon; communicant* became *cantant, interfectio* became *intentio,* and
Nichomachia, the Nicomachean Ethics of Aristotle, became *necromagia.*
To be sure, the punctuation, about which Johann Buxtorf the Younger
complains with so much indignation, is neither worse nor better than that
of the manuscripts and printed editions of the Latinobardians (who were
always skipping over difficulties); it is more or less the opposite of everything we would expect of diacritical marks. Nevertheless, given the nature
of manuscripts, the Giustiniani edition is preferable in some respects to
the Munich codex; hence the former will always possess reference value
for the establishment of the correct Latin text.

Thus there is no such thing as a "first" or "second" medieval Latin translation of the *Guide*. There is only this one anonymous translation, which Giustiniani prepared for printing with only slight finishing touches, but in which he had no more share and is entitled to no more credit than Jacob Mantino, the respected physician and late Renaissance translator, whose name has also been associated with that translation.[33] In view of the variety of Latin titles under which the book is listed, one is easily tempted to assume that there were a large number of Latin translations. However, all these titles have turned out to be based on varying transmissions and groping efforts to find a better title for one and the same book. The *Guide* is mentioned under an even dozen of Latin titles: *Directio neutrorum; Director neutrorum; Directio perplexorum; Demonstrator errantium; Ductor nutantium; Directio nutantium; Director nutantium; Director dubitantium aut perplexorum; Dux neutrorum seu dubiorum; Doctor perplexorum; Doctor titubantium; Doctor dubitantium.* These titles are used by Raymond Martin, Paulus Burgensis, Alphons de Spina, Giustiniani, Albertus Magnus, and in a Latin manuscript produced in Paris[34] as variants of one and the same thing.

A second translation of the *Guide* did not appear until 1629, if we do not count Vatican MS 4274, which has not yet been examined but which, judging by its title, *Dux neutrorum,* might be identical with the old translation, and if we also omit a Latin version cited by J. Chr. Wolf, which supposedly was prepared by a German Jew during the seventeenth century.[35] The new translation was prepared and published by Johann Buxtorf the Younger, the famous Basel Hebraist. He found that the earlier Latin translation was useless to him because some parts of it were completely at variance with the Hebrew translation by ibn Tibbon, from which Buxtorf worked since he had not been able to get a copy of the original book. He noted thousands of arbitrary changes, discrepancies, and similar problems which he could not explain because he did not know that the Latin *Guide* edited by Giustiniani was not based on the ibn Tibbon version, but the al-Ḥarizi translation. It remained for Perles to make this discovery. Buxtorf was enough of an expert and sufficiently familiar with Latin philosophical terminology, which was still in everyday use at the time, to be able to do without the help of the earlier Latin version. His work rapidly gained such a reputation that, as early as 1634, Jacob Roman,[36] the scholarly book collector in Constantinople, was ready to issue a tripartite polyglot edition of the *Guide,* including the Arabic text in Hebrew characters, the Hebrew translation by ibn Tibbon, and Buxtorf's Latin translation. It was through this translation that no less a figure than Leibniz became acquainted with the *Guide.* His admiration for the author and his work was exceeded only by that of Justus Scaliger. The Royal Library in Hannover still has the precious copy covered with Leibniz's own handwritten Latin notes,[37] showing how the greatest polyhistor of modern times traced, step by step, the workings of an intellect whom he describes on the back cover of the book as a distinguished philosopher, outstanding mathematician, and highly erudite physician and student of the Scriptures. It may be that Leibniz first learned about the *Guide* from Spinoza, who had, among the few Hebrew books in his personal library, a copy of the Venice (1551) edition of the Tibbonite translation.[38]

However, Buxtorf's work did not make the earlier Latin translation obsolete. Giustiniani's edition has become rare, almost like a manuscript, and is virtually unavailable for the study of the sources for the history of medieval theology and philosophy. Accordingly, scholars actively interested in obtaining that version in which the *Guide* was read in medieval Christendom ever since it first became known to the Christian world are now faced with a pressing task: to locate all the available manuscript material relating to the anonymous Latin version. This search will surely yield much material which is at present still buried in various libraries, waiting for someone to stir it to new life. In this connection one's thoughts turn almost spontaneously to Professor Clemens Baeumker of Breslau, the distinguished promoter, patron, and reawakener of the history of medieval philosophy who, together with Count Georg von Hertling, founded the *Journal of the History of Medieval Philosophy* [*Beiträge zur Geschichte der Philosophie des Mittelalters*] as an organ for critical editions, based on manuscripts and incunabula, of fundamental texts. In numbers 2–4 of volume 2 of this journal, Baeumker himself, working with exemplary accuracy and selfless devotion, has presented the Latin version of the other masterpiece of medieval Jewish thought, the *Fountain of Life* by "Avencebrol," the appellation which hid from the Scholastics the true identity of that prince of Jewish poets, the philosopher Solomon ibn Gabirol.[39] In this work, Baeumker made use of all the pertinent manuscripts known to date and added an exhaustive index of terminology and sources. Thus he also would be qualified to undertake the second task now confronting his branch of scholarly endeavor: the preparation of the other basic text of medieval Jewish philosophy, the presentation of the authentic version of that old, anonymous Latin translation of the *Guide,* for which the faulty Giustiniani edition can be no more than one of many sources, and an inferior one at that. The Munich manuscript is no longer the sole extant basis for the preparation of such a text, because fragments of this book have been turned up in other libraries (that of Cambridge [University], for instance), and the manuscript discovered in the Vatican may well contain the complete translation. Future research will yield additional manuscript sources and uncover new, unexpected information about the character and perhaps also the origin of that older piece of work which is certainly a monument to the skill of medieval translators. Then the day may come when al-Ḥarizi's Hebrew translation—which, in the course of history, has suffered enough for the sins of its creator—will also be cleansed of the blemishes and imperfections that various copyists added to later editions. One may hope that in this endeavor, too, conclusive new findings will help lift the veil of anonymity and obscurity which still hides the origins of the Latin *Guide*.

IV
Translations of the *Guide* into Modern Languages

The Castilian Translation of Pedro of Toledo

One of the strangest facts in the glorious history of the *Guide* was only brought to light very recently. During his studies at the Biblioteca Nacional in Madrid, Mario Schiff, an alumnus of the École des chartes in Paris, was the first modern scholar to examine the beautiful KK-9 manuscript, richly ornamented in gold and many colors, which he identified as a Castilian translation of the *Guide*. He has just published the results of his research.[40] Until now, hardly anything has been known about this work except its title; it was like a fleeting shadow which had been briefly called to the attention of the scholarly world only by Menendez Pelayo. But we know now that in the very year in which Vincente Ferrer, the terror and scourge of Spain's Jewish communities, died, the memory of that greatest of Jewish thinkers, a native son of Spain, was still held in such undisputed high esteem that there was a demand for a Castilian translation of the *Guide*. During this tragic period, when on all sides the seeds were sown that eventually came to fruition in the expulsion of the Jews from Spain, we see the work of the Jew Maimonides, clad in a new garb, deeply influence the intellectual life of his native land and enter the sanctuary of his mother tongue. The initiator and moving spirit of this undertaking was Gomez Suares de Figueróa, scion of one of Castile's most prominent noble families, which subsequently produced numerous statesmen, generals, poets, and scholars. A man of philosophical bent and training, de Figueróa was the son of the knight Don Lorenço Suares de Figueróa, grand master of the Order of Saint James of the Sword (also called the Knights of Santiago), who, on the pattern of the Knights Templar, had been charged with the responsibility of keeping the road to the tomb of Saint James in Santiago de Compostela open to pilgrims who flocked to the shrine. Here, then, we still note that medieval open-mindedness which made it possible for a scion of old nobility, the son of a paladin of Spanish Christendom, to wish to study the work of a Jewish theologian. The noble task of preparing the Castilian translation—the "romanization" of the *Guide*—was entrusted to Pedro of Toledo, the son of Master John of Castillo. We know that he completed the second volume of his work in 1419 in Zafra, a town in the province of Badajoz. According to a note at the end of the finished work, the translation of Part III was not completed until February 8, 1432, in Seville. Schiff therefore assumes that the work was completed after the death of Pedro's patron, de Figueróa, who died in 1429. However, it is possible that the 1432 date refers not to the completion of the translation but only to that of this particular manuscript. Its copyist was Alfonso Peres de Caceres, whose name recalls that of Spinoza's brother-in-law, and who probably was a member of a Jewish family which had escaped death by undergoing baptism during the persecutions of 1391 or 1412–14.

Pedro of Toledo, too, must have been a baptized Jew or the son of a Jewish convert to Catholicism. (Schiff also credits him with a treatise on the question why angels cannot be in more than one place at the same time.) Despite his day-to-day occupational pursuits, he must have had sufficient leisure to study not only the philosophical literature of the ancients in their Arabic and Hebrew translations, but also that of the Muslims and the Jews. Contrary to the assumption of his publisher or editor, it seems that Pedro must have known Arabic, for he refers to the pertinent authors only by their Arabic names. Thus he calls Maimonides "El Cordovi" ("the man from Cordova") and Alexander of Aphrodisias (whom he names following chapter 31 of Part I of the *Guide*) "Alixandre Alfaradosi." He refers to Ghazali by his given name, Abu Hamid, to ibn Badja as "Mahomet Abuzecaria" ("son of Yaha"), and to al-Farabi as "Abunacer Alfaravi." He quotes Aristotle in an Arabic translation (*morisca*) and probably also read Ghazali's well-known *Balance of Custom or Conduct,* to which he refers as *El Peso de Las Costumbres,* in the Arabic original. Probably the only reason why he did not translate the *Guide* from Maimonides's Arabic original was that it was practically impossible to obtain a copy of the original Arabic text in the Spain of his day.

On the other hand, Pedro was well informed about the Hebrew translations of the *Guide.* In fact, unless the "four" in his manuscript represents an error in writing or transcription, he must have known as many as four Hebrew translations that were then circulating in Spain. If one wanted to press the point, one could interpret this information to mean that he also knew Mattatiyah ben Ghartom's Hebrew verse rendering of the *Guide.*[41] The fourth translation, in fact, is not in Hebrew at all, but in Latin translation from the Hebrew. This seems to be borne out by his remark about translations based on other translations.

Be that as it may, it is certain that he was thoroughly conversant with the work of Samuel ibn Tibbon and Judah al-Harizi, and that he correctly considered the former as the greater expert on the subject matter and the latter as the more distinguished linguist. Nevertheless, he used al-Ḥarizi rather than the ibn Tibbon version as the basis for his own translation. One glance into Maimonides's dedication to ibn Aknin is sufficient to answer the question as to which of the two translators Pedro had followed. Indeed, the al-Ḥarizi version shimmers through every turn of phrase in Pedro's translation. The extent of his dependence on the al-Ḥarizi text is revealed by the way in which the Castilian translator blundered at the very beginning of the work in connection with a place name. Unlike ibn Tibbon, who rendered it as "Alexandria," al-Ḥarizi, the affected purist, translated it (as did the Egyptian Jews) as the biblical "No Amon," causing the unsuspecting Castilian to come to grief because he did not know that this was a geographical name. Pedro's "hand of separation" (*la mano de tu separamiento*) reflects the poetic imagery of speech by the *maqamat* poet who had felt it necessary to improve upon the dry style of the original. Indeed, the Castilian translation leaned so heavily on the al-Ḥarizi version that it can in many instances be consulted for improving or determining the proper reading of the text.

Pedro of Toledo is fully aware of the difficulty of his task. He never tires of pointing out the possibilities for errors that lie in wait for the novice as a result of the mistakes by previous translators, who were frequently unreliable, or by copyists, who were generally ignorant of the subject matter. . . . Yet Pedro was firmly convinced that he would extricate himself honorably from the thousands of pitfalls along his road because, enthusiastic admirer of Maimonides that he was, he knew his subject matter well and was a conscientious worker.

Pedro's manuscript version is divided into 178 chapters. This fact alone indicates his reliance on the al-Ḥarizi version, for ibn Tibbon's translation was divided into 177 chapters, alluding to the numerical value of the letters in the Hebrew term for "paradise." Pedro's manuscript has survived in its entirety; some of its pictorial ornamentation also is still intact. Moreover, the existence of a manuscript which is now lost but was at one time in the Colombina indicates that this was not the only specimen of its kind. The attention and expertise with which it was studied can be seen from the sharp and abusive comments by a former owner of the manuscript, which cover almost every margin and empty space on the first twenty sheets and show that their author was well qualified to engage in a critical analysis both of the linguistic aspects and of the contents of the translation.

This Castilian translation and the anonymous Latin translation have one common feature: both abridge the quotations from rabbinical texts which the translators felt would not be understood by Christian readers, either because of their epigrammatic terseness or because the concepts to which they referred would be alien to Christian audiences. Extensive paraphrasing therefore would be required to explain them properly to the uninitiated. However, in every other respect the Castilian translation is objective throughout, so that the translation as such does not permit any inference about the translator's Christian origin. A more detailed characterization of Pedro's work must await the publication of additional excerpts from his work.

The Italian Translation by Jedidiah ben Moses (Amadeo de Moise di Recanati)

More than 160 years were to pass before the appearance of the next known translation of the *Guide* into a modern European language—this time Italian. Prior to the recent discovery of the older Castilian version, this translation had gloried in being regarded as "the oldest translation of this work in any living language."[42] Only two copies of this Italian translation, both of them written in Hebrew characters, have survived, one in the manuscript collection of the Königliche Bibliothek in Berlin, and the other in the collection of J. B. de Rossi, who listed this item in his Italian catalogue as early as 1803. The translator, who entitled his work *Erudizione de' Confusi,* introduces himself as Jedidiah or Amadeo, son of Moses of Recanate. He dictated the translation (in 1581 or 1583) to his brother Elijah, who explains, in the words of Jer. 36:18, that he "wrote them with ink in the book."[43] Amadeo was adequately qualified for his task by virtue of his thorough knowledge of Hebrew literature and his training in philosophy and mathematics. His name appears in many a work of Jewish literature, not merely as a manuscript copyist but also as an author in his own right, and he is particularly known for his facility in Hebrew prose and poetry. On Sunday, November 8, 1580, he entered the household of Isaac ben Judah of Urbino as a tutor for the latter's twenty-three-year-old son, Moses. The extent of his secular education is indicated by the fact that he knew Latin, from which he translated, for example, the apocryphal Book of Judith. At the end of the translation, he briefly recapitulates its contents in a Hebrew acrostic poem which consists of the entire Hebrew alphabet and his full name, Jedidiah ben Moses.[44] A statement (which is in fact a nonattributed quotation) in his introduction to his Italian translation of the *Guide* shows that he was also familiar with the works of Tasso, and the fact that in most instances he correctly translated Maimonides's scientific terminology by terms conventionally employed in Latin and in the modern languages proves that he was conversant with the scientific literature of his era. He dedicated the book to Emanuel da Fano with effusive expressions of admiration. [Moritz] Steinschneider held that Emanuel de Fano was identical with Menaḥem Azariah de Fano, one of Italy's most renowned rabbis and Kabbalists.

The association of such a personality with the translation would make it exceptionally significant in the history of Italian Jewish culture. But as long as we are not completely certain of the identity of the person to whom the translation was dedicated, it should be admissible to presume that the patron was some other member of the da Fano family, someone who, unlike the future rabbi of Reggio, was more prominent in practical affairs than in the realm of scholarship.

Amadeo of Rimini, as Jedidiah is frequently called, resembles Pedro of Toldeo in his admiration for Maimonides, in his rejection of unqualified faultfinders, and in his gratitude for his teachings. Amadeo considers the author of the *Guide* to be a consummate master in the humanities; in his eyes, Maimonides was a new Euclid in mathematics and a new Galen in the natural sciences, more divine than Plato and a better astronomer than Ptolemy. Yet Amadeo feels that despite Maimonides's masterly skills and his ability to shed light on even the most obscure issues, his *Guide* presupposed such an extensive scholarly background that the average reader, not endowed with Maimonides's universality, is forced to stay away from it. This realization, and his desire to have as many readers as possible refresh and edify their minds with this wonderful book, impels Amadeo to translate the *Guide* into the "common Italian language with which all are familiar." Nevertheless, regardless of the faults one may find in his work, it is obvious from the samples transcribed into readable Italian and published by Sacerdote[45] that this translation need not fear comparison with any of its precursors and most of its successors with regard to fluidity of language and simplicity of style, which are coupled with a rare lucidity of syntax and sentence structure. It is certain that Amadeo's translation made the *Guide* accessible to many a reader to whom the ibn Tibbon version, from which he worked, would have remained quite literally a closed book.

Nineteenth-Century Translations of the Guide

Another two-and-a-half centuries were to pass before the publication of the next known translation of the *Guide,* but there then appeared a whole series of translations which introduced Maimonides's book into the newer languages of the civilized world. The interval appeared quiet; nevertheless, the *Guide* continued to be studied and admired in Jewish and non-Jewish circles, no less and perhaps even more than it had been in an earlier era. There was a recurrent demand in the scholarly world for the Arabic original of the book. As early as December 10, 1690, Thomas Hyde (d. 1703), chief librarian of the Bodleian Library at Oxford, recommended publication of the original Arab text accompanied by a Latin translation and annotations. Even earlier, in 1654, the noted British Arabist Edward Pococke (d. September 10, 1691) had successfully dealt with the original texts of Maimonides's other writings in his *Porta Mosis*. The *Guide* was destined to exert a new historical influence comparable to its impact at the time it first appeared. It was this book that kindled the spark of light which radiated from Moses Mendelssohn to his coreligionists. This book, too, accomplished the amazing transformation of Salomon Maimon into a German philosopher who set forth his Kantian philosophy in his Hebrew commentary on the *Guide*. The never-ceasing influence and steadily widening distribution of this old but by no means outdated book gave rise to a demand for more modern translations that would be understood by larger numbers of readers.

In 1829 a new Hebrew translation of almost all of Part I of the *Guide*, based on the ibn Tibbon version but showing the new translator's concern for readability and intelligibility, was published in Zolkiev by Mendel Lewin of Satanow. This development is indicative of the circles in which the demand for this difficult book initially arose and then spread during the nineteenth century. Yet only a decade later the demand for this basic work of Jewish literature became so great in the German-speaking countries also that two scholars began to work on a German translation independently but almost simultaneously. In 1838 Dr. Simon B. Scheyer in Frankfurt am Main published a German translation of Part III, the portion of the *Guide* that is particularly significant for Jewish theology. Eminently qualified for this task by his knowledge of the Arabic original, his philosophical training, and his familiarity with the ancient sources, Scheyer was guided by the Arabic original but meticulously checked his understanding of the text against the two old Hebrew translations. Notwithstanding some indications that he was a novice in this field, Scheyer's translation will have enduring value and significance as a scholarly work in its own right.

The following year, 1839, saw the publication of a German translation of Part I by Raphael Fürstenthal (d. Breslau, February 16, 1855) in Krotoshin. With all due respect for Fürstenthal's knowledge of the subject matter and his devotion to the task, it must be said that his work fell far short of Scheyer's because he did not rely on guidance by the original text. The Fürstenthal translation contains not a few comical misinterpretations. Thus, at the very beginning of the book, Fürstenthal's misinterpretation of a salutation caused him to translate the name of Maimonides's favorite disciple as if that scholar had been the cantor of a congregation. Throughout the translation, the *mutakallimûn,* the theologians or dogmatists of the Muslim faith, are rendered as dialecticians [*Wortphilosophen*], and we are not even going to attempt to list the other inadequate renderings and labored turns of phrase with which the work is replete.

Part II of the *Guide* was not translated into German at the time because other would-be German translators were intimidated by the news that a scholar of the caliber of Salomon Munk was about to come to the book's rescue. When the first samples of his version were published, the tidings spread that Munk (b. Glogau, Silesia, 1803), a distinguished expert in the Arabic language who had been trained at the school of Silvestre de Sacy, had made it his life's work to prepare a new edition of the Arabic original and a French translation. This tireless student, who had immersed himself in Maimonides's own sources and the philosophy of the ancient Greeks and their Arab disciples, and who had made the study of the manuscript copies of the original and its two Hebrew translations his field of concentration, became the natural interpreter of his author. He had acquired such a thorough mastery of his text and evolved such a clear and unquestionable conception of his task that even the most terrible tragedy which can befall a scholar—the loss of his eyesight—could not deter him from completing the work he had set out to do. Yet the darkness that had settled over his eyes was brightened by the vision of his patrons, Baron and Baroness James de Rothschild, who assumed the expenses for publishing his monumental work. From that time on, nothing could stop him in his firm determination to see his Arabic and French edition of the *Guide* through the press. In April, 1856, he was able to complete his translation of Part I and his introduction, in which he touched, briefly and with dignified restraint but with all the more moving moral greatness, upon his personal tragedy. It does not require the reverence so beautifully depicted in the painting *The Blind Man and His Guide* to look upon Munk's creation with sympathy and amazement. The work is informed with the spirit of genuine scholarship, with a loving devotion of the subject matter free of all affectation and superficial motivations, and coupled with solid philological training and discipline directed only toward the search for truth. Its elegant format reflects the mentality with which the work was begun and finally presented to the public. Here, for the first time, we have the Arabic text prepared on the basis of a careful, exhaustive study of extant manuscripts, side-by-side with a French translation whose faithfulness and elegance meet the most exacting standards of the present level of scholarship. The work is accompanied by instructive annotations taken from the domain of Arabic philology and philosophy. The other two parts of the translation appeared in 1861 and 1866. Given the circumstances under which the work was done, its successful completion must be regarded as a memorable literary event. It may be that a study of details that were overshadowed by the magnitude of the completed work will reveal the need for emendations and improvements both in the Arabic text and in the French translation. Nevertheless, the book as a whole will always be regarded as one of the most distinguished achievements in the study of the history of medieval philosophy.

Now at last the floodgates had been opened through which the contents of the *Guide* could flow into other European languages. A German translation of Part II was published as early as 1864 by the modern Hebrew poet M. E. Stern, but it is inferior to Scheyer's translation of Part III and even to Fürstenthal's translation of Part I, inasmuch as it is merely a translation of the French version rather than an independent rendering of Maimonides's ideas.

The year 1870 saw the publication of an Italian translation of Part I of the *Guide* by Rabbi David Jacob Maroni of Florence.[46] Printed in Leghorn and entitled *La Guida degli Smarriti,* this work too somewhat timidly follows Munk's footprints, but it also reflects independent work on Maroni's part. Unlike Munk, Maroni, who was addressing himself to a lay public, felt it necessary to enlarge upon many subjects, and he therefore added his own ample notes to the annotations he had taken over from the French translation. As a result his book, the balance of which appeared in 1876, is far thicker than any of the other translations. The translation is prefaced by a reverent biographical tribute to Munk, who had died suddenly on February 6, 1867, . . . and who had been honored while still a young student, by a one-hour interview with Goethe.

In 1878, Dr. Moritz Klein, who now holds a pulpit in Nagybecskerek, published the first part of a Hungarian translation of the *Guide*. Completed in 1890, it was the first addition of a major work of medieval Jewish literature to the burgeoning literature in Hungarian. Klein's translation also relies on Munk's exemplary work and incorporates translations of his most essential notes.

The most independent work among the translations inspired by Munk is the English translation by Dr. Michael Friedländer, begun in 1881, completed in 1885, and published in London as *The Guide of the Perplexed*. Only a few segments of this translation utilize the efforts of other scholars. The introductory biographical chapter on Maimonides and the translation, as well as the footnotes and supplementary annotations, reflect the editor's independent work, marked by a familiarity with the subject matter and personal devotion to the task.

To sum up: this study yields the curious conclusion that, among the literatures in the modern languages, German literature alone lacks a standardized and coherent translation of all of this memorable book. Only Scheyer's work merits serious attention. That three translators of unequal qualifications, differing among themselves even with regard to basic issues of translation, worked independently on a book of such philosophical concentration and stringent terminology tended to impede this vital but difficult task from the very outset. Yet the fact that this fragmented effort has made it difficult for individual readers to get hold of all parts of book at the same time may well stimulate and facilitate the preparation of a new translation. Such a translation would provide German literature with an edition of its own, independent of Munk, of a book that is important not only as a source of knowledge for the history of medieval thought, but also as an effective weapon in today's struggle of ideas, and which therefore can contribute immensely to the enrichment of modern religious thought. In addition to gaining from the continued study of the manuscripts of the Arabic original that have been discovered since Munk's days, as well as of their translations, this German translation would benefit from recent research in the major works of the Arab thinkers to whom modern scholarship has rightfully begun to give increased attention. It would equally benefit from the growing knowledge of Hebrew commentaries on the *Guide* that have been so carefully cultivated through the centuries. These scholarly advances will provide the new translator with an abundance of useful material which should promise a finished work even more perfect than Munk's. Our hope is that the felicitous hand and mind which can both master the material and handle, with consummate art, the noblest of the translator's tools—the German philosophical language—will not keep us waiting much longer.

Notes

"Maimonides's *Guide* in World Literature," translated by Gertrude Hirschler, first appeared as "Der 'Führer' Maimunis in der Weltliteratur," *Archiv für Geschichte der Philosophie* 11 (1898):314ff.; reprinted in *Gesammelte Schriften*, ed. Marcus Brann (Frankfurt am Main, 1910), 2:152–89; reprinted in Kurt Wilhelm, ed., *Wissenschaft des Judentums im deutschen Sprachbereich* (Tübingen, 1967), 2:407–30.

1. *Die hebräischen Übersetzungen des Mittelalters und die Juden als Dolmetscher. Ein Beitrag zur Literaturgeschichte des Mittelalters, meist nach handschriftlichen Quellen* (Berlin, 1893), 1077 pp.
2. Menendez Pelayo, *Historia de los Heterodoxos Españoles* (Madrid, 1877), 1:404, n. 1. Steinschneider makes no mention of this fact. On the other hand, he mentions (ibid., p. 986) another Jewish translator of the Koran, William Raymond de Moncada, who was active during the second half of the fifteenth century.
3. Wilhelm Bacher, *Die Bibelexegese Moses Maimûnis* (Strasbourg, 1896).
4. See David Kaufmann, *Geschichte der Attributenlehre in der jüdischen Religionsphilosophie des Mittelalters von Saadja bis Maimûni* (Gotha, 1877), pp. 428–70.
5. Kurt Lasswitz, *Geschichte der Atomistik*, 1:134–46.
6. *Zeitschrift der Deutschen Morgenländischen Gesellschaft*, vol. 16.
7. *Relation de l'Égypte, p. 466.*
8. Steinschneider, *Übersetzungen*, pp. 410n, 344.
9. Salomon Munk, *Notice sur Joseph Ben-Jehouda* (Paris, 1842), p. 27, n. 1.
10. Steinschneider, *Übersetzungen*, pp. 361ff.
11. Ignaz Goldziher, in *Jewish Quarterly Review* 6:218ff.
12. *Taam Zekeinim* (Frankfurt am Main, 1854). *Mitzrim* is a printer's error. The correct term is *Notzrim* (that is, Christians).
13. Cf. August Müller, in *Actes du huitième congrès international des orientalistes*, sec. I, 1, pp. 17–33.
14. Steinschneider, *Übersetzungen*, p. 420.
15. Kaufmann, *Attributenlehre*, p. 500.
16. M. Steinschneider, *Kobetz al Yad* (Berlin, 1885), 1:1–32, 2:33–37.
17. Cf. the edition of Hariri's translation by Thomas Chennery (London, 1872), editor of the London *Times*, and Steinschneider, *Übersetzungen*, pp. 851–52. Jacob Roman had

already prepared an edition of this book which included the original; see *Revue des études juives* [hereafter *REJ*] 8:89.
18. Kaufmann, *Attributenlehre*, p. 493, n. 182.
19. Cf. the comment by Rabbi Yomtov ben Abraham in his *Sefer HaZikkaron*, 1:55a.
20. Jakob Guttmann, in *REJ* 19:224–34.
21. Guttmann, ibid., 18:243–55.
22. M. Joël, *Das Verhältnis Alberts des Grossen zu Moses Maimonides* (Breslau, 1863).
23. Jakob Guttmannn, *Das Verhältnis des Thomas von Aquino zum Judentum und zur jüdischen Literatur* (Göttingen, 1891).
24. Jakob Guttman, *Monatsschrift für die Geschichte und Wissenschaft des Judentums* [hereafter *MGWJ*] 39 (1895):207–21.
25. *Lettres choisies*, 3:108, no. 16.
26. Georg Bülow, *Des Dominicus Gundissalinus Schrift von der Unsterblichkeit der Seele* (Münster, 1897), p. 103, n. 1.
27. Jakob Guttmann, *MGWJ* 38 (1894):37ff.
28. Cf. references in M. Güdemann, *Geschichte des Erziehungswesens und der Kultur der Juden in Italien* (Vienna, 1884), pp. 104ff.
29. Steinschneider, *Übersetzungen*, p. 433.
30. Ibid.
31. Menendez Pelayo, *Historia*, p. 509, n. 1.
32. *Die in einer Münchner Handschrift aufgefundene erste lateinsche Übersetzung des Maimonidischen "Führers"* (Breslau, 1875).
33. Cf. the author's refutation of this assumption, *REJ* 27:39, n. 5.
34. Perles, *Münchner Handschrift*, "Notes," pp. 1, n. 2; 3, n. 5; 6; 9.
35. *Bibliotheca Hebraica*, 1:858.
36. M. Kayserling, in *REJ* 8:93.
37. Edited by Count Foucher de Careil in *Leibniz, la philosophie juive et la cabale* (Paris, 1861).
38. A. J. Servaas van Rooijen, *Inventaire des livres formant la bibliothèque de Bénédict Spinoza* (The Hague, 1889); Kaufmann's note, ibid., p. 204.
39. Avencebrolis [ibn Gabirol], *Fons Vitae: Ex arabico in latinum translatus ab Johanne Hispano et Dom. Gundissalino* (Münster, 1892–95).
40. *Revista critica de Historia y Literatura* (Madrid, 1897), 2:160–76.
41. Steinschneider, *Übersetzungen*, p. 428, n. 411.
42. Moritz Steinschneider, *Die Handschriftenverzeichnisse der Kgl. Bibliothek zu Berlin*, 2:34.
43. Erroneously interpreted by Gustavo Sacerdoti in *Rendiconti* of the R. Accademia dei Lincei (1892), p. 315, n. 2.
44. Despite an error in the succession of the verses (indicated by the copyist of the Ghirondi MS [21–22] which is in the author's possession), the acrostic reads in the proper order.
45. Sacerdoti, *Rendiconti*, pp. 318–25.
46. Schiff, p. 164, erroneously identified him as a Jesuit priest.

11
SCIENTIFIC ALLEGORIZATION DURING THE JEWISH MIDDLE AGES

Isaak Heinemann

Based on a more precise definition of the nature and motives of allegory than earlier studies have provided,[1] the following essay sets out to write a new page in the history of biblical exegesis.

Allegories are figuratively expressed composites of meaning, in contrast to metaphors, which express only a single phrase in figurative language. An allegorist, therefore, is someone who views larger units, in particular whole narratives and laws, in a figurative manner; he is not someone who interprets individual words, especially attributes of God, in a metaphorical way. This difference is basic to the investigation of medieval interpretations of Scripture, and the right to metaphorical interpretation is undisputed in this study. Allegorization alone is under discussion. Whoever calls the interpretations of words "allegorical"—as is often done—makes it impossible to pose a clear question.

Admittedly, allegory and metaphor have in common that, in addition to their literal meaning, they contain another; the very word "allegory"—"other speech"—expresses this clearly. What is the relationship between the figurative and the literal meaning? In the case of metaphor it is, as a rule, inimical. Whoever understands God's attributes metaphorically says, in effect, that God has no "countenance," that he does not "descend," and so on. This negative aspect of interpretation, the removal of the literal meaning of the word, is at least as important to the exegete as is the positive aspect, the discovery of the figurative meaning. In exceptional cases, the meaning of the word remains and is in fact taken for granted by the deeper meaning. Rachel says to Leah: "Let Jacob, then, sleep with you in the night." According to the Midrash (Gen. R. 72:3), these words really allude to the sleep of death; yet Rachel's separation from Jacob in death is a punishment for having treated the pious man so slightingly in the literal meaning of her words. Therefore we will have to define "metaphor" here as *polysemous interpretation,* whereas in the majority of instances it represents reinterpretation. Allegory, too, called "the continuous metaphor" (Quintilian), disputes the semantic meaning of the word. Philo often emphasizes its impossibility. But is this valid without exception? Or are there allegorical polysemous interpretations as well as reinterpretations? Our investigation will at least have to allow for this possibility.

We shall also have to guard against the danger of imprecision about the motivations of allegorization.

According to the prevalent view, each allegorization serves only the apologetic purpose of appearing to bridge the gap between advanced understanding and the holy documents. It is, therefore, considered to be "an art as indispensable as it is useless" (Dilthey). If this view were correct, we would have no right to speak of "scientific" allegorization.

In reality, however, this view is completely one-sided and can be attributed to the above-mentioned failure to distinguish between allegorism and metaphorism. The oldest allegorical interpretations do refer in part to texts which required no reinterpretation: for instance, to the Greek story of the race between Achilles and Hector (sun and moon) and to the Jewish warning in Proverbs not to commit adultery, which the Septuagint, in accordance with the well-known biblical figurative language and also according to more recent critical exegetes, regards as a warning against religious defection. The Jew Philo sanctions allegorization of Hera and Hestia, surely not for apologetic reasons, but because he regarded it as scientifically justified in view of the character of Greek natural religion.

But even though allegorization served the cause of the poets well, it was of doubtful value to religion, inasmuch as the latter was largely based on belief in a literalism which allegory annulled. It is not surprising that among the first allegorists in Greece were students of Anaxagoras, who had to leave Athens because he was considered an enemy of the people's religion. Plutarch knows of Greeks who see "the abyss of godlessness" in atomizing allegorization of the gods' personalities; in Alexandria pious Jews protested against allegory which abolished the creation story, the personality of the patriarchs, and the validity of the ritual laws.

These facts demonstrate that an account of medieval allegorization will have to reckon with the possibility that scientific motivations played a part in allegorization, whereas apologetic motivations played a part in the fight against it. Moreover, the joy in intellectual games could be fully realized in all these reinterpretations, a fact whose significance in religious life also is becoming increasingly clear.[2]

The following investigation will not cover all of Jewish medieval exegesis. On the one hand, the Karaites, who of course did not tend to deviate from literalism to any substantial degree, have been excluded;[3] on the other hand, so have the Kabbalah and its precursors, in whose case a particularly strong tendency toward esoteric reinterpretation may be assumed. Our attention will focus mainly on philosophical exegesis.

I

Historical Presuppositions

Unlike Greek allegory, Jewish allegorization during the Middle Ages should not be regarded as an original creation, nor, like the hellenistic-Jewish allegory, as a transference of Homeric exegesis to the Bible. Philo, the Midrash, Christianity, and Islam had preceded it in reinterpretation of the Bible. All these precursors share a belief in the divine origin and esoteric meaning of biblical documents. This belief, of course, provided a much more favorable soil for allegorization than does modern rationalism, with its tendency to regard the Bible as one literary document among others, and with its need for precision and clarity.

To what extent Philo influenced medieval allegory—whether directly or through the agency of the Catholic church—will become apparent only in the course of our investigation. But from the very first one has to reckon with the influence of the Midrash. However, medieval interpreters did not regard the ancient rabbinic exegesis as absolutely authoritative, not even in the Halakhah,[4] let alone in the Aggadah.[5] An interpreter like Rashi, who certainly tends to associate himself with tradition, relates Kohelet's call to enjoy life to moderation in eating and drinking; he cites the aggadic reinterpretation of 8:15 together with his own explanation;[6] he relates only the words *v'ra'ah tov* ["and enjoy pleasure"] (cf. 5:17) to religious activity. On the other hand, he goes further than most Aggadists when he interprets not only the "Woman of Valor" in Proverbs as an allegory of Torah, but also the evil woman as a symbol of heathen worship or of unbelief (5:3).[7] Apparently he concluded from the title of the book that it contained parables. But one can also assume that, in his view, the allegorization of the good woman necessarily also required that of the seductress. Rashi clearly demands such deductive interpretation in the introduction to his commentary on the Song of Songs: he had found some midrashic interpretations which were complete in themselves and some which were fragmentary and did not follow the sequence of the

Bible; he does not completely reject the latter because he acknowledges the manifold interpretability of Scripture. Methodologically, however, he adheres to the former, thus following the example of the Targum inasmuch as his commentary also is meant to be read consecutively, whereas the Midrashim constitute only a collection of fragments.[8] In essence, he does not deviate from the rabbis. We cite his posture here merely to show that the medieval exegete, for all his attachment to the ancient Aggadah, had plenty of free play.

Most Jewish philosophers take their terminology from the Arabs. This terminology is not free of ambiguity. The allegorists are designated as *bāṭiniyah;* but *beten* applies in general to the "inner meaning" of Scripture, which many interpreters considered valid in addition to the manifest meaning (ظهر). تاويل can be used to designate any kind of reinterpretation, especially metaphor; this is usually rendered in Hebrew as *perush,*[9] rarely as *derash.*[10] Sometimes it is distinguished from تطبيق, "parallelization,"[11] designating manifold interpretability (defined below) of the literal and allegorical kind.

The justification to spiritualize was based upon a *hadîth* according to which each verse of the Koran has "a manifest and an inner" meaning.[12] But Old and New Testament passages were allegorized too.[13] A deeper meaning is attributed to heathen rites, and the acuity of the allegorists demonstrates itself even in a nursery rhyme.[14] I hope it is not necessary to prove that Islamic allegory did not arise solely from apologetic motives.

However, radical reinterpretation of laws and narratives was uncommon, especially in circles that affected Judaism. To be sure, according to the Brethren of Purity, the literal meaning is meant for the masses and the inner meaning for the initiates who waited for the beyond.[15] But even mystical circles upheld Ghazali's reproof of the "one-eyed" *bāṭiniyah* who, by limiting themselves to the inner meaning, were just as one-sided as the "boors" who rejected all secrets.[16] Hence it is small wonder that Jews paid little attention to them. Only Maimonides [in the *Guide for the Perplexed (Moreh)* II,25] takes a not exactly respectful look at the reinterpretation of biblical miracles by the "devotees of inner meaning."

Christian allegorization was taken much more seriously. How was it regarded by Jews?

The New Testament was well known in Jewish philosophical circles. Maimonides, of course, knows that Christians interpret the Torah "in contradiction to Halakhah," and even goes so far as to say that Jesus explains it in a manner which had to lead to its abrogation.[17] But it is hardly likely that he found allegorization in the Gospels; he may have had in mind the antitheses in the Sermon on the Mount. Paul also is far removed from the allegorisms of the Jewish Alexandrians who regarded biblical characters as symbols of states of the soul, and laws as indicating processes of the soul (circumcision, for instance, as "the excision from the soul of everything excessive"). That hereditary sin was transmitted from the man Adam to us and that the man Abraham was "justified" through his faith are fundamental to Paul's dogma. The laws too he regarded as having to be fulfilled literally until the coming of the redeemer. The exception, namely the reinterpretation of the prohibition to muzzle the mouth of the threshing ox (1 Cor. 9:9) proves the rule because of its special explanation ("Is it for oxen that God is concerned?").[18] Furthermore, the description of the Christians as "Israel in spirit" (Rom. 9:7) was not an allegorization,[19] as Judah Halevi knew (*Kuzari* I,4). But some early Christian documents, and especially the Letter of Barnabas, declare, in a sharp polemic against the Jews, that certain laws of the Torah (for example, the sacrificial laws condemned by the prophets) could not have been meant literally.[20] Origen frequently used allegorization for apologetic reinterpretation of offensive biblical passages. Within the circle of his influence, the literal meaning was, in fact, called *sensus iudaicus,* and the Jews *carnalis populus* and *amici literae.*[21] Even a man like Pascal, who knew Maimonides's *Guide* and its allegorical interpretations, accuses the Jews of completely rejecting allegory.[22] Such exaggeration of the doubtlessly existing contrast is understandable if one is aware that allegorization of the Bible greatly helped missionaries. A twelfth-century Premonstratensian boasts of having refuted a Jew with the help of allegoric reinterpretation.[23] When the convert William of Burgos displays particular joy in allegoric reinterpretations even where there is no need for apologetics (for instance by interpreting the children in Thracians 1:5 as symbols of the senses[24]), one is correct in assuming that he considered Christians' allegoric interpretation of Scripture in general superior to the "carnal" scriptural interpretation of his people, even in instances where it lent support to Christian diacritical teachings.

Allegory among the Jews in the Middle Ages is, then, to be understood in connection with ancient Jewish, Muslim, and Christian allegories and their respective countercurrents.

II

Methodological Approach

During the Middle Ages it was not possible to seek rigorously for the justification of allegorism because a technical term for this form of reinterpretation was not available. But with the framework of a general inquiry into the justification of reinterpreting biblical passages, important methodological comments need to be made.

Saadiah, in the seventh book of his main philosophical work [*Kitab al-Amanat w'al I'tiqadat*], deals with the question of resurrection. He feels he is duty-bound to justify the literal view of the relevant biblical passages.

> We Israelites always keep to the literal sense unless it is contradicted by the observation of the senses (Eve is not the mother of all life, but only of human beings); by reason (God is not fire, but His punishment has the effect of fire); by other biblical passages ("Prove me," Mal. 3:10, is to be restricted with a view to Deut. 6:16); or by tradition (the "forty stripes" of Deut. 25:3 is a rounding-off of thirty-nine). If one were to admit other interpretations one could, on the basis of parallels, apply the prohibitions of lighting a fire on the Sabbath to the drawing up of troops, of leavening to unchastity, and of killing the mother bird together with its young to cruelty in war. The account of the Israelites reaching the middle of the sea could signify their penetration into the enemy army; the standing still of the sun and moon could be taken to mean enduring dominion; the account of creation could indicate the restoration of a people.[25]

Saadiah, then, objects to the allegorizing of Ezek. 37 on the grounds that the unrestrained reinterpretation of biblical passages leads to impossible consequences and that a departure from the literal meaning was admissible only for very compelling reasons. This is what "we Israelites" think; he apparently regards Arabs like the Brethren of Purity, as well as Christians, as his methodological opponents. But he must have known that limitations quite similar to the *ta'wil* existed in Islam,[26] and that, for instance, Augustine admitted the literal meaning alongside the allegorical to a much greater extent than did Origen.[27] If one follows Saadiah's train of thought, there still remains a limited but not inconsiderable amount of freedom for allegorization. If, however, one looks at his examples, one finds that all admissible and proffered reinterpretations concern merely details, whereas the allegorizations he mentions are all wrong. One should, of course, not yet conclude from this that he rejected all allegory. One could even argue that he expressly attributes an inner meaning (*bātin*) to Proverbs and that he applies 31:10ff. to a woman of valor according to the literal meaning, but also allegorically to an exemplary sage.[28] Still, presumably like Rashi, he may have been stimulated by the title "parables,"[29] for allegorization could not exert any kind of stimulus on an exegete as sober as he was.

This point explains the relationship of Abraham ibn Ezra to Saadiah. Ibn Ezra turns against the allegorists in the rhymed prefaces to his two Torah interpretations.

According to the well-known commentary, the third way of interpretation is a way of darkness, the way of those who arbitrarily impute a secret meaning to all things and regard laws and ordinances as riddles.[30] After a few denigrating words against them he admits that "they are correct in one thing," namely, in that "every word and law, large or small, has to be weighed on the scales of the heart" with the aid of that reason which is rooted in divine wisdom. And if a word contradicts either this reason or sense perception, then we look for a secret meaning (*sod*). But whatever reason does not reject, we interpret according to its simple meaning. Why change something obvious into something concealed? And if something obvious and something concealed are in places connected with one another, then the one can be compared to the body and the other to thought—for example, like the circumcision of the flesh to that of the heart and the precious secret (*sod yin'am*) of the tree of knowledge. Here too the words are true in the literal sense, just as nose, tongue, and legs serve dual purposes.

According to the incompletely preserved Torah commentary,[31] the first way is that of the Christian sages, according to whom the whole Torah—the narratives of the first Book of Moses as well as the ordinances and statutes—contains only riddles and similes. Canaanite people are supposed to mean the seven inner organs which we have to subdue; the woman in childbed means the Catholic church and the number of days of impurity furnish the proof;[32] the number of the twelve tribes is said to point to the "apostles of error." This is all vain talk. Each law and each story must be expounded according to its literal meaning to the extent that it is plausible. But it is, of course, true that some things have a secret meaning; they are true in themselves and yet puzzling, like the story of Paradise and of the Tree of Knowledge. The wisdom of the heart must always link itself with the wisdom learned from the mouth of the father.[33] The sure guarantor for all our explaining is the "reason of the heart" which the Holy One has implanted within us. Whatever is opposed to reason equals that which contradicts the senses.[34] . . . If, then, we find something in the Torah that reason cannot support, we have to enlarge or correct the meaning of the word according to the laws of language coined by the first man.[35] We proceed in the same manner with laws if the literal meaning of the wording seems unthinkable (as, for instance, with "circumcise the foreskin of your heart"), for the Torah says concerning all laws that one should do them and live by them. Moreover, God could not possibly frown upon the murder of others and condone suicide in the most cruel manner. . . . And if one were to ask how sentences can be right according to both their literal and their secret meanings, then we answer that precisely this shows the magnificence of the words of the living God vis-à-vis the sages of the people, the authors of books of riddles picturing the blind and the dumb. By contrast, what God did as

He created man can illumine what He did as He gave the Torah. The nose, too, has four functions: to ventilate the brain, to drain it of mucus, to make smell possible, and to enhance our appearance.

Both passages show that the author takes only the Christian allegory seriously, not the Islamic, and this not so much because of its reinterpretation of the stories (to which only the second passage alludes briefly), but because it denies the literal meaning of the laws. Now, ibn Ezra admits on behalf of Judaism first, that everything which contradicts either the senses or reason (which, like the Torah, is God-given) is to be reinterpreted; and second, that many passages of the Torah contain an esoteric meaning. But it does not follow from these two points that the arbitrarily assumed esoteric meaning is to replace the literal sense.[36] Where reinterpretation is accepted, the true meaning has to be established according to the laws of language as coined by Adam—that is, on the basis of the sentence, "The Torah speaks in the language of the sons of Adam"—not according to the whim of the interpreter. This sentence is not applied by Aggadah[37] nor by Saadiah,[38] but is by his successors wherever they reinterpret anthropomorphic turns of phrase. Nor would Saadiah, whose views the author apparently follows, object to this requirement of methodological caution; after all, he indicates that even the allegorical interpretations which he rejects can be attributed to biblical metaphors. Ibn Ezra goes beyond Saadiah by admitting to his pleasure in profound interpretations; however, he thinks this esoteric meaning interferes with the literal meaning as little as the law of circumcision is abrogated by being interpreted as a symbol for the circumcision of the heart's inclinations. Similarly, the story of Paradise is to have, together with its literal meaning, a deeper meaning—which the author, however, does not specify further. Ibn Ezra probably knew that in the writings of many Christian exegetes, among them Augustine, the *sensus mysticus* does, in principle, not invalidate the *sensus literalis*. Nonetheless, he represents the radical allegorists among them, whom he opposes, as raising the question how such ambiguity is possible. He does this for the sake of challenge, not apologetics, for the double meaning is certainly ruled out in texts like Rev. 5:6: "A lamb with seven horns and seven eyes which are the seven Spirits of God sent forth into all the earth." Such beings do not exist for anyone who knows how to use his eyes and tongue.[39] But the divine narratives of Torah nowhere contain such impossibilities. In this way they are superior to the writings of the Christians, who commit the methodological error of applying to the exegesis of the true word of God principles which may be appropriate to their human documents—a remark which pulls the rug out from under his opponents by explaining their standpoint from their own suppositions.[40]

Ibn Ezra and his secret-filled depth must have been much more sensitive to the lure of allegory than Saadiah's dispassionate sobriety. Someone who liked so much to talk in riddles himself must have been greatly attracted by Christian efforts to regard the whole Bible as a book of riddles. Yet he too approves of eliminating the literal meaning only in special emergencies. Furthermore, he does not tell us whether only individual phrases are to be reinterpreted, like "circumcision of the heart" (which no one has ever taken literally), or possibly also complete units of meaning. Because clear technical terminology is lacking, we do not receive a completely unambiguous answer to the question of allegorization here either. Only this much is clear: he rejects reinterpretative allegorization in by far the majority of cases. However, his successors have found that his critical remarks against the Christian method of interpretation, which he sets forth in these short rhymed introductions, need much supplementation.

Crescas confronts the Christians with the fact that they practice baptism in the literal sense although it points to cleansing from sins: the laws concerning the levirate and holidays must be understood analogously.[41] Albo explains that "Torah" means "testimony."[42] And just as the statement "A killed B on Sunday" admits of no figurative interpretation, so figurative language or reinterpretations are not acceptable for the laws of the Torah.[43] This testimony means "truthful," true in the literal sense. It will not do to say that the prohibition of pork was limited to a particular period (according to Paulus) or that it refers only to the evil inclination (according to allegory).[44] Whereas, in the opinion of all the sages, stories like that of Paradise and its rivers contain allusions to higher, more spiritual subjects, nonetheless their existence has not been called into question. The Tabernacle exists in reality while pointing to something higher and more precious; man's tongue, teeth, and lips serve for eating as they do in animals, yet also serve a higher purpose as instruments of speech.[45] Thus the sages have identified the earthly Jerusalem as a simile for the heavenly Jerusalem, without, however, disputing the existence of the earthly one.

Maimonides does not cast an apologetic glance in the direction of Christianity, as do all these exegetes. As he says in his introduction to the *Guide* (6bff.), the biblical verse "Apples of gold in settings of silver" is fundamental to him: "It is a saying that has two meanings." (Thus he understood the difficult '*al 'ofnav.*) The words of the prophets, even if taken literally, contain very useful things, but in their deeper meaning they contain the complete scientific truth. Thus "the strange woman" in Prov. 7:5 ff. designates matter (according to III,8, bad, unreceptive matter in contrast to good matter, the symbol of which is the good woman in Prov. 31:10ff.).[46] The literal meaning is in no way meant to be disdainful. Indeed, Solomon wrote the book "as a warning against unchastity and gluttony" (III,8). But there is a good connection between this literal and the deeper significance, for it is matter which degrades the spirit. The interpretation is based on Plato's comparison of matter with a woman.[47]

Of course, these sentences do not mean that the literal sense is acceptable everywhere. In fact, Maimonides candidly admits (II,25) that in very many passages we must rely on a metaphorical reinterpretation in order to remove anthropomorphisms, and he does not shrink from reinterpreting factual accounts as visions. But in his view, allegorization apparently is admissible only as multiple interpretation, not as reinterpretation. This stance of Maimonides the exegete strikes us as all the more noteworthy because Maimonides the author did not despise the genuine, unambiguous allegorical interpretation. He sent a reply in this very style to his student Joseph ben Yehudah, who had complained of the unfaithfulness of Maimonides's "daughter," who was entrusted to him.[48] In his case, retention of the literal meaning alongside the deeper meaning does not stem, as it does with Saadiah, from uneasiness over the fact that arbitrary reinterpretation cuts the ground from under our feet, as it were, nor, as with ibn Ezra and his successors, from essentially apologetic reasons (else he above all also would allude to interpretation of laws).[49] Rather, it grows from his conviction, which distinguishes him from many philosophers, that the true teacher of his people may and can proclaim the ultimate secrets only to the select, but that he must also transmit the basic teachings of wisdom and morality to the people at large.[50]

Were the philosophers able to follow through with this methodological approach to allegorization in their exegeses?

III

Allegorical Interpretations of the Philosophers

Only wisdom literature and narratives of a certain kind, not laws, are being allegorized by the philosophers.

We saw already that Proverbs, according to the philosophers, contains "parables" and that Saadiah interpreted the two women ethically, while Maimonides and his followers did so according to natural philosophy. But Canticles, too, could be the "Song of Songs" to them only if it were taken to be allegorical wisdom literature. Nevertheless, in accordance with the belief that multiple allegorical interpretations are justified, the spiritual interpretation in no wise excludes the literal interpretation. Ibn Ezra offers a literal interpretation. Gersonides would take some specifics exclusively as literal and exempt them from allegorization,[51] altogether in the spirit of his master Maimonides, who had expressly warned against the danger of converting every detail into an image while interpreting biblical parables.[52] Ibn Ezra follows the basically national interpretation of Aggadah and rejects the psychological (which joins the loftier aspects of the soul to the body) and the astronomical [interpretations].[53] Maimonides mentions the national interpretation in his "Epistle to Yemen" [Iggeret Teman] (3b, 4d, 7c,), but he himself sees in the relationship of the two lovers the symbol of the love between man and God.[54] Since the time of his student ibn Aknin, the metaphysical interpretation, pointing to the connection of the human spirit with the "active spirit" emanating from God, has been very popular.[55]

As in the interpretation of the Song of Songs, philosophy follows the method of Aggadah by understanding the Satan of the Book of Job and the great king of Eccles. 9:14 as symbols of the evil inclination (III,22).[56] The praise of the king who brings the foreign king's daughter home as his bride (Ps. 45) poses difficulties to Catholic exegesis even today.[57] Maimonides sees the king [as a personification of] intellect, and the powers of the thinking soul in the king's daughter. Zor [Tyre] (v. 12) is interpreted as zur ["rock," "fortress"].

Preeminent among interpretations of narratives is the story of Paradise. It is with good reason that it serves ibn Ezra as a prototype of allegorization.[58]

According to Gabirol,[59] Eden is the divine element, the upper sphere, while the garden is the *pleroma* [the highest spiritual sphere].[60] The river is the "mother" of bodies, that is to say, primordial matter. Its four "heads" are the four "roots," or elements. Adam, who names things, stands for the rational soul, Eve for the animal soul, and the serpent for the craving soul (both [of the latter interpretations are] etymologically justified).[61] The Tree of Knowledge symbolizes the sex drive and garments, the body.[62] The spirit, debased through what is lowly, can share in eternal life by partaking of the Tree of Life, that is, through knowledge of God. This way, however, is blocked for the unworthy by the flaming sword, the sun.[63]

Maimonides interprets the Paradise story twice. He stays close to the Bible in the exoteric part of the *Guide* (I,2), but finds, following the Targum, that eating from the Tree of Knowledge could not possibly have endowed man with a likeness to God; he had already been created in the image of God. Indeed, because of his surrender to his imaginings and to physical pleasures, man sinks to levels corresponding to the "measures of the earth," and his punishment is not meted out through the will of God but is rather the inevitable consequence of his defection.[64] At the same time the Fall may well, according to this interpretation, appear as an illustration of the eternal, supratemporal defection of man from his destiny. And Maimonides finds precisely this aspect appropriate for a book written as "a signpost for the earlier and the later"—that is, as a proclamation of supratemporal truths and not only as a historical chronicle. But the outward course of the biblical narrative is not touched by this explanation. One could call it typological;[65] it is not allegorical.

Maimonides's explanation in II,30, where he reckons with mature readers, is quite another matter. He does not "give" this explanation but lets it shine through darkly by using midrashic quotations which he finds altogether excellent but wants to leave without comment so as not to "reveal secrets." According to these quotations, Adam and Eve formed only one being, the serpent was as large as a camel, and on it rode Samael, who did not speak directly to Adam, but to Eve. The serpent defiled her with its dirt, and this was lifted off Israel at Mount Sinai, but never off the heathen. This last saying would be unthinkable, as Maimonides stresses, if the narrative were to be understood literally. But even the further remark that the Tree of Life had a circumference of 500 days' journey Maimonides surely transmits only to show that these Aggadists did not believe in the literal existence of this tree.

Obviously Maimonides sees the allegorical representation of a purely psychic event in the Paradise story. In the Midrashim he cites, "Samael" always means Satan, who tempts Abraham and Isaac. The Tree of Knowledge which God neither has nor will reveal to man of course designates the possession of the ultimate truths which are denied us. But the expression *vayaniḥehu* ["and He placed him"; Gen. 2:15], according to the Aggadah, intimates that God elevated man's rank [among the existent things] and granted him rest such as is denied to beings tied to forms of existence which imply forever coming into being and passing away. Maimonides makes a remark in this connection without referring to anything in the Aggadah. It was, he says, wise that Adam's sons were called Cain and Abel and perished at the same time, although God shows forbearance towards the murderer, but that Seth achieved true existence. Obviously he sees in the first sons the allegorization of striving after possessions and trifles, but in Seth a striving after knowledge which guarantees enduring life.

Levi ben Gershom in his Torah commentary follows Maimonides. The purpose of the Paradise story is instruction concerning the tools which God has given man to achieve happiness (14a). According to Gersonides, this happiness means that our hylic [material] intellect (that is, our intellectual capacity) receives ideas which have emanated from God's "active intellect" and thus achieves an actual existence which outlasts the body.[66] Accordingly, "garden" means the material and "Eden" the active intellect (14b). The Tree of Life is the intelligible order of the lower world. "Good and Evil" signify, as in the Guide (I,2), that which men regard as good and evil, the pleasant and the unpleasant. The rivers designate the impact of the hylic intellect on the other faculties of the soul; the serpent the faculty of imagination; the angels the forms through which we comprehend the intelligible; and the flaming sword which, according to the Bible, blocks the way to Paradise the influence of the active intellect which often strikes like lightning.[67]

Abrabanel, too, understands the Tree of Knowledge in a literal sense, as a transmitter of conventional values, and erects on it a peculiar, culturally pessimistic view of history.[68] His allegorical interpretation (*Comm.* 28; see also 34b) combines Gabirol's essentially cosmological and Gersonides's psychological interpretations. The Garden of Eden signifies the lower world which, with its changing forms, is located within the "comprehensive sphere"; trees and plants in general denote man's requirements which God satisfied; the Tree of Life the perception of the intelligible; and the Tree of Good and Evil the perception of the political sphere. The four rivers designate the four elements as well as the four realms of nature, which are also operative in man as mineral, vegetable, animal, and spiritual powers. And the obligation to cultivate Eden means that man must cultivate his soul[69] and, in particular, guard it against the influences of the Tree of Good and Evil. The consumption of the fruit results from the seduction by the serpent, that is, the powers of imagination and desire.

Most of these allegorizations can certainly be regarded as multiple interpretations. Ibn Ezra says explicitly, as we saw above, that the literal meaning is not canceled. Gersonides takes the narrative of the creation of Eve literally, deducing from it that man is the purpose and cause of woman and therefore entitled to her subservience. But he also sees in the four rivers the known rivers of the earth and recognizes "an especial wisdom in this parable [*mashal*] in that its literal meaning corresponds to reality" (14d). Gabirol's understanding is in doubt. According to ibn Ezra to Gen. 3:1, Saadiah had disputed that the serpent spoke, and in this Gabirol had agreed with him. Did he appropriate the nonallegorizing interpretation of Saadiah, according to which an angel spoke instead of the serpent, or did he totally reject the literal meaning? Maimonides, it seems to me, has certainly done the latter. The omission of the allegorical interpretation in the first book, the deliberate obscurity in the second, and the constant entrenchment behind recognized rabbinic authorities show clearly how aware he was of the boldness of this interpretation. And the reference to the Aggadah concerning the enormous circumference of the Tree of Life can only denote that, in his view, the literal meaning had already seemed unacceptable to the rabbis.

Maimonides's interpretation of the prologue of Job (III,22), too, is to be regarded as reinterpretation, not as multiple interpretation. For Maimonides refers expressly to Resh Lakish in order to maintain that Satan does not exist as a personality. Maimonides believes just as little in personal angels. Both the "Sons of God" and Satan, who is connected to earth and only accidentally among the higher spirits, are nothing but personifications. According to Maimonides's well-known explanation of the name "Uz," they are at home only in the "land 'guess'!"[70]

The allegorization of a law is, indeed, found in the writings of Samuel ben Meir, who was not a philosopher, who referred Exod. 13:9 to the enduring memory of the Exodus from Egypt, not to *tefillin* [phylacteries]. However, ibn Ezra expressly rejects this interpretation.

IV

Semiphilosophical Allegorization of the Post-Maimonidean Period

In the battle over Maimonides's writings, men are repeatedly mentioned who, though they owe their philosophical views primarily to him, go far beyond Maimonides in their use of allegory.[71] "Whatever is contained in the Torah, from creation to the giving of the Law at Sinai, is, according to them, only parable." Abraham and Sarah are said to represent matter and form; the story of the birth of Moses could not be meant literally, else Jochebed had given birth at 130, which would be an even greater miracle than Sarah's—rather, "the house of Levi" [Exod. 2:1] designates "composite man."[72] But they also "shake off the yoke of the practice of the laws and do not take an interest in their literal meaning."[73]

There is a grain of truth in the bitter complaint of the opponents of philosophy that "since wisdom has spread out, piety and fear of sin have come to an end."[74] Contact with Greek philosophy and communication with Christian freethinkers as well has certainly led to a serious questioning of traditional belief. But from these allusions by staunch opponents of science it would be hard to determine to what extent serious men espoused a type of allegory so radical that it denied the historical foundations of Judaism, including the Exodus from Egypt, and disputed the binding nature of the religious laws. A man like Jacob ben Abba Mari Anatoli does show pronounced interest in allegorization; together with his patron, the very freethinking Hohenstaufen Frederick II (died 1250), he examined the philosophical content of the cosmology of *Pirkei de Rabbi Eliezer,* and he thought that snow (par. 3) designated original matter which assumes all forms, just as white assumes all colors.[75] But his very influential *The Instruction of Students* [*Malmad ha-Talmidim*] shows him to be a follower of Maimonides to the extent that in principle he pleads for an allegory of multiple interpretation, not reinterpretation.[76] "The manifest meaning of Scripture benefits all; the hidden meaning is of particular use for the few" (33a). Throughout, the patriarchs are personalities for him (for example, see 14ff.), even though he reads their history essentially because of its religious content. And if, according to him, one can properly fulfil the laws of Shofar and Tallit only with an understanding of their meaning (Foreword, 5a), then this shows his opposition to representatives of a naive, unthinking piety as well as to the denigrators of life under the Law.

One will have to suspend judgment over Levi ben Abraham ben Ḥayyim (ca.1300) until his *Chaplet of Grace* [*Livyat Ḥen*] is generally available. If it is correct that, in his penchant for philosophy, he was even "more moderate than Anatoli,"[77] his allegorization of patriarchal narratives can have been intended only homiletically and not as a denial of their historical existence. This is completely certain in the case of Isaac Arama (d. 1494) who, as an opponent of philosophy, compared it to Hagar, but compared the Torah to her mistress Sarah.[78] And if a man like Moses Isserles, who is primarily devoted to Halakhah, interprets the Purim story allegorically,[79] this is of course no more than a sophisticated game, in consonance with those instances of boldness which the festive mood already occasioned in rabbinic times.[80] Solomon ben Ephraim Luntschitz (d. 1619) even went so far as to allegorize the Ten Commandments (murder means abstention from learning Torah, which is tantamount to sinning against one's soul),[81] but he aimed, of course, only at an edifying game, not at destroying the historical and legal content of Judaism.

Summing up, one might say that those thinkers of the later Middle Ages whose views found an echo in Judaism remained far removed from the [more] radical allegorists of Philo's time. But it is also evident that the radical Christian allegorization which had already impressed ibn Ezra significantly determined the taste of the post-Maimonidean period, just as Christianity exerted a growing influence on Jewish intellectual life while Islam increasingly was displaced, especially from Spain. To what extent this tendency was connected with the fact that the Jewish spirit progressively turned away from the strictly rational methods of philosophy and towards the mysterious depths of kabbalistic interpretations of the world and Scripture cannot be examined within the framework of this monograph.

V

Extent, Motivations, and Content of Medieval Jewish Allegorization

Allegory during the Jewish Middle Ages limits itself, as we have seen, mostly to a narrow range of texts. Even these it does not deprive of their literal meaning, but merely places a deeper meaning alongside. The complaint of the Catholic church concerning the Jews who would have nothing to do with allegory, therefore, is surely somewhat exaggerated but essentially justified.

The church was concerned precisely with that which Judaism rejected: the reinterpretation of historical and legal passages. If, as we indicated in our introduction, allegorization in general threatened historical religion by suspending literalness, the church welcomed this suspension. It could retain the Old Testament in principle, yet drop the historical and legal character of religion. To this extent, [Christian] allegory served to harmonize the biblical text not with the "progressive" ideas of science, but with the norms of its own religion.

Nevertheless, Dilthey's previously mentioned opinion of allegory does not apply to ecclesiastical allegorization. It is neither "indispensable" (Paul managed without it) nor "useless" (that is, in conscious or unconscious opposition to scientific truth, thought up for apologetic purposes). Medieval thinkers believed in a secret meaning of ancient documents—a meaning which only etymological-allegoristic interpretation would reveal—far transcending apologetic interests. Otherwise they would not have "sought gold in Virgil's mire"[82] by means of allegory, nor would Christian allegory have been successful in persuading individual Jews either to appreciate its methods and findings (see above, sec. IV) or even to alienate them from Judaism (see above, sec. I). The allegorical method also was considered to be scientifically superior to "the carnal method of interpretation" and could appear as basically justified to outsiders, just as Philo's interpretation of Homeric gods found approval.

In Jewish allegorization, too, religious motives act in unison with scientific motives but point in an essentially different direction.

In Judaism, allegorization has not served the harmonistic purposes for which it is supposed to have been created. In order to reconcile the biblical and the Aristotelian world views, [the Jewish allegorist] has recourse to metaphor or views events as visions.[83] Probably nowhere is allegorization used to "get rid of" an inconvenient text: the literal meaning of the Paradise story is allowed to stand in addition to its deeper meaning. Even Maimonides, in the first book of the *Guide,* does not regard it as insupportable, as he does the anthropomorphisms. It is true that allegorization was cultivated also for religious purposes; the fact that polysemy could be ascribed to the sacred texts endowed them, in prevailing medieval opinion, with superiority over human documents.[84] Moreover, allegorization, including the polysemous kind, bestowed a higher value on the wisdom literature—above all on the Song of Songs—and conferred a religious sanction upon the philosophical world view. Precisely for this reason one should note how firmly allegorization was restricted [in Judaism] in contrast to Christianity, and how cautiously Maimonides, the only one whose reinterpretations have come down to us, documents his opinion. Obviously there were no illusions concerning the grave threat to the continued existence of Judaism inherent in the reduction or even the removal of the literal meaning of the biblical laws and narratives. Consideration for the religious interests which, according to prevalent opinion, should be the sole rationale of allegorization did as much to restrict allegorization as to promote it in medieval Judaism.

Just as religious motivations went hand-in-hand with scientific ones in Christian allegory, so also in Jewish allegory. The restriction which it imposed certainly was in the interest of preserving the Jewish faith, but it also corresponded to the doubtlessly correct insight that the historical and legal sections of the Bible were meant literally. Allegorization was limited to precisely those sections whose content called for a more profound interpretation—like the stories of the Trees of Knowledge and of Life— or which, as their authors seemed to indicate, were capable of more than one interpretation.[85] This fact proves that the right to engage in allegorical multiple interpretations was made scientifically legitimate. Today the right to allegorize is, in principle, not contested. If the Jewish Middle Ages interpreted this right more broadly than we do, the question can justifiably be raised whether the stronger tendency of that time to ascribe a deliberate ambivalence to biblical passages is not scientifically tenable.[86] It is, at any rate, understandable that people saw, in the very possibility of pursuing an allegorical interpretation into every detail, proof for the assumption that the interpreted passages were polysemous. Maimonides is so convinced of the truth of his interpretation of Job and Ps. 45 that he avers that his recognition of them overcame him like a divine revelation.[87] His semiscientific continuators, who would see the senses symbolized in the sons of Leah, surely felt supported in their view because one of the sons of Dan is called Ḥushim [here understood as the plural of ḥush, "the senses"].[88]

Of course, it is not easy to determine to what extent the need for artistic play operated concurrently with religious belief in the inner meaning of the Bible and the scientific justification of allegory. It may not be a coincidence that the very free interpretations of the post-Maimonidean period were delivered specifically at weddings,[89] occasions when the desire to entertain the guests was surely as much a motivation as were religious edification or scientific instruction.

Yet allegory, including its playful aspect, permits a very serious insight into the thinking of the Jewish Middle Ages if we inquire after its ideological content. What we mean is this: each allegorization projects the given text into another world, which is somehow felt to be more lofty. Which world is this?

The few allegorical interpretations of the Aggadah show a strong tendency to be related to Israel's fate. When even the dreams of Pharaoh's officials are given a national Jewish meaning,[90] it is surely understandable that the Song of Songs is primarily interpreted as a dialogue between God and Israel. Such interpretations are completely absent in Philo; he knows only "ethical" or "physical" allegorization. They are occasionally found among the Karaites,[91] the later homiletes, and especially among the Kabbalists,[92] but almost never among the philosophers.[93] Maimonides does mention the national interpretation of the Song of Songs, but he prefers the psychological; in general the cosmic allegorizations prevail. The philosophers of the Middle Ages, then, side with the rabbis against the Hellenists as far as the volume of allegory is concerned (they reject reinterpretation of laws and narratives), but with the Hellenists against the rabbis regarding its supranational content.

How can this paradoxical fact be explained?

Source criticism offers no solution. That the medieval philosophers were acquainted with Jewish Hellenism is not attested to before Abrabanel,[94] and a comparison of the allegoristic interpretations of both [Hellenism and Abrabanel] argues not for but against their use of Philo's writings. Ibn Ezra's remark that the internal and external meanings of scriptural passages correspond like body and soul could have been taken from Philo (*De migratione Abrahami* 93) through the mediation of Origen (*De principiis* IV.173),[95] but the interpretations of the Paradise story rest completely on systems handed down by the Middle Ages, and Philo has no parallel for the interpretations of wisdom literature. Of course, the methods of "physical" and "ethical" interpretation were known through the church. But why could they crowd out the national interpretations found in traditional rabbinic writings which, despite some opposition to details, were nonetheless venerated?

There is only one answer: because the philosophers' attempt to base Jewish piety on supranational [universal] metaphysics must naturally relegate the historico-Jewish element to the background—not, indeed, with respect to piety, but with respect to theology. It is the same issue which we encounter when the problem of the election of Israel recedes into the background. The election of Israel (in which, of course, the philosophers also believe) is, according to their theology, based on its special share in supranational truths, not on the historical act of the covenant.[96] Hence Scripture, in a philosophic-allegorical interpretation, is only a herald of eternal truths, not a proclaimer of the special historical relationship between Israel and God.

These brief suggestions should suffice to indicate that the investigation of Jewish allegorization during the Middle Ages is valuable as more than a contribution to the history of Bible exegesis. It bears witness to the transformation which, under the influence of Greek scientific teaching, took place in the depth of Jewish group sentiment. This testimony is unconscious, but the halakhic sentence to the effect that the unconscious statement often deserves preference over the conscious is also valid in science.[97] This testimony is to be obtained only from allegorization, not from other forms of reinterpretation. It therefore justifies the separate consideration which we have devoted to allegory, as distinct from other methods.

Notes

"Scientific Allegorization during the Jewish Middle Ages," translated by Elizabeth Petuchowski, first appeared as "Die wissenschaftliche Allegoristic des jüdischen Mittelalters," *Hebrew Union College Annual,* vol. 23, pt. 1 (Cincinnati, Ohio, 1950–51), pp. 611–43. Whenever possible, the bibliographical references in the notes have been completed editorially; other sources are listed in the author's original abbreviated forms.

1. "Die wissenschaftliche Allegoristik der Griechen," *Mnemosyne,* ser. 4, vol. 2, pp. 5–18; האליגוריסטיקה של היהודים ההלניסטים מחקרים ... לזכרון של יוחנן לוי ז"ל (ירושלים תש"ט) ואילך. "Altjüdische Allegoristik," supplement to *Jahresbericht des jüdisch-theologischen Seminars* (Breslau, 1936). Documentation of facts cited below can also be found in these articles.
2. See esp. Johann Huizinga, *Homo Ludens: A Study of the Play Element in Human Culture* (London, 1949).
3. Cf. Samuel Poznanski, "Allegorische Gesetzesauslegung bei den älteren Karäern," in *Studies in Jewish Literature issued in Honor of K. Kohler* (Berlin, 1913). pp. 244ff. They follow the rabbis in the sexual interpretation of laws (see "Altjüdische Allegoristik," p. 42; see also H. L. Ginzberg in S. W. Baron and A. Marx, eds., *Jewish Studies in Memory of G. A. Kohut* [New York, 1935]). Here too the motive is not apologetics but an excessive biblical tendency, already noted by the rabbis, to achieve a tactful circumscription.
4. Ḥanokh Albeck, in *Benjamin Manasseh Lewin, Sefer Hayovel* (Jerusalem, 1939), pp. 2ff.
5. About the smaller authority of the Aggadah, see *Darkhey ha-'Aggadah* (1950), pp. 187ff.
6. "Altjüdische Allegoristik," p. 58.
7. Ibid., p. 54. Cf. passage about view of the Midrash.
8. Ibid., p. 62; *Darkhey ha-'Aggadah,* pp. 137ff.
9. Israel Efros, *Philosophical Terms in the "Moreh Nebukim"* (New York, 1924), p. 100; Jacob Klatzkin, *Thesaurus Philosophicus Linguae Hebraicae,* vol. 3 (Berlin, 1926), p. 210.
10. Baḥya, *Ḥovot ha-Levavot* XI, toward end.
11. Ibn Arabi (thirteenth century; Ignaz Goldziher, *Die Richtungen der islamischen Koranauslegung* [Leiden, 1920], pp. 242ff.). According to him, the Flood signifies the sea of matter from which one has to take refuge in the ark of the divine law; nonetheless, the narrative is to be taken literally and to be believed in all its details. According to the same mystic, Moses' ark of bulrushes designates his human constitution; the water designates the highest knowledge; the wet nurse whom the infant rejects (according to the Midrash) designates previously given laws which the Torah repeals.
12. Goldziher, *Richtungen,* p. 215. Ghazali also cited a verse from the Koran (ibid., p. 246).
13. See, for instance, n. 11.
14. Goldziher, *Richtungen,* pp. 196, 235.
15. Ibid., pp. 196, 210; but cf. p. 192.
16. Ibid., p. 237. There is ample material about mystics on pp. 259ff. In addition, David H. Baneth has kindly drawn my attention to W. Ivanow, *Kalami Pir* (Bombay, 1935), p. xxxiv; Persian text, p. 55.
17. *Iggeret Teman,* pp. 18ff., Holub; for Christian biblical exegesis, see Wilhelm Bacher, "Die Bibelexegese Maimunis," *Jahresbericht der Landesrabbinerschule* (Budapest, 1896), p. 16; also published as *Die Bibelexegese Maimunis* (Strassburg, 1897).
18. The typological interpretation of 1 Cor. 10:11, Gal. 4:22, and Heb. 9:9 and 11:9 also do not surrender the literal meaning.

19. Of course, this comparison has been taken as a point of departure for reinterpretation, even for the words of Jesus saying that he had been sent only to the lost sheep of the house of Israel (Hans Joachim Schoeps, *Theologie und Geschichte des Judenchristentums* [Tübingen, 1949], p. 300).

20. In the *Epistle to Flora,* Ptolemy counts circumcision, the Sabbath, and fasts among the "typical" parts of the Bible; with the appearance of the truth, their literal sense was taken from them, while the spiritual sense remained.

21. Adolf Harnack, *Der kirchengeschichtliche Ertrag der exegetischen Arbeiten des Origenes* (Leipzig, 1919), 2:47; Schoeps, *Theologie und Geschichte.*

22. Pascal still denies that Jews practice allegorization, although he knows Maimonides (information from my student Seidmann, of blessed memory).

23. Wilhelm Bacher, in Jakob Winter and A. Wünsche, eds., *Die jüdische Literatur seit Abschluss des Kanons* (Trier, 1894–96), 2:29, n. 3.

24. Moritz Güdemann, *Geschichte des Erziehungswesen und der Kultur der Juden während des Mittelalters und der neueren Zeit* (Vienna, 1884), 2:29.

25. Shortened account of the philosophical magnum opus, 8:211ff.

26. Goldziher, *Richtungen,* pp. 134, 201; about the Islamic polemic against Christian allegory, see Erdmann Fritsch, *Islam und Christentum im Mittelalter* (Breslau, 1930), p. 135.

27. Even in the account of David's guilt, which is troublesome for him, he lets the literal meaning stand (*Doct. chr.,* 3:21f.).

28. Heller, *Revue des études juives* [hereafter *REJ*] 37:227, 247.

29. Wilhelm Bacher, *Die Bibelexegese der jüdischen Religionsphilosophie des Mittelalters vor Maimuni* (Strassburg, 1892), p. 26.

30. David Rosin, "Reime und Gedichte des Abraham ibn Esra I," *Jahresbericht des jüdischen-theologischen Seminars* [hereafter *Jahresbericht*] (Breslau, 1885), pp. 35ff.

31. Ibid., II, *Jahresbericht* (1887), p. 57.

32. According to Rosin, the woman in childbed is meant to designate the Virgin Mary because no father is mentioned; this does not seem to me to correspond to what the text suggests.

33. Rosin applies the following remarks only to the previously mentioned multiple interpretations, but they also apply generally to the reinterpretations.

34. The reverse is meant: whatever runs counter to the senses is on the same level as that which tends against reason.

35. No allusion to the divine origin of language (Rosin); for explanation, see below.

36. According to the second passage (Rosin, II, *Jahresbericht* (1887), p. 58), the Christians interpret Scripture "as it occurs to them, with additions or omissions."

37. Bacher, *Bibelexegese Maimunis,* p. 72 and passim. Arthur Marmorstein's objection (*The Old Rabbinic Doctrine of God* (London, 1927), 2:120 seems to me in no way justified.

38. My former student Hochmann, of blessed memory, saw the reason for this in the fact that Saadiah did not yet know the sharp separation between the broad masses and the educated.

39. This is probably the meaning of the words המשלים על פי עורים אלמים.

40. Abrabanel, in his commentary on the Paradise narrative (21d, ed. Hanau), explains in greater detail that it is the particular merit of the Torah, above all works of human wisdom, that these contain either exclusively the manifest meaning without any pointer toward higher teachings, or only the inner meaning, while the outer remains empty and without essence. But in the Torah the outward meaning is in accord with the events and full of allusions to a higher truth. The contradictions which are fully admitted by Saadiah (see above) and his successors and which exist between the letter of Scripture on the one hand, and experience or reason on the other, can be removed if one assumes a not too careful manner of expression. They are therefore hardly comparable to instances of boldness such as are found in the Apocalypse.

41. בטול עקרי הנוצרים.

42. *Ikkarim* III,21.

43. *Zurah* is too literal a rendition of *figura.*

44. According to the Epistle of Barnabas 10:2, the prohibition of pork means not to mix with people who resemble pigs.

45. Skillful continuation of Ibn Ezra's concluding thought (superiority of the Torah).
46. His father had already held this opinion (David Rosin, "Die Ethik des Maimonides," *Jahresbericht* [1876], pp. 52, 54). Levi ben Gershom sees the capable woman in 31:10ff. as matter faultlessly in the service of the spirit, but in 2:16 and (less definitely) 5:6 the evil woman is the craving soul. But he too expressly holds fast to the literal meaning.
47. Likewise ibn Rushd (Adolf Abraham Schmiedl, *Studien über jüdische Religionsphilosophie, insbesonders jüdische-arabische* [sic] [Vienna, 1869], p. 231).
48. Edited and discussed in detail by David H. Baneth, *Iggeret ha-Rambam*, vol. 1 (Jerusalem, 1946), pp. 17ff.
49. Maimonides quite incidentally rejects the reinterpretation of the laws (*Sefer ha-Mitzvot*, ed. Bloch, p. 193).
50. I have thoroughly demonstrated Maimonides's attitude toward the question of enlightenment of the people in *Monatsschrift für die Geschichte und Wissenschaft des Judentums* [hereafter *MGWJ*] 79 (1935):26ff. For amplification, see Simon Rawidowicz, *Kneset* 4 (1938), esp. pp. 330ff. He justly emphasizes that Maimonides also believed that the mass of people was not able to apprehend spiritual matters.
51. Siegmund Salfeld, *Das Hohelied bei den jüdischen Erklärern des Mittelalters* (Berlin, 1879), p. 99.
52. As continued in the passage cited above, before n. 46. Concerning such "mixed allegories," see Eduard König, *Stilistik, Rhetorik, Poetik in Bezug auf die biblische Literatur* (Leipzig, 1900), p. 275.
53. Introduction to explanation of the Song of Songs; Wilhelm Bacher, *Abraham ibn Isras Einleitung zu seinem Pentateuchkommentar* (Vienna, 1876), p. 67.
54. Particularly beautiful *Hilkhot Teshuvah* X; Bacher, *Bibelexegese Maimunis*, p. 17, brings further documentation from *Mishneh Torah* and *Moreh*.
55. Salfeld, *Hohelied*, pp. 80ff.
56. The interpretation of the king is already found in Baḥya, *Duties of the Heart* V,5, towards the beginning, and that of Satan in an anonymous Job commentary (Wilhelm Bacher, "Arabische Übersetzung und arabischer Kommentar zum Buche Hiob von Mose ibn Ciquitilla," *REJ* 31 [1895]:307–18; *Festschrift zu Ehren des Dr. A. Harkavy*, ed. D. v. Günzburg and I. Markon [Saint Petersburg, 1908], p. 222).
57. Jacob Anatoli, *Malmad ha-Talmidim* (Lyck, 1866), pp. 19ff., however, maintains the literal sense alongside the deeper meaning.
58. Cf. Wilhelm Bacher, *Jewish Quarterly Review* [hereafter *JQR*] 9:280ff.
59. Cited in ibn Ezra's fragmentary commentary to Genesis (printed in Michael Friedländer, *Essays on the Writings of Ibn Ezra* [London, 1877], p. 40 of the Hebrew part).
60. Dominion of light according to gnostic views. David Kaufmann, *Studien über Salomon Ibn Gabirol* (Budapest, 1899), p. 68, does not use the expression here rendered as *hamon*, but he recognizes the significance and proves that *pleroma* was often rendered as *melo*. For an explanation of the passage, see also David Rosin, *MGWJ* 42 (1898):484ff.
61. For the distinction, cf. Saul Horovitz, "Die Psychologie bei den jüdischen Religionsphilosophen des Mittelalters," *Jahresbericht* (1900), p. 115.
62. Goldziher, *Richtungen*, pp. 227, 233 documents interpretations of passages in the Torah and in the Koran concerning physical and spiritual powers in Islam.
63. Julius Guttmann, *MGWJ* 80 (1936):180ff.
64. Cf. *MGWJ* 82 (1938):389ff.
65. According to Thomas Aquinas, *Summa* I.1.10, God can predict the future not only through words but also through historical events (arranged by Him).
66. Cf. Goldziher, *Richtungen*, p. 184 about such allusions to material and active intellect in the Koran interpretation of Avicenna.
67. Concerning these lightning insights according to Maimonides, see Julius Guttmann, *Die Philosophie des Judentums* (Munich, 1933), p. 178. About Plato as a source for this thought, see Stenzel, *Die Antike*, 2:238 and my note in *MGWJ* 77 (1933):395. There is more about Gersonides's interpretation in Schmiedl, *Studien*, p. 227.
68. I have discussed them thoroughly in *MGWJ* 82 (1938):384ff.
69. Although Eden had been understood previously to be the soul!

70. Other interpretations of whole narratives by Maimonides are not known to me. In *Sefer ha-Mitzvot*, ed. Bloch, p. 14, he mentions the interpretation according to which the conquest of Kiryat Sefer signifies the winning back of ancient Halakhot (Temura 16a; related matter in "Altjüdische Allegoristik," p. 36, but this comment does not mean much). He is more intent on facts concerning the history of tradition than upon their exegetical connection. For interpretation of Exod. 3:6, "Moses hid his face," and 33:21, "Behold, there is a place by Me," see Bacher, *Exegese Maimunis*, p. 12. Both verses should, indeed, point to Moses' reluctance at coming forward to be recognized and to his elevation in rank, but they should not lose their literal meaning—just as a detail of the thorn bush episode (reference to the two shoes of Moses) was metaphorically interpreted in Islam, both with and without abolishing the literal meaning (Goldziher, *Richtungen*, pp. 199, 232, 236). In no wise is it here a matter of allegorizing the meaning of the whole.

71. Main source: *Minḥat Qenaot* and a testimonial which David Kaufmann has issued in Curatorium der Zunzstiftung, ed., *Jubelschrift zum neunzigsten Geburtstag des Dr. L. Zunz* (Berlin, 1884), p. 143 of the German section and p. 142 of the Hebrew section. Further details also in S. Horovitz, *Die Stellung des Aristoteles bei den Juden des Mittelalters* (Leipzig, 1911), p. 17. This work and those listed below give due recognition to the influence of Christianity.

72. רמז לכלל הרכבת האדם, Kaufmann, in *Jubelschrift Zunz*, p. 160, Hebrew section.

73. *Minḥat Qenaot*, p. 153.

74. Kaufmann, in *Jubelschrift Zunz*, p. 157, Hebrew section.

75. Salomon Munk, *Mélanges de philosophie juive et arabe* (1859), p. 145.

76. Something similar probably applies to the presumably oldest document of this allegory, the treatise found among Maimonides's letters (*Qobez*, II, pp.38ff.), briefly discussed by Bacher, *Exegese Maimunis*, pp. 18ff. According to this, for instance, Egypt is the body (Philo, *Leg. all.*, II,59 and passim), the good kings signify reason, and Shomrom signifies cursed matter. With the last interpretation the author expressly links up with Maimonides. Moreover, he refers to Ibn Ezra, who similarly advocates multiple interpretation, not reinterpretation of passages understood allegorically. But the superior value of the spiritual idea is quite apparent when Abraham is said to have taught circumcision of the flesh and Moses that of the heart. Here that advance which, according to Christian teaching, is said to have occurred in the transition from Judaism to Christianity is viewed as an internal Jewish process.

77. Leo Baeck, "Zur Charakteristik des Levi ben Abraham ben Chajjim," *MGWJ* 44 (1900):28; in contrast to Heinrich Gross, "Zur Geschichte der Juden in Arles," ibid., 28 (1879):430, according to which Levi "seems to dissolve the Bible into allegories." For the narrative of the patriarch cf. Suler, *Encyclopedia Judaica*, 10:847.

78. חזות קשה. par. 11. Schmiedl, *Studien*, p. 217, draws attention to a relationship with Philo but underestimates the difference; for Philo, philosophy is mistress of encylical studies.

79. Concerning the work מחיר יין, see Glenn, *The Jewish Forum* (1948), pp. 48ff.

80. Wilhelm Bacher, *Die Aggada der palästinensischen Amoräer*, 3:553.

81. For typical examples see S. Bäck, in Winter and Wünsche, *Jüdische Literatur*, 2:675ff.; see also Schmiedl, *Studien*, p. 236, with notes by L. Löw about Christian parallels.

82. Konrad Müller, *Pauly-Krolls Realenzyklopädie der Altertumswissenschaft*, Suppl. 4, p. 22.

83. Jacob Kramer, *Probleme des Wunders in Zusammenhang mit dem der Providenz* (Strassburg, 1903), pp. 74ff.

84. "Altjüdische Allegoristik," p. 75.

85. Cf. par. 2 concerning Maimonides's interpretation of Prov. 7:6, and the introduction to *Malmad ha-Talmidim* concerning the comparison of the words of the wise with *darvonot n'masmerot* (Eccles. 12:11).

86. For an understanding of the ancient evaluation of the mysterious ("Altjüdische Allegoristik," pp. 9, 15), see esp. Huizinga, *Homo Ludens*, p. 110, who even sees in the riddle "a ritual element of highest importance."

87. Bacher, *JQR* 9:282, 286.

88. Cf. Bacher, in Winter and Wünsche, *Jüdische Literatur*, 2:317.

89. Kaufmann, in *Jubelschrift Zunz*, p. 148 of German section.
90. *Darkhey ha-'Aggadah* 83, also about related matters.
91. Nahawendi interprets Eccles. 1:5, "The sun also ariseth and the sun goeth down," as referring to the kingdom of Israel, and 12:3, "The keepers of the house shall tremble," to the Temple and Levites (Poznanski, "Allegorische Gesetzesauslegung," p. 247).
92. Ephraim S. Luntschitz, *Ir Gibborim* (Basel, 1580), pp. 11d ff. applies the law of the man who sells his daughter in some detail to God and the soul, but then, in accordance with the Midrash, to God and Israel ("Altjüdische Allegoristik," p. 68). Both interpretations are also found in the Zohar II,94.
93. Only as an exception are predictions about cosmic changes interpreted geographically (*Moreh* II,29).
94. He refers to Josephus for the interpretations of the Tabernacle.
95. In the introduction to the accessible commentary, "Third Way," toward the end. Also, the exegesis according to Maimonides is only tenuously connected with Philo; see above, n. 78; Kaufmann, in *Jubelschrift Zunz*, p. 145.
96. To what extent Judah Halevi differs cannot be discussed here.
97. Of the *mesiaḥ lefi tumo* [one who talks innocently, in ignorance of the implications of his statement].

12
LEONE EBREO, RENAISSANCE PHILOSOPHER

Hiram Peri (Heinz Pflaum)

he rhythm of Jewish history is so totally at variance with that of the history of western nations that even those great movements and events, those true turning points which thoroughly altered the intellectual face of Europe, left virtually no traces on the Jewish spirit. Vice versa, the truly fateful moments of Jewish history frequently coincided with periods of tranquility in European history. Even the Renaissance, that great and complex movement which completely reshaped every aspect of Europe and of European culture between the fourteenth and the sixteenth centuries, had no real effect on the internal history of the Jewish people. It is true, of course, that their external history was crucially affected (but even here, the impact was only indirect) by . . . the founding and vigorous expansion of the Dominican Order, which, like the [Franciscan], was specifically a product of the early Renaissance. The chiliastic unrest of that period led to the Spanish Inquisition, and the centralization of military-political power, along with the strengthening of national consciousness, led to the expulsion of the Moors from Spain. At the intersection of these two lines of development, as it were, is the destruction of the center of Jewish culture that flourished on the Iberian peninsula. But Jewish culture—literature, philosophy, education, language, law, and social order—remained unaffected. From its core almost to its periphery, Judaism adopted neither the specific cultural contents of the Renaissance nor its mental attitude, neither the importance it attached to antiquity and nature nor its passion for renewal, *reformatio*.

Significant contemporary Jewish developments occurred in speculative thought in the renewed flowering of Kabbalah, which from then occupied a dominant place in the minds of the people for a long time; politically, in the messianic agitation, which crystallized into great and partly schismatic movements; and sociologically, in the concentration of Jewish settlement in urban centers, which paved the way for the emergence of the ghetto. But none of these had even the most tenuous connection with the dominant social forces or the significant phenomena and personalities of the European history of the period. The conceptual scheme of western history—the Renaissance as a bridge between the Middle Ages and the modern era—is completely irrelevant to the history of the Jews.

True, Jews occasionally attempted to use the newly discovered treasures of their host nations for the benefit of Jewish culture. Thus, about 1490, Messer Leon (Judah ben Jeḥiel) in Italy composed a Hebrew rhetorical work patterned after Cicero. However these attempts had no significance and gradually ceased without stimulating further efforts.

As far as we can see, there was only one instance of a genuine, meaningful encounter between the spirit of Judaism and that of Renaissance, and even this encounter remained merely an isolated episode in Jewish intellectual history. We are referring to the *Dialogues on Love* [*Dialoghi di Amore*], by Leone Ebreo. This work had a profound impact on Renaissance philosophy, yet it never became part of the Jewish literary tradition. Nonetheless, the life and the teachings of the man who embodied this significant encounter are worthy of our interest.[1]

I

Leone Ebreo's life reflects the fate which befell the entire last generation of Spanish Jewry. First the glory and tranquility of the happiest of all stations of Jewish exile, a period of power, wealth, influence, and culture; then the storm warnings of impending catastrophe, followed by the catastrophe itself with all its horrors; and finally, a continuous alternation of flight, brief respite, renewed flight, and peace regained in a fate of homelessness. These elements constituted the lives of this entire uprooted generation, including the life of Judah Abrabanel, known as Leone Ebreo.

We know that the Abrabanels were among the most distinguished families of Sephardic Jewry; they were able to trace their descent to the Davidian dynasty. The members of this family who lived during the fourteenth and fifteenth centuries enjoyed high esteem, both as powerful financiers and as patrons of Jewish learning. Rabbi Don Isaac Abrabanel, Leone Ebreo's father, was equally famous as chief minister to several kings and as author of theological and exegetical works which occupy an important place in rational biblical exegesis to this day. His primary interest, of course, was the study of rabbinic tradition. However—and it is important to remember this in order to understand the cultural environment in which Leone grew up—it seems that even at an early age Isaac Abrabanel acquired much more western (Christian and classic) culture than was usual for Jewish scholars of his day. It comes as no surprise, of course, that Isaac Abrabanel's writings should reveal a thorough knowledge of Jewish literature—Talmudic and exegetical, philosophical and apologetical—but it is worthy of note that he was also familiar with and utilized the works of Aristotle, the Pythagoreans, Empedocles, Plotinus, Pliny, Seneca, and Cicero, as well as with those of Saint Augustine, Duns Scotus, Saint Thomas Aquinas, and a number of other Christian authors. A letter he wrote to a nobleman of his acquaintance shows that he was thoroughly at home in the Portuguese language and the rhetorical style of his era.

Isaac also held a prominent position in Portuguese society. Several unpublished documents, preserved in the Arquivo Nacional in Lisbon, show that he received special favors and privileges from Alfonso V, who conferred upon him the title of *morador* (which gave him the right to be presented at court), gave him a house (which was confiscated after Isaac fled from Portugal in 1484), permitted him the privilege of riding on a mule (which Jews were forbidden to do under the old Ordinaçoes Alfonsinas), and exempted him from having to wear the "Jewish badge."

Isaac's eldest son, Judah, was born about 1460. It could hardly have been a later date, because it is known that he practiced medicine even prior to 1485, the year he settled in Castile. A contemporaneous register of physicians in Lisbon mentions one "Yehuda ben Ishay Abarbanel de Lisboa" who practiced medicine (*a chinica geral*), and the first page of a manuscript edition of Yosef Hayyim's commentary on the Book of Psalms (first printed in Salonica in 1522) shows the inscription, "Presented to the nobleman (*sar*) Don Judah Abrabanel."

Leone must have received this gift while he was still living in Lisbon. Thus it was in Lisbon that he acquired the foundations of his education, whose scope and thoroughness later became a source of widespread amazement. His education no doubt was based on Jewish thought and religious philosophy, especially that of Maimonides. It was particularly during this period that Portuguese Jewry experienced a remarkable spiritual flowering which made the synagogue of Lisbon a rival of the famous rabbinical schools of Toledo and Cordova. The ideas of the medieval philosophers, Jews and Arabs alike, occupy a prominent place in Leone's works; he regarded the "sacred theology of the Hebrew" [*santa teologia degli ebrei*] as the highest authority. Much later, when he had already concentrated his studies on western thought, the study of the law and the language of Judaism retained undiminished importance for him. In verses 92–93 of his great elegy (ca. 1505) lamenting the fate of his son, who had been kidnapped and baptized, he admonishes the latter, above all, to learn Hebrew, to read the Bible, and to study the Mishnah and the Talmud.

In addition to pursuing his general philosophical studies, Leone studied medicine. Medicine was not merely the profession that enabled the philosopher to earn a livelihood. Biological and anatomical theories were among the basic constituent elements of his philosophy. According to Aristotle's teachings—ancient yet still considered valid—botany and zoology were components of philosophical speculation. Moreover, Leone's specific view of the bonds of love that link all things in creation required a foundation of mineralogy and astronomy. These subjects were then part of the study of medicine, which was much broader in scope during that period than medical studies are today. Incidentally, Leone was to give evidence of outstanding proficiency as a physician in Naples.

In 1484, his activities and studies were suddenly interrupted by his father's downfall. The reign of John II, who had succeeded the kindly Alfonso V, had given rise to a conspiracy which involved the country's highest nobility and led to bloody persecution. Thanks to the records of the conspiracy trial, published in the *Archive Historico Portuguez*, vols. 1, 2, and 4 (Lisbon, 1903–6), we are in a better position than earlier Jewish historiographers (Grätz, Schwab, and others) to evaluate Isaac Abrabanel's role in this conspiracy. We can see from these records that Isaac had indeed given financial support to the leader of the conspiracy, the duke of Braganza, and to his friends, that he had attended their meetings, and that he had assisted them with his counsel. He escaped the king's wrath by fleeing posthaste to Spain, but all his Portuguese property was confiscated. He and his family found a haven in Seville. His son Leone settled there too, in 1484, and began to practice medicine. In this city, the center of Spanish culture, Judah probably found even more cultural stimulation and resources than in Portugal, where the waves thrown up by the great intellectual revolution that was then sweeping Europe did not run quite so high. In 1491 he had a son, whom he named Isaac. By that time the elder Isaac had regained his position as minister of finance at the royal court of Castile.

However, this happy existence came to an end with the expulsion of the Jews from Spain in 1492. The Abrabanels moved to Naples. In the confusion of the mass exodus, Leone suffered the misfortune of losing his son, who was then just one year old. He had secretly sent the infant to Portugal, where John II, as an act of revenge, had him seized. In 1495, John's successor had the boy forcibly baptized along with thousands of other Jewish children and arranged to have them raised in the Christian faith. Leone Ebreo was never able to overcome this sorrow, which he movingly expressed in his elegy. However, it would appear that eventually the younger Isaac Abrabanel managed to flee from Portugal and to return to his original faith, for a son of his (in other words, a grandson of Leone's) turned up in Salonica about the middle of the sixteenth century.

In 1494, Leone Ebreo's name occurs for the first time in an Italian source, in the records of the Aragonian State Chancellery in Naples. I was able to inspect these documents by kind permission of the administration of the Reale Archivio di Stato. Volume 36 of the *Commune della Sommaria,* fols. 97ff., contains a decision by King Alfonso II of Aragon (1494–96) "in favorem jude Abramanel Ebrey filii Don Ysac Abramanel." According to this document, Judah (Leone) had lodged a complaint with the chamber to the effect that, although he was legally domiciled in Naples, he had been discriminated against as a foreigner by the state treasury in violation of the patent granted to the Jews by King Ferrente I. Alfonso ruled that all official authorities were to treat the complainant with punctilious correctness as a citizen of Naples and to accord him all the privileges to which he was entitled by virtue of his status and of the royal patent, on pain of royal disfavor and a fine of 100 ounces of gold. A copy of this decree, which is dated July 28, 1494, was to be handed to the complainant for his protection.

Yet, only two years after his arrival, political chaos once again uprooted Leone from his place of refuge, exiling him along with his aged father. Ferdinand of Aragon, who had retained Isaac Abrabanel as his chief minister and Leone as his personal physician, had died in 1494, and Isaac Abrabanel had entered the service of Ferdinand's successor, Alfonso II of Aragon. Late that year, Charles VIII of France drove the Aragonians out of Naples. After entering the city, the French troops looted the Jewish homes. The elder Abrabanel, who had lost all his possessions, including his priceless library, to looting and arson followed his sovereign, Alfonso II, to Messina. After Alfonso's death, Isaac moved again, first to Corfu and from there to Monopoli in Apulia, where he devoted himself entirely to his literary work. Leone and his wife moved to Genoa, where Leone established a medical practice. His intellectual isolation in this city of merchants to whom the arts were alien must have deeply frustrated this versatile philosopher. His mood is reflected in the melancholy undertone that pervades his *Dialogues,* most of which he composed there.

We do not know how long Leone remained in Genoa, but in May, 1501, we find him in Barletta, Apulia, probably together with his father. We have this information from a letter which I was permitted to inspect in the archives of the city of Naples. Dated May 10, 1501, this letter was addressed by King Federigo of Naples to the municipality of Barletta. In it the king, who had assumed sovereignty over the Kingdom of Naples following the expulsion of the French in 1498, calls upon the city to be at the service of Isaac Abrabanel and his son Leone in all things, "havendo noi cari li dilecti nostri Don Isach abrauanel et Maestro Leone physico suo figliolo per le loro virtù et desiderando se transferiscono con la loro famiglia in questa nostra città de napoli a nostri serviti" ("holding in high esteem the precious Don Isaac Abrabanel and his son, Master Leon, [who] desire to transfer with their family to our city and to enter our service"). It is probable that Leone had moved to Naples at that time at the king's request. During this period another son was born to Leone, but this child died at the age of five (see the "Elegy," verses 18–20). Overwhelmed by despondency and by a sense of utter isolation, Leone once again began to travel; he visited his father in Venice, where the latter had finally found a peaceful haven. There Leone composed several dedicatory poems for his father's works, including *Sebaḥ Pesaḥ* [a commentary on the Passover Haggadah], *Rosh Amanali* [refutations of some of Maimonides's theses], and *Naḥlat Abot* [which dealt with the Pirke Avot]. The poems were published along with the books in Constantinople in 1506. After his return to Naples, Leone became personal physician to the city's governor. It was during this period that he composed the "Elegy," which expresses in the most intense terms his own despondency, the misery of the homeless exile, and the messianic hopes of the believing Jew. It is probable that at the same time he worked on his masterpiece, the *Dialogues on Love,* which he had begun in Naples but was never to complete. However, the governor, Leone's employer, was recalled to Spain in 1506, and Leone, once again left without a protector, returned to his father in Venice. On the way to Venice he was stricken with a raging fever and arrived at his father's house sick and weak. That the Jews of the time held Leone in high esteem as a philosopher may be seen from a letter addressed by one Saul Cohen to the elder Abrabanel, inquiring about the views of the "noble Rabbi Judah," who had "set out upon a remarkable path of thoughtful research."

In 1508, the elder Abrabanel died in Venice, weary and broken. A note by David Kaufmann, "Un manuscrit de Mischné tora" (*Revue des études juives* 36:64) yields a final document, touching in its intimacy. It is a moving testimony to the personality and mood of this man who had been driven about so much. A priceless illuminated manuscript of the *Mishneh Torah,* dating from the first half of the fourteenth century, it begins with a record of births, entered into this valuable document in accordance with time-honored Jewish custom. The record opens with a Hebrew sentence in almost completely faded script: "I am writing this here in Venice, my heart broken as I recall the (former) blessed days, I, Isaac Abrabanel, the least among men." Leone marked his father's death with a Hebrew poem which is a beautiful memorial to the latter's outstanding qualities.

We do not know where Leone lived during the years that followed. It seems that he spent some time with his brother, who lived in Ferrara. According to information from one of my Israeli friends, a parchment manuscript, dated 1516 and found in a private collection in Haifa, contains the statutes of a Ḥevra Kaddisha in Ferrara. Among the signers of these statutes is one Don Judah Abrabanel; his name is the second on the document, following the signature of another individual named Abrabanel. The next documentary evidence of his whereabouts is found in the Pesaro (1520) edition of his father's commentary to the Minor Prophets. This book is prefaced with a poem by Leone in praise of his father, which shows that Leone himself supervised the printing of the volume. It seems that he moved back to Naples once again at that time. A decree enacted by Charles I of Castile, dated December 28, 1520, now in the Naples archives, conferred upon "maestro leon abrauanel medico" special privileges and complete exemption from the tax imposed upon Jews. This decree was reissued on May 15, 1521. The *Diaries* of the Venetian Marino Sanudo (a kind of journal in Venetian dialect dating from the first half of the sixteenth century), have preserved for us a third document from the same period, indicating the high esteem in which this Jewish physician was held, his influence on the then viceroy, and, at the same time, his concerned and vigorous espousal of the interests of his oppressed coreligionists. On April 1, 1521, Sanudo received a report from Naples that, following some inflammatory sermons by a Franciscan friar, the representatives of the Estates requested the viceroy to require Jews to wear such distinguishing apparel as yellow headgear, as they did in Venice. However, "maestro Lion hebreo medico" managed to persuade the viceroy not to accede to that request, on the grounds that the requirement to wear a Jewish badge would constitute not only a personal affront but also a threat to the safety of all those concerned.

Sanudo records still another incident which caused considerable stir in Naples during the spring of 1521. Here we again see Leone in action, this time as a physician of outstanding ability. It seems that Cardinal Riario, one of the foremost princes of the church, had contracted a disease which Sanudo does not name, but indicates only by a series of dots. The cardinal's physician had already given him up, but "maestro Lion hebreo medico dil vicerè" was able to cure him in short order.

These are the last direct sources on Leone's life. According to a note in the prologue to Carlos Montesa's Spanish translation of the *Dialogues* (Saragossa, 1584), Leone was later employed as personal physician to the pope (Julian III?), but this information cannot be verified. The year of his death is unknown. The date of 1542 given by Edmondo Solmi in *Giornale Storico della Letteratura Italiana,* vol. 53 (1909), pp. 446ff., based on information in a seventeenth-century encyclopedia, has turned out to be incorrect and historically unjustifiable. The error resulted from a confusion of names with the Swiss reformer Leo Jud (Meister Leu, 1482–1542). All we know for certain is that by 1535, the year in which the *Dialogues on Love* was published—"brought to light from the obscurity in which they had lain buried," as the publisher put it—the troubled life of the physician Don Judah Abrabanel, called Maestro Leone, had already come to a close. In addition to several Hebrew occasional poems, Leone left a beautiful elegy, which appeared in translation for the first time, and an unfinished philosophical work, the *Dialogues on Love,* the most widely published and translated philosophical book of the period.

II

The philosophy of Leone Ebreo contained in the *Dialogues* does not represent a system; its structure is not architectonic but organic. It is the unfolding of an idea through the totality of that which exists: the idea of love as the principle of being and as an ethical-religious norm. The ground for this universal conception of love had already been prepared in the philosophy of the period. It goes, of course, back to Plato's *Symposium.* The turn toward Platonism which took place in fifteenth-century philosophy resulted not only from a change in speculative tendencies, but also from the aesthetic trends of the period. The *Symposium* had moved into the foreground of interest because the vivid beauty of its form and the grace of its philosophical posture satisfied, more than anything else, the prevailing taste. Neoplatonism had moved the Platonic concept of love so close to the tendencies of Christian philosophy that a new syncretistic *Weltanschauung* could evolve from it. This pagan-Christian teaching found expression in Marsilio Ficino's commentary on the *Symposium,* which, like Leone Ebreo's *Dialogues,* was composed in dialogue form. It was followed by a series of philosophical works with similar tendencies and views which were shared by the literary circles around Lorenzo de Medici, and the religiously motivated groups around Savonarola.

Thanks to Leone Ebreo, these ideas acquired a new form which, through countless popular philosophical works published during the decades that followed, spread throughout the educated stratum of Renaissance society and penetrated into every branch of culture, poetry, and thought. This popular tradition, however, was lost in the middle strata of culture, remaining clearly discernible only here and there—for instance, in French Renaissance lyricism and in the aesthetics and religious poetry of Spain. The impact of this conception of philosophy itself, however, was much more evident. We encounter it as a clear trend in Giordano Bruno and Campanella as well as in Bacon and Spinoza. It is intimately related to the shift from speculation (focused originally on the purely metaphysical) to natural philosophy and, finally, to natural science.

The seeds of this development can already be found in Leone Ebreo himself. He sees the idea of love as an ontological principle. According to Leone, all created things, the inanimate no less than the animate, are bound to one another by mutual love. He eliminates the problems entailed in this view by merging, as the need arises, the concept of love into that of a general act of will, or else he imparts to it a quite specific meaning. While love represents a vital bond linking all creatures of the same species, it is also seen as operating between the individual existential spheres of the cosmos. Leone Ebreo adopts unchanged the medieval physical image of the world, the concept of a strict hierarchy of existence. However, his conception of love imparts a new meaning to that image. It is no longer a fixed, static structure, but rather a form which is motivated by love and thus a living thing. The distinctiveness of this dynamic principle yields the specific differences between the spheres of existence. Medieval substantialism is transformed into functionalism.

What makes Leone's book important is primarily this new attitude—its determination to derive a world view from a single principle, to grasp philosophically the whole of being. This universalist feature gives Leone's philosophy a singular place amidst the turbulent ferment of ideas which made his century extraordinarily fructifying yet philosophically little productive. Leone's era still lacked the firm foundation needed for the speculative formulation of a well-rounded and generally accepted view of the world, the foundation which alone mattered from then on: man as the center of and the measure for all being. The era still had not attained an all-embracing framework of experience to give material support and substance to the concept of the world. Hence all philosophers of the Italian Renaissance are bold, contentious, unsystematic, contradictory, vague, fanciful, rich in ideas, and yet lacking one central idea. In the midst of this chaotic deluge of ideas, Leone Ebreo occupies a unique place. He is still sufficiently a son of the Middle Ages to be able to believe in the possibility of achieving a universal philosophy, yet also close enough to the spirit of modernity to be able to replace the rigid, spherically graduated cosmos of medieval speculation with a vital world structure held together by emotion. Thus Leone's conception of the world took from Scholasticism the hierarchical structure of the doctrine of emanation; from the spirit of the new era it derived the concept of ensoulment through the universal principle of love; from Judaism it drew the speculative ingredients (the theory of attributes, the doctrine of creation, eschatology); and from Plato it adopted the theory of ideas.

However, this ontological doctrine of love constitutes only the pre-condition for that ethical-religious conception which is the primary theme of Leone's book and the goal of his philosophy. This conception is a mystical one. It seeks to achieve a union of the universe and of the individual soul with God, without, at the same time, surrendering God's transcendence. It is in this striving for union that Leone sees both the foundation and the motivating law of the world; everything that exists seeks to return to God, not each creation for itself, but together, as a whole, as a universe. For this reason the ethical postulate is not a world-denying love of God, but the permeation of the world by love. The spiritual intelligences which Leone, in the manner of Scholasticism, accepts as nonmaterial but real, perfect, and above all material things, turn lovingly to lower matter in order to draw it up to themselves, for the imperfection of the latter means an imperfection in the world and is, therefore, incompatible with the ultimate goal of the return flow of all things to God, in whom there can only be perfection. Thus there is movement in two directions through the universe—down from above and up from below. The bridge between the higher and the lower worlds is the human soul: in it the universe becomes one.

In order to deduce the idea of God's love for His creatures—a concept which medieval Jewish theology avoided postulating philosophi-cally—Leone developed from the concept of love a transcendental aes-thetics which occupies a prominent place in the history of aesthetics. This is the first idealistic theory of beauty, closely linked with a theory of ideas built on Platonic foundations. A graduated structure of beauty leads up to one Sublime Beauty which is inherent in God Himself. It is the Neopla-tonic *logos* given an aesthetic turn. The distinguishing feature of this concept is "multifarious unity" (*multifaria unità*). This term, which may have been derived from Gabirol's *Fountain of Life* [*Fons Vitae*], is ap-plied both to beauty as such and to God. Thus aesthetics leads directly to the idea of God. By contemplating the "first" beauty, the Sublime Beauty in Himself, God encompasses the whole world in intellectual love. Man, insofar as he contemplates the pure idea of beauty, attains an intellectual love of God (*amore intellettuale di Dio*). Here, in the third dialogue of Leone Ebreo, Spinoza found the concept basic to his own philosophy.[2]

This is the path mapped out by Leone Ebreo's philosophy of love. The goal of all human desire is pleasure in union with the desired object. The object of the love of the universe for God is the ultimate perfection of the universe. It consists in the reunion of all creation with the Creator. The highest activity aiming at perfection is intellectual love. The universe yearns for infinite delight in keeping with the infinite beauty of God, and God, in turn, derives pleasure from the perfection of His creation. Thus all that exists is united in one circle of love (*circolo amoroso*) which, moving down from God to the *materia prima* below, implies a begetting, while moving again upward implies a union with God.

> Without love and the desire to return to the Sublime Beauty, it would be impossible for things to emerge in creation and move away from the Deity. For without a fatherly love and procreative desire similar to God's, it would be impossible for one sphere of being to be begotten by another, higher sphere, and for each to move farther away from the Deity, following one another, sphere by sphere, down to the *materia prima*. In the same way, it would also be impossible for created things to achieve a reunion with the Deity and attain that sublime delight in which the bliss and perfection of the entire universe consists, and from which they would remain infinitely remote in the *materia prima*, were it not for love and the desire to return to the Deity as their final sphere of perfection. It is this desire that leads them to that ultimate blissful act of the universe—intellectual gratification [Italian ed. (Venice, 1549), fol. 201a].

This philosophy occupied a singular borderline position between the world of Jewish thought and that of Christianity and Platonism; in it the traditional Jewish concept of God merged into the flow of a Neoplatonic mysticism. As a result, Leone's strange and beautiful book enjoyed a long and significant influence in European philosophy but had no impact on Jewish intellectual history, and in fact did not come to light in a Hebrew version until the nineteenth century. However, its mystical fervor and spiritual nobility make this work worthy of being recalled in our day. It is the monument to a significant encounter between the spirit of Judaism and that of the western world.

Notes

"Leone Ebreo, Renaissance Philosopher," translated by Gertrude Hirschler, first appeared as "Der Renaissance Philosoph Leone Ebreo—Jehudah Abarbanel," *Soncino Blätter* 1 (1926–27):213–21; reprinted in Kurt Wilhelm, ed., *Wissenschaft des Judentums im deutschen Sprachbereich* (Tübingen, 1967), 2:471–81.

1. On Leone Ebreo, see Bernhard Zimmels, *Leo Hebraeus, ein jüdischer Philosoph der Renaissance* (Breslau, 1886). A monograph entitled "Leone Ebreo," by the author of the present study, appeared as vol. 7 of *Heidelberger Abhandlungen zur Philosophie und ihrer Geschichte*, ed. Ernst Hoffmann and Heinrich Rickert.

2. Cf. E. Solmi, *Benedetto Spinoza et Leone Ebreo Modena* (1903) and C. Gebhart, "Spinoza und der Platonismus," in *Chronicum Spinozanum*, vol. 1 (The Hague, 1921), pp. 178ff.

13
RELIGION AND SCIENCE IN MEDIEVAL AND MODERN THOUGHT

Julius Guttmann

[Julius Guttmann's original study consists of six sections: 1. The Concept of Religious Truth in the Middle Ages: Reason and Revelation; 2. The Content of Religion According to Arabic and Jewish Philosophy; 3. The Concept of Universal Revelation in Arabic Philosophy; 4. The Concept of Religion in Christian Scholasticism as Compared with the Arabic-Jewish Concept; 5. Revelatory Religion and Religion of Reason in Modern Philosophy; 6. Religious and Theoretical Truth in Kant and Schleiermacher. This English version omits section 4, in which Guttmann points out that Christian Scholasticism has large areas of agreement with medieval Arabic-Jewish philosophy with regard to the formulation of the problem of faith and reason, yet differs radically from them with regard to the solution of the problem. Their differences emerge from the different ways in which each religion confronts the world of Greek science. Islam and Judaism are keenly aware of the autonomous power of scientific cognition, against which religion must vindicate and assert itself. This stance is hardly discernible in Scholasticism, in which the task of the philosophy of religion is to incorporate the existing scientific traditions into the given system of faith. A thinker who acknowledges the truth of the Christian articles of faith is required to acknowledge a sphere of truth that is inaccessible to reason. Faith belongs to the domain of grace and mystery becomes a doctrine; it is no longer the distinctive expression of the immediacy of religious certitude. The subsequent sections and the corresponding notes have been renumbered to reflect the omission of this section.]

To have made religion the problem of philosophy is the distinctive achievement of the Middle Ages. In all other respects

281

medieval thought is wholly dependent on ancient tradition, being productive only in the elaboration and continuation of traditional ideas; there, however, it introduces a new area of investigation and provides philosophical consciousness with a new theme.

Ancient philosophy is, of course, also profoundly affected by religious impulses. From its beginnings in the philosophies of nature, in which the religious experience of nature is intimately intertwined with the scientific concept of nature, to Plato's ethical religiosity and to Neoplatonism, which makes religion central to its structure and which employs the results of all previous logical development to indicate the path leading from thought to religious intuition, the religious motive remains a potent ingredient in the development of philosophy. The more philosophy becomes imbued with religious life, however, the less it knows of religion as a proper object of study. Religious philosophy among the ancients absorbs religion, and for this reason does not become a philosophy of religion. Even at the beginning of its development, Greek popular religion leaves philosophy so far behind that philosophy no longer has to deal with religion as a problem. Neither the early criticism of the popular belief in the gods nor the later philosophical reinterpretation of this belief gives the slightest indication that such a problem exists. To be sure, there was no lack of speculation in ancient times concerning the origin of the belief in gods. Men were deeply interested in the genesis of religion, as in that of all other cultural phenomena. The Stoics in particular turned their attention to specific aspects of religious life. All this, however, remains in the sphere of psychology, or possibly of speculative history. Nowhere does it touch upon the central problem, the problem of religious truth.

The step from ancient religious philosophy to the philosophy of religion becomes possible only as philosophic consciousness comes into contact with the monotheistic religions and their sacred writings. These religions, by virtue of the strength of their claims to truth and the profundity of their spiritual content, confront philosophy as an autonomous spiritual power. They believe that they possess the ultimate and unconditional truth that needs no validation by science, and that they provide a consistent and conclusive answer to the questions with whose solution philosophy is wrestling. The meeting of these two spiritual worlds that differ so completely in their origin creates the philosophy of religion in the scientific sphere and theology in the religious sphere, although the distinction between the two was of course not clearly perceived at first.

Initially, the relation of religious truth to scientific truth is considered only from the standpoint of content: religion and philosophy compete with one another with respect to the content of their teachings. Posed in this form, the problem makes for a highly superficial understanding of religion. In fact, religion initially does not develop beyond this stage. Yet the significance of the problem must be judged neither by the question whether the first attempts to find a solution are adequate, nor by the relative unimportance that is at first attached to the problem itself. The formulation of the problem from the standpoint of content must necessarily lead to the question of the concept of religious truth and of its relationship to the concept of scientific truth; this objective necessity is paralleled by the historical continuity in which the methodological formulation emerges from the substantive formulation. The step from one formulation to the other, which of course never means the displacement of one by the other, characterizes the methodological development of our problem, from which alone we can gain an understanding of the solutions relating to the content.

These considerations determine the starting point for the analysis that follows. I merely wish to preface it with one comment concerning the selection of the material. This study begins with the Middle Ages in its more restricted sense, that is, as the period in which the relation of religion to philosophy is first discussed at length; it does not treat the earlier history of the problem as it appears in the works of Philo and the Church Fathers. Within this medieval period, our study will deal primarily with Muslim and Jewish philosophy. One reason for this approach is personal: it is in the direction of my own special interests. However, from the standpoint of the subject itself, it may well be advantageous to include these hitherto little considered sources within the historical framework of the problem, especially since this approach eliminates a whole series of complicating factors that were conspicuous in Scholasticism. Certain typical problems thus may appear in a simpler and more transparent form.

I

The presuppositions on which the development of our problem rests are the belief in revelation common to the monotheistic religions, on the one hand, and the idea that philosophy [can provide] absolute metaphysical knowledge of the world, on the other. These presuppositions imply that the question of the relationship between religious and scientific truth is identical with that of the relationship between the truth of revelation and the truth of metaphysical knowledge. The exclusive claim to truth inherent in the idea of revelation, however, necessarily restricts the problem to the relationship between a particular religion and the general truth of science. The concept of religion as a tendency of consciousness encompassing the various individual religions is completely foreign to the formulation of this problem. Admittedly the diversity of historical religions, which in Islam in particular, even in its early days, was the subject of a comparative study of religion, necessarily leads to the construction of a general concept of religion. This general concept, however, was at first taken from prescientific thought without being demonstrated, and it was only later that the need arose to formulate it methodologically. At any rate, as far as the question of religious truth is concerned, this general concept of religion, which the study of comparative religion is able to develop merely as an empirical class concept, recedes completely behind the concept of revelatory truth. As long as the concept of revelation is adhered to in its original, pure form, true religion is a phenomenon sui generis, whose genuine divine nature has nothing in common with that claimed by the other religions—except, of course, that of those religions recognized by the revealed religion itself as its preliminary stages, such as Christianity's recognition of Judaism and Islam's recognition of both. The only bond that unites these religions is their claim to the character of revelation, the very claim that makes them mutually exclusive. Rationalistic criticism, however, which rejects all these claims, finds itself without any authoritative power with which it can contend after the disintegration of the individual religions.

This formulation of the problem also suggests the manner in which religious truth may be compared to scientific truth. That the two spheres are compared in terms of their content lies in the nature of the motive that prompts the comparison. The need of the religious as well as of the scientific person to know the truth first requires that content of the religious and scientific consciousness be harmoniously reconciled. From this point of view, methodological determination of the various concepts of truth is significant only insofar as it involves the reconciliation of their substantive contradictions. This direction of interest to the content is not dependent on the identification of a particular religion with the truth of revelation. The influence of this identification manifests itself only when religion as revealed metaphysics confronts the metaphysical knowledge of science. Religious truth as such is characterized not by its inner essence, but only by its character as revelatory knowledge. Where this point of view alone is dominant, the consequence is that every single statement of the revealed document is an autonomous revelatory truth, regardless of whether its content is rational or historical; and this truth as such, independent of its specific meaning, is valid for the whole of religious consciousness. This basic conception of religion as revealed doctrine is expressed with sharp precision by Thomas Aquinas, for whom human knowledge of the content of revelation is dependent on the knowledge of the revealing God, just as in the sphere of human consciousness a derived science is founded on a basic science under which it is subsumed.[1] The atomizing consequence of a one-sided mode of thinking, oriented solely to a formal concept of revelation, is clearly seen in the writings of the Jewish philosopher of the late Middle Ages, Isaac Abrabanel, who rejects the notion that Judaism has fundamental doctrines on the ground that every statement in the Torah is a truth revealed by God. Hence there is no scale of values by which these truths can be ranked.[2]

All certitude concerning the content of revelation thus rests on the certitude that is given to us with the fact of revelation itself. The rivalry among the various positive religions, as well as their need to assert themselves against science, requires that the fact of revelation be safeguarded against all possible doubt. Thus Jewish, Christian, and Muslim theologians strive equally to remove the fact of revelation from the sphere of purely subjective conviction and to demonstrate its historicity objectively. This demonstration follows a somewhat different line of reasoning in each religion. Jewish theology bases its claim chiefly on the circumstances that the revelation at Sinai was imparted to the entire people, and that the tradition of such a revelation could never have become deeply rooted had it not been confirmed by the recollection of the people itself.[3] For Christianity revelation is based on the testimony of miracles, on the agreement among the various witnesses of the revelation, and on the fulfillment of the prophecies contained in the sacred Scriptures.[4] In addition to the miracles performed by Muhammad, Islam cites as especial proof of its divine origin the literary perfection of the Koran, which could not have been achieved by human skill alone.[5]

The aim of all these proofs is, of course, the same: to provide historical verification of the fact of revelation. The belief in revelation is thus raised to the rank of factual knowledge. It is verified by the evidence of historical knowledge, and thereby also guarantees the truth of the metaphysical doctrines that belong to the content of revelation. In Islamic and in Jewish theology, this concept of faith is set forth with unmistakable clarity, while Christian Scholasticism makes the doctrine more complex by the fact that it must, at the same time, interpret faith as one of the basic Christian virtues. It thus has to establish the validity of the nonintellectual elements involved in the act of faith. There is a constant struggle within Scholasticism between the desire to understand faith as an act of confidence in a living God who reveals Himself in His action to man (*fiducia*) and the need to endow faith with the character of objective certainty (*fides*). Only the latter is relevant in our present context since we are not dealing with the psychology of faith, but only with the doctrine of religious truth. From this point of view faith acquires in Christian Scholasticism, too, the character of historical knowledge, accessible to all who are willing to examine the historical evidence without prejudice. Regarded from the standpoint of certitude, religion is related to philosophy as historical knowledge is related to metaphysical knowledge.

The supranatural intellectualism of this faith stance hardly exhausts the understanding of religion among its adherents—something that happens, no doubt, only in exceptional cases. In general we see it bound up with a profound understanding of all the inwardness of religious consciousness. The deepest awareness and redeeming virtue of the content of revelation can be united with the most rigorous intellectualism in the perception of the concept or revelation. All this will be duly treated in its proper place. In no way does it affect the understanding of the concept of religious truth itself. On the contrary, the purely intellectual comprehension of religious certitude becomes even clearer when contrasted with an interpretation that stresses the more vital aspects of the total religious consciousness.

From a formal point of view, the truth of revelation is thereby made independent of verification by philosophical knowledge. It does not matter, contrary to what some people contend, that a clearly irrational assertion can in no way be made acceptable on the evidence of miracles and that a doctrine containing such assertions is to be rejected ipso facto, without historical examination. For every such obstacle can be removed by interpretation. Substantively, however, the most far-reaching accommodation of the doctrine of revelation to philosophy is still possible, and it is precisely the interpretation of the sacred text which, by formally acknowledging the authority of revelation, makes it possible to accommodate the content of revelation completely to philosophy. The principle that is prevalent throughout the Middle Ages—that reason and revelation cannot contradict one another, for both are derived from God, the source of all truth—obviously can be applied in entirely different ways. The traditional views of faith are essentially maintained in Christian Scholasticism, indicating the basis on which the unity of reason and revelation can be achieved. A reinterpretation of basic doctrines is impossible because they had already been formulated as fixed dogmas; philosophy is faced not with the flexible text of a sacred document, but with an unequivocally formulated principle of faith. The formal recognition of the Koran in Arabic philosophy makes for radical reinterpretations of the basic religious views which, because of the more flexible nature of Muslim dogmatics, are much more free. Even the complete abandonment of personalistic religiosity in favor of the Aristotelian conception of the necessary interrelation of the world and God can be defended by ibn Rushd on the ground that it represents the real meaning of the Koran's teachings; and it appears, indeed, that this recognition of the Koran, in complete contradiction to its actual content, is sincerely meant.[6] The Jewish philosophy of religion stands halfway between these two tendencies. In spite of the far-reaching accommodation of its religious ideas to Aristotelianism and Neoplatonism, it still adheres to the basic attitude of biblical religiosity by leaving the freedom of the divine act of creation—and with it the place of the Creator as the sovereign master of the universe—untouched. This differentiation, posited at first simply as a fact, is later developed in a highly interesting manner from the concept of revelation itself. The presuppositions concerning the nature of God and man, without which the idea of revelation is meaningless, are to be recognized as the universally binding basic principles of Jewish teaching. As such they also set definite limits to the philosophical interpretation of the Bible. The concept of revelation thus creates out of itself the material content of the religious doctrines that are to be recognized as binding.[7]

The basic relationship of religion and reason is not affected by these differences. Within the framework of the problem as it has been formulated up to this point, the sole variable factor is clearly that of cognitive knowledge. Medieval theories concerning the relationship between faith and knowledge deal chiefly with the ability of cognition to create out of itself the truths of revelation, and these theories differ from one another according to their evaluation of the cognitive faculty. Psychologically, this evaluation is determined decisively by religious motives. Attempts to restrict the competency of the cognitive faculty obviously are motivated by the need to secure for religion the possibility of free movement, regardless of whether this is done solely in the interest of religious traditionalism or as a spontaneous reaction by religion to protect itself against all rationalistic efforts to restrict its power. As an attitude of the spirit this criticism, directed against science and generated by a religious impulse, is a completely new phenomenon. It represents the breakthrough of a voluntarist criticism of reason which is completely alien to antiquity, and which prefigures modern irrationalism in its religious as well as its secular gestalt. It is an irrationalism which, in sharp contrast to Skepticism in the ancient world, negates reason in order to make room for a supralogical conception of reality.

Recognition of the role of knowledge, however, can well be the expression of a definite religiosity that seeks to express its relationship to God also in the form of cognitive knowledge. The objective solution of the problem, however, is something that has to be achieved by examining and defining "knowledge." It is in connection with this question that the Middle Ages develops its interest in the problem of knowledge, and especially in the problem of metaphysical knowledge. The justification of cognition basically follows the ancient tradition; in its essential aspects, it does not advance beyond the ancients, either in the form of Aristotelianism or in the stricter a priori form of Neoplatonism, which is dominant especially in the Augustinian school of Christian theology.

A more independent attitude is adopted by the criticism of metaphysics undertaken in the interest of faith. This criticism, to be sure, is directed more against the prevailing metaphysical systems than against the concept of metaphysics. Even when it asserts the impossibility of metaphysics as such, it bases its criticism on the collapse of all previous metaphysical attempts and on the unresolved antagonisms among the metaphysical systems, rather than on proofs derived from the concept of knowledge designed to demonstrate the futility of the metaphysical enterprise. [In other words,] the severity and at times profundity of the criticism is directed not so much against the presuppositions as against the argumentations of the metaphysicians. This accounts for the fact that in principle no line is drawn between metaphysics and legitimate cognition, and that the criticism for the most part results in a mere restriction of metaphysical knowledge. This is plainly evident in the writings of the first Jewish critic of metaphysics, Judah Halevi. His sharp polemic against philosophy concludes with the admission that the existence of a Supreme Being can be rationally demonstrated, and it is only the closer determination of the relationship of God and world that is beyond human cognition. Similarly, Duns Scotus, in his criticism of metaphysics, is content to restrict himself more or less to marking the limits of metaphysical knowledge.[8]

The criticism of metaphysics in the Middle Ages does not move beyond this barrier, even where a starting point for a basic change seems to be available. This is evident in Arabic philosophy in the case of Ghazali, who is distinguished by the originality of his thought as well as by the depth of his religious consciousness. His refutation of philosophy seeks its starting point in the concept of knowledge which is to serve as the criterion for judging all cognition. When he compares the clear evidence of mathematical knowledge with the unsure gropings of metaphysics, his objective is not only to exhibit the futility of all previous metaphysical attempts, but also to determine the norm that all genuine cognition must satisfy. We may reasonably assume that his criticism of causality is an application of this requirement. The well-known principle of this criticism—that cause and effect are not correlated and that, therefore, positing the one does not necessarily require positing the other—would appear to represent a judgment of causality from the standpoint of cognition based on mathematics. But quite apart from this context, the criticism of the principle of causality deprives the knowledge of reality in general and metaphysical knowledge in particular of their logical basis, thus nullifying the possibility of metaphysics in principle.

The elements of such a position, which is not far from that of Hume, are no doubt present in Ghazali. However, he does not realize the full import of his isolated insights himself and, in fact, approaches the problem from an altogether different angle, as far as we can judge his position from his concept of cognition. In his *Incoherence of the Philoso-*

phers [*Tahafut al-Falasifah*] the criticism of the causal principle does not occupy the central place that would correspond to its logical importance. It occupies a place beside the broad mass of ideas that seek to expose the fallacies of the prevailing system of metaphysics, not above them as the principle that constitutes the basis for criticism of the individual points. Above all, however, the meaning of this criticism of causality seems far less radical than the argumentation discussed above would lead us to surmise, for beside it we also find an argument which affirms causality in principle—namely, that only the causality of the will is understandable, whereas physical causality is simply inconceivable. On the basis of this argument Ghazali himself deduces from the existence of the world a creator who brought it forth. This deduction would be impossible if his criticism were directed against the principle of causality itself. Considering the direction of Ghazali's thought, his criticism can only refer to the necessity of a connection between a specific cause and a specific effect. Since cause and effect are not correlated, the effect that proceeds from a thing cannot be deduced from its essence, and it is only the will of God that established the connection between them. The aim of this criticism of causality thus is to negate any empirical causal connection in favor of the sole causality of the divine will. Hence it is precisely the metaphysical application of the causal principle that remains unaffected by Ghazali's criticism—except that in his case it leads to a metaphysics of the will instead of to the Aristotelian system of necessity.[9]

In Christian philosophy a basic criticism of metaphysics can be found only in the nominalism of the late Middle Ages. Indeed, metaphysics is hardly compatible with the theory of knowledge derived from this concept as it is understood by this philosophical movement. It therefore adopts Ghazali's criticism of causality and extends it to the problem of substance and of physical reality in general. However, this extension makes not only metaphysics but all knowledge of reality impossible. The ban of skepticism that condemns metaphysics also covers the empirical knowledge of reality. For this very reason the force of skeptical arguments becomes blunted: it negates only the logical evidence of the principles assailed but not their validity as probable assumptions. On this basis, room can once again be found for a metaphysics of probability, and, as a result of this restriction, at least some of the traditional proofs for God are recognized.[10] In any case, even these phenomena in no way affect the conclusion that the various medieval theories concerning the relation of faith and knowledge differ quantitatively from one another in their evaluation of cognitive knowledge.

In terms of the principles involved, the details of these theories are of no particular interest. We merely emphasize those elements that contribute to our understanding of the concept of religion. The rationalist, who assumes that the entire metaphysical content of the doctrine of revelation is rationally demonstrable and that religious truth is completely identical with philosophical truth, can conceive the purpose of revelation solely as pedagogical, designed to make the truth of reason accessible to those who are unable to grasp it scientifically.[11] In Arabic and Jewish philosophy, largely dominated by an unrestricted rationalism, this conception of religion extends to its entire content. Christian theology, which even in its rationalistic forms withdraws its mysteries of faith from the scrutiny of reason, restricts it to the rational part of the doctrine of revelation. Within this limitation, however, it remains an integral element of Christian theology well into the Enlightenment of the eighteenth century. Even in its radical form, this theory is motivated by the conviction that it confers on revelation the dignity of the highest wisdom and that, by showing its congruity with metaphysical knowledge, it demonstrates the profundity of its entire truth. However, all this applies only to the objective content of the doctrine of revelation. As far as the understanding of this content is concerned, scientific knowledge is clearly superior to mere knowledge derived from revelation. Rooted in the soil of the concept of supranaturalistic revelation, religion gradually grows into a description of philosophical truth for the people. Religion is such a description, not according to its objective content, but according to the manner in which this content is comprehended.

The development of this conception of religion becomes even more apparent when the literal meaning of the revelatory document is distinguished from its deeper meaning, which is comprehended only by the philosophically trained. The literal meaning that is meant only for the simple believer constitutes in reality the metaphysical truth in a form adapted for the understanding of the common folk, even though the truth of revelation in its deeper sense includes, of course, the entire content of metaphysical knowledge.

The resulting concept of religion is thus that of an enlightenment that believes in a revelation fusing the rational character of religious truth with acknowledgment of its supranatural origin. Islam and Judaism, lacking mysteries of faith, are more hospitable to this concept than Christianity, where it develops a pronounced polemical character. But even in the culture of Islam this concept is possible only because of a general tendency to subordinate all areas of spiritual life to the rule of the intellect. There too the enlightenment that believes in revelation—insofar as this belief is sincerely held—springs from an apologetic tendency; it seeks to safeguard the possibility of revelation against the radical criticism of the enlightenment. In fact, we find clear traces of such a freethinking enlightenment even in the early days of Islamic culture, and we may assume that its influence is considerably greater than the reports that have come down to us from their opponents' writings might lead us to assume. This enlightenment fully develops the idea of natural religion, in its deeper meaning if not in its literal sense, and we shall later encounter in it all essential aspects of this idea.

In this conception of the relationship of revelation to cognitive knowledge, however, enlightenment meets its most extreme antithesis: the mystical tendency of medieval philosophy. Medieval Neoplatonism also teaches that the truth of revelation coincides with that of knowledge, but it regards the act of cognition itself as determined by religion, and it conceives the knowledge of the divine as the union of the soul with its divine source. This Neoplatonism is dominant in Arabic and Jewish philosophy, especially in its fusion with the Aristotelian system. In the view of this neoplatonically tinged Aristotelianism, the union of the human spirit with the divine in the act of cognition constitutes the apex and consummation of the cognitive process. In metaphysical knowledge the individual soul is raised to the divine spirit.

The Neoplatonism of the Christian Middle Ages is determined by the Augustinian spirit which, especially in its earlier phases, tends to broaden the sphere of validity of rational knowledge as far as possible. According to this Augustinian conception of Neoplatonism, the union of the human soul with God is not brought about by cognitive knowledge; it regards knowledge rather as the expression of the original unity of the human and divine spirit. The fact of knowledge testifies to the human spirit's participation in divine truth. The proofs for the existence of God in this Augustinian view express in conceptual form the connection with the divine that is innate in consciousness. In both forms cognition is an unmediated union with the divine, and in the interpretation of the process of cognition the religious nature of the soul is both exhibited and determined in its specificity. This determination, however, applies only to the religious attitude and does not touch the concept of religious truth. Despite all mystical interpretation, the truth of cognition retains its intellectual character; its certitude remains that of logical insight. It is not the mystical but the intellectual aspect of this conception that requires consideration with respect to the problem of religious truth.

We have already indicated the different motives prompting opposition to complete rationalization of the truth of revelation. The competency of reason can be restricted either in the interest of the authority of religious faith or in order to assure the untrammeled spontaneity of religious life. This variety of motives has no objective significance, however, as long as the limits of metaphysical knowledge are determined solely by logical analysis. Occasionally we encounter an attempt to deduce the unknowability of objects of belief from their very nature, a position sharply formulated by Judah Halevi, according to whom it would mean a deficiency in God if we were able to know Him.[12] That God cannot be known is not deduced from the nature of our knowledge, but is required by the dignity of the divine. It is a positive factor, as it were, in the determination of the nature of the divine, and it is a necessity demanded by the religious relationship of God and man. Although this point is not systematically pursued by Judah Halevi or any similarly oriented thinker, it nevertheless gives rise to a conception of religious truth that leaves the opposition between the knowledge of reason and the knowledge of revelation far behind. Religious truth is not the content of the doctrine of revelation, but of revelation in an altogether different sense, whereby the secret depths of the divine within it are revealed to consciousness.

The problem described thus far also constitutes the basis of the paradoxical doctrine of "double truth" which appears in different places in the late Middle Ages. Its origin has so far remained obscure. The assumption that the thirteenth-century Christian Averroists took this doctrine from ibn Rushd is no doubt inaccurate, since the latter posits the complete identity of the content of revelation and philosophical truth. The distinction he makes between the literal sense of the Koran, which is meant for the masses, and its real truth, which is reserved for the learned, stems from a tendency that is the very opposite to that of the double truth. Nor can this doctrine be regarded as a creation of the Christian Averroists themselves, for we already find it at the end of the thirteenth century in the writings of the Jewish philosopher Isaac Albalag, not only in its practical application, as is the case in Christian Averroism, but in a coherent theoretical development.[13] That this is merely a coincidence is hardly conceivable; it is probable that a hitherto unknown Arabic reconstruction of ibn Rushd's theory served as the common source. Objective understanding of the doctrine of the double truth is hardly affected by this hiatus in our knowledge, although it could be affected by our uncertainty whether we are to regard this theory as having been held in all seriousness or merely as a disguised denial of the authority of revelation. The doctrine of the double truth has, to be sure, often been used to conceal freethinking radicalism, yet it is not likely that it is merely meant to be a diplomatic strategy. It is, rather, meant to express the difficulty that arises from the juxtaposition of two authorities claiming equal validity, the authority of revelation and that of metaphysical knowledge. If both are retained as absolutes, their differences can be reconciled only through mutual adjustment and accommodation, for it is impossible to conceive of an even higher stage of truth that would permit a resolution of such differences in principle. Where the awareness of the specific nature of the two opposing worlds resists such an accommodation, nothing remains but to acknowledge their duality. Here we have, reduced to its basic form, the notion that the idea of truth has various autonomous spheres, a notion which demolishes the unity of the concept of truth. Vice versa, the equation of the truth of revelation with that of reason is able to comprehend the unity of truth only as the identity of its various forms. The unity of the concept of truth and the autonomy of its various spheres struggle in vain to achieve a synthesis.

This struggle continues, of course, when the concept of religious truth is anchored not in the authority of revelation, but in the inwardness of the religious consciousness. To be sure, according to this conception we can no longer speak of the identity of religious and scientific truth. But even when religion ceases to be a kind of metaphysical knowledge, its declarations concerning the divine still apply to the same sphere of absolute reality that constitutes the object of metaphysical knowledge. As long as religious and scientific consciousness aim at the same sphere of absolute being, it remains difficult to safeguard the autonomy of both and at the same time to combine them into a unity of a consciousness of truth. The full import of this problem was comprehended only after a long and complicated development. The significance of the doctrine of the double truth is that the problem appears in it for the first time.

II

Besides their metaphysical elements, reason and revelation also encompass the sphere of ethical norms, and the question of their reciprocal relationship applies equally to the ethical and metaphysical elements. The difference between the validity of the ethical and of the theoretical [epistemological] spheres need not be considered here. Especially in the sphere of religious truth the ethics of revelation does not occupy a position different from that of the theoretical content of the doctrine of revelation. Hence the viewpoints from which the question of religious truth is discussed remain unchanged when applied to the ethical component of the doctrine of revelation. In the ethical sphere, however, they lead to entirely different consequences, which raise problems about ethical lawfulness in its profoundest aspects.

The tensions between the statements contained in the religious documents and the results of rational insight, which must be properly reconciled in the theoretical sphere, are greatly reduced in the ethical sphere. The difference between the ethos of Greek philosophy and that of the monotheistic religions, at least in the orbit of Arabic and Jewish culture, is never perceived as acutely as are the differences in the sphere of religious doctrines. In the ethical sphere the proper subject of discussion is the question of the autonomy of the moral consciousness. Whereas the only disputed subject in the theoretical sphere is the power of reason to penetrate the metaphysical depths of the truths of faith, in the ethical sphere the concept of moral reason as such is questioned. Rationalism asserts that the meaning of the moral law and its necessity are innate in human consciousness and accessible to reason. According to the exclusive standpoint of revelation, there is no inner criterion of moral truth. The validity of moral norms is based solely on the authority of revelation.

In its most extreme form, this heteronomous point of view is expressed in the thought that it is not the weakness of our reason that prevents it from comprehending moral truth, but rather that rational insight is not possible in the moral sphere because the source of moral laws is hidden in an uncaused act of the divine will. Our actions are good and evil not because of their intrinsic nature, but solely because they are demands of the divine will which can arbitrarily make good evil and evil good. This view actually has its deepest roots in the desire to elevate the sovereignty of the divine will above all criteria of moral judgment, and not in the question concerning the relationship between reason and revelation. A God-consciousness that is totally imbued with the feeling of divine majesty resists any attempt to limit the divine will; it makes the Sovereign of the world also the Ruler over good and evil. It negates the idea of moral reason, which seeks to measure God's actions, even as it does human actions, with its own criteria.

Thus, the real source of this view is to be found in the problem of theodicy. Every rational theodicy becomes superfluous, for we no longer have a criterion that can serve as a justification of God. Next to this, the negation of moral reason, even in the sphere of human morality, is of secondary importance. The fact that it is applied to this sphere confirms the unity of the idea of ethical validity, which must be acknowledged absolutely or else wholly abandoned.

The history of the idea [of the sovereignty of the divine will over all criteria of moral judgment] still requires some clarification. Its first and most significant expression is found in Islam, whose conception of God is dominated by the sovereign power of the divine will. The Ash'arite school of the Kalām elaborates this idea in detail; even a thinker such as Ghazali, despite his differently oriented concept of God, cannot escape its influence.[14] In the Christian Middle Ages we see the initial outlines of this idea in Duns Scotus, but it is fully developed only in Occam's school, which, as mentioned before, is also close to Ghazali in its criticism of causality. The assumption that there is a historical connection [between the two] ought not to be dismissed, although it has until now not been possible to examine and demonstrate the problem in detail. The same basic themes recur in modern theology and philosophy, although in a different form, but again it has not yet been possible to demonstrate the definite existence of a historical continuity. In theology, the Calvinist doctrine of predestination adopts the idea of divine sovereignty in all its grandiose severity; every criticism of a divine judgment that elects one man to damnation and another to eternal bliss is met by the argument that the divine will is superior to every moral norm which it has itself established. In philosophy we find, even in Descartes's rationalism, the idea that all truth, moral as well as logical, is dependent on the divine will, although this is only a passing thought, aside from which Descartes maintains his view of moral and logical reason. It is in Pascal's thought, however, that the idea of God's sovereign will is treated with the utmost seriousness: reason cannot do enough to humble itself, and it is deprived of every moral criterion in order to make submission to the incomprehensible divine will the sole norm of moral conduct.[15] It is not too difficult to show a relationship here to similar views in the Christianity of the Middle Ages. The criticism of causality by Ghazali and by the Nominalists of the late Middle Ages reappears in Occasionalism, which is in many ways close to Pascal's thinking (although it does not appear in Pascal's own writings) and, similar to what we find among the Arabs, the immanent causal connection with nature is negated in favor of the sole causality of the divine will. Whether this is a purely parallel development in the history of thought or whether these remarkably similar voluntarist systems are united in a historical continuity is a question that cannot be answered on the basis of our present-day knowledge.

In the medieval tradition, the idea of moral reason means that moral laws are rooted not in God's will but in His reason. This view does not affect the rootedness of moral lawfulness in the idea of God. It teaches the autonomy of moral reason over against revelation but not over against a natural God-consciousness. Rational justification of the moral law can thus assume many different forms: individual and social eudaemonism, an ethic of perfectibility, duty, and love are all possible in the framework of this view. The only indispensable element is that the moral law permit rational insight into the idea of morality.

This view finds its sharpest expression in the demand that every doctrine laying claim to divine origin should be examined with respect to its moral content before its external authority is verified; a doctrine's offensiveness to moral reason precludes its divinity from the outset, and no external confirmation, however strong, can offset this rejection or compensate for it. We have already indicated that this criterion is practically of little significance for the authenticity of revelation, since any contradiction can be interpreted away. However, this does not affect its basic significance; indeed, it is confirmed anew when the demands of the moral consciousness are made the norm for interpretation of the document of revelation.

Although the philosophic idea of moral reason carries a good deal of weight in this view, it would be one-sided to regard it only as the expression of philosophical rationalism. It is just as much the philosophic formulation of the fundamental religious affirmation of ethical monotheism. In its view too, God is will, but, in conformity with His nature, moral will. The basic religious experience is that of God as the beneficent power from whom all religious categories receive their ethical character. Reverence for God is not directed to the unbounded sovereignty of the divine will, but to God's moral majesty as the quintessence of the good. To regard the divine demands as mere commands requiring nothing but unconditional obedience is incompatible with this religious attitude, which presupposes that there is evidence for the divine demands, and which makes sense only when the inner truth of these demands is plainly evident. The notion that ethical precepts are clearly evident is one of the basic ideas of Israelite prophecy; it runs through the entire history of Jewish piety. It belongs no less to Christian religiosity, and even where the Christian morality of grace represents a higher stage than the natural morality of reason, the essential idea need not be lost. Moral values can also be clearly revealed to someone who is infused by the power of grace and whose reason cannot reach these moral values by its own strength. We thus have two different forms of religious consciousness that confront each other in the two medieval theories concerning the relationship of God and the moral law. The methodological question regarding the relationship between reason and revealed morality represents the form in which the objective contrast of two essentially different views of the divine is expressed.

For the determination of the concept of religion, however, this analysis does not lead us beyond what has already been established. From the perspective of the concept of truth, the exclusive criterion of religion is the fact that it has been revealed. Yet this formal characterization of religious truth, particularly when seen from the standpoint of the moral content of religion, can in no way exhaust the understanding of religion. That religion is distinguished from science by its revelatory character is self-evident to the Middle Ages; but just as evident is the fact that revelation, according to its content, is an instrument of the divine will to clarify the purpose of man's life, and that the content of doctrine should include a revelation concerning God's being and essence. That all religions deal with a doctrine regarding God and God's will belongs to the content of that general prescientific concept of religion of which we have already spoken. Philosophy, too, ultimately seeks to arrive at a doctrine of the nature of God and the vocation of man. Yet these more or less specific ideas regarding the nature of religion are irrelevant for the medieval theory of religion; they acquire philosophical significance only when methodologically formulated. This is done in the philosophy of religion, which is primarily interested in the comparison of reason and revelation, by raising the question of the purpose of revelation. Where religion is conceived as a doctrine of revelation, its substantive content manifests itself as a theory concerning the purpose of revelation. This makes it possible to distinguish between the basic and the derived, between the central and the peripheral, within the content of revelation, which, because of its divine origin, is of equal value in all its parts. Both the ritual and ceremonial duties prescribed in the sacred writings and their historical components thus become the means that either serve the moral purpose of revelation or are meant to lead to knowledge of its external truths.

Two types of purpose must be clearly distinguished in the concept of revelation: one is in the ethical sphere, the other in the speculative sphere. The ethical interpretation of religion is dominant especially among the early Arab thinkers and, influenced by them, among the first representatives of Jewish religious philosophy. In this view, which found its purest expression in the Mu'tazalite Kalām, the observance of God's commandments is the way to attain the highest good and eternal bliss. To provide guidance to this goal is the ultimate purpose of revelation: the presuppositions of this conception of man's vocation are basic truths of religion—the existence of a Divine Law-giver, man's ability to fulfill the divine demands, and God's retributive justice, which also includes the idea of a future life.[16] The affinity of this view with that of modern Enlightenment, previously emphasized from another perspective, becomes evident in this interpretation of religion. The basic religious truths articulated here as the fundamentals of the religion of revelation are completely congruous with those of the natural religion in the era of the Enlightenment: God, freedom, and immortality. In both the divine origin of the moral law and God's retributive justice constitute the real core of religion. The eighteenth-century Enlightenment which believes in revelation is in all its essential points prefigured in this medieval conception of religion.

The speculative interpretation of religion predominates in the Aristotelian and Neoplatonic systems. That there are also numerous different intermediate and transitional forms needs no special emphasis. In its pure and fully developed form, this speculative interpretation posits that the real purpose of revelation is to impart to men true knowledge of God and of the supraterrestrial world and to illumine and clarify the minds of believers. The criterion distinguishing a divine from a human law consists, according to Maimonides, in the fact that it is not content to regulate men's actions and their interrelations, but also desires to achieve man's spiritual perfection by teaching him the true conception of God and His acts. As he explains at the end of the *Guide for the Perplexed* [*Moreh*], man's closeness to or distance from God is determined by the degree of his knowledge. The hierarchial order among the different classes of people is constructed wholly from this intellectual point of view.[17] The emotion-filled religiosity of Baḥya ibn Paquda, too, is deeply influenced, although in milder form, by the same intellectualizing approach. The deepening of religious inwardness presupposes for him a deeper penetration of the intellectual content of religious truth.[18] The Greek origin of this high evaluation of the cognitive faculty is obvious. We have before us in religious form the Aristotelian conception of the intellect as the ultimate distinction of the human personality. Strangely enough, this hellenic idea takes a peculiar turn from time to time, not only in the religious but also in the dogmatic sphere: the dogmatic conception that every deviation from correct belief endangers the salvation of the soul is equated with the philosophical idea that only true knowledge can lead the spirit to perfection.

This rigorous intellectualism is alleviated by the thought that knowledge of God must necessarily lead to love of God. Not the mere knowledge of God but the love of Him resulting from it thus becomes the real meaning of religious conduct. However, this is only an inadequate and exoteric presentation of the true religious content of this view. It conceals an interpretation of knowledge in the sense of that Neoplatonic mysticism already discussed in another context. When the knowledge of God is glorified as the ultimate goal of revelation, and the metaphysical absorption in the divine truth as the highest form of life, knowledge is understood as union with the Divine Spirit. To place knowledge above moral conduct, whose ultimate goal is to liberate the spirit from the coils of sensibility, and to endow it with the strength to behold the pure vision of truth is in the last analysis tantamount to placing contemplative religiosity above moral conduct.

In these two interpretations of religion we find the expression of two different forms of religious life. In the moral interpretation there is an ethical religiosity which is rooted and alive in the monotheistic religions; in the intellectualizing interpretation there is a contemplative piety that finds its speculative expression in Neoplatonism, which then penetrates the more learned strata of the Arabic cultural orbit. In neither theory, however, does the specifically religious element find adequate expression. The moral interpretation of religion understands ethical religiosity as a morality that is closely bound up with the belief in divine justice; the intellectual interpretation conceives contemplative religiosity as an act of theoretical cognition which as such binds man to God.

The religious ideal of Neoplatonism is by its very nature accessible only to a narrow circle of initiates. Within a religious community comprising all stages of education, therefore, it must be supplemented with an ideal designed for the believing masses. The Arabic Neoplatonists met this requirement by conceiving the moral interpretation of religion as the exoteric dimension of their system. The ultimate purpose of revelation is religion in the sense of knowledge of God; its preliminary stage—designed for the masses—is religion as belief in morality and in reward and punishment.

In Jewish philosophy this consequence, which is contrary to the innermost character of Jewish piety, is rarely drawn,[19] except [for instance] by ibn Rushd, who makes a very precise distinction between esoteric and exoteric piety in the sense just mentioned. According to him, popular religion also contains both morality and truth, although only as much of the latter as is commonly understood to be required for the purpose of morality. The basic religious truths, which, in his view, must also be understood by those on the lowest level of knowledge and which represent the binding dogmas of Islam, are identical with the presuppositions of the moral belief in retribution.[20]

The content of religion which we have attempted to describe is rationally determined in both forms. Nothing essential is changed when, for example, the moral type appears in conjunction with the antirationalistic, exclusive doctrine of revelation. However, among some representatives of this antirationalistic view we find a conception of the purpose of revelation which, side-by-side with knowledge and morality, shows an autonomous sphere of religious life. This view, which penetrates to the depths of the religious life, is developed for the first time by Ghazali. The complexity of his motives, however, make it advisable to proceed from Judah Halevi's simpler and clearer interpretation and then, for the sake of completeness, to return to Ghazali's more comprehensive but also more diffuse theory of religion.

The distinctiveness of Judah Halevi's conception of religion does not lie, as is often assumed, in his doctrine of the autonomy of religious certitude over against philosophical cognition. His conception of religious certitude is the medieval view identifying religious faith with belief in the divine origin of the doctrine of revelation. What distinguishes Judah Halevi is simply the vigor with which he emphasizes that the fact of revelation is historically provable. Only when we proceed from his proof of religious truth to his interpretation of the phenomena of religious life do we come closer to the essential element in his view. For him, the ultimate purpose of revelation is to show man the way to make contact with God. This life with God, as it unfolds itself under the influence of divine revelation, consists in religious conduct, whose distinctive nature Judah Halevi attempts to elucidate. The concept "life with God" is to be taken literally. All religious life involves a genuine communion with God which is removed from the realm of natural existence and which can only be understood as the effect of God's acts. The miraculous events in which God makes Himself known to the prophets are merely an intensified form of the communion with God that is also found in everyday religious experience.

The conviction that religious life constitutes a world that is wholly sui generis is expressed most clearly in the teaching that a special spiritual power is required to achieve contact with God, a power that was conferred in ancient times only upon chosen individuals, and which became the possession of a larger group only in Israel. This special faculty, which is basic to all religious life, is added to man's natural faculties as something completely new. It is, of course, a mere disposition that enables man to receive the divine influence. Its realization can only be the work of God, for all activity in the religious relationship between man and God is initiated by God. The purpose of the doctrine of revelation is to intensify the original religious disposition so as to render it capable of receiving the divine influence. All religious and cultic precepts given to Israel serve this end.

The medieval context in which this view of the religious life appears may at first tend to obscure its profundity and inwardness. A genuine life with God is possible, according to Judah Halevi, only within the Jewish religious community; everywhere else there is only the illusion of such a life, born out of longing. The dogmatic conception of religion, according to which there can be no genuine religious life outside of revealed religion, has a restrictive severity which is much more noticeable in Judah Halevi than in the other medieval Jewish philosophers of religion, since for them knowledge is the path to God accessible to everyone. The harshness of this particularism becomes even more evident when the specific religious disposition is restricted to the members of the Israelite people. To be sure, this national particularism is progressively modified in the course of his exposition (whose theme is the conversion of a heathen prince to Judaism), and then wholly negated by the idea of the messianic future. The dogmatic exclusivity remains, however, and with it the peculiar reification of the religious life which ascribes the power to achieve contact with God to the cultic and ceremonial rites and attributes this effect to the mysterious power that inheres, as if by nature, in the duties prescribed by God.

All this, however, refers only to the theory designed to explain the religious phenomena; it does not point up these phenomena themselves. The distinction between life with God and knowledge about God, the conception of this life with God as being seized by a God who reveals Himself to man—all these are the result of observing the religious occurrences which are subsequently interpreted partly according to specific traditional views, partly according to the Neoplatonic conception of the influence of the upper upon the lower world. The distinctiveness of religious phenomena is made especially clear by Judah Halevi's comparison of the prophetic experience of God with the philosophical knowledge of God. In this comparison the intuitive immediacy of the prophetic God-consciousness is first contrasted with the mediated and hence always relative nature of the philosophical knowledge of God. He then points out that the effect of this direct experience of God is the soul's devotion to God, a devotion that can never be derived from conceptual thought. For science, God is merely one object of cognition among others, distinguished from them only by its superior logical significance in the cognitive context. No other logical distinctions among its objects are recognized by science, as Judah Halevi points out with remarkable insight. The greatness, glory, and majesty of God are known only where God is experienced directly, and from this experience alone spring the joy and bliss of communion with Him. This idea is at first developed only in connection with the extraordinary God-experiences of the prophet, but is then extended to the God-consciousness of the pious man in general. He too possesses an immediate certitude of God, although not in the graphic imagery of prophetic revelation, and is seized and enraptured by God's glory. At this decisive point, however, Judah Halevi is not equipped to define the immediate certainty of the pious man which, after all, lacks the intuitive character of the prophetic experience of God. He does not possess the psychological categories he needs to describe the distinctive characteristics of the religious consciousness. This lack, which frequently also is a vexing problem for the modern philosophy of religion, makes for a certain lack of precision in his description of that stage of religious life which has not risen to the level of the prophetic stage, though he does not miss its basic intent. Nevertheless, despite this struggle for psychological clarity, Judah Halevi's description of the God-consciousness which the pious man possesses, even without prophetic illumination, clearly expresses the principle of the autonomy of *all* religious experience in relation to philosophical cognition. However, he does not use the immediacy of this God-consciousness as a proof for the certainty of religious truth. The objectivity of the certitude of faith demands, in his view, validation by an objective argument of compelling force. The subjectivity of the immediate experience of God cannot be used for this purpose. Hence a revelation whose historical factuality can be clearly demonstrated remains the criterion of religious truth.[21]

This theory of religion goes back to Ghazali, especially in its basic intention to describe the phenomena of religious life as completely different from [something attained by] cognitive reasoning. Judah Halevi's description of the pious man's immediate certitude of God is borrowed from Ghazali, as is his polemic against the pseudoknowledge of metaphysics. According to Ghazali, the certitude of God dwells in the heart, not the intellect. It is absurd to try to attain it by way of argument, not only because metaphysical knowledge is inadequate for this purpose, but also because the pious man's consciousness of God is not simply a knowledge of God. Rather, his soul is permeated with God. Both Judah Halevi and Ghazali clarify the essential difference between religious and scientific consciousness by contrasting prophetic illumination with philosophic speculation. The intuitive knowledge of the prophets differs in principle just as much from discursive understanding as the conceptual faculty of the intellect differs from sense perception. By characterizing prophecy as the experience of the divine, this contrast emphasizes the receptivity of the religious consciousness, which distinguishes it from the spontaneity of cognition.[22]

To base all religious life on the union of the soul with God, however, appears to be foreign to Ghazali's thought. Such a union occurs only in the ecstasy of the prophet and of the Ṣūfī, while Ghazali recognizes no such relationship in the ordinary phenomena of religious life. In his view, revelation is not a constitutive fact of religious life in the same way it is for Judah Halevi. The immediacy of religious consciousness for him resides chiefly in the fact that certainty of God and devotion to Him are native to the soul. All that is necessary to develop this religious faculty is a proper mode of life. With respect to details, however, the distinction between the two conceptions is often considerably blurred. In his statements on the evident and doubt-free faith of some favored natures, Judah Halevi conceives this faith wholly in the spirit of Ghazali, and almost in his very words, as an innate tendency of the soul towards God, without mentioning a presence of the divine in the soul. On the other hand, Ghazali frequently expresses the concept of the pious man's certitude of God as divine illumination. Despite these blurrings, however, the difference in their basic attitudes remains clear. Judah Halevi's idea of seeking the differentiating criterion of the religious life in the soul's union with God is foreign to Ghazali. The divine illumination which, in the language of all pious people, he ascribes to the believer manifests itself in nothing but the certitude of God experienced by the perfect soul.

This line of argument alone enables Ghazali to view all the advanced spiritual aspects of man's life as an expression of this tendency of the soul; in all consciousness which rises above the senses and strives to reach out beyond them, he sees the manifestation of the soul's hidden longing for the divine. The spirit, in its need to seek knowledge beyond the perception of the senses and to pursue truth regardless of benefit or profit, ultimately strives to reach only God. All love impulses of the soul are expressions of a love force whose essence is directed to God in Whom alone it finds its rest. The example of causality provides the clearest illustration of this point. We have already seen that for Ghazali only the causality of will is comprehensible. Wherever we seek the cause of a thing, we actually—if we understand ourselves rightly—refer to the will from which the thing proceeds. The spirit's instinctive search for the cause of things is thus an initially subconscious search for God, to Whom alone true causality may be attributed. Thus, the tendency to seek God is inborn in human consciousness as its ultimate motive power, and all we need to do is to raise this hidden sense of our spiritual life to consciousness. The religious consciousness thereby becomes the source and, at the same time, the consummation of our spiritual life in general. It is its source insofar as all functions of the spirit are moved by a power which, in the last analysis, is directed toward God, and it is its consummation in that all spiritual life reaches its goal only when its inborn tendency to seek God is realized.[23]

While Ghazali's initial concern is to separate religious life from the theoretical dimension of consciousness, all of consciousness is now included in the religious sphere. At first the autonomy of religion is established by the separation of religion from philosophical cognition; then the autonomy of religion is guaranteed by its being seen as encompassing the entire life of the intellect. Although these views can be reconciled, the basic tensions between them are evident. According to the religious interpretation of the intellect as a whole, the religious character of its functions is only latent at first, and an intermediate development is necessary to raise it to consciousness. The immediacy of the certitude of God, which is the true criterion of religious consciousness in Ghazali's original position, is thereby lost. The two different conceptions of religion obviously stem from two different points of view. The separation of the religious from the cognitive consciousness originates in the description of the data of consciousness. The attempt to discover a relationship to God in all forms of spiritual life serves as a kind of psychological proof of religious truth. Similar to the Augustinian tendency in Scholasticism, although employing other means, Ghazali, in seeking to find the path to God, bases himself on the nature of the human soul. Since all functions of the spirit point to God, man becomes certain of the truth that the consciousness of God is the necessary consummation of our spiritual life, the fulfillment of life's innate tendencies. This description indicates that every fully developed human consciousness contains the religious element. Ghazali is well aware of the universalistic implication of this idea. Each individual bears within himself the consciousness of God—not as a member of a particular religious community, but simply as a human personality. Ghazali's description of the pious man who is filled with God's presence depicts the life of piety in such general terms that again the universalistic tendency seems implicit. Thus it seems that his struggle against metaphysics and its encroachments on the religious sphere is conducted not in the interest of the historical authority of revelation, but of the inwardness of this universal religious consciousness. It thus would seem that Ghazali breaks through the limitations of the medieval formulation of the problem of the relationship of reason and revelation and arrives at a concept of religion that would make religion an autonomous sphere, distinct from cognition and morality. There is no doubt that such conclusions may be drawn from Ghazali's ideas emphasized here, and that his conception of religion takes us very close to the limits of the medieval modes of thought. But he does not go beyond those limits, and the conclusions we could possibly draw remain foreign to him. For him too, religious truth is represented by the doctrine of revelation whose final stage is the Koran. To be sure, he seeks to base the divine origin of revelation more on internal evidence than on external signs and miracles. According to him, we can be fully convinced of the divine mission of a prophet and the distinctive nature of prophetic illumination only when we immerse ourselves in the specific spiritual world of the prophets and recognize that it is a coherent world of phenomena defying natural explanation. It is this truth alone that is revealed to the prophet, however, which Ghazali sets up as an autonomous authority in contrast to rational knowledge. He constantly reproaches the Arabic Aristotelians for abandoning the fundamental teachings of the Koran and desiring knowledge obtainable solely from the word of God, but he does not complain about their opposition to the inner certainty of the believer. For him the pious man's immediate certainty of faith is, as little as it is for Judah Halevi, an independent source of truth as opposed to cognition. It is one of the forms in which the distinctiveness of religious life reveals itself, but which, because of its subjectivity, is unable to guarantee the truth of its beliefs.

Ghazali's great achievement is to have revealed the specific sphere of religious life and not a new formulation of the problem of religious truth. However, we must carefully distinguish between the real content of his teaching and its implicit consequences. The fact that his description of religious experience exhibits the fundamental principles of every higher form of piety does not mean that it applies to phenomena outside the limits of Islam. He is consciously universalistic only in the idea that the possession of a religious disposition is a general human phenomenon, but he obviously conceives of its realization only through Islamic forms. Judah Halevi's belief that only the forms of religious practice prescribed by God can influence man's proper conduct goes back to Ghazali, who supports it with medical and astrological analogies. [According to Ghazali,] these practices, which cannot be understood rationally, are effective only if very specific procedures are followed. The matter-of-fact faith of favored souls—a faith that cannot be diverted by doubt—consists not only of the soul's devotion to God; it is completely imbued with the truth of divine revelation. The pious man's consciousness of God is for Ghazali synonymous with that of the Islamic believer. He seeks to comprehend its essence and interpret it in the sense of a spiritualistic ideal of religion. His universalism therefore sees in Islam, as he understands it, the fulfillment of that for which human nature is destined and equipped. The idea of a religious consciousness transcending particular religions or of a religious inwardness autonomous of the historical authority of revelation is completely foreign to him. The spiritualism of his religious view remains wholly within the bounds of Muslim orthodoxy.

Further consequences, however, are clearly implicit in Ghazali's ideas, especially in his descriptive determination of religious phenomena. He not only describes religious experiences, as mystical and spiritualistic writers before him and after him have often done, but he differentiates these experiences in principle from the facts of cognition by confining them to a special sphere of psychic facts, thus arriving at a concept of religion determined by purely inner criteria. The establishment of an independent sphere of religious facts implies a new definition of the concept of religion, although this is by no means his intention; it is, at the same time, a definition of the concept of religion as such, even though such a generalization is remote from his views. That the problem of religious truth, too, is thereby placed on a new basis could of course only be discovered on the basis of an entirely new view of the concept of truth and validity. To understand the personal certitude of the believer—described with great precision by Ghazali as a fact of religious consciousness—as the specifically religious manifestation of the consciousness of truth presupposes that the intellectually restricted concept of objectivity has been transcended. The Middle Ages, thoroughly dominated by this concept, can comprehend the nature of religion in terms of its inwardness. Nevertheless, the only authorities of religious truth at its disposal are the objectivity of knowledge or the supernatural authority of revelation.

III

The rationalistic philosophy of medieval religion, as we have seen, substantively developed the idea of the religion of reason. We were able to establish the methodological and substantive affinity of this philosophy with the rationalism of modern Enlightenment. The medieval religion of reason, however, is distinguished from the natural religion of the Enlightenment in that philosophical knowledge is its sole bearer. Outside the sphere of revelation, religious truth is accessible only to the thinker, and in this form it is called rational knowledge, not religion. The belief in revelation can, of course, acknowledge that its truth is also accessible to cognition and rejoice in its congruence with this source of truth which likewise comes from God. [Because it claims] exclusivity, however, it cannot accept that there can be a religious truth outside its own sphere. In this respect the rationalistic tendency of Muslim and Jewish theology takes the same position as the school of thought that is hostile to science; it is distinguished from it only by its evaluation of philosophy. A similar position is that of the freethinking critics of religion who reject revelation, replace it with reason as the sole source of truth (beside which revelation is superfluous), and thus together with revelation dispense with religion altogether.

Medieval free thought, however, is also familiar with an entirely different attitude to religion. Side-by-side with the basic negation of all religion, we also find a relative recognition of the different religions. The bold words concerning the three swindlers serve the late Middle Ages as a description of one tendency of this popular criticism of religion, and the anecdote of the three precious stones as a description of the other. In the Christian countries of the West these tendencies do not appear until the second half of the Middle Ages. We meet them as early as the tenth and eleventh centuries in the cultural sphere of Islam. Islam's direct contact, not only with the Judaism and Christianity which preceded it in time, but also with the Persian and Indian religions, creates a climate of enlightenment at a very early date, leading to significant beginnings in the scientific study of comparative religion and, in the sphere of religion, to a critical attitude with respect to one's own faith. Adherents of the different religions, according to a well-known report, frequently came together for amicable conversations on religion, in which an appeal to the dogmatic authorities of any of the positive religions was frowned upon and in which all claims to truth on the part of a particular religion were to be examined freely and impartially.[24] In this setting, adherence to the authority of revelation gave rise to an enlightened mode of belief in revelation, whose nature we have already analyzed. From ibn Hazm, an author who lived not much later, we learn how many different forms of skepticism existed with respect to the belief in revelation. Yet the two types—the rejection in principle of all religions and the relativistic recognition of the various religions—can be clearly distinguished. The latter tendency demands that every man confess adherence to some religion, for without religion there can be no moral life. The notion that all positive religions are equally valid becomes especially evident in the rejection of religious conversion: according to ibn Hazm, conversion is regarded by many as rebellion against God, who has assigned to each man his religion. This view is not contradicted (although it appears to be in ibn Hazm's report) by the fact that there are others who teach that adherence to one's inherited religion is no excuse for opposing what all religions as well as human understanding acknowledge to be good and right—namely, the basic ethical commandments, which are at first enumerated singly and then summarized in the rule to treat one's fellow man as one would like to be treated by him.[25] The two views are not contradictory but complementary. The tolerant attitude to the positive religions reaches its limit where they are found to contradict basic ethical demands. It is, of course, of utmost importance that these basic ethical demands are defined as postulates of reason as well as that [core] which all religions have in common. The manner in which this agreement among the religions is cited as proof for the validity of these demands is equally important. Here we have all the elements from which the idea of natural religion will later arise: the assumption of a common core that is to be found in all religions and constitutes their most essential and significant component; the identity of this core with the teachings of reason; and, finally, the view that this core consists in the postulates of human morality. Yet regardless of how clearly the thought of a universal human religion—a religion that is essentially identical with morality—is stated, this thought is more the expression of a particular religious mentality that it is the development of a theory of religion. Indeed, ibn Hazm's report emphasizes only the factual agreement of the positive religions about their basic ethical demands and the congruence of these demands with those of the intellect; there is no further discussion of the origin of the common core or of its relationship to the intellect.

Arabic Aristotelianism, on the other hand, which provides a philosophical foundation for the freethinking tendencies within the orbit of Arabic culture, uses its metaphysical presuppositions to develop an interpretation of religious phenomena that contains, at least in its beginnings, the basis of a universalistic concept of religion. Nevertheless, even for this school of thought the criterion of religion remains its revelatory character, which it fully acknowledges and endeavors to explain metaphysically. But it is precisely this metaphysical theory of revelation that deprives revelation of its exclusive character and makes the development of a universal concept of religion possible. Prophetic inspiration, according to the Arabic Aristotelians, is a function of the active intellect which, as the lowest of the intelligences emanating from God, provides the forms for the terrestrial world. Prophecy is but another phenomenal form of the impact of this active intellect on the human mind; it occurs in every act of conceptual cognition. In the act of cognition, however, this impact affects only man's rational faculty, whereas in prophetic inspiration it also acts upon the imagination and thus creates figurative visions which embody in sensual form what the intellect comprehends conceptually. This difference stems from differences in the disposition of the receptive spirit. A purely intellectual disposition leads only to conceptual cognition; prophetic illumination originates in the union of the intellectual and imaginative faculties and their corresponding development. This theory reflects the intent to interpret prophecy as a natural fact and to deduce it from the general principles of the cognitive process. It acknowledges the fact of revelation, but divests it of its supernatural and miraculous character.[26]

The concept of revelation is central to the medieval view of religion and therefore has important consequences for the understanding of the concept of religion. It extends the identity of philosophical and revealed truth to the psychological sphere by attributing these two ways of conceiving truth to the same principle. The prophet as bearer of the doctrine of revelation is, according to this theory, necessarily also a philosopher, although he is distinguished from the mere philosopher by a special disposition which enables him to apprehend truth in a special form. This theory, however, introduces psychology to explain the difference between religious and philosophic truth. Religious revelation is philosophical truth in the form of imaginative intuition. Its figurative and intuitive character no longer is explained merely as something that is needed to make revelation comprehensible to the masses; it is comprehended and deduced from the nature of the process of revelation itself. Religion is thus granted a measure of autonomy, which is possible only in a speculative-metaphysical conception of its nature. Religion may be defined, somewhat in the late Hegelian manner, as comprehension of the ultimate metaphysical truth in the form of intuition. Religion is thus granted its own form of consciousness within the framework of the doctrine of revelation.

This natural explanation of prophecy negates the exclusive character of the concept of revelation and in fact widens it. In its broadest sense, revelation also encompasses philosophical cognition, since the active intellect imparts this faculty to the individual soul too. But revelation also is deprived of its exclusivity in terms of its specific religious significance. Where the [metaphysical] theory is carried to its conclusion, it must permit prophetic revelation to appear wherever man's spirit possesses the appropriate disposition. Hence prophetic illumination is no longer bound to a particular religion, but can appear in various religions. What is even more important, different religions can equally be based on divine revelation. This does not preclude differences in their value and perfection; for, just as we do among the philosophers, we find among the prophets different grades and stages of ability corresponding to different degrees of prophetic illumination. The differences between the various religions based on inspiration, however, thereby become more relative, more a matter of degree. True religion, revealed by God, no longer confronts everything outside of itself as human delusion; instead, we have a multiplicity of divine revelations, among which even the highest and most perfect is of the same character as the others.

The relativistic consequences of this theory of revelation, as far as we know, are nowhere systematically developed or candidly expressed by its originators. There is no doubt that they are aware of these consequences and even desire them. This is indirectly proved by the restrictions that Maimonides places on the theory. Whereas in all other cases he accepts prophecy with a proviso (irrelevant in our present context), he declares the prophecy of Moses to be sui generis and altogether different from all other prophecy, not in degree but in essence, and inaccessible to natural explanation. It is obvious that Maimonides wishes to preserve thereby the absolute character of the Jewish doctrine of revelation and to avert the consequences of a theory that would relativize revelation. The natural explanation of prophecy stops short of the Mosaic revelation so as not to impair its absolute and unique character. A clear acknowledgment of this relativity, on the other hand, is to be found in ibn Rushd's well-known dictum that the philosopher should associate himself with the most perfect religion of his age.[27]

This dictum is not to be understood, as has generally been the case, in the sense of an external accommodation to religions which, although indispensable for the masses, are in themselves not binding on the philosopher, who should select for himself the relatively most perfect religion. On the other hand, we fail to grasp ibn Rushd's intent if we understand him wholly in the sense of Muslim orthodoxy, which recognizes Judaism and Christianity in addition to Islam, and which regards Islam only as the culmination of these earlier stages of revelation. When he speaks of the philosopher's relationship to the positive religions he surely does not have in mind, as the generalizing form of his dictum clearly shows, only the sequence of revelations recognized by Islam. What he has in mind . . . is the generalized concept of religion that is the product of his concept of revelation. He does not inform us of which particular historical phenomena he may be thinking, since it is objectively not relevant. Of decisive importance, however, is the fact that he is able to formulate the problem in a conceptually generalized form since revelation, just as philosophy, represents for him a general phenomenon. This enables us to understand why ibn Rushd's attitude to Islam must have appeared ambiguous and how it could have been understood in such different ways: he acknowledges the revelatory character of Islam but not in the exclusive sense of the supernatural concept of revelation, even though he speaks of it in these terms. Islam is for him the most perfect of the existing prophetic revelations, just as Aristotelian philosophy is the most perfect embodiment of philosophical truth. But just as Aristotelianism is not simply philosophy in its absolute form [schlechthin], Islam is not simply religion in its absolute form. Both are links in a series that includes other phenomena of a similar nature and in which there exists only relative and not absolute perfection.

It is difficult to reconcile the view of revelation discussed above, according to which the purpose of revelation is to make divine truth accessible to those who are untrained in philosophy, with this natural interpretation of revelation. Nevertheless, the Arabic Aristotelians retain this teleological explanation which, strictly speaking, is only possible by assuming [that] freedom of will [is operative] in divine revelation.[28] This retention is due in part to the strong influence of the antinomy resulting from their interpretation of prophecy with respect to the gradations in the relation between prophetic and philosophical doctrine: whereas prophetic revelation, in conformity with its nature, stands above philosophical cognition and is based on the highest and most complete form of communication of the active intellect, speculative truth, the ultimate content of prophecy and philosophy, finds its pure and adequate expression in the form of conceptual thought. This truth must first be translated from the cryptic and figurative language of prophetic intuition into the form of a concept so that the deep wisdom of revelation may be fully comprehended. The teleological view of revelation leads us out of this difficulty by explaining that the figurative form of expression has a specific purpose, thus making it an excellent device for revelation. Nevertheless, despite revelation, the final goal of men—speculative perfection—remains unattainable for those untrained in philosophy. As we have already seen in another context, Arabic Aristotelianism regards the purpose of divine revelation to be the moral perfection of the masses. To this end it integrates the moral interpretation of religion into its theory of religion as the preliminary stage to its speculative interpretation, which is its final goal. Maimonides restricts this double interpretation to the Mosaic revelation which, in his view, retains its supernatural character; it alone is revelation in the absolute sense of the word. For ibn Rushd, on the other hand, this twofold definition of revelation is as valid as the concept of revelation itself: every revelation is, in accordance with its *esoteric* character, a disclosure of metaphysical truth; in accordance with its *exoteric* intent, it is an instrument of moral education by proclaiming the moral law and the doctrine of reward and punishment.

This brings us back to the general concept of religion which we have already met among the popular freethinking movements of the Arab world. The different religions share the same ethical goal; morality constitutes their common core. For ibn Rushd, however, this [communality of goal] applies only to religion in the popular sense, whereas the [truly] enlightened [thinker] believes he has captured the final truth of religion in morality. In ibn Rushd's view, religion conceived merely as morality is intended only for the masses of people. This aspect of his teaching gives the impression that he regards religion only as a means to maintain discipline among the masses; therefore the philosopher must respect it outwardly without being bound by it inwardly. Ghazali had already interpreted ibn Sina's identical conception in this sense. Yet neither ibn Sina [Avicenna] nor ibn Rushd recognize religion merely as an external accommodation. They take the idea of the divinity of religion very seriously, and they also acknowledge the truth of the moral law, even though it does not exhaust the full depth of religious truth. According to ibn Rushd, the basic doctrines of the moral belief in retribution belong to those parts of the doctrine of revelation in which the philosophical interpretation agrees with the literal meaning of the text; they are just as binding for the philosopher as they are for the uneducated masses. External accommodation occurs not where revelation as such is acknowledged, but only where there is an acknowledgment of its literal meaning intended for the masses, in order to prevent them from becoming confused by the philosopher's criticism.

Ibn Rushd develops the conviction that religions are identical in their moral content into a theory of their common character. His generalization of the concept of revelation enables him to define the common content of religions formally at first, and then to use this formal definition to distinguish religion from the teachings of reason. To the moral postulates and precepts of the religions he adds the moral belief in retribution in the form in which it had been developed by Muslim and Jewish Mu'tazilites as a basic doctrine of Islam and Judaism. The existence of a retributive God and belief in a future life are articles of faith common to all positive religions. Ibn Rushd occasionally refers to the factual agreement of religions with regard to these doctrines. Of paramount importance for him, however, is the idea that religion requires these doctrines in order to accomplish its task and purpose, and hence they necessarily belong to its essence. He expresses this thought in a form that might easily permit religion to appear as a purely human creation. Every founder of a religion, he states, must know in what form to present these basic religious doctrines to the people so that they will have the strongest possible impact. In the course of his exposition, however, it appears that the founder of a religion is for him identical with the prophet, and that it is the prophet's intuition that gives his religious teachings their individual form. The various religions differ in the realization of their purpose depending on the degree of perfection of this intuition in their founders. The differences among the individual religions, however, can only refer to the form in which these basic truths are presented—as, for example, the way the doctrine of retribution in the world to come is worked out—but they can never extend to the truths themselves, which belong to the concept of religion. Ibn Rushd does not yet formulate this idea so as to indicate that a definite system of dogmas belongs to the common essence of all religions; nevertheless, he develops the dogmas of religion in general with great precision.

The profound influence of these ideas is clearly seen in the Jewish philosophy of the later Middle Ages. We encounter them in as radical a thinker as Isaac Albalag, who enumerates the dogmas that are common to all religions: reward and punishment, immortality of the soul, a God who rewards and punishes, and a providence that watches over the affairs of men.[29] But even thinkers such as Simeon ben Ẓemaḥ Duran and Joseph Albo—men deeply imbued with faith—cannot escape these influences and, relying even more on ibn Rushd, define the existence of God, the belief in reward and punishment, and revelation as the principles of every possible religion.[30] This formulation of the idea of a universal religious truth, grown out of the concept of revelation, might perhaps be also considered as the latent source of the tale of the three precious stones. The enlightenment of the late Middle Ages abandons the idea of an exclusive revelation and regards the various religions as a series of revelations of the same divine truth.

IV

In modern philosophy it is a new science that enters the debate with religion. The scientific and philosophical productivity that arises in the Renaissance replaces the ancient traditions that dominated science in the Middle Ages with a new image of nature which, gradually leaving fanciful and unbridled speculations behind, eventually coheres in methodological conceptions of nature. In philosophy, this creativity produces a plethora of new systems which, although initially (consciously or unconsciously) remaining tied to the basic themes of the ancient systems and able to express their own content only in revived forms of ancient thought, gradually begin to comprehend the entire scope of the philosophical issues from a new starting point and coherently. Religion now has to come to terms not with an independent, self-contained scientific tradition, but with a science that is in the midst of a vital development. Even where this science uses ancient forms of thought, their meaning is changed into something substantially different from what it was in the Christian Middle Ages. They are detached from the theological distortions of the Middle Ages and are pursued to conclusions which collide harshly with religious tradition. Beyond all objective contradictions resulting from this process, however, it is the consciousness of the autonomy of science that above all separates the two periods. Even among thinkers who believe in revelation [*Denker positiver Gläubigkeit*], it no longer is theology that determines the place of philosophy, but philosophy which seeks to define its relation to religious truth. This movement also leads beyond the limits the Arabic Middle Ages imposed on the notion of autonomy. Then philosophy had the task, at least formally, of confirming the truth of revelation existing independently, in its own right, and philosophy was capable of asserting its own freedom only by adapting the contents of revelation to its own results. [In the Renaissance] it is only the results of philosophical activity that will decide whether philosophy accords with the teachings of religion. Even when the result turns out to be in favor of religion, it is obtained on the basis of a new method.

These differences refer only to the understanding of science and do not affect that of religion. However much the relationship between reason and revelation changes, the concept of revelation continues to be the authority of religious truth, and the belief in revelation the specific form of religious certitude. Luther's new concept of faith has little influence on the philosophical treatment of the problem of religion, because (in addition to several external causes) the profundity of Luther's doctrine of faith unfolds exclusively in the struggle for personal certitude of salvation and not in the search for religious truth. The function of faith, according to Luther, is not to vouch for the truth of the Christian doctrine, but to transmit the certitude of grace to sinful man. The influence of this concept of faith on the definition of religious certitude is, therefore, confined to the narrower circle of Lutheran theology, which no longer bases the revelatory character of God's word on external historical evidence, but on its faith-awakening power. The general philosophical discussion of religion is hardly affected by this influence.

This discussion takes over from medieval philosophy not only the concept of religion and with it the whole problem of reason and revelation, but also many of the ideas that the Middle Ages acquired while occupied with these problems. It has often been pointed out that the rationalistic conception of the relationship between religion and cognitive knowledge takes a considerable number of its arguments from the rationalistic substructure of Scholasticism. What is taught there only with respect to the rational lower stage of religion is transferred to the whole sphere of religious truth. We often cannot distinguish where the arguments for the religious claims of reason go back to scholastic tradition and where they reach back directly to the ancient sources of this tradition, and especially to Stoicism. The view of those thinkers who insist on maintaining the distinction between natural and supranatural truth is even closer to Scholasticism. Only a painstaking examination reveals the methodological difference.

The affinity to the rationalism of Arabic and Jewish philosophy is still closer, though it is not clear to what degree this relationship reflects a historical connection. Just as the relationship of Renaissance philosophy to Arabic philosophy is in need of further historical clarification, so its relationship to the Middle Ages needs to be investigated more exhaustively before the philosophical development of the Renaissance can be understood historically. The external differences among the various schools and factions teach us surprisingly little about the actual course of the development. The differences often revolve around the academic formulations of the various schools, even where the intellectual content is the same. Thus, the vehemence with which Averroism was attacked in the Renaissance by no means indicates that its ideas were not influential. In fact, this philosophy was studied with great interest, as is evident from numerous sources. A thinker as far removed from ibn Rushd as Pico della Mirandola was not content with the knowledge of Latin Averroism; he also studied ibn Rushd's philosophy with the help of a Jewish philosopher with whom he was on friendly terms. Similarly, a familiarity with this philosophy on the part of important Jewish thinkers can be traced throughout the early period of modern philosophy, from the Italian Renaissance down to the English Platonism of the seventeenth century. There are thus no external difficulties to prevent us from assuming that the religious-philosophical views of these thinkers influenced modern philosophy.

Although the relationship between reason and revelation is also the central concern of modern philosophy in its study of the concept of religious truth, this concept is, from the very beginning, closely connected with the idea of a universal *religious* truth. Where autonomous reason is also granted the power to encompass religious truth, this idea is imperceptibly transformed into the notion that religious truth is the common possession of mankind. Both motives are indissolubly combined in universal theism, whose significance for the culture of the Renaissance gained wide recognition through the works of Burckhardt and Dilthey. The bearers of the universal knowledge of God are, above all, the great thinkers of the pagan world; but the truth they teach appears not only as cognitive truth but simultaneously as the content of a religious consciousness that also exists outside of revealed religion. This idea appears in numerous shadings. In the Platonic school of Florence, general religious truth is completed as well as superseded by Christian revelation. Very soon, however, the idea emerges that universal religion contains within itself all of religious truth, and this idea is soon worked out formally with great precision. Thomas More in his *Utopia* also describes the religion of his ideal people as one that contains nothing more than the general teachings of a theistic religion. Jean Bodin gives this thought its finishing touch in his *Heptaplomeres,* where he describes an assembly of representatives of the various positive religions who seek to convince each other of the truth of their respective faiths, among them the adherent of natural religion who declares, amid general approbation, that his religion is the oldest of all religions and the common basis of all individual confessions.[31]

In the concept of *lex naturalis*, scholastic tradition finds a basic point of departure for the idea of a universal religion. The natural moral law and the natural knowledge of God, which come together in this concept, directly offer the content for such a universal religion. There is no doubt that humanism has borrowed much from this scholastic tradition, whose influence is clearly reflected in the rational formulation of the concept of a universal religion. Completely new, however, is the motive that gives this idea its central importance. The idea of a universal religious truth necessarily implies the idea of the universality of the path to salvation, thus nullifying the notion that the non-Christian world is excluded from the benefits of salvation. Those humanists who sincerely adhered to Christianity and the Catholic church go their own way in this respect, too. That the entire ancient world should be excluded from salvation is an intolerable thought for the humanistic consciousness, and it is from its resistance to this thought that universal religion derives its greatest strength. Of course, this interpretation is not necessary in order to permit the ancient teachers of wisdom to partake of salvation. The affirmation of reason does not have to take the form of the universal idea of religion for their sake. In this form, however, the non-Christian path to salvation is not restricted to the spiritual aristocracy of thinkers and sages, but is accessible to all. A humane morality that yet rests on a religious basis is the way in which all men can find favor in God's sight.

The teaching of a universal religion does not appear only in the rationalistic formulation in which we have so far described it. Its original formulation within humanistic and Renaissance philosophies emphasizes other motives. Universal religion is there conceived as the effect of a universal revelation in which God made Himself known to the whole of mankind. Church tradition provides a starting point for this concept in its teaching of a primal revelation [*Uroffenbarung*] that was imparted to the ancestors of the human race. This teaching is elaborated by rabbinic tradition into the Noachide legislation and is used by medieval Jewish philosophers as a biblical basis for their acceptance of a universal religious truth. Renaissance philosophy, too, uses this teaching in the same sense and combines with it the idea of secret wisdom borrowed from the Kabbalah, an idea that goes back in an uninterrupted tradition to the earliest progenitors of mankind. Greek philosophy also is said to have sprung from this source, and the same great tradition is said to be the nexus in which the idea of religious and philosophical truth originated.[32] Even where this last developmental stage is absent, the common religious possession of mankind is at any rate traced back to this primal revelation.[33]

It has been justly emphasized that side-by-side with this conception we find in many authors an altogether different conception, which seeks the common source of truth in the common power of human reason, not in a coherent historical tradition. The same truths are attributed now to revelation and now to reason. As the universal religion, in accordance with its content, is identified with the general truths of morality and of reason, it appears sometimes as the effect of divine revelation and sometimes as a component of the natural insight of reason.[34] Individual authors reconcile these elements in various ways. In the general development of the problem, however, the connecting link is likely to be an extension of the concept of revelation, similar to the one already known to us from medieval philosophy. Florentine Platonism, whose significance for the development of the idea of universal religion is well known, shares with the Arabic and Jewish Aristotelians the view that cognition means to have a share in divine truth. In the act of cognition the individual consciousness rises to the eternal realm of truth whose bearer is divine reason.[35] The activities of reason, despite their spontaneity, are affected by divine illumination. Knowledge can only grow from the harmonious union of man's natural disposition, which is capable of receiving the divine influence, and the divine influence itself. This is especially true of moral and religious truth which, as the possession of reason, also remains the effect of divine revelation. This suprahistorical concept of revelation mediates between the conception of universal religion as a teaching of revelation and its conception as a teaching of reason. Original revelation rationally conceived and knowledge interpreted as revelation approach each other so closely that they become only two phenomenal forms of the same basic process.

. . . The Platonism of the early Renaissance which, on epistemological grounds, seeks to emphasize the idea of the a priori over against Aristotle, also comprehends the concept of revelation as an original illumination of the soul and not as the terminal stage of the discursive activity of cognition. In accordance with its Christian tendency, it gives a Christian mystical coloration to the concept of revelation. This explains the fact that it later develops in an entirely different direction. The religious element in it often is separated completely from the stricter epistemological motives and transformed into the spiritualistic notion of inner illumination. Universal revelation thus is presented as the general human process of divine illumination of the soul, conceived as the essence of all religious life and raised above all dogmatic and ritualistic externals. Sebastian Franck, for instance, understands the concept of universal religion in this spiritualistic sense, and he traces the diverse forms of the historical religions back to this basic mold.[36] In the specifically philosophical development of the Renaissance, the intellectual motives in the idea of revelation once again gain the upper hand. The pantheistic philosophy of nature and of metaphysics sees in cognition the act in which the union of the human and the divine spirit is consummated, and insofar as the concept of universal religion is still retained, it is also interpreted in this sense.

The gradual fusion of universal revelation with the Stoic concept of *lumen naturale* is even more significant for the development of the philosophy of religion. The revelatory character of cognition becomes progressively weaker as man's innate possession of reason comes to be understood as the divine light of the soul. The idea of a genuine union of human and divine consciousness disappears, and the idea of revelation becomes merely a religious and theological formula for the concept of reason itself. It is in the form of the idea of revelation that rationalism now expresses itself and gives universal religion its characteristic stamp. The confluence of both points of view can be seen at a relatively early stage of humanism and of Renaissance philosophy, insofar as the latter is not dominated by Neoplatonism. To pursue the individual aspects of this process lies outside the scope of our interest, but its effects are still evident in Herbert of Cherbury, whose concept of cognition rests completely on Stoic premises, and whose interpretation of the idea of universal religion reflects the same spirit. Although in his works the idea of universal religion is clearly formulated as the rational concept of natural religion, he attributes an element of intuitive immediacy to the certainty of God in which Dilthey detects Jacobi's religious concept of intuition. We have here the dying echoes of the Neoplatonic idea of revelation within the framework of an essentially Stoic view of religion.

Even before the idea of universal revelation undergoes this process of dissolution, it exhibits signs of wavering indetermination that clearly distinguish it from related conceptions, especially those of the Arabic Middle Ages. As a result of this indetermination, these generalizations of the idea of revelation lack the precision with which the Middle Ages distinguish between the religious and the philosophical forms of revelation.

It is difficult to find an analogy to the medieval theories concerning the relation of philosophical and prophetic illumination. Some Jewish and Arabic authors, like Bodin, utilize this doctrine of prophecy, but they fail to find a central place for it in their concept of religion.[37] Insofar as universal religious revelation is distinguished from scientific knowledge at all, it is presented mostly in the form of the historical original revelation, which is generally understood to be the source of religious insight. As a rule, however, the concept of revelation, as soon as it goes beyond the limits of revelation as interpreted by the church, encompasses both philosophical and religious illumination without distinction. The philosophers whom the humanists admired are raised to prophetic heights and considered to be proclaimers of religious truth and hence also the bearers of revelation in the ancient world. Thus, no hard and fast distinction can be made between general religion and philosophy in terms of their origin. Sometimes reason is drawn completely into the sphere of revelation, and sometimes religion is integrated into the sphere of reason. Sometimes reason is counterposed to the church's truth of revelation and sometimes to universal religion, depending on the direction of the prevailing interest. It is clear that the concept of religion, insofar as it goes beyond the concept of the truth of supranatural revelation, is thus determined only by its content. Universal religion is religion because of its content, which consists in the knowledge of God and directives regarding the manner in which He is to be served. It is a segment of the total area of the truth of reason, an area that is distinguished as religion only by its relation to God.

The interpretation of the content of religion is once again divided into the two well-known types—the speculative and the moral ideals—but they can approach each other more closely than in the Middle Ages. The speculative ideal of religion dominates the sphere of Neoplatonism and the systems imbued with its motives. The development of this ideal proceeds along the same lines as that of the concept of revelation discussed above. The Platonism of the Florentine school understands and praises cognition as the union of the soul with God, but places above it the specific Christian form of perfection in which knowledge is subordinated to love. The distinction between the two stages, however, is merely quantitative. The communion with God attained through knowledge is understood basically in the mystical sense, while, on the other side, the element of contemplative bliss is predominant in the Christian love of God.[38] The various motives of Christian and general religious mysticism, of the intellectual and religious union of the soul and God, of personalistic and pantheistic religiosity, whose mutual opposition is here still concealed, separate and gradually become distinct. On the one hand, the union of the soul and God is understood in the sense of spiritualistic religiosity and Christian mysticism. The soul aspires to the love and contemplation of God; cognition, as a form of union of the soul with God, is relegated to the background. In the philosophy of the Renaissance, on the other hand, it is precisely cognition that becomes the ideal medium for union with God. Religious contemplation is essentially conceived as an intellectual process, a definition that gains increasing clarity the further religiosity is removed from personalism and the more purely its pantheistic character is expressed. The forms in which this union of the cognitive spirit with the divine are conceived follow all the transformations of the concept of cognition which, from this point of view, could be illustrated by highly informative examples. However, the religious content of the idea is only slightly affected by these transformations, which need not detain us except for the last stage of this entire development in Giordano Bruno. His religious ideal is totally dominated by the notion of cognition. For him the philosopher is the man who is truly filled with the spirit of God, and philosophy is the form in which the divine depth of human nature becomes conscious of itself. His *Heroic Enthusiasms* [*De gli eroici furori*] are wholly directed to demonstrating that philosophy is the true religion, and that the felicity of cognition is the proper form of religious bliss.[39] Spinoza's religious ideal is essentially the same. Only the concept of cognition, which provides the theoretical form [for his religious ideal], and the conception of nature with which his religiosity must fuse itself are completely changed.

From the beginnings of humanism on, the moral ideal of religion appears alongside the speculative ideal. The two coalesce in manifold transitional forms, yet in its essence each remains clearly separated from the other. As much as moral perfection is bound up with the ideal of the perfect knowledge of God—and the pure knowlege of God with the pure worship of God—the emphases differ. The essential consideration for the moral ideal of religion is ethical conduct, and it is quite sufficient for ethical conduct to be associated with a simple description of God and His rule. The mystical element in the speculative ideal of religion is as foreign to the pure form of this view as is the contemplative ideal. Piety is not directed to the union of the soul with God; soul and God are two even when their ethical relationship is conceived as one of love and experienced with fervent passion. Accordingly, the personalistic character of religiosity remains intact.

The simple basic notions of this ideal of religion are set forth so clearly even by its first modern representatives that we can speak of progress in its development only with great reservation. The fundamental doctrines of this conception of religion can already be found complete in Thomas More's *Utopia*. They are doctrines known to us from the Middle Ages—God, immortality, and retribution—but [in More] set forth at greater length. In More they are already listed as the fundamental ideas of religion in general. The same conception of religion appears in many different combinations with [the notion of] positive ecclesiastical piety, sometimes as a rational lower stage of Christian piety based on grace, and sometimes as an interpretation of the essence of the Christian religion. The gradual progression of these ideas, their growing power in the theological sphere, the compromises and adjustments between them and Christian religiosity—all these are of the highest interest culturally and historically. The genesis and growth of the modern spirit can be followed in all its refinements and subtleties. However, from the standpoint of the history of ideas, the results of this movement are disproportionately small. Moral rationalism remains essentially unchanged, regardless of the transformations in which it appears and the combinations into which it enters. The only thing that changes is its position in the whole range of conceptions of religion, the extent of its influence within the theological and philosophical systems, as well as the [specific] philosophical basis for the religious concept of reason—a basis which each individual system develops in accordance with its epistemological foundations.

These ideas reached a certain degree of completion in Herbert of Cherbury before their development was temporarily retarded by the age of religious wars. The originality of his achievement consists essentially in his attempt to find a place for the religious idea of truth in the system of cognition, which he accomplishes by means of the Stoic doctrine of cognition. While his approach represents a forward step in the systematic classification of types of cognition and in the discussion of the relation of cognition and object, his conception of religion does not add anything to the ideas with which we are already familiar. In this connection, what is significant is merely the definiteness with which the moral ideal of religion is developed as the content of natural religion. Herbert of Cherbury assembles all these ideas into a system of principles of the religion of reason which, in a preliminary formulation, he specifies as belief in God, divine providence, and retribution. His [final] authoritative formulation expands this list to include belief in God, the duty to serve Him, acknowledgment that morality is the proper form of serving God, repentance of sin, and acknowledgment of retribution in the world to come.[40]

Spinoza presents a similar system of basic religious principles in his *Theologico-Political Treatise*. His description of religion, however, is the exact opposite of that which we find in all his predecessors. Contrary to their approach, he does not seek to identify religious truth with rational truth, but aims at the complete separation of religion from science. It does not matter whether religious doctrines are true; what alone matters is whether they promote obedience to God. Truth is the sole concern of philosophy; religion knows only piety—that is, the obedient worship of God. The individual doctrines of faith are deduced from this religious goal.[41] [Spinoza's] separation of religion from philosophy has often been admired as an original insight into the basic distinction between religious and scientific consciousness, but just as often it has been interpreted as merely a diplomatic attempt to free philosophy from all ties to religion. The first view surely misses Spinoza's intention, for even though he makes a distinction between faith and cognition, the latter remains his true religion. Faith forgoes the truth value of cognition, but cognition does not dispense with the religious content of faith. It is clear that for the external form of Spinoza's theory the opposite interpretation seems to be more correct. The ambiguity characteristic of the entire *Theologico-Political Treatise* here reaches its highest point. Though apparently recognizing the authority of biblical revelation, Spinoza still interprets the Bible from a philosophical point of view that consciously excludes the concept of revelation and then applies the result of this reinterpretation to the Bible itself. This process reaches its climax when he reads the surrender of faith's claim to possess the truth into the biblical documents themselves and then defines mere "pious" faith as the faith of the Bible. Doubtless Spinoza reads his concept of faith into the Bible solely as a defense against religious intolerance. The concept itself, however, springs from deeper motives. Because of its aristocratic exclusiveness, Spinoza's speculative interpretation of religion requires completion by a religious form that is also accessible to the common people. Here we have the same problem that we encountered in the Arabic Aristotelians, and the solution, by and large, is the same as theirs: the moral ideal of religion serves as the popular preliminary stage of the higher form of union with God that is attained through cognition. In their concept of prophecy, the Arabs find the means that enable them to attribute both forms to one source and to relate them to one another internally. They are related to one another as the exoteric is related to the esoteric meaning of revelation. In Spinoza's system, the concept of revelation no longer has any place even in the "natural" form the Arabs gave it. The popular form of religion loses its logical place, as it were. Philosophical religion is severed from morality, and popular piety from ethical conduct. The system has no way of bridging the gap. Spinoza clothes the idea of popular religiosity in this peculiar biblical form and thereby makes it internally ambiguous.

The connection between the *Theologico-Political Treatise* and the Jewish philosophy of the Middle Ages is therefore clarified from a new and more profound perspective. Where the relation between religion and philosophy becomes a problem for Spinoza, he sees it in the light of the categories of Arabic philosophy with which he is familiar, though in an attenuated form, through his study of Maimonides's *Guide*. The solution, too, is the same insofar as he conceives the religion of the masses as moral religion in the same way the Arabs did and defines this religion of the common people as a preliminary stage of the speculative religion of the philosophers. The only difference appears in the attitude to the Bible, which, for the Jewish Aristotelians, is in truth a divine revelation containing both forms of religion, whereas for Spinoza the Bible loses its apparently immutable character as revelation and is relegated to the sphere of popular religion. That there is a direct historical connection is evident from Spinoza's attitude to the problem of prophecy. His criticism of the theories of the Arabic and Jewish Aristotelians is explicitly designed to remove the basis of the union they had established between religion and philosophy. His own theory—in which he takes Maimonides as his starting point (in spite of opposing him in many particulars)—is structured in accordance with his own concept of religion. The prophet is for him the bearer of a revelation that dispenses with philosophical truth, aiming solely at morality and worship of God.[42] The basic religious dogmas he sets forth can conceivably also be traced to Jewish sources. He finds the principles of moral faith developed especially clearly by Joseph Albo, to whom the system that Spinoza erects can easily be traced back.[43]

Giordano Bruno occupies a position between Spinoza and the Arabs, a particularly interesting fact since a historical connection between him and Spinoza in this point is out of the question. Like Spinoza, he divorces religion from philosophy and demands that religion, which is indispensable for the common people, leave philosophy its freedom; philosophy, in turn, must acknowledge the necessity and importance of religion. In his view, the two are clearly distinguished with respect to their purpose, for religion is concerned solely with the refinement of our morals and the promotion of the common good. His formulation of these ideas, for which Bruno explicitly refers to his Arabic predecessors, reminds one of the well-known view that religion is necessary solely as an instrument of discipline for the common people and possesses no truth value. Nevertheless, though Bruno seems to come close to this view, his conception of religion (like Spinoza's) is never identical with it. Both men also regard the content of popular religion as the truth that is found in philosophy; in religion, however, this truth is found as an inadequate form adapted to the comprehension of the common people. The nonphilosopher, of course, is incapable of comprehending this truth as such and must forego the blessedness of cognition. But the practical conduct which religion teaches him is, in accordance with the essence of religion, identical with the truth of reason. Nevertheless, for Spinoza as for Bruno, the theistic idea of God—as well as all religious views of the hereafter—belong to the popular form of religion. That this interpretation of Giordano Bruno is correct can be deduced from his attitude to prophecy, which was true reality for him. Like the Arabs, he places it side-by-side with philosophy as the two forms of divine revelation. Of the two, however, it is not prophecy but philosophy that represents the higher stage. Prophetic illumination no longer presupposes philosophical cognition as the highest stage of knowledge; it is the form in which the divine dwells in the untrained intellect, unbeknown to itself. The analogy to Spinoza's thinking is plain. But it is just as obvious that Bruno's vitalistic and teleological system has room for such a [concept of] prophecy, whereas Spinoza's mechanistic view of the world excludes it and reduces the idea of prophecy to a mere fiction.[44]

These ideas initially had little influence on the further development of philosophical rationalism. The identification of religious and philosophical truth remained the dominant view, and the moral conception of religion gained virtually undisputed acceptance. The period of the Enlightenment stood completely under its influence in the way in which God, freedom, and immortality were set forth as the principles of religion. In view of everything that has already been said, no further proof is needed to show that the Enlightenment was completely based on the earlier rationalism and added nothing new to its theory of religion. It merely made previously developed views generally acceptable, something it was able to do because it imbued theology with its spirit, causing theology to acknowledge the autonomy of reason. The English rationalistic theology of the seventeenth century gradually prepared the ground for the emergence of this position. It praised the reasonableness of Christianity as its characteristic superiority over all other religions, and it made reason the judge not only of the historical evidence of revelation, but also of its content.[45] John Locke, the real father of the Enlightenment, gives a précis of this position when he assigns to reason the double function of determining the certainty of the fact of revelation and of comparing the content of revelation with its own teachings. In this double sense, reason is for him the basis of revelation, and his work *The Reasonableness of Christianity* is entirely concerned with demonstrating that Christianity is identical with the religion of reason. What is left of the Christian mystery is a quantitative completion of the natural findings of reason. Locke's theory concerning the relation of reason and revelation reminds us almost word for word of the formulation of the Muslim and Jewish Mu'tazilites. Wholly in their spirit, he demands that the evidence of revelation be demonstrated by compelling historical proof, and in the rationality of the content of revelation he sees the guarantee of its divine origin. Thus the question about the purpose of the coexistence of reason and revelation remained in its old form and continued to be answered in this form until Lessing's *Education of the Human Race* [*Die Erziehung des Menschengeschlechts*, 1780]. Only a slight nuance distinguishes Locke from the medieval theologians. He not only teaches that revelation must coincide with reason, but requires proof of this coincidence as the precondition of acknowledging revelation. This shift, of which only slight intimations can be found in the Arabic Middle Ages, is of utmost importance despite its seeming insignificance. Severing reason from the authority of revelation culminates in the idea that reason may judge the validity of revelation.

The Enlightenment also did not treat the idea of the historical verification of revelation in the spirit of the Middle Ages. Although [medieval thinkers] emphasized the conclusiveness of the historical proof of revelation, the concept of historical experience in its strict sense was foreign to them. The Enlightenment applied the criteria of historical criticism to the biblical accounts as well, demanding that the traditional proof of revelation be subject to strict historical demonstration. In addition, however, it raised the question how historical certainty in general can be methodologically established and sought to determine the degree of certitude in historical knowledge, its position within the system of sciences, and the presuppositions of historical proof. This sharpening of historical consciousness overpowered the traditional line of argument, and gradually the awareness emerged that the factuality of revelation cannot be historically demonstrated. Even where the belief in revelation remained intact, it no longer served as the basis of religious conviction, but rather was supported and sustained by a conviction arising from a different basis. Hence the historical result produced by the criticism of revelation also is of highest importance from a systematic point of view. It imposes the task of determining the different bases on which religious conviction rests.

The relationship to history becomes a problem for natural religion too. The full import of this problem was only gradually recognized. The concept of natural religion implies that it is to be, at one and the same time, the basis of the historical religions and the norm by which they are measured. Natural religion is both the general religion that has become embodied in the multifariousness of the different historical religions and the true religion that constitutes their criterion. In the concept of the "natural," the general factor which underlies all historically conditioned differences intersects with the factor of value which is free of the accidentalness that characterizes these differences. However, signs of attempts to overcome this concept of nature can already be found among the founders of the Enlightenment. In his struggle against innate ideas, Locke attacks the foundations of this concept from the empirical point of view and adduces the data of historical experience against it. The historical authorities that he cites against innate ideas are primarily in the religious and moral spheres. This aspect of Locke's train of thought is also recognized by Leibniz when he makes a distinction between the innate possession of reason and that which is psychologically acquired.

The consequences of this initial effort to deal with the concepts of natural truth in general and of natural religion in particular were, however, not fully developed even by these thinkers, and the ambiguous concept of nature remained the key concept in the further course of the Enlightenment. The Enlightenment's view of history sometimes places the one and sometimes the other aspect in the foreground. Sometimes it seeks to show how all historical religions express the same fundamental truths in various forms and symbols, and sometimes it criticizes the historical data by using the criterion of reason. The contradiction between these two points of view, insofar as one is conscious of it, can be reconciled only by assuming that there is a state of natural perfection at the beginning of history which deteriorates until the effects of this pristine state are distorted and blurred in the existing historical structures. This notion disappeared, however, toward the end of the Enlightenment. As a result, the concept of natural religion as it had been understood until then became untenable. The religious development of mankind then was viewed—Hume clearly sees this—as an ascent from the most primitive and barbarous social structures to perfection. The rational value of the religion of reason does thereby become questionable, but the identification of natural and rational religion becomes impossible. The concept of an ideal religion ceased to be identical with the common core of the different religions and to constitute their general concept. What the different religions have in common could no longer be sought in all-inclusive religious truths as determined by their content, and the task became to go beyond the differences in the content of the individual religions and penetrate to their essence.[46] This formulation of the question, however, goes beyond the limits of the Enlightenment, for it is characteristic of the Enlightenment to regard the essence of religion as determined by its content and to equate it with the quintessence of definite religious truths which themselves are among the truths of reason in general. The ideas of God and immortality are truths of theoretical reason. They are distinct from all other truths of reason, not because of their logical structure, but because of their significance for morality. Possessing the character of truth, religious principles belong to the theoretical sphere; only the moral consequences that arise from them give them their religious character.

In all these theories, the Enlightenment merely summarized the results of the development up to that point, though it accentuated them differently since the basic struggle against religion had acquired a significance it did not possess before. The religion of reason no longer simply wanted to assert the rational character of these truths as opposed to revelation; it wanted to defend the truth of religion in general against irreligious reason. The concept of religion was removed from the sphere of rational truth and acquired a new prominence, for the right of religion itself had become the subject of dispute.

V

The decisive turn which Kant gave to the philosophy of religion was wholly the result of his critique of the theory of knowledge. His achievement in this area is even greater than it is in the other philosophical disciplines, for it was his method, rooted in his epistemology, that gave all areas of philosophy their new form. This transcendental method connected his ethics and aesthetics with his theory of knowledge. Beyond this, it was only a most general idea of the autonomy of truth that had a liberating effect on these disciplines. This idea makes it possible to comprehend the validity of the autonomy of the ethical and aesthetic spheres and to place them side-by-side with theoretical validity as equals.

Kant's philosophy of religion, however, also rests on the individual results of his critique of reason. His critique of metaphysics destroys the earlier foundation of the philosophy of religion. Not only does it oppose the attempt to prove the truth of religious doctrines, but it also attacks the very concept of religious truth upon which these doctrines are based. The concept of religion as theoretical knowledge is negated by his criticism. Kant's attempt differs from all previous attempts to remove religious truth from metaphysical cognition by virtue of the wholly different character of its critique of metaphysics, which is directed against the presuppositions of metaphysical thought, not its results. No less significant from the viewpoint of the philosophy of religion is that this critique of metaphysics no longer has anything in common with the tendency of those earlier attempts. The idea of eliminating knowledge in order to make room for faith—understood as belief in revelation—is foreign to Kant. He not only adopts as his own the Enlightenment's critique of the historical proofs of revelation, but his concept of experience removes the methodological presuppositions of all such proofs. Thus both forms of the religious concept of truth which we have followed throughout the history of the problem are equally negated: religious truth can be based neither on metaphysical cognition nor on historical knowledge.

It is of fundamental importance to the Kantian philosophy of religion that it arrives at the separation of religious and theoretical truth not by an analysis of religion, but by a critique of cognition. Since it follows from the determination of the theoretical concept of truth that it is unable to serve as a basis of religion, a new verification has to be found for the latter. Kant thus liberates analysis of religion from the difficulty that results from equating the religious with the metaphysical concept of truth, and in his removal of this oppressive burden he performed his greatest service for the philosophy of religion. Kant himself is more conscious of this liberating effect in the ethical sphere than in the sphere of the philosophy of religion. He sees that his criticism of metaphysics removes the danger which a theologically based idea of morality poses to the idea of ethical autonomy. In his *Dreams of a Visionary* [*Träume eines Geistersehers*], Kant already states that to exclude all thoughts of other-wordly retribution from the proof of morality enhances the purity of ethical consciousness. This consciousness also governs his critical ethics, which are no longer restricted by any metaphysical derivation from the laws of ethics. It is only in this connection that he is aware of the importance of the religious-philosophical consequences of his critique of metaphysics. This is clearly evident in his own construction of the philosophy of religion, which is simply appended to his ethics rather than developed as an independent methodological investigation of religious consciousness. This judgment also applies to Kant's *Religion within the Limits of Reason*

Alone, which is not an independent investigation of the religious facts, but an interpretation of Christian religiosity from the standpoint of his ethical concept of religion. He also arrives at corresponding conclusions. The truths of religion are guaranteed by the validity of the moral law, which demands belief in the power of morality over reality. Just as religious truth is a conceptual consequence of ethical truth, so can its content be deduced from the moral law. The deduction of the concept of religion, in turn, leads to a concept of the religion of reason that is determined by its content, a concept that presents the suprahistorical character of religion and that coincides with the moral interpretation of religion. This interpretation of religious certitude is in agreement with the interpretation of the objective content of religion. Faith, as the specific form of this certainty, is the conviction of the validity of the moral postulates. This faith is based on the consciousness of ethical validity, just as religious truth itself arises from the validity of the moral law.

This interpretation of religion, despite its deductive character, comes infinitely closer to the essence of the religious phenomena than does the metaphysical conception of religious truth which is demolished by Kant. It differs from Kant's conception primarily by virtue of the fact that the religious object does not belong to the sphere of mere being, as it does in metaphysics, but principally and originally also to the sphere of value. The value content of the religious object is not added to it subsequently, but is inherent in it from the outset as the quintessence of the highest values. This transformation is most clearly expressed by the concept of faith. Faith is a certitude which is directed to the value character of the religious object, whose reality it affirms by virtue of its value. That this value is conceived as a moral value is deeply rooted in the religiosity of ethical monotheism. But this rootedness does not demand that the meaning of religiosity be completely dissolved in morality, as is the case with Kant. This [separatedness of morality and religiosity] applies both to the religious object and to the act in which this object is apprehended and affirmed by consciousness. While his insight into the "practical" character of faith leads Kant close to the essence of religious certitude, his faith does not become an independent apprehension of the religious value content, but rather remains the psychological equivalent of the deduction of the moral proof of faith. His faith remains the form in which moral consciousness demands religious completion; it does not lead out of the sphere of want and need to the possession of religious truth.

The full effect of Kant's methodology on the philosophy of religion is first evident in Schleiermacher's philosophy. His system on the whole is far removed from Kant's, yet the achievement which constitutes his enduring philosophical significance—his analysis of religion—is, in its final methodological intent, the application of the Kantian formulation of the issue to the problem of religion. Just as Kant starts from the fact of scientific consciousness in order to develop the concept of objective knowledge, and then uses the same method to question the foundations of moral and aesthetic consciousness, so [Schleiermacher addresses] the same question to the religious consciousness. The central task of the philosophy of religion is no longer to investigate the truth of specific ideas and teachings found in the historical religions, but instead to determine their place in the religious consciousness and to comprehend the inner structure of this consciousness. The subject of investigation is not a particular religion with its claim to exclusive validity, but religious consciousness itself, as expressed in the multifariousness of religious phenomena. That there is such an autonomous world of religion can of course only be established by the investigation itself, but here too the problem is that which confronts Kant in his ethics and aesthetics: the autonomy of the ethical and aesthetic spheres of validity can be demonstrated only by an analysis of the facts in both spheres. The point of departure in such an investigation has to be the problem of their autonomy. This investigation must show whether ethical and aesthetic truth are identical with that of theoretical knowledge or are based on an independent principle of validity. The demonstration of their independence is accomplished by a constant comparison with the sphere of theoretical knowledge. The passionate and enthusiastically overflowing tone of Schleiermacher's *On Religion—Addresses to its Cultured Despisers* [*Reden über die Religion*] makes it difficult to recognize the methodological point of view on which these addresses are based. But closer examination shows unmistakably that Schleiermacher's method is the same as Kant's. The concept of religion is worked out by drawing the lines of demarcation that separate it from theoretical knowledge on the one hand and from ethics on the other.

The first step in this procedure involves a negation: religion is neither metaphysics nor morality. Every disclosure of a new basic philosophical fact is possible only with the help of such negations. In making a distinction between religion and metaphysics, Schleiermacher agrees with Kant. Yet the two philosophers attach different meanings to this distinction, and an understanding of this difference illuminates the difference in their methods. Kant separates religion from metaphysics because his critique of metaphysics demonstrates that it cannot serve as a basis for religion. Schleiermacher arrives at the same conclusion because religious consciousness exhibits a character different from that of metaphysics. This conclusion remains unchanged even when metaphysical knowledge is possible, and Schleiermacher actually undertakes to establish a new metaphysics. A similar line of demarcation is drawn vis-à-vis morality. The essential problem is not the impossibility of deducing the content of religion from morality, but of demonstrating that the religious consciousness cannot be conceived as a mere appendage to morality.

The decisive authority in both [religious consciousness and morality] is the immediacy of the religious consciousness, which permits us neither to identify religion with the conceptual cognition of metaphysics nor to deduce it from moral postulates. Schleiermacher's well-known definition of religion as feeling and as consciousness of the universe expresses this position in several ways. Sometimes he emphasizes the immediacy of the religious conception of the object, at other times the relation of the religious subject to its object. Or, seen differently, the immediacy of the religious consciousness resides in its passivity, which differentiates it just as much from science and ethics. Both the productivity of scientific cognition and the activity of moral conduct are manifestations of spontaneous creativity. Religion knows neither the spontaneity of the intellect nor the activity of the will; it is but a serene surrender to the universe.

This conception of religion corresponds essentially with the descriptions of religious experience found in the literature of mysticism and the religious views closely related to it. Its originality lies not so much in the treatment of individual experiences—although here, too, Schleiermacher goes beyond such individual data—as in the methodological significance which he attributes to it. What was formerly the expression of a personal religious experience now defines the character of religion in general. Schleiermacher finds that the same basic traits of religious consciousness constitute the soil from which religious thoughts and ideas emerge in all their variety. He interprets religious ideas and doctrines as the expression of the basic powers of religious consciousness. However, he does not identify these powers with the phenomenal form they assume in a particular mode of religiosity, but conceives them as variables, as shapable elements that can manifest themselves in the most varied concrete phenomena. The multiplicity of religious types is based on a variety of such expressions of the religious primal consciousness. Thus these views, though previously known, acquire a new significance because he sees them in the light of the theory of religion, not as statements of religion.

It is even more significant that this conception of religion also encompasses the problem of religious truth. In Schleiermacher's thought, the autonomy of religion also includes the autonomy of the consciousness of religious truth. This removes the barrier which we encounter where the description of religious experience, as in Ghazali, leads to a theoretical consciousness of the peculiar nature of religious conduct. Until Schleiermacher, the verification of religion had to be based either on the supranatural authority of revelation or on the certitude of reason. Schleiermacher was the first to base the claims of religion on the inner certitude of religious consciousness. His development of the concept of religion is, of course, not systematically designed to remove the idea of religious truth from the sphere of religious consciousness and to demonstrate its fundamental significance; it acquires the concept of religion by describing religious experience in every detail. This development, however, is entirely dominated by the thought that religious experience contains a peculiar certitude on which all religious conviction is based. Religious consciousness has a unique claim to truth. Schleiermacher sees clearly that this claim cannot be validated on compelling objective grounds. He considers personal certitude to be the essence of religious conviction, and he demands of the believer the inner strength to entrust himself to this certitude.

Schleiermacher's ideas gave the religious-philosophical work of the last century its principal direction. To be sure, the dominant trend in the philosophy of religion during the first decades of the nineteenth century is the constructive method of the Hegelian dialectic, which attempts repeatedly and in an infinitely profounder way to comprehend religion as a phenomenal form of theoretical knowledge. Side-by-side with it, however, we find from the very beginning a continuous development of Schleiermacher's ideas which, after the decline of Hegelianism, made him the most powerful influence on religious-philosophical studies. Current attempts to develop a religious-philosophical system also keep going back to Schleiermacher, from whom they receive their basic direction. Schleiermacher's lasting, epochal influence, however, does not rest on the objective results of his analysis of religion, but rather on what underlies these results— namely, the methodology he uses for his investigation of religion. Even where later research in the interpretation of the content of religion has gone far beyond his views, its method is determined by his. The discussions in the past decades of the methodological foundations of the philosophy of religion constantly return to Schleiermacher, and they may to a large extent be understood as an attempt to realize the program of the religious-philosophical task he outlined, as they try in ever new ways to find a method of studying religion systematically. But it is precisely these constantly renewed attempts which show that no satisfactory method has yet emerged from Schleiermacher's initial methodology. Indeed, the widely divergent attempts to make his program fruitful for the philosophy of religion reveal that he did not clearly indicate how this program was to be carried out. Only his basic definition of the philosophy of religion as an analysis of the religious consciousness remains free of doubts and vacillation, as does his insistence on defining the truth character of religion and on its autonomy in relation to knowledge and ethics.

The principal difficulty, however, revolves around the question as to the kind of analytical procedure that the philosophy of religion should adopt. Schleiermacher's vagueness does not permit the concept of religious truth to emerge with full clarity. This is not the place for a discussion of the problem of the religious-philosophical method, and we shall only briefly indicate the obstacles that still stand in the way of a clear definition of the concept of religious truth.

We have described Schleiermacher's analysis of religious consciousness as an application of the Kantian method to the problem of religion. Just as Kant subjects ethics and aesthetics, after having dealt with cognition, to philosophical analysis, so Schleiermacher makes religion the subject of a similar analysis. But this parallel has a definite limit. In spite of numerous intricacies and complications, Kant's analysis of the moral or the aesthetic consciousness has as its real object moral and aesthetic objectivity—the moral validity content on the one hand and the aesthetic value content on the other. The object of the Kantian investigation is not the experience of the moral will, but the content of the postulates and laws with which our moral consciousness confronts us. Similarly, it is the character of value in the aesthetic consciousness to which the Kantian aesthetic directs its investigation. The distinction that Kant makes between his own transcendental method and the psychological method proceeds from an entirely different point of view than the distinction between the acts of consciousness and their meanings which now dominates the analysis of consciousness. When we view the Kantian procedure from the standpoint of these modern distinctions, there can be no doubt that its object is the meaning-content that confronts consciousness, though it is analyzed in the transcendental method from a particular and special point of view.

Schleiermacher's analysis of the philosophy of religion differs from Kant's precisely in this point. The object of religious consciousness recedes completely behind the religious experience, and religion itself is characterized principally from the standpoint of experience, as is clearly evidenced by Schleiermacher's definition of religion as feeling or intuition or a sense of dependence. Thus the truth character of religion is warranted essentially by the certainty of the religious subject. Of course, this does not completely eliminate the religious object, since it is by definition impossible to speak of a religious experience without at the same time taking its object into account. But Schleiermacher never reaches an explicit consciousness of the object-dimension of religious experience, and it often seems as if the objective religious content is merely a by-product of a consciousness which, from the very outset, dispenses with every object relationship. This point can once again be corroborated by some of Schleiermacher's general definitions. His view of the universe lacks every specific religious element with respect to the object. The same universe that is grasped conceptually by the intellect becomes the subject of religion as the object of intuition. Similarly, the object of the sense of dependence is devoid of any specific religious element. Thus we finally reach the certitude of religious consciousness without having a clear notion of the truth to which it is directed, and only subsequently does this vague and indeterminate religious consciousness reach the stage of objectification. What must be seen, however, is that none of these experiences is possible without an objective relation, and that which distinguishes religious consciousness of dependence from other experiences of being bound and conditioned is precisely the relationship to an object that is religiously determined. The world of religion can be comprehended as an autonomous world only when we can demonstrate the existence of an autonomous realm of objective religious content. The analysis of religious consciousness must, therefore, be primarily an analysis of religious objects (as research in recent years has gradually begun to realize), however much the form of experience in which these objects appear in consciousness deserves special consideration. A methodological line of demarcation against the psychology of religion is thereby drawn clearly and without difficulty, and the world of religious truth appears objectively as an independent realm among the objects of consciousness. The relationship of scientific to religious truth can ultimately be clarified only in this sphere of objectivity.

Another obstacle in Schleiermacher's analysis can perhaps be overcome from this point of view. His analysis aims to exhibit the essence of religious consciousness, which constitutes the basis of the various phenomenal forms of religion in its full universality. Schleiermacher actually achieves this goal with brilliant intuition, but he indicates no universally valid method that would lead from the concrete religious facts to the concept of religion. Later research, following in his path, time and again experiences this difficulty and, by holding fast to the analytical approach, is compelled to use empirical generalization in order to arrive at the basic form of general religious consciousness. The concept of religion thus becomes an empirical class concept and ceases to be a philosophical system concept.

The Kantian analysis of consciousness is not affected by these difficulties. It overcomes them by making a distinction between the form of consciousness and its content. The question arises, however, whether this distinction can also be applied to the problem of religion, and whether a form of religious objectivity in the general sense of the Kantian concept of form is possible at all. Without attempting to give a final answer to this difficult problem, we shall merely indicate the difficulties involved in transferring the Kantian concept to the religious sphere.

Kant's concept of form, in its strict sense, has as its correlate the concept of validity [Geltungsbegriff]. The concept of religious form thus would describe the specific validity value of the religious view, but would be unable to incorporate the value content common to all religious phenomena. Yet in its validity aspect, religion differs from all other spheres of consciousness by virtue of its specific relationship to reality. How the reality character of the religious object is to be understood in detail may be subject to dispute, but there is no doubt that religious objects, in contrast to validity values, are invested with the character of reality. This claim to reality on the part of religion can be included in the form concept only if one can speak of a form of reality indigenous to religion. But it is precisely this possibility that is placed in doubt by the relationship of religious to nonreligious reality. Hence the question of what can be extracted from Kant's concept of form for the problem of religion continues to require serious consideration. We encounter here an issue relevant to all philosophical movements of today—the problem of the [possible] extension of the concept of apriority beyond the limits of the sphere of form. The phenomenological school in present-day philosophy has posited this problem in its most general form and provoked a discussion that is still going on. The new motives that have been introduced into philosophy, even when restricted to narrower limits than their representatives imagine, will continue to concern philosophers. At the very least, they will enable the philosophy of religion to discover the basis of religious consciousness and enable it to proceed from concrete religious phenomena to the concept of religion itself.

If a sound and reliable methodology for analyzing religious consciousness can be developed, it will distinguish religion from all other realms of objects and modes of consciousness and thus establish a secure and independent world for it and its truth with greater precision than Schleiermacher was able to do. Yet even the most thorough dissection of religious consciousness cannot exhaust the total task of the philosophy of religion. The separation of individual realms of objects can never signify their isolation from one another. On the contrary, their methodological separation makes their mutual interrelationship possible. Kant has already fully clarified the necessary relationship of these two points of view. He does not permit these two methodologically distinct spheres of validity to coexist without any connection, and he completes his critique of knowledge with the idea of their systematic interrelationship by demonstrating their mutual dependence. This [principle of connectedness] applies to the religious sphere in a special way. If the meaning of religion is to present a final and absolute truth, then religion cannot be a segment of truth side-by-side with all others; it must be able to subsume and incorporate them in one form or another. The task of the system of philosophy—to correlate all areas of objective truth—coincides in a certain sense with the requirement of religious consciousness to include within itself all spheres of truth as a unified whole. The highest truth, the highest morality, and the highest beauty are understood to originate in one common source. The religious value must, at the same time, be a value beside and above all others, the *fons et origo* of all value contents. Analysis of the religious consciousness must be able to point up this duality. At the same time, it is also necessary to delineate the relationship of the other realms of objects and values to religion. This does not mean that religion is deduced from these realms; it is meant to indicate the place where they point to religion. Kant's treatment of the religious problem is thus restored to its proper place. Moral consciousness, more than any other sphere of consciousness, requires that it be completed in religion. Insofar as it reveals this completion, the Kantian position is fully justified. However, religion cannot be derived in this manner, for it needs its own sphere of religious consciousness in order to occupy the indicated place and to transform the postulates of morality into religious certainties.

To be sure, religion's relationships to other spheres of consciousness also contain the strong possibility of conflict. This possibility is especially clear in the relationship of religion to scientific truth, a relationship that has formed a limited subject of our presentation. The relation of religious to scientific truth differs from that of the other spheres of value to theoretical knowledge. Ethics and aesthetics claim value that has objective validity without demanding reality in the sense of existence. The notion of such an existence is irreconcilable with their meaning. "Being" and "being valid" coincide in them. In comprehending their specific nature every conflict with the "being" of theoretical knowledge is avoided. The possibility of such conflicts can arise only in connection with the question of the realization of these values.

In religion, however, the situation is completely different. Here the distinction between religious and theoretical truth does not eliminate conflict; on the contrary, it opens the possibility, for the awareness of religious truth not only posits the validity of value, but also asserts the existence of a bearer of value. In the God of religion the highest value and the highest reality coincide. The God of religion is certainly different in essence from the God of metaphysics, since the specific religious content of the concept of God can never be derived from the theoretical conception of the world: nevertheless, both reside in the same sphere of reality, and it is not possible to affirm religiously that which is negated metaphysically, and vice versa. In principle, religion contains a definite mode of judging reality that is compatible with every theoretical conception of the world, but just as it posits some kind of reality in a divine being, so it also incorporates certain presuppositions about reality which are not compatible with every theoretical conception of reality. Theoretical materialism and religion are absolutely and unconditionally mutually exclusive.

The analysis of religious consciousness is unable to reconcile such differences. It can define the meaning of religion, but it cannot establish the unity of religious and theoretical knowledge: this can only be accomplished on a systematic philosophical basis. Kant removes these difficulties with his critique of metaphysical knowledge, and it now becomes clear which function Kant's separation of religion from metaphysics performs as compared with Schleiermacher's. Schleiermacher deduces the distinction between religion and metaphysics from the nature of religious consciousness, and, as mentioned before, he permits a metaphysical system to exist side-by-side with religion, thus making it possible for their assertions to contradict one another. Kant eliminates the possibility of such a contradiction by positing theoretical knowledge only as experience. It is Kant's concept of cognition and not his concept of religion that makes this conciliation possible. Whereas the result of the analysis of the philosophy of religion is independent from the results of all other philosophical disciplines, at least in theory, the final decision about the truth of religion remains bound to the totality of the philosophical enterprise. This is illustrated with particular clarity by the history of the concept of religion within Kantianism. According to the traditional Kantian conception—which denies that we have knowledge of transcendental reality but affirms its concept—the objects of religious consciousness retain their character as absolute realities and fill, as it were, the space left vacant by cognition. If, however, the possibility of a transcendent reality is negated, the objects of faith also lose their character as absolute reality. Our interpretation of the concept of the thing-in-itself [*Ding-an-sich*] thus determines the truth value of religious ideas. This determination frequently involves an interpretation of the existential suppositions of religion in accordance with a concept of existence derived from a specific theory of knowledge, but it often also takes the form of criticizing and correcting these presuppositions from the standpoint of the concept of existence. Thus the determination of the relationship of religion to cognition acquires different meanings depending on the changes in the total perception of Kantian principles. Indeed, the metaphysical trend in philosophy, which has once again become influential in our day, penetrates the content of the sphere to which the objects of religion also belong, thereby demanding that its results be harmonized with the claims of religious consciousness.

Thus the question concerning the relationship of religion and theoretical knowledge retains its significance even in our time. But it is in a new form that this problem now appears, chiefly because the question is based on a new concept of religion. The philosophical analysis of religion, which goes back to the religious motives and contents in which the ideas and doctrines of religion are grounded, can use this basis to identify and clarify the points where religion touches the sphere of theoretical knowledge. At the same time, the philosophical position that now confronts religion has changed. Whereas in the past metaphysics was the basic philosophical discipline that served as a criterion for religion, its place is now taken by the theory of knowledge, which defines the concept of religious as well as theoretical knowledge and thus establishes the firm foundation on which all objective disputes have to be based. Nor can the metaphysical trend in present-day philosophy avoid this kind of epistemological justification if it is not to revert to outmoded ways of thought. The general theory of truth, whose complete unfolding is the principal function of today's philosophy, is also the authority that decides the place which religion is to occupy within the whole sphere of consciousness. The fate of the philosophy of religion is necessarily bound up with the basic conception of truth and its object, and it is wholly dependent on the formulation and solution of the general philosophical problem of truth. The question of the relationship of religious truth to scientific truth must attend philosophy in all phases of its development. Like all central problems of philosophy, this question will remain essentially unchanged, and yet will continue to stimulate a growing depth and clarity [of understanding].

Notes

"Religion and Science in Medieval and Modern Thought," translated by Noah J. Jacobs and Alfred Jospe, first appeared as "Religion und Wissenschaft im mittelalterlichen und im modernen Denken," in *Festschrift zum fünfzigjährigen Bestehen der Hochschule für die Wissenschaft des Judentums* (Berlin, 1922), pp. 146–216; also published as an offprint (Berlin, 1922), 72 pp.

1. *Summa Theologica*, Ques. 1, art. 2.
2. *Rosh Amanah*, chap. 23; cf. Jacob Guttmann, *Die religionsphilosophischen Lehren des Isaak Abravanel* (Breslau, 1916), pp. 113ff.
3. Already found in Saadiah, in his introduction to *Emunot ve-De'ot* (ed. Slucky, p. 12). Judah Halevi (*Kuzari* I,25; I,87 and elsewhere) attaches the greatest importance to this argument. Taking the same view as Saadiah, he considers the miracle of the manna which fed the whole people for forty years as especially convincing proof. Maimonides, *Hilkhot yessodei ha-Torah*, chap. 8, emphasizes the distinction between the unconditioned certainty of the Sinatic revelation and the usual, never completely reliable, proofs of miracles.
4. This proof keeps recurring in Scholasticism with many modifications, which, however, do not affect the essence of the matter. See, for example, Thomas, *Summa contra Gentiles* I,6; Duns Scotus, *Sententiarum prologus*, Ques. 2, reproduced in detail in Johannes Seeberg, *Die Theologie des Johannes Duns Scotus* (Leipzig, 1900), pp. 116ff.
5. See the instructive additional material in Martin Schreiner, "Zur Geschichte der Polemik zwischen Juden und Muhammedanern," *Zeitschrift der Deutsch Morgenländischen Gesellschaft* [hereafter *ZDMG*] 42:663ff.
6. The following basic works agree with this conclusion and support it with ample evidence: Léon Gauthier, *La Théorie d'Ibn Rochd sur les rapports de la religion et de la philosophie* (Paris, 1909); Gallus Manser, "Das Verhältnis von Glauben und Wissen bei Averroes," *Jahrbücher für Philosophie und spekulative Theologie* 24 (1910):398–408; 25 (1911):9–34, 163–79, 250–77.
7. This derivation is developed in detail by Crescas, in whom we find, in addition to dogmas required by the concept of revelation, those of secondary importance which are not conditions of the possibility of revelation. Simeon ben Ẓemaḥ Duran, in the Introduction to his commentary on Job, chap. 10, uses only the derivation of the concept of revelation (cf. Jacob Guttmann, *Monatsschrift für die Geschichte und Wissenschaft des*

Judentums 53 [1907]:6). See also Albo, *Ikkarim*, 1, chap. 10. Neither goes beyond the dogmas set forth by ibn Rushd, as we shall show later, but interpret them in a distinctly personalistic sense from the standpoint of the concept of revelation.

8. For Judah Halevi, see my essay, "Das Verhältnis von Religion und Philosophie bei Jehuda Halewi," in Marcus Brann and Israel Elbogen, eds., *Festschrift zu Israel Lewys 70. Geburtstag* (Breslau, 1911); for Duns Scotus, see Parthenius Minges, *Das Verhältnis von Glauben und Wissen, Theologie und Philosophie nach Duns Scotus* (Paderborn, 1908).

9. See Joel Julian Obermann, *Der philosophische und religiöse Subjektivismus Gazzalis* (Vienna, 1921). This comprehensive and informative description has the merit of giving prominence to Ghazali's voluntarist causal concept and correcting the one-sided emphasis generally given to the logical necessity of causal succession, but in contrast to this, Obermann's theory ignores the contradiction of the two theories and harmonizes them in a manner that yields no clear picture of Ghazali's general position. I have sought to go somewhat further than this in the text, but cannot here give the details.

10. See Baumgartner's revised edition of Überweg, *Grundriss der Geschichte der Philosophie*, 1:45, 46. As stated in the text, the source of Nicholas of Autrecourt's criticism of causality is to be found in Ghazali. This had already been surmised by S. Horovitz in "Der Einfluss der griechischen Skepsis auf die Entwicklung der Philosophie bei ben Arabern," *Jahresbericht des Breslauer Seminars* (Breslau, 1915), pp. 46ff. He bases his surmise on the surprising affinity between the general position of late scholastic Skepticism and Ash'arite ideas, a similarity that extends to the problem of substance, atomism, and, above all, the positivist view of morality. It can be proved with certainty that Ghazali's *Destructio* was used for the causal problem. The passage cited in Baumgartner, p. 617, is almost a literal reproduction of Ghazali's words, and even repeats his example of the burning of coarse flax. Dependence on Ghazali is in this point beyond doubt; other points may also be traced to his *Destructio*, of which, as far as we know, only those excerpts that appear in ibn Rushd's refutation have been translated into Latin.

11. Cf. Saadiah, *Emunot ve-De'ot*, Introduction, pp. 11ff.; Maimonides, *Moreh* I,34, which was used by Thomas Aquinas (as shown by Jacob Guttman, *Das Verhältnis des Thomas v. Aquino zum Judentum und zu der jüdischen Literatur* [Göttingen, 1891], pp. 34–37).

12. Cf. *Kuzari* V,21.

13. The teaching of the double truth among the Christian Averroists of the thirteenth century is exhaustively treated by Pierre F. Mandonnet, *Siger de Brabant et l'averroisme latin au XIII siècle*, 2 vols. (Louvain, 1908, 1911). This teaching is not developed in detail in the texts that he published, but only used here and there (vol. 2, pp. 154, 157, and elsewhere). Isaac Albalag's theory, which receives far more extensive treatment, derives the opposition of philosophical and religious truth in an interesting manner from the contrast between the philosophers' conceptual form of knowledge and the prophets' intuitive form (cf. Schorr, *He-Ḥalutz*, 4:85–86). It is clear that the distinction ibn Rushd makes between the literal interpretation of the Koran that is meant for the masses and the speculative one that is permitted only to the philosopher presupposes the unity of philosophical and religious truth. However, it is possible that this view had already been reinterpreted by Arabic thinkers in the sense of the double truth.

14. For the Ash'arites, see Horovitz, "Einfluss der griechischen Skepsis," pp. 25ff.; for Ghazali, see Hans Bauer, *Die Dogmatik Al-Ghazalis* (Halle, 1912), pp. 67ff., where the relation to the problem of theodicy is clearly established.

15. Cf. Ernst Cassirer, *Das Erkenntnisproblem in der Philosophie und Wissenschaft der neueren Zeit*, 2 vols. (Berlin, 1922, 1923), 1:444ff.

16. It is not difficult to extract these ideas as the central core of the Mu'tazilite conception of religion. All Mu'tazilite systems revolve around the question concerning the unity of God and His justice. At the center of the theory of divine justice we find the doctrine of the freedom of the will as a presupposition of divine retribution, so that we are left with God, freedom, and retribution as the total of all religious teaching.

17. Cf. *Moreh* II,40; III,51.

18. See esp. the Introduction to Baḥya's *Duties of the Heart*, which is completely dominated by this tendency.
19. In any case, Maimonides implicitly comes close to this view when he requires a minimal knowledge of God of the nonphilosophers, which amounts to the basic idea of the belief in retribution and is for the most part content with the observance of the divine commandments.
20. Cf. Markus Joseph Müller, *Averroës, Philosophie, und Theologie* (Munich, 1859), pp. 14, 66, and elsewhere, translated from the Arabic.
21. In "Verhältnis von Religion und Philosophie," I have treated Judah Halevi's theory of religion in detail; I refer the reader to it for all that is said here on this subject.
22. The basic features of Ghazali's concept of religion have often been described. The latest and most complete description is to be found in Obermann, *Subjektivismus Gazzalis,* esp. pp. 31ff., 86–110. Ghazali made a summary of the essential ideas in his *Munkid,* translated in Schmölder's "Essai sur les idées philosophiques chez les arabes," where see esp. pp. 63–87.
23. See Obermann, *Subjektivismus Gazzalis,* chap. 3, pp. 3, 4.
24. Cf. Alfred von Kremer, *Geschichte der herrschenden Ideen des Islams* (Leipzig, 1868), pp. 241ff. The report deals with a period in which the Mu'tazilite enlightenment had already passed its highest development. It is highly probable that this period of enlightenment was preceded by a strong tendency of free thought, and not only because of internal evidence. Saadiah's related point of view in the Jewish philosophy of religion has a pronounced apologetic tendency, and the biblical criticism of Chivi of Balch which ibn Rushd attacked already represented such an advanced stage in the criticism of religion that an extensive development must necessarily have come before it.
25. Cf. Schreiner, "Geschichte der Polemik," pp. 615ff., and the reproduced text of ibn Hazm, pp. 657ff.
26. The most detailed description of the theory is to be found in Maimonides, *Moreh* II,32ff., who first presents it as it is and then introduces reservations that are later discussed in the text. In essential agreement with it, although less clearly presented, is Shahrastani's report on ibn Sina (German translation, 2:317ff.). Ibn Rushd, as far as we can judge, adopted it unchanged.
27. Cf. Gauthier, *Théorie d'Ibn Rochd,* p. 121.
28. Already found in ibn Sina; cf. Shahrastani, German translation, 2:283, where the moral interpretation of religion is also clearly developed. The same view is the basis of ibn Rushd's writings, published and translated by Müller.
29. Cf. Schorr, *He-Ḥalutz,* 4:92.
30. Cf. the passages cited at n. 7, above.
31. For all this, see Jacob Burckhardt, *Die Kultur der Renaissance* (Leipzig, 1901), 2:283ff.; Wilhelm Dilthey, *Gesammelte Schriften* (Leipzig and Berlin, 1921–), 2:39ff., 145ff.
32. Cf. Cassirer, *Erkenntnisproblem,* 1:155ff.
33. Bodin, *Heptaplomeres,* ed. Guhrauer, pp. 57, 154ff.
34. Cf. Cassirer, *Erkenntnisproblem,* vol. 1.
35. Ibid., pp. 105ff.
36. Moriz Carriere, *Die philosophische Weltanschauung der Reformationszeit,* chap. 3. For Franck, see also Dilthey, *Gesammelte Schriften,* 2:81–90.
37. Cf. Jacob Guttmann, *Jean Bodin in seinen Beziehungen zum Judentum,* p. 52.
38. Cf. Zeller, "Über Ursprung und Charakter des Zwinglischen Lehrbegriffs," *Baur-Zellers Jahrbücher,* vol. 16, pp. 52ff.
39. Hermann Brunnhofer, *Giordano Brunos Weltanschauung und Verhängnis,* pp. 265ff.
40. On Herbert of Cherbury, see Güttler's comprehensive work. Excerpts from his writings were published by Heinrich Scholz, who describes Herbert's historical place in his introduction. For a general characterization, see Dilthey, *Gesammelte Schriften,* 2:248ff.
41. Spinoza, *Theologisch-politischer Traktat,* chap. 14.
42. For the problem of prophecy, see Manuel Joël, *Spinozas theologische-politischer Traktat* (Breslau, 1870), pp. 16ff.
43. A derivation from Jewish sources had already been attempted by David Neumark in "Crescas and Spinoza," *Yearbook of the Central Conference of American Rabbis,* vol.

18, pp. 277ff. But it is precisely in Crescas's case that there is no clear relationship, and Neumark's derivation, instead of developing basic relationships, attempts to piece together the unified structure of Spinoza's system from isolated statements taken from Crescas.

44. For Giordano Bruno's conception of religion, see Brunnhofter, *Giordano Brunos Weltanschauung und Verhängnis,* pp. 217, 270. In the quotation cited in the latter place from "Cena della cenere" (Wagner, 1:172), Bruno refers to Ghazali for the view that religion does not serve the attainment of the knowledge of truth, but rather the inculcation of moral education. This is not the place to investigate how Bruno came to attribute this Averröistic view to Ghazali; in any case, quoting Arabic predecessors is very characteristic. For the opposition of prophecy and philosophy, see the above-mentioned work, pp. 265–66, and the passage cited there from *Eroici Furori* (Wagner, 2:329–31). Bruno's relation to Averroism is touched upon by Barach, "Über die Philosophie des Giordano Bruno," *Philosophische Monatshefte,* vol. 13, pp. 55–56. Unfortunately, the author does not substantiate his views as adequately as he had promised.

45. Cf. Georg F. Hertling, *John Locke und die Schule von Cambridge* (Freiburg im Breisgau, 1892), pp. 102ff., 169ff.

46. For the relationship of the philosophy of religion of the Enlightenment to history, see the ample proof in Ernst Troeltsch, *Das Historische in Kants Religionsphilosophie* (Berlin, 1904).

REVELATION
AND REASON:
THE CHALLENGE
OF MODERNITY

14
MENDELSSOHN'S CONCEPT
OF JUDAISM

Fritz Bamberger

oses Mendelssohn's reformatory impact on Judaism undoubtedly was strong and lasting. Yet surely this effect was not intentional, not due to any ideas of reform (in whatever sense of this term) he may have entertained from the start. Mendelssohn's influence on Judaism was of a practical, personal nature. This becomes evident in the easily ascertainable fact that his concept of Judaism did not significantly affect later discussions about Judaism's idea and form. One thought alone was accepted: that Judaism has no dogmas. But because this notion was taken out of its organic ideational context and accepted only in and by itself, it assumed a meaning it had not had for Mendelssohn. If one wishes to understand his Jewish accomplishments, one must first ask why his own theory of Judaism played no role in them.

To answer that Mendelssohn's concept of Judaism—presented mainly in *Jerusalem*—is paradoxical and strange, if not erroneous (since it omits essential factors), in its distinction between and evaluation of the different "divisions" of Judaism is to give merely a provisional answer. One gets closer to the core of the problem by asking how Mendelssohn came to develop his notion and whether its genesis might not explain why his concept was not only unproductive for all ensuing discussions of religious theory, but also useless for those dealing with religious practice. Even the way in which *Jerusalem* affected contemporary readers says something about the meaning of Mendelssohn's theory in the context in which it had developed, and, as we have said before, we are concerned more with its meaning than with its correctness.

Jerusalem, published in 1783, is divided into two parts. The first part examines in depth the rights of state and church with regard to law and coercion; it delimits the respective claims of state and church, as well as the right of the individual to self-determination in a manner that is still classic. All in all, it constitutes a well-reasoned defense of man's right to the most far-reaching and inviolable freedom of conscience. The second part offers a definition of Judaism by drawing a distinction between "supranatural legislation" and "supranatural religious revelation."

> Judaism knows nothing of a *revealed religion* in the sense in which Christians define this term. The Israelites possess a *divine legislation*—laws, commandments, statutes, rules of conduct, instruction in God's will and in what they are to do to attain temporal and eternal salvation. Moses, in a miraculous and supernatural way, revealed to them these laws and commandments, but not dogmas, propositions concerning salvation, or self-evident principles of reason. These the Lord reveals to us as well as to all other men at all times through the nature of things, but never through the spoken or written word.[1]

This two-pronged definition was rejected *a limine* by his contemporaries in quite the same way and for the same reasons it was later (roughly, between 1830 and 1850) rejected in publications concerned with establishing a theoretical foundation for Judaism. It is interesting to see from what completely contradictory points of view this rejection was justified and how differently Mendelssohn's presentation was comprehended, not so much as to its motives, which could be understood easily, but as to its objective content.

Mendelssohn was not surprised; in fact, he had expected that his definition of Judaism would please no one. "My notions of Judaism can, really, justify neither the orthodox nor the heterodox," he said in a letter to Herz Homberg on March 1, 1784. This letter is most revealing. In it Mendelssohn speaks of the effect of *Jerusalem* and of the fact that he was not surprised to learn that a Leipzig professor had said that the first part of the work showed him to be a sophist, and the second one an arch-Jew (as [Johann Georg] Hamann, too, had asserted in his *Golgatha und Scheblimini*, the polemic he wrote against *Jerusalem*). Nor does Mendelssohn find it astounding that someone in Wittenberg accused him of being a "sacrilegist" and "naturalist." Indeed, it seems barely possible to find a common denominator for the general principles of the first part of *Jerusalem*, the discussion of state and church rights, and those of the second part, his definition of Judaism, merely by interpreting the text. Yet it is amazing how Mendelssohn takes these reproaches in stride and is barely touched by them. Reading this particular letter, one gets the definite impression that he was aware of the theoretical difficulties inherent in his work, but that he did not wish to discuss them for reasons connected with the circumstances under which *Jerusalem* had been written. These reasons are not expressly mentioned in the work; in fact, they are glossed over as much as possible. But they were the cause for the discrepancies pointed out by his critics.

Mendelssohn could not enter a discussion which, doomed to failure on philosophical grounds, would have had to disclose his real motivations; a public debate of them was impossible. One can therefore understand both his unconditional refusal to be drawn into such a discussion of *Jerusalem* and his request that anyone wishing to voice his objections should do so in print. This view also is supported by some remarks which show the orientation of the motives underlying his theory.

> I am far from reacting as favorably as you do to the mood of tolerance so prevalent in all our newspapers. As long as the proponents of a unification system continue to lurk in the background, this falsely glittering, tinseled tolerance seems to me more dangerous than open persecution. Unless I am mistaken, the devious notion that kindness and tolerance rather than harshness and persecution constitute the best means to achieve conversion has already been mentioned in Montesquieu's *Lettres persanes*. And it is my impression that our time is dominated by this principle rather than by wisdom and brotherly love. If so, it would be so much more urgent for the handful of people who wish as little to convert others as to be converted by others to consolidate, united by a firm bond. And what should constitute this unifying bond? This leads me to point out once again the need for observing the ceremonial law, unless we wish to see mere hypotheses turned into law, or books turned into symbols.[2]

The resigned spirit of these remarks shows what Mendelssohn saw in the ceremonial law and, according to *Jerusalem,* in "law" as such: a means to ensure Judaism's continued existence. Moreover, and apart from pointing out this specific purpose, his words seem clearly to indicate that the status he assigns to law in Judaism (as he conceives of it) is not merely a matter of interpretation. True, taken by themselves they furnish no convincing proof that his concept of Judaism is based on assumptions which are incompatible with an objective determination or interpretation of the facts. Nevertheless, they do suggest a direction for further investigation, and this suggestion is not misleading.

Until [Johann Kaspar] Lavater's attempt to convert him, apologetic considerations (one can hardly refer to them as inclinations, given Mendelssohn's often expressed abhorrence of having to defend Judaism against attacks, be they gentle or spiteful) play no role in his writings. This was due neither to any reluctance to take an aggressive stand (and with it the risk of giving offense) in religious matters, nor to any uncertainty or sense of insecurity, and certainly not to an indifference which would not contemplate a religious commitment, let alone consider such a decision worthwhile. It was, rather, a result of his conviction that there was no need to declare and justify his religious commitment in a milieu dominated by the ideals he, his friends, and the "enlightened age" itself proclaimed.

His conviction was, of course, predicated on certain concepts which can always be cited in its support. For Mendelssohn had made sure that all was well on the part of religion, without denying that

> I have discovered certain human additions to and abuses of my religion which, alas!, badly tarnish its original luster. . . . If I may say so, it is not just yesterday that I started studying my religion, having recognized early in life my obligation to examine my views and actions. . . . If my decision after all these years of study had not been absolutely in favor of my religion, I should have considered it necessary to proclaim this fact publicly. . . . But since my studies served to corroborate the validity of my religious heritage, I was able to continue quietly on my path, without any need to justify my beliefs before the world.[3]

This view is formulated with increasing clarity in the course of Mendelssohn's dispute with Lavater and [Charles] Bonnet, as well as in his responses to questions others addressed to him concerning his attitude towards religion. Thus one can see how his investigation of his "religious heritage" served to protect him, once and for all, against anything that might disturb his philosophy. And since it was this philosophy which had equipped him with the means to undertake these investigations, he was subsequently able and permitted to enter the circle of philosophers, unencumbered and capable of their own mode of philosophizing.

The philosophy of those men was rooted in their belief in the sovereignty of reason, that is to say, in the view that man can autonomously develop all notions of truth as well as formulate all principles necessary for leading a rational and happy life. This fundamental capacity, possessed by all men, makes the demand for tolerance self-evident, and the fact that by dint of this capacity man can arrive at a universal religion, through his own rather than through revealed ideas, makes the problem of particular religions, and of membership in them, irrelevant from the perspective of philosophy.

To be sure, the German philosophy of Enlightenment did not reject all concrete religion and the questions centered on it, nor was it unaware of them. On the contrary, it even developed a specific theology. But there was no room for theological considerations in the objective foundations and emotions or attitudes surrounding this philosophy's basic beliefs and their consequences. Of course, the problem of revealed religion did exist; that is, it could and probably even had to arise, but it was not constantly present. It became a problem only for those who were interested in incorporating religious issues into the system of philosophy or in a critique of such issues by philosophy.

Mendelssohn's confessional letter to the hereditary prince of Brunswick shows that things were different for him. His personal situation and development make this easy to understand. The fundamentally autonomous character of philosophy, in which religion may become a subject for philosophical concern (though not in any modern sense), of course remains untouched. Nevertheless, the philosopher Mendelssohn always kept his sight trained on his religion, constantly and legitimately using philosophical means to question not the justification of its particular existence (which he regarded as self-evident) but its content. Thus, while his intellectual point of reference was purely philosophical, for him it represented the identity of philosophical and Jewish notions.

This presented no substantive difficulty. The ideas of a universal religion—God, freedom, and immortality—could be found in Judaism, too. And Leibniz's conception of the universe, particularly its strong emphasis on teleology, contrasted so little with Judaism's world view that Leibniz himself could refer to Maimonides.

The world view of aesthetics, however, which no longer concentrated exclusively on universal teleology but rather was psychologically oriented (a development to which Mendelssohn's essays on the theory of art contributed significantly) seemed less compatible with a Jewish point of view. It is characteristic that Mendelssohn sees and sharply formulates the contrasts between a merely aesthetic and a religious position. Shaftesbury is "dangerous" for religion. Lessing too had written in his twelfth *Literaturbrief*: "Shaftesbury is the most dangerous enemy of religion, because he is the most refined."

Yet Shaftesbury's and Mendelssohn's positions are not identical. Mendelssohn neither agrees with the Englishman's pantheism nor forces psychological aestheticism into the immoral stance Shaftesbury occasionally assumes. Mendelssohn's Judaism may even serve as a restraining force obviating certain consequences of his aesthetic thinking, while reducing some subjective utterances to views which ultimately go back to Leibniz's teleology and thus present no religious difficulties.[4] Mendelssohn's position is strengthened by the multifarious meanings of the concept "perfection," in which religious and aesthetic moods flow together, coinciding in the idea of human happiness which is as much the goal of man's striving and the object of the beautiful as it is a gift of divine goodness.

It was in this idyllic situation that Mendelssohn was jolted by Lavater's attempt to convert him and thrown into a state of philosophical consternation. The challenge of the Swiss preacher presented him with a problem that never let go of him, and it is his attempt to solve it which resulted in his definition of Judaism.

Lavater's challenge certainly was an imposition and an indiscretion. But had it been only those, it would have been taken care of by his apology and their mutual assurances of loyalty. Lessing's attitude in this matter seemed strange and was occasionally criticized. But is it not understandable? He minimizes the importance of the affair, considering it one of the great many trespasses and arrogant acts habitually committed by the adherents of any particular religion. He even welcomes what has happened, hoping that it will move Mendelssohn to abandon his customary reserve and unrestrainedly tell those orthodox religionists the truth. "Above all, though, I beg you to respond to it as freely as possible, and with all conceivable emphasis. You alone can and must speak up in this matter or write about it. Actually, you are infinitely more fortunate than other decent people, who can work for the overthrow of that despicable edifice of nonsense only under the pretext of providing it with new foundations."

Lessing sees Lavater's letter as an attack on the adherents of a universal religion, and he would be satisfied if Mendelssohn were to destroy the "despicable edifice of nonsense" and expound anew the splendor and truth of universal religion. But to Mendelssohn, the challenge to convert must appear as an attack on Judaism, on the natural union he sees between Judaism and rational religion. If, therefore, he is to defend himself at all, he must justify that union.

At first Mendelssohn did not intend to do so. His *Letter to Deacon Lavater of Zurich* [*Schreiben an den Herrn Diakonus Lavater zu Zürich*] asserts that long ago and after much study, he won clarity about the worth of his religion. "There comes a moment in a man's life when he has to make up his mind about certain issues in order to be able to go on from there. This happened to me several years ago with regard to religion. I have read; I have compared; I have reflected; and I have made up my mind."[5] He feels no need to examine Bonnet's arguments in favor of Christianity and evaluate his own stand in their light. Judaism is not interested in proselytizing, and the Law of Moses is binding for Jews alone. "We act in accordance with our convictions and do not mind if others question the validity of our laws which, as we ourselves emphasize, are not binding on them. . . . As long as we do not convince or convert others, we have no quarrel with them."[6]

But Mendelssohn could not stay indifferent to the task Lavater forced upon him, the challenge to furnish compelling reasons for his decision to remain a Jew despite his philosophical views. Lavater replied to Mendelssohn's response with a new question, and with a reprimand that could not be ignored. In his letter, Mendelssohn had also been casually critical of Bonnet's arguments. "I have the impression that M. Bonnet's personal convictions and laudable religious zeal led him to ascribe to his arguments a cogency that no one else can see in them. Most of his conclusions do not follow from his premises; moreover, I would venture to defend *any religion whatever* with the identical arguments."[7]

Lavater read into this quite harmless passage a meaning it never had and which Mendelssohn rejected. Still, the sting remained. Mendelssohn, Lavater writes, speaks of religious doctrine to which he had never referred. What Mendelssohn should have done was to refute the *factual evidence* for [the truth of] Christianity. "For the time being, it was nothing but *history* I wanted investigated by an impartial philosopher. I must say, though, that I simply could not imagine, and that I find inexplicable even now, how you, with your absolute conviction of [the truth of] your religion's fundamental principles, could 'venture to defend *any religion whatever* with the identical arguments' used by Bonnet to prove [the truth of] Christianity." He then appeals to Mendelssohn, the adherent of a "revealed religion," to state his "philosophical reasons" in support of the "divine character [*Göttlichkeit*] of the Jewish religion." He is not satisfied with Mendelssohn's explanation that he had found no contradiction between the fundamental teachings of religion and of philosophy. Instead, he sharply accentuates the question of Judaism's claim to truth, to its divine character, a claim to be weighed by philosophy against the counterclaim of Christianity. "To be sure, I will not insist that you, my sincere friend of truth, refute either Bonnet or Christianity (for I have no right to do so); nor will I ask you to explain why you are a Jew and not a Christian."[8]

In his "Postscript" ["Nacherinnerung"] to Lavater's reply, as well as in *Bonnet's "Palingénésis": A Counterinquiry [Gegenbetrachtungen über Bonnets Palingénésie]*, Mendelssohn reacts to Lavater's challenge, citing his reasons for validating the claim of the Sinaitic revelation. With this, Mendelssohn's defense turns in a different direction, and the turn is significant: the philosophical exposition of Judaism assumes a new dimension.

Lavater's "insistence" refers to the implications of Mendelssohn's thinking, for the considerations and convictions which had led Mendelssohn, according to his own report, to deal with the problem of religion before the Lavater dispute left certain questions unanswered. Mendelssohn had been convinced that his religion and his philosophy could coexist without difficulty, since it had never occurred to him that his philosophical theory contradicted his religion in any way. Until the Lavater dispute, therefore, he had not even hinted at an attempt to apply the criterion of philosophy to the claims of religious tradition as such.

There are several reasons why the idea had never occurred to Mendelssohn. First, there was no Jewish theology in the sense in which Christian theology constitutes a compilation or system of religious truths claiming to represent a specifically religious source of knowledge [*Erfahrungsquelle*]. Moreover, the Jew felt that his religion was not a system of creedal or salvific truths and only to a very limited degree a transmitter of cognitive knowledge. The Jew encountered the reality of religion by deriving from it all rules of conduct, ranging from divine commandments to regionally determined customs.

Mendelssohn could have rejected Lavater's question in the more pointed and provocative but also more philosophical form it assumed in the *Reply* with equally objective arguments, or he could have evaded it. He would have had to explain that Judaism, because of its totally different character, can provide no evidence corresponding to that cited by Bonnet, for reasons which, as we mentioned before, determined Mendelssohn's pre-Lavater attitude towards Judaism. But in the interest of apologetics, he did nothing of the kind, instead embarking on an undertaking which then had to follow its prescribed course. Still, and within the given limitations, he did try to present these arguments. His concept of Judaism, developing in his writings during the Lavater dispute and maintained until the publication of *Jerusalem*, represents an attempt to define Judaism's unique character from a religiously and philosophically determined position.

> M. Bonnet (Mendelssohn replies in his *Postscript*) makes the working of miracles into incontrovertible criteria of truth, on the assumption that a prophet's divine mission can no longer be doubted where there is creditable evidence for the fact that he has wrought miracles. And he goes on to prove—actually with perfectly sound logic—that the performance of miracles is not impossible, and that evidence of the occurrence of such miracles may indeed be creditable. However, according to the teachings of my religion, miracles neither constitute a criterion of truth, nor can they furnish us with the moral certainty that a given prophet really did have a divine mission. In our view, it was the public revelation of the Law alone that provided us with such assurance. For here the emissary needed no accreditation, since all the people heard with their own ears the divine mandate given to him. Here, there was no need to confirm certain truths and precepts by miraculous acts and wondrous deeds. Instead, it was evident to the people that this prophet had indeed been appointed God's emissary: every one of them had heard his being summoned.[9]

The concept of legislation already appears here in Mendelssohn's argument, a concept he later used to define Judaism as such. However, he does not discuss it at this point. The specific character of the Jewish revelation—the fact that it manifested itself as legislation—serves here to substantiate its claim to truth, as it does in Maimonides, whom Mendelssohn quotes and whose arguments he takes over literally. The argument combines several motives. The fact that the Law was given publicly—the starting point of tradition—furnishes evidence for the historicity of the Sinaitic revelation, as Judah Halevi had pointed out before Maimonides in his *Kuzari*. Mendelssohn too makes this point. But since a miracle also can be performed publicly, it is the legislative character of the revelation (that is, its directness) which was more significant for him and for Maimonides. As he puts it, "Every revelation is perpetuated through tradition and monuments; on that we are agreed. But according to the principles of my religion, it is not the performance of miracles alone, but a public act of legislation, that constitutes the source of this tradition."[10]

Mendelssohn obviously wants to avoid having to argue against Bonnet's "factual evidence." Hence he divests it of its absolute character as ultimate proof and submits it for verification to a higher court: the Law which commands us to acknowledge the authenticity of such factual evidence.

> The admonition in Deuteronomy 18:15 to obey miracle-working prophets is, according to our rabbis, nothing but a positive commandment. As such, it reflects the will of the Lawgiver rather than any verifying power inherent in miracles. By way of analogy, we might cite another positive commandment that asks us to base legal decisions on the testimony of two witnesses (Deuteronomy 17:6), though this testimony is thereby not regarded as absolutely conclusive evidence. In one word, our rabbis hold that the belief in miracles is grounded in the Law alone, on the premise that this Law represents an incontrovertible truth.[11]

This reply is obviously very skillful apologetics. The same holds true for and is still more evident in Mendelssohn's letters to Bonnet and his *Counterinquiry* to the latter's *Palingénésis*. There it is apparent that his statements regarding the primary character of the Law render the miracles of Christianity questionable without attacking them, while at the same time establishing a strong position both for Mendelssohn and for Judaism. This position could hardly be attacked by his opponent's arguments, to which he had already responded. And it is also apparent that his conception is philosophically well thought through.

Mendelssohn's letters to Bonnet and his *Counterinquiry* also take his criticism of Bonnet's evidence for [the historicity of] miracles as their point of departure, reiterating his statements concerning the evidence, which is based on the Law, for the Old Testament miracles. But the philosophical valence of the Law had become more manifest.

> According to the teachings of our religion, any belief in miracles must itself be founded on law and not on subjective conviction. Anyone referring to miracles must take as his basis the law authorizing this belief. But when

someone attempts to impose upon us, by logic, the belief that miracles are a conclusive evidence of truth, or when someone, out of unlimited trust in the infallible proof of miracles, wishes to annul our law and to replace it with a new one, we shall be justified in falling back upon our disbelief. We then compare the miracles of which numerous religions boast, contrast each with the other, and deny all of them our approval.[12]

One can easily see Mendelssohn's point: any facts serving as grounding for a religion must be so incontestable that all criticism of their inherent truth becomes superfluous and nonsensical. Or, to put it more correctly, the concept of revelation on which Judaism is predicated is placed beyond the reach of criticism and verified by different arguments. Moreover, this procedure has an obvious consequence: the foundations of Christianity must crumble once it is recognized that any proof by miracle is, as a matter of principle, delimited if not altogether impossible, since it lacks that other kind of verification, the Law. The *Counterinquiry* only hints at this fact, while the confessional letter to Brunswick's hereditary prince points it up more explicitly.

Mendelssohn's position was absolutely congruent with that of the Enlightenment. His criticism of religion, in which he was engaged willy-nilly, was no more backward than that of the general religious criticism of his time. Both proceed in two ways: first, as critiques of religious doctrine as such; second, as critiques of the fact of revelation by which this doctrine was transmitted. Logically, this sequence is not justifiable; historically, it is. The medieval equation between rational and revealed truths does not acknowledge one source of knowledge as superior to the other, at least not in principle. It is only with the emergence of the subsequently self-evident conviction of the autonomy of reason that rational truths gain an advantage; all revealed truth must submit to the judgment of reason. This judgment recognizes no claim derived from any other source. As Mendelssohn put it in his letter to the prince, "I cannot repeat it often enough: what is of utmost importance is not the historical truth of a [religious] mission but the logical truth of a [religious] precept."[13]

Judaism can stand up under the scrutiny of reason; Christianity cannot. The doctrines of the Trinity, of a deity's incarnation, of Christ's human suffering and his sacrificial death "diametrically counter to the fundamental principles of man's rational understanding," as Mendelssohn expresses it most openly [in his letter].

Reimarus had been consequent: he had rejected all claims to and doctrines of truth that went beyond reason, and he had exposed the alleged miracles of the Bible as natural events. And he had asked for a pure Deism which was hostile to all religion, in distinction to Leibniz and Wolff, who resorted to the mediating notion of the supranatural as opposed to the antinatural [*widernatürlich*]. These thinkers explained the miracle of revelation—and certain dogmas which, as the content of revelation, had to be believed—as something which, though incomprehensible to our reason, cannot be disproved. The antirational contradicts all reason and therefore cannot exist. The suprarational is beyond the grasp of our reason, yet it need not contradict divine reason or the quintessence of eternal verities.

Mendelssohn, however, does not have to resort to such an expedient, which can be worked out only at the expense of philosophical principles, for the content of Judaism's religious revelation remains within the limits of the rational. A legislating God naturally poses no problem inasmuch as He belongs to the realm of rational basic truths. All in all,

> As far as its main principles are concerned, my fathers' religion knows no mysteries which we must accept on faith rather than comprehend. Taking as its point of departure the primary and certain basic principles of cognition, our reason can quite easily start on its way and be assured of meeting religion at the end of the same road. Here, there is no conflict between faith [*Religion*] and reason, no revolt of our natural cognitive faculty against the oppressive power of religion [*Glauben*]. . . . Essentially, the religion of the Israelites has only three fundamental principles: God, Providence, and Legislation.[14]

In a similar vein, but in a formulation that indicates his awareness of the philosophical significance of his concept of Judaism, Mendelssohn says in his July 22, 1771, letter to Elkan Herz:

> We have no dogmas that go beyond or against reason, nor do we add anything but commandments, statutes and straightforward rules to natural religion. Our religious principles and tenets are grounded in reason, and therefore not in conflict with it. Rather than contradict the findings of rational investigation, they are fully congruent with them. This actually constitutes the pre-eminence of our religion, our true and divine religion, over all other confessions of faith.[15]

The philosophical correctness of Mendelssohn's concept of Judaism, however, did not suffice; he also had to be able to meet the needs of apologetics. For it was of course obvious that a religion which based its very existence and claim to truth on historical evidence could be told that this evidence had been superseded and thus invalidated by another truth. Mendelssohn had based Judaism on a historical event—in the language of philosophy, on a contingent truth. But such a truth lacks the necessity which remains untouched by time. He therefore had to protect himself against the objection of those who, while acknowledging the validity of such evidence, would assert that it had been obliterated and replaced by the coming of Christ.

This need probably also accounts for Mendelssohn's determined rejection of Lessing's interpretation of revealed religions. For Lessing, the different religions were but stages in the education of the human race. When Judaism had fulfilled its historical and pedagogical destiny, Christianity took its place. For this reason Mendelssohn emphasizes the point that the Law has not yet been annulled, not even by Christ, who came to fulfill, not to abrogate.

> Did the Lawgiver abrogate these laws? Not at all. He proclaimed them audibly in a great public manifestation; He would proclaim their abrogation equally audibly in another great manifestation. . . . As long, then, as this most exalted Lawgiver does not proclaim His will to an entire nation in an equally great, public manifestation, no evidence of miracles will suffice to convince me that God has abrogated these laws, and I must continue to regard them as inviolable.

Another formulation expressing essentially the same ideas in all likelihood also serves an apologetic purpose. It defines Judaism as a religion in which necessary, hence universally binding, truths coincide with the Law whose origin constitutes a unique historical truth. And just as it is evident that the universality of the rational truths of religion is intrinsic to their necessary character, so it is evident that the historical character of the Sinaitic revelation makes the Law it proclaimed incumbent only upon those to whom it was addressed at that time. The idea of Israel's election here becomes peculiarly constricted: election, in the sense of being set apart, is valid for all time, unless and until a new revelation changes the law—that is, the ceremonial law—an event that is possible but hardly probable. Israel's election is to be in effect until messianic times.

The concept of mission—that the Israelites have been called to proclaim divine truths—is completely obviated by the exclusively legislative character of the revelation. The purpose of the Law is limited to one nation alone, even and indeed especially as far as universal truths are concerned.

> The ceremonial laws of the Jews seem to have the incidental purpose (among other intents we do not always fully comprehend) of visibly distinguishing this nation from all others by reminding it unceasingly of those sacred truths none of us should ever forget. . . . They serve to remind us that God is One; that He has created the world, ruling it with wisdom; that He is the absolute Lord of all nature; that He liberated the people from oppression by extraordinary acts; that He gave them laws, et cetera.[16]

Our presentation of Mendelssohn's view of Judaism so far has been derived only from the writings of the seventies, and quite deliberately so.

In this way it can be seen that all categories which later on constitute the concept of Judaism had been present from the start, but that their original position was different. At first, the purpose of "legislation," regardless of its content, was merely to shield the revelation from which it issued from the kind of criticism to which no other miracle is impervious. In this way, the existence of Judaism can be traced back to a *vérité de fait* which is subject only to "historical" accreditation; moreover, this *vérité de fait* has demonstrably never been invalidated.

With the transition to the content of revelation thus established, the line of reasoning proceeds from a validation of Judaism's claim to legitimacy [*Existenzanspruch*] to its substantive definition as a religion of which the Law is an essential component. Nothing further is said. Here Mendelssohn's exposition becomes inadequate. However, he did not have to anticipate the problems that would subsequently arise, for in the writings we have so far discussed he had found solutions to the questions put to him and to the difficulties they engendered. And these solutions, admittedly, do prove adequate in their perfect combination of philosophical validity and apologetic skill.

Mendelssohn repeatedly attacked what he called *Konsequenzerei* [insistence on purely formal reasoning] in religious matters. He referred to an intellectual attitude that, dissatisfied with the inadequacy of solutions worked out for certain purposes, pits logical consequences against each other or demonstrates their inherent absurdity beyond any actual need. Thus he would quite possibly have declined to answer the question whether the very notion of a divine law to which a nation must submit is compatible with the concept of man as such—that is, whether the notion of religious coercion can be made to accord with the idea of freedom.

The same problem existed for the eighteenth-century philosophy of the state insofar as it was predicated on the concept of natural right. As an easy solution, this philosophy resorted to explaining that the state's delimiting power was merely a means of providing the greatest possible freedom for its citizens. This power is an organizing principle which brings under one denominator individuals who, with their conflicting human inclinations, would destroy each other if left to their free pursuits.

Mendelssohn shared this view, as evidenced by some of his statements. He gave it added depth in his Preface to Manasseh ben Israel's *Vindiciae Judaeorum* by contending that the state is entitled to this right of coercion, but that religious coercion may never be used. In reply to this contention, August Friedrich Cranz, the anonymous author of the pamphlet *The Search for Light and Right* [*Das Forschen nach Licht und Recht*] raised the obvious question how Mendelssohn could bring this assertion into accord with the factual existence of the revealed Sinaitic

Law. "How can you, my dear Mr. Mendelssohn, persist in the faith of your fathers, and at the same time shake its very foundations by disavowing the ecclesiastical law given by Moses from divine revelation?"

Mendelssohn replied to this question, which he said went to his very heart, in 1783 in *Jerusalem*. In presenting and evaluating the view expressed in this response, one must keep in mind that it is similar to his position in the Lavater correspondence. Cranz's question was prompted by the same interest which Lavater's dedication had disclosed: "Can the peculiar step you have just taken really present your answer to the request Lavater made of you?" The positions he took in *Jerusalem* remain basically the same, though a change in orientation, necessitated by Cranz's objection, also produces some new views.

Mendelssohn had to show that the Mosaic Law constitutes neither a law of coercion nor an ecclesiastical law. "The state commands and coerces, religion teaches and persuades. The state issues laws, religion issues commandments. The law of coercion belongs to the state alone; religion can only mold conviction, can only teach and comfort. The power of religion consists in love and charity."[17] This division is due to one overriding maxim. "Principles are free. Neither church nor state has the right to make privileges, rights, or claims to persons or things contingent upon principles and convictions."

Faced with this dilemma, Mendelssohn draws a distinction between religion and Judaism. He equates Judaism with law, and demonstrates that Judaism's legislation, which is its essence, does not concern truths or convictions. It comprises only "laws, commandments, statutes, rules of conduct, instruction in God's will and in what they [the Jews] are to do to attain temporal and eternal salvation" but no "dogmas, propositions concerning salvation or self-evident principles of reason."

On the whole, this is formally correct; and one need not make too much of such details as the fact that he uses the terms "law" and "commandment" as homonyms, which means that the distinction made in the first part of *Jerusalem* is here forgotten. The question, however, is what is the relationship between religion and this Judaism?

Mendelssohn explains that the Law—that is, by his definition, Judaism—"is closely linked to speculative insights of religion and ethics." This linkage is established because every law and custom has "significance" and a "genuinely profound meaning," and that in itself makes it conducive to intellectual speculation. "The Law, to be sure, did not impel man to contemplation; it merely prescribed his acts, what he was to do or not to do. The great maxim of this constitution seems to have been: Men must be driven to action but merely stimulated to contemplation."[18]

This is the decisive passage in Mendelssohn's exposition of Judaism, which could cancel out that paradoxical division between religion and a legislative Judaism. The linkage between law and speculative truth—which in Mendelssohn's terminology means [the sphere of] the religious as such—could be conceived of as substantive. But Mendelssohn admits this only to a very limited extent. The Law continues to be defined merely as a "stimulus" to contemplation, even where it serves as an easily grasped, pedagogical introduction to Judaism's teachings, or where it is understood as a symbolic way of pointing to religious truths.

With this position, religious practice and religious teaching are being kept apart after all. Yet it is by no means necessary to insist on the division between revealed religion and revealed Jewish legislation which Mendelssohn uses as his point of departure, if only because it becomes untenable when religious revelation as such is regarded as superfluous. The relation of Judaism's different components to each other becomes particularly clear towards the end of *Jerusalem,* where Mendelssohn briefly summarizes his "views of the Judaism of the past," enumerating as its constitutive components religious doctrines or eternal truths concerning God, historical truths, and laws. He depicts Judaism as it was "in times past" when "state and religion were not unified but identical, not joined together but one and the same."[19]

In this Jewish nation, rational conviction and law are related in the only way that is legitimate within the system of a state: convictions must not be made into law, for man's reason, from which they have evolved, must remain free. Yet law exists legitimately, for it constitutes a national bond without which the state cannot exist. The Sinaitic law was given so as to ensure Judaism's inner cohesion, and it is for this end that Mendelssohn wants to preserve it. He writes to Homberg on September 22, 1783:

> Even if they [the laws] had lost their significance as a kind of script and symbolic language, they would still be needed as a unifying bond. And this bond, I feel, will have to be preserved in the plan of Providence as long as polytheism, anthropomorphism and religious usurpation still hold sway over our world. As long as these vexatious offenders of reason are banded together, all genuine theists must also unite in some manner, lest the others trample us underfoot.[20]

Does that mean that Mendelssohn regards only Jews as genuine theists? If this passage really indicates an attempt to widen, at least in theory, the circle of those who are subject to the Law (which does not seem very likely), this would not have been the way to do it. Nor was it his intent to establish a "church" of all true theists. The same letter to Homberg objects to such [proposals by so-called] Unitarians in unusually sharp language. "[This] is the 'unification system' of wolves which, in their great desire to be 'united' with some sheep or lambs, try their best to turn them into wolves' flesh."[21] And in a letter of October 4, 1783, he says:

" 'Thanks' to all tolerance as long as it persists in working for a unification of faiths."

Jerusalem concludes with a challenge expressing the same sentiment. "Brothers, if you care for true godliness, let us not pretend that conformity exists where diversity is obviously the plan and goal of Providence."[22]

The preservation of this diversity was threatened from two sides: by the religion of reason which, as such, is characterized by universality; and by those who saw in Christianity the best, the true, expression of this universal religion. Mendelssohn wished to be a theist and remain a Jew. He fully understood—and emphasized vis-à-vis Lavater or Bonnet—that a universal religion and its rationale make commitment to a particular revealed religion impossible. In other words, he recognized the unhistorical, "finished" character of a religion of reason and juxtaposed it to Lessing's concept of [historical] development. And since the God of reason (the "metaphysical" God) gave no evidence that there was any need for particular religions, Mendelssohn created a synthesis between him and the God of Judaism (the "political" God). "God, the Creator and Keeper of the world, was at the same time the King and Administrator of this nation. He is a unique Being who admits of no division or plurality in the political or metaphysical spheres."[23] This [divine] arrangement is not subject to revision by the passage of time; only God Himself can make any revision known by another public proclamation. And this cannot happen until the Law is absolutely annulled, that is, at the messianic time.

As has already been mentioned, Mendelssohn hardly spoke of that time. To what extent he may have hoped for it and for the concurrent abrogation of the Law remains his secret. Not wishing to engage here in the *Konsequenzerei* he so detested, we shall not ask whether, given his philosophical view, he should have desired its immediate coming. The intent of this essay was precisely to show that Mendelssohn's Jewish position neither is nor ought to be tied to his basic philosophical view; that his Jewish position becomes manifest only as an apologetic tendency; and that he arrived at his definition of Judaism under the pressure of these two forces.

However, he did not achieve a perfect conceptual harmonization of these forces. He himself said that "our rationalizations cannot free us from the absolute obedience we owe to the Law," and with this he described the break in his system. "Reverence for God draws a line of demarcation between [theoretical] speculation and [practical] observance which no one who has a conscience may cross."

This, then, is the reason *Jerusalem* is divided into two parts. In the first it is the enlightened philosopher or, to use Hamann's designation, the "sophist" who speaks; in the second it is the arch-Jew [*Stockjude*].

The paradox lies in the fact that the determined rationalist, when he undertook to validate the specific religion of Judaism philosophically, retained for it merely the nonrational elements. This is not the place to expound the general philosophical significance of this result; Ernst Cassirer has dealt with the philosophical structure of Mendelssohn's concept of religion in the *Festgabe zum zehnjährigen Bestehen der Akademie für die Wissenschaft des Judentums*. Nor do we wish to examine the correctness of this concept; Hermann Cohen has contributed some important points to this question in his essay "Deutschtum und Judentum." All we wanted to do was to render explicable the strange nature of this concept. Its demonstrated contingency on certain philosophical and personal constellations makes understandable why it could not be accepted by anyone who did not share Mendelssohn's premises.

None of the Jewish contemporary critics whom Mendelssohn mentions in his letters did share those premises; his detached Christian critics were probably more likely to understand the motivations for his view. Jewish theology after Mendelssohn, whether reformed or orthodox, understood his concept in absolute terms and therefore did it an injustice. We still have no full evaluation of Mendelssohn's attempt to validate Judaism philosophically, nor of the attempts by Jewish philosophers who preceded him. We consider the present study as a preliminary effort, which, because it exposes the temporally conditioned features of Mendelssohn's Jewish philosophy, may facilitate a presentation of its universal and lasting elements.

Notes

"Mendelssohn's Concept of Judaism," translated by Eva Jospe, first appeared as "Mendelssohns Begriff vom Judentum," *Korrespondenzblatt des Vereins zur Gründung und Erhaltung einer Akademie für die Wissenschaft des Judentums* 10 (1929):4–19; reprinted in Kurt Wilhelm, ed., *Wissenschaft des Judentums im deutschen Sprachbereich* (Tübingen, 1967), 2:521–36.

1. Moses Mendelssohn, *"Jerusalem" and Other Jewish Writings* [hereafter *Jerusalem*], trans. and ed. Alfred Jospe (New York, 1969), p. 61.
2. Moses Mendelssohn, *Moses Mendelssohn: Selections from his Writings* [hereafter *Mendelssohn*], trans. and ed. Eva Jospe, with an introduction by Alfred Jospe (New York, 1975), p. 144.
3. Ibid., pp. 133, 132.
4. For details, see my introduction to Moses Mendelssohn, *Gesammelte Schriften, Jubiläumsausgabe* (1971–   ) [hereafter *JubA*], 1:xxxiv ff.
5. *Jerusalem*, p. 116.
6. Ibid., p. 117.
7. Ibid., p. 121.
8. *Mendelssohn*, p. 128.
9. *JubA*, 7:31ff.
10. *Mendelssohn*, pp. 129–30.
11. Ibid., pp. 128–29.
12. *Jerusalem*, p. 132.

13. *Mendelssohn*, p. 118.
14. *JubA*, 7:95.
15. *Mendelssohn*, p. 121.
16. Ibid., p. 126.
17. *Jerusalem*, p. 23.
18. Ibid., p. 90.
19. Ibid., p. 99.
20. *Mendelssohn*, p. 147.
21. Ibid., p. 148.
22. *Jerusalem*, p. 109.
23. Ibid., p. 99.

15
MENDELSSOHN'S *JERUSALEM* AND SPINOZA'S *THEOLOGICO-POLITICAL TREATISE*

Julius Guttmann

pinoza's philosophical system, as is well known, began to influence European thought only more than a century after the philosopher's death. True, his younger contemporary E. W. von Tschirnhaus derived some of his views from Spinoza, and even a thinker of Leibniz's stature was significantly influenced by him. But then his impact waned, and it was only in the muddled heads of some religious enthusiasts that one could find versions of Spinoza's ideas, usually torn out of context.[1]

Yet at the very time when Spinoza's *Ethics* was bypassed and ignored by the emerging philosophical systems, his *Theologico-Political Treatise* exerted a strong influence on the history of religious enlightenment. His historical critique of the Bible was widely used in the literature of English Deism and, as a consequence, had a significant impact on the French and the German Enlightenment.[2] We cannot trace here every detail pertaining to the importance of the *Theologico-Political Treatise* for eighteenth-century Deism. One point may suffice to show the strength of this influence. Spinoza's conception of Judaism—his thesis that the Mosaic legislation had a purely political, not a religious character—was decisively influential on the self-definition of Judaism in the eighteenth century. Its impact on English Deism was equally strong, and it was the source for the central idea of the fourth of Lessing's *Wolfenbütteler Fragmente,* which claimed "that the books of the Old Testament were not written to reveal a religion."[3] Yet nowhere can a clearer agreement with Spinoza be found than in Kant's view of Judaism, which strikes the reader as if it were a brief summary of Spinoza's theory.[4] Precisely because one may assume that Kant did not know the *Theologico-Political Treatise*, this similarity shows even more clearly the extent to which Spinoza's views had permeated the intellectual trends of the century.

That Mendelssohn's *Jerusalem*, too, was influenced by the *Theologico-Political Treatise* becomes evident as soon as one considers the peculiar way in which both works establish connections between dissimilar problems. It can hardly be an accident that both Mendelssohn and Spinoza combine in a single work a legal and philosophical validation of the principle of freedom of thought and belief, a general theory of religion, and a specific theory of Judaism. Saul Ascher, one of Mendelssohn's younger contemporaries, had already noted the connection between Mendelssohn's and Spinoza's theories of Judaism.[5] This connection has also been mentioned repeatedly in more recent years but has not been analyzed further.[6]

Jerusalem itself does not mention the *Theologico-Political Treatise*. When Mendelssohn explicitly deals with Spinoza or refers to him, he is primarily concerned with his ethical system. The public tends to recall Mendelssohn mainly as Spinoza's bitter enemy, who used his last ounce of strength in his controversy with Jacobi to clear Lessing of the suspicion that he was a Spinozist. Yet the enormous stir created by this controversy obscured the fact that Mendelssohn was the first German thinker to try to secure Spinoza his proper place in the history of thought.[7] In his first work, *Philosophical Dialogues* [*Philosophische Gespräche*], he praises Spinoza as the discoverer of the doctrine of "preestablished harmony," which was later taken over by Leibniz.[8] Nevertheless, he cannot but regard the system which Spinoza erected on this basis as a repudiation of all religion. He considers Spinoza's position to be a frightful error, though necessitated by history. "Before there could be a transition from Cartesian to Leibnizian wisdom, someone had to tumble into the chasm separating them. This was Spinoza's unhappy lot. How much his fate is to be regretted! He was a sacrifice to the human intellect, but a sacrifice that deserves to be decorated with flowers. Without him, human wisdom could never have expanded its frontiers as far as it did."[9] These words reveal not only the young thinker's pride in his ability to rise to an unbiased appreciation of the reviled heretic, but also his firm conviction to possess, in the Leibniz-Wolffian philosophy, the truth which vouchsafes protection against Spinoza's religion-shattering errors.

He maintained this attitude toward Spinoza throughout his life, not deviating from it even in his controversy with Jacobi. The vehemence of his defense is a reaction to Jacobi's imputation that Lessing had relapsed into Spinoza's long-corrected error and had identified himself with Spinoza's atheism. Mendelssohn's own judgment of Spinoza remained unaffected. Indeed, his *Morning Hours* [*Morgenstunden*] attempts to work out the notion of a "purified pantheism" as the kernel of the Spinozist system, a clarity which, he feels, Spinoza himself had been unable to achieve.[10] In *Jerusalem* he maintains the same attitude toward Spinoza that he had expressed in his earlier work. Indeed, in his desire to see that justice be done not only to Spinoza but also to Hobbes—allegedly just as great a heretic—he sums up his views in the statement, "Hobbes did for moral philosophy what Spinoza had done for metaphysics. His subtle fallacies stimulated further inquiry."[11]

This is the only reference to Spinoza in *Jerusalem*. In view of the direction of Mendelssohn's thought, it is important to note that he refers exclusively to Spinoza's metaphysics, completely ignoring his approach to ethics and legal philosophy in the *Theologico-Political Treatise,* despite its affinity to that of Hobbes. Nor does he mention the *Theologico-Political Treatise* anywhere else, except in *Bonnet's "Palingénésis": A Counterinquiry* [*Gegenbetrachtungen über Bonnets Palingénésie*], where we find an occasional reference to Spinoza's criticism of miracles.[12]

However, the enumeration of such external links between *Jerusalem* and the *Theologico-Political Treatise* is hardly needed, considering their strong inner connection. This connection does not, of course, imply that Mendelssohn simply appropriated Spinoza's theses. The two works differ far too strongly in their fundamental orientation. The philosophical basis of the *Theologico-Political Treatise* is pantheism, to which Mendelssohn is diametrically opposed. Spinoza seeks to dissolve the concept of revealed religion because it is incompatible with the presuppositions of his system; Mendelssohn seeks to safeguard the validity of the concept of revelation side-by-side with the concept of reason. The exposition in the *Theologico-Political Treatise* is meant to deprive Judaism of its religious significance, whereas *Jerusalem* is conceived as an apologia for it. The two thinkers also define the relationship between religion and state differently, notwithstanding the similarity of their points of departure.

Thus Mendelssohn stands in opposition to Spinoza on every fundamental question. This contrast defines the limited extent to which one is justified in speaking of the dependence of his work on Spinoza's. For this reason, it is particularly instructive to see how a number of Spinoza's essential themes reappear in Mendelssohn, yet used in a completely different way. In exploring this connection, we can gain new insight into the continuity of the treatment of religion by various schools of modern rationalism, despite the differences in their systems. And by placing Mendelssohn's views in their historical context, we can clarify those aspects of his thought that must otherwise appear strange and paradoxical.

I

Judaism as Revealed Legislation

The central theory of *Jerusalem* is at the same time the point which shows Mendelssohn's connection with Spinoza most clearly. Mendelssohn's diverse lines of argument flow together in the assertion that Judaism is not a revealed religion but revealed legislation. The famous chapter on the election of the Hebrews in the *Theologico-Political Treatise* reaches the same conclusion: what was revealed to the Jewish people through Moses was not a religion but a law.

At first glance, the agreement here seems to be more verbal than substantive; the two thinkers differ widely in the meaning of their thesis and in the reasons for it. First of all, they differ in the meaning they ascribe to the concept of law. Mendelssohn, in defining Judaism as revealed legislation, wants it to be understood as a religious phenomenon. For Spinoza, the Mosaic legislation is a purely political phenomenon. The legislative interpretation is intended to prove that the Jews were called by God solely to establish a particular state and set up a particular kind of society. The law they received is nothing but a political law, serving no religious or moral purpose. Its sole aim is the social and political welfare of the Jewish people.[13] The doctrine of a special call to, or vocation of, the Jewish people can be understood only in this political sense. Religiously, the people neither possessed any special advantages over other nations nor were such advantages intended for it. The Hebrews excelled neither in knowledge nor in piety. As to their cognitive powers, Spinoza asserts they had "only ordinary perceptions of God and nature," above which even Israel's prophets did not rise, and he makes the same judgment with regard to their piety.[14]

The thesis that the biblical legislation has a purely political character and no religious content recurred repeatedly in the literature of the English and German Enlightenment. The undervaluation of the religious significance of the Old Testament [Guttmann's terminology has been retained here] by the radical wing of the Enlightenment is largely due to Spinoza's influence.

Spinoza's meaning is also clarified by the reasons he gives for his thesis. The principal and decisive argument for his claim that Israel's election was a purely political act is the fact, which he mentions time and again, that the Bible offers only terrestrial rewards or punishments (for instance, the destruction of the Jewish nation) for obedience or disobedience to the Law, but never mentions immortality as a reward for its fulfillment.[15] Christian theologians had long cited the absence of the promise of immortality in the Hebrew Bible as a major proof for the superiority of the New Testament revelation. The Socinians in particular had made this point the focus of their criticism of the Old Testament.[16] Spinoza, however, gives this familiar criticism an entirely new turn by using it to insist that the Mosaic legislation possesses no religious character whatsoever. His thesis and his arguments for it recur constantly among his successors in Enlightenment philosophy up to Kant.

Mendelssohn could not identify himself with Spinoza's thesis or the reasoning behind it. For him, biblical legislation is religious legislation, whose ultimate purpose is religion's ultimate aim—attainment of the soul's eternal bliss. His arguments that Judaism is not a revealed religion but revealed legislation, therefore, proceed along different lines.

His initial "proof" is his assertion that the notion of a revealed religion is in itself untenable. No external revelation can disclose the ultimate religious verities to the human intellect, for man could not possibly understand such a communication unless he had first arrived at these truths by his own reasoning. The ultimate truths originate solely in our reason, which neither needs nor can be replaced by revelation.[17] Affirmation of a complementary religious revelation is possible only on the basis of reason's capacity to perceive religious verities.

These profound differences seem to rule out any inner connection [between Spinoza and Mendelssohn]. Yet further analysis yields a different picture. Mendelssohn's just-mentioned train of thought turns out to be a development of one of Spinoza's thoughts; moreover, the similarity between the two statements is so great that it cannot be considered accidental. Mendelssohn writes about the Sinaitic revelation:

> Who could have needed the sound of thunder and the blast of trumpets to become convinced of the validity of these eternal verities? Surely not the unthinking animallike man whom his own reflections had not yet taught to acknowledge the existence of an invisible being that governs the visible world. The miraculous voice could not have instilled any such concept in this kind of person, and consequently could not have convinced him. Nor could it have affected the sophist whose ears are buzzing with so many doubts and brooding questions that he can no longer hear the voice of common sense.[18]

Compare this with Spinoza's statement on the voice that proclaims the Decalogue to the people of Israel at Sinai:

> It seems hardly reasonable to assume that a created thing, depending on God in the same way all other created things do, would be able to express or explain God's essence or existence de facto or verbally by applying God's words to himself, declaring in the first person, "I am the Lord, your God" etc. . . . . I fail to see how such a verbal assertion, "I am God," by a creature whose relationship to God is not different from that of any other created

thing, and which is not part of the divine essence, can satisfy the desire of
people who previously knew nothing of God except His name and who
wished to commune with Him in order to be assured of His existence.[19]

The context of this statement points, of course, toward Spinoza's
apparent conclusion that the sounding of the divine voice must have been
associated with a visible manifestation of God Himself in order to convince the people of His existence. Thus Spinoza uses the fundamental
Jewish concept of revelation as proof for his assertion that the Bible
presents God in corporeal terms.

Spinoza again refers to the Sinaitic revelation in a later section
which shows even more clearly that his theory serves as Mendelssohn's
point of departure. Spinoza defines faith as a doctrine of obedience,
designed to lead to a devout way of life, not to knowledge of theoretical
truth. The introductory paragraph to the discussion of this theory contains an argument embodying the kernel of Mendelssohn's thought. [Ac-
cording to Spinoza,] that one must believe in God's attributes, even
though one does not understand them, is nonsense. What is invisible and
can be perceived only through the mind cannot be comprehended except
through [logical] proofs. Merely to repeat words which one has heard is
no more meaningful than the prattling of a parrot.[20] Then in a section in
which he gives his definition of faith, Spinoza declares that faith contains
those notions about God which are indispensable preconditions for obedience. Our other notions about God should not be regulated by faith.
Every person should be entitled to think of God according to his intellectual capacity.

These arguments are also meant to provide a solution to the earlier
difficulties regarding the Sinaitic revelation.

> For although the voice heard by the Israelites could not give them any
> philosophical or mathematical certitude regarding God's existence, the ex-
> perience was sufficient to overwhelm them with admiration for God, as they
> already knew Him, and to stir them to obedience—the objective of the
> dramatic event. For God did not intend to teach the Israelites the absolute
> attributes of His essence (none of which He revealed at that time), but to
> break down their obstinacy and to lead them to obedience.[21]

Consequently, the knowledge of God attained through revelation is
not taught but assumed here. Israel's idea of God is not changed by the
revelatory event. The people are merely admonished to be obedient to
the God who is already known to them. In exactly the same way, Spinoza
had said in an earlier chapter that God always appeared to the prophets
in a manner which corresponded to their conception of Him, thus imply-
ing that their conception existed prior to the revelation.[22] There appears

to be one exception: Spinoza's definition of faith ascribes to revelation those aspects of God that lead to obedience. But this exception cannot disrupt the cogent inner logic of Spinoza's thesis; and it is in this thesis that Mendelssohn discovered the clearly developed positions that neither God nor His essence can be revealed and that the sole purpose of revelation is man's obedience, be it political or moral. The impact of this thesis on Mendelssohn was not diminished by the fact that he, like the modern reader of the *Theologico-Political Treatise,* saw clearly that Spinoza's faith in revelation was, and was meant to be, nothing but a fiction.

The congruity between Mendelssohn and Spinoza is especially significant because both were opposed to the entire tradition of theological rationalism. To the extent to which religious rationalism can affirm the factuality of a revelation at all, it defines the relationship of revelation to reason by claiming that both contain the same truth. Revelation is the divine validation of the truth attained by reason. This, for instance, was the common conviction of the medieval Jewish rationalists, who considered it the purpose of revelation to make the fundamental religious verities (which are rationally verifiable by the philosopher) accessible to the common people who cannot perceive them rationally.[23] The Christian Scholastic held the same view of the rational foundation of religious truth, and the philosophy of the Enlightenment assigns even greater significance to it. Christianity's congruity with reason is the decisive proof for its divine origin, and for Christianity the purpose of revelation is to make the eternal religion of reason universally known in the simplest and clearest manner. Relatively conservative thinkers such as Leibniz[24] and Locke shared this view with the leading exponents of Deism, such as [John] Toland and [Matthew] Tindal, as exemplified for instance in the title of Tindal's dialogue, *Christianity as Old as the Creation or the Gospel: A Republication of the Religion of Nature.*

Both Spinoza and Mendelssohn objected to the basic assumption of this theory: that it is possible to communicate metaphysical truths through revelation. For both, religious truth is the exclusive property of reason; hence a revelation existing beside reason can reveal only laws, not truths.

Behind Mendelssohn's formal, almost formalistic, objections to the possibility of a revealed religion, however, lies a deeper religious motive which calls for further consideration of his relationship to Spinoza. He is opposed less to the *possibility* of a religious revelation than to the *necessity* of such a revelation. The truths of natural religion that are required for man's felicity and eternal bliss, and the canons of morality based on these truths, must be equally accessible to all people. It is incompatible with God's goodness to assume that the perception of these truths should have required a particularistic revelation inaccessible to a large segment of mankind.

I do not believe that human reason is incapable of perceiving those eternal truths which are indispensable to man's happiness, or that, therefore, God had to reveal these truths in a supernatural way. Those who cling to this notion subtract from God's omnipotence the very thing they are adding to His goodness. . . . Moreover, those who take this position consider the necessity of a supernatural revelation more significant than revelation itself. If mankind without revelation cannot but be corrupt and miserable, why should by far the larger part of mankind have been compelled to live without benefit of true revelation from the very beginning? Why should the two Indies have to wait until it should please the Europeans to send them missionaries with a message of comfort, without which, according to this opinion, the Indians can live neither virtuously nor happily?[25]

His concern for the universality of religious truth—which can already be found in his *Counterinquiry* in a formulation that is virtually identical with these sentences in *Jerusalem*—induced Mendelssohn to claim religious truth exclusively for natural religion.[26] Even the Jewish people possess [religious truth] only as natural religion. Hence Jewish distinctiveness must be established on entirely different grounds. In taking this position, Mendelssohn believed he was in complete harmony with the Jewish doctrine which assigns a share of eternal life to the righteous of all nations and which considers "the law of nature and the religion of the patriarchs" as the norm of piety. They are identical, as he indicated in his letter to Lavater. For him, the Noachide laws coincided with the demands of natural law, and in the very next sentence he identifies the religion of the patriarchs with "the religion of nature and of reason."[27] He dissolves the historical meaning of the concept of the Noachide laws, gives them a purely rational meaning, and thus is able to rediscover his concept of the universal religion of reason in the Talmud. Mendelssohn probably merely wishes to object to a statement in the *Theologico-Political Treatise* when he rejects Maimonides's interpretation of the "pious of all nations." "Maimonides adds the limitation [that the righteous of other nations are entitled to eternal salvation] only if they observe these [Noachide laws] not merely as a requirement of natural law, but as laws specifically promulgated by God. However, this addendum is not validated by the Talmud."[28] Spinoza, on the other hand, wanted to use Maimonides's statement to prove that, according to Judaism, "true opinions and a true way of life are no help in attaining felicity as long as people accept them only as products of reason and not as doctrines that were prophetically revealed to Moses."[29]

One can understand why Mendelssohn emphasized the fact that only Maimonides's personal opinion, not a talmudic precept, is involved here. His deep concern to safeguard the correct meaning of the talmudic statement against Maimonides's restrictive interpretation is evident in the extensive Hebrew inquiry he addressed to Jacob Emden, in which he says in connection with Maimonides's views:

These words are harder for me than gravel. Are all the inhabitants of the earth from sunrise to sunset, except for us, condemned to perdition if they do not believe in the Torah, which has been granted as an inheritance solely to the congregation of Jacob, especially in connection with a matter which is not explicitly mentioned in the Torah, which can be found only in the tradition of the Chosen People, and which is an interpretation of the Torah by the sages? . . . What then are those nations to do that are not reached by the radiant rays of the Torah and do not possess a tradition except for what came to them from unreliable ancestors on whom they could not lean? Does God act like a tyrant when He deals with His creatures, destroying them and extirpating their names, although they have done no wrong?[30]

Thus the universality of reason is even more significant for Mendelssohn on moral than on logical grounds. It is this point which explains how he transforms the concept of reason. In the medieval tradition, rational truth, based on scientific methods and conceived as the product of strictly philosophical cognition, stands as a universal criterion, in sharp contrast to revealed truth. Religious truth can be perceived independently of revelation, but only by the scholar, not by the unschooled masses. This kind of intellectual elitism fails to do justice to Mendelssohn's ethical convictions. For him, the fundamental religious and moral truths require a universally accessible source of knowledge. Here we have the basis of his faith in the soundness and naturalness of man's common sense.

It would be an injustice to Mendelssohn to assume that he wanted to make common sense the criterion of scientific knowledge. He demanded strict methodical reasoning in scientific matters, and especially in metaphysics, and he liked to emphasize German thoroughness as contrasted to French superficiality.[31] Plain common sense is a source of religious, not scientific, knowledge. Its function is to assure the independence of religious certainty from metaphysics and the quarrels of its various schools of thought. Similar considerations motivated Rousseau to base religion on emotion and Kant to ground it in practical reason. Such radical negations of an intellectualized conception of religion were, of course, impossible for Mendelssohn, an Enlightenment thinker. Religion was and remained a matter of theoretical knowledge for him. However, he attempted to reach the same goal by making plain common sense, innate in every human being, the bearer of religious truth within the sphere of the intellect.

Here too is the real reason for Mendelssohn's objection to Lessing's views on the education of the human race. Mendelssohn did not object to the notion of historical progress as such. He asserted, with Enlightenment-nourished pride, that such progress does take place and that the science and especially the philosophy of his age had risen far above the level attained by the Greeks.[32] However, he was disturbed that Lessing also applied his theory of progress to religious truth, thus excluding previous generations from complete possession of it. It was axiomatic for him that the religious truths required for human felicity must be accessible to all people at all times. Consequently, he could not approve of any idea of progress which included the religious sphere. In this area he preserved a static conception of reason, rejecting Lessing's dynamic one.[33]

There is an interesting change of position in his attempt to reconcile this rational postulate with historic reality. He admits in his *Counterinquiry* that mankind's development began with a phase of superstition and bias. However, even this stage did not lack "the concepts and moral conviction of the truths of natural religion" that are indispensable to man's felicity. For the common people, superstition and prejudices themselves become the basis of faith in these truths, although their first discoverers had no proof and "could only feel [them] inwardly without being able to communicate them."[34] When Mendelssohn speaks here of superstition and prejudices, he seems to refer to the religious notions of paganism, which he sees as possessing the most significant principles of natural religion, though not yet fully clarified. Thus, in this limited and weakened form, he comes near to Voltaire's and Hume's view that the history of religion began with primitive superstition and does not yet possess rational truth. However, a later statement in the *Counterinquiry* returns to his earlier view that paganism is a degeneration of the originally pure religion of reason. This view is dominant in *Jerusalem,* where the postulate of natural religion—that eternal verities are universally given and accessible—finds its logical place and expression.[35]

This postulate is so widespread in deistic literature that it proves nothing about a special relationship between Mendelssohn and Spinoza. Yet no other exponent of Deism drew from it the conclusions Mendelssohn did. Later, more radical, epigones of Deism used this postulate as an argument for rejecting revelation unconditionally.[36] But as long as the belief in revelation was maintained, the traditional doctrine of the congruence of reason and revelation was retained. Religious truth is not bound to revelation, but must be independently attainable by all peoples at all times. Nevertheless, the notion that religious truth finds clarification and confirmation through revelation is not considered objectionable.

Mendelssohn accepts the conclusion of the radical branch of Deism that there cannot be any special, separate revelation of universal truth. However, he combines it with belief in revelation by conceiving revelation as the disclosure of legislation. In the fusion of these motives he comes closer to Spinoza's view than to anyone else's. Spinoza also uses the notion that general human doctrines of religion must be equally accessible to all people in order to separate these doctrines from the Mosaic revelation, thus justifying his political interpretation of Judaism. His definition of Mosaic legislation as a purely political phenomenon leads logically to the conclusion that Jews were in no way preferred by God over other nations in moral and religious matters. Spinoza too justifies this view by asserting that God's benevolence is extended to all peoples alike, and that He therefore granted the means to attain felicity to all of them.[37] He seeks to prove his point by quoting Job 28:28 to show that "God ordained for the whole human race the law to revere God and to refrain from doing evil, that is, to act morally." Furthermore, he invokes numerous verses from the Hebrew Bible and also Paul's statement that heathens [Gentiles] and Jews were equally prone to sin in order to prove that the universality of the moral is a biblical doctrine.[38] This thought is later worked out systematically on the basis of the assertion that there is a universally valid faith embodying the religious notions that constitute the indispensable foundation of moral obedience. This faith is just as independent of the historical and ritual components of Judaism as it is of the dogmatic components of Christianity.[39] In contrast to Mendelssohn, Spinoza defines revelation, not reason, as the source of this universal faith. Following the chapters in the *Theologico-Political Treatise* in which he deals with the concept of faith, he develops [what he considers] the central position of Scripture: it is God's word precisely because it contains the true religion. The universality of this concept of religion requires a corresponding universalization of the concept of revelation. For this purpose Spinoza employs the traditional notion of a general human archetype of revelation but maintains, in the chapter on Israel's election, that prophets who taught the transmitted true religion existed not only in Israel, but also among all other peoples.[40] Just as true religion is a universal phenomenon, so is its wellspring, prophecy. We consider prophecy as being limited to Israel simply because our historical tradition is one-sided.

Spinoza's concept of reason necessitates this linkage of universal religion to revelation. There can be no rational perception except in the sphere of scientific cognition, nor any road to truth except that of science. Therefore only the metaphysician can have true knowledge of God, and a notion such as "common sense" as this term is used by Mendelssohn—claiming a knowledge of God that is attained by metaphysics yet without sharing its scientific cognition—is plain nonsense for Spinoza. The sentence in the *Ethics* (II,47) saying that the human mind has an adequate knowledge of the eternal and infinite essence of God of course implies that the true concept of God is "known to all." This is the basis of the position in the *Theologico-Political Treatise* that the Law, which is identified with religion in general and described as "the word of God," is divinely inscribed in the human mind.[41] However, neither Spinoza's theory of reason nor his theory of religion elaborate this point. He wanted to develop the concept of God that is immanent in the human mind methodically in his metaphysics. He is convinced that it is only in metaphysics that the true concept of God is disclosed and can be discovered. The concept of God which in principle should be adequately known by all men is in reality an idea possessed only by the metaphysician; the masses are mired in superstition and prejudices.

Here we see how the divine Law and the rationally conceived universal religion of the *Theologico-Political Treatise* must be understood. Spinoza's theory of the immanence of the knowledge of God in the human mind has nothing in common with Mendelssohn's thesis of a popular common sense. Spinoza's theory is meant to provide adequate knowledge based on the evidence of strict rational cognition. Inasmuch as Spinoza feels that only the metaphysician possesses adequate cognition, for him true knowledge of God remains, as it does for the rationalists of the Middle Ages, something which is reserved for the philosopher. The religion of the people cannot be based on reason.[42]

Above all, it is the content of reason which makes it impossible for the people's religion to be based on it. For Spinoza, the God of reason can only be the God of his system, from whom the world emerges with mathematical necessity. This God cannot be the God of popular religion because He cannot be the foundation of popular morality. Spinoza's system knows neither an absolute distinction between good and evil nor the concept of an absolute moral commandment. No law originates in God except the unbreakable law of nature. God cannot be the source of any law prescribing the "ought"—that is, a law man can obey or violate. Morality has a place in Spinoza's system only as an attitude by which man attains his highest perfection. Its rules are not laws, but the means to reach this goal. They can be understood only by the wise person who can penetrate the inner connections and interrelationships of human actions, an especially important precondition because the true perfection of mankind lies solely in cognition. Strictly speaking, moral perfection is merely a consequence of intellectual perfection.[43] Speculative cognition is life's ultimate ideal. It encompasses true virtue, the virtue of the philosopher. The common people, of course, cannot attain it. If they are not to be completely excluded from [attaining] virtue, the philosophical concept of virtue must be replaced by a popular concept. Their content is identical, but the philosophical proof for the ideal of virtue is something incomprehensible to the popular consciousness. Hence virtue, uncomprehended in its ultimate meaning, can be nothing but [the product of] commanded law for the common people. Their moral deportment is grounded in obedience. But that this obedience leads to felicity is something which also cannot be grasped by the people. In fact, the virtue of obedience cannot be comprehended rationally at all. Obedience is motivated not by cognition but by faith.

This popular form of morality requires a corresponding religious form. The virtue of obedience is validated by being grounded in the concept of a personal law-giving God.[44] Spinoza's dogmas of "pious faith" are nothing but the dogmatic presuppositions necessary for the idea of obedience. He deduced his dogmatics from the concept of obedience in the same way in which medieval Jewish philosophy deduced its dogmatics from the concept of revelation.[45] It is self-evident that these dogmas are merely "pious dogmas" (*pia dogmata*), not true dogmas. They define the world of popular religion, which stands in radical contrast to true metaphysical cognition. Since these pious dogmas do not belong to reason, Spinoza assigns them to revelation. The metaphysical presuppositions of his system make it quite evident that he did not grant metaphysical reality to revelation, and the *Theologico-Political Treatise* clearly reveals his true position: general religion is a product of popular thought. That he nevertheless makes it appear as if he were retaining the idea of revelation—although he had uprooted it historically and metaphysically—is not solely due to his accommodation to churchly doctrine. He wants to salvage the idea of revelation for the popular consciousness because he sees no other ground on which to base the morality of the people except the ideas of a personal God and a divine revelation. He therefore appropriates the concept of revelation of historical religion but expands it, in accordance with the general character of the popular concept of virtue, into the concept of universal revelation.

Thus his theory of religion distinguishes three levels: 1) the metaphysical truth of philosophy, which includes the ultimate religious truth; 2) the universal religion of obedience; 3) the merely political Mosaic legislation.

The Bible contains elements of all three. Some of its books, especially those ascribed to Solomon, rise to the height of philosophy, whereas the teachings of the prophets remain in the sphere of popular religion, which also reflects the prophetic concept of God. However, this sphere contains the pure religion of obedience as well as the Mosaic political legislation destined for the Jewish people alone.[46]

Nothing of the complexity and artificiality of this train of thought, nothing of the twilight of the *Theologico-Political Treatise* which obscures Spinoza's actual views, is found in *Jerusalem*. Here we find no conflict, but full harmony between the esoteric truth of philosophy and popular faith. Here the personal God of religion is also the God of metaphysics, and the concept of morality is identical in the religious and metaphysical spheres. Natural religion and the religion of reason coincide for Mendelssohn, and he can dispense with Spinoza's notion of a universal revelation as the source of religion in general. What connects him with Spinoza is the severance of religion from its historical basis in the specific revelation of the Bible, not the positive concept of religion. Like Spinoza, he maintained that revelation cannot disclose theoretical truth. Like Spinoza, he affirmed the universality of morality and of its religious foundations. And like Spinoza, he concluded that Judaism's specific revelation was not the revelation of a universal human religion, but solely that of a specific Jewish law. Yet by transforming Spinoza's political law into religious law, Mendelssohn gave this thesis an entirely new direction.

Spinoza's aim in interpreting Judaism as purely political legislation had been to deprive it of its religious significance. All eighteenth-century authors influenced by Spinoza pursued the same aim in their exclusively legalistic conception of the Mosaic revelation. Mendelssohn also adopted this conception, but in a form which he considered to be the most effective instrument of Jewish apologetics. He saw in it the possibility of harmonizing Judaism with the ultimate consequences of the rationalistic concept of religion.

A radical religious rationalism cannot tolerate the coexistence and parity of any revelation of religious truth. It posits that man's felicity is based solely on reason and is not connected to any particular revelation. Judaism can affirm this position without surrendering its identity. It presupposes the religious truth of reason. Hence its revelation is that which alone is possible according to these assumptions: the disclosure of a [system of] law whose function is the actualization of religious truth. Jewish apologetics before and after Mendelssohn has frequently emphasized that Jewish particularism is grounded in a deeper universalism. The revelation of the Torah is intended only for the people of Israel and does not claim to be the sole path to God. The other nations are not obligated to observe the mandates of the Torah. Precisely for this reason the Torah cannot constitute the only path to salvation. Non-Jewish nations can find their way to God without Torah through piety and moral conduct.

Mendelssohn fused this notion with the idea of Enlightenment rationalism and presented it as a renunciation of any claim that [Judaism] possesses any particular distinctive truth. It is not despite but because of its legalistic character that Judaism is the religion that is completely grounded in reason. Faith in the universality and self-sufficiency of reason is Judaism's faith as well. The Jew qua Jew demands no other certitude than the universal human certitude provided by reason. He claims for himself the religious law alone, given only to him. In other words, Mendelssohn wanted to defeat the deistic critique of Judaism with its own weapons. His interpretation of Judaism can be understood only in this historical context.

In order to complete this analysis of Mendelssohn's interpretation of Judaism, we must discuss his concept of religious law or, as he puts it, the commandments of religion. The Sinaitic revelation is a revelation not of truths but of laws, yet of laws which are based on eternal verities and which are to serve as incentives to reflection on these verities. They hide the most profound insights, and the divine compendium of laws "has become a source of cognition for a large segment of mankind, on which mankind draws for new insights or to correct old ones." "These daily acts were to be closely linked to religious and moral insights," and their "profound significance" was to provide an incentive "to reflect upon these sacred matters or to seek instruction from men of wisdom."[47] This method of transmitting religious truths was intended to protect the Jewish people from sliding into paganism. The errors of paganism were not inborn in the human mind, but rather originated in an erroneous presentation of ideas that in themselves are true. The human mind functions in such a way that man expresses his ideas through symbols. Yet he is in constant danger of mistaking the symbol for the actual object it represents. Thus, the symbols which were meant to represent man's conception of God have turned into "sensualized" bodily images of God.[48] Here is the root of all erroneous pagan religious beliefs and especially of their moral atrocities.

As already mentioned, in *Jerusalem* Mendelssohn returned to the traditional view of paganism as a degenerated form of an originally pure religion. But while he previously felt that the prejudices and superstitions of paganism were merely a way station in man's development toward the perception of indispensable truths, he had come to view "godlessness as no less godless than such a religion."[49] Deeds and practices—which were not liable to such a misinterpretation—were to replace the symbols for the Jewish people. The ceremonial law was the instrument of preserving the pure truth of the religion of reason among them.[50]

Despite the skillful construction of his argument, its faults and structural stresses are very evident. On the one hand, Mendelssohn insists that the doctrines of natural religion are self-evident to common sense; on the other, he critically weakens this notion by ascribing to man's mind a natural tendency to obscure the truth it originally possessed, with the psychologically inevitable result that the vast majority of mankind succumbs to the errors of paganism. After all, it makes little difference whether people cannot grasp the truth required for their felicity because they are incapable of comprehending it from the very beginning, or whether their own or their ancestors' rational faculty was obscured.

The same difficulty occurs once more when Mendelssohn assigns the possession of a preventive against paganism to only one people. He cannot reconcile God's goodness with the notion that He is supposed to have revealed the verities required for man's felicity to the Jews alone. Yet the same contradiction exists in his concept of the revelation of the Law, which keeps only one people on the road to truth. Insofar as a religious meaning is ascribed to revelation at all, it is inevitable that revelation must raise its recipient to a higher religious level. There surely cannot be a revelation that reveals nothing. Hence the meaning of the divine plan for mankind's history can no longer be seen in the undifferentiated sameness of all people and ages. When Mendelssohn attempted to resolve this contradiction by accepting and affirming the notion of the priestly vocation of Israel—which, by its very existence, unceasingly teaches, proclaims, preaches, and seeks to sustain the correct conception of God—he introduced a theory different in principle.[51] Even in its weakened form, the notion of Israel's election cannot be fitted into his scheme.

It should also be pointed out that these difficulties can be found not only in Mendelssohn's theory but also in his total religious orientation. The distinction between the universal religion of reason and Jewish religious law is the intellectual expression of the two spheres between which Mendelssohn's life, too, oscillated. He did not accept a division by which he would, religiously, be identified exclusively with Judaism, while sharing the general intellectual and cultural trends of his time in everything else. His identification with these general trends actually had a religious basis for him. He felt himself to be a member of a transdenominational religious community whose credo consisted of the eternal verities of natural religion. For his Enlightenment religiosity, natural religion was not abstract, but a living reality which had captured men's minds in his century. In view of the complete congruence of its ideas with those of Judaism, Mendelssohn saw no contradiction in feeling associated with both with equal fidelity. The idealism of reason placed him in the religious community of the Enlightenment, the matter-of-fact naturalness of his Jewish emotions into that of Judaism. His Jewish world was structured by the regimen of life prescribed in Jewish law, which be observed scrupulously. Thus he avoided every possible conflict—but at the price of a peculiar split, which can be traced in every detail. Such a divorce between a religious idea and a religious regimen of life does violence to both. If Judaism's religious regimen is not to be demoted to a purely formal observance of the Law, it demands a religious meaning which simultaneously gives meaning to the existence of the Jewish community. Mendelssohn expresses this very thought when, in a well-known letter to Herz Homberg, he justifies the necessity of Jewish ceremonial law by arguing that "genuine theists" require "a unifying bond . . . as long as polytheism, anthropomorphism, and religious usurpation are rampant in the world."[52] The Jews constitute the community of the genuine theists, and the need to maintain this basic religious conviction demands the preservation of Judaism. This makes good sense, but can hardly be reconciled with Mendelssohn's concept of a religious community that is not bound to any credo. Mendelssohn has not succeeded in fusing the idea of a universal religion and that of the historic religion of Judaism—both of which he affirms—into an organic whole. To achieve this goal would require a different conception of religion.

II
The Principle of Freedom of Religion

The connection between *Jerusalem* and the *Theologico-Political Treatise,* as already indicated, is evident above all in the fact that the two works combine their interpretation of Judaism—viewed in the light of the philosophical concept of religion—with the treatment of freedom of thought and religion. However, whereas the religio-philosophical parts of *Jerusalem* are closely connected with the *Theologico-Political Treatise,* notwithstanding their differences in tendency and position, Spinoza's influence is far less noticeable in that part of *Jerusalem* which deals with legal and political philosophy and establishes the principle of freedom of religion.

Spinoza's position was very different from Mendelssohn's notion of unconditional freedom of religion and his rejection of any coercion in matters of religion. According to Spinoza, the public [*äussere*] exercise of religion is subject to regulation by the state, which has a right in sacred matters (*ius circa sacra*).[53] His exposition of the relationship between state and church belongs completely to the seventeenth-century world of ideas, whose dominant concern was to safeguard the independence of the state and to free it from any connection with ecclesiastical authorities. He grants the state final authority in all matters pertaining to the exercise of religion and rejects any autonomous ecclesiastical power. Only man's freedom of thought is not limited by state authority, and to demonstrate this fact is the second major concern of the legal-philosophical part of the *Theologico-Political Treatise.* That the state should have the right to control thought as such is an impossible concept. The expression of thought can, of course, be subjected to governmental regulation; however, it is contrary to the reasonable interest of the state to limit freedom of expression, provided the exercise of this freedom does not endanger the foundations of state authority.[54] He demands freedom of thought primarily in the interest of philosophy, whose domain is thought. To control the cognition of truth transcends the task of the state.

An analogous freedom exists for the religious attitude: for piety and the private worship of God.[55] Only public religious observance is subject to state regulation. Nevertheless, the relationship between conviction and action is not as clear and precise as it might at first appear. The exercise of religion involves not only ritual observance, but also the fulfillment of the moral commandments, which are the essential ingredients of Spinoza's religion of obedience. It is this aspect of religious practice in which the state is directly interested: the moral doctrine of religion demands control by the state. Thus, for Spinoza, the obedience demanded by religion must be legitimized by the state in order to attain legally binding power. Hence, subordination to the power of the state becomes a commandment of piety itself.[56] Precisely because the state has final authority over the actions of its citizens, it must claim the right to determine the moral doctrine of the churches, and one of its tasks is "to establish and determine the foundations of the church and of its doctrine."[57] But in this case too, it is in the state's interest to permit free expression in everything unrelated to the political order and to grant freedom to the religious communities as long as they respect the requirements of the state.

Mendelssohn conceives of the relationship between state and church in accordance with entirely different notions, which were introduced into eighteenth-century thinking primarily by Locke. The seventeenth century's battle to establish the sovereignty of the state vis-à-vis the church was no longer relevant. The central issue had become the independence of religious conviction vis-à-vis the state. The same freedom which Spinoza had proclaimed for thought was now claimed for religious faith, which was not a mere doctrine of obedience but a doctrine of truth for men like Locke and Mendelssohn. Mendelssohn draws the conclusion, already inherent in Locke's views, that the enjoyment of civic rights must be wholly independent of a person's faith, inasmuch as any attempt to tie civic advantages to a religious creed represents an intrusion of the state into the sphere of religious conviction.[58]

However, it was not only in connection with his concern for the civic equality of the Jews that he pursued the principle of freedom of faith to its ultimate conclusions. Whereas Locke denied tolerance to atheism, Mendelssohn eliminates this restriction, although he considers it proper that the state should, in a restrained way, remain concerned that atheistic doctrines threatening its moral foundations not be disseminated.[59] Above all, however, he denies to the state—just as he does to the church—the right to impose any kind of coercion upon religious conviction. In contrast to Locke, he denies the churches' right to discipline or banish their members; they may not refuse religious instruction to anyone desiring it.[60] With a radicalism never known before, he establishes the spontaneity of conviction as the basis of religious life.

Methodologically, too, Mendelssohn stood in complete opposition to Spinoza. In his opinion, Hobbes had failed to make the proper distinction between physical and moral power, between might and right,[61] and the same was even more true of Spinoza. Indeed, Spinoza repudiated the fundamental principle of his *Ethics* on the basis of this distinction. Inasmuch as he did not recognize any law except the law of nature, he could not recognize any basis for right except the natural order, according to which every individual possesses right to the degree that he possesses power. Natural law refers to nothing but every individual's sphere of power.

This concept of right as power is the sole basis on which the right of the state can be established. Although the state's value lies in its actions to safeguard human life, its right is derived from the power which the individual has ceded to it, either willingly or under compulsion, and its laws are laws only to the extent to which the state has the power to enforce them.[62] Hence the fundamental concern of politics must be to secure a maximum of stability and constancy for the power of the state, and the freedom of its citizens is justifiable as a political goal only because and insofar as it strengthens the state.

These considerations also define the state's relationship to religion and church. The sovereignty of the state over them is coextensive with its power, and considerations of power alone determine the extent to which the state uses its right to sovereignty and grants freedom to those facets of religious life which it has the authority to regulate.[63]

Mendelssohn, in contrast to Spinoza, based natural law completely on a teleologically conceived ethic. "Law" was a moral concept for him. He defines right as the "faculty (the moral capacity) to use a thing as a means for promoting happiness," and he defines this capacity as moral "if it is compatible with the laws of wisdom and goodness."[64] In this way he develops a [concept of] natural law that coincides with ethics. From this in turn he deduces the moral validity of contracts and is thus able to use the notion of the social contract to establish the authority of the state. Formally, this authority rests on the morally binding force of the social contract; substantively, it rests on the moral necessity to submit [conflicts arising from] the collision of the rights of individuals to arbitration by an impartial legal authority. Both the state's rights and the limitations of it are morally circumscribed. The contract on which the state is founded can transform an imperfect into a perfect right, but it can never create a right where there is not [at least] an imperfect right, that is, a conditional moral claim on the person who is under obligation [to fulfill the conditions of the contract]. In other words, the state never has the right to compel its citizens to do something which they are not also at least conditionally morally obligated to do. A breach of this principle cannot be justified by invoking the authority of a social contract.[65]

The most important use Mendelssohn makes of this principle is to establish the principle of freedom of belief. Precisely because the law rests on moral foundations, neither the state nor any other corporate institution possesses the right to coercion in matters of religion.

Despite these fundamental differences between Mendelssohn and Spinoza, they agree in some areas, which, while not very important in themselves, have some significance for the whole argument. They agree about freedom of thought and belief, insofar as each deduces from the concept of law the limits of the state's rights in matters of religious conviction. Mendelssohn's analysis of this issue has just been discussed; Spinoza similarly deduces the right to freedom of thought from the notion that, according to the highest law of nature, each person is master of his thought because he cannot surrender the freedom to judge and think according to his will.[66] In Spinoza's case, of course, this means nothing more than that the state cannot force the individual to change his conviction—a self-evident notion which reappears throughout the literature of the "tolerance period." Yet what makes Spinoza's approach distinctive is not the idea itself, but its conceptual formulation, which alone is significant in relation to Mendelssohn's thinking. Locke, who expressed the same idea as Spinoza, merely drew from it the conclusion that coercion is useless in matters of religious conviction,[67] whereas Spinoza insists that the state has no right to coercion with regard to an individual's thinking because it lacks the power to do so.

Still another of Locke's notions illuminates Spinoza's and Mendelssohn's distinctive approach in this matter. Locke declared that the social contract has never deprived people of their freedom of conviction because they have never wanted to give it up.[68] Each in his own way, Mendelssohn and Spinoza declared that people could never have renounced their freedom of conviction because such a renunciation is legally impossible. Of course, they based their views on different premises, leading to the different conclusions we discussed before. Spinoza, who proceeds from the equation of right and might, limits inalienable freedom to those convictions which are inaccessible to the coercive power of the state, and he determines the right to free expression of conviction by considering whether it is useful for the state. Mendelssohn's concept of the moral law requires that both religious conviction and religious conduct be exempt from state coercion.

This formal agreement of Mendelssohn's and Spinoza's thought is accompanied by a substantive agreement. Locke attempted to validate freedom of conscience by defining the state as a society whose purpose is to promote the collective temporal welfare of its members. Mendelssohn rejected this definition because he considered it inadequate and arbitrary:[69] it did not show why people could not also band together to promote their eternal welfare—and to promote it by coercive measures. Above all, he did not regard temporal and eternal welfare to be two unrelated spheres. Mankind's temporal and eternal weal were inseparable for him; both have their origin and basis in the "fulfillment of our obligations." The obligation to associate ourselves with others [for the promotion of our common well-being] refers to what is collectively best for us in every respect.[70] Hence Locke's concept of the state required correction. The state is concerned not only with men's deeds, but also with the convictions behind them. But where the state cannot generate the right conviction, it must remain satisfied with the right action alone. It can compel people to perform the right deed, but right conviction can be achieved only through education. Education is also among the state's tasks, and in this sphere the state is assisted by religion. Religion thus becomes a support of civic felicity [*bürgerliche Glückseligkeit*].[71]

Spinoza comes to a similar conclusion, but by a different road. Although he bases the state's right on its power, he does not want power to be understood narrowly as being grounded merely in its citizens' fear. Obedience, essential for the state, can also arise from inner motives, and the sovereignty of the state will be strongest where it has captured the hearts of its subjects. Their loyalty is the most secure foundation of the state's authority.[72] To acquire this loyalty, the state also utilizes the religious obligation of obedience, and this is the reason why the state claims to be the supreme authority in religious matters.[73]

In contrast to Mendelssohn, Spinoza held that convictions should be influenced solely in order to solidify the authority of the state. However, this difference is far less significant than their agreement that conviction must be included in the sphere of the state's interests and functions. Both think that the state attaches importance only to the moral will of its subjects. The [interest of the] state extends beyond regulating external conduct, without, however, transforming it once again into a servant of religion, in the sense in which the role of the state traditionally had been conceived. To the extent to which the state is interested in religion at all, its interest lies in the moral sphere. For this reason, Mendelssohn let the state invoke religion as an educative force, while Spinoza thought that the state claims ultimate authority in religious matters in order to gain control over religion as a moral influence. In either case, religion becomes a means for [realizing] the moral aims of the state.

Both thinkers came even closer to each other's position as they applied their theories concerning the relationship of state and religion to Judaism. However, Mendelssohn faced an extraordinary difficulty. By rejecting every kind of coercion in religious matters, he appeared radically to oppose biblical legislation, which threatens harsh punishment for the violation of strictly religious commandments. When he first expressed this view in his introduction to the German translation of Manesseh ben Israel's *Vindiciae Judaeorum,* he was emphatically reproached for it. In *Jerusalem* he came to grips with this objection, which went "right to [his] heart."[74] According to the original constitution of Israel, state and reli-

gion were not only united but identical, and God was the king and administrator of this nation. All civil laws were simultaneously religious laws;
vice versa, the religious content of the revealed Law also became state
law. Every offense against God as the Law-giver of the nation was a
"crime against the sovereign and, therefore, a political crime," and what
was punished was not unbelief or doctrinal error, but rebellion against the
Law-giver and the constitution of the state.[75] This has nothing to do with
"ecclesiastical rights and ecclesiastical power" or with state persecution of
heresy. Though the power to banish [ecclesiastical authorities possessed]
in postbiblical times seems to intimate something else, it was merely a
later abuse of power.

Spinoza took the same fundamental position, though he differed
sharply from Mendelssohn in his hostile interpretation of the motives of
the biblical legislation. After the Exodus from Egypt, the Israelites transferred their rights to God and made Him their king. Therefore, civil law
and religious law are identical in their state, the dogmas of religion are
not doctrines but legal statements and ordinances, Godlessness is injustice, and he who renounces his religion ceases to be a citizen.[76] Like
Mendelssohn, Spinoza uses the Sabbath as an illustration: observance of
it was required by state law; violators were therefore punished by and for
the sake of the state.[77]

However, Spinoza's purpose differed radically from Mendelssohn's.
It was not an anomaly for Spinoza that the state also regulated religious
matters in [ancient] Israel; it accorded fully with his principle of the
state's authority in religious matters. When he insisted that God issued
the Mosaic legislation solely in His capacity as sovereign, he meant to
legitimize the state as the sole authority for religious legislation in Israel
and to refute the claim that there was an autonomous religious legislation. In fact, he could cite the Israelite state as proof for his thesis,
inasmuch as he conceived the kingdom of God as merely ideational and
wanted Moses, who proclaimed God's commandments, and his successors
(though they did not command the same authority) to be considered the
actual rulers of the state.[78]

Such a transfer of conditions unique to ancient Israel to other states
is precisely what Mendelssohn wanted to prevent. For him, the biblical
legislation is absolutely unique. Religious laws can be state laws only
when God rules the people, but even then the state can be concerned
with them only as far as they relate to the state. Locke had already
similarly justified his principle of toleration against the opposite principle
inherent in the biblical legislation,[79] and it is conceivable that he drew on
Spinoza's construction of the argument to support his own position.

It need hardly be pointed out that Mendelssohn's position was a
compromise dictated by necessity [Notausgleich]. It is obvious that rec-

ognizing God as sovereign of the state presupposes the metaphysical conviction of His existence and that one can no longer speak of freedom of belief if the citizens of the state are expected to affirm metaphysical notions. Nevertheless, Mendelssohn sought to resolve the dilemma as well as he could. The modern concept of freedom of belief is something entirely different from the traditional authoritative religious attitude. Until modernity, detachment from the communal faith constituted for Judaism, just as for other religions, a punishable desertion of God and His commandments. The change in religious consciousness even among believers who unconditionally accepted the authority of the tradition is nowhere evident as sharply as it is in this point, and the conflict involved cannot be resolved without force and coercion. Mendelssohn was the first modern Jewish thinker to experience the sharpness of this conflict, but he was not the only one to abandon the attempt to reach a logically tenable solution in order to maintain the authority of the Bible against freedom of belief.

His *Jerusalem* has enduring significance as a first attempt to justify Judaism before the cultural consciousness of modernity. No wonder that, in this effort, he was mindful of the work of the thinker who had undertaken to validate his dissociation from Judaism with the help of the new scientific thought. Mendelssohn was convinced that advances in metaphysical thought would overcome Spinoza's criticism of the basic ideas of the traditional religious world view and restore them to their proper place. In the same way he felt that, on the basis of their common rationalist orientation, he would be able to defeat Spinoza's attack against Judaism and legitimize Judaism philosophically with the help of Spinoza's own principles.

Notes

"Mendelssohn's *Jerusalem* and Spinoza's *Theologico-Political Treatise*," translated by Alfred Jospe, first appeared as "Mendelssohns *Jerusalem* und Spinozas *Theologisch-Politischer Traktat*," in *Achtundvierzigster Bericht der Hochschule für die Wissenschaft des Judentums* (Berlin, 1931), pp. 33–67.

1. See Jakob Freudenthal, *Spinoza, sein Leben und seine Lehre*, vol. 2 (Stuttgart, 1927), pp. 219–25.
2. See Leslie Stephen, *History of English Thought in the Eighteenth Century* (London, 1881), 1:33; Ernst Troeltsch, *Gesammelte Schriften*, 4:440.
3. See my essay, "Kant und das Judentum," p. 61, n. 3. The details given there show only a few of the proofs, selected from the vast material. As we have already mentioned there, Reimarus is not connected with the English Deists but with their opponent Warburton, who uses the data given by the Deists as the basis of his proof for the divine origin of the Old Testament. In rejecting this paradoxical proof, Reimarus reestablishes the deistic position.
4. Guttmann, "Kant und das Judentum," pp. 50ff. Cf. Hermann Cohen's concurrence in "Innere Beziehungen der Kantischen Philosophie zum Judentum," in *Jüdische Schriften*, vol. 1 (Berlin, 1924), p. 294 and *Die Religion der Vernunft* (Leipzig, 1919), pp. 385ff.

5. Saul Ascher, *Leviathan oder über Religion in Rücksicht des Judentums* (Berlin, 1792), pp. 157ff.
6. Kayserling, *Moses Mendelssohn*, 2d ed. (Leipzig, 1888), pp. 385, 393, 396; Guttmann, "Kant und das Judentum," p. 51; A. Lewkowitz, "Das Judentum und die geistigen Strömungen der Neuzeit II," in *Festschrift zum 75 jährigen Bestehen des jüdisch-theologischen Seminars Fraenckelscher Stiftung*, vol. 1 (Breslau, 1929), p. 226.
7. See Freudenthal, *Spinoza*, 2:229ff.
8. Moses Mendelssohn, *Gesammelte Schriften, Jubiläumsausgabe*, 1:8ff. Hereafter Mendelssohn's works are quoted according to the available volumes of this edition [hereafter *JubA*]; the remainder are quoted according to the earlier edition prepared by G. B. Mendelssohn: *Gesammelte Schriften*, 7 vols. (Leipzig, 1843–45) [hereafter *GS*].
9. *JubA*, 1:14.
10. *GS*, 2:350; see also *JubA*, 1:17.
11. *GS*, 3:260.
12. *JubA*, 7:78. In a comment on this passage, the editor, S. Rawidowicz, points out that Mendelssohn, in his "Postscript" to Lavater's reply, utilizes the *Theologico-Political Treatise* [hereafter *TPT*]. Although the thrust of his comment refers to a passage of Maimonides mentioned by Mendelssohn in the text, its formulation would seem to indicate that he used Spinoza.
13. *TPT*, chap. 3, pars. 17, 22, 26, 42; chap. 4, par. 31. (The numbering of the paragraphs follows the edition by Bruder.)
14. Ibid., chap. 3, pars. 18, 26.
15. Ibid., pars. 19, 20; chap. 5, pars. 8, 10.
16. The theology of the Catholic church and of orthodox Protestantism usually did not claim that the concept of immortality could not be found in the Hebrew Bible (though it was found only in veiled form) and that this concept was clearly enunciated first in the New Testament. The significance which the absence of the promise of immortality had in the anti-Jewish polemics of the Middle Ages can be seen, for example, in Albo's *Ikkarim*. Regarding Socianism, see Leo Strauss, *Die Religionskritik Spinozas als Grundlage seiner Bibelwissenschaft* (Berlin, 1930), pp. 34ff. Regarding the rejection of this claim by the "Unitarians," see Mendelssohn's *Gegenbetrachtungen über Bonnets Palingénésie*, *GS*, 7:101, where he claims the doctrine of immortality specifically for the Hebrew Bible by referring to Job, the Psalms, and the prophetic books, and counts this doctrine among the articles of faith of Judaism.
17. *Jerusalem*, *GS*, 3:315ff., 319ff.
18. Ibid., p. 319.
19. *TPT*, chap. 2, par. 16.
20. Ibid., chap. 13, par. 17.
21. Ibid., chap. 14, par. 34. The clearest exposition of this thought is found in his *Short Treatise on God, Man, and His Well-Being* (known only since the nineteenth century). There Spinoza explains that God cannot reveal Himself through words because people would already have to be familiar with the words in order to understand them. He continues: "If God had, for instance, said to the Israelites, 'I am YHWH, your God,' it would have been necessary for them to know even without words that He was God before they could be assured that it was indeed God who was speaking. Hence we consider it impossible that God could have manifested Himself to human beings by means of any external symbol."
22. *TPT*, chap. 2, pars. 31ff.
23. See my essay, "Religion und Wissenschaft im mittelalterichen und im modernen Denken," in *Festschrift zum fünfzigjährigen Bestehen der Hochschule für die Wissenschaft des Judentums* (Berlin, 1922), pp. 155ff. [See also the present volume.]
24. Cf. the introduction to his *Theodicy*, with its formulation, pregnant with meaning, that Christianity has transformed the religion of the wise into the religion of the people.
25. *GS*, 3:315ff.
26. *JubA*, 7:73. The passage in *Jerusalem* according to which God punishes the sinner for his own good and, for this reason, cannot impose punishment in an afterlife is taken with minor modifications from *Gegenbetrachtungen*, ibid., p. 72. The same is true of

other notions, although they are not taken over literally. When Mendelssohn wrote *Jerusalem*, he utilized the still unfinished and unpublished draft of *Gegenbetrachtungen*. In fact, *Jerusalem* largely uses concepts which were first clearly defined in the controversy with Lavater and Bonnet. See Fritz Bamberger, "Mendelssohns Begriff vom Judentums," *Korrespondenzblatt der Akademie für die Wissenschaft des Judentums* 10 (1929):4–19, esp. p. 15. [See also the present volume.]

27. *JubA*, 7:11; see also *Gegenbetrachtungen*, pp. 75, 98.
28. *JubA*, 7:11, n.c.
29. *TPT*, chap. 5, pars. 47ff.
30. Letter of October 26, 1773, *JubA*, 16:178. Mendelssohn mentions there that he had already addressed the same inquiry to Emden much earlier. It can be assumed that this first inquiry was made during the time of his conflict with Lavater. It is interesting to see how Mendelssohn attempts to trace Maimonides's strange view to the latter's conviction that ethics cannot be grounded in principles of reason, but only in generally held convictions (cf. David Rosin, "Die Ethik des Maimonides," *Jahresbericht des jüd.-theol. Seminars Breslau* [Breslau, 1876], p. 37), which, according to Mendelssohn's erroneous interpretation, must be based on tradition.
31. *JubA*, 1:30ff.; ibid., p. 43; ibid., 2:313, 328; *GS*, 2:306ff.
32. *JubA*, 2:269ff.
33. See Ernst Cassirer, "Die Idee der Religion bei Lessing und Mendelssohn," in *Festgabe zum zehnjährigen Bestehen der Akademie für die Wissenschaft des Judentums*, pp. 31ff.
34. *JubA*, 7:74ff.
35. *JubA*, 7:98; *GS*, 3:337ff. On pp. 316ff., one can still sense the opposite view. However, the condition of "raw nature" is virtually idealized à la Rousseau, and the subsequent excesses of paganism are not attributed to it.
36. The second of the *Wolfenbüttler Fragmente* contains a detailed exposition echoed by several passages in *Jerusalem* (p. 316): "According to the true concepts of Judaism, all inhabitants of the earth are destined to felicity, and the means to attain it are as widespread as the means to overcome hunger and other natural needs." Compare this with Reimarus's statement: "God certainly acts differently in matters of the body. He offers through nature in abundance what people and especially children require to live. . . . How, then, can He possibly have placed the means to attain spiritual and eternal life and well-being so far beyond the reach of man that they are partly unattainable and partly left to chance?" (*Lessings Werke*, ed. Julius Petersen and Waldemar v. Olshausen, vol. 22 [Berlin, 1925], p. 75).
37. *TPT*, chap. 3, pars. 27–31.
38. Ibid., pars. 30, 43–46.
39. Ibid., chap. 12, pars. 19ff.; chap. 14, pars. 23ff.
40. Ibid., chap. 3, pars. 31–38; see also chap. 11ff.
41. Ibid., chap. 12, pars. 2, 19, 22.
42. *Ethics*, Appendix to Book I; Introduction to *TPT*. There is a conflict between the assumption of a true knowledge of God, which is necessary, essential, and immanent in the human mind, and the assumption that the masses are governed by superstition. This conflict cannot be resolved by assuming a darkening of the originally clear consciousness of God, for an adequate cognition cannot, according to Spinoza, be darkened [obscured]. Cf. *Ethics* II,43. Spinoza's suggested solution in the scholium to II,43 is obviously inadequate. Leo Strauss, *Religionskritik Spinozas*, p. 245, wants to see the general religion as penetration of the opacity of superstition by the illuminating radiance of the original knowledge of God. In this way he wants to explain the virtuousness of the masses. But it is difficult to see how these two extremes can be reconciled and produce a middle position on the "general religion" and how, especially, one can arrive at a concept of God as the giver of the moral law—a concept that is alien to both extremes. Spinoza's repeated explanation that philosophy is not competent to deal with the notion that obedience can lead to felicity is hardly compatible with this approach (see chap. 15, pars. 22, 26). Even if one wants to explain the origins of the popular religion and morality this way, there remains what the text itself says: logically it is not grounded in reason.

43. *TPT*, chap. 4, pars. 1–15.
44. Ibid., pars. 25ff., 37; chap. 14, pars. 24ff.
45. Ibid., chap. 14, par. 10. The dogmas of the general religion were substantively taken over by Herbert of Cherbury. His method of derivation reminds one strongly of that of the Jewish philosophers, especially Albo, whose three basic dogmas could easily be expanded to those of Spinoza.
46. Strauss, *Religionskritik Spinozas*, pp. 252ff.
47. *GS*, 3:321, 340ff.
48. Ibid., pp. 332–39.
49. Ibid., p. 337.
50. Ibid., pp. 339ff.
51. Ibid., p. 340.
52. Letter of September 22, 1783, *GS*, 5:669.
53. *TPT*, chap. 19. It hardly seems necessary to mention the connection of these views with those of Hobbes and probably also of Hugo Grotius.
54. Ibid., chap. 20, esp. pars. 1–7.
55. Ibid., chap. 7, pars. 90ff.; chap. 19, par. 3.
56. Ibid., chap. 19, pars. 6ff., 21ff.
57. Ibid., par. 39.
58. *GS*, 3:269.
59. Ibid., p. 287. *Re* Locke, cf. "A Letter Concerning Toleration," in *The Works of John Locke*, vol. 5 (London, 1824) [hereafter *Locke*], p. 47.
60. *GS*, 3:297ff. For Locke's opposite view, see *Locke*, p. 17.
61. *GS*, 3:260.
62. *TPT*, chap. 16, par. 208.
63. Ibid., chap. 19; chap. 20, pars. 1ff., 7ff.
64. *GS*, 3:269.
65. Ibid., pp. 276–81, 283ff.
66. *TPT*, chap. 7, par. 91; chap. 19, par. 3; chap. 20, pars. 1–3.
67. *Locke*, p. 11.
68. Ibid., pp. 10–11.
69. *GS*, 3:261ff. Locke does not speak of "temporal well-being" but of "civil interests." However, according to his further exposition, this difference does not seem significant, although Mendelssohn's statements regarding temporal and eternal weal lose their formal point of origin.
70. *GS*, 3:263ff.
71. Ibid., p. 267.
72. *TPT*, chap. 17, pars. 5–8, 13.
73. Ibid., chap. 19, pars. 39–43.
74. *GS*, 3:307.
75. Ibid., pp. 350ff.
76. *TPT*, chap. 17, pars. 26–32.
77. Ibid., chap. 19, par. 12.
78. Ibid., chap. 17, pars. 36ff.; chap. 19, pars. 11ff., 35ff.
79. *Locke*, pp. 37ff.

16
MOSES MENDELSSOHN ON EDUCATION AND THE IMAGE OF MAN

Alexander Altmann

hen philosophy paints its grey in grey, a gestalt of life has grown old; it cannot be rejuvenated but merely known by this 'grey in grey.' The Owl of Minerva begins its flight only at the approach of dusk." The fact that reflection on a form of culture can set in only at the end of its course, as Hegel asserts in this famous utterance, is probably most clearly illustrated by the German Enlightenment. It was not until its decline, when there were already indications of the rise of Romanticism, that men began to discuss the meaning of the term "enlightenment." Johann Friedrich Zöllner, provost and senior councillor of the Consistory of Berlin, casually posed the question of its meaning in an essay published in 1783 in the *Berlinische Monatsschrift*. It was answered by two important thinkers: by Moses Mendelssohn in September, 1784, and by Immanuel Kant in December of the same year.[1]

Kant defined "enlightenment" as "man's release from his self-incurred tutelage" and as "the courage to use one's own reason." If the question "Do we currently live in an enlightened age?" were raised, the answer should be, "No, not in an enlightened age, but in an age of enlightenment." Frederick the Great's century had opened a path for man's enlightenment by granting him freedom of conscience. Now it was up to the people to make use—within the framework of law and order—of the freedom offered to them. To relinquish enlightenment and permit oneself to be held in intellectual tutelage would be to violate the sacred rights of humanity.

If Kant's reply to Zöllner was a flaming manifesto for freedom, Mendelssohn's essay constituted a carefully deliberated disquisition which went beyond the original question. He discussed not merely "enlightenment" but the more general concept of *Bildung* ("education"; literally, "formation" of mind, spirit, character), and one can sense his awareness of the crisis in which the Enlightenment then found itself. It was precisely because of his unwavering identification with Enlightenment philosophy that Mendelssohn was much more affected by its crisis than Kant.

For Kant, the pioneer of German Idealism, enlightenment was no longer anything but a motto for freedom of conscience, though as such it was surely of the highest significance. For Mendelssohn, "enlightenment" meant a definite, clearly circumscribed philosophy, to which he tenaciously adhered despite his early awareness of its crisis. It was this awareness that compelled him to distinguish between "enlightenment" and "culture" and to subsume both under the concept of education.

Let us, then, analyze the double-tracked notion of education. This analysis will lead us from Mendelssohn's concept of *Bildung* to the image of man on which this concept is predicated. Nowhere in his work are the features of this image systematically presented, since by his own admission he did not dare to undertake the systematic form of presentation which he admired in his models, Christian Wolff and Alexander Gottlieb Baumgarten. The easy, natural style of dialogue, letter, and essay suited him better. Even his prize-winning composition *Essay on Evidence in the Metaphysical Sciences* [*Abhandlung über die Evidenz in Metaphysischen Wissenschaften*, 1764], which comes close to being a systematic treatise, is basically an elaborate essay; his last great work, *Morning Hours* [*Morgenstunden*] is based on lectures and discussions.

We encounter Mendelssohn's view of man in many variations, but without vacillations or inconsistencies, throughout his rich oeuvre. Though no systematizer as far as the presentation of his thoughts is concerned, Mendelssohn can justly be called a systematic thinker. Neither an eclectic nor an expounder of popular philosophy, he had struggled for many years with the teachings of the Leibniz-Wolff-Baumgarten school and as a result developed into a strict metaphysician whose graceful style all too easily belies the precision and conciseness of his thought. The cohesiveness of his image of man is derived, as will soon become evident, from the clear conceptual structure of his metaphysics.

Mendelssohn opens his essay on Zöllner's question with an interesting linguistic observation. "The terms 'enlightenment' [*Aufklärung*], 'culture' [*Cultur*], and 'education' [*Bildung*]," he says, are still newcomers in our language. As of now, they are part of the literary language alone. Ordinary people hardly understand them."[2] A look into the first edition of Johann Christoph Adelung's *Grammatical-Critical Dictionary of the*

High German Vernacular [*Grammatisch-kritisches Wörterbuch der Hochdeutschen Mundart*], published in 1774, proves that the term *Cultur* is altogether missing there, and that *Bildung* is noted solely in the sense of molding [*bilden*], depicting [*abbilden*] the form [*Gestalt*] of an object, and, especially, in the sense of "the shape of a person, especially . . . of his face." "A person possessed of fine *Bildung*," it says there, "is one whose face has fine features" (col. 912). The entry of *Bildung* is unchanged in the second edition, published in 1793, while the term *Cultur* is introduced (cols. 1354–55) for the first time and, what is more, in a literal appropriation of Mendelssohn's definition of *Bildung*. Yet the term *Bildung* had already won a place in literature, as Mendelssohn emphasized. Thus, to cite only one example, the well-known pedagogue Joachim Heinrich Campe had written an article, "On Early Childhood Education" ["Über die früheste Bildung junger Kinderseelen"] in the *Berlinische Monatsschrift*.[3] The novel terminology, Mendelssohn remarked, did not mean that the things it described were new. But linguistic usage had not yet had time to establish clear distinctions in the meanings of *Aufklärung*, *Cultur*, and *Bildung*.

According to Mendelssohn's definition, "education is divided into culture and enlightenment." The distinction between these two elements, he argues, is that culture is concerned with practical and enlightenment with theoretical matters. Culture has to do with the crafts, arts, and mores of society; the degree of culture is determined by the self-evident refinement and beauty of its objects, much in the way in which the degree of cultivation and tillage of a plot of land is determined by the number of useful things it yields to human industriousness. Gradations in skills, propensities, inclinations, and habits are the subjective correlates to the various degrees in the objective qualities of the products of culture. The more refined these aptitudes become, the higher will be the level of human culture. Enlightenment, on the other hand, in objective terms means rationally gained insights; subjectively, it means man's aptitude to think rationally about all human concerns and to do so in a way commensurate with their significance for, and impact upon, his destiny.

Mendelssohn's concept of man's destiny is more clearly stated in the third discussion of *Phaedo:* progression to ever greater perfection.[4] In the essay on Zöllner's question, he says, "I always posit man's destiny as the measure and goal of all our strivings and endeavors, as the point on which we must train our sight lest we become lost."[5] We shall have to discuss the metaphysical meaning of this progression toward perfection later on. Here it suffices to note Mendelssohn's differentiation between culture and enlightenment, between practical and theoretical reason, within the concept of education. Some people, he explains, possess both culture and enlightenment. This was true of the ancient Greeks. "They were an educated people [*eine gebildete Nation*], just as their language is an educated language." Altogether, a people's language is the best indicator of the level of its education in the sense of both culture and enlightenment. The Chinese, he contends, have much culture but little enlightenment (a judgment contradicting Voltaire's).[6] Nuremberg's population has more culture, and Berlin's more enlightenment; Frenchmen have more culture, and Englishmen more enlightenment.[7]

Mendelssohn reflected on culture and enlightenment in both their splendor and their potential corruption. The nobler a thing is in its perfection, he says, quoting "a Hebrew author,"[8] the more repulsive it is in its decay.[9] Misuse of enlightenment weakens man's moral sense and leads to obtuseness, egotism, irreligion, and anarchy. Misuse of culture engenders voluptuousness, hypocrisy, effeminacy, superstition, and enslavement. It is noteworthy that Mendelssohn traces superstition not to a lack of enlightenment but to a decline of culture—that is, to a deterioration of man's moral fiber. An educated [*gebildete*] nation, he holds, is threatened by nothing as much as by a "superabundance of national prosperity," which, as is also true for the most perfect physical health, might actually be called a disease.

The very fact that a people has reached the highest possible level of education poses a threat. It may go into a decline simply because it cannot climb any higher. In the fragment titled "The Affinity of the Beautiful and the Good" ["Verwandtschaft des Schönen und Guten"],[10] Mendelssohn had already pointed out the dangers inherent in a people's affluence. Opulence has frequently ruined the fine arts. Once man's character is deteriorating, even the good changes its nature and turns into poison. Nothing does more harm to a people on the verge of falling into decadence than license and a reckless [*heroische*] youth. What he meant by the dangers of affluence is most clearly expressed in his remarks on Ernst Ferdinand Klein's essay "On the Best Constitution of the State" [*Über die beste Staatsverfassung*]:[11]

> Without exercising their faculties, neither states nor individuals can be happy. One's faculties must, however, meet resistance if they are to be activated. As soon as a spring has overcome its coil's resistance and has unwound itself, its tension is gone and it stops working. It follows that it is the nature of things to move in a cycle. Once the fathers leave whatever status and wealth they have gained to the children, nothing is left to the latter but a dispirited consumption, without any prior effort. Once the fathers have struggled for freedom and made it secure against all attack, their children become indolent and their minds slavish. Once all prejudice has been fought and eradicated, love of truth grows dim and dies, and the children have no longer any incentive to enlightenment.

The dubious value of an enlightenment that has become stereotyped and, having reached its goal, has lost its authentic ethos, seems to have disturbed Mendelssohn profoundly. In an article published in 1785 in the *Berlinische Monatsschrift,* he distinguishes between genuine and pseudo enlightenment.[12] Shaftesbury had said that the best means for counteracting enthusiasm [*Schwärmerei*] and superstition were wit and humor. This prescription, Mendelssohn remarks, would prove ineffective unless it were used in moderation. Trying to exorcise superstition and enthusiasm by scorn and derisive laughter rather than by gentle irony would produce no genuine enlightenment. Fear of being ridiculed may make people conceal, but not get rid of, their follies. In fact, some people may even join the scoffers whenever this seems indicated by the dictate of fashion. Inwardly, though, they will not have changed at all. They will remain hidden enthusiasts. "Nothing is more detrimental to the true weal of man," Mendelssohn says, "than this pseudo enlightenment which has everybody declaim some stale truism from which the spirit has long since evaporated, a pseudo enlightenment that makes everybody scoff at certain biases [*Vorurtheile*] without distinguishing between their true and erroneous components." Ridicule is not the means by which to advance true enlightenment. The only effective means is enlightenment itself. Man is not meant to repress prejudices, but to shed light on them. Indeed, Mendelssohn goes further: instead of mocking preconceived notions, one ought to distinguish whatever truth they may contain from their fallacies. He acknowledges that there also is a kernel of truth in enthusiasm. To him, as to the Enlightenment as a whole, *Schwärmerei* is a collective term encompassing crass superstition as well as mysticism.[13] Bewildered by both shallow philosophies and immorality and therefore nostalgic for the naiveté of their childhood, people revert to puerile follies. They prefer the company of ghosts to walking among the corpses of a lifeless nature.[14]

True, Mendelssohn's characterization of *Schwärmerei* as a kind of infantile regression bears the typical features of an enlightenment that looks down from reason's lofty heights. Yet his assertion that even *Schwärmerei* contains a kernel of truth points in a new direction: to esoteric interpretation. In contrast to the customary stance of the Enlightenment, Mendelssohn had kept, or else regained, a certain respect even for so-called prejudices. "Do not let us submit to any prejudice against prejudices," he wrote in 1779 to Hennings, in the same spirit in which Lessing had written to him in 1771: "I am afraid that in discarding certain prejudices, I may have discarded a bit too much of what I shall now have to fetch back."[15]

Lessing's esoteric interpretation of the eternality of punishment in hell as taught by the church and defended by Leibniz exemplifies well

what Mendelssohn meant when he spoke of reinstating discarded prejudices. There was no way in which Mendelssohn could come to terms with
this particular doctrine, which he considered contrary to all rational theology; he could merely shake his head about Lessing's attempt at interpretation. He himself, however, developed a theory of tolerance for
prejudices which seemed no less dubious to such sworn adherents of the
Enlightenment as Hennings and the Reimaruses. In the essay on Zöllner's
question he discusses the possibility that enlightenment could become a
threat to the moral order of society. Given such circumstances, should one
curb the spread of it? His answer reads: "As long . . . as one cannot
disseminate certain truths which are useful and becoming to man without
demolishing whatever religious and moral principles he, for better or
worse, may cling to, any proponent of enlightenment who loves virtue will
proceed with care and caution. He will tolerate a bias rather than exorcise
along with it any truth with which it may be tightly interwoven." In other
words, wherever a conflict of interests exists between enlightenment as
theoretical reason and culture as practical, religio-ethical reason, it is advisable to give the latter priority. Wherever a close link exists between a
moral system and any sort of theology, it would be an unkind act to
endanger the practical efficacy of a prejudice-supported morality for the
sake of theoretical truth. The interpretation he gave in his *Phaedon* to the
fact that Socrates tolerated and, from an esoteric perspective, even approved of the cultic worship of the gods was derived from this particular
view. What is more, he candidly admitted in the course of his dispute with
Lavater that he, as a philosopher of the Enlightenment, could see no need
for attacking the dogmas of Christianity, inasmuch as they were intricately
interwoven with the morals of Christian society and infused that society
with the strength it needed for its moral stability.[16] And in his *Causa Dei*,
he cautioned against eliminating naive popular notions of retribution in the
beyond.

> It amounts to misanthropic malice to take from some sinful wretch that
> common fear which might prevent him from carrying out some evil design,
> as long as his soul is still incapable of grasping the great truth that evildoing
> as such constitutes damnation. What would you call a mischievous boy who
> breaks a lame man's crutch because he himself has no need of it? You are
> doing the very same thing if you destroy the popular system as long as the
> common man has not yet developed a sense for your higher principles.[17]

To this pedagogic consideration is added, however, an esoteric one.
"Secondly, and at bottom, even the popular system contains much that is
true. Its notions need to be refined but not reformed." Mendelssohn asks
not that dogmas be abolished, but that their meaning be given the profundity consonant with the principles of rational theology. Thus he sets him-

self far apart from that radical fight against prejudice which, starting at the end of the seventeenth century, had been carried on within the ranks of the French Enlightenment. He regards as destructive—and he is not alone in this view—an attitude which rejects all tradition as prejudice, an attitude such as we encounter in, say, Fontenelles, de La Motte, and especially in d'Holbach. The obsession to think of all inherited beliefs and practices as prejudices had already, in 1751, led Duclos to call for caution, and had, in 1755, induced Chevalier d'Arq to utter this warning: "The proposition to eradicate some prejudice is a very delicate matter. Unless one brings to it an enlightened mind along with the necessary firmness, one will undermine the truth instead of dealing a blow to error."[18] Mendelssohn's moderate position originated, as we have seen, not merely in his fear of undermining the truth, but primarily in moral considerations. On the other hand, he was not inclined to join Justus Moeser, the Osnabrück patriot and historian revered by Goethe, in a serious defense of superstition. Had he lived to see it, Mendelssohn would not have praised Moeser's 1790 essay, "In Defense of Our Ancestors' So-called Superstition" ["Etwas zur Vertheidigung des sogenannten Aberglaubens unserer Vorfahren"], as unreservedly as Goethe did.[19]

If one wishes to understand Mendelssohn's concept of education as derived from his philosophical premises, one must consider his image of man. His differentiation between enlightenment and education in the larger sense is rooted in the distinction between reason [*Vernunft*] and sensuousness [*Sinnlichkeit*], between the higher and lower faculties of the soul, to use the designation customary in the German Enlightenment. Enlightenment, if we may paraphrase Mendelssohn, consists in the perfection of the soul's higher faculties, in that clear, scientific, abstract cognition which, in Wolff's terminology, is termed "symbolic" cognition—that is, a purely intellectual function, free of all intuitive representation.[20]

In distinction to that abstract or symbolic cognition which furnishes the basis of enlightenment, education in the pregnant sense of *Bildung* is the harmonious development of all psychic faculties; to put it more precisely, it is the accord between sensibility and reason, between sensory-intuitive and abstract knowledge, between the lower and higher faculties of the soul. How essential it is to bring about this accord may be illustrated by the fact that one can have a clear, logically determined cognitive notion of God's existence, or of the validity of the moral law, without leading a religious or moral life. Man's enlightened attitude alone, we may say in line with Mendelssohn's thinking, does not yet guarantee the harmonious development of his character [*Bildung des Menschen*]. Only where there is accord between symbolic-abstract and sensory-intuitive cognition does rational discernment gain the necessary momentum to break through its isolation and turn into a vital, effective insight.

How to create this accord presents a psychological problem which occupied Mendelssohn quite early in his career. It furnished the topic of his essay, "On Controlling the Inclinations" ["Von der Herrschaft über die Neigungen"], which originated in 1756 during his famous correspondence with Friedrich Nicolai and Lessing concerning the nature of tragedy. In December, 1756, he wrote to Lessing: "I have had some entirely new ideas about the struggle between the lower and higher faculties of the soul, and shall submit them to you as soon as possible for your critical appraisal."[21] The psychological theory he develops in his essay, being closely linked to his aesthetic views, doubtless had been suggested by this epistolary discussion of aesthetic questions.

Briefly, the theory runs as follows. The factors which are instrumental in bringing about a certain action are 1) the number of motivations which stimulate that action; 2) the clarity of the notions which the soul forms of the good it considers desirable; and 3) the time needed for forming those notions. It is possible, Mendelssohn maintains, to be completely convinced, on the basis of rational considerations, of the moral imperative for a certain course of action and still to act differently if obscure motivations, suggested to us by our lower psychic faculties, impress upon us a multiplicity of different desirable objects more rapidly than rational considerations do. In other words, clear, rational cognition—which takes more time to obtain—may be overwhelmed by the admittedly dark, and frequently even unconscious, power of passion. If one wishes to ensure virtue, it is therefore not enough soberly to demonstrate how laudable it is. One must also awaken a great many moral motivations in one's soul by reflection, and one must learn to sort them out quickly in one's mind. To do so requires both practice and concretization [konkrete Veranschaulichung]— that is, intuitive, not merely abstract, cognition. Mendelssohn says with regard to practice: "As the artist must keep following certain prescribed rules until he is no longer aware of doing so, so must moral man follow the laws of nature (that is, of rational morality), if he wishes to harmonize the lower and higher faculties of his soul."[22] We gain intuitive cognition [anschauende Erkenntnis] by experience, by examples learned from history, and by poetry, and Mendelssohn would not have the last moralize in a "frosty" manner, but rather present man's actions and inclinations in a way that is true to life.[23]

He again takes up the psychological theory, in a particularly impressive manner, in "Rhapsody; or, Additions to the Letters on the Sentiments ["Rhapsodie oder Zusätze zu den Briefen über die Empfindungen"], first published in 1761. In it he charmingly recounts Xenophanes' tale of Panthea, Cyrus' beautiful prisoner, and Araspes, the young hero who trusts the strength of his rational will to resist the power of his natural inclination. Finally succumbing to his violent passion, however, he recognizes that man's practical will is decidedly not controlled by his reason. Araspes could have said, as Medea did say in Ovid, "Desire counsels one thing, the mind another; I see and approve of the better, yet follow the worse" ("Aliud cupido, mens aliud suadet; video meliora proboque, deteriora sequor").[24] In his "Rhapsody" and the prize-winning *Essay on Evidence in the Metaphysical Sciences,* Mendelssohn speaks in poetic terms of the means by which to achieve harmony between the soul's higher and lower faculties. Moreover, he adds a number of new observations. Thus he says in the "Rhapsody" that the important thing about an increase in one's motivations is not merely their quantity but also their weight. "One must learn to recognize man's true dignity, and see the loftiness of his moral nature in the proper light." And in order to accelerate the mental process of sorting out one's motives for virtuous conduct, one must continue to practice until the theoretical principles, once they are recognized as such, have been transformed into inclinations and virtue seems the product more of a natural drive than of reason. The purpose of such practice, he says in "Essay on Evidence," is to make the recognition of moral duties part of our temperament.[25]

Christian Wolff also had emphasized the importance of moral practice, and the notion of virtue as habit of the soul actually goes back to Aristotle's *Ethics.* What distinguishes Mendelssohn from his predecessors is his novel view of moral perfection as an ability to fulfill the moral law effortlessly and unconsciously, as if it were one's second nature. His almost hymnic description of an individual who, having transcended the struggle with his passions, practices the highest virtue without vanity introduces a new tone into moral theory. It is well known how profoundly this new tenor touched Schiller. He spoke in his "Kallias Letter" ["Kalliasbrief"] of 1793 of the man for whom duty had become second nature and in whom moral beauty had found its representative. Influenced by Mendelssohn's thinking, he also had spoken in favor of inclination when taking issue with Kant's rigorous ethics of duty.

Mendelssohn himself derived the idea that the individual who acts morally out of inclination is superior to one who merely bows to the demands of duty from Jewish tradition, as Ernst Simon has shown in a sensitive study.[26] Schiller's essay "On Grace and Dignity" [Über Anmut und Würde," 1793], whose close resemblance to Mendelssohn's "On the Sublime and Naive in the Fine Arts" ["Über das Erhabene und Naive in den schönen Wissenschaften"][27] has given rise to several literary-historical speculations, may also be mentioned in this context. Schiller, like Mendelssohn before him, drew on Lord Henry Home Kames's *Elements of Criticism* (1762), but it seems likely that Schiller also used Mendelssohn's

treatise.[28] What interests us above all is the connection Mendelssohn
establishes between grace—to which he refers also as "sublime beauty of
movement"—and morality when it has become natural inclination.
Again the unconscious plays a decisive role. "Grace," he says, "is . . .
related to the naive, since the movements of the graceful slide naturally,
flowing easily and gently one into the other, making us realize, without
intent or conscious deliberation, that the mainsprings of the soul and the
stirrings of the heart from which these free movements flow are at play
equally naturally, harmonize with each other equally gently, and unfold
equally artlessly. Hence, the idea of innocence and moral simplicity [*Ein-
falt*] is always tied to sublime grace."[29]

We have endeavored to show that Mendelssohn's concept of *Bildung* is grounded in his psychological view of man. And we have also
referred, if only briefly, to the relationship between this concept and his
aesthetics. However, Mendelssohn was not only a psychologist and aes-
thetician; his main interest was metaphysics, and the concluding section
of our reflections will therefore deal with the metaphysical grounding of
his concept of education.

It seems best to take as our point of departure a notion which is
closely linked to that of practice as the means for gaining moral perfection. This is the notion of *bon-sens,* of taste, and it occupied Mendelssohn
again and again. He had already contrasted this notion with the theory of
Francis Hutcheson, who had drawn a sharp demarcation between reason
and moral sense, in his early essay, "The Affinity of the Beautiful and the
Good" ["Verwandtschaft des Schönen und Guten"]. We approve of an
action, Hutcheson had asserted (and Hume as well as Adam Smith had
taught the same thing) not because reason makes a valid statement about
it, but because our moral sense approves of it. By the same token we
consider beautiful whatever our aesthetic sense approves of. An action is
always determined by some purpose [*zweckbedingt*], and purposes presuppose desires and effects. The quality of these desires and effects is
evaluated by the moral sense, but this quality is not subject to the judgment of reason, since reason can recognize only relations but can neither
set nor evaluate purposes.

As had Hutcheson, Alexander Gerard assumed an entire scale of
senses in order to demonstrate the imagination's capabilities in all their
differentiation ("Essay on Taste," 1759). Mendelssohn refuses to embrace this theory of the diversity of the senses. He criticizes it as being
conducive to an arbitrary cutting short of rational investigation.[30] He does
not wish to see the rational character of morality violated. But he also
does not wish to do violence to psychological facts. Thus he arrives at a
kind of compromise with the help of the concept of *bon-sens.* In his
formulation, *bon-sens* is "practiced (skilled) reason." Reason and *bon-*

sens operate according to similar rules, the one more slowly, the other more quickly. It is our reason that makes us distinguish between truth and error, good and evil, the beautiful and the ugly. In addition, we possess *bon-sens*, sentiment and taste which also present us with an immediate awareness of the true, the good, and the beautiful, though not with the distinctness of a logical demonstration. While our taste must guide our reason in judging the beautiful, in matters of morality our *bon-sens* is subordinate to reason.[31]

The *Essay on Evidence* defines the somewhat vague statements about *bon-sens* more precisely. The concept "conscience" is introduced, and *bon-sens* is no longer regarded as a combination of sentiment, taste, and the ability to draw instant if indistinct conclusions, but as that latter ability alone. Taste as such is confined to the realm of aesthetics; conscience and *bon-sens* together are defined as that "inner sense" which must do duty in urgent moral decisions in place of time-consuming demonstrative syllogisms. However, despite this differentiation of concepts, Mendelssohn's basic attitude remains unchanged. "Conscience" is by no means a hidden moral sense à la Hutcheson, nor has a special moral principle been smuggled in by the introduction of "inner sense" as denoting both conscience and *bon-sens*. Conscience is the product of continuous practice of our rational faculties. Mendelssohn combines his exposition of the inner sense with an indication of the means by which a theoretical comprehension of the moral law is turned into a vital, effective insight.[32]

What is most important about these conceptual definitions is the metaphysical view that gave rise to them, a view going back to Leibniz. Mendelssohn's "Affinity of the Beautiful and the Good" discusses this metaphysical aspect. What marks the difference between reason and sensibility, between thought and sentiment, is not a sharp contrast, but a graduation in the mode of perceiving the same object. Mendelssohn holds that rational concepts are to sense perception what, say, the sound of a distinctly heard musical chord is to the roaring of the sea. The soul thinks when it perceives distinctly; it feels when it surrenders itself to impressions, that is, when it lets itself be affected by the total impact of notions.

In thinking, we comprehend the reality of things by perceiving their particular details distinctly. In sense perception, reality appears in a kind of indistinct mirror image, or, as Mendelssohn calls it in a Leibnizian designation, as a mere phenomenon. To illustrate this difference, he cites the example of the phenomenon of physically perceivable colors, which corresponds to the reality of a certain kind of light-ray refraction. In the reality-oriented, scientific way of thinking, no colors actually exist, but merely certain refractions. To the feeling human being dealing with phenomena, the world is radiant in its variegation of colors. This fact accounts for the difference between the liveliness of sense perception and the abstractness of grey theory. Mendelssohn desires both the one and the other. To him, sensibility is the fragrance of life's blossom and reason its perfect fruit. In art we possess that "sensibly perfect" representation which, as an imitation of nature, delights, elates, or shakes us. Aesthetic taste has its own laws. Neither abstract reason nor theory of art, it corresponds to the mode which theory seeks to formulate. Taste, as Mendelssohn (along with Baumgarten, the founder of German aesthetics) defines it, is something analogous to reason. Similarly, *bon-sens,* moral taste, is an *analogon rationis,* so to speak. The term "analogy" denotes neither contrariness nor complete identity. It is the most suitable expression with which to describe the two levels [*Zweistufigkeit*] of reality and phenomenon.

To render a comprehensive description of Mendelssohn's thinking about the relationship between sensibility and reason, one would have to analyze his aesthetic writings and critiques, starting with his *Letters on the Sentiments,* and, in conclusion, deal once more with his epistemological-metaphysical views, which he developed toward the end of his life in a particularly appealing essay, "The Statue" ["Die Bildsäule"], where he discusses Condillac's sensualism and Berkeley's idealism.[33] This analysis would show how staunchly he defended the autonomy and irreducibility, not of reason alone, but also of the senses in their relationship to reason and to one another. Failure to recognize this autonomous and irreducible character, he says at the end of his essay, means not only "to imagine, as that blind man did,[34] the color of scarlet as the sound of a trumpet, but to imagine the soul itself as a violin . . . and to forget the virtuoso [that is, the rational faculty] that must produce a . . . harmonious sound if we are to evaluate the quality of the instrument."

However, the task remains of reducing the variety of faculties which comprise the totality of man to a basic metaphysical principle. Like Leibniz, Mendelssohn regards every being, from inorganic nature to God, as a system of units, or monads, which are equipped with a nucleus of potencies [*Kraftzentrum*]. These nuclei possess perception as well as conatus [*Zielstrebung*], but they differ in the degree of consciousness, clarity, and distinctness of these faculties. From the dormant monad of the inorganic to the cognitive alertness of man and the omniscience of God as the central monad, there stretches an infinite sequence of gradations. Human perception or, as Leibniz calls it, "apperception," is, ideally, the comprehension of eternal and necessary truths—clear and distinct cognition. But not all cognition possessed by the human soul is marked by clarity and distinctness. Only God's thought is *actus purus,* perfect and unimpeded. Leibniz points out quite incidentally that music generates pleasure in the soul, though the soul is not aware of beating time while listening. Indeed, there is much that the soul does in a state of confused or unconscious perception [*in perceptionibus confusis seu insensibilibus*]; hence it is erroneous to believe, as some people do, that nothing occurs in the soul of which it is not conscious [*cuius ipsa non scit conscia*].

This passage furnishes important evidence for Leibniz's acknowledgment of the role the unconscious plays in psychic processes.[35] On the other hand, according to Leibniz, the human soul is not a *tabula rasa* which depends completely on sense impressions, as Locke taught. It is independently capable of spontaneity and creativity, and it possesses a wealth of innate ideas which, however, are originally confused and imperfect. Here we have the beginnings of a theory of the collective unconscious, although it was not further developed. Mendelssohn cites approvingly a saying of Heraclitus, quoted by Plutarch: "We share a single, common world only while we are awake; in his sleep or dream, each individual lives, as it were, in a world of his own."[36] Kant quotes the same passage, attributing it to Aristotle, in his "Dreams of a Spirit-Seer" ["Träume eines Geistersehers," 1766],[37] adding: "It seems to me that one may well reverse the latter part of this statement, and say: 'If of several individuals each has a world of his own, one must assume all are dreaming.' " Obviously neither Mendelssohn nor Kant considered the possibility of a collective subconscious in dreams. For Mendelssohn, the Leibnizian, increasingly clear cognition of objective reality constitutes a kind of increasing awakening from the dream of subjective, let alone merely individual, association of ideas.[38] Since he sees man's destiny and ultimate bliss in an "uninterrupted progression to higher perfections,"[39] rational cognition is for him the pinnacle of everything worth striving for. He is, however, far from entrusting the achievement of man's perfection to reason alone, nor does he wish to see merely a few of the soul's faculties developed and the rest repressed. What he advocates is a harmonious unfolding of the total human being: an enlightened mind, a righteous heart, and an acute sense for genuine beauty.[40] This comprehensive ideal of perfection is expressed in his favorite motto, which he wrote more than once into his friends' autograph albums: "Man's destiny: to seek truth; to love beauty; to will the good; to do his best."

Mendelssohn was one of the first to state that the true, the good, and the beautiful constitute the essence of humanism. And it is characteristic of the spirit of the Enlightenment not to grant any distinct validity to the holy as denoting a religious apperception of the world. Mendelssohn holds that the light of reason is adequate for disclosing the truths man needs to know in order to attain salvation, for showing him the way of the God-pleasing good, and for motivating him to extol hymnically the Creator's majesty. To Mendelssohn, reason itself is holy, for it is a reflection of divine wisdom.[41] The revelation documented in the Bible signifies a vivification of a rationally gained insight through the law which orders and sanctifies life, not an overarching of reason by a mystery. There is nothing of the blasé character of Deism about this attitude, which has found its classic expression in his *Jerusalem* (1783). The image of man is not secularized. Man continues to be seen as created in the image of God. He is a God-oriented, God-related being. But he is freed from the bonds of an intolerant confessionalism, for the image man associates with God has undergone a change during the Enlightenment. God, the archetype of perfection, will neither inflict the eternal punishments of hell nor exclude the heathens from eternal felicity, as the Sorbonne still asserted when it condemned Marmontel's novel *Bélisair* (published in 1767) for advocating tolerance. The seventeenth and eighteenth centuries had discovered man as a human being, and Mendelssohn allowed full scope to this view. God could be no less tolerant than the Enlightenment asked man to be.

Mendelssohn sees the progression toward perfection, which he terms man's destiny, as continuing ceaselessly even in the beyond. Each individual is to follow his own way, pursuing an infinite succession of goals providence has set for him alone. The development of all human faculties and capacities is not simply good in itself; it constitutes man's ultimate purpose.[42] Here Mendelssohn has made progress as such absolute, even though he defines it as ordained by providence and by the decree of God. Like Lessing in his *Nathan,* Mendelssohn prefers the striving for truth to its possession. He offers no *visio beatifica* beckoning to the restless wanderer as a final resting place, no *unio mystica*, and no cleaving to God. There is no roundelay of the righteous, with God at its center, as Jewish eschatology depicts Paradise. Medieval man aimed at a vision of God. This goal is now relinquished, replaced by the concept of infinite progression, of continuous movement toward human perfection. Herder asked Mendelssohn what fruit the faculties we acquired on earth might bear in the life to come.[43] Mendelssohn answered in merely general terms: the thread is never broken, and we shall continue there whatever we have begun here, for everything about man implies infinity. Each of his sensory perceptions contains something capable of ceaseless development; each of his desires persists beyond all measure.[44] Here, as also in Kant, belief in infinite progress has become religion.

In contrast to Kant and Lessing, however, Mendelssohn believes in the progress of the individual, and not in that of mankind as a whole. His viewpoint is determined by Leibniz's monadology. It is the individual soul which, out of darkness and unconsciousness, strives for the light of reason. Mendelssohn's perspective lacks a historical dimension. To put it more precisely, he rejects this dimension as irreconcilable with his concept of progress.[45] True, he acrimoniously objects to Rousseau's critique of culture, but not because it turns historical progress into its opposite—rather, because it runs counter to the traditional concept of natural law.

What Mendelssohn approves of in Rousseau is the notion of perfectibility, though he gives it a Leibnizian orientation which Rousseau had not intended and which Lessing had already felt to be wrong.[46] It is characteristic of Mendelssohn that he makes use in one of his essays [47] of Rousseau's thesis concerning the corrupting effect of the arts and sciences on man's morals only to the extent of individualizing the historical problem it poses. Every rational human being should ask himself the question which Rousseau wished to answer for entire nations: will man's appreciation of the beautiful detract from his love of the good?

With this we have returned to our point of departure, the question concerning enlightenment and culture. The cultural crisis Mendelssohn sensed in the world around him surely presented, as he had to admit, a collective phenomenon. But he saw its solution in the individual's conscious affirmation of his own destiny. Genuine education derives its sustenance from the self-image man carries in his soul. That Mendelssohn's contemporaries understood well what he meant by this assertion is shown by some humorous verses in which Goethe's friend Merck presents two schoolboys discussing Mendelssohn's treatment of suicide. "Through Mendelssohn and his *Letters on the Sensations,* they showed how, all considered, a suicide proves that *in extremis* man lets his sensibility gain control over his soul's higher faculties."[48] Indeed, harmony between the lower and higher faculties of the soul constitutes the core of Mendelssohn's philosophy; and only where such harmony reigns, he taught, is the will to live secure.

Notes

"Moses Mendelssohn on Education and the Image of Man," translated by Eva Jospe, first appeared as "Das Menschenbild und die Bildung des Menschen nach Moses Mendelssohn," in Cécile Lowenthal-Hensel, ed., *Mendelssohn Studien,* vol. 1 (Berlin, 1972), pp. 11–28.

1. Mendelssohn's answer is titled "Über die Frage: Was heisst Aufklären?," *Berlinische Monatsschrift* 4:193–200; Kant's answer is "Beantwortung der Frage: Was ist Aufklärung?," ibid., pp. 481–94. [On the debate of this issue within the Berlin Wednesday Society (Mittwochsgesellschaft), see Alexander Altmann, *Moses Mendelssohn: A Biographical Study* (University, Ala., 1973), pp. 660–64; Norbert Hinske, ed., *Was ist Aufklärung?* (Darmstadt, 1973), and the Postscript ("Nachwort") to the 2d ed. (1977), pp. 519–88, where the present essay is discussed. See also Ehrhard Bahr, ed., *Was ist Aufklärung? Thesen und Definitionen* (Stuttgart, 1974), pp. 71–84. On the indebtedness of Kant's essay to a passage in Mendelssohn's *Jerusalem,* see Eberhard Günther Schulz, "Kant und die Berliner Aufklärung," in *Akten des 4. Internationalen Kant-Kongresses Mainz 6.–10. April 1974,* vol. 2, no. 1 (Berlin, 1974), pp. 60–80.]
2. Moses Mendelssohn, *Gesammelte Schriften,* ed. G. B. Mendelssohn, 7 vols. (Leipzig, 1843–45) [hereafter *GS*], 3:399. [See now Otto Brunner et al., eds., *Geschichtliche Grundbegriffe, Historisches Lexikon zur politisch-sozialen Sprache in Deutschland,* vol. 1 (Stuttgart, 1974), pp. 243–342 (reference to Mendelssohn, pp. 272–74).]
3. *Berlinische Monatsschrift* 3 (1784):217ff.
4. *Moses Mendelssohns Gesammelte Schriften, Jubiläumsausgabe* [hereafter *JubA*], 3:102–15.

5. *GS*, 3:400.

6. According to Voltaire, who repeats an argument widespread during the Enlightenment, a clear and simple rational religion and a highly developed moral doctrine, hence a state of enlightenment and an advanced level of culture, had existed in China since the appearance of Confucius, long before the advent of Christianity (see Friedrich Meinecke, *Die Enstehung des Historismus* [Munich, 1959], pp. 88ff.).

7. Mendelssohn's view of the English character was contested by his friend August Hennings and further explained in Mendelssohn's reply (*JubA*, vol. 13, Letters 660 and 664). For a more elaborate characterization of various nations, see Immanuel Kant's *Anthropology (Werke*, ed. Cassirer, 8:207–14).

8. He obviously had in mind *Mishna Yadayim* IV,6; see Judah Moscato, *Nefuşot Yehuda* (Lemberg, 1850), fol. 94c (quoting Isaac 'Arama, *'Aqedat Yiṣḥaq*, chaps. 79, 94).

9. Similarly, Hume said in his *Essay on Superstition and Enthusiasm* (1741): "Corruption of the best produces the worst."

10. *JubA*, 2:181.

11. *GS*, 4:150ff.

12. Ibid., 5:133–37.

13. See Hermann Bausinger, "Aufklärung and Aberglaube," in *Deutsche Vierteljahresschrift für Literaturwissenschaft und Geistesgeschichte* 37 (1963):345–62.

14. *GS*, 3:314. Cf. Goethe's verdict on d'Holbach's *Système de la nature:* "How hollow and empty we felt in this sad atheistic seminight!" *(Dichtung und Wahrheit*, bk. 11).

15. *JubA*, vol. 12.1, no. 357, p. 1.

16. Ibid., 7:13ff.

17. Ibid., 3.2:237ff.

18. See Werner Krauss, *Studien zur deutschen und französischen Aufklärung* (Berlin, 1963), pp. 274ff., 527ff.

19. Goethe, *Werke*, Insel Verlag ed., 13:84ff.

20. Christian Wolff, *Psychologia Empirica*, sec. 289.

21. *JubA*, vol. 11, no. 38, p. 84.

22. Ibid., 2:152.

23. Cf. Ludwig Goldstein, *Moses Mendelssohn und die deutsche Aesthetik* (Königsberg, 1904), pp. 25–40.

24. *JubA*, 1:408–15.

25. Ibid., 1:422ff.; 2:325.

26. Ernst Simon, *Brücken, Gesammelte Aufsätze* (Heidelberg, 1965), pp. 184–204.

27. *JubA*, 1:453–94.

28. See Goldstein, *Moses Mendelssohn*, p. 122.

29. *JubA*, 1:488.

30. Ibid., p. 169.

31. Ibid., 2:182ff.

32. Ibid., pp. 325–30.

33. *GS*, 3:385–99.

34. Of whom Locke speaks in his "Essay Concerning Human Understanding," 3.4.11.

35. Cf. my *Moses Mendelssohns Frühschriften zur Metaphysik untersucht und erläutert* (Tübingen, 1969), p. 128, n. 59.

36. *GS*, 4.1:127; cf. Diels, *Fragmente*, p. 75.

37. *Werke*, ed. Cassirer, 2:357.

38. *GS*, 3:128.

39. Cf. *GS*, 4.1:67 and passim.

40. Ibid., p. 68.

41. *JubA*, vol. 12.1, no. 241, p. 32.

42. *GS*, 5:380–84; 398–99.

43. *JubA*, vol. 12.1, nos. 322, 327, pp. 174–81, 197–201.

44. *GS*, 5:383; cf. Johann Joachim Spalding, *Die Bestimmung des Menschen*, 9th ed. (Leipzig, 1768), p. 55.

45. Cf. *GS*, 3:317ff.; *JubA*, vol. 13, no. 571.

46. *JubA*, vol. 11, no. 18, p. 34.

47. *GS,* 4.1:78ff.

48. "Die zeigten durch den Mendelssohn / und die Empfindungsbriefe, / Dass aller Selbst-
mord in der Welt / am Ende dahin liefe: / Dass man im Unglück sich so liess / Durch
Sinnlichkeiten rühren, / Die höh'ren Seelenkräfte nicht / Das Ruder liesse führen"
(quoted in Martin Sommerfeld, *Friedrich Nicolai und der Sturm und Drang* [Halle/
Saale, 1921], p. 259).

MOSES MENDELSSOHN AND THE RELIGIOUS FORMS OF JUDAISM IN THE NINETEENTH CENTURY

Max Wiener

xploring Moses Mendelssohn's connection with the history of ideas in German Judaism of the nineteenth century means seeking an understanding of a highly intellectual development. This essay attempts to delineate the forces that motivated and shaped this development.

The new era in Jewish intellectual life was not brought about by a development within Judaism itself, but by the influx of alien—Enlightenment—ideas that could be found throughout Europe. This struggle with external forces was the characteristic mark of the entire period. Whether these external forces were actually absorbed and internalized by Judaism, or whether an innate sense of Jewish worth rejected their influence and achieved a more profound understanding of itself by itself, is a question of little importance. What is important is the fact that the development is not linear; the intellectual trends and currents do not follow each other in logical succession, driven as it were by their inner logic, but represent a synthesis of Judaism and the spirit and changing movements of the time.

"Synthesis" is, indeed, the most appropriate term to describe the Jewish historical experience in every period in which Judaism is compelled to defend itself against the powerful impact of an alien culture to which it has, willingly or unwillingly, exposed its soul. Yet [the nineteenth century] has a unique character which deserves special attention. Never before had Judaism been equally conscious of the practical problems involved in the task it had set for itself: to absorb the culture of the surrounding world and to enter into its political, social, and intellectual life, while at the same time holding fast to its ancestral heritage. This task may or may not have been realizable. At any rate, however, it forced Judaism to turn its attention to the ideas and developments in the larger society in which it lived and moved.

The dynamics of this development is of great significance for the evolving modes of Judaism, inasmuch as it constitutes a criterion that enables us to assess the influence of outstanding personalities on later generations. They are not so much exponents of an autochthonous inner development as they are striking examples of the impact of alien ideas on the Jewish spirit. Hence it is hardly possible to establish clear-cut boundaries for each of the successive stages of development, or to determine with complete certainty where one stage ends and the other begins. The forms and ideas in which the Jewish spirit expressed itself and sought to render an account of itself seemingly stem from the environment and generally share the fate of the ideas in the surrounding world. Thus we have the strange phenomenon that the attempts to examine Jewish life and thought and to present the results systematically, however admirable in themselves, are insular. They hardly influence one another, rarely take notice of each other, and generally fail to penetrate Jewish consciousness. The great intellectual achievements of [Salomon] Steinheim, Samuel Hirsch, [Solomon] Formstecher, and others may be compared to erratically dispersed, unconnected blocks, representing only the last stage of the process by which external ideas affected Jewish thought.

An additional factor aggravated this peculiar lack of inner continuity. The need to clarify Judaism's position philosophically, as part of a theoretical world view, could be at best of secondary importance; primary importance was still assigned to the traditional religious law that governed the lives of its adherents or prompted critical reactions leading to changes. This situation imposed a heavy burden on Jewish life and inevitably retarded the tempo of changes. We must remember that the earliest comprehensive efforts to modernize religious institutions, attempted by the rabbinical assemblies of the 1840s, hardly differ in content and purpose from the synodal attempts almost a generation later; indeed, the guidelines of 1912 still struggled to reach practically the same goals. The issues that were of absorbing interest to the entire Jewish community and the manner in which they were treated had remained essentially unchanged for seventy years. Inasmuch as the internal issues that had engaged the attention of the Jewish people before the rise of Jewish nationalism were few and unvaried (because the daily regimen of an individual's religious life remained basically unchanged), the theoretical response to such an unvaried life obviously also failed to produce significantly different reactions. Moreover, the nuances and differences that did exist were nourished more from without than from within, and therefore could hardly be expected to have any influence in shaping the ideas of the community through the creation of new forms.

These facts indicate why Moses Mendelssohn, who ushered in the new era, did not create a new school of thought with his religio-philosophical exposition of Judaism. Nevertheless, his views are highly significant as typical and representative of the trends during the century that followed. Hence we want to show how his interpretation of Judaism enables us to isolate and identify the various trends and facets of Jewish life that found expression in the nineteenth century.

At a very early date, Mendelssohn was suspected—and not only by his ultraorthodox rabbinic opponents—of advocating a conception of Judaism that tended to dissolve its very essence, its religious law. The unusual phenomenon of a philosophizing Jew could lead a malicious Christian like [Johann Balthasar] Kölbele to conclude that Mendelssohn was not to be taken as a wholly authentic Jew, since he "neglected the talmudic customs"[1]—an imputation against which Mendelssohn himself felt compelled to protest. This incident is interesting only because it shows that, according to an outsider's evaluation of Judaism, this remarkable combination of a Jewish way of life and philosophical enlightenment was inconceivable. More significant are the misgivings with which a learned Jewish opponent viewed him even in the early days of the Emancipation. In his *Leviathan; or, Concerning Religion in Respect to Judaism* [*Leviathan oder über Religion in Rücksicht des Judentums;* Berlin, 1794] and in his pamphlet *Germanomania* [*Die Germanomanie;* Leipzig, 1815], Saul Ascher characterizes Spinoza's and Mendelssohn's view of Judaism as disastrous. He clearly recognized that Mendelssohn's position, which he defines as a rupture between religious doctrine and revealed law, was untenable. It should be noted that Ascher's criticism is not based on a specific view of the character of Judaism; rather, it is derived from a concept of religion that is grounded in a dogmatic position, in this case a specific theoretical world view. His criticism, which was directed against Mendelssohn but applies to the Enlightenment as a whole, is that Mendelssohn regarded positive religion as the sole means for educating the people. He accuses Mendelssohn of deliberately advocating more education so as to make his coreligionists forget or discard their traditional religion as completely as possible. Although Ascher holds fast to the Enlightenment's liberal-rational conception of the state, he rejects the view of men like Fichte and Rühs that Jews should completely renounce their "nationality" in order to be accepted as Germans. His political ideal was America, whose role as a melting pot of immigrants from many countries could, of course, not be anticipated at the beginning of the new century. At any rate, it was precisely because he regarded traditional Law and its particular religious world view as a unified whole that the Jews remained for him the bearers of a special religio-national ethos; the goal of the specific Jewish world view, although by no means identical with Mendelssohn's religion of reason, was not to establish its validity against dogma as such, but merely to function as an antidote against excessive dogmatism.

Ascher's suspicions no doubt did an injustice not only to Mendelssohn's personality but also to his system. Yet his perception of one particular point was correct. His criticism reveals for the first time the ambiguity of Mendelssohn's position. What was Mendelssohn's central point? Simply the dualism of religious belief and religious law! Ascher's interpretation was, of course, slanted and based on a wholly subjective sentiment, but in it we have *in nuce* the manifoldness that vitalized the various movements within German Jewry during the nineteenth century. The multifarious facets of modern Judaism can trace their origin to Mendelssohn intellectually, though of course not historically. For the various strands—the religious as well as the national, the orthodox as well as the liberal—out of which the total fabric of Jewish consciousness is woven were clearly recorded and anticipated in Mendelssohn's views.

That Mendelssohn spoke everywhere of the "nation" of Jews and took for granted the separate existence of his people as a concrete and vital fact is of no particular significance. The political and social incorporation of the Jews into the surrounding world was still far off, even in the final days of the ghetto. It was religion that led Mendelssohn to view Judaism as a self-contained national entity. Ceremonies and rites constitute its specific character. They were disclosed to the Jewish people in a positive, supernatural revelation. Here we encounter once again the view, emphasized in rabbinic-talmudic Judaism and by so authentic a Jewish thinker as Judah Halevi in particular, of the divine revelation as the foundation of the religious-national existence of the Jewish people; accepted by the entire people at Sinai, it is Israel's basic and binding law for all time. Mendelssohn rejected all conversion, whether to or from Judaism. In his translation of Manasseh ben Israel's *Vindiciae Judaeorum*, he vigorously rejects the notion that Jews pray for the conversion of other nations. Conversion, he adds sarcastically, was also something for which people prayed fervently at every auto-da-fé. He considers it impossible to abolish or change the divine law regulating the life of Jews down to the smallest detail, unless God Himself were to revoke it with a new revelation that would make His will known to His children with the same clarity with which it was first promulgated to their fathers at Sinai. He is conscious of the isolating effect of the ceremonial law, but sees it as a providential, preordained means of preventing the disappearance of the Jews amidst the nations around them. He therefore rejects symbolic and allegorical interpretations that are calculated to relax the strict observance of the law, such as we find in the New Testament, and he characterizes them as sentiments that have no practical effect.[2]

It is important to bear in mind that Mendelssohn made no serious attempt—something which was frequently done in early rabbinic literature and favored by Neo-Orthodoxy—to interpret Jewish statutes ethically or to claim that they are the best and shortest road to moral perfection. The revealed law is binding "on our nation alone."[3] Mendelssohn's fervent faith in reason inevitably led him to the conclusion that as far as morality is concerned there could be no distinction, no inequality, between "the best Christians and the best Jews," in whose lives and deeds the divinely ordained felicity of the human race becomes realized.[4]

Hence that which makes the Jew a Jew, namely a life lived in accordance with the inviolable divine law, is not a universal value, valid for all people in the same manner. It is precisely this emphasis on national exclusiveness that appears to be the ineradicable, unchangeable element in Judaism. This conclusion is not invalidated by the fact that there have been occasional interpretations of revelation which assert that the basic intent of the ceremonial system is to protect the Jews from idolatry by deterring them, as far as possible, from fashioning images of the supernatural.[5] But even if this rationale of the law were no longer considered valid, Mendelssohn still did not want to see the law abolished, just as it did not occur to him to impute pagan motives to his educated Christian contemporaries. To be sure, he considered Judaism superior to Christianity, because Judaism easily can be harmonized with the religion of reason, whereas Christian dogma, and especially its core, Christology, resists such a harmonization. But pagan idolatry was by no means the only alternative to a dogmaless religion of reason for Mendelssohn. He was well aware of Jewish attempts to freeze religion into rigid doctrines and to urge the faithful to accept their authority as binding. If, as he assumed, Maimonides, Albo, and Crescas were not successful in this attempt, it mattered little whether their definitions of "reason" turned out to be true or false, even though they contradicted one another. The essential point was that at the heart of Judaism is not a system of metaphysics, but a life devoted to the fulfillment of the law.[6]

Mendelssohn's struggle against dogma must be understood essentially as proceeding from his opposition to a certain kind of speculative metaphysics. His primary concern was to prevent the substance of Jewish life, its religious laws, from evaporating into vague articles of faith. This is the "national" tendency of his thinking and especially of his emotions—both prompted by his concern for the concrete existence of the Jews. In addition, however, we must also consider the self-sufficiency of his Enlightenment-motivated speculation concerning the things man needs to know in order to attain felicity. Mendelssohn himself was a speculative philosopher, but the reasonableness of enlightened religion, of which he was the ardent herald, is from the very outset hostile to all metaphysical speculation that goes beyond the holy trinity of God, soul, and human felicity. The more he found these and no other elements clearly expressed in Jewish teaching as self-evident presuppositions and as the exclusive meaning of all true piety, the brighter did the law shine forth as the essence of Judaism, and with it the living religious community as its bearer and guardian.

These basic views should, of course, not be pressed too far; nor should we overlook the fact that Mendelssohn had tendencies which point in the opposite direction. For Mendelssohn the enlightened individualist, the devoutly hoped-for state of felicity was something attained solely by the individual, and the idea of [the progress of] mankind disappeared behind the notion of individual progress. In the same way, the idea of a people destined to realize specific cultural values vanished completely. It was wholly beyond his scope to imagine the possibility of a secularization of Judaism that would put nonreligious values in the place of revelation and make them the authentic spiritual and intellectual core of Jewish peoplehood. Nor [did he express] any trace of nationalism in its modern sense. An interesting light is thrown on this subject in a letter to Herz Homberg (September 22, 1783) in which, in connection with a discussion of *Jerusalem,* he comments on the validity of the ritual law.

> [The ritual laws] may have lost their significance and usefulness as script or sign language. But their necessity as a unifying bond of our people has not been lost. And this unifying bond will have to be preserved in the plans of providence as long as polytheism, anthropomorphism, and religious usurpation are rampant in the world. As long as these tormentors of reason are united against us, genuine theists must also create some kind of unifying bond among themselves. . . . which can only be acts and, indeed, significant acts, that is, ceremonies. Abuses that have crept in should of course be remedied, the ceremonies be given genuine significance, and the Scriptures, corrupted by hypocrisy and priestcraft, again be made readable and understandable.

Mendelssohn here sharply rejects compliance with the "desire of others for unity." He compares it with the wolf who wishes to unite with the lamb—which merely means that the flesh of the lamb becomes that of the wolf. Unity, he felt, could only lead to a return to barbarism within fifty years.

In the light of these considerations, ceremonial observance in Judaism did not seem to be unimportant for the religion of reason; theism still emerged as the special heritage of Judaism. This was indeed in harmony with Mendelssohn's original position, but it did not quite agree with his often proclaimed faith in the power of reason. This subtle shading of his views probably resulted from Mendelssohn's desire to bring the radical recipient of the letter to a more moderate position. However, the other point he made in his letter was expressed more clearly: his conviction that the content of Judaism, the meaning of the separateness and distinctiveness of the Jewish nation, is identical with the Jewish religion. There are no other reasons, or at least none of which Mendelssohn was conscious, to preserve the Jewish way of life.

One can readily see the lines of development which inevitably led to a denationalization of Judaism and its transformation into a denomination, a "confession." It is beyond the scope of this study to discuss the significance of Mendelssohn's educational efforts on behalf of the German Jews; the practical consequences of his work on the Bible, which he translated or arranged to have translated into the German language; or his numerous efforts to make the culture and social manners of his day more accessible to his degraded coreligionists. We are only concerned with his conception of Judaism.

Here we see, however, how Mendelssohn's strictly observed ritualism had to lead, in theory and in practice, to a definite displacement of the center of gravity. His interpretation of Judaism as revealed legislation shatters the structure of Jewish life as a whole and would eventually destroy it by reducing it to the observance of ritual laws. This is, after all, the meaning and intent of his *Jerusalem*. If, as this work explains, state and religion formerly constituted an absolute unity which permitted no separation between the secular and the sacred law in God's community and which regarded even the most insignificant police ordinance as sanctioned by God, then this unity, as the rabbis expressly state, should have been suspended with the destruction of the Temple. All corporeal chastisement, capital punishment, and even pecuniary penalties, insofar as they are based merely on national laws, were no longer legally valid.[7] Moreover, after church and state were separated, religious transgressions were no longer regarded as civil offenses. Religion as such knows of no other penalty than that which the penitent sinner imposes upon himself.

Mendelssohn, however, did not seem to regard the separation of the religious and the national-political spheres as a historical fact which gave the Jewish people its particular stamp after it had lost its state and land. He projected this condition back into the ancient biblical history of Israel as one of its essential elements. [According to his conception], a pure theocracy existed only from the earliest days until the period of the judges, and it began to decline as soon as the people demanded that Samuel establish a secular kingdom. The national and the political elements were clearly identical; the latter constituted the full content of the former. This notion gives rise to a strange historical judgment: the separation of an independent secular-political life from the theocratic structure of the nation's earliest period became more acute as foreign rulers reigned over the people and imposed burdens that had to be borne just as those that had been imposed by God.

At any rate, Mendelssohn did not believe that the isolation of a specific religious element in the totality of Judaism was the result of Israel's fate in the Diaspora. Rather, the seeds of this division were inherent in Israel's history from the very beginning—a premise from which several conclusions for both the present and the future can be drawn. The House of Jacob might conclude from its reflections on its character and history that it had to adapt itself to the practices and the constitution of the land into which it had been transplanted, while at the same time remaining true to the religion of its fathers.

Here we have the motto that Israel was to follow throughout the Emancipation period: unreserved participation in the life of the surrounding world and faithfulness to its ancestral religion. However, in his Enlightenment-nourished individualism, Mendelssohn failed to notice (or if he did notice he may not have considered it harmful) that this path would at best lead to a highly individualized religiosity, whereas Jewish religious law, of which not one tittle or iota was to be surrendered, demands a style of communal life which it was becoming extremely difficult to preserve. Mendelssohn occasionally sensed that his apparently pure and clear theory might in practice encounter grave obstacles. Whenever this occurred, his Jewish instinct turned out to be superior to his intellectual propensity for assimilation, as, for instance, when he counseled his coreligionists to forego civil equality rather than abandon observance of the religious law. Nevertheless, he hoped that the growth of tolerance would generate that degree of love among men which would enable Jews to participate in the general culture without being accused of faithlessness to their own heritage.

Yet this faithfulness was almost immediately subjected to a severe test as challenges arose which required the existence of the Jewish people as a whole in order to be met. A case in point is the way in which he dealt with the belief in the Messiah, which had not yet been converted into an abstract Messianism. Mendelssohn treats the question in a particularly characteristic manner in his answer to "Count Michaelis's Assessment of the First Part of Dohm's *On the Civic Improvement of the Jews*" ["Des Ritters Michaelis Beurteilung des ersten Teils von Dohm *Über die bürgerliche Verbesserung der Juden*"]. Mendelssohn was undoubtedly correct in believing that the hope for a return to Palestine, which had caused so much concern to Michaelis, ought to have no influence on the status of the Jews. Most of them, however reluctantly, would follow the dictum "ubi bene ibi patria" as a practical policy dictated by prudence. Mendels-

sohn's problem is further clarified by the consideration that, according to
our sages, the return to the Holy Land is not a matter for arbitrary
decision, but will be announced by God with signs and miracles. Although Mendelssohn's argument is calculated to silence the anti-Semitic
Michaelis, it is merely an expedient dismemberment of Judaism, inasmuch as it abandons a fundamental religious doctrine which is as basic to
Judaism as is the observance of the law which, for Mendelssohn, was an
inviolate duty of the individual Jew. We can already see the beginning of
that typical twilight atmosphere in which the character of Jewish teachings, traditionally based on the affirmation both of the concrete existence
of the Jewish people and of its divine guidance, is becoming blurred.

Mendelssohn's conclusions lead inevitably to a denationalization or,
as Mendelssohn himself might have put it more adequately, to a depoliti-
cization of Judaism. Judaism seems to become a "religious community,"
a "confession," even though there are people who raise basic objections
to the *confiteor* or reject religious affiliation and belief altogether.

As a religious community, Judaism serves as the common denominator for several conflicting eighteenth-century trends. How does a Judaism so defined deal with them?

The extent to which the core of Mendelssohn's theory, the dualism
of law and faith, permits multiple (religious and national) interpretations
of Judaism was pointed out before. The example of his personal life, his
personal fealty to the religious law, and its designation as the specifically
Jewish element in the Jewish religion suggest that Mendelssohn must be
understood as being close to the spirit of Torah-true Judaism. The classical exponent of Neo-Orthodoxy, Samson Raphael Hirsch, though he
would hardly be inclined to accept Mendelssohn as his Jewish mentor,
clearly adopts the same position when he defines the relationship of faith
to law: "The acknowledgment of the One God makes of the heathen a
human being; the fulfillment of the law, as transmitted in Scripture and
tradition, makes of the human being a Jew."[8]

As a consequence of this view, the gap between Hirsch's orthodox
position and that of the neologist is felt to be far greater than that between Catholicism and Protestantism[9]—again corresponding to Mendelssohn's uncompromising opposition to all attempts to fragmentize the law.
To the renewer of orthodoxy it appears just as certain as it does to the
enlightened philosopher that those divine matters which are at all accessible to human consciousness are as uncompounded (simple) as their
object, God. The doctrine of man and of human matters, however, is
manifold and rich in relationships, even as life itself.[10] Hirsch wrote these
sentences in connection with pedagogical considerations, according to
which a thorough study of the Hebrew language and of Jewish "national
literature" is indispensable for every Jew in order to deepen his under-

standing of Jewish life and, indeed, even make such a life possible. At any rate, Mendelssohn and Hirsch used the same means to ensure the existence of a palpable Jewish reality that neither thinker believed could be created by specific theological teachings or particular world views.

This accounts for the fact that Torah-true Judaism, although fundamentally opposed to nationalism as a force that secularized Judaism, was generally better able to make its peace with nationalism than the early Reform movement. Whether the motivation was to safeguard life under the law or to struggle for the achievement of a full national [Jewish] culture, the [common] aim was to preserve the particularity of Jewish existence. Hirsch preferred to avoid altogether the use of the word "religion" to denote the totality of legitimate Jewish concerns; he wanted to restrict it specifically to the Torah, which finds fulfillment in the life-long realization of its precepts in every aspect of man's life in accordance with God's unquestioned will. Rightly or wrongly, he regarded religion as an isolated sphere in the totality of human existence, and he declared emphatically that it possesses an inwardness which, if defined merely as an idea or vague emotional experience, might easily evaporate into nothingness when faced by a reality demanding action.[11]

This is certainly an authentic Jewish view, expressive of the biblical-rabbinic spirit. However, we can also discover in it pietistic ideas of the Enlightenment that had found their way into Jewish thinking: for example, the idea voiced in the dictum in Lessing's *Nathan* that it is much easier to indulge in pious sentimentality than to act decently.

All religious currents in modern Judaism share the view that the ultimate meaning of religiosity, of Torah and law, is the moral perfection of Israel and through it (depending on the degree of universalistic thinking) of mankind as a whole. They all equate the religious with the ethical or regard it as the only true and unfailing path to moral perfection. However, this emphasis on ethical rationalism, which has always been a seminal force in Judaism, also makes Mendelssohn, a child of the Enlightenment, the prototype of religious liberalism, although his fidelity to the religious law, which constituted for him the core and substance of Judaism, seems to distance him from the antinomian tendencies of liberalism.

What then was the deep-rooted feeling in which his personal piety was anchored? When he denied that Judaism is a revealed faith, he did so not because he failed to find in Jewish consciousness what he regarded as the core of belief in God, but because he saw his people as the loyal guardian and preserver of that which alone is always needed—pure reason reflecting on the eternal truths concerning God, the soul, and man's fate under the governance of divine providence.

What did he understand by "dogma"? Evidently [he did not mean] merely definite formulations promulgated by an unconditionally legitimate church authority, but every theoretical article of faith drawn up as a doctrine. It seems to have been remarkably blind on his part to assume that the beliefs in the divine origin of the Torah, prophetic inspiration, the Messiah, and resurrection—even granted that they are not formulated as dogmas—lack the doctrinal character that give them their specific Jewish stamp. If Mendelssohn failed to see or did not wish to see this, it was primarily because his personal piety and religious fervor sprang from his ardent devotion to faith in reason. The compatibility of Judaism with this reason, its identity with such pure perception, its freedom from all turbid irrational elements—these constituted for him the spiritual essence of the religion of his fathers and the heritage that irresistibly drew his mind and heart to the teachings of his forefathers.

He was orthodox in the modern sense insofar as he assumed the entire corpus of the law to be binding and inviolable. His position reflects the deeply rooted self-evident nature of the ancient national-religious way of life which, as a son of the congregation of Jacob, he considered himself bound to follow. His personal piety, however, and the soaring of his intoxication with God flowed from a different source, from the truths of reason. These truths therefore occupied the first place in the scale of values in the Jewish consciousness. Mendelssohn's notion of tolerance and humanity originated in the same rational universalism that made him reject conversion from one religion to another.

To the extent to which these views stood in the foreground of his thinking, he clearly anticipated the appraisals of the nature of Judaism that are characteristic of nineteenth-century liberalism. To be sure, the diverse liberal attitudes to the law differ profoundly from Mendelssohn's. But the fervor of his certainty that Judaism is *the* ethical religion of reason, the very certainty which also gives liberal Judaism its strength and meaning, anticipates liberalism and was proclaimed with similar ardor.

In this matter there is complete unanimity, whether we are dealing with the various great systematic attempts down to Hermann Cohen or with the popular conceptions of the common man. But the emphasis on Judaism as the religion of ethical universalism emerges with particular clarity when there is a need to define the distinctive values of Judaism in contrast to those of Christianity. The focal point of these analyses usually is the question of Jewish universalism, which is always regarded with suspicion because it is proclaimed by a religion that is restricted to one people. Hence Jewish thinkers seek to rescue Jewish universalism by citing the Jewish teaching that embodies the most radical universalism, that of moral reason. Thus, in the views of men such as Abraham Geiger, Ludwig Philippson, and Leopold Stein, we encounter a fusion of Judaism and the Enlightenment ideas of humanity, first made by Mendelssohn, which are characteristic of nineteenth-century Judaism.

The emphasis on ethical universalism is even more pronounced among those spokesmen of liberal Judaism who either relegate the law . . . to the periphery of the systems of Judaism they constructed or pass over it in silence. Basically, however, Mendelssohn can also be taken as a forerunner of liberalism with regard to this attitude to the law, inasmuch as he did not include it as an organic part of his religious consciousness.

Only one characteristic difference strikes us as significant. It concerns the interpretation of the doctrine of the Messiah. The linking of this idea with that of a world-historical progress, excluding a personal Messiah sent by God, was reserved for a post-Mendelssohn period. Such an interpretation would have made no sense for Mendelssohn, for he believed in the perfection of the individual, but not in the progress of the human race as a whole. The development spurred by Lessing and Herder passed him by. Nevertheless, if modern man considers it important to transform the concept of the Messiah into the idea of the messianic kingdom and, finally, into the concept of general human progress, he is acting in accordance with the spirit of that religion of reason which, according to Mendelssohn, is identical with Judaism.

Notes

"Moses Mendelssohn and the Religious Forms of Judaism in the Nineteenth Century," translated by Noah J. Jacobs, first appeared as "Moses Mendelssohn und die religiösen Gestalten des Judentums im 19. Jahrhundert," *Zeitschrift für die Geschichte der Juden in Deutschland* 1 (October 1929):201–12.

1. Moses Mendelssohn, *Gesammelte Schriften,* ed. G. B. Mendelssohn, 7 vols. (Leipzig, 1843–45), 3:72.
2. Ibid., p. 160.
3. Ibid., pp. 42ff.
4. Ibid., p. 70.
5. Ibid., pp. 340ff.
6. Ibid., pp. 322ff.
7. Ibid., p. 353.
8. S. R. Hirsch, *Gesammelte Schriften,* 2:372.
9. Ibid., p. 374.
10. Ibid., p. 434.
11. Mendelssohn, *Gesammelte Schriften,* 1:83.

CONTRIBUTORS

Authors

Alexander Altmann (born Kassa, Hungary, 1904; now living in Newton Centre, Massachusetts).

Alexander Altmann, leading historian of Jewish philosophy, studied at the Berlin Rabbinical Seminary and the University of Berlin, was rabbi in Berlin from 1931 to 1938, and taught philosophy at the seminary. From 1939 to 1958 he served as communal rabbi of Manchester, England, where he founded the Institute for Jewish Studies. From 1959 to 1976 he was professor of Jewish philosophy and director of the Philip W. Lown Institute of Advanced Jewish Studies at Brandeis University. His major works include *Saadya Gaon: The Book of Doctrines and Beliefs* (abridged English translation and commentary, 1946); *Isaac Israeli: A Neoplatonic Philosopher of the Early Tenth Century* (translated with comments and an outline of his philosophy, with S. M. Stern, 1959); *Moses Mendelssohns Frühschriften zur Metaphysik* (1969); *Studies in Religious Philosophy and Mysticism* (1969); and *Moses Mendelssohn: A Biographical Study* (1973). He was editor (1954–59) of the *Journal for Jewish Studies* (London), edited *Between East and West: Essays Dedicated to the Memory of Bela Horovitz* (1958), *Studies and Texts of the Philip W. Lown Institute* (4 vols., 1963–67), and has been serving as general editor of the new edition of *Moses Mendelssohns Gesammelte Schriften, Jubiläumsausgabe* (1971–   ). He has contributed numerous articles to leading scholarly journals, festschriften, anthologies, and encyclopedias.

Leo Baeck (born Lissa, Posen, 1873; died in London, 1956).

Leo Baeck has been called "the last great teacher of German Jewry." After studying at the Jewish Theological Seminary at Breslau, at the Hochschule für die Wissenschaft des Judentums in Berlin, and, under Wilhelm Dilthey, at the University of Berlin, he served as rabbi in Oppeln, Düsseldorf, and from 1912 on in Berlin, where he also taught Midrash and homiletics at the Hochschule. He was deported to Theresienstadt in 1943; after being liberated in 1945, he lived in London but taught part of every year at the Hebrew Union College in Cincinnati, Ohio.

Baeck emerged as the leading personality of German Jewry long before Hitler's rise to power, but he was especially influential during the Hitler years. He headed a number of communal and international agencies, including the Reichsvertretung der Juden in Deutschland and the World Union for Progressive Judaism. His central concern as a rabbi, religious thinker, and scholar was the exposition and clarification of the distinctiveness of the Jewish world view, of "the essence of Judaism," for which he named his first (1905) and most widely known book and which was the implicit theme of much of his later work. His approach resulted not so much in a theology or philosophy of Judaism as in a phenomenology of the Jewish spirit.

His numerous publications, besides *The Essence of Judaism* (original title *Das Wesen des Judentums*), include *This People Israel* (New York, 1964; original title *Dieses Volke: Jüdische Existenz,* 2 vols. [Frankfurt am Main, 1955, 1957]), written in Theresienstadt; essays published as *Judaism and Christianity* (Berlin, 1938; rprt. Tübingen, 1958); and two volumes of major essays, *Wege im Judentum* (Berlin, 1933) and *Aus drei Jahrtausenden.*

Fritz Bamberger (born Frankfurt am Main, Germany, 1902; now living in New York, New York).

A scholar and author in the field of Jewish philosophy, Fritz Bamberger studied at the Hochschule für die Wissenschaft des Judentums and the University of Berlin, was a research fellow at the Forschungs–Institut der Akademie für die Wissenschaft des Judentums (1926–33), lectured on Jewish philosophy at the Hochschule (1933–34), and directed the Jewish Teachers' Seminary and the Berlin Jewish community school system. Following his emigration to the United States in 1938, he taught at the

College of Jewish Studies in Chicago and served both on the staff and as chief editor of *Coronet* magazine (1942–61). In 1962 he became professor of Jewish intellectual history and assistant to the president of the Hebrew Union College-Jewish Institute of Religion. With Simon Bernfeld, Bamberger edited volume 5 of *Die Lehren des Judentums* (1930); he coedited several volumes of the Jubilee edition of *Moses Mendelssohns Gesammelte Schriften* (1929–32) and published *Das System des Maimonides* (1935). In addition to his studies of Mendelssohn, he has published essays on Spinoza, Leopold Zunz, Leo Baeck, and Julius Guttmann.

David Hartwig (Zvi) Baneth (born Krotoschin, Poland, 1893; died Jerusalem, Israel, 1973).

David Hartwig (Zvi) Baneth studied Semitic and classical languages and was associated with the Forschungs-Institut der Akademie für die Wissenschaft des Judentums until 1924, when he settled in Jerusalem. There he served as librarian of the Jewish National Library and as a lecturer and then professor of Arabic language and literature at the Hebrew University. He was chiefly interested in the study of Jewish thought in Arabic and medieval literature. He published a critical text edition of Maimonides's letters *(Iggerot ha-Rambam,* 1946) and analyzed Maimonides's Hebrew usage and the Hebrew translation of his treatise on resurrection (in *Tarbiz* 6 [1934–35]; 11 [1939–40]; 13 [1941–42]; 23 [1951–52]). Baneth's contributions to the study of the language and contents of the Cairo *Genizah* documents are of major importance.

Ismar Elbogen (born Schilda, Germany, 1874; died New York, New York, 1943).

Ismar Elbogen studied at the Jewish Theological Seminary and at the University of Breslau and taught Jewish history and biblical exegesis at the Collegio Rabbinico in Florence, Italy, before joining the faculty of the Hochschule (then Lehranstalt) für die Wissenschaft des Judentums in Berlin in 1903. He taught there until 1938, when he left for the United States in order to serve as research professor simultaneously at the Jewish Theological Seminary, Hebrew Union College, the Jewish Institute of Religion, and Dropsie College. Although deeply involved in the organizational life and cultural affairs of German Jewry and the administration of the Hochschule in addition to his teaching responsibilities, he was an enormously productive scholar, chiefly in Jewish history and the history of Jewish liturgy. His bibliography lists 15 books and pamphlets, 225 articles in scholarly journals, and more than 270 contributions to various encyclopedias. He served as one of the editors of the periodical *Devir* (1923–24); *Germania Judaica* (2 vols., 1917, 1934); *Zeitschrift für die Geschichte der Juden in Deutschland* (1929–38); *Jüdisches Lexikon* (5 vols., 1927–30); *Encyclopaedia Judaica* (vols. 1–9, 1928–38); and the *Universal Jewish Encyclopedia* (10 vols., 1939–43). His major works include *Der jüdische Gottesdienst in seiner geschichtlichen Entwicklung* and *A Century of Jewish Life* (1944), planned as a sequel to Heinrich Graetz's *History of the Jews*.

Julius Guttmann (born Hildesheim, Germany, 1880; died Jerusalem, Israel, 1950).

The son of a well-known historian of medieval Jewish philosophy, Julius Guttmann was ordained at the Jewish Theological Seminary at Breslau, taught philosophy at the University of Breslau, and held the chair in Jewish philosophy at the Hochschule für die Wissenschaft des Judentums in Berlin from 1919 to 1934. From 1922 on, he also served as director of the Forschungs-Institut für die Wissenschaft des Judentums, until accepting an appointment as professor of Jewish philosophy at the Hebrew University in Jerusalem. Guttmann combined studies in sociology and economic history with wide-ranging philosophical investigations, but his primary area of research was the history of Jewish philosophy, to which he devoted not only numerous studies but his major work, *Die Philosophie des Judentums*, which appeared in 1933 (Hebrew edition, *Ha-Filosofyah shel ha-Yahadut*, 1951; English edition, *Philosophies of Judaism*, 1964, based largely on the Hebrew translation). This standard work deals with the attempts made through the ages to explain and justify the Jewish religion. A selection from Guttmann's most important publications on Jewish philosophy was issued in Hebrew translation as *Dat u-Madda* in 1955.

Isaak (Yizhak) Heinemann (born Frankfurt am Main, Germany, 1876; died Jerusalem, Israel, 1957).

Isaak Heinemann studied philosophy and classics in Strassburg, Göttingen, and Berlin, taught Jewish philosophy and literature at the Jewish Theological Seminary in Breslau (1919–38), lectured on the intellectual history of Hellenism at the University of Breslau (1929–33), and served as editor of the *Monatsschrift für die Geschichte und Wissenschaft des Judentums* (1920–38). After moving to Jerusalem in 1939, he continued to write extensively on Jewish philosophy and religious thought. He was awarded the Israel Prize for Jewish Studies in 1955.

Heinemann's mastery of Greek, hellenistic, and medieval Jewish sources is evident in his writings. In addition to essays and monographs that appeared in the *Monatsschrift,* the annual reports of the Breslau seminary, and other journals, he prepared and partly edited the German translation of Philo's works (Parts 2–6) and edited the *Festschrift für Immanuel Löw* (1934). He also published *Zeitfragen im Lichte jüdischer Lebensanschauung* (1921); *Poseidonios' Metaphysische Schriften* (2 vols., 1921, 1928); *Ta'amei ha-Mitzvot be-Sifrut Yisrael* (2 vols., 1942, 1957); an abridged edition of Judah Halevi's *Kuzari,* with an introduction and commentary (1947); and *Darkhei ha-'Aggadah* (1950).

David Kaufmann (born Kojetan, Austria, 1852; died Karlsbad, Czechoslovakia, 1899).

David Kaufmann studied at the Jewish Theological Seminary and the University of Breslau, received a Ph.D. from the University of Leipzig, and taught Jewish history, religious philosophy, and homiletics at the Landesrabbinerschule in Budapest from 1877 until his death. Kaufmann was a scholar of unusual versatility and extraordinary productivity. His bibliography, compiled by Markus Brann (in *Gedenkbuch zur Erinnerung an David Kaufmann* [Breslau, 1900]) lists 546 titles, including numerous articles and book reviews in German, Hungarian, and Hebrew, as well as more than 25 books. Most important among the latter are *Geschichte der Attributenlehre in der jüdischen Religionsphilosophie des Mittelalters von Sa'adja bis Maimuni; Die Theologie des Bachia Ibn Pakuda; Die letzte Vertreibung der Juden aus Wien: ihre Vorgeschichte (1625–1670) und ihre Opfer;* and *Aus Henrich Heines Ahnensaal.* After his death, his major essays were published in *Gesammelte Schriften,* edited by Markus Brann.

Hiram Peri (Heinz Pflaum) (born Berlin, Germany, 1900; died Jerusalem, Israel, 1962).

Hiram Peri studied Romance languages at several European universities. He was assistant librarian at the Hebrew National and University Library in Jerusalem, and from 1928 served as lecturer and from 1948 as professor of Romance languages and literature and of the history of Renaissance literature at the Hebrew University. Among his publications are *Die Idee der Liebe: Zwei Abhandlungen zur Geschichte der Philosophie in der Renaissance* (1926), *Deux hymns judeo-français du moyen âge* (1934), and numerous articles in Hebrew, German, French, English, Italian, and Spanish. He also edited and annotated Jacob Burckhardt's *Kultur der Renaissance in Italien* and served as an editor and contributor in his field to the *Encyclopaedia Judaica.*

Max Wiener (born Oppeln, Germany, 1882; died New York, New York, 1950).

Max Wiener received his rabbinical training at the Jewish Theological Seminary in Breslau and at the Hochschule (then Lehranstalt) für die Wissenschaft des Judentums. He held pulpits in Düsseldorf (as an associate of Leo Baeck), Stettin, and, from 1926 to 1939, in Berlin, where he also taught Jewish philosophy at the Hochschule after Julius Guttmann emigrated in 1934. After coming to the United States in 1939, Wiener was first associated with the Hebrew Union College in Cincinnati, Ohio, and later held several rabbinical posts, in which he combined congregational work with research and writing. His publications, primarily in the fields of theology and Jewish religious thought, include numerous contributions to festschriften and scholarly journals and several books, among them *Die Anschauungen der Propheten von der Sittlichkeit* (1909); his important major work, *Jüdische Religion im Zeitalter der Emanzipation* (Berlin, 1933); and *Abraham Geiger and Liberal Judaism* (compiler and editor; Philadelphia, 1962).

Leopold Zunz (born Detmold, Germany, 1794; died Berlin, Germany, 1886).

Leopold Zunz was educated at the famous Samson Schule in Wolfenbüttel, Germany, and attended the universities of Berlin and Halle. He was one of the founders and leading spirits of the Wissenschaft des Judentums. A man of unusually broad learning and a very productive scholar, Zunz was primarily interested in Jewish liturgy and medieval religious poetry. His first major work, *Die gottesdienstlichen Vorträge der Juden* (1832), was written in response to a Prussian governmental decree forbidding innovations in Jewish religious affairs and services, including the introduction of sermons in German. Zunz demonstrated that liturgical addresses in the vernacular were not an innovation, but had been an integral part of Jewish services since ancient times. Among his numerous other writings are a historical study of Jewish names, a history of the Jewish liturgy, several volumes on the religious poetry of the Jewish Middle Ages, and a thirty-page essay, "Etwas über die rabbinische Literatur," which represents the first programmatic statement on the Wissenschaft des Judentums.

Translators

Gertrude Hirschler (New York, New York): author, translator, and editor.

Noah J. Jacobs, Ph.D. (Jerusalem, Israel): former head of the translating division at the Nuremberg war crimes trials.

Alfred Jospe, Ph.D. (Washington, D.C.): editor; former international director of B'nai B'rith Hillel Foundations, Inc.

Eva Jospe (Washington, D.C.): lecturer in modern Jewish thought at The George Washington University and Georgetown University.

Elizabeth Petuchowski, Ph.D. (Cincinnati, Ohio): author, translator, and member of the faculty of the University of Cincinnati.

Karl Richter, D.D. (Sarasota, Florida): former lecturer in philosophy at Purdue University.

INDEX

Abdallatif, al-Baghdadi, 224
Abrabanel, Isaac, 259, 264, 271–72, 273, 274, 275, 285
Abrabanel, Judah. *See* Ebreo, Leone
Abraham, 75
Abraham ben David (Rabed), 166
Abulafia, Abraham, 163, 171, 201, 203, 206, 207–9
Action, doctrine of purpose and, 130, 138, 150, 155
Adelung, Johann Christoph, 388
Affinity of the Beautiful and the Good (Mendelssohn), 396, 397
Affluence, dangers of, 390
Aggadah, 11, 48, 50, 58, 59, 86, 249, 257, 258, 259, 263
Akiba ben Joseph, 48, 67, 208
Albalag, Isaac, 292, 312
Albertus Magnus (Albert the Great), 227, 229, 231
Albo, Joseph, 60, 255, 322, 408; doctrine of purpose and, 149–51
Alexander of Hales, 230
Al-Farabi, 224, 238
Alfonso II of Aragon, 274
Alfonso V of Portugal, 272
Alfonso the Wise, 233
Al-Ghazali (Abu Hamid), 116, 120, 121, 136, 147, 238, 250, 311; causality and, 189; free will and, 189; fundamental views of, 192–95, 196; God's activity and, 189; Israel and, 192; rejection of philosophers by, 183–88; religious truth and, 288–89, 294, 299, 301–5; universalism and, 191; works of, 182–83
Al-Harizi, Judah, translation of the *Guide* and, 228–30, 235, 238–39
Allegory, 12, 223; Christian, 250–51, 254–55, 261–63; defined, 247–48; historical presuppositions of, 249–51; Maimonides and, 255–58, 259–60, 262, 263–64; med-

ieval, 248–49, 261–65; methodological approach to, 251–56; motivations of, 248; Paradise story and, 257–59, 262; philosophers and, 256–60; semiphilosophical, 260–61; the Torah and, 253–54
Alphabet, numerical value of letters in, 159, 165
Altmann, Alexander, 12
Amadeo of Rimini (Jedidiah ben Moses), 240, 241
Anaxagoras, 115, 154, 248
Andrew, Master, 221
Antigonus of Sokho, 92–93
Aquinas, Thomas, 12, 227, 231, 284
Arabs. *See* Islam; Muslims
Arama, Isaac, 261
Aristotle, 94, 183, 190, 222, 231, 395, 399; purpose and, 115, 120–21, 136, 140–41, 143, 144, 152, 154, 156, 157
Aristotelianism, 12, 93, 135, 140, 143–44, 156, 309; Arab, 121, 133, 190, 304, 309–10, 316, 321–22; Jewish, 97, 101; rejection of, by al-Ghazali and Judah Halevi, 182, 183–88
Asceticism, 194, 197, 325, 328, 331, 334, 347, 397, 398
Ascher, Saul, 406–7
Asclepius, 121
Assimilation, 107–8
Astrology, 201
Atheism, 363, 378
Atomism, 223
Augustine, Saint, 252, 254
Avencebrol. *See* Ibn Gabirol, Solomon
Averroës (Ibn Rushd), 143, 286, 292, 309, 314; religion and, 310–12
Averroism: Christian, 292; Latin, 314
Avicenna (Ibn Sina), 224, 311
Azriel. *See* Ezra ben Solomon

425

Baeck, Leo, 11; dogma and, 54–55, 56, 63–64

Baeumker, Clemens, 236

Baḥya, ibn Pakuda, 116, 123–29, 142, 147, 148, 152, 153, 157

Baneth, David, 12

Baptism, 255

Basic Principles (Albo), 149, 151

Baumgarten, Alexander Gottlieb, 388, 398

Bélisair (Marmontel), 400

Ben Gerson, Levi. *See* Gersonides

Bernays, Isaac, 159

Bible, 159, 287, 352, 373, 374, 383, 410; allegory and, 249–50, 251, 252, 255, 260, 262, 263; interpretation and reinterpretation of, 65–66; monotheism in, 98–102; purpose of man and, 118–19, 123, 137, 155; Spinoza and, 320–21, 361, 364–65, 366. *See also* Creation; Paradise story

Bodin, Jean, 314, 317

Bonnet, Charles, 358; Mendelssohn and, 346, 348–49, 350–51

Bon sens, Mendelssohn on, 396–97

Bradwardine, Thomas, 231

Brethren of Purity, 250, 252

Bruno, Giordano, 318–19, 322

Brunswick, prince of, 347

Buddhism, 89–90

Burckhardt, Jacob, 314

Buxtorf, Johann the Younger, 234, 235, 236

Casaubon, Isaac, 234

Caspi, Joseph, 225

Cassirer, Ernst, 359

Catholicism, 164; dogma and, 45–46, 55; ecclesiastical law and, 79. *See also* Christianity

Causality, 189, 190–91, 213; religious truth and, 288–89, 294, 295, 302

Cause and effect, 288

Century of Wissenschaft des Judentums, A (Elbogen), 10; excerpts from, 26–36

Ceremonial law. *See* Law, ceremonial

Chaplet of Grace (Levi ben Abraham ben Ḥayyim), 261

Charles I of Castile, 276

Charles VIII of France, 274

Chateaubriand, François René de, 159

Chelo, Isaac, 172

Chosen People, Jews as. *See* Divine election of the Jewish people

Christ, 353–54

Christianity, 42, 65, 66, 80, 92, 109, 156, 350, 358, 371, 408; allegory and, 250–51, 254–55, 261–63; Bonnet and, 348, 349; denomination and, 50, 78; ecclesiastical writings and, 101; miracles and, 351, 352;

piety and, 101, 319; religious truth and, 289, 290, 295; revelation and, 75, 285–86, 314, 316, 323, 367; the Trinity and, 101, 108, 352. *See also* Catholicism; Protestantism

Church: dogma and, 49; Mendelssohn on, 378, 379–83; rights of, 344; Spinoza on, 377–79, 380, 382. *See also* State

Cicero, 45

Clemens, Bishop, 120

Cognition, 41, 186, 350, 353, 375, 398, 399; al-Ghazali and, 193–95; doctrine of purpose and, 132, 147, 150, 154; faith and, 320; intuitive, 394; Judah Halevi and, 195–96; metaphysical, 211, 326; rational, 394; religious truth and, 287–88, 289, 291, 298, 299, 303, 305, 307–8, 316, 317, 318–19, 320, 322, 326, 335; the soul and, 318; Spinoza on, 320–21, 371, 372; symbolic, 393

Cohen, Hermann, 97, 135, 359, 414

Collective subconscious, 399

Colors, perception of, 397–98

Community, Jewish sense of. *See* Judaism, as religious community

Consciousness: moral, religious truth and, 293–98, 331; religious, analysis of, 328–32, 333–35, 383; religious and cognitive, 303

Constantinus Africanus, 221

Conversion: Maimonides legend, the Kabbala and, 200–201; Mendelssohn on, 345, 407; as rebellion against God, 306

Counterinquiry (Mendelssohn), 370

Cranz, August Friedrich, 355–56

Creation, 58, 66, 103, 122, 186, 188, 223. *See also* Bible

Crescas, Ḥasdai, 60, 255, 408; doctrine of purpose and, 144–49, 151, 152, 158

Culture: literature and, 22; Mendelssohn's definition of enlightenment and, 388–90; Wissenschaft des Judentums and, 30, 33. *See also* Greek culture; Jewish culture

D'Argentières, Bonafoux, 225

D'Arq, Chevalier, 393

David ben Judah Ḥasid, 169

De Caceres, Alfonso Peres, 238

De Fano, Emanuel, 240

De Figuerôa, Gomes Suares, 237–38

Deism, 105, 367, 400; Spinoza and, 361, 370

De Rétines, Robert, 221

De Rossi, J. B., 240

Descartes, René, 295

Dialogues of Love (Ebreo), 271, 275, 277–80

Dilthey, Wilhelm, 248, 262, 314, 317
Diaspora, 80, 106, 411
Divine election of the Jewish people, 71, 73, 75, 76–77, 79, 81, 82, 85, 191–92, 264, 354, 364, 366, 371, 376
Divine revelation. *See* Revelation
Doctrine of purpose: Albo and, 149–51; Baḥya and, 123–29, 152, 153; Crescas and, 144–49; eschatology and, 122–23; ethics and, 152–54; Gabirol and, 129–34, 152; Greek-Jewish thought and, 153–60; Greek thought and, 118–19, 121, 122; hermetic concepts and, 125–28; Ibn Daud and, 135–36; ibn Zaddik (Saddiq) and, 134–35, 152; Isaac Israeli and, 123, 151; Islam and, 121, 124–29, 152–53; Judaism and, 118; Maimonides and, 136–44, 145, 146; man's self-perception and, 120; Neoplatonism and, 122; Saadia (Saadiah) ben Joseph and, 123; the soul and, 124–28, 130–32, 134, 138, 150; theory of obligation and, 117–18
Dogma, 10, 60, 63, 66, 97, 300; articles of faith and, 44–45; assimilation and, 107–8; authority and, 47–49, 55, 56–58, 61, 63, 64; Christian, 392, 408; confession of faith and, 50; defined, 41, 44, 45–47, 54, 55–56; divine revelation and, 41–43; divinity of the Torah and, 67; Jewish piety and, 70; Judah Halevi and, 186; "liturgically sanctioned," 43–44; Mendelssohn on, 41–42, 45, 47, 50, 343, 353, 408, 413–14; obligatory tenents and, 54–55; pious, of Spinoza, 373; Reform Judaism and, 42, 43
Dornseiff, Franz, 116
Dreams, 399
Dreams of a Visionary (Kant), 326
Duclos, Charles Pinot, 393
Duns Scotus, John, 231, 288, 294
Duties of the Heart (Baḥya), 123, 157, 160

Ebreo, Leone (Judah Abrabanel), 12; *Dialogues of Love* and, 274, 275, 277–80; life of, 271–77
Education: changes in Jewish, 27–28; Lessing's views on, 369–70; Mendelssohn and, 388–90, 393, 396, 401, 406, 410; Wissenschaft des Judentums and, 30
Education of the Human Race (Lessing), 323
Effect. *See* Cause and effect
Einhorn, David, 43
Elbogen, Ismar, 10; Wissenschaft des Judentums and, 26–36
Eleazar of Worms, 164
Election. *See* Divine election of the Jewish people

Emanation, 184, 211–14, 278
Emden, Jacob, 368
Enelow, H. G., 163
Enlightenment: defined, 387–88; esoteric, 203; Mendelssohn on, 389–94; religious truth and, 290–91
Enlightenment, the (movement), 105, 326, 352, 367, 376, 406; German philosophy of, 346–47, 361, 364, 387; religious truth and, 297, 305, 322–25
Eschatology, 400; doctrine of purpose and, 122–23, 133, 135, 151, 155, 156
Essay on Evidence in the Metaphysical Sciences (Mendelssohn), 388, 395
Ethics, 90, 92, 327, 328, 331; doctrine of purpose and, 152–54; doctrines of, and religious groups, 82; dogma and, 45; Judah Halevi and, 196; of philosophers, 185; religion and, 306–7; religious truth and, 293–97, 298, 319, 325, 334; Spinoza and, 362
Ethics (Aristotle), 395
Ethics (Spinoza), 371, 378
Evil, 210, 212, 213, 257
Exalted Faith, The (Ibn Daud), 136
Ezekiel, 205
Ezra ben Solomon (Azriel), 167–68

Faith: articles of, 10, 44, 47, 48, 70, 102, 103, 281; of the Bible, 321; cognition and, 320; confession of, 50; dogma and, 41, 44, 45, 47, 48, 50; doubt-free, 302; Kant's religious philosophy and, 327–28; Luther and, 313; monotheism and piety and, 96–97; reason and, 353; revelation and, 285–86, 290; Spinoza and, 266–67, 373
Farabi, al-. *See* Al-Farabi
Federigo, king of Naples, 274–75
Ferdinand of Aragon, 274
Ferrente I of Naples, 274
Ferrer, Vincente, 237
Ficino, Marsilio, 277
Form, 187–88; religious truth and, 304, 332–33
Formstecher, Solomon, 405
Fountain of Life (Gabirol), 130, 131, 133, 279
Franck, Sebastian, 316
Frankel, Zacharias, 29
Frederick II (the Great), king of Prussia, 231–32, 233
Freedom, 107, 355; of belief, 58; of religion, 377–83
Freethinkers, 306, 307, 310
Free will, 189–90

428INDEX

Friedländer, Michael, 244
Fürstenthal, Raphael, 242, 244

Gabirol. *See* Ibn Gabirol, Solomon
Gamliel, Rabban, 171
Geiger, Abraham, 29, 30; dogma and, 44–45, 50; lectures of, 31–32
Gerard, Alexander, 396
Gerard of Cremona, 221
German Jews, 9, 11, 407, 410; rabbinic literature and, 20
Gersonides (Levi ben Gerson), 58, 144, 256, 258–59
Gfrörer, August Friedrich, 31
Ghazali. *See* Al-Ghazali
Gikatilla, Joseph, 170–71, 174
Giustiniani, Bishop Augustinus, 234–35, 236
Gnosis, 210
Gnosticism, 120, 126, 156, 210–11, 212
God: activities of, 188, 189; allegory and, 253–54, 258; attributes of, allegory and, 247; Christianity and, 101, 108; communion with, 196–97; conceptions of, 85, 184–85, 294, 371–72; consciousness of, 79–80; creation and, 103; divine sovereignty and, 294–95; emanation and, 212, 213; goodness of, 367–68; grace of, Judah Halevi on, 196; images of, 375, 400; intuition and, 317; invocation of, 80; Israel and, 73, 75, 76; Judaism and, 75; the kavvanah and, 162, 164, 165, 166; knowledge of, 58, 136, 193–94, 298, 300, 314–15, 319, 371; the law and, 353, 358; love of, 279, 280; name of, mysticism of, 170, 207; nature of, philosophy and, 296; omnipotence of, reason and, 368; piety and, 304, 319; prophetic experience of, 301–2; prophets and, 299–300; purpose of man and, 119, 121–22, 123–24, 127, 134, 136, 141, 142, 143, 144, 145, 146, 147, 148–49, 150–51, 154, 158–59; reason and, 372; the soul and, 193, 291, 302, 318, 319; speculative sphere of revelation and, 297–98; supernatural events and, 190–91; symbolic cognition and existence of, 393; thought of, 398; truth and, 334; unity of, 187–88; as will, 296
Goethe, Johann Wolfgang von, 117, 244, 393
Goldmann, Felix, 11, 67–68
Golgatha und Scheblimini (Hamann), 344
Goodness, 188–89, 297; doctrine of purpose and, 147; God's, 367–68
Grace, 94, 313, 396; Christian piety and, 319; doctrine of, 92; election principle and, 77; God's, Judah Halevi on, 196; the Torah and, 86

Grätz, Heinrich, 34
Greek culture, 11; allegory and, 248; Judaism and, 109; purpose and, 115, 118–19, 121, 122, 140–41, 153–60. *See also* Culture; Hellenism; Jewish culture
Gregory of Nyssa, 45
Guide for the Perplexed (Maimonides), 321; discussion of contents, 223–24; doctrine of purpose and, 141–42, 146; Hebrew translations of, 225–30; Moses' translation of, 240–41; Latin translations of, 230–37; the Muslims and, 224–25; nineteenth-century translations of, 241–45; Pedro of Toledo's translation of, 237–40; "secrets" and, 202–3, 204, 206–7; speculative interpretation of revelation and, 297. *See also* Maimonides
Guide for the Perplexed of the Time (Krochmal), 31
Gundisalvi, Dominicus, 221
Gutschmid, Alfred von, 223
Guttmann, Julius, 11, 12

Hakohen, Jonathan, 225
Halakhah, 48, 59, 205, 249
Halevi, Judah. *See* Judah Halevi
Hamann, Johann Georg, 344, 358
Harnack, Adolf, 46, 49, 55
Hasidism, 31, 163, 164
Hebrew language. *See* Language, Hebrew
Heinemann, Isaak, 11, 12
Hellenism, 11; al-Ghazali and Judah Halevi and, 183–88; Greek-Jewish thought and, 153–60; Jewish, 264; man's purpose and, 118–19, 121, 122. *See also* Greek culture
Hennings, August Adolph, 391, 392
Heptaplomeres (Bodin), 314
Heraclitus, 116, 399
Herbert of Cherbury, 317, 320
Herder, Johann Gottfried von, 400, 415
Hermannus Dalmata, 221
Hermeticism, doctrine of purpose and, 115, 124, 125–28, 131, 142, 143, 152
Heroic Enthusiasms (Bruno), 319
Hertling, Georg von, 236
Herz, Elkan, 353
Hillel, 94
Hippocrates, 184
Hirsch, Samson Raphael, 159, 412–13
Hirsch, Samuel, 405
Hirzel, Rudolf, 116
History, 11; Jewish, 31, 33; religious significance of, 110
History of Philosophy (Überweg), 223
Hobbes, Thomas, 363, 378
Holdheim, Samuel, 43

Holy Land, return to, Mendelssohn and, 411–12. *See also* Israel
Homberg, Herz, 344, 357, 409
Home, Henry (Lord Kames), 395
Horodetzky, S. A., 200
Human purpose. *See* Doctrine of purpose
Hume, David, 189, 370
Hutcheson, Francis, 396
Hyde, Thomas, 241

Ibn Abi Bekr al Tebrizi, Abu Abd Allah Muhammad, 225
Ibn Daud, Abraham, doctrine of purpose and, 135–36, 140
Ibn Ezra, Abraham, 58, 252–53, 254–55, 256–57, 259, 261, 264
Ibn Gabirol, Solomon (Avencebrol), 116, 222, 236, 257, 259; doctrine of purpose and, 123, 129–34, 140, 147, 152, 153, 156, 157; piety and, 109–10
Ibn Gaon, Shemtov, 203
Ibn Hazm, 306, 307
Ibn Hûd, al Mursi, Abu Ali, 225
Ibn Rushd. *See* Averroës
Ibn Saddiq (Ẓaddik), Joseph, doctrine of purpose and, 134–35, 141, 152
Ibn Tibbon, Judah, 226, 232
Ibn Tibbon, Samuel, 224; translation of the *Guide* and, 225–27, 227, 228, 229, 232, 235, 238–39, 242
Immortality, 58, 61, 103–4, 186, 319, 364–65; doctrine of purpose and, 127–28, 132, 150
Incoherence of Philosophers, The (al-Ghazali), 183, 288–89
Individualism, religious, piety and, 82–84; piety and, 105; tradition and, 63
Instruction of Students (Eliezer), 260
Intellect, contemplation and, 318
Intellectualism, religious truth and, 286, 298
Intolerance, monotheistic religion and, 85
Introduction to the Talmud and Midrash (Strack), 34
Intuition, 317
Isaac of Acre, 163
Isaac ben Judah of Urbino, 240
Isaac ben Nathan of Cordova, 225
Isaac the Blind, 164–66, 170, 174
Islam, 80, 191, 198, 284; allegory and, 250, 252, 254; conception of God and, 294; doctrine of purpose and, 121, 124–29, 147, 152–53; piety and, 299, 304–5; prophecy and, 321; revelation and, 285, 286, 290, 291, 298–99, 309–11, 321; study of, 35. *See also* Muslims
Israel, 86, 119, 154, 374, 381–82; as God's

people, 73, 75, 76, 191–92, 264, 354, 364, 366, 371, 376, 413; Mendelssohn and, 411. *See also* Divine election of the Jewish people; Holy Land
Israeli, Isaac ben Solomon, 184, 222; doctrine of purpose and, 122, 123, 151
Isserles, Moses, 261

Jacob ben Abba Mari Anatoli, 221, 260
Jacob ben Asher, 144
Jacobi, Friedrich Heinrich, 317, 362
Jedidiah ben Moses. *See* Amadeo of Rimini
Jerusalem (Mendelssohn), 13, 350, 356, 358, 368, 370, 373, 375, 383, 409; concept of Judaism in, 343–46; Spinoza and, 362, 363
Jesus Christ. *See* Christ
Jewish culture, 11; the Diaspora and, 106; purpose and, 115, 118, 153–60. *See also* Culture; Greek culture
Jewish denomination (*Konfession*), 78, 108
Jewish race. *See* Race, Jews as a
Jews as the Chosen People. *See* Divine election of the Jewish people
Joël, Manuel, 44–45
John Hispanus (John of Seville), 221
John II of Portugal, 273
Jonas, Hans, 210
Joseph ben Yehudah, 256
Judah ben Barzilai, 207
Judah ben Jehiel, 271
Judah Halevi, 12, 79, 109, 116, 127, 141, 142, 147, 155, 158, 251, 407; al-Ghazali's works and, 182–83; causality and, 190–91; essence of Judaism and, 181–82, 187; free will and, 190; fundamental views of, 195–99; God's activity and, 189; Israel and, 191–92; rejection of philosophers and, 182, 183–88; religious truth and, 288, 291–92, 299–301, 304; supernatural events and, 190–91
Judaism: assimilation and, 107–8; dogma and, 41–50, 54–57; essence of, 67–69, 181–82, 187; ethical universalism and, 75–77; ethical aspects of, 71–72, 78; forms of, in nineteenth century, 404–15; living, science and, 34–36; Mendelssohn's concept of, 343–59, 364–65, 367–68, 399, 406, 407, 408, 412, 414; modernizing religious institutions and, 405; national sense of, 32, 70–72, 85, 86, 89, 90, 405, 407, 409, 413; religious beliefs and, 56–69; as religious community, 32, 49, 56–57, 63–64, 78, 79, 81–82, 104, 376, 411, 412; scientific study of, 9, 10, 19–24, 26–36. *See also* Reform Judaism

Kabbalah, 11, 110, 249, 264, 271; kavvanah and, 164–74; Maimonides and, 200–201, 207, 210, 213; mysticism and, 162–63, 166, 167–68, 169, 170, 171
Kalām, 11, 140, 223, 294, 297
Kames, Lord (Henry Home), 395
Kant, Immanuel, 152, 362, 369, 395, 399; enlightenment and, 387–94; religious truth and, 325–28, 331, 332–33, 335
Kaufmann, David, 12, 14, 275
Kavvanah of prayer. See Prayer, kavvanah of
Klein, Ernst Ferdinand, 390
Klein, Moritz, 244
Knowledge: doctrine of purpose and, 130–31, 141, 146; God's, as universal, 58; Kant on, 325–26, 328; religious and scientific truth and, 287–89, 290, 292, 298, 336, 369
Kölbele, Johann Balthasar, 406
Konfession. See Jewish denomination
Koran, 121, 140, 194, 250, 286, 304; translation of, 221
Krochmal, Nachman, 31
Kuzari (Judah Halevi), 182, 184, 187, 190, 195, 197

Language: Arabic, 35; German, use of, 20; Hebrew, revival of, 28–29
Lavater, Johann Caspar, 358, 392; Mendelssohn and, 345, 348–50
Law, 79, 223, 405; allegory and, 250, 251, 253, 260–61; ceremonial, 345, 354, 375, 376, 407–8; divine, 371–72; interpretation of divine, 64, 65; Mendelssohn's concept of religion and, 344, 345, 350–51, 354–58, 364–65, 375–76, 381–82, 406, 408, 412; Mosaic, 356, 364–65, 371, 373, 382; natural, 379; piety and, 93–96, 102–3, 108; purpose and, 144; religious, 66; revealed, 65; ritual, 409; the Torah and, 73–74, 92; validity of religious, 59. See also Revelation, the law and
Lazarus, Moritz, 32
Learning, Jewish. See Scholarship, nature of Jewish
Leibniz, Gottfried Wilhelm von, 188, 235–36, 347, 362, 367, 391, 398–99, 400
Lessing, Gotthold Ephraim, 347, 348, 354, 358, 361, 367, 391, 394, 400, 413, 415; education and, 369–70
Letter to Deacon Lavater of Zurich (Mendelssohn), 348–49
Leviathan; or, Concerning Religion in Respect to Judaism (Ascher), 406
Levi ben Abraham ben Ḥayyim, 261
Levi ben Gerson. See Gersonides

Lewin, Mendel, 242
Literature, 97; Arabic, 35, 221–22; hellenistic, purpose and, 124; holy, authority and, 101; Jewish, 19–24, 28, 34, 220–21; kabbalistic, 162; prophetic, 205; purpose and, 151, 152; talmudic, piety and, 93
Locke, John, 323, 324, 367, 378, 380–81, 399
Love, 93, 257; doctrine of purpose and, 147, 148; Ebreo's dialogues and, 274, 275, 277–80; the soul and, 318
Löw, Leopold, 43–44
Lumen naturale, the soul and, 317
Luther, Martin, 313

Magic, 197; the kavvanah and, 171, 174; Maimonides and, 201
Maimon, Solomon, 242
Maimonides (Moses ben Maimon), 12, 26, 100, 321, 347, 350, 408; allegory and, 250, 255–58, 259–60, 262, 263, 264; doctrine of purpose and, 136–44, 145, 146, 147, 148, 149, 152, 153, 157, 158; dogma and, 65; Kabbalah and, 200–201; the kavvanah and, 168–69; mysticism and, 200–214; piety and, 93–94, 96, 102–4, 368; purpose of revelation and, 297–98, 310; resurrection and, 66; Thirteen Articles of Faith of, 57, 60, 91. See also Guide for the Perplexed
Man: doctrine of purpose and, 115, 117, 118, 119–21, 122, 130, 134, 135, 137, 140, 141, 142, 143, 144, 149, 155–56; image of, Mendelssohn on, 388, 389; Judah Halevi on, 196; progress and, Mendelssohn on, 369–70, 400, 401, 409; surrender to God and, 193
Manasseh ben Israel, 355, 381
Man's existence, purpose of. See Doctrine of purpose
Mantino, Jacob, 235
Marmontel, Jean François, 400
Maroni, David Jacob, 244
Martin, Raymond, 233
Master-disciple relationship, 202, 204
Mattatiyah ben Ghartom, 238
Matter, 187–88
Medici, Lorenzo de, 277
Mehlis, George, 170
Meir ben Simeon of Narbonne, 167
Mendelssohn, Moses, 13, 97, 242; Asher's analysis of, 406–7; bon sens and, 396–97; church and state and, 378, 379–83, 390, 409; concept of Judaism and, 343–59; dogma and, 41–42, 45, 47, 50, 343, 353, 408, 413–14; education and, 388–90, 393, 396, 401, 406, 410; enlightenment and,

389–94; image of man and, 388, 389; Israel and, 411; the law and religion and, 344, 345, 350–51, 354–58, 364–65, 375–76, 381–82, 406, 407, 408, 409, 414; man's progress and, 369–70, 400–401, 409; Messianism and, 411–12; metaphysical speculation and, 408–9; opinion of Spinoza and, 362–63; piety and, 409; reason and, 352–53, 355, 357, 374, 396–97, 399–400, 408, 414; religious truth and, 368, 369–70; return to Palestine and, 411–12; revelation and, 41–42, 45, 47, 50, 54, 344, 349, 350–53, 355, 357, 364–65, 367–68, 399, 406, 407, 408, 412; ritual law and, 409; sense perception and, 397–98; the soul and, 394–95, 398–99, 401; talmudic customs and, 406; universalism and, 357–58

Messiah, 61, 104, 415
Messianic era, 66–67, 95, 300
Messianism, 76, 105; Mendelssohn and, 411–12
Metaphor, allegory and, 247–48, 256
Metaphysics, 185, 186, 187, 205, 207, 284, 303, 396; concept of truth and, 326; knowledge and religious truth and, 287–90, 291, 292; Mendelssohn and, 408–9; rejection of, 183; religion and, 328; revelation and, 307, 308, 367
Michaelis, Count, 411–12
Miracles, 66, 190, 250, 350–53
Mishnah, 80, 120, 136, 142, 146, 205; dogma and, 47–48, 56
Moeser, Justus, 393
Monotheism, 72, 75, 193, 223, 283, 293, 298; as article of faith, 96–97; ethical, 82, 327; piety and, 96–102; self-righteousness and, 85; true meaning of Jewish, 91; universalism and, 86–87
Montesa, Carlos, 276
Morality: prejudice-supported, 392; religious truth and, 293–98, 307, 319, 320, 322, 327, 331; retribution and, 311; Spinoza and, 372–74
More, Thomas, 314, 319
Morning Hours (Mendelssohn), 363, 388
Moses, 62, 86, 102, 344
Moses ben Maimon. *See* Maimonides
Moses ben Solomon of Salerno, 232
Munk, Solomon, 223, 242, 244, 245
Murder, 253
Muslims, Maimonides's *Guide* and, 224–25. *See also* Islam
Mysticism, 11, 12, 191, 192, 193, 298, 318, 329, 391; Kabbalah and, 162–63; Maimonides and, 200–214; piety and, 72–73, 74–75

Naḥmanides (Moses ben Nahman), 174, 201
Nathan the Wise (Lessing), 400, 413
Neoplatonism, 93, 184, 211, 277, 279, 287, 298, 300; purpose and, 115, 122, 127, 132, 135, 141, 143, 144, 147, 152, 156
Neumark, David, 152, 210
Nicolai, Friedrich, 394
Nicolo de Giovenazzo, 232
Nietzsche, Friedrich Wilhelm, 117
Norden, Eduard, 116, 120, 154
Nous (mind, intellect), 125, 126, 131, 141, 146, 147, 184
Numerology, 163; letters of the alphabet and, 159, 165

Obedience, 366–67, 372–73, 378, 381
Obligation (theory of), purpose and, 117–18, 129, 155
Occam, William of, 295
On Controlling the Inclinations (Mendelssohn), 394
On Grace and Dignity (Schiller), 395
On Rabbinic Literature (Zunz), 9, 10; Wissenschaft des Judentums and, 19–24, 29, 30–31, 33
On Religion—Addresses to its Cultured Despisers (Schleiermacher), 328
Oral tradition. *See* Tradition, oral
Origen, Adamantius, 251, 252
Orthodox Jews, 348
Orthodoxy, 43, 412; education and, 27–28
Or Zaru'a (David ben Judah Ḥasid), 169
Otto, Walter, 157

Paganism, 370, 375
Palestine, 198; return to, Mendelssohn and, 411–12. *See also* Israel
Pantheism, 193, 316, 318, 347, 363
Paradise story, allegory and, 254, 257–59, 262, 264. *See also* Bible
Particularism, 81, 300, 374; Messianism and, 76–77; piety and, 105; universalism and, 88–90, 191
Pascal, Blaise, 251, 295
Pedro (Petrus) of Toledo, 221; translation of the *Guide* and, 237–40
Pelayo, Menendez, 237
Perception. *See* Sense perception
Peri, Hiram, 12
Perles, Josef, 233, 235
Philo, 10, 48, 152, 157, 159, 202, 248, 262, 264
Philosophers, 12, 141–42, 160; allegory and, 256–60; rejection of, 183–88
Philosophical Dialogues (Mendelssohn), 362

Philosophy, 26; Arabic, 288, 313–14; Kant's religious, 326–28; nature of God and, 296; reason and, 346; religious impulses and ancient, 282; religious truth and, 309–14, 321, 322, 335; Schleiermacher's religious, 331; truth of reason and, 290, 291

Pico della Mirandola, 314

Piety, 11, 154, 157, 158, 377, 413; assimilation and, 107–8; basic elements of, 65; Christian, 101, 319; dogma and, 70; ethical aspects of, 71–72; Gabirol and, 109–10; individualism and, 82–84; Jewish theology and, 97–98; Judah Halevi and, 195, 197–98; the law and, 93–96; Maimonides and, 93–94, 96, 102–4, 368; Mendelssohn and, 409; monotheism and, 82, 85, 86–87, 91, 96–102; mysticism and, 72–73, 74–75; nature and, 368; particularism and, 88–90; philosophers and, 264; reform and, 105–6; religious truth and, 296, 299, 301–2, 303, 304, 319, 320; Spinoza and, 373; the Torah and, 73–75, 85–86, 91–92; universalism and, 75–77, 86–87, 88–90, 93–94

Pirkei de Rabbi Eliezer, 208, 260

Plato, 115, 126, 148, 157, 277

Platonism, 316

Plotinus, 125, 131, 156, 194, 211

Plutarch, 248, 399

Pococke, Edward, 241–42

Porphyry, 119, 131, 152

Posidonius, 119, 129, 154, 156

Prayer, 10; communal, 56–57; definition of, 168; kavvanah of, 11, 164–74

Predestination, 295

Prejudice: against Jewish literature, 23; tolerance for, Mendelssohn and, 392–93

Prophecy, 91, 102, 192, 223, 225, 371; the Arabs and, 321; Bruno's attitude toward, 322; God and, 301–2; illumination and, 317; religious truth and, 322; revelation and, 307–10, 322; Spinoza and, 321

Prophets, 142, 150, 157, 194, 255, 304, 311, 371, 373; authority and, 62; contact with God and, 299–300; Maimonides on, 204–5; piety of, 75–76; revelation and, 350–51

Protestantism, 92; dogma and, 46, 50, 55. *See also* Christianity

Pure Brethren. *See* Brethren of Purity

Purpose of man's existence. *See* Doctrine of purpose

Rabbinism, 73

Race, Jews as, 36. *See also* Judaism, national sense of

Rade, Martin, 46, 55

Rashi (Shelomo Yitshaki), 249

Rashid Abu'l Kheir, 224

Rationalism, 105, 182, 296, 313, 374; moral, 319; philosophical, 322–23; purpose and, 135, 140; theological, 367

Raymond, archbishop of Toledo, 221

Reason: God and, 372; Judah Halevi and, 196; Mendelssohn and, 41–42, 352–53, 355, 357, 374, 396–97, 399–400, 408; moral, 294, 295; purpose and, 125, 126, 135–36; religious truth and, 287–88, 290, 304, 305–6, 314, 316–18, 320, 323; revelation and, 286, 297, 304, 313, 314, 316, 317, 318, 323, 367–68, 414; scientific truth and, 287–88; Spinoza and, 367, 371–72; tolerance and, 346

Redemption, 49–50, 83

Reform Judaism, 42, 43, 44, 50, 66, 106, 413. *See also* Judaism

Reimarus, Hermann Samuel, 352, 392

Religion: comparative, religious truth and, 289–91, 298–99, 306–7; defined as metaphysical truth, 308; ethical aspects of, 72; historic, 148; Mendelssohn and, 413; natural, 307, 324–25, 367, 368, 370, 373, 376; philosophy and, 309–14, 322; philosophy of, 282

Religion within the Limits of Reason Alone (Kant), 326–27

Religious community. *See* Judaism, as religious community

Resurrection, 56, 61, 66, 83

Retribution, 63, 83, 93, 150, 297, 311, 319, 326, 392

Revelation, 65, 79, 86, 91, 97, 157, 168, 185, 190, 191; al-Ghazali and, 194; authoritative character of, 60–61, 62–63; Christianity and, 75, 314; as divine, 43; dogma and, 42–43, 45, 46, 47; Einhorn on, 43; the Enlightenment and, 323–24; historical view of, 62–63; Holdheim on, 43; Islam and, 285, 286, 290, 291, 298–99, 309–11, 321; the law and, 42–43, 45, 73–74; Mendelssohn on, 41–42, 45, 47, 50, 54, 344, 349, 350–53, 355, 357, 364–65, 399, 406, 407, 408; philosophy and, 312–13; piety and, 72, 73–74; primal, 315; prophecy and, 307–10, 322; prophetic, 307–10; reason and, 41, 42, 43, 286, 297, 304, 313, 314, 316, 317, 318, 323, 367–68; religious truth and, 59–60, 63, 283–87, 290–91, 292, 293, 295, 296–97, 299–300, 304, 307–10, 311, 312, 313, 314, 315–18, 322, 323; scientific truth and, 283–87; speculative interpretation and, 297–98; Spinoza and, 363, 364–69, 370–71, 373, 374; supernatural

concept of, 66, 305; theory of, for all religions, 309
Rhapsody (Mendelssohn), 395
Riario, Cardinal, 276
Ritschl, O., 55
Ritual, 195. *See also* Law, ritual
Roman, Jacob, 235
Roscher, Wilhelm, 116
Rothschild, James de, 243
Rousseau, Jean Jacques, 369, 400–401
Royal Crown (Gabirol), 130, 131, 134, 157, 160
Rubaschoff, Salman (Zalman Shazar), 14

Saadia (Saadiah), ben Joseph (Gaon), 100; allegory and, 252, 254, 256, 259; doctrine of purpose and, 123, 155, 158
Sabbath, 382
Sachs, Hans, 116
Sacrifice, 174
Sacy, Antoine Isaac Silvestre de, 224, 243
Sages, 204–5, 206, 253, 255
Salvation, 65, 75, 98, 193; non-Christian, 315; piety and, 104–5
Samuel, 410
Samuel ben Meir, 260
Sanhedrin, 47–48, 64
Sanudo, Marino, 276
Scaliger, Justus, 234, 235
Scheftelowitz, Isidor, dogma and, 11, 46, 54–55, 57
Scheyer, Simon B., 242, 244
Schiff, Mario, 237, 238
Schiller, Johann Christoph Friedrich von, 395
Schleiermacher, Friedrich Ernst Daniel, religious truth and, 328–32, 335
Scholarship, 221; biblical, 34; Hebrew language and, 28–29; nature of Jewish, 26–27; study of Jewish literature and, 19–24
Scholasticism, 100, 278, 281, 285, 303, 313, 367
Scholem, Gershom, 11, 200
Science, 371; doctrine of purpose and, 135, 137, 143–44, 146, 147, 148, 151, 154, 155, 159; Gabirol and, 132–34; Greek, 12; Jewish scholarship and, 27; religious truth and, 290, 296, 312–13, 369
Scientific Study of Judaism. *See* Wissenschaft des Judentums
Scot, Michael, 221, 233
Scriptural authority, 62–63
Search for Light and Right (Cranz), 355
Secret, concept of, in Maimonides, 201–4, 206–9, 258
Self-consciousness (Jewish), 85
Seneca, 119
Sense perception, 397–98

Sermons of the Jews (Zunz), 31
Shaftesbury, Anthony Ashley Cooper, third earl of, 347, 391
Shazar, Zalman. *See* Rubaschoff, Salman
Simeon bar Yoḥai, 139
Simeon ben Ẓemaḥ Duran, 60, 225
Simon, Ernst, 395
Simon, Richard, 231
Sin, 119
Skepticism, 287, 306
Socrates, 392
Solmi, Edmondo, 276
Solomon, 137, 255, 373
Solomon ben Ephraim Luntschitz, 261
"Solomon ben Isaac, called Rashi" (Zunz), 30
Song of Songs, 256–57, 264
Sophists, 358
Soul, 105, 185, 186, 192–93, 303, 316; cognition as union with, 318; doctrine of purpose and, 124–28, 130–32, 133, 134, 138, 150; God and, 193, 291, 302, 318, 319; *lumen naturale* and, 317; Mendelssohn and, 394–95, 398–99, 401; union of, with divine source, 291, 302
Spheres, 184, 192, 209, 212
Spinoza, Baruch, 109, 148, 236, 406; church and state and, 377–79, 380, 382; Deism and, 361, 370; *Jerusalem* (Mendelssohn) and, 363; Mendelssohn's opinion of, 362–63; morality and, 372–74; "preestablished harmony" and, 362; reason and, 367, 371–72; religious truth and, 320–22; revelation and, 363, 364–69, 370–71, 373, 374
State, the, 357; coercion and, 355; Mendelssohn on, 378, 379–83; rights of, 344; Spinoza and, 377–79, 380, 382. *See also* Church
Statue, The (Mendelssohn), 398
Steinheim, Solomon, 405
Steinschneider, Moritz, 221, 240
Steinthal, Heymann, 36
Stern, M. E., 244
Stoicism, 313, 317
Strack, Hermann, 34
Suares, de Figuerôa Gomes. *See* De Figuerôa, Gomes Suares
Subconscious, 399
Suffering, 127
Sucide, 253, 401
Supernatural, 190–91, 198; nature of revelation, 66, 305, 344, 352; revelation-legislation and, 42
Superstitition, 370, 375, 391, 393
Symbolism, 257, 375; of God's name, 170; of light, 174; mystical, 207
Symposium (Plato), 277

Taitazak, Joseph, 163
Talmud, 34, 95, 102, 205; dogma and, 47–
  48; immortality and, 58; the law and, 64;
  oral tradition and, 59; piety-natural law
  and, 368; study of, 30
Talmudism, 73
Teleology, 115, 120, 129, 140, 143, 148,
  156, 159, 264, 279, 347
Theodicy, 294
Theodotus, 120
Theologico-Political Treatise (Spinoza), 13,
  320, 321, 361–64, 368, 371, 372, 373, 377
Timaeus (Plato), 147
Tindal, Matthew, 367
Toland, John, 367
Tolerance, 382, 411, 414; conversion and,
  345; for prejudices, 392–93; reason and,
  346; unification of faiths and, 358
Torah, 168, 174, 369, 374, 413; allegory
  and, 249, 250, 253–54; belief norms and,
  65; divine origin of, 58–59, 61, 64, 67,
  94, 414; dogma and, 48, 56; interpreting
  vs. questioning the truth in, 60–61; piety
  and, 73–75, 80, 85–86, 91–92, 93–94,
  102; purpose and, 119, 144–45, 149, 150,
  151, 152; revelation and, 43; science and,
  28; "secrets" of, 202, 205–6; study of,
  27, 83
Tradition, 106; authority of, 61, 63; historical,
  62; oral, divine origin of, 59, 65, 66, 205
Trinity, 101, 108, 352
Troeltsch, Ernst, 46, 55
Truth, religious, 57, 282; al-Ghazali and,
  288–89, 294, 299, 301–5; analyzing religious consciousness and, 328–32, 333–35;
  causality and, 288–89; cognition and,
  287–88, 291, 298, 299, 303, 305, 307,
  316, 317, 318–19, 320, 322, 326, 335; duality of truth and, 292–93; enlightenment
  and, 290–91; the Enlightenment and,
  297, 305, 322–25; form and, 332–33; intellectualism and, 286, 298; Judah Halevi
  and, 288, 291–92, 299–301; Kant and,
  325–28, 332, 335; knowledge-cognition
  and, 287–89, 290–91, 292; Mendelssohn
  on, 368, 369–70; moral truth and, 293–
  93; philosophy and, 309, 310–14, 322; piety and, 296, 299, 301–2, 303, 304, 319,
  320; prophecy and, 322; rational truth
  and, 369; reason and, 287–88, 290, 304,
  305–6, 314, 316–18, 323; revelation and,
  59–60, 63, 283–87, 290–91, 292, 293,
  295, 296–97, 299–300, 304, 307–10, 311,
  312, 313, 314, 315–18, 322, 323, 367–68;
  Schleiermacher and, 328–32, 335; science
  and, 312–13; Spinoza and, 320–22; study
  of comparative religion and, 289–91,
  306–7; universal, 314–17

Truth, scientific, 282–83, 293, 296; comparative religion and, 306; knowledge-
  cognition and, 287–89; reason and, 287–
  88; revelation and, 283–87
Tschirnhaus, E. W. von, 361

Überweg, Friedrich, 223
Underhill, Evelyn, 170
Universalism, 374; al-Ghazali and, 304–5;
  causality and, 191; Ebreo's dialogues on
  love and, 278; Jewish, 414–15; Mendelssohn and, 357–58; particularism and, 88–
  90; piety and, 75–77, 81, 86–87, 105; religious truth and, 314–17; Spinoza and, 371
Unknown God (Norden), 154
Utopia (More), 314, 319

Venerabilis, Petrus, 221
Vincent of Beauvais, 231
Vindiciae Judaeorum (Manasseh ben Is-
  rael), 355, 381
Virtue, 372, 395
Visionary act, 208
Voltaire, 370

Water, forms of, 208, 212, 213
Weltanschauung, 70–71, 74, 75, 90, 94, 98,
  105, 106
Wendt, H. H., 46
Werner, Z., 159
Wiener, Max, 11
Wilhelm, Kurt, 9
Will, freedom of. *See* Free will
William of Auvergne, 222, 230–31
William of Burgos, 251
Wisdom: divine, 188; doctrine of purpose
  and, 134, 137–39
Wissenschaft des Judentums (Scientific
  Study of Judaism), 13; *A Century of Wis-
  senschaft des Judentums* (Elbogen) and,
  26–36; classic statements on, 10; compo-
  nents of, 33–34; defining, difficulty of,
  31–33; Judeocentric, rejection of, 26;
  On Rabbinic Literature (Zunz) and, 19–
  24; origin of term, 9, 29–31; roots of,
  29–31; scholarship and study of, 19–24
*Wissenschaft des Judentums im deutschen
  Sprachbereich* (Wilhelm), 9
Wolf, Immanuel (later Wohlwill), 33
Wolf, J. Chr., 235
Wolfenbütteler Fragmente (Lessing), 361
Wolff, Christian, 352, 388, 395
Writing (written communication), 118–19

Zöllner, Johann Friedrich, 387
Zunz, Leopold, 9, 10, 26, 27; Wissenschaft
  des Judentums and, 19–24, 29, 30–31,
  33, 34, 35

Alfred Jospe received his rabbinical training and ordination at the Jewish Theological Seminary of Breslau, Germany, and holds a Ph.D. from the University of Breslau and a D.D. from the Hebrew Union College-Jewish Institute of Religion. Before emigrating to the United States, he served as rabbi of the "New Synagogue" and as lecturer in Jewish history and thought at the School of Jewish Social Work in Berlin.

Associated with the B'nai B'rith Hillel Foundations since 1940, he directed the Hillel program at West Virginia and Indiana universities until 1949, when he joined the Hillel executive staff as director of programs and resources and, from 1971 to 1974, as international director. He is a member of the B'nai B'rith Hillel Commission and of the Board of Directors of the Leo Baeck Institute.

Dr. Jospe has lectured before university and community audiences in every part of the North American continent and in Europe, Israel, Australia, and Latin America. He has edited a number of Hillel publications and is the author or editor of several books. He has also published articles in the fields of philosophy, religion, and education, and is among the contributors to the *Encyclopaedia Judaica*.

The manuscript was edited for publication by Sherwyn T. Carr. The book was designed by Don Ross. The typeface for the text is VIP Times Roman, designed by Stanley Morison about 1932. The display face is Melior, designed by Hermann Zapf about 1952.

The text is printed on International Paper Company's 60 lb. Bookmark Natural text paper, and the book is bound in Holliston Mills' Roxite cloth over binder's boards. Manufactured in the United States of America.